Catholic Dictionary

Revised

**Reverend
Peter M.J. Stravinskas,
Ph.D., S.T.D.**

OUR SUNDAY VISITOR PUBLISHING DIVISION

OUR SUNDAY VISITOR, INC.

HUNTINGTON, INDIANA 46750

Cover design by Monica Haneline
Interior design by Sherri L. Hoffman

PRINTED IN THE UNITED STATES OF AMERICA

Table of Contents

EDITOR
The Rev. Peter M. J. Stravinskas

CONTRIBUTORS
The Rev. Robert Batule
The Rev. John Michael Beers
The Rev. Joseph A. DiNoia, O.P.
The Rev. Thomas P. Doyle, O.P.
The Rev. Charles M. Mangan
The Rev. Christopher Phillips
The Rev. Peter J. Scagnelli

Acknowledgments

It is astonishing to find how often the ancient pagans "got it right." A case in point is on the importance of saying "thanks." Seneca notes that "there is as much greatness of mind in acknowledging a good turn, as in doing it." Cicero asserts that "gratitude is not only the greatest of virtues, but the parent of all the others."

With that in mind, it is a happy duty for me to renew my thanks to those who worked on the first edition of this dictionary and to express my sincerest appreciation for the revision task entrusted to Brother Joshua Kibler and completed so well. Furthermore, the patient, efficient, and good-humored support of Mr. Michael Dubruiel at Our Sunday Visitor was likewise key to the successful outcome of the project.

May the work of all redound to a profitable experience for our readers, so that as their knowledge of the Lord deepens, so may their love and service.

Rev. Peter M. J. Stravinskas, Editor

Foreword

"Jesus Christ is the same yesterday, today, and forever," the Scriptures assure us. The same can be said of the truths of our Catholic Faith, entrusted to the Church. This means that a true following of Christ requires knowledge of the Church, which is His body. We continue to realize the necessity of catechesis in the process of evangelization, as witnessed by the publication of the *Catechism of the Catholic Church*. In this light, *Our Sunday Visitor's Catholic Dictionary* appears as a timely reference for explaining the terms in which the Church speaks of the various aspects of her teaching and practice.

With the publication of this volume, Our Sunday Visitor completes a trilogy — *Our Sunday Visitor's Catholic Almanac, Our Sunday Visitor's Catholic Encyclopedia,* and, now, the revision of *Our Sunday Visitor's Catholic Dictionary* — which provides access to materials for that ongoing catechesis necessary for all members of the Church. I am sure this work will be of use at home, in the rectory, and in the classroom as a handy reference due to the accuracy of its contents and the clarity of its presentation.

It is my hope and prayer that the efforts of Father Peter Stravinskas and the other contributors to this volume will bear much fruit by drawing us ever more deeply and faithfully into the Church.

✠ *Seán O'Malley, O.F.M. Cap.*
Bishop of Fall River, Massachusetts

Guide to Pronunciation

Adapted from the "respelling" method of Joseph M. Staudacher in *Lector's Guide to Biblical Pronunciations* (Our Sunday Visitor Publishing, 2001).

Our alphabet has twenty-six letters to express as many as thirty-nine sounds; it is, therefore, incomplete. Sometimes the same letter has to play several roles. For example, the letter "A" is used to express six different sounds: PLATE, CAROL, PAT, FATHER, ALL, and SOFA.

Strictly speaking, our alphabet does not have twenty-six separate letters. C is either S or K; Q is K; and X is EKS. Therefore our alphabet has only twenty-three letters to express as many as thirty-nine sounds.

A second disadvantage in our limited alphabet is found in the pronunciation of some letter combinations. One example among many is the letter combination OUGH. These letters are pronounced differently in words like THOUGH, ROUGH, THOROUGH, and COUGH.

To solve the problem of the inconsistency in pronouncing these and other letter combinations, three systems are possible: phonetics, diacritical markings, and respelling.

Phonetics, a system using a separate symbol for each vowel and consonant sound, was established by a group of international scholars in 1888. The same symbol always stands for the same sound, and the same sound is always represented by the same symbol whether the language be English, German, French, or any other. As a result, phonetics may be considered the most accurate way of representing vowel and consonant sounds for accurate pronunciation. The only difficulty is the fact that the system of phonetics is not generally taught in our schools, as are reading, writing, and arithmetic, and therefore few persons are able to read phonetics.

A second method of indicating speech sounds with visual symbols is the system of *diacritical markings* found in dictionaries. These markings are helpful, but unfortunately they vary from one dictionary to another. This lack of consistency can be confusing.

A third method is *respelling,* a system which this pronunciation guide follows. An attempt is made to spell the words in such a way that the acceptable pronunciation is immediately clear and obvious. For example, Deuteronomy is listed as Dyöö-ter-AH-nuh-mee.

To standardize the sounds of the words to be visualized, the following *pronunciation key* is offered. Two basic assumptions underlie the use of the key in its application to pronunciation:

1. No sounds foreign to American speech are introduced; e.g., no rolled or glottal "r" or German or Scottish "ch," as in *ich* or *loch*.
2. The pronunciations are based on standard or "generic" American speech. Those who speak with Eastern or Southern accents are encouraged to make their own adjustments wherever needed.

Finally, in the following pronunciation key, notice that ØØ is a short vowel sound as in BØØK, while ÖÖ is a long vowel sound as in MÖÖN. Notice, too, that the italicized *TH* sound is the voiced TH as in *TH*EE, while the plain TH is the breathy TH sound as in THREE. And last, notice that the accented syllable is in capital letters as in UHN-der-graund.

A Key to Pronouncing Words in Respelling

Vowel Sounds

A as in "pat, slab, map": PAT, SLAB, MAP
AH as in "farmer, car, heart": FAHR-mer, KAHR, HAHRT
AI as in "ice, fly, side": AIS, FLAI, SAID
AU as in "out, how, down": AUT, HAU, DAUN
AW as in "law, taught, appall": LAW, TAWT, uh-PAWL
AY as in "ace, aid, deign": AYS, AYD, DAYN
EE as in "eat, beat, shriek": EET, BEET, SHREEK
EH as in "ebb, wreck, bread": EHB, REHK, BREHD
EHR as in "air, fare, square": EHR, FEHR, SKWEHR
ER as in "bird, hurt, earn": BERD, HERT, ERN
IH as in "bit, myth, build": BIHT, MIHTH, BIHLD
O as in "home, coat, abode": HOM, KOT, uh-BOD
OI as in "boy, coin, voice": BOI, KOIN, VOIS
ØØ as in "book, pull, woman": BØØK, PØØL, WØØ-muhn

ÖÖ as in "moon, food, do": MÖÖN, FÖÖD, DÖÖ
UH as in "cut, love, nut": KUHT, LUHV, NUHT

Consonant Sounds

B as in "better, rub, blubber": BEH-ter, RUHB, BLUH-ber
D as in "dome, bad, redder": DOM, BAD, REH-der
DZH as in "Jim, John, edge": DZHIHM, DZHAHN, EHDZH
F as in "from, leaf, muffle": FRUHM, LEEF, MUH-fuhl
G as in "gun, lug, nugget": GUHN, LUHG, NUH-geht
H as in "hat, ahead, who": HAT, uh-HEHD, HOO
K as in "king, link, lucky": KIHNG, LIHNK, LUH-kee
L as in "leap, pool, allow": LEEP, PÖÖL, uh-LAU
M as in "man, name, mummy": MAN, NAYM, MUH-mee
N as in "not, ran, sinner": NAHT, RAN, SIH-ner
NG as in "sing, running, bank": SIHNG, RUHN-ihng, BANGK
P as in "push, oppose, nap": PØØSH, uh-POZ, NAP
R as in "run, car, arrow": RUHN, KAHR, EHR-o
S as in "sum, pace, lesser": SUHM, PAYS, LEH-ser
SH as in "sure, hush, gusher": SHØØR, HUHSH, GUH-sher
T as in "tin, bit, letter": TIHN, BIHT, LEH-ter
TH as in "thin, myth, zither": THIHN, MIHTH, ZIH-ther
TH as in "then, this, mother": *TH*EHN, *TH*IHS, MUH-*th*er
TSH as in "church, chance, chipper": TSHERTSH, TSHANS, TSHIH-per
V as in "vine, move, lover": VAIN, MÖÖV, LUH-ver
W as in "win, won, weather": WIHN, WUHN, WEH-*th*er
Y as in "you, onion, canyon": YÖÖ, UHN-yuhn, KAN-yuhn
Z as in "zoo, topaz, easy": ZÖÖ, TO-paz, EE-zee
ZH as in "azure, garage, mirage": AZH-yer, guh-RAHZH, mih-RAHZH

Pronunciation Defined

Pronunciation is the expression of sounds and accents of words in connected speech and in conformity with acceptable standards. (See *Laymen, Proclaim the Word* by Joseph M. Staudacher: Chicago, Franciscan Herald Press, 1973, pp.

11

47-49.) From this definition of pronunciation, four key elements arise: sounds, accents, connected speech, and acceptable standards.

a. *Sounds:* The basic ingredients of spoken words are vowel and consonant sounds. Mispronunciations occur when vowel or consonant sounds are added, omitted, or substituted.

Words can be mispronounced when sounds are added.

	Wrong	*Correct*
Arthritis	ahr-ther-AI-tihs	ahr-THRAI-tihs
Athletics	ath-uh-LEH-tihks	ath-LEH-tihks
Chicago	tshih-KAW-go	shih-KAH-go
		(or shih-KAW-go)

Words can be mispronounced when sounds are omitted.

	Wrong	*Correct*
Aluminum	uh-LÖÖM-nuhm	uh-LÖÖM-ih-nuhm
Honorable	AH-ner-bool	AH-ner-uh-bool

	Wrong	*Correct*
Library	LAI-behr-ee	LAI-brehr-ee

And words can be mispronounced when sounds are substituted.

	Wrong	*Correct*
February	FEHB-yöö-ehr-ee	FEHB-röö-ehr-ee
Them	dehm	*th*ehm
Until	ohn-TIHL	uhn-TIHL

b. *Accents:* As used here, the word does not refer to foreign intonations but to the stress placed upon certain syllables of a word. Some words admit of differently accented syllables. A word can be mispronounced, therefore, by misplacing the accent.

	Wrong	*Correct*
Detroit	DEE-troit	dee-TROIT
Museum	MYÖÖ-zee-øøm	Myöö-ZEE-uhm
Theater	thee-AY-ter	THEE-uh-ter

c. *Connected speech:* This refers to the pronunciation of words, not as single words, but in sentences as used in combination with other words. For example, the word BECAUSE is usually pronounced bee-KAWZ as an individual word, but in connected speech, unless the speaker wishes to emphasize BECAUSE, he or she may acceptably pronounce it bee-KUHZ. The purpose of speech is communication, and not to call attention to itself. Readers who pronounce every syllable of every word in connected speech the way they pronounce words singly fail to follow Shakespeare's wise advice in *Hamlet:* "Speak the speech, I pray you, as I pronounced it to you, trippingly on the tongue, but if you mouth it as many of your players do, I had as lief the town-crier spoke my lines."

Connected speech permits no pauses in the sentence "Pat takes science." Pausing after "Pat" or "takes" would sound affected or overdone.

Examples of other pronunciation variations in connected speech involve the simple words A (UH) and THE (*TH*UH). Don't say AY MAN. Say UH MAN. Use AY only for emphasis. For example, "I didn't ask all of you to help. I asked for AY (one) helper." Don't say *TH*EE MAN. Say *TH*UH MAN. Say *TH*EE only for emphasis; for example, "He is *TH*EE man of the hour." Or say *TH*EE before a vowel sound. For example, *TH*EE APPLE or *TH*EE F.H.A. (Even though the "f" in F.H.A. is called a consonant, it begins with a vowel sound.)

d. *Acceptable standards:* An acceptable standard is a model agreed upon by experts for imitation. There is no one pronunciation standard acceptable for all words in the English language. Variations are easily discernible in the speech of cultured British, Canadian, Australian, and American persons. In the speech of cultured Americans we find three general classifications: Eastern, Southern, and "Generic" American, and even in these categories we recognize acceptable variations.

While it may be emotionally difficult for some persons to be tolerant of pronunciation of different areas, it must be admitted that language is the result of usage and not of preconceived rules. This is not to say, because thousands of persons say "toity-toid" for "thirty-third," or "dis" for "this," or "hep" for "help," that these pronunciations are correct. Each locality has its unacceptable provincialisms. What we are looking for is a more general acceptability and uniformity.

Abbreviations
Used in the Dictionary

Acts: Acts of the Apostles (N.T. [New Testament]).
A.D.: *Anno Domini*: in the year of Our Lord.
Am: Book of Amos (O.T. [Old Testament]).
b.: born.
B., Bl.: *Beata, -us*; Blessed.
Bar: Book of Baruch (O.T.).
B.C.: Before Christ.
Bp.: Bishop.
Bro.: Brother.
c., ca.: *circa*: about.
Can., cc.: Canon, canons.
CCC: *Catechism of the Catholic Church*.
Ch., Chs.: Chapter, Chapters
1 Chr: First Book of Chronicles (O.T.).
2 Chr: Second Book of Chronicles (O.T.).
C.I.C.: *Codex Iuris Canonici*: Code of Canon Law.
Col: Letter to the Colossians (N.T.).
1 Cor: First Letter to the Corinthians (N.T.).
2 Cor: Second Letter to the Corinthians (N.T.).
d.: died.
Dn: Book of Daniel (O.T.).
Dt: Book of Deuteronomy (O.T.).
Eccl: Book of Ecclesiastes (O.T.).
e.g.: *exempli gratia*: for example.
Eph: Letter to the Ephesians (N.T.).
Est: Book of Esther (O.T.).
et. al.: *et alii (aliae, alia)*: and others.
Ex: Book of Exodus (O.T.).
Ez: Book of Ezekiel (O.T.).
Ezr: Book of Ezra (O.T.).
f., ff.: following.
Fr.: Father or Friar.
Gal: Letter to the Galatians (N.T.).
Gn: Book of Genesis (O.T.).
Hb: Book of Habakkuk (O.T.).
Heb: Letter to the Hebrews (N.T.).

Hg: Book of Haggai (O.T.).
Hos: Book of Hosea (O.T.).
ibid.: *ibidem*: in the same place (book or periodical).
i.e.: *id est*: that is.
Is: Book of Isaiah (O.T.).
Jas: Letter of James (N.T.).
Jb: Book of Job (O.T.).
Jdt: Book of Judith (O.T.).
Jer: Book of Jeremiah (O.T.).
Jgs: Book of Judges (O.T.).
Jl: Book of Joel (O.T.).
Jn: Gospel According to John (N.T.).
1 Jn: First Letter of John (N.T.).
2 Jn: Second Letter of John (N.T.).
3 Jn: Third Letter of John (N.T.).
Jon: Book of Jonah (O.T.).
Jos: Book of Joshua (O.T.).
Jude: Letter of Jude (N.T.).
1 Kgs: First Book of Kings (O.T.).
2 Kgs: Second Book of Kings (O.T.).
Lam: Book of Lamentations (O.T.).
Lk: Gospel According to Luke (N.T.).
Lv: Book of Leviticus (O.T.).
Mal: Book of Malachi (O.T.).
1 Mc: First Book of Maccabees (O.T.).
2 Mc: Second Book of Maccabees (O.T.).
Mi: Book of Micah (O.T.).
Mk: Gospel According to Mark (N.T.).
Mt: Gospel According to Matthew (N.T.).
n., nn.: number, numbers.
Na: Book of Nahum (O.T.).
Neh: Book of Nehemiah (O.T.).
Nm: Book of Numbers (O.T.).
N.T.: New Testament.
Ob: Book of Obadiah (O.T.).
O.T.: Old Testament.
Phil: Letter to the Philippians (N.T.).
Phlm: Letter to Philemon (N.T.).
Prv: Book of Proverbs (O.T.).
Ps(s): Book of Psalms (O.T.).
1 Pt: First Letter of Peter (N.T.).

2 Pt: Second Letter of Peter (N.T.).

q.v.: *quid vide*: which see (reference).

Rom: Letter to the Romans (N.T.).

Ru: Book of Ruth (O.T.).

Rv: Revelation to John (Apocalypse or Book of Revelation, N.T.).

S. or St.; SS. or Sts.: Saint; Saints.

Sg: Song of Songs (Canticle of Canticles, Song of Solomon, O.T.).

Sir: Book of Sirach (or Ecclesiasticus, O.T.).

1 Sm: First Book of Samuel (O.T.).

2 Sm: Second Book of Samuel (O.T.).

Tb: Book of Tobit (O.T.).

1 Thes: First Letter to the Thessalonians (N.T.).

2 Thes: Second Letter to the Thessalonians (N.T.).

Ti: Letter to Titus (N.T.).

1 Tm: First Letter to Timothy (N.T.).

2 Tm: Second Letter to Timothy (N.T.).

v., vv.: verse, verses.

Ven.: Venerable.

viz.: *videlicet*: namely.

vs.: *versus*: against.

Wis: Book of Wisdom (O.T.).

Zec: Book of Zechariah (O.T.).

Zep: Book of Zephaniah (O.T.).

A

Aaron (EHR-uhn): Brother of Moses, three years his senior; serving as his spokesman (Ex 4:14; 7:1), he sought the release of the Israelites from Pharaoh (Ex 5:1); thus, a significant figure in Israel's liberation. At God's instruction, he brought the plagues upon Egypt by stretching out his hand (Ex 7:19-20, 8:1-7, 12-13). He was the first priest of the Levites (Ex 28:41; 29:9-21; Lv 8), thus, the ancestor of the Aaronite priests; for this reason, the priestly source of Exodus minimizes his responsibility for fashioning the Golden Calf for the Israelites (Ex 32). In the N.T., this imperfect priesthood is contrasted with the perfect priesthood of Christ (Heb 5:4; 7:11). Like his brother, Aaron was denied entrance into the Promised Land (Nm 20), with his death either on Mt. Hor (Nm 20:29) or at Moserah (Dt 10:6). **CCC 1541-1542**

Abaddon (AB-uh-dahn): (Hebrew *ábaddon:* destruction) The dwelling place of the dead (Ps 88:11-12; Jb 26:6; 28:22), a synonym for Sheol (Prv 15:11; 27:20); in postbiblical Judaism, it is associated with Gehenna; in the N.T., it occurs only in Rv 9:11, for the name of the angel of the underworld (Greek *Appollyon:* destroyer). **Cf. CCC 633, 1034**

Abandonment (uh-BAN-duhn-mehnt): The spiritual practice of yielding in trust and acceptance to God's loving providence in every event and experience of daily life. The recommendation of this practice was a characteristic feature of the spiritual teaching of the French Jesuit Jean-Pierre de Caussade (1675-1751). The practice is meant to engender attitudes of peace, spiritual tranquillity, and the allaying of anxiety. **CCC 305, 322**

Abba (AB-uh): (Aramaic emphatic form of *áb:* father) The familiar form of address used by children in calling out to their father; it appears that Jesus used it in just this sense in invoking His Father in the great crises of His life (Mk 14:36); in this same sense, the term was appropriated by the early Church: "It is the spirit of sons, and it makes us cry out

'Abba, Father' " (Rom 8:15; cf. Gal 4:6). Many scholars believe that this Semitic use underlies the opening words of the Lord's Prayer, "Our Father, who art in heaven" (Mt 6:9; Lk 11:2). While in the O.T. God is often identified as Father (cf. Jer 31:9; Ps 89:27), it is never with the intimacy of the N.T. *Abba.* CCC 2777; cf. 683, 742, 1303

Abbacy Nullius (AB-uh-see nöö-LEE-øøs): An extra-diocesan territory, with an abbot having jurisdiction as the ordinary of clergy and faithful within the abbacy. Cf. CCC 833, 1672

Abbé (ah-BAY): Title used in French-speaking countries for a member of the secular clergy.

Abbess (A-behs): Female equivalent of an abbot; the temporal and spiritual superior elected by a community of nuns, especially in the Benedictine or Cistercian tradition (later extending to the Franciscan Poor Clares and other communities that profess or observe the monastic ideal of stability to a particular place). Cf. CCC 1672

Abbey (A-bee): A monastery of monks or nuns governed respectively by an abbot or abbess elected by the community. Cf. CCC 1672

Abbey Nullius (A-bee nöö-LEE-øøs): An abbey belonging to no diocese, with separate territorial and jurisdictional boundaries set by the Holy See. The abbot may or may not be a bishop but has ordinary authority and jurisdiction over the inhabitants of the territory similar to a bishop in his own diocese. Its origin is found in the large and influential monasteries of the Middle Ages, but following the Second Vatican Council Pope Paul VI decreed that no more such abbeys should be erected, except for extraordinary reasons. Cf. CCC 833, 1672

Abbot (A-buht): The male superior of a monastic community of religious men; e.g., Benedictines, Cistercians, some others. Elected by members of the community, an abbot has ordinary jurisdiction and general authority over his community. Eastern Rite equivalents of an abbot are a hegumen and an archimandrite. A regular abbot is the head of an abbey or monastery. An abbot general or archabbot is the head of a congregation consisting of several monasteries. Cf. CCC 1672

Abbot General (A-buht DZHEHN-er-uhl): In men's monastic orders, like Trappists, Carthusians, and Benedictines, which are composed of independent abbeys headed by abbots, the abbot general functions as a kind of superior general with limited powers; he may act as a visitator, as representative of the Order to the Holy See (usually maintaining a residence and office in Rome), and as presider at general chapters of abbots. The powers of the abbot general vary from order to order. Cf. CCC 1672

Abbot, Titular (TIH-tshoo-ler A-buht): A retired abbot of an active monastery who has been named abbot of a suppressed or defunct monastery. Cf. CCC 1672

Abdication (ab-dih-KAY-shuhn): The act of relinquishing a position of authority.

Abduction (ab-DUHK-shuhn): The unlawful carrying away of a woman for purposes of marriage or intercourse. Also, a diriment impediment to marriage in the Code of Canon Law (cf. Can. 1089). Cf. CCC 2297

Abel (AY-buhl): The second son of Adam and Eve (according to Gn 4:2), a shepherd, killed out of jealousy by his brother Cain (Gn 4:3). Christ mentions him as the first of a line of prophets who were killed (Mt 23:35). The Fathers of the Church regarded Abel as a type of Christ. One of the prayers of the Roman Canon (Eucharistic Prayer I) refers to him along with Abraham and Melchizedek, CCC 58, 401, 2259

Abib (ah-VEEV): Originally, the name of the first month of the Hebrew calendar (March-April), later known as Nisan. Cf. CCC 1170

Abiogenesis (AY-bai-o-DZHEHN-uh-sihs): The scientific term for "spontaneous generation," the emergence of living from nonliving matter.

Abjuration (AB-dzhøø-RAY-shun): The formal disclaiming under oath whereby a person renounces or recants a heresy. CCC 2089; cf. 817

Ablution (uh-BLØØ-shuhn): 1. Ritual purification with water (or wine and water) of the sacred vessels or the priest's (or other authorized minister's) fingers following contact with the Sacred Species of the Lord's Body and Blood. 2. The wine/water that has been poured into the chalice and drunk by the priest (or other minister) who purifies the sacred vessels.

Ablution Cup (uh-BLÖÖ-shuhn kup): The small bowl-shaped vessel with cover, kept with a small linen towel near the tabernacle to permit cleansing of the thumb and index finger of those who have assisted with the distribution of Holy Communion or who are returning Hosts to the tabernacle following Communion to the sick.

Abnegation (AB-nih-GAY-shuhn): The spiritual practice of self-denial or mortification, through fasting, abstinence, or refraining from legitimate pleasure, in order to make up for past sins or in order to join oneself to the passion of Christ. CCC 37, 908

Abomination of Desolation (uh-BAH-mih-NAY-shuhn uhv deh-so-LAY-shuhn): Phrase descriptive of the defiling of the Temple of Jerusalem by Antiochus Epiphanes (168 B.C.), who erected an altar to Zeus, thus driving away the Jewish worshippers and even God from that desecrated place, as foretold by Daniel (Dn 11:31; cf. Dn 9:27; 12:11; 1 Mc 1:48). The N.T. applies this prophecy to the siege of Jerusalem (A.D. 70), which signals the nearness of the end of this world and Christ's second coming, or *parousia* (Mk 13:14; Mt 24:15; cf. Lk 21:20; 2 Thes 2:3).

Abortion (uh-BOR-shuhn): The removal of a nonviable embryo or fetus from the womb or the direct killing of such.

Abortion may be "direct" (i.e., when the death of the child is intended) or "indirect" (i.e., when the death is a side effect of another morally good action). The Church has always taught the gravity of direct abortion. The penalty of excommunication may be incurred by anyone cooperating with the act; however, the Sacrament of Penance is always available for anyone connected to this sin (cf. Can. 1398). On December 5, 1989, the Pontifical Commission for the Authentic Interpretation of the Code of Canon Law — with the approval of Pope John Paul II — asserted that abortion is any killing of an immature fetus (which may result from the use of abortifacient drugs like the Pill, RU-486, and the implants placed under the skin of a woman's arm). **CCC 2270-2275**

Aboulia or Abulia (uh-BÖÖ-lee-uh): (Greek: literally, loss of will) A psychological illness characterized by a pathological inability to make decisions or to act.

Abraham (AY-bruh-ham): The Hebrew patriarch who, according to the account presented in Genesis 12-25, was born at Ur in Chaldea and was inspired by God to go to Haran and then to Canaan. In promises confirmed by a covenant, God assured Abraham an innumerable posterity by his wife Sarah. Abraham's fidelity and obedience to God were such that he was willing to sacrifice his son Isaac. As heir to the promises made to Abraham, the Church numbers herself, with the people of Israel, as among the spiritual descendants of Abraham, who is our father in faith (see Rom 4:11, Gal 3:7, Heb 11:8-10). **CCC 59-60, 72, 705-706, 762, 144-146, 2570-2572**

Abraham's Bosom (AY-bruh-hamz BÖÖ-zuhm): Phrase used in Lk 16:19-31 in the parable about the rich man and Lazarus; when both die on the same night, Lazarus is carried to "the bosom of Abraham," while the rich man finds himself in great suffering in Hades. In the late intertestamental literature, "just ones" are depicted as being received at death by Abraham, Isaac, and Jacob into a heavenly banquet (cf. 2 Mc 1:2; Mt 8:11); in the ancient Near East, honored guests were invited to recline at the host's right (or bosom) side. In the parable, Lazarus can be understood as enjoying a high place of honor and esteem in paradise. **CCC 633**

Abram (AY-bruhm): (Hebrew: *ab ram,* exalted father, possibly a shortened form *of abi ram,* my father is exalted) The name given to the patriarch Abraham by his father Terah; he is called Abram in the narrative of Gn 11:26—17:4; in Gn 17:5, God changes his name to Abraham as a sign of the divine promise that he is to become "the father of many nations"; by God's choice of a new name for Abraham, He shows His particular Fatherly care for him as His son. **CCC 59**

Abrogation (a-bro-GAY-shuhn): Abolishing or eliminating a law by official action. In Canon Law, abrogation takes place through a direct decree of the Holy See or by the enactment of a later or subsequent law contrary to the former law.

Absence, Ecclesiastical (eh-klee-zee-AS-tih-kuhl AB-sehns): Nonparticipation (authorized or not) in an activity in which one's presence is required (e.g., elections, deliberations, judicial proceedings, or religious functions). The term may also refer to long periods of nonresidence in the locations where ecclesiastical offices are held (e.g., dioceses or abbeys).

Absolute (AB-so-lööt): 1. The philosophical term, introduced at the end of the eighteenth century and employed by Scholasticism, signifying "perfect being," i.e., God, Who does not rely upon anyone for existence. Modern philosophy has added two new notions: (a) the Absolute is the sum of all being; (b) it has no relationship with other things, thereby making the Absolute unknowable. This agnostic stance is contrary to Catholicism, which holds that God is the cause — not the sum — of all being and that He is knowable, at least in part, by His creatures. 2. Certain truths, revealed by God, which cannot change. These principles are absolute because their divine Source is absolute. **Cf. CCC 36, 50, 213**

Absolution (ab-so-LÖÖ-shuhn): The forgiveness of a debt either by the remission of sin in the Sacrament of Penance or the lifting of a canonical penalty. Christ gave the Church the authority to "bind" and "loose" (Mt 16:19); the power to forgive sin was also granted (Mt 18:18; Jn 20:22-23). CCC 979, 1446

Absolution, General (DZHEN-er-uhl ab-so-LÖÖ-shuhn): Absolution conferred by a priest on a group of persons who are unable to confess their sins individually. Circumstances where such absolution is appropriate include situations where there is danger of imminent death (such as wartime when soldiers are on their way to battle) or where there is habitually no opportunity for confession. After the danger passes and when there is a priest available, one who has received general absolution is nonetheless bound to the individual confession of serious sins. CCC 1483

Absolution of an Accomplice (ab-so-LÖÖ-shuhn uhv an uh-KAHM-plihs): The sacramental absolution of sin by a priest of a person with whom he had committed a sexual sin. This constitutes a crime in Canon Law that results in the automatic penalty of excommunication, reserved to the Holy See (cf. Can. 1378.1). Cf. CCC 1463

Abstinence (AB-stih-nehns): 1. Penitential: Depriving oneself of meat or of foods prepared with meat on days prescribed by the Church as "penitential": Ash Wednesday, Good Friday, and all Fridays of the year that are not solemnities (in the United States, not all Fridays of the year but only the Fridays of Lent). The discipline binds those fourteen years of age and above. 2. Sexual: To refrain from sexual intercourse, completely (total abstinence) or periodically (periodic abstinence or periodic continence). Total abstinence is observed in obedience to the Sixth Commandment by single persons and couples whose marriages are not recognized by the Church as valid. Periodic abstinence is observed by a married couple for regulating conception by natural means or for ascetical motives.

Abstinence, Day of (DAY uhv AB-stih-nehns): In current Church practice, a day on which the faithful, above the age of reason, must refrain from eating meat. Ash Wednesday and Good Friday are days of abstinence, as are at least the

Fridays of Lent in the U.S. The practice of abstinence is intended to remind Christians of their sins and the need to repent, and in this way to enter more deeply into the mystery of Christ's passion and death. CCC 2043

Abstinence, Penitential (peh-nih-TEHN-shuhl AB-stih-nehns): Depriving oneself of meat or of foods prepared with meat (sauces, gravies, soups from meat stock) on days prescribed by the Church as "penitential." According to the 1983 Code of Canon Law (cc. 1249-1253), the universal Church designates as penitential days all Fridays of the year that are not solemnities, as well as Ash Wednesday and Good Friday. Each national conference of bishops, however, may adapt this universal law for particular regions. Accordingly, in 1966 the bishops of the United States determined that in their jurisdiction, abstinence would be obligatory only on the Fridays of Lent, Ash Wednesday, and Good Friday. While strongly recommending that abstinence be observed on *all* Fridays of the year as the privileged and traditional way of commemorating the day of the Lord's passion, the United States' bishops permitted Catholics to substitute other works of charity and devotion on Fridays outside Lent. When issuing their pastoral letter on peace, the bishops recommended abstinence (and fasting, when possible) on all Fridays for the intention of world peace and as an act of solidarity with the world's hungry. CCC 1438, 2043

Abstinence, Sexual (SEHK-shöö-uhl AB-stih-nehns): Refraining from sexual intercourse completely (total abstinence) or at certain times for specific reasons (periodic abstinence or periodic continence). CCC 2349, 2370, 2520; cf. 1650

Abstract (AB-strakt): In contrast to "concrete," the consideration of some quality apart from application to or instantiation in some object or circumstances.

Abstraction (ab-STRAK-shuhn): In the theory of knowledge, the intellectual process by which concepts are formed in the mind. As the term itself suggests, abstraction takes place as the individuating material characteristics of a particular object are left behind, in order to form a general concept that can cover an indefinite number of similar entities in the world. Thus, for example, the concept of "dog" is applicable to many kinds and individuals that are in reality distinguishable and particular beings.

Abuna (uh-BŌŌ-nuh): (Geez: literally, "our father") Term used to refer to the patriarch of the Abyssinian Church.

Abuse (uh-BYŌŌS): The wrong or improper use of ecclesiastical power or authority by a cleric or layperson. A crime in the Code of Canon Law (cf. Can. 1389).

Abyss (uh-BIHS): A term sometimes used by spiritual writers and mystics to describe the infinite being and love of God, His power continually and unendingly to draw the soul into union and rest in Him. **CCC 1439**

Abyssinian Church (a-bih-SIHN-ee-uhn TSHERTSH): The Abyssinian, or Ethiopian, Church dates back to the missionary work of St. Frumentius in the fourth century. Although at one time entirely dependent on the Monophysite patriarch of the Coptic Church in Egypt, the Abyssinian Church is independent today and is not in communion with Rome. Geez is the official language of the liturgy.

Acacianism (uh-KAY-shuhn-ihz-uhm): A fifth-century heresy, named after the Patriarch Acacius, which held that the Father and Son were one Person.

Academies, Pontifical (pahn-TIH-fih-kuhl uh-KA-duh-meez): Societies founded under the direction of the Holy See to promote scholarship in the sciences, the fine arts, music, archaeology, literature, and diplomacy; their members are appointed directly by the Pope. Among them are the Pontifical Academy of the Sciences, founded in 1603, with membership drawn from distinguished mathematicians and experimental scientists, regardless of creed, and the Pontifical Ecclesiastical Academy, which is charged with training priests who will serve in the diplomatic corps of the Vatican Secretariat of State.

Academy of Sciences, Pontifical (pahn-TIH-fih-kuhl uh-KA-duh-mee uhv SAI-ehn-sehz): Founded in 1603 by Frederico Cesi, Giovanni Heck, Francesco Stelluti, and Anastasio Dei Feliis, with the title *Linceorum Academia* (Academy of the Lynx), the academy was devoted to the scientific study of nature, mathematics, philosophy, and literature. After a period of decline, the Academy was restored by Pope Pius IX in 1847, enlarged by Pope Leo XIII in 1887, and refounded with new statutes under its present title by Pope Pius XI in 1936. Through its long evolution, the Academy has come to concentrate on the natural and mathematical sciences. Its core membership consists of eighty *accademici pontifici,* in addition to permanent and honorary members.

Acadians (uh-KAY-dee-uhns): French colonists on the island of Nova Scotia who were deported by the British in the mid-eighteenth century. Some returned to France, others fled to Canada, and still others were quartered in British colonies. The best-known group went to French Louisiana where their descendants are known as "Cajuns" (from "Acadians").

A capella (AH kuh-PEH-lah): (Italian: In chapel style) A style of singing characterized by the absence of the accompaniment of musical instruments.

Acathist Hymn (AH-kuh-thihst HIHM): (Also Akathist, from Greek *akathistos:* standing) An office in the form of a prayer-poem celebrated by the Eastern Church in honor of the Virgin Mary, originally on March 25 (Annunciation), now officially as part of the vigil service for the fifth Saturday of Lent and popularly (in some Eastern usages) at other times as a Lenten devotion. CCC 2678

Access (AK-sehs): In Canon Law, the right of entry into a cloister of religious men or women. Also, the ability to present a case to a Church tribunal or court.

Accessory (ak-SEH-so-ree): One who culpably assists another in the performance of an evil action. This may be done by counsel, command, provocation, consent, praise, flattery, concealment, participation, silence, or defense of the evil done. CCC 2480; cf. 1869

Accident (AK-sih-dehnt): A quality, quantity, or relation that is dependent on another entity ("substance") for its existence. An accident is real and objective; it serves as the medium through which the human mind can know a substance. A car, for instance, is a substance, while the color and weight of the vehicle are accidents.

Acclamation (AK-luh-MAY-shuhn): A liturgical response (ideally, sung) by the congregation giving strong assent to the words of the Lord and/or the prayer of the celebrant. CCC 2760; cf. 2589, 1345, 559

Accommodation (uh-KAH-mo-DAY-shuhn): The application of a Scripture text with a meaning remote from the original context and not necessarily intended by the sacred author; this accommodation does not represent the literal sense of Scripture and therefore cannot be used as a proof in establishing doctrine that requires a biblical base. In general, this use of Scripture is more rhetorical than soundly exegetical or theological and should be avoided.

Acculturation (a-KUHL-tsher-AY-shuhn): The process of socialization by which the members of one culture become accustomed to life in another culture. In Catholic usage, the term refers to the efforts by missionaries to learn the language and to adopt the customs of a society, in order to be more effective in the communication of the Faith.

Acephalic [Acephalous] (ah-seh-FAL-ihk) [uh-SEH-fuh-luhs]: (Greek: without a head) Any Christian group without a determinate leader in communion with a recognized hierarchy; this was the status of some ancient groups who separated themselves in schism from the recognized central authority of the Church, as the Nestorians, e.g., who refused to accept the teaching of the Council of Ephesus (A.D. 431) that Mary is truly the Mother of God. Since the term is seen as derisive and ecumenically insensitive, it is generally avoided today.

Achiropoetos, -ta (ay-KAI-ro-po-EH-tos, -tah): (Greek: not made by a human hand) The term used to designate the archetypal Icon, Jesus Christ, as the incarnate Son of God; as Christ appeared on earth in the flesh, so too the representation of the divine in visible form is seen as justification of the use of sacred images. With the Incarnation, the invisible becomes visible, and in Christ we have the prototype Image or Icon; thus the Second Council of Nicaea (A.D. 787) maintained that the veneration given to sacred images by kissing or kneeling before them is in fact referred to Christ and His saints, represented by the icons. Cf. CCC 1159

Acolouthia (AK-uh-LÖÖ-thee-uh): (Greek: hearing) The arrangement of all the Divine Praises, except for the Divine Liturgy itself, in Offices of the Eastern Rites, especially that of the Byzantine Rite; it is so called for the participation of the faithful who hear the Offices chanted, structured as they are for public liturgical celebration. The sequence begins with Vespers before sunset, followed by Compline at midnight and Matins at dawn; four of the liturgical hours are followed in a simple numerical sequence: First, early morning; Third, midmorning; Sixth, early afternoon; and Ninth, midafternoon.

Acolyte (A-ko-lait): 1. Previously a "minor order," but since Vatican II a "ministry" into which men are instituted on a permanent or transitory basis to assist the celebrant at Mass and to distribute Holy Communion when necessity demands. 2. Commonly used as the equivalent of "altar server" to denote anyone who serves the Mass or who assists at other church services. CCC 903, 1672

Acquired Rights (uh-KWAIRD RAITS): Rights obtained through a completed legal transaction or as a result of the assumption of ecclesiastical authority (cf. Can. 6).

Acta Apostolicae Sedis (AHK-tuh ah-po-STAHL-ee-tshay SAY-dihs): (Latin: Acts of the Apostolic See) The journal of

30

record of the Holy See, containing official texts of papal pronouncements and decrees and the means of formal promulgation of Canon Law.

Acta Sanctae Sedis (AHK-tuh SAHNK-tay SAY-dihs): (Latin: Acts of the Holy See) The journal of record of the Holy See until 1909, when the name was changed to *Acta Apostolicae Sedis.*

Acta Sanctorum (AHK-tuh sahnk-TO-røøm): (Latin: Acts of the Saints) The title of the series of saints' lives collected, edited, and published by the Bollandists. The series of critical editions was begun by the Jesuit John van Bolland (1596-1665) and continues, in a modified form, to this day.

Action Française (ahk-see-ON frahn-SEHZ): A French social and political movement founded in 1908 by Charles Maurras to promote royalist and nationalistic ideals. It sought to use the Church in carrying out its agenda, but when it advocated an overthrow of the government and expressed racist ideas, it was condemned in 1926 by Pope Pius XI. When the movement underwent some reform, the ban was lifted by Pope Pius XII in 1939; it has no real influence today.

Actions, Human (HYÖÖ-muhn AK-shuhnz): Actions are specifically human when they proceed from deliberation and issue in choice. Such actions are distinguished from the whole range of spontaneous, instinctual, and biological processes and activities that are not deliberative and voluntary. In addition, human actions are distinguished from actions undertaken by agents without the use of reason or under compulsion. Strictly speaking, then, human actions are those over which the agent is master. Only proper human actions can be moral or immoral. Factors conditioning the knowledge (e.g., ignorance) and will (e.g., passion or violence) of the agent influence the moral character of one's actions. CCC 1749; cf. 1732

Active Life (AK-tiv LAIF): Often synonymous with "active orders," this term can also refer more broadly to any forms

— including lay — of living the Christian life that involve a particular dedication to the corporal and spiritual works of mercy. The term implies a contrast with "contemplative life," where the primary emphasis is upon prayer and silence. In fact, all authentic Christian life must involve active and contemplative dimensions, although in some states of life one or another dimension attains a primacy. Cf. CCC 900, 928-929

Active Orders (AK-tiv OR-derz): An expression used to describe those religious institutes in which the members (priests, Brothers, or Sisters) engage in some form of activity such as teaching, nursing, and missionary work. Communities of this type are distinguished from contemplative institutes, in which the monks and nuns remain within their cloisters to chant the Liturgy of the Hours and to engage in works for the support of their communities. CCC 925-927

Act of God (AKT uhv GAHD): The legal term designating an occurrence beyond the control of man. A natural disaster, like a tornado, is allowed by God and therefore is spoken of as an act of God.

Act of Supremacy (AKT uhv söö-PREH-muh-see): Enacted by Parliament under Henry VIII in 1543, then renewed and modified by Elizabeth I in 1559, this law established the reigning sovereign as the earthly head of the Church of England. Communion with Rome was thereby brought to an end. All clerics, ecclesiastics, and public officials were required to acknowledge the royal supremacy by oath.

Act of Toleration (AKT uhv tah-ler-AY-shuhn): An act of the British Parliament (1689) granting freedom of the practice of religion to all but Catholics and certain sects denying the Trinity. It has since been repealed.

Act of Worship (AKT uhv WER-shihp): Any act by which glory and honor are given to God, Who is properly the object of worship. To accord such honor to a creaturely object is in effect to engage in idolatry. Thus, an act of worship is an act in which the creature prayerfully acknowledges his or her Creator. The sacred liturgy of the Mass and of the Divine Office are the official acts of worship of the Church. **CCC 1069-1070**

Acts, Canonical (ka-NAH-nih-kuhl AKTS): 1. The official record of any process taking place according to Canon Law. 2. Actions having a legal effect in Canon Law.

Acts of Faith (AKTS uhv FAYTH): Any actions — whether prayers or confessions of faith — by which the theological virtue of faith is exercised and cultivated. **Cf. CCC 1816**

Acts of Paul (AKTS uhv PAWL): One of a series of apocryphal (noncanonical) works that purport to provide information not given in the Acts of the Apostles. Tertullian is the first to mention the Acts of Paul, but it was not until the twentieth century that the contents of this work could be determined. The Acts of Paul contains the story of Paul and Thecla, alleged correspondence of St. Paul with the Corinthians, and a legendary description of the martyrdom of St. Paul. Although these Acts were never accepted as part of the canon of Sacred Scripture, they exerted a considerable influence on Christian art and liturgy.

Acts of Pilate (AKTS uhv PAI-luht): An apocryphal work dating from the fifth century, though comprising older materials. The Acts of Pilate contains a legendary account of the trial, crucifixion, and burial of Jesus, as well as a description of debates held by the Sanhedrin after the resurrection of Christ, and finally, an allegedly eyewitness account of Christ's descent into hell.

Acts of Settlement (AKTS uhv SEH-tuhl-mehnt): Two official acts of the Irish and British Parliaments, respectively. The first sought to restore lost property to Protestants and Catholics, while the second requires the monarch of England to be a member of the Church of England.

Acts of the Apostles (AKTS uhv *th*ee uh-PAH-suhlz): The fifth book of the N.T., written by St. Luke in Greek, ca. A.D. 63, which serves as the sequel to his Gospel. The work of the

Hellenistic Church, it is written in the style of biographies of famous men, such as Alexander the Great and Hannibal, but is much closer to biblical histories, such as Kings and Maccabees. As a historical narrative, it seeks to chronicle the important events in the life of the early Church: the founding of the Church on Pentecost; the Holy Spirit's guidance of the Church's missionary activity; the preaching of Peter, Paul, and Barnabas; the persecution of the Christians; the miracles worked in confirmation of their faith; and the rapid expansion of Christianity throughout the Mediterranean world. Acts describes in detail the universal mission of the Church — in particular, God's desire to save and reconcile the world to Himself through His Son within the context of His Church; this divine will is in no way impeded by ethnic, linguistic, or cultural barriers. In this sense, it is apologetical as well as historical.

Acts of the Martyrs (AKTS uhv *th*uh MAHR-terz): A large and disparate collection of writings from various sources detailing the lives of the Church's earliest martyrs.

Acts of the Saints (AKTS uhv *th*uh SAYNTS): An extensive collection of the saints' lives compiled by the Bollandists.

Actual Grace (AK-tshöö-uhl GRAYS): The divine assistance that heals one of sin, elevates the faculties of the intellect, the will, and the memory, and gives an action a "supernatural" character. Without actual grace, one cannot observe the natural law. The Church contends, in opposition to Jansenism, that one must have an assisting grace in order to perform a supernatural act. **CCC 2000, 2024**

Actual Sin (AK-tshöö-uhl SIHN): An action, not synonymous with moral evil, which is contrary to God's love. Not loving one's enemy is a sin against charity and, therefore, an actual sin, but it may not be a moral evil, which contravenes a natural moral norm like justice or truth. One may commit an actual sin against God, one's neighbor, or oneself that is grave or venial. For an actual sin to be culpable, it must be voluntary and done with full knowledge and consent. Culpability for actual sins is limited by insufficient consent, restricted freedom, or inadequate knowledge. CCC 1849-1864

Acus (A-kuhs): (Latin: pin, needle; pl. *aci*) The pin used by the Pope and all metropolitan archbishops to fasten the pallium to the chasuble. Most often it is made of gold and decorated with precious or semiprecious stones and liturgical symbols.

A.D. (AY DEE): The abbreviation for the Latin *Anno Domini,* translated "in the year of the Lord," and used in the system of dating in effect since the sixth century to count the years since the birth of Christ.

Adam (A-duhm): The first man, who, together with his wife, Eve, lived in the Garden of Eden. Blessed with many gifts — including immortality — from the hand of God, Adam yielded to the temptation proposed by Satan and so committed the Original Sin as a result. Jesus Christ is the "Second Adam," Who was promised after the Fall. Jesus' "yes" to the Father repairs the damage done by the refusal of Adam and Eve to obey the Lord. CCC 399, 402-405; cf. 359

Adamites (A-duh-maits): An obscure group that appeared first in the second century and from time to time until the fifteenth century, espousing everyday nakedness.

Ad Bestias (ahd BEHS-tee-ahs): (Latin: To the beasts) Expression for the condemnation of Christians to mortal combat with wild animals in the arena during the Roman persecutions.

Address, Papal (PAY-puhl uh-DREHS): Any formal or semiformal allocution or speech made by the Pope.

Adeste Fideles (uh-DEHS-tay fee-DAY-lehz): A Latin Christmas carol whose text and music were composed by John Francis Wade (c. 1711-1786). The carol was translated into English with the title "O Come All Ye Faithful" by Frederick Oakeley (1802-1880) and others.

Ad Gentes (ahd DZHEHN-tehz): The Decree, promulgated on December 7, 1965, by the Second Vatican Council, outlining the doctrine and nature of the missionary activity of the Church. This Decree reaffirms the fundamental missionary character of the Church; the norms for its implementation were promulgated by Pope Paul VI on August 6, 1966, in *Ecclesia Sancta III.*

Ad Hominem (ahd HAW-mee-nehm): This Latin expression refers to two kinds of arguments, one logically fallacious and the other valid. A fallacious argument *ad hominem* is one that seeks to draw general implications from a premise concerning a single individual. A valid argument *ad hominem* is one in which an arguer moves from a premise that the other party accepts (while the arguer may not) to a conclusion rejected by the other party.

Adjuration (A-dzhuh-RAY-shuhn): An appeal or command to act in God's name. In Mt 26:63, the High Priest adjured Christ to declare whether or not He was the Messiah. Adjuration should be used only when the adjurer is seeking the truth and when the command is just. **Cf. CCC 2147**

Ad Libitum (ahd LIH-bee-tøøm): A Latin expression indicating that the manner of performing some task is at the discretion of the one acting.

Ad Limina [Apostolorum] (ahd LIH-mih-nuh) [uh-PAHS-to-LAW-røøm]: (Latin: To the threshold of the Apostles' [tombs]) The visit that each diocesan bishop (Ordinary) must make, at five-year intervals, to pray at the tombs of Sts. Peter and Paul in Rome and to report to the Pope and curial officials regarding the state of his diocese.

Administration, Apostolic (a-pah-STAH-lihk ad-mih-nih-STRAY-shuhn): An officially established territorial division of the Church lacking the stability of a diocese. Not headed by a bishop but by an apostolic administrator.

Administration of the Sacraments (ad-mih-nih-STRAY-shuhn uhv *th*uh SA-kruh-mehnts): The act of conferring, according to the proper canonical, liturgical, and pastoral norms, one of the seven sacraments. A valid administration of the sacraments requires that the duly appointed minister, who acts in the name of Christ and the Church, use the proper matter and form, and have the correct intention (i.e., "to do what the Church does"). Neither lack of faith nor state of sin on the part of the minister militates against validity. An ordinary minister possesses authority by virtue of his office; an extraordinary minister has delegated authority.

Administrative Act (ad-mih-nih-STRAY-tihv AKT): A decree, precept, or order issued by one having executive power of governance according to Canon Law, usually in writing (cf. cc. 35-47).

Administrative Recourse (ad-mih-nih-STRAY-tihv REE-kawrs): A process of appeal in Canon Law against administrative decrees of superiors (cf. cc. 1732-1739).

Administrator (ad-mih-nih-STRAY-ter): 1. An office in Canon Law. One who is officially appointed for a temporary period to perform the duties of the person holding the permanent office. There are diocesan, parish, and apostolic administrators. 2. Also, a cleric or layperson charged with the management of church property or other temporal goods (cf. cc. 1281-1289).

Admonition (ad-muh-NIH-shuhn): Official warning required by Canon Law that must be issued to a person accused of a crime before a penalty is imposed (cf. cc, 1339, 1348).

Ad Nutum Sanctae Sedis (ahd NÖÖ-tøøm SAHNK-tay SAY-dihs): (Latin: At the will of the Holy See) The phrase indicates that a person holds an office at the discretion of the Pope.

Adonai (A-do-nai): The O.T. Hebrew term for God, meaning "Lord" or "my Lord." It was used as a substitution for the unspeakable name "Yahweh," in order to demonstrate profound reverence. **CCC 209**

Adoption, Canonical (ka-NAH-nih-kuhl uh-DAHP-shuhn): A diriment impediment to marriage. In Canon Law (cf. Can. 1094), it refers to the legal relationship that arises in the direct line (parent and child) or in the second degree collateral line (siblings).

Adoptionism (uh-DAHP-shuhn-ihz-uhm): The heresy that claims that Jesus Christ, in His humanity, is not the true Son of God, but is only adopted. Its roots are found in the Monarchian, Ebionite, and Nestorian heresies, and became more defined in the eighth century, when it was condemned by the Second Council of Nicaea (787) and the Council of Frankfort (794). **Cf. CCC 465**

Adoption, Supernatural (söö-per-NATSH-er-uhl uh-DAHP-shuhn): The state of being a child of God by virtue of our status as brothers and sisters of Christ — the Great Reconciler of all things to the Father. Before Original Sin, we were "natural" children of God, but the Fall destroyed that close relationship to the Lord, which was finally repaired through the Incarnation. **CCC 460**

Adoration (a-do-RAY-shuhn): An outward act of giving worship to a person or object. Both the Old and New Testaments give clear indications that God requires exclusive adoration from His creatures. The most perfect form of worship is the Holy Sacrifice of the Mass because it is the re-presentation of Christ's paschal mystery. Adoration may also be internal (e.g., contemplative prayer). **CCC 2096-2097**

Adoration, Perpetual (per-PEH-tshöö-uhl a-do-RAY-shuhn): The practice of the continuous exposition of the Blessed Sacrament, usually in the monstrance, for the purposes of uninterrupted vigil and adoration on the part of the faithful. Exposition and adoration of the Blessed Sacrament are seen by Catholics as means of focusing the heart and mind in prayer, with attention fixed on the mystery of the Eucharistic presence of Christ in the Church. **Cf. CCC 1418**

Adorer (uh-DAW-rer): Usually, one who engages in adoration of Christ as He is present in the Blessed Sacrament.

Adult (uh-DUHLT): In civil and Canon Law, an adult is one who has reached maturity.

Adultery (uh-DUHL-ter-ee): Sexual intercourse between a married person and one who is not a spouse. In Canon Law, it is considered sufficient reason for a separation of spouses but is not in itself a sufficient cause for nullity of marriage. CCC 2380-2381

Advena (AHD-veh-nuh): (Latin: temporary resident) The term used in Canon Law to designate one who resides for a time in a place where he has quasi-domicile. The term distinguishes such a person from: (1) a permanent resident *(incola)* in the place of domicile; (2) a traveler *(peregrinus)* when away from the place of domicile or quasi-domicile; (3) a transient *(vagus),* who has neither domicile nor quasi-domicile anywhere.

Advent (AD-vehnt): 1. In the Latin (Roman) Rite, the liturgical season of approximately four weeks before Christmas during which the themes of joyful expectation and devout conversion combine to prepare the faithful for the remembrance of the Lord's first coming in His Incarnation and for His glorious coming at the end of time. 2. In the Ambrosian Rite (Milan and Northern Italy), a similar liturgical season of six weeks. 3. In the Byzantine Rite, an unofficial term sometimes used popularly to designate the corresponding but shorter "Nativity pre-feast" period. CCC 524

Adventist (ad-VEHN-tihst): Doctrinal position advanced by the Seventh Day Adventists and other small Protestant groups that Christ's Second Coming is imminent and that the exact time and place can be determined by their interpretation of specific biblical passages, such as Rom 13:12, 1 Pt 1:20, and Rv 20:3. The Adventist movement originated in the work and writings of William Miller (1782-1849), who preached in the Dresden, New York, area in the mid-nineteenth century.

Advent of Christ (AD-vehnt uhv KRAIST): This expression refers to the Incarnation of the Second Person of the

Blessed Trinity in human flesh. The Incarnation is thus Christ's coming among us, or His advent. Cf. CCC 461-463

Advent Wreath (AD-vehnt REETH): A decorative table wreath, usually composed of holly or fir branches. The wreath is constructed to hold four candles (of which three are purple and one is rose-colored) standing for the four Sundays of Advent. In a paraliturgical service, either in the home or at the beginning of the Sunday Eucharist, the candles are lighted on the consecutive Sundays of Advent until, by the fourth Sunday, all of the candles are burning. The practice is meant to cultivate a deeper sense of the liturgical season of Advent.

Advocate (AD-vo-kuht): A cleric or layperson appointed by a bishop to represent a person and safeguard his/her rights in a canonical court process (cf. cc. 1481-1490).

Advocate of God (AD-vo-kuht uhv GAHD): In the process of beatification and canonization, the title of the official whose responsibility is to promote the cause of the person under consideration for sainthood.

Advocate of the Church (AD-vo-kuht uhv *th*uh TSHERTSH): A discontinued office, once held by laymen who were appointed to defend the temporal interests of the Church in civil courts.

Advocatus Diaboli (ahd-vo-KAH-tøøs dee-AH-bo-lee): (Latin: devil's advocate) Whimsical term that formerly designated the official in a process of canonization whose duty was to advance evidence and arguments against the elevation of the person in question to sainthood.

Advocatus of the Roman Congregations (ahd-vo-KAH-tøøs uhv *th*uh RO-muhn kahn-greh-GAY-shuhns): (Latin: advocate) An attorney especially trained and allowed to practice before the Roman congregations and tribunals.

Advowson (ad-VAU-suhn): A benefactor of the Church who had donated property and was allowed to nominate clerics to hold canonical positions over that property. Today the practice is defunct.

Aeon (EE-ahn): A long period of time, perpetuity (Rom 16:27; Jn 6:51, 58); a historical epoch or period (Mt 12:32); material reality (Heb 1:2); powerful beings hostile to God (1 Tm 4:1; Eph 2:2; Col 2:15). In Greek philosophy, the term represents an element of cosmology that the Gnostics applied to those spiritual beings that emanated from the Divine Being and constituted the *pleroma* (invisible spiritual world). In some Gnostic heresies, the term is applied to Christ Himself.

Aequiprobabilism (eh-kwee-PRAH-buh-bih-lih-zuhm): One of a number of methods for arriving at certainty concerning the morality of a projected course of action when the agent is in doubt. According to aequiprobabilism, when conflicting opinions are equally or almost equally probable, it is lawful to follow the more favorable opinion if the doubt concerns the existence of a law. But if the doubt concerns the cessation of a law, then one must observe the law. St. Alphonsus Liguori (1696-1787) developed this method in opposition to the probabilism favored by some Jesuit moral theologians of his day.

Aer (EHR): In the Byzantine Rite, the large veil used to cover both the chalice and the diskos.

Aesthetics (ehs-THEH-tihks): The study or philosophy of beauty, and the theory of people's response to it. St. Thomas Aquinas taught that the principal ingredients of beauty were integrity of form, proportion, and radiance. Cf. CCC 2500-2503

Aestimative Sense (eh-STIH-muh-tihv SEHNS): In the theory of knowledge, the internal power by which one discerns, at the level of sense perception, the useful or offensive character of particular objects.

Aeterni Patris (ay-TEHR-nee PAH-trihs): The encyclical of Pope Leo XIII, promulgated on August 4, 1874, in which the study of philosophy, and especially of St. Thomas Aquinas, was commended to the Church. This important encyclical marked the beginning of a revival of the study of the great figures of scholastic philosophy, including (in addition to St. Thomas) St. Albertus Magnus, St. Bonaventure, and Bl. John Duns Scotus. The influential neo-scholastic and neo-Thomistic movements date from this revival.

Aetianism (EE-shuhn-ih-zuhm): An obscure fourth-century heresy founded by Aetius. A brand of Arianism. **Cf. CCC 465**

Affability (A-fuh-BIHL-ih-tee): The virtue of affability or politeness is related to the cardinal virtue of justice. As social beings, we are required in justice to conduct ourselves in a courteous and agreeable manner in our dealings and association with others. The vices opposed to affability are flattery (excessive praise of others to obtain special favors) and contentiousness (frequent contradiction of others). **Cf. CCC 1807**

Affectio Maritalis (uh-FEHK-see-o mah-ree-TAH-lihs): (Latin: marital affection) A legal term found in Roman Law and medieval Canon Law. In Roman Law, it referred to the attitude or continuous state of mind of being married. In medieval Canon Law, there exists no official definition, yet it was used in various decrees and texts and generally refers to the attitude whereby one treats a spouse as a spouse ought to be treated.

Affections (uh-FEHK-shuhnz): Emotional responses of delight or revulsion to particular objects of sense perception. Christian spiritual life involves the discipline of affection or the training of the heart, so as to cultivate an ordered response to the good things of life and to grow in virtue. **Cf. CCC 2545**

Affective Prayer (uh-FEHK-tiv PREHR): The lifting of the heart to God in words and silent longings expressive of loving devotion. **Cf. CCC 2563, 2717**

Affinity (uh-FIH-nih-tee): In Canon Law, a diriment impediment to marriage. It is the canonical relationship between a spouse and all relatives in the direct line of the other spouse (parent, grandparent, child). Such marriages are prohibited (cf. Can. 1092).

Affusion (uh-FYÖÖ-zhuhn): The practice of baptizing by means of pouring water over the head of the baptizand. Cf. CCC 1239-1240

Africa, Church in (TSHERTSH ihn AF-rih-kuh): Although it is not exactly known how Christianity spread to North Africa (present-day Morocco, Algeria, Tunisia, and Libya), there is evidence that the Church was well organized by the end of the second century. Even while Greek was the general language of the Church, a Latin Bible and liturgy were being used in Africa. Alexandria, long a center of pre-Christian philosophy and religious thought, saw the development of Coptic Christianity and produced many of the early Church's best-known theologians, both orthodox and heretical, including Clement, Origen, Apollinaris, and Cyril. Persecution by the Emperor Decius (250) led to controversy and schism, but the Church recovered strength under the leadership of St. Cyprian of Carthage, as it faced new persecution under the Emperor Valerian (258). The fourth century saw further struggles against heresies, especially Donatism, but the rise of saints like Augustine of Hippo (d. 430) led to a period that included the growth of monasticism and the series of African Councils that produced canons incorporated into Greek and Latin Canon Law. This era of growth was brought to a close by the Vandal invaders (429), and the weakened Church was reduced to a shadow of its former glory through Muslim dominance of the area. A resurgence of faith began once more in the fifteenth century by Portuguese missionaries, who worked mostly in sub-Saharan Africa. The Catholic Faith gained a foothold in most parts of Africa, including North Africa, and by the post-World War II era the Church was developing rapidly throughout the continent. The first two native African bishops were ordained in 1939, and now most dioceses are led by native bishops.

African Liturgy (AF-rih-kuhn LIH-ter-dzhee): An extinct Latin Rite liturgy in use in North Africa prior to the Arab invasion in the seventh century.

African Methodist Episcopal Church [A.M.E.] (AF-rih-kuhn MEH-tho-dihst ih-PIHS-kuh-puhl TSHERTSH [AY EHM EE]): Dating from the withdrawal in 1787 of a group of Methodists from St. George Methodist Episcopal Church in Philadelphia, the A.M.E. Church today ranks as one of the three largest Methodist bodies in the U.S., with over two million members and more than six thousand churches. Racial discrimination led Richard Allen to organize the first members of the church in Bethel Chapel. The A.M.E. Church was officially organized in 1816 when Allen was consecrated bishop. Its membership is composed primarily of African Americans.

Agape (ah-GAH-pay): Greek word for love that has come to possess a uniquely Christian sense in referring to the deep and active care God has for the world, and the selflessness appropriate to Christian love of others. It occurs twice in the Synoptics (Mt 24:12; Lk 11:42). The term was also used in the early Church to designate a common meal held either before or after the celebration of the Eucharist. **Cf. CCC 1823**

Age, Canonical (ka-NAH-nih-kuhl AYDZH): An age established by Canon Law required for the reception of certain sacraments or ecclesiastical offices. The canonical age for marriage, for instance, is fourteen for girls and sixteen for boys.

Age Impediment (AYDZH ihm-PEH-dih-mehnt): In Canon Law, a diriment impediment to marriage. A male must be sixteen and a female fourteen to marry validly (cf. Can. 1083).

Age of Consent (AYDZH uhv kuhn-SEHNT): The age at which a person is competent to contract marriage. Also, in civil law, sexual relations with a female below this age constitutes the crime of statutory rape on the part of the male partner.

Age of Discretion (AYDZH uhv dihs-KREH-shuhn): The age under law at which a person can be considered to possess sufficient knowledge to be held responsible for his actions.

Age of Reason (AYDZH uhv REE-zuhn): 1. The time when a person reaches a level of moral responsibility that enables him to choose between right and wrong and to observe various obligations (e.g., to attend Mass on Sundays and holy days of obligation). The end of the seventh year is considered to be the age of reason (later for the mentally retarded). 2. The term designating the eighteenth century's philosophies, consisting of Deist, Encyclopedist, and Rationalist principles, especially in British and French circles.

Aggiornamento (uh-DZHORR-nuh-MEHN-to): An Italian word used to describe the renewal and revitalization of the Church, especially as a result of the Second Vatican Council. Popularized by Pope John XXIII, it seeks new ways of expressing the unchanging truths of the Faith.

Aggregation (AG-gruh-GAY-shuhn): In Canon Law, the process by which one religious institute may become affiliated with another religious institute. For example, in nineteenth-century America, numerous newly founded congregations of religious women became aggregated to the Franciscan and Dominican Orders.

Aggression, Defense Against Unjust (dih-FENS ah-GEHNST uhn-DZHUHST uh-GREH-shuhn): The Church teaches that every person has the strict right to protect himself against an unjust aggressor, even to the point of killing him, provided that the injury done does not exceed what is necessary for the defense of oneself or one's property. CCC 2263-2267

Agility (uh-DZHIHL-ih-tee): One of the qualities supposed to be possessed by a glorified body, permitting passage from one place to another with great speed. Cf. CCC 645

Aglipayan Schism (A-glih-PAI-uhn SIH-zuhm): A splinter, or schismatic, church founded in the Philippines in 1902 by Gregorio Aglipay, who was reconciled to the Church. Now practically insignificant.

Agnet (AG-neht): In Byzantine liturgical celebration of the Eucharist, the agnet is the first piece of bread cut from the prosphora, signifying the action of the Lamb of God (hence *agnet*) Who "takes away the sins of the world."

Agnosticism (ag-NAH-stih-sih-zuhm): The view that it is impossible to know whether or not God exists, since human knowledge cannot reach to any realm beyond sense perception. In opposition to agnosticism, the Church teaches that the human mind is capable of attaining certain basic truths about reality, including that God exists. CCC 2127-2128

Agnus Dei (AHN-yøøs DAY-ee): (Latin: Lamb of God — i.e., Jesus Christ; cf. Jn 1:29, Rv 5:12) 1. Chant sung at Mass during the breaking of the Sacred Host prior to the reception of Holy Communion. 2. A small disc made from wax blessed by the Pope and upon which is imprinted the seal of the Lamb of God.

Agony of Christ (AG-uh-nee uhv KRAIST): The mental anguish and physical distress suffered by Christ when He prayed in the Garden of Gethsemane in the interval between the Last Supper and His arrest. In His prayer, Christ was both drawn by His determination to accomplish the divine will for our salvation and at the same time repelled by His anticipation of the suffering this would entail. The Agony in the Garden, as it is called, is the first Sorrowful Mystery of the Rosary. Cf. CCC 612

Agrapha (AG-ruh-fuh): (Greek: unwritten things) Sayings of Jesus not found in the four canonical Gospels, some of which appear as glosses in various N.T. manuscripts or as commentaries in the writings of Church Fathers; most are apocryphal. Many are sound, edifying sentiments, wholly compatible with the genuine spirit and teaching of Jesus;

several are, in fact, variations or the joining together of words found in the canonical Gospels. Cf. **CCC 120**

A.I.D. (AY AI DEE): Abbreviation for "Artificial Insemination by a Donor," referring to a man's using artificial means to inseminate a woman who is not his wife. From Pope Pius XII to Pope John Paul II, the Church has consistently condemned A.I.D. because the act is adulterous, because conception must occur within the loving act of marital intercourse, and because each child has the right to be reared by its natural parents. **CCC 2376; cf. 2380 2381**

AIDS (AYDZ): Acrostic/abbreviation for "Acquired Immune Deficiency Syndrome," the name of the disease from HIV, an accompanying virus that attacks the human immune system and leaves one susceptible to infectious diseases. AIDS is spread through exchange of bodily fluids — e.g., sexual intercourse, blood transfusions, and intravenous injections — and is sometimes passed from a mother to her preborn child. The virus can remain latent for years; those who die from AIDS-related complications suffer long, painful deaths.

A.I.H. (AY AI AYTSH): Abbreviation for "Artificial Insemination by the Husband," referring to a woman's insemination by her husband through artificial means. The Church has not officially taught that this procedure is immoral when it tries to assist conception after a married couple has engaged in a natural act of intercourse. **CCC 2377; cf. 2379**

Air (EHR): Since in the Bible God's breath signifies His gift of life, breathing out air has sometimes figured in Christian liturgy as a sign of blessing. **CCC 691; cf. 362**

Aisle (AIL): In church buildings, the passageway between sections of pews or seats.

Aitesis (ai-TEE-sihs): In the Byzantine Rite, litany of petition to which the people answer, "Grant this, O Lord."

Akathist Hymn (AK-uh-thist HIHM): (From Greek for "without sitting") Dating from the seventh century or before, the most profound expression of Marian devotion in Eastern Rite churches, consisting of twenty-four sections, which relate to the Infancy Gospel, to the Incarnation, and to the virginal motherhood of Mary. It is sung in part during Byzantine liturgies on the first four Saturdays of Lent and wholly on the fifth Saturday. **CCC 2678**

Akeldama (ah-KEHL-dah-muh): (Aramaic: field of blood or field of sleeping) The plot of ground bought by the Sanhedrin with the money that Judas had received in exchange for his betrayal of Jesus and that Judas then returned to the Council; the term *akeldama* occurs only once in the Scriptures (Acts 1:19). The field, previously known as the "potter's field" (Mt 27:7), is traditionally identified as that outside the city walls of Jerusalem, south of the Ben-Hinnom valley.

Akolouthia (ah-kah-löö-THEE-uh): Greek for "sequence," this term may refer to any ceremony in the Byzantine Rite, but usually designates the recitation of the Liturgy of the Hours or Divine Office.

Alais, Treaty of (TREE-tee uhv ah-LAY): A treaty between the French Huguenots and Catholics in 1629 that removed the Huguenots as rivals to the French throne and resulted in their civil disability.

Alamo (AL-uh-mo): The site of a Franciscan mission, the Alamo was a fortresslike enclosure in San Antonio, defended against an army of Mexicans by a small group of Texans in a fierce battle on March 6, 1836. The Mission of San Antonio de Valera had been founded at San Pedro Springs, Texas, in 1718, and moved to its present location in San Antonio in 1746. It consisted of a friary, church, and hospital surrounded by a wall.

Alb (ALB): White robe that must be worn by deacons and priests and may be worn by other ministers during Mass and other liturgical functions according to rubrics and local custom.

Albania, Church in (TSHERTSH ihn al-BAY-nee-uh): Christianity in Albania dates from the fourth century. In 1054, the Albanian Church followed Byzantium into schism. After Albania became part of the Ottoman empire in the fifteenth century, many Christians were forced to convert to Islam. While over half the population was Muslim, Catholicism prevailed in the northern part of the country. The Communist takeover in 1945 was calamitous for all religions in Albania where persecution was systematic and unrelenting — so much so, that in 1967 the regime proclaimed Albania to be the first truly atheistic State in the world. With the worldwide collapse of Communism, the right to practice religion was restored in Albania in 1990, and in 1991 the Holy See revived diplomatic relations with the country. The effort to rebuild the Church in Albania is now under way.

Albany (AWL-buh-nee): The present capital of New York State and a diocese since 1947, Albany grew from the early Dutch settlement called Fort Orange. The settlement provided refuge for St. Isaac Jogues when he escaped from the Mohawk Indians.

Albigensianism (al-bih-DZHEHN-see-uhn-ih-zuhm): A heresy founded in Southern France in the eleventh century that rejected the sacraments and Church authority, adopted vegetarianism and promiscuity, and repudiated the right of the State to punish criminals. Named after the city of its inception, Albi, in France, it was eradicated by the fourteenth century.

Alcantara, Knights of (NAITS uhv ahl-KAHN-tuh-ruh): A twelfth-century Spanish military order organized to combat the Moors, the Knights of Alcantara is today an honorary order of laymen.

Alcoholism and Related Drug Problems, National Catholic Council on (NA-shuh-nuhl KATH-uh-lihk KAUN-sihl awn AL-kuh-hawl-ih-zuhm and re-LAY-tehd DRUHG PRAH-blehmz): The national agency located in Washington that promotes treatment for those priests, religious, and laity suffering from chemical dependency. Those who work with the addicted are provided with education by this council. Cf. CCC 2211, 2290

Aleph (AHL-ehf): The first letter of the Hebrew alphabet.

Alexandria, Church of (TSHERTSH uhv al-ehg-ZAN-dree-uh): The home of the ancient Catholic Coptic Church in Egypt. The seat of one of the ancient and traditional patriarchates of the East.

Alexandria, Patriarchate of (PAY-tree-AHR-kayt uhv al-ehg-ZAN-dree-uh): The foundation of the Church in Alexandria is ascribed by tradition to St. Mark. At the Council of Nicaea (325), the preeminence of the Church at Alexandria was acknowledged when the patriarchate was ranked second only to Rome and even before Antioch. But subsequently, Constantinople was accorded precedence over Alexandria. The patriarchate gradually lost its influence, especially after the Muslim invasion of Egypt in 642. At the division between the Eastern and Western Churches, Alexandria sided with Constantinople. In addition to the Greek Patriarch of Alexandria, there are also Coptic and Latin patriarchs. Cf. CCC 247, 1203

Alexandria, School of (SKÖÖL uhv al-ehg-ZAN-dree-uh): The history of the once-flourishing School of Alexandria closely tracks that of the Church of Alexandria. In a tradition already well-placed in Hellenic and Judaic studies, Christian thinkers of the caliber of Cyril, Clement, and most notably perhaps, Athanasius, combined to place the ancient city at the center of Catholic scholarship, too. Although acclaimed for its pioneering catechetical techniques, the best-known work of its academicians doubtless was the Septuagint version of the Bible, so named because a team of some seventy scholars had contributed to it. With the lapse of the city into various heresies, however, its schools and academic reputation slowly disintegrated.

Alexandrian Rite (al-ehg-ZAN-dree-uhn RAIT:) Liturgy attributed to St. Mark and codified by St. Cyril in the fifth century. Elements of this ancient use are still to be found in the Coptic Rite, which is the present liturgy for the Catholic Patriarchate of Alexandria.

Alexandrine Liturgies (al-ehg-ZAN-drihn LIH-ter-dzheez): Three liturgies in use in the Coptic Church: those of St. Cyril, St. Gregory Nazianzen, and St. Basil. The ancient liturgy of St. Mark survives now only in the anaphora of the liturgy of St. Cyril.

Alexian Brothers (uh-LEHK-see-uhn BRUII-therz): A religious congregation of Brothers dating from an association of pious laymen founded in Belgium in 1365 by Brother Tobias to care for the victims of the Black Death. They took St. Alexis as their patron. The Alexian Brothers (C.F.A.) are dedicated to all aspects of health care, such as nursing and pastoral care; in the U.S., they operate a variety of facilities, including hospitals, life care centers, and a residential home for persons with AIDS.

Algeria (al-DZHIH-ree-uh): Prior to the eighth century, the Roman provinces of Numidia and Mauretania — modern-day Algeria — were areas of flourishing Christianity, centered especially in Carthage. St. Augustine was born in this area. Today the area is mainly Muslim, with a population of perhaps one million Catholics.

Alienation (AY-lee-uh-NAY-shuhn): The canonical term for the sale, gift, or other form of transfer of ownership of church goods or property from official church ownership to another person or entity (cf. cc. 1290-1298).

Alimentation (a-lih-mehn-TAY-shuhn): Today, used to describe artificial feeding. Formerly used to describe supplies and support offered to priests and religious in the course of their duties.

Aliturgical Days (AY-lih-TER-dzhih-kuhl DAYZ): Days on which the celebration of Mass is forbidden, e.g., in the Roman Rite, Good Friday and Holy Saturday.

Allah (AH-lah): The name of God in Islam. The Koran teaches that God is the Creator. Emphasis on the absolute unity of God is such that to disbelieve it came to be regarded as an unforgivable sin. Among the Ninety-nine Names of God are the Dominant, the Compassionate, the Provider, and the Loving.

Allatae Sunt (ah-LAH-tay SØØNT): The title, after its first two words (Latin for "they were carried away"), of Pope Benedict XIV's encyclical (1775) addressed to missionaries in Syria and Asia Minor. The encyclical provided guidelines for the missionaries' relations with the Eastern Churches and enunciated the principle that converts should be initiated, not into Latin Rite communities, but into Eastern Rite communities in union with Rome.

Allegorical Interpretation (AL-uh-GAW-rih-kuhl ihn-TER-pruh-TAY-shuhn): A method of interpretation of Sacred Scripture whereby persons, places, events, and things are seen as signifying other persons, places, events, and things, usually with a spiritual significance; though found in the N.T. and rabbinic literature, it was especially popular among the patristic writers of both East and West. For example, Richard of St. Victor made popular in the twelfth century the interpretation of Noah's ark as an allegory of the Church, also described as the "bark of Peter." The blessing of Easter water alludes to a number of allegories for the saving waters of Baptism, among them the waters after the flood, the Red Sea parted by Moses, and the water that came from the rock at his touch. **CCC 117-118**

Allegory (AL-uh-gaw-ree): (Greek *allegoria:* symbolic representation) Literary device of the Stoic and Cynic philosophers to explain the names of various mythological figures, adapted in Hellenistic Judaism as a means of figurative biblical exegesis, especially employed by Philo of Alexandria. It generally describes one thing under the image of another by way of an extended comparison. In the N.T., Paul alone uses the word "allegory" (Gal 4:24).

Alleluia (AH-lay-LÖÖ-yuh): (Hebrew: Yahweh be praised) Used extensively as a doxology in the Psalms (Pss 104-106, 135), the N.T., and early Church liturgical texts, as well as in the liturgy today, where it is ordinarily required as a sung preparation for the proclamation of the Gospel at Mass. **Cf. CCC 2589**

Allocution (AL-lo-KYÖÖ-shuhn): 1. An address given by the Pope to the College of Cardinals during a secret consistory. If relevant to the faithful, the allocution is later published. 2. The address by the Legion of Mary spiritual director to the Legionaries at each weekly meeting.

All Saints (AWL SAYNTS): Liturgical feast observed on November 1 to honor all saints, canonized and unknown. **CCC 2177**

All Souls (AWL SOLZ): Liturgical observance on November 2 to offer Masses and intercessory prayers on behalf of the faithful departed.

Alma [Almah] (AHL-muh): (Latin: *alma*, nourishing; Hebrew: *almah*, maiden, young woman) A title of the Blessed Mother in Latin, in recognition of her role as the nurturing Mother of God's Son, as in the title *Alma Redemptoris Mater*; it further derives from Isaiah's prophecy that "a young woman *(almah)* shall conceive and bear a son, and shall call his name Immanuel" (Is 7:14). In the Septuagint, *almah* is further specified by its translation as *parthenos* (virgin).

Alma Redemptoris Mater (AHL-muh ray-dehmp-TO-rees MAH-tchr): Latin for "loving Mother of the Redeemer," the title of one of the seasonal antiphons in honor of Our Lady to be sung at the end of Compline (Night Prayer) from the vigil of the First Sunday of Advent until the vigil of the Feast of the Presentation (February 2).

Almighty (awl-MAI-tee): A term used to refer to God, sometimes serving as a name that substitutes for the term "God," as in the case of "the Almighty." More usually, "almighty" refers to God's omnipotence. **CCC 268-278**

Almoner (AL-muh-ner): An official within the Church or other charitable organization appointed to oversee the distribution of alms to those in need.

Alms (AHLMZ): (From Greek: *eleemosyne,* mercy, pity) Material or financial offerings for the poor, prompted by charity. Provision for the needy is admonished throughout the O.T. (cf. Prv 3:27; 22:9; 28:27; Tb 4:6-11; Sir 3:30—4:10; Dn 4:24). Giving all that one has to the poor is a condition for discipleship (Mt 6:24, 19:21; Mk 10:21; Lk 18:22); thus the early Church cared for the needs of the poor in the community (Acts 4:32-37; 2 Cor 8—9). In Christian tradition, almsgiving is a corporal work of mercy. Cf. **CCC 1434, 1438, 1969, 2447, 2462**

Almuce (AL-myöös): (Latin *almutia:* cowl or hood) Cowl or hood covering the head and shoulders; the forerunner of the mozzetta. A modified almuce is found as part of the habits of the Orders of Canons Regular, such as the Norbertines and the Augustinians.

Alpha and Omega (AL-fuh and OH-meh-guh): The combination of the first (alpha) and last (omega) letters of the Greek alphabet as a symbol of Christ, Who is "the first and the last, the living one" (Rv 1:17-18). Jesus says of Himself: "I am the Alpha and the Omega, the beginning and the end, who is, who was, and who is to come, the Almighty" (Rv 1:8; cf. Rv 21:6, 22:13); those three passages from Revelation are in fact the only occurrences of this combination of letters in all the N.T. The biblical foundation for the expression in Revelation can be found in such O.T. texts as "I, the Lord, the first, and with the last, I am He" (Is 41:4; cf. Is 43:10; 48:12). These letters frequently occur in church art and architecture, most notably as an integral part of the ornamentation of the paschal candle.

Alphabetic Psalms (AL-fuh-BEH-tihk SAHMZ): Psalms in which individual parts (verses, strophes, or stanzas) begin

54

consecutively with one of the twenty-two letters of the Hebrew alphabet. The arrangement apparently is an aid to memory, with no theological significance. Most notable among Psalms of this sort is Psalm 119 (cf. Pss 9, 25, 34, 111, and 145); the Lamentations of Jeremiah are another example of this form in Hebrew poetry (cf. Sir 51:13-30). Also called acrostic psalms.

Altar (AWL-ter): Sacred table, set apart (immovable and consecrated, or movable and simply blessed) for the celebration of the Eucharistic Sacrifice and, as local custom may suggest, for Eucharistic exposition and adoration. **CCC 786, 1182, 1364, 1366-1368, 1383, 1589, 2570, 2655**

Altar Bread (AWL-ter BREHD): Bread destined for consecration during the Sacrifice of the Mass, made of pure wheat flour and water, unleavened in the Latin rite but leavened in most of the Eastern rites.

Altar Cards (AWL-ter KAHRDZ): Memory aids, usually three in number, introduced into the furnishing of the altar in the sixteenth century, with two smaller cards placed at the sides and the larger at the center of the altar, inscribed with some of the prayers used at those locations; not generally used since the liturgical reforms following the Second Vatican Council.

Altar Cloths (AWL-ter KLAWTHZ): Pieces of cloth, traditionally white and made of linen or other durable and worthy material; at least one is required to cover the altar during the celebration of the Eucharistic Sacrifice.

Altar, Consecration of an (KAHN-seh-KRAY-shuhn uhv an AWL-ter): When a permanent altar is installed in a new or renovated church, it can be consecrated by the bishop according to the elaborate rite provided for this in the pontifical ritual. Perhaps the most striking feature of this rite is the rubbing of oil and chrism into the mensa, or table. **CCC 1672**

Altar, Gregorian (greh-GOR-ee-uhn AWL-ter): An altar to which the privilege enjoyed by the main altar of the Roman church of St. Gregory had been extended. According to this privilege, a plenary indulgence was granted to the soul of some faithful departed person upon the celebration of Mass at the altar.

Altar Linens (AWL-ter LIH-nuhnz): When used in distinction from altar cloths, the term refers to those that are used during the Eucharist itself, in particular the corporal, the purificator, and the finger towel. These cloths are treated with special reverence after Mass, since they may have come into contact with the Sacred Host or the Precious Blood.

Altar, Papal (PAY-puhl AWL-ter): An altar reserved for use by the Pope or his delegate. Such altars are to be found in the major Roman basilicas.

Altar, Privileged (PRIHV-ih-lehdzhd AWL-ter): An altar enjoying the privilege of specially designated indulgences.

Altar Societies (AWL-ter suh-SAI-uh-teez): Organizations within parishes for the care of the altar and those things used at the altar, such as vestments, sacred vessels, and linens. In addition to the practical work, there is some form of common devotional practice among members.

Altar Stone (AWL-ter STON): 1. The permanent, or immovable, table of the altar made of one piece or slab of natural, solid stone into which are deposited the relics of martyrs or other saints. 2. A smaller stone slab, containing relics, which is mortised or imbedded into a larger altar table or (formerly) carried about for the celebration of Mass outside a sacred place.

Altar, Stripping of the (STRIHP-ihng uhv *thee* AWL-ter): Removal of the altar cloth(s) following Holy Thursday's evening Mass of the Lord's Supper and Good Friday's Communion rite during the "Celebration of the Lord's Passion," accompanied by the chanting of Psalm 22 prior to the liturgical reforms of 1970, but now performed in silence and without ceremonial.

Alternation (AWL-ter-NAY-shuhn): A manner of reciting or singing prayers, psalms, litanies, or hymns, according to which a congregation alternates with a single voice, or two choirs or sides of the church alternate with each other.

Altruism (AL-trȫ-ih-zuhm): Completely unselfish service of others or regard for their concerns and needs. Altruism may, but need not, be practiced for religious reasons. In a sense, the Christian law of love of neighbor comprises a basically altruistic attitude toward others.

Ambo (AM-bo): Pulpit from which the Scriptures are read and the homily may be delivered, and at which the petitions of the general intercessions may be announced and the *Exsultet* (Easter Proclamation) chanted. **CCC 1184**

Ambrosian Chant (am-BRO-zhuhn TSHANT): Melodies ascribed to St. Ambrose or his followers for use in the Ambrosian Rite of Milan, as distinguished from the Gregorian chants of the Roman Rite.

Ambrosian Hymnography, also Ambrosiani (am-BRO-zhuhn hihm-NAH-gruh-fee, am-BRO-zee-AH-nee): Hymn texts ascribed to St. Ambrose and his followers for use in the daily offices and festal celebrations of the Ambrosian Rite of Milan, many of which gradually came to be used throughout the Western Church. Also called simply *Ambrosiani.*

Ambrosian Rite (am-BRO-zhuhn RAIT): The rite of the Mass and Divine Office prevailing for centuries in the territory of the Archdiocese of Milan and attributed to St. Ambrose. After the reform of the liturgy mandated by Vatican Council II, the Ambrosian Rite was brought into conformity with the Roman Rite (1976), but in a way that respected its traditions. Thus, certain variations in the Divine Office and the Mass (notably, the offertory procession before the profession of the Creed) perdure. Cf. **CCC 1203**

Ambry: See Aumbry

Ambulatory (AM-byȫ-luh-taw-ree): 1. Aisle extension, generally forming an arc, behind the high, or main, altar, used for processions. 2. Covered walkway between the main church and auxiliary buildings or along the sides of a cloister.

Amen (ay-MEHN, ah-MEHN): Hebrew word of assent found in Old and New Testaments, generally left untranslated but meaning "So be it," "Truly," "Certainly," or even "I do believe." CCC 1062-1064, 1348, 1396, 2856, 2865

Amendment, Purpose of (PER-puhs uhv uh-MEHND-mehnt): On the part of the penitent in the Sacrament of Penance, the purpose of amendment is the firm resolution not to sin again. This resolution is required for the validity of the sacrament. Usually, it is implicit in the act of sincere contrition that is essential to a true confession, but it can be made explicit, particularly in regard to some specific sin that has been the subject of confession. Cf. CCC 1451-1453

American Board of Catholic Missions (uh-MEHR-ih-kuhn BORD uhv KATH-uh-lihk MIH-shuhns): A committee of the United States Conference of Catholic Bishops that makes grants to needy Catholic parishes and organizations within the United States and its dependencies, for the planning and building of the Church where it is either absent or weak.

American Cassinese Congregation (uh-MEHR-ih-kuhn KAS-sih-NEEZ Kahn-gruh-GAY-shuhn): A confederation of Benedictine abbeys in the United States and Canada, dating from the first Benedictine abbey — St. Vincent Archabbey in Latrobe, Pennsylvania, founded in the U.S. in 1846 by Fr. Boniface Wimmer, O.S.B., in order to serve the growing German immigrant population here. Among the congregation's more than twenty abbeys and priories, the best known are St. John's, Collegeville, Minnesota (1856), and St. Anselm's, Manchester, New Hampshire (1889).

Americanism (uh-MEHR-ih-kuhn-ihz-uhm): A movement, originating in the United States during the latter part of the nineteenth century, which stated that the Catholic Church should adapt its teaching to the surrounding culture. In its acceptance of democratic principles when dealing with matters of faith and morals, Americanism contained the seeds of anticlericalism and a rejection of obedience to ecclesiastical authority. It was condemned by Pope Leo XIII in his apostolic letter *Testem Benevolentiae* (January 22, 1899), which was addressed to James Cardinal Gibbons of Baltimore.

American Protective Association (uh-MEHR-ih-kuhn pro-TEHK-tihv uh-SO-see-AY-shuhn): A society dedicated to the exclusion of Catholics from public office, the A.P.A. attained notoriety in the late nineteenth century when it tried and failed to block the nomination of William McKinley. It attacked Catholicism through tactics such as the circulation of bogus documents and other slanders.

Amice (A-muhs): Rectangular linen cloth with long strips of linen tape attached at two corners, to be worn under the alb at liturgical functions if the alb does not completely cover street clothing at the neck.

Amish (AH-mihsh): Followers of Jakob Ammann, who broke away from the Mennonites in late seventeenth-century Switzerland. They shared fundamental Mennonite beliefs, but desired a more strict separation from the wider culture and a more uncompromising enforcement of shunning (avoidance of the excommunicated). In the eighteenth century, a large number of Amish migrated to America where they formed communities in Pennsylvania, Ohio, Indiana, and elsewhere. The so-called "Pennsylvania Dutch" customs and language, which the Amish in Pennsylvania have retained, are a distinctive mark of their communities.

Ammonian Sections (a-MO-nee-uhn SEHK-shuhns): Divisions found in the margins of most Greek and Latin manuscripts of the four Gospels, meant to show the parallelism between and among corresponding passages in the Evangelists' writings. Originally thought to be the work of Ammonius Saccas (d. 242), they are more likely the work of Eusebius of Caesarea (d. 340) and were widely used before the later division of Scripture into chapters and verses.

Amos, Book of (BØØK uhv AY-muhs): The oldest book of the prophetic literature and the first collection of prophecy in the O.T. isolated as a separate book; while there were earlier prophets, e.g., Elijah and Nathan, none merited a book of his own. Amos (c. 750 B.C.) was a shepherd and trimmer of sycamores in Tekoa, a village south of Bethlehem; without any special training or inclination for a religious mission, Amos was abruptly called (Am 7:15) from his work to preach against abuses in the north, in Bethel and Samaria. He specifically indicts the attitudes of those people in Israel who had grown affluent, to the detriment of the poor. He issued a sobering reminder to the people that the covenant they shared with God demanded that God be all the more exacting in His demands of Israel (Am 3:2).

Amovability (A-möö-vuh-BIHL-ih-tee): In the 1917 Code of Canon Law, a term that referred to the ability of the bishop to remove a person from an ecclesiastical office.

Amphibology (AM-fih-BAHL-uh-dzhee): A form of mental reservation in which the actual truth of the matter in question is concealed by an ambiguous statement. Moral theologians regard this broad form of mental reservation as permissible, since a necessary or reasonable concealment of the truth is accomplished by a statement that has more than one meaning, though not by an actual lie or a more strict mental reservation. Cf. CCC 2482-2487

Ampulla (am-PØØ-luh): (From the Greek *ampho-phero:* to carry by both) Literally, a little vessel with a small neck and two handles. *Ampule* refers to the oil "stocks," or vessels used to carry the holy oils; *ampullae* to the wine and water cruets at Mass.

Amula (AM-yuh-luh): In the early Church, a vessel for the Eucharistic wine that was presented by the people.

Amulet (AM-yöö-leht): A charm, carrying some inscription, that is worn in order to protect the wearer from evil or to aid in some endeavor. Anyone who seriously credits the power of amulets sins against the virtue of religion and against the First Commandment. The wearing of amulets for more than purely ornamental purposes is regarded by the Church as a form of idolatry. Cf. CCC 2117

Anabaptists (a-nuh-BAP-tihsts): Dating from the sixteenth century, members of a Protestant movement of many sects that denied the necessity and validity of infant Baptism. Cf. CCC 1250-1252

Anagni (ahn-AHN-yee): An ancient city of central Italy where, in 1303, Pope Boniface VIII was held prisoner by Guillaume de Nogaret, at the order of King Philip IV of France, in defiance of Boniface's claim to papal hegemony. Though freed by the local citizenry, Boniface emerged so weakened that this "Crime of Anagni" hastened his death and has come to symbolize the decline in the power of the medieval papacy.

Anagnostes (an-ag-NAH-steez): (Greek: reader) The person, usually a cantor, who publicly reads or chants the lessons prescribed at liturgical services in the Byzantine Church; after tonsure, the first step to priesthood in the sequence of Holy Orders.

Anagogical Sense (a-nuh-GAH-dzhih-kuhl SEHNS): (Greek *anagein:* to raise or lead up) The spiritual sense of Scripture that foreshadows or otherwise anticipates the blessings hoped for and to be realized in the beatific vision; for example, Paul refers to the earthly city of Jerusalem as the heavenly city that is our mother, thus the anagogical anticipation of the heavenly reality. CCC 117-118

Analecta (a-nuh-LEHK-tuh): (Greek *ana-:* up + *legein:* to gather) The gathering of various excerpts or fragments of texts into one collection.

Analogy (uh-NAL-uh-dzhee): According to the theory of analogy, statements like "God is good" or "God is wise" express true predications about God even though terms like "good" and "wise" arise from our knowledge of the created order and cannot apply to God in the same way they apply to things in our experience. The truth of such statements rests in the fact that whatever goodness or wisdom there is in the world is caused by God and must therefore exist in Him in an unlimited manner. The same is true for all the perfections we attribute to God on the basis of our knowledge of the world He has made and the redemption He has wrought for us in Christ. CCC 41, 2500

Anamnesis (a-nam-NEE-sihs): Greek word meaning "remembrance," "commemoration," "memorial," referring specifically, in the Latin Rite, to the prayer that follows the institution narrative and memorial acclamation and commemorates the death and resurrection of the Lord. CCC 1103, 1106, 1354, 1362

Ananias (an-uh-NAI-uhs): 1. In Acts 5:1-5, a man by that name and his wife, Sapphira, were struck dead by God because they held back from the community a portion of the money they had gained from the sale of some property while pretending to hand it all over to the Apostles for distribution. 2. In Acts 9:10-17, the name of a Christian man who was instructed by God in a dream to receive Paul into fellowship after the latter's conversion on the road to Damascus. 3. In Acts 23 and 24, the name of a Jewish high priest before whom St. Paul was tried, and who later accused Paul before the Roman governor Felix.

Anaphora (uh-NA-fo-ruh): Greek term taken from the Byzantine liturgy and used in the Latin Rite as a synonym for the Eucharistic Prayer or Canon of the Mass. CCC 1352

Anastasis (uh-NA-stuh-sis): Greek word for "resurrection" used to refer to the Church of the Holy Sepulcher in Jerusalem.

Anathema (uh-NA-thuh-muh): The excommunication of a person, usually for apostasy. In 1 Cor 5:5, St. Paul uses this term to describe those who have separated themselves from the Christian community by sins such as teaching a false gospel. An anathema, which was abolished following the Second Vatican Council, designated a complete departure from the Faith, whereas an excommunication signifies an exclusion from the sacraments.

Anchor (AN-ker): An ancient symbol of hope, courage, safety, and confidence, as in the N.T.: "Hold fast the hope set before us which we have as the anchor for the soul" (Heb 6:19). It was used as a symbol for the cross of Christ, to be kept secret among the Christians and unrecognizable by the unbelievers. It appears on early Christian sarcophagi as a symbol of hope in the resurrection.

Anchor Cross (AN-ker KRAWS): A symbol that combines the anchor, as a sign of safety, with the cross, as a sign of salvation, to symbolize the Christian hope in eternal salvation. It appears as early as the second century in the catacombs of Rome, indicating the hope that the faithful departed had reached the "port" of heaven. The anchor is mentioned in the Epistle to the Hebrews (6:19-20) in relation to the hope of the Christian.

Anchoret: See Anchorite

Anchorhold (AN-ker-hold): The cell or dwelling of an anchorite.

Anchorite (AN-ker-rait): A person who lives in almost total seclusion for religious purposes.

Ancient of Days (AYN-shuhnt uhv DAYZ): A metaphorical name for God, signifying His eternity. God's being is without beginning or end, for He possesses His life in all its fullness always.

Andrew, St. (SAYNT AN-droo): One of the Apostles, and the brother of St. Peter, with whom he is often paired in the Gospels, where he figures in several accounts (e.g., Mt 4:18-20 and Jn 1:35-42). According to tradition, he was crucified on an X-shaped cross. His feast is observed on November 30. Since the eighth century, he has been venerated as the patron saint of Scotland.

Angel, Guardian: See Guardian Angels

Angelic Doctor, The (*thee* an-DZHEH-lihk DAHK-ter): A traditional title for St. Thomas Aquinas, arising probably from the penetrating brilliance of his mind.

Angelic Hymn, The (*thee* an-DZHEH-lihk HIHM): A title given to the *"Gloria in excelsis,"* opening words of the hymn sung by the angels who announced the birth of Christ to the shepherds at Bethlehem (Lk 2:14).

Angelic Salutation, The (*thee* an-DZHEH-lihk sal-yöö-TAY-shuhn): The angel's greeting to Mary beginning with the words "Hail Mary," or *Ave Maria* (Lk 1:28). Along with the salutation of Elizabeth (Lk 1:42), and the words "Holy Mary, mother of God. . ." added in the sixteenth century, the Hail Mary is the most common and popular prayer addressed to the Blessed Virgin Mary. See also *Ave Maria*.

Angelicum, The (*thee* an-DZHEHL-ih-kuhm): The popular title for the Pontifical University of St. Thomas Aquinas in Rome, administered and staffed by professors drawn from the Dominican Order. The Angelicum dates back to the College of St. Thomas founded in 1577 by Juan Solano with the approval of Pope Gregory XIII. Although it is renowned primarily for its faculties of theology, philosophy, and Canon Law, it also maintains significant humanities and social sciences divisions. Pope John Paul II is numbered among its distinguished alumni.

Angel Lights (AYN-dzhehl LAITS): The smaller section of glass situated throughout the larger patterns found in church windows.

Angels (AYN-dzhehlz): (Greek *angelos:* messenger) Pure created spirits without bodies who have keen intellects and resolute wills. Angels were created good by God. Some, now called the devils, disobeyed God and presently make their home in hell; they tempt humans to commit sin. The good angels continue to serve God and to act as His messengers to humankind. There are nine choirs of angels: seraphim, cherubim, thrones, dominations, virtues, powers, principalities, archangels, and angels. CCC 328-336

Angels, Evil: See Devil and Evil Spirits

Angels, Names of the (NAYMZ uhv *thee* AYN-dzhehlz): Michael, Raphael, and Gabriel are the only angels mentioned by name in the Bible. Uriel and Jeremiel are the names of angels occurring in Jewish apocrypha. By tradition, Raphael and Gabriel are accorded the rank of archangel, along with Michael (Jude 9).

Angels of the Churches (AYN-dzhehlz uhv *thuh* TSHERTSH-ehz): Seven angels instructed by the Lord, in Revelation 2-3, to record His dictation that He might thereby address the Churches of Ephesus, Smyrna, Pergamum, Thyatira, Sardis, Philadelphia, and Laodicea; these angels could also be understood as the guardian angels of given Churches, or metaphorically as their bishops.

Angelus (AHN-dzheh-løøs): Term derived from the first word of the prayer formula in Latin to describe a daily prayer recited morning, noon, and evening to commemorate the Incarnation of Jesus Christ, conceived by the Holy Spirit and born of the Virgin Mary.

Anger (ANG-ger): Anger is a complex passion, characterized especially by the desire to gain revenge or redress because of some evil that has been committed. But anger becomes sinful when the desire for revenge is uncontrolled and leads to offenses against justice and charity. It is in this latter sense that anger is numbered among the seven capital, or deadly, sins. The vice of anger gives rise to indignation, the loss of interior tranquillity, harsh speech, and quarrels. The spiritually mature Christian seeks to control anger through prayer, through consideration of the example of Christ, through understanding its causes, and by prompt resistance to its development. CCC 1772, 1866, 2302

Anglican, Anglicanism (AN-glih-kuhn, AN-glih-kuhn-ih-zuhm): The Anglican Church is a worldwide community of churches, all descended from the Church of England, which was separated from the Roman Catholic Church in the sixteenth century when King Henry VIII declared himself to be the head of the Church and so rejected the spiritual authority and jurisdiction of the papacy. Until recently, the defining characteristic of Anglicans consisted of being in communion with the Anglican See of Canterbury; however, with the development of the Continuing Anglican Movement (resulting from certain doctrinal changes, such as the ordination of women), there are those who call themselves Anglican while lacking formal communion with other Anglicans. The theology of Anglicanism is comprehensive, including the full spectrum from Calvinism to Catholicism, and is claimed to be based upon the combination of Scripture, Tradition, and reason. Historically, Anglicanism has seen itself as the "bridge" between Protestantism and Catholicism, with a special sympathy toward the position of the Eastern Orthodox Churches; however, as a result of the increasingly controversial positions taken by Anglicanism, particularly in the area of certain moral issues, its place in ecumenical dialogue has been considerably weakened.

Anglican Church: See Anglican, Anglicanism; Anglican Communion; Episcopalians

Anglican Communion (ANG-glih-kuhn kuh-MYÖÖN-yuhn): Those autonomous churches that acknowledge the spiritual leadership of the Archbishop of Canterbury and are in communion with the Church of England comprise the Anglican Communion. The Anglican Church dates from Henry VIII's promulgation of the Act of Supremacy in 1543 (and confirmed by Elizabeth I in 1559), which declared the reigning British sovereign to be the head of the Church of England. With British colonization and emigration, the church spread beyond the territory of the original Church of England, Ireland, and Wales. The first autonomous Anglican church in communion with the see of Canterbury was the Protestant Episcopal Church in America (founded in 1787). The Anglican Communion today includes similarly established autonomous churches in the former British colonies and in present British Commonwealth countries, e.g., in Canada, Hong Kong, and Australia. Since 1867, the Anglican episcopate has gathered for periodic meetings in the Lambeth Conference, but without authority to promulgate legislation for the worldwide Anglican Communion. Although the Anglican Church is not in communion with the See of Peter, since Vatican Council II, ecumenical discussions (including meetings between the Pope and the Archbishop of Canterbury) have taken place. The Anglican Church maintains membership in the World Council of Churches.

Anglican Orders (ANG-glih-kuhn OR-derz): The Holy Orders of the Church of England. They were declared invalid by the Holy See in 1896 and remain officially considered such.

Anglican Use Parishes (ANG-glih-kuhn YÖÖS PA-rih-shihz): In line with Vatican-approved developments since 1980, several Anglican Use parishes have been established in the United States with the right to maintain some elements of Anglican usage in their liturgical celebrations. A Vatican document dated March 31, 1981, said: "In June, 1980, the Holy See, through the Congregation for the Doctrine of the Faith, agreed to the request presented by the bishops of the United States of America in behalf of some clergy and laity formerly or actually belonging to the Episcopal (Anglican) Church for full communion with the Catholic Church. The Holy See's response to the initiative of these Episcopalians includes the possibility of a 'pastoral provision' which will provide, for those who desire it, a common identity reflecting certain elements of their own heritage."

Anglo-Catholics (ANG-glo-KATH-uh-lihks): Since the eighteenth-century Oxford Movement, a minority within Anglicanism that has sought to restore Catholic belief and practice within the Anglican Church. Usually, although not always, members of this group have favored corporate reunion with the Roman Catholic Church. Although there has been a steady number of converts to the Catholic Church from this group (perhaps the most famous being John Henry Cardinal Newman), the numbers have increased in recent years with the establishment of the Pastoral Provision, commonly known as the Anglican Use, in 1981 in the United States. This provision allows for the ordination of former Anglican clergy (even if married) and the establishment of parishes for the continuation of traditional Anglican liturgical practice within the Roman Catholic Church.

Anima Christi (AHN-ee-muh KRIHS-tee): From the first words of the prayer formula in Latin, a prayer traditionally used as a private act of thanksgiving after Holy Communion; known also as "Prayer to the Most Holy Redeemer," and sometimes attributed to St. Ignatius of Loyola.

Animals in Church Art (A-nih-muhlz ihn TSHERTSH ART): Animals and their characteristics have been used to symbolize various truths, persons, virtues, etc., within Christian art from the earliest years of the Church, as is evidenced in the paintings found in the catacombs.

Annates (AN-nayts): In Latin, the *"annata,"* the term for a tax payable since the thirteenth century to the papal Curia, deriving from the first year of the revenue of an ecclesiastical benefice.

Ann or Anne, St. (SAYNT AN): Traditional name for the wife of Joachim and mother of the Blessed Virgin Mary.

Anne de Beaupré, St., Shrine of: See Canadian Shrines

Anniversary (an-nih-VER-suh-ree): 1. Annual or special liturgical commemoration of an event in the life of the Church or of persons within the Church (dedication, election, ordination, profession, marriage). 2. Commemoration of the faithful departed, observed traditionally after the first month (month's mind) and thereafter annually.

Anniversary Mass (an-nih-VER-suh-ree MAS): Any Mass celebrated to mark the anniversary of a special occasion. Commonly, the term refers to Masses offered on the anniversary of a person's death (one week or one month after the date of death, or annually on that date). Anniversary Masses are also often celebrated to mark the silver or golden jubilees of marriage, religious profession, or ordination. Cf. CCC 1687

Annuario Pontificio (ahn-nöö-AHR-ee-o pahn-tih-FEE-tshee-o): Published annually, this official directory contains the birthdates, dates of ordinations and elevations, addresses, and telephone numbers of all cardinals, bishops, major religious superiors, and those who work for the Holy See. This compendium enjoys "official status" and has been published since 1716 — presently by the Vatican's Central Office of Church Statistics.

Annulment (uh-NUHL-mehnt): A decree issued by an appropriate Church authority or tribunal that an ecclesiastical act or sacrament is invalid and therefore lacking in all legal or canonical consequences. Cf. CCC 1629

Annunciation of Mary (uh-nuhn-see-AY-shuhn uhv MEH-ree): (Latin *annuntiatio:* announcement) The announcement in Nazareth by the angel Gabriel to Mary that she "will conceive . . . a son," Who in fact will be the Son of God (without a human father, born of her, remaining a virgin), the Messiah (Lk 1:26-38); after her initial hesitation, Mary responds with her *fiat,* "Let it be [done] to me according to your word." The liturgical solemnity of the Annunciation is celebrated on March 25. Cf. CCC 430, 484, 490, 973, 1171

Anointing (uh-NOIN-tihng): Pouring oil on a person, thing, or place to single the anointed one out as one made sacred. A common religious practice in the ancient Near East, and in many other cultures and ages, anointing with oil was also a sign of joy and honor, often occurring at festivals. In the O.T., the ark of the covenant, the tent of meeting and its furniture, priests, and kings were all anointed. In the N.T., anointing refers to messianic joy, honor, healing, and the forgiveness of sins. In the Catholic Church, anointing is employed in the celebration of the Sacraments of Baptism, Confirmation, Anointing of the Sick, and Holy Orders; the oils for these sacraments — oil of the catechumens, oil of the sick, and chrism — are blessed by the bishop at Mass on Holy Thursday, usually called the Chrism Mass. Bishops are also anointed during the rites of their episcopal consecration. CCC 91, 438, 690, 695, 698, 786, 1241-1242, 1289, 1291, 1293-1295, 1300, 1574, 2769

Anointing of the Sick (uh-NOIN-tihng uhv *th*uh SIHK): Sacrament instituted by Christ and administered by a priest or bishop to offer God's healing grace to the infirm and aged, to remit sin, and to make known the prayerful solicitude of the entire Church for those beset by illness or advanced age. CCC 1499-1525

Anointing, Rite of: See Anointing of the Sick; Sacraments, Seven

Anomeans (a-NO-mee-uhns): A fourth-century group that broke off from Arianism, denying any similarity between the Father and the Son.

Antediluvian (an-tee-dih-LÖÖ-vee-uhn): (From Latin: "before the deluge") Term referring to the time period from the Creation until the Great Flood. Today, "antediluvian" has acquired the meaning of being old-fashioned or passé.

Antependium (an-teh-PEHN-dee-uhm): (From Latin: "to hang before" or "in front of") A liturgical parament used as a frontal tapestry to adorn the altar of sacrifice.

Anthem (AN-thehm): This term, or antiphon (of which it is the anglicized form), designates a piece of sacred choral music, usually with a scriptural text.

Anthropomorphism (an-thro-po-MOR-fih-zuhm): (Greek *anthropomorphos,* of human form) Depiction of God in human terms and in possession of human emotions, such as love, compassion, anger, and kindness, a common literary device to depict God's dealing with humanity in a vivid fashion. To counter the error that comes from a literal understanding of this metaphorical or analogous way of depicting God, the Church teaches that God is a pure spirit with no physical or spatial dimensions. Similarly, the prohibition of Leviticus against making images of God attempts to preserve God's absolute transcendence, and thus His uniqueness as distinct from the created order.

Anticamera (AHN-tee-kah-meh-ruh): The anteroom to the papal office in the Vatican that serves as a waiting room for visitors scheduled for private audiences with the Pope.

Anti-Catholicism (in America) (AN-tee-ka-THAH-luh-sih-zuhm [ihn uh-MEIIR ih-kuh]): The "deepest bias in the history of the American people" (Arthur M. Schlesinger), anti-Catholicism has its origins in the strongly Protestant European roots of the first colonists to populate eastern America. Catholics were proscribed in every colony except Pennsylvania and early Maryland. Throughout the nineteenth century, Catholics faced the charge that they could not be loyal citizens. Anti-Catholicism reached a pitch in the 1830s movement known as "Nativism," which provoked riots that caused the destruction of Catholic property and the loss of life. Prejudice against Catholics was fostered by such organizations as the American Protective Association, the Ku Klux Klan, and Protestants and Other Americans United for the Separation of Church and State. Despite the election of a Catholic president in 1960, anti-Catholicism has remained endemic. It has taken two forms in particular: (1) religious animosity on the part of some Fundamentalists who regard Catholicism as a perversion of true Christianity, and (2) cultural hostility on the part of liberal intellectuals who consider the Church as backward and repressive. Catholic opposition to abortion has provoked anti-Catholic sentiment in various quarters, notably in the media and among radical feminists.

Antichrist (AN-tih-KRAIST): (Greek *antichristos:* against Christ, adversary of Christ) The principal antagonist of Christ in a final war of cosmological proportions that will occur immediately prior to Christ's Second Coming and the final judgment of the world; the term "antichrist" occurs only in 1 Jn 2:18, 22; 4:3; 2 Jn 7. The Gospels speak of false prophets (Mt 24:5-23; Mk 13:21); Paul speaks of the man of lawlessness (2 Thes 2:3-12). **CCC 675-676**

Anticipate (an-TIH-sih-payt): Liturgical term meaning to observe a feast or to celebrate an office earlier than the time officially appointed (e.g., Sunday Mass on Saturday evening; the Office of Readings or Vigils on the evening before the feast).

Anticipated Mass (an-TIH-sih-pay-tehd MAS): The proper Mass for a Sunday or Feast of Obligation that is celebrated on the eve of the day and that fulfills the obligation to attend Mass (cf. Can. 1248.1).

Anticlericalism (an-tee-KLEH-rih-kuhl-ih-zuhm): An opposition to the clergy, or to the Church in general, especially concerning any influence the Church has upon society. Its effect ranges from mere dislike to the outlawing of the Church and clergy.

Antidicomarianites (an-tee-dai-co-MEH-ree-uh-naits): (Latin *anti* + *dicere* + *Maria:* speak against Mary) Members of a fourth-century heretical sect who maintained that the Blessed Virgin Mary gave birth to other children after Christ's nativity, thus denying her perpetual virginity. **Cf. CCC 499-501**

Antidoron (an-tee-DAW-rahn): (Greek: that which replaces the gift) Particles taken from the unconsecrated portion of the bread used for the Eucharist, distributed to the faithful after Divine Liturgy in the Eastern Rite.

Antigonish Movement (an-TIHG-uh-nish MÖÖV-muhnt): A social action and education movement originating in 1930 at St. Francis Xavier University in Antigonish, Nova Scotia. The movement organized trade unions, cooperative retail stores, and credit unions worldwide.

Antilegomoena (an-tee-leh-GAH-meh-nuh): (Greek: disputed writings) Name given by Eusebius of Caesarea (A.D. 340) to those texts whose place in the N.T. canon was disputed; among them he distinguished two categories: those generally recognized as part of the canon (e.g., James and 2 and 3 John) and those definitely excluded (e.g., the *Didache*).

Antimension or Antimensium (an-tih-MEHN-see-ahn, an-tih-MEHN-see-uhm): (Greek: that which replaces the table) Linen cloth imprinted with an icon of Christ's burial and into which is sewn the relic of a saint.

Antinomians (an-tih-NO-mcc-uhnz): (Greek *antinomos:* against the law) Adherents of an early heresy that Christians, by their faith in the person of Christ, were exempt from following all the prescriptions of the law, natural or positive, biblical or ecclesiastical, even, in the extreme, from observing the Ten Commandments. They based their antagonism to the law on an erroneous interpretation of Paul's theology of justification and the law. In antiquity, this position was advanced among Gnostic groups. During the Reformation, some Protestants held that "justification by faith" reduced all acts, good or bad, to moral irrelevancy, a position that was condemned by the Council of Trent.

Antioch (AN-tee-ahk): Capital city of the ancient Roman province of Syria, the third largest city of the Roman Empire, a center of Greek culture that ranked alongside Rome and Alexandria. It became an early center of Christian evangelization, with many of the followers of Christ fleeing there after Stephen's martyrdom (Acts 7); in time, the initial conversion of the sizable Jewish population was augmented by Gentile converts. Antioch became a major support for Paul's first missionary journey (Acts 13:2—14:28), which would take him on his mission to the Gentiles. It was in Antioch that followers of Christ were first called Christians (Acts 11:26); the episcopal see of Antioch, early distinguished by St. Ignatius, is considered one of the original apostolic sees of the ancient Church.

Antiochene [or Antiochian] Liturgy (an-TAI-o-keen [an-tee-O-kee-uhn] LIH-ter-dzhee): An ancient liturgy represented today in East Syrian (Chaldean and Malabarese) and West Syrian (Syrian and Malankarese) liturgies. The *Didascalia Apostolorum* (third century) provides a glimpse of the ancient Antiochene liturgy. In the fourth century, elements of the Jerusalem liturgy (e.g., the prayer of St. James) were incorporated at Antioch.

Antiochene Rite: See Antiochene Liturgy; Rite, Antiochene

Antioch, Patriarchate of (PAY-tree-ahr-kayt uhv AN-tee-ahk): In the fourth century, the Patriarch of Antioch ranked only after those of Rome and Alexandria. St. Peter is traditionally regarded as the first bishop there. Antioch receded in importance with the rise of Constantinople and, later, with the Nestorian and Monophysite controversies. In the schism with the West, Antioch joined with Constantinople. Today the Orthodox Patriarch of Antioch resides in Damascus. The Monophysite bishop also claims the title of Patriarch of Antioch, as do the Catholic patriarchs of the Melkite, Syrian, and Maronite Rites.

Antioch, School of (SKÖÖL uhv AN-tee-ahk): Although not a school or institution in the physical sense, it was a type of theological attitude beginning around the third century, which used Aristotelian and historical methods of interpreting Scripture, rather than the Platonic and allegorical methods of Alexandria. In its Christological understanding, the school tended to emphasize the humanity of Christ, even leading to a belief in a "loose" union of the divine and human natures of Christ; it lost its credibility after the Council of Ephesus in 431.

Antiphon (AN-tih-fahn): (From Latin: "sounding against," "singing opposite," "alternating") Short verse from a psalm or other, usually biblical, source, sung or recited before or after a psalm or between verses.

Antiphonal (an-TIH-fuh-nuhl): A style of singing the psalms in which a group is divided into two alternating sections. Cantor/congregation or half congregation/half congregation are the usual divisions.

Antiphonal Chants (an-TIH-fuh-nuhl TSHANTS): Liturgical songs at the Eucharist or the Liturgy of the Hours that are sung by alternating voices or choirs.

Antiphonary (an-TIH-fuhn-eh-ree): Book containing antiphons with accompanying melodies. See Antiphon.

Antiphons of Our Lady, The (thee AN-tih-fahnz uhv aur LAY-dee): A series of ancient liturgical hymns in honor of the Blessed Virgin Mary, usually recited or sung in the setting of the hours of the Divine Office or during the Eucharist. The best-known are the *Salve Regina*, the *Angelus*, and the *Regina Coeli* (q.v.).

Antipope (AN-tee-pop): A pretender to the papal throne. One claiming to be Pope in opposition to the one canonically elected.

Anti-Semitism (AN-tai-SEH-mih-tih-zuhm): A prejudice against Jews, and often accompanied by persecution. The prejudice has existed historically from the time of the ancient Persian Empire and survives even to the present day. It has been condemned consistently by the Church as being in opposition to scriptural principles and Christian charity. Cf. CCC 597-598

Antistes (an-TIHS-teez): (Greek and Latin: overseer, similar in meaning to the Greek *episcopos*) In liturgical use, the title of a bishop as the chief priest of a diocese, as in the Roman Canon *"et antistite nostro";* it also appears in LG, n. 27, with reference to bishops in their governance of the particular churches assigned to them.

Antitrinitarians (an-tai-trih-nih-TEHR-ee-uhnz): Followers of various heresies that deny the reality of the Blessed Trinity.

Antitype (AN-tih-taip): (Greek *antitypos:* a corresponding model) The O.T. anticipation of an N.T. "type" whereby a person, event, or thing foreshadows or prepares the way for a corresponding one that will come later. In typological interpretation, Christ is seen as the type anticipated by such figures as Moses and David; Mary is the type prefigured by Eve; the Eucharist is the type for which the manna is the antitype.

Apocalypse: See Revelation, Book of

Apocalypticism (uh-PAH-kuh-LIHP-tih-sih-zuhm): (Greek *apokalypsis:* revelation or uncovering) 1. Movement, widespread in the Jewish world between 600 B.C. and A.D. 200, which attempted to discern God's intention for the immediate future. With its roots in O.T. prophecy, apocalyptic literature is preoccupied with the power of sin and its hold on the world; it prophesies impending catastrophic war of a cosmic nature, a final and climactic conflict between God and evil in which God wins, and creation is restored to its preternatural state. 2. Cluster of beliefs, expectations, and practices recurring in Church history up to the present.

Apocalyptic Number (uh-PAH-kuh-LIHP-tihk NUHMber): The number 666, also known as the "number of the beast," from Rv 13:18, which is commonly thought to refer to the Antichrist.

Apocatastasis (A-puh-kuh-TA-stuh-sihs): The belief, known as "universalism" and propagated by Origen (d. 254), that all rational creatures are saved, including the fallen angels and unrepentant sinners. Origenism was first condemned by a synod at Constantinople (543). The Church holds that such a doctrine denies the reality and possibility of damnation and belittles the effect of one's good and evil actions. Cf. CCC 1033-1036

Apocrisiarius (A-puh-krih-zee-EHR-ee-uhs): (Greek *apokrisis:* answer) The term used for an ambassador, nuncio, or representative sent from one prince (even the Pope) to another head of State, often requesting an answer to important business. The apocrisiarii were the forerunners to the Vatican Diplomatic Corps, which functions throughout the world today.

Apocrypha (uh-PAH-krih-fuh): (Greek: secret, hidden) Various types of literature (e.g., gospels, acts, epistles, and apocalypses) that imitate the style and content of O.T. and N.T. books, falsely asserting divine inspiration by claiming authorship by a noted patriarch, prophet, or apostle, thus implying the transmission of "true revelation" previously hidden from others but now revealed to clarify what is found in the canonical Scriptures. **Cf. CCC 120**

Apodeipnon (A-po-DAYP-nahn): (Greek: after the evening meal) referring to the Compline service, the concluding portion of the Divine Office in the Byzantine Church.

Apodosis (uh-PAH-do-sihs): (Greek: giving back) The conclusion of the period of time during which a feast is observed in the Byzantine Church; e.g., the Nativity of the Mother of God, September 8, has its apodosis on September 12; in the West, called an octave.

Apollinarianism (uh-PAH-lih-NEH-ree-uhn-ih-zuhm): The heresy advocated by Apollinarius in the fourth century, which taught that Jesus possessed only a human body with a sensitive soul but not a rational human intellect and free will (those replaced by divine intellect and will). This opinion was condemned by two Roman councils and the Council of Constantinople in 381.

Apologetics (uh-PAHL-uh-DZHEH-tihks): The theological discipline concerned with the defense of the Christian Faith. The principal functions of apologetics are defense against those who challenge the reasonability of the Faith and persuasion of those who are potential converts to the Faith. Although apologetics works from general principles, it is most effective when it is developed with reference to specific objections or difficulties.

Apologist (uh-PAHL-uh-dzhihst): Originally a title of honor for those who wrote or spoke in defense of orthodox or true Christianity. Today, it refers to anyone who speaks or writes on behalf of the teachings of the Church.

Apology (uh-PAH-lo-dzhee) or Apologia (A-puh-LO-dzhee-uh): The Christian literary genre used to defend the truths of the Faith against objections, which dates from the early centuries and was used by such early martyrs as Justin Martyr.

Apolusia (a-pah-löö-SEE-uh): (Greek *apolousis:* washing) The ritual, uncommon today, preceding Baptism in the Byzantine Rite. Apolusia was performed eight days before one's Baptism and symbolized the eighth day ("eschaton") on which Jesus will arrive "to make all things new."

Apolysis (uh-PAHL-ee-sihs): (Greek: dismissal) Dismissal prayer said by the priest at the conclusion of a liturgical ceremony in the Eastern Church.

Apolytikion (uh-pah-lih-TEE-kee-yahn): (Greek: dismissal) Final prayer or hymn that concludes a liturgical service in the Byzantine Church, after which the congregation is dismissed.

Apostasy (uh-PAH-stuh-see): (Greek *apostasis:* standing away) Rejection of the Christian Faith previously professed by a baptized person, thus incurring automatic excommunication (cc. 205, 751, 1364). In the O.T., Israel's unfaithfulness to God is an apostasy (Jer 2:19; Jos 22:22). In the N.T., it refers to the abandonment of the life of faith and grace given at Baptism (Heb 6:1-8). **CCC 675, 817, 2089, 2577**

Apostate (uh-PAH-stayt): One who repudiates the Christian Faith after having freely professed it. Apostasy incurs automatic excommunication.

Apostle (uh-PAH-suhl): (Greek *apostolos,* one sent off or commissioned) One who represents the sender with authority; related to the Hebrew *siliah,* with similar meaning. While in the N.T. an apostle may be any one of Christ's disciples, the term more specifically designates the Twelve chosen by Jesus as His immediate followers (Mt 10:2-4; Mk 3:16-19; Lk 6:13-16; Acts 1:13). After the ascension, the Twelve are always called Apostles; chosen by Jesus (Acts 1:2), they taught and presided over the early Church (Acts 2:42), spoke in the name of Jesus (Acts 5:40), and performed signs and wonders in His name (Acts 5:12). Cf. **CCC 688, 756, 857, 865, 869, 1342, 2032**

Apostles' Creed (uh-PAH-suhlz KREED): The statement of belief, not written by the Apostles but inspired by their teachings, containing the fundamentals of Christianity in twelve articles. It reads: "I believe in God, the Father Almighty, the Creator of heaven and earth, and in Jesus Christ, His only Son, our Lord, Who was conceived by the Holy Spirit, born of the Virgin Mary, suffered under Pontius Pilate, was crucified, died and was buried. He descended into hell, the third day He rose again from the dead. He ascended into heaven, sitteth at the right hand of God, the Father Almighty, from thence He shall come to judge the living and the dead. I believe in the Holy Spirit, the Holy Catholic Church, the Communion of Saints, the forgiveness of sins, the resurrection of the body and life everlasting. Amen." Cf. CCC 184

Apostles, Dispersion of the (dih-SPER-zhuhn uhv *th*ee uh-PAH-suhlz): The missionary journeys of the Apostles after Pentecost. Nothing is known of the activities of James the Less, Philip, Thaddeus, Simon, and Matthias. According to Eusebius's *Ecclesiastical History,* Matthew stayed in Palestine, Andrew went to Scythia, Bartholomew to India, and Thomas to Parthia (though Malabar Christians insist that he reached India). About Peter, James, and John we possess more reliable information. Peter certainly went to Rome and was martyred there, while James the Elder remained in Jerusalem and was martyred there in A.D. 44 under Herod Agrippa. According to Tradition, John — the only Apostle not to die a martyr's death — left Palestine after the passing of the Blessed Virgin and went to Ephesus.

Apostles, Teaching of the Twelve: See Didache; Didascalia Apostolorum

Apostleship of Prayer (uh-PAH-suhl-shihp uhv PREHR): Universal Catholic organization, associated with the League of the Sacred Heart founded by Fr. F. X. Gautrelet, S.J., in 1844, promoting devotion to the Heart of Christ and seeking prayers for the Pope's monthly general and mission intentions.

Apostleship of the Sea (uh-PAH-suhl-shihp uhv *th*uh SEE):
Organized in Glasgow, Scotland, in 1920, this Catholic society serves Catholic seamen by uniting them in a worldwide community. In important ports, the apostleship maintains clubs served by chaplains. These local clubs are organized nationally and internationally. Pastoral care, education, and social activities are the focus of the society's work.

Apostles of Places and Peoples (uh-PAH-suhlz uhv PLAY-sehz and PEE-puhlz): These are similar to the patron saints of the various countries and are as follows:

Alps: St. Bernard of Menthon
Andalusia (Spain): St. John of Ávila
Antioch: St. Barnabas
Armenia: St. Gregory the Illuminator; St. Bartholomew
Austria: St. Severine
Bavaria: St. Killian
Brazil: Bl. José Anchieta
California: Bl. Junípero Serra
Carinthia (Yugoslavia): St. Virgil
Colombia: St. Luis Bertrán
Corsica: St. Alexander Sauli
Crete: St. Titus
Cyprus: St. Barnabas
Denmark: St. Ansgar
England: St. Augustine of Canterbury; St. Gregory the Great
Ethiopia: St. Frumentius
Finland: St. Henry
Florence: St. Andrew Corsini
France: St. Remigius; St. Martin of Tours; St. Denis
Friesland (Germany): St. Swithbert; St. Willibrord
Gaul: St. Irenaeus
Gentiles: St. Paul
Georgia (Russia): St. Nino (or St. Christiana)
Germany: St. Boniface; St. Peter Canisius
Gothland (Sweden): St. Sigfrid
Guelderland (Holland): St. Plechelm
Highlanders (Scotland): St. Columba
Hungarians (Magyars): St. Stephen, king; St. Gerard; Bl. Astricus

India: St. Thomas, Apostle
Indies: St. Francis Xavier
Ireland: St. Patrick
Iroquois: St. François Picquit
Italy: St. Bernardine of Siena
Japan: St. Francis Xavier
Malta: St. Paul
Mexico: The twelve apostles of Mexico (Franciscans), headed by Fra Martin de Valencia
Negro Slaves: St. Peter Claver
Netherlands: St. Willibrord
Northumbria (Britain): St. Aidan
Norway: St. Olaf
Ottawa Indians: Fr. Claude Jean Allouez
Persia (Iran): St. Maruthas
Poland: St. Hyacinth
Portugal: St. Christian
Prussia (Slavs): St. Adalbert of Magdeburg, St. Bruno of Querfurt
Rome: St. Philip Neri
Rumania: St. Nicetas
Ruthenia: St. Bruno
Sardinia: St. Ephesus
Saxony: St. Willibald
Scandinavia (North): St. Ansgar
Scotland: St. Palladius; St. George
Slavs: Sts. Cyril and Methodius; St. Adalbert
Spain: St. James; Sts. Euphrasius and Felix
Sweden: St. Ansgar
Switzerland: St. Andeol
Tournai (Belgium): St. Eligius; St. Piaton

Apostolate (uh-PAHS-tuh-luht): Term, derived from the N.T. word "apostle," referring to labors done in the name of Christ. Laypersons have for their apostolate the responsibility to preach Christ in their homes and workplaces. Pope John Paul II treated the lay apostolate in his 1988 post-synodal exhortation, *Christifideles Laici,* and concluded that the laity have their vocation by virtue of their Baptism. Religious orders, too, have a specific apostolate in which they expend the majority of their energies, e.g., education of youth and health care. **CCC 863-864, 900, 905, 940, 1324**

Apostolate of Lay People, Decree on the: See Apostolicam Actuositatem

Apostolate of Suffering (uh-PAH-stuh-luht uhv SUH-fer-ihng): Founded in 1926, this "pious association" strives to inculcate, especially in the terminally and chronically ill, a sense of the Christian meaning of suffering.

Apostolic (a-pah-STAH-lihk): 1. Describing anything having its origins or roots in the Apostles. **2.** A term in Canon Law and Church tradition that refers to the papal see or offices, and other matters related to the papacy. **Cf. CCC 857**

Apostolicae Curae (a-po-STAH-lee-tshay KÖÖ-ray): Papal brief of Leo XIII (issued in 1896) in which Anglican Orders are declared to be "absolutely null and utterly void" due to defects of form and intention.

Apostolicam Actuositatem (ah-po-STO-lee-kahm ak-töö-o-see-TAH-tehm): Decree issued by the Second Vatican Council on November 18, 1965, defining the mission of the Church to which the members of the laity are called by virtue of their Baptism. This apostolate is exercised by evangelizing and sanctifying those in the world, by working to influence all things with the Gospel, by bearing witness to Christ, and by helping people to be saved. **CCC 900**

Apostolica Signatura (ah-pah-STAH-lihk-uh SIHG-nuh-TÖÖ-ruh): (Latin: Apostolic Signature) The formal title for the Supreme Court of the Roman Catholic Church, based in Rome. It deals with questions of the authority of lower courts and also deals with appeals of the clergy in disputes against their superiors.

Apostolic Canons (a-pah-STAH-lihk KA-nuhnz): Set of eighty-five canons, contained in the seventh book of the fourth-century *Apostolic Constitutions,* which influenced

Church law pertaining to clerical life. The author claimed that the canons had "apostolic authority"; however, there is no proof for such an assertion.

Apostolic Constitution (a-pah-STAH-lihk kahn-stih-TÖÖ-shuhn): The highest form of ecclesiastical legal, or legislative, pronouncement issued by the Pope himself.

Apostolic Datary (a-pah-STAH-lihk DAY-ter-ee): The office, functioning by the fifteenth century and suppressed in 1967, which granted favors, dispensations, and benefices in the name of the Holy See.

Apostolic Delegate (a-pah-STAH-lihk DEL-eh-geht): The official representative of the Holy See to the Church in a country that does not have official diplomatic relations with the Holy See.

Apostolic Fathers (a-pah-STAH-lihk FAH-therz): A select group of Catholic writers who learned their doctrine directly from the Apostles or from those close to the Apostles.

Apostolici (a-po-STO-lee-tshee): Latin word for "apostolic."

Apostolicity (uh-pahs-to-LIH-sih-tee): One of the four marks of the Church referring to the fact that the Church was founded by Jesus Christ and given to the Apostles in order that the Gospel be proclaimed; the doctrines of the Church — which are to be defended as being from Christ Himself — and the validly ordained bishops (because of apostolic succession) are traceable back to the Apostles and the Apostolic Age. **CCC 857-865**

Apostolic Ministry (a-pah-STAH-lihk MIH-nihs tree): The work of the Church from the time of the Apostles, now carried on by their successors, the Pope and bishops united with him. The apostolic ministry, which is the basis for and has primacy over other apostolic endeavors, is threefold: *sanctifying* (through the sacraments); *teaching* (preaching the Gospel); *governing* (guiding the Church's order and internal and external life). **CCC 873, 888-896**

Apostolic Preacher (a-pah-STAH-lihk PREE-tsher): Also known as the preacher of the papal household, this position is always held by a member of the Capuchin Franciscan Order. His duties include preaching to the papal household on special occasions during Advent and Lent.

Apostolic Prefecture, or Prefecture Apostolic (a-pah-STAH-lihk PREE-fehk-tsher): A territorial division of the Church, erected by the Holy See, comprised of mission parishes. It lacks the stability of a diocese and is headed by one possessing many of the juridical powers of a bishop but who is not a bishop.

Apostolic See (a-pah-STAH-lihk SEE): (Greek *apostolos,* one who is sent; Latin *sedes:* seat) The diocese of Rome, as the See of Peter and his successors, the Popes; also known as the Holy See.

Apostolic Succession (a-pah-STAH-lihk suhk-SEH-shuhn): Bishops of the Church, who form a collective body or college, are successors to the Apostles by ordination and divine right; as such they carry on the mission entrusted by Christ to the Apostles as guardians and teachers of the deposit of faith and as principal pastors and spiritual authorities of the faithful. The doctrine of apostolic succession is based on N.T. evidence and the constant teaching of the Church, reflected as early as the end of the first century in a letter of Pope St. Clement to the Corinthians. A significant facet of the doctrine is the role of the Pope as the successor of St. Peter, the vicar of Christ and head of the college of bishops. The doctrine of apostolic succession means more than continuity of apostolic faith and doctrine; its basic requisite is ordination by the laying on of hands in apostolic succession. **CCC 861, 1087; cf. 815, 77, 1209**

Apostolic Union (a-pah-STAH-lihk YÖÖN-yuhn): The association of diocesan priests, initiated by Venerable Benedict Holzhauser and begun in Bavaria in the seventeenth century, who follow a rule of life intended to enhance their spiritual and pastoral activities.

Apostolic Vicariate: See Apostolic Prefecture, Prefect

Apostolos (ah-POS-to-los): 1. An apostle of Jesus Christ, usually referring to the Chosen Twelve. 2. The book containing the epistles in the Byzantine Rite or the epistles themselves.

Apparel (uh-PEHR-ehl): (From French *appareiller:* to make fit) The small panel of embroidery, gold, silver, or the liturgical color of the day (except black), on the cuffs and the bottom of the alb, along with the top section of the amice.

Apparitions (a-puh-RIH-shuhnz): Visions of Jesus, Mary, angels, and saints, which are investigated by the Church in order to verify their authenticity. Scripture has recorded many apparitions, such as the visit of the Archangel Gabriel to Mary. Apparitions often contain messages that are "private revelation" as opposed to the "public revelation" of Scripture and Tradition. Cf. CCC 67

Appeal (uh-PEEL): 1. A canonical action whereby one has recourse from the decision of a lower Church court to a higher, or recourse against an administrative decree. 2. Verb: To take up the act of making an appeal.

Appellant Controversy (uh-PEHL-uhnt KAHN-truh-ver-see): A dispute that arose in the sixteenth century over the naming of a successor to Cardinal Allen, founder of the Douai College in Rome.

Appellants (uh-PEHL-unts): In Canon Law, persons who file an appeal against a judicial or administrative decision. Also, historical term for a group of eighteenth-century French clergy who supposedly filed an appeal against a papal condemnation of certain Jansenistic materials.

Appetite (A-puh-tait): A philosophical term designating the capacity of a thing to seek its good (and to avoid evil things). In human beings, appetite is both sensitive (viz., the passions or emotions) and intellectual (viz., the will). In addition to natural appetites (the basic tendency to be and to function according to one's nature), there are elicited appetites that respond to awareness or knowledge of certain objects of desire or avoidance. For this reason, appetite is understood to follow upon knowledge — according to the maxim "You can't love what you don't know." Among sensitive appetites, one group is called "concupiscible" (e.g., love, desire, hatred, sorrow), whose object is the simple sense-perceptible good; while another group is called "irascible" (e.g., hope, anger, courage), whose object is the difficult sense-perceptible good. Scholastic philosophy introduced the notion of appetite into Christian Tradition, and it remains central to all discussion of the principles of the moral life. Cf. CCC 1763-1775

Appetite, Concupiscible (kahn-kyöö-PIH-sih-buhl A-puh-tait): Term designating emotions whose object is simple sense-perceptible goods; i.e., food, drink, comfort, pleasure, etc. Cf. CCC 2514-2557

Appetite, Irascible (ihr-A-sih-buhl A-puh-tait): term designating that group of emotions (sense appetites) that are aroused by good objects that are difficult to attain. Irascible or contending emotions are hope, despair, courage, fear, and anger. Cf. CCC 2514-2557

Appropriation (uh-pro-pree-AY-shuhn): The attributes or characteristics of one of the Three Divine Persons that are common to all Three Persons. For instance, the Father is often termed "Creator," the Son "Redeemer," and the Holy Spirit "Sanctifier." Cf. CCC 257-260

April (AY-prihl): The month dedicated to fostering devotion to the Holy Eucharist.

Apse (APS): The semicircular end of a church, where the altar is often located, common in basilican-style churches.

Apsidiole (ap-SIH-dee-ol): A small apse. The term is used particularly in churches with more than one apse, in order to distinguish the smaller from the main apse.

Aquamanile (ah-kwa-mah-NEE-lay): Medieval bronze water pitchers for washing the celebrant's hands at Mass.

Aquarians (uh-KWEHR-ee-uhnz): An obscure second-century heretical sect that held that use of wine in the Eucharist was sinful.

Aquileian Rite (ah-kwih-LAY-uhn RAIT): Rite of the ancient patriarchal See of Aquileia in Northern Italy, superseded by a variant of the Roman Rite during the Carolingian period, and finally suppressed in 1597.

Ara Coeli (AH-ruh TSHAY-lee): One of the great churches of Rome, Santa Maria in Ara Coeli is located on the Capitoline Hill on the site of an ancient temple in honor of Jupiter. A legend has it that the Emperor Augustus beheld a vision of the Blessed Virgin standing on an altar of heaven (or *ara coeli*).

Aramaic (ehr-uh-MAY-ihk): The common Semitic dialect spoken in the time of Jesus, Hebrew being spoken only by the learned, rabbis, and priests. Named from Aram, a country of Southwest Asia, with its origins after the Babylonian Exile, ca. 536 B.C. The Hebrew Bible was paraphrased into Aramaic Targums, available to the common people. In the N.T., there are several Aramaic words and phrases: *talitha koumi; ephphata; eloi, eloi, lama sabachthani; marana tha; Akeldama; Golgotha; Bethesda; Gethsemane.* A modern form of Aramaic is still used in a few Christian villages of Lebanon.

Arca (AHR-kuh): Box or pyx in which the Eucharist was reserved by early Christians in their homes for daily Communion outside Mass.

Arch (AHRTSH): An architectural term for a form spanning a space and supporting the structure above. Arches of various types (e.g., round, horseshoe, Tudor, and trefoil) are a fundamental feature of all styles of church architecture and are in fact among the distinctive marks of particular styles.

Archabbot (ahrtsh-A-buht): The superior of an archabbey (i.e., a major abbey so designated by reason of its size, pre-eminence, or historic distinction).

Archaeology, Christian (KRIHS-tshuhn ahr-kee-AHL-uh-dzhee): The study of Christian monuments and shrines in order to uncover fresh insights about the early Church. Archaeological finds can present new information about Scripture, the Liturgy, the early governance of the Church, etc.

Archaeology, Commission of Sacred (kuh-MIH-shuhn uhv SAY-krehd ahr-kee-AHL-uh-dzhee): Established on January 6, 1852, by Blessed Pius IX, its purpose is to study ancient Christian monuments and art in order to understand better the life and thought of the early Church. This commission is also responsible for the Vatican State museums.

Archangel (ahrk-AYN-dzhehl): (Greek *archangelos:* chief messenger) High-ranking angel with a unique role as God's messenger to people at critical times in salvation history (Tb 12:6; Lk 1:26; Jn 5:4; Jude 9; 1 Thes 4:16; Rv 12:7-9). More strictly speaking, archangels belong to the eighth of the nine orders of angels. Three archangels are named in the Scriptures: Michael, Gabriel, and Raphael.

Archbishop (ahrtsh-BIH-shuhp): Title of a bishop with jurisdiction over an archdiocese, which is the principal see of a region; he has a certain limited supervisory jurisdiction over the other dioceses in his province. However, some archbishops may be created *ad personam,* with no authority over an archdiocese, as a personal honor bestowed by the Pope.

Archbishop-Elect (ahrtsh-BIH-shuhp eh-LEHKT): The proper title of a prelate in the interval of time between the date of the Holy See's announcement of his elevation to an archiepiscopal see and the day of his actual consecration and/or installation in that see.

Archbishop, Titular (TIH-tshöö-ler ahrtsh-BIH-shuhp): The archbishop of a suppressed or defunct see.

Archconfraternity (AHRTSH-kahn-fruh-TER-nih-tee):
The confederation of local chapters of confraternities, approved by the Church, which foster Christian teaching and piety. The Holy Name Society is an example of one such confraternity.

Archdeacon (artsh-DEE-kuhn): Dating from the third century, the office of archdeacon was held by one appointed by the bishop to help him in the liturgical and administrative affairs of the diocese. The Council of Trent suppressed this office. The vicar general and the vicars forane of a diocese do much of what the archdeacon had done.

Archdiocese (ahrtsh-DAI-o-sees): A territorial division of the Church governed by an archbishop. It is the primary see of an ecclesiastical province having one or more other dioceses.

Archetype (AHR-keh-taip): The original pattern according to which something is modeled and produced. In Christian thought, the term is sometimes used for the so-called "divine ideas" in order to affirm that everything that exists is caused by God and therefore reflects His being and wisdom. The term has many other uses in philosophy and psychology.

Archiepiscopal Cross (ahr-kee-uh-PIIIS-kuh-puhl KRAWS): The plain crucifix, stemming from medieval times, which is mounted on a staff and carried (with the crucifix facing the Pope) before the Pontiff in solemn processions. Today the Roman liturgy does not call for a specific archiepiscopal cross.

Archimandrite (ahr-kee-MAN-drait): In the Eastern Rite, originally title of the superior of a monastery, but now a title of honor conferred by a patriarch upon a deserving priest.

Architecture (AHR-kih-tehk-tsher): The design of ecclesiastical buildings including churches, monasteries, priories, convents, and colleges. Church architecture dates from 313, when Emperor Constantine granted privileges to the Church.

Gradually, architecture has developed and has encompassed many styles: Byzantine, Romanesque, Gothic, Renaissance, Baroque, and neo-Gothic.

Archives (AHR-kaivz): The place where records, documents, and other historical material is stored. Church organizations such as dioceses and religious communities have archives.

Archives, Diocesan (dai-AH-seh-suhn AHR-kaivz): The official storage place for records and documents pertaining to a diocese as prescribed by Canon Law (cf. cc. 486-491).

Archivist (AHR-kih-vihst): The official of a diocese who is charged with gathering, organizing, and safeguarding the documents and records of a diocese. Traditionally, this position was held by the chancellor (Can. 482).

Archpriest (AHRTSH-preest): 1. The priest chosen to assist the bishop or to substitute for him in the performance of priestly tasks. 2. The superior over secular priests; this usage dates from the sixteenth century in England. 3. The priest who assists a newly ordained priest at his Solemn Mass of Thanksgiving, or the priest, dressed in cope, who attends to the prelate at a Pontifical Mass.

Arcosolium (ahr-ko-SO-lee-øøm): An arched niche with a flat bottom, common in Roman catacombs, upon which Mass was offered during the persecutions of Christians. From the Latin *arcus* and *solium* ("seat of the arch"), the arcosolium's flat slab was used to seal the tomb and mark the graves of Christians.

Arculae: See Arca

Areopagite (ehr-ee-AH-puh-gait): (Greek *areopagus:* hill of Mars or Ares) In general, anyone who speaks at the Areopagus, a small hill northwest of the Acropolis, in Athens; it was the site of a public court where cases were heard regarding complaints brought against teachers and other public lecturers; thus, Paul was summoned there on the charge that his teaching was "startling" (Acts 17:16-34); his defense is noteworthy for its more philosophical style and his appeal to the altar there dedicated to the "unknown god." One of the court members, Dionysius, converted to Christianity; he is usually called the Areopagite.

Arianism (EHR-ee-uh-nih-zuhm): The heresy propagated by the Alexandrian monk Arius, originating in the fourth century and claiming that Jesus Christ was created and, therefore, not divine. Arius was excommunicated in 319. The Council of Nicaea (325) condemned Arius's proposition and developed a creed that used the Greek *homoousios* (Latin *consubstantialis)* to teach that Christ is the Son of God and of the same substance as the Father. The Council of Constantinople (381) reaffirmed Nicaea's definition and also taught the consubstantiality of the Holy Spirit. Cf. CCC 232-242, 249-256

Aridity (uh-RIH-dih-tee): Literally, "dryness." In spiritual theology, the term is used to designate experiences of prayer that carry no emotional warmth or affection. Such experiences are understood to be permitted by God in order to deepen the faith and trust of the contemplative. Cf. CCC 2731

Ariel (EHR-ee-uhl): A Hebrew name meaning "the lion of God" or the "hearth of God." In Is 29:1-2, 7, the term is used to designate Jerusalem.

Aristotelianism (A-rih-stuh-TEEL-ee-uhn-ih-zuhm): The philosophical system originating in the writings of the Greek thinker Aristotle (384-322 B.C.) and developed through the centuries by his commentators and followers. Aristotle wrote on a wide range of topics, stretching from logic through all the branches of natural science to psychology and metaphysics. His logic exercised an influence on Christian thought from the time of the Fathers of the Church. The rest of his philosophy became known in the West in the Middle Ages and helped to shape the characteristic positions of Christian philosophy and theology that emerged in that period. Perhaps the most thoroughgoing Aristotelianism is to be found in the thought of St. Albert the Great and St. Thomas

Aquinas; it continues to influence theology through the Thomistic tradition.

Ark (AHRK): 1. The vessel in which Noah and his family took refuge from the Deluge (Gn 6-8). The ark was 450 feet in length, 75 feet in width, and 45 feet in height with three decks. 2. A kind of Baptism (1 Pt 3:20 f.) through which one attains salvation by virtue of water. 3. The basket in which Moses was kept safe from the Nile River. 4. The receptacle or tabernacle made of acacia wood, called the Ark of the Covenant, which Moses built to house the tablets of the Mosaic Law. Cf. CCC 845, 1094, 1219, 2058, 2578, 2594, 2676

Arles, Councils of (KAUN-suhlz uhv ARL): The fifteen Church-sponsored gatherings dedicated to address disputed questions of doctrine and pastoral practice held in Arles, France. The first was convened in 314 by Constantine to address the Donatist schism in northern Africa, while the last was convoked in 1275.

Armageddon (ahr-muh-GEH-duhn): Site of the final battle between God and Satan, where good will triumph over evil, commonly identified with the ancient city of Megiddo; it is named only in Rv 16:16. It has come to be synonymous with the chaos and destruction associated with the end-times. Cf. CCC 668-677

Armagh, Book of (BØØK uhv ahr-MAH): The eighth- or ninth-century volume, now housed at Dublin's Trinity College, containing several important manuscripts. Attributed to Ferdomnach of Armagh (d. 846), the Book of Armagh includes two lives of St. Patrick and St. Martin of Tours, along with a non-Vulgate Latin translation of the N.T.

Armenian Church (ahr-MEE-nee-uhn TSHERTSH): One of the Oriental Churches (q.v.). The Armenian Church has its own patriarch.

Armenian Rite: See Rite, Armenian

Armenian Rite, Catholics of the (KATH-uh-lihks uhv *th*ee ahr-MEE-nee-uhn RAIT): In the fourteenth century, during the period when Little Armenia, or Cilicia, enjoyed independence, the Christians there entered into union with the See of Peter and later sent representatives to the Council of Florence (1438-1439). Today, Armenian Catholics are centered mainly in Germany and the United States, under the leadership of their *Katholikos* in Cilicia. Since 1981, an Armenian exarchate has been based in New York.

Arms of Christ, The (*th*ee ARMZ uhv KRAIST): The symbolic representation of the instruments used during the passion of Christ; viz., the nails, the scourge, the lance, the cross, and so on.

Art, Christian (KRIHS-tshuhn AHRT): The depiction of Christian subjects in the various artistic media, having its beginning in the catacombs; throughout the centuries many of the greatest artistic works have been created under the patronage of the Church. CCC 1159-1162; cf. 2500-2503

Art, Liturgical (lih-TER-dzhih-kuhl AHRT): The branch of Christian art that is concerned principally with the design of the objects and fabrics used in worship. This field includes the design and manufacture of sanctuary furniture, vestments, sacred vessels, candles, altar cloths, linens, and hangings. Statues, church design, and decoration may also fall within the competence of liturgical artists. CCC 1161-1162

Art, Sacred (SAY-krehd AHRT): An umbrella term for the whole range of depictive, ornamental, decorative, and sculptural arts that center on religious subjects and purposes. CCC 1159-1162; cf. 2500-2503

Articles of Faith (AHR-tih-kuhlz uhv FAYTH): An article of faith is "a perception of divine truth that leads us to the truth itself" (St. Thomas Aquinas). Our faith has God Himself as its object: we believe in God and in the promises He reveals to us. Given the richness and deep intelligibility of God and His promises, our faith in Him comes to be "articulated" or formulated in a number of connected propositions. In Christian theology, the term "article" has been used to designate a proposition by which the divine reality is attained.

Artificial Insemination (ahr-tih-FIH-shuhl ihn-SEHM-ih-NAY-shuhn): The implanting of human semen by some means other than consummation of natural marital intercourse. In view of the principle that procreation should result only from marital intercourse, donor insemination is not permissible. **CCC 2376-2379**

Artoklasia (ahr-to-kluh-SEE-uh): (Greek: bread-breaking) The ceremony in the celebration of Vespers on a feast (e.g., Pentecost) in the Byzantine Church, when five loaves of leavened bread, symbolic of the loaves and fishes blessed and multiplied by Our Lord in feeding the five thousand, and containers of wheat, wine, and oil are blessed for distribution on the feast day to the faithful, who are anointed with the blessed oil. The ceremony originated in the need for actual sustenance of the faithful during the all-night vigil.

Artos (AHR-tos): 1. In the Eastern Rite, any bread used in a liturgical ceremony, corresponding to the term "host" in the Roman Rite. 2. The special Paschal (Easter) bread shared on Thomas Sunday (the Sunday after Easter).

Arts, The Liberal (*th*uh LIH-ber-uhl AHRTS): Usually, a term for humanistic studies, as distinct from vocational or occupational expertise. In this sense, the liberal arts include literature, history, languages, philosophy, and science. In modern higher education, such studies are understood to cultivate general knowledge and culture, and to provide a broad background for subsequent specialization.

Ascension of Christ (uh-SEHN-shuhn uhv KRAIST): The going up to heaven of Christ's risen and glorified body forty days after His resurrection (Lk 24:50 ff.; Acts 1:9 ff.), so that He exists in corporeal form with the Father outside time and space, thus the concluding work of redemption and the pledge of our own eventual ascension into heaven. **CCC 659-667**

Ascetical Theology (uh-SEH-tih-kuhl thee-AHL-uh-dzhee): The science concerning the "ordinary" ways of reaching Christian perfection, based on Scripture and Tradition. Ascetical theology considers how one is able to respond to God's grace by engaging in certain practices of self-denial such as fasting and "custody of the eyes." The three stages of perfection dealt with in this science are the purgative, the illuminative, and the unitive.

Asceticism (uh-SEH-tih sih-zuhm): The rule of life, based on disciplinary practices (fasting, vigilance of the tongue, etc.), that aims at controlling desires and reparation for past sins, which one accepts as an aid in realizing Christian perfection. Asceticism enables one to deny oneself pleasures and to strive to follow Jesus perfectly. Cf. CCC 1734, 2015, 2043, 2340, 2733, 2755

Aseity (uh-SAY-ih-too): (Latin, *a:* from + *se:* itself) The truth stating that the existence of God is received from Him alone. The Divine Godhead is not created, and He is His own reason for existing, with no need for creation. It also excludes any notion of God "becoming" or developing. CCC 212-213

Ashes (ASH-ehz): In Christian practice, the remains of burnt palm branches, blessed and used to mark the foreheads of the faithful on the first day of Lent (Ash Wednesday), as a reminder of mortality and as a penitential sign of turning away from sin.

Ash Wednesday (ASH WEHNZ-day): In the Roman Rite, the first day of Lent, on which ashes are blessed and imposed upon the heads of the faithful as a sign of penitence and mortality.

Aspiration (A-sper-AY-shuhn): Short exclamatory prayer; e.g., "My Jesus, mercy!" See Ejaculation.

Asperges (uh-SPEHR-dzhehz): (From Latin: to sprinkle) 1. A ceremony in which the faithful are sprinkled with holy water, formerly celebrated before Mass, now an optional replacement for the penitential rite as a reminder of Baptism. 2. The Latin chant that may accompany this ceremony.

Aspergillum (A-sper-DZHIHL-uhm) or Aspergill (A-sper-dzhihl): Liturgical instrument used for the sprinkling of holy water, usually consisting of a silver, brass, or wooden handle with a hollow multipierced orb or (especially in Eastern Europe and the Eastern Rites) brush.

Aspersion (uh-SPER-zhuhn): A form of Baptism in which the candidate is sprinkled with water. The term has the additional sense of sprinkling with holy water in blessings.

Aspersorium (AS-per-SO-ree-uhm) or Aspersory (uh-SPER-suh-ree): A bucketlike vessel for holding the holy water used in blessings, along with an implement for sprinkling (the "aspergillum").

Aspirancy (AS-per-uhn-see): An interval of time prior to entrance into the novitiate of a religious order or congregation.

Aspirant (AS-per-uhnt): One who has signaled his or her desire or intention to join a religious community, but who must undergo a period of candidacy before admission to the novitiate.

Aspirations (AS-per-AY-shuhnz): Short prayers, often called "ejaculations," which offer to God adoration, atonement, thanks, and supplication, all in a spirit of charity (e.g., "Jesus is Lord," "Come, Holy Spirit," "Jesus, Mary, Joseph").

Ass (AS): The domesticated ass was employed as a work animal and for riding as early as the third millennium B.C. The animal figures frequently in the Bible. According to the prophets, the future king of Zion would come riding on an ass (rather than on horseback or in a chariot) to underscore the peaceableness of his reign (Zec 9:9) — a prophecy fulfilled in Christ's entry into Jerusalem amidst the waving of palms. Cf. CCC 559

Assemblies of God (uh-SEHM-bleez uhv GAHD): Largest of the Pentecostal bodies in the U.S., the Assemblies of God date from the General Council of Pentecostal Saints held in April 1914 in Hot Springs, Arkansas. The purpose of this general council was to bring greater unity to the Pentecostal movement and to affirm its basic teachings. Extremely conservative in doctrine, the Assemblies affirm the inerrancy of Scripture, Baptism in the Holy Spirit (manifested in speaking in tongues), and premillennialism. Assemblies of God polity combines Presbyterian and Congregational elements.

Assent (uh-SEHNT): The assent of faith consists in the acceptance of all that is contained in Scripture and Tradition, in the one deposit of faith entrusted to the Church and proposed in either her solemn or ordinary Magisterium. In addition, religious respect, though not strictly the assent of faith, is to be accorded to the authentic Magisterium when it teaches on faith and morals, even if this teaching is not intended as definitive. Cf. CCC 143, 150, 156-175, 891-892, 1993

Assent, External (ehks-TER-nuhl uh-SEHNT): Outward acceptance of the deposit of faith, exhibited in teaching, preaching, and writing that is in accord with the content of the Faith. External assent could coexist with interior, unexpressed doubts about some element of the deposit. But in matters of faith, the Christian is obliged to seek guidance to resolve such doubts.

Assent, Internal (ihn-TER-nuhl uh-SEHNT): Interior acceptance of all that is proposed for belief in Scripture and Tradition, and taught as divinely revealed by the authentic Magisterium of the Church.

Assessor (uh-SEHS-ser): An officially appointed consultant to judge in a canonical trial.

Assistant at the Pontifical Throne (uh-SIHS-tuhnt at *th*uh pahn-TIH-fih-kuhl THRON): An episcopal member of the papal court who ranks after the cardinals, but who is seated in a place of honor around the papal throne.

Assistant Priest (uh-SIHS-tuhnt PREEST): A priest who aids another priest in ecclesiastical duties. The term refers to a parochial vicar (i.e., associate pastor), the priest who assists the bishop during the liturgy or the priest who helps a newly ordained priest in celebrating Mass for the first time.

Assist at Mass (uh-SIHST at MAS): An expression used to describe active participation in the celebration of the Eucharist on the part of the faithful. Presence at Mass should never simply be a passive, noninvolved attendance, but an active participation in which all join in (i.e., assist in) the offering of the Sacrifice by prayerful attention, singing, and responding to the various prayers, as well as by the appropriate postures of standing, sitting, and kneeling. CCC 2178, 2180

Associate Pastor (uh-SO-shee-uht PAS-ter): Term for a priest assigned to a parish to assist the pastor. It was replaced in the 1983 Code of Canon Law by the term "parochial vicar."

Associations of the Christian Faithful (uh-so-shee-AY-shuhns uhv *th*uh KRIHS-tshuhn FAYTH-fuhl): A term in Canon Law referring to a wide variety of organizations to which Catholic faithful, lay, religious, and clerical, may belong. The code contains certain provisions for the foundation, rights, and duties of associations. It is divided into private and public associations of the faithful (cf. cc. 278-302).

Associations, Pious: See Associations of the Christian Faithful

Assumptionists (uh-SUHMP-shuhn-ihsts): The Augustinians of the Assumption (A.A.), as they are officially known, were founded by Emmanuel d'Alzon in 1845 at Nîmes, France. They engage in teaching (e.g., at Assumption College, Worcester, Massachusetts), parish ministry, mission work, and other apostolic activities.

Assumption of the Blessed Virgin Mary (uh-SUHMP-shuhn uhv *th*uh BLEH-sehd VER-dzhihn MEH-ree): Defined as a doctrine of the faith on November 1, 1950, by Pope Pius XII, stating that Mary was taken up body and soul into heaven after the completion of her earthly life (in theological terminology, her dormition, or falling asleep in the Lord), since, by reason of her Immaculate Conception, she should not suffer the consequences of Original Sin. With no direct biblical evidence for the Assumption, the Church has long held, on the basis of theological reasoning and Tradition, the implicit belief in Our Lord's taking His mother to Himself from the moment of her passage from this life. In the Eastern tradition, the argument is advanced from the doctrine of the Incarnation that Christ took His Mother into heaven so that He Who was perfectly human might gaze forever upon at least one other with a human nature, glorified like Himself (Lk 1:28, 35; Rv 12:5-6; LG 59, 68-69). The feast of the Assumption has been celebrated by Christians since as early as the seventh century; today it is celebrated as a holy day of obligation in the United States on August 15. CCC 966

Assyrian Church, The (*th*ee uh-SEER-ee-uhn TSHERTSH): Known officially in the U.S. as the Holy Apostolic and Catholic Church of the East, the Assyrian Church is also known as the Nestorian Church, the Chaldean Church, or the Church of Persia. It claims St. Thomas the Apostle as its founder and is comprised of Christian groups originating in Iraq and Persia (modern-day Iran). It broke communion with other Christian patriarchs when it welcomed Nestorius. The church declines to call Mary the Mother of God, yet accepts the unity of the two natures of Christ in one Person. Among its liturgies is the ancient rite of Addai and Mari, celebrated in a form of Syriac related to Aramaic. The Assyrian patriarch ("Catholicos Patriarch of the East") has resided in the U.S. since 1940. There is a small branch of the Assyrian Church that has been in communion with the Holy See since the sixteenth century.

Asteriskos (ahs-ter-EES-kos): In the Eastern Rite, a liturgical implement consisting of two arched strips of metal joined together in the middle to form a cupola from which a small star is often suspended, representing the star of Bethlehem and placed on or over the diskos (paten) with the Holy Bread to hold the veils away from it.

Astrology (uh-STRAHL-uh-dzhee): The practice of determining the future by measuring the position of the stars. It is condemned by the Church because it demonstrates a distrust in God's providence and concern for the welfare of His children. **CCC 2116**

Asylum, Right of (RAIT uhv uh-SAI-luhm): The custom, dating from medieval times, of giving refuge, in churches or ecclesiastical buildings or territories, to criminals, debtors, or anyone fleeing from capture. Also known as the right of sanctuary, it is generally accepted that a person who has been given this right cannot be forcibly removed.

Athanasian Creed: See Creed, Athanasian

Atheism (AY-thee-ih-zuhm): The belief that the Supreme Being does not exist. There have been various categories of atheists: philosophical agnostics, who contend that there is insufficient evidence to affirm or deny God's existence; and materialists, who believe that spiritual realities must be excluded from consideration. Atheism can be speculative (i.e., the theory that God truly does not exist) or practical (one's words and actions suggest that he does not believe in God or in following His will). **CCC 2123-2128**

Atonement (uh-TON-mehnt): The Christian doctrine that Christ's redemptive act brought about reconciliation between God and man. Jesus' obedience renders infinite satisfaction to the Father and repairs for the sin of Adam and Eve. The Sacrifice of Christ, renewed at each Holy Mass, surpasses the mere human significance of the Old Law. Some theories of atonement stress that Jesus appeased the wrath of the Father through His death; however, theologians today underscore the perfect humility and subservience of Jesus in His salvific act. **CCC 606-618**

Atonement, Day of (DAY uhv uh-TON-mehnt): (Middle English: at-one-ment) The highest of Jewish holy days, *Yom Kippur,* which occurs on the tenth day of the seventh month of the Jewish calendar. Ritual is designated for the reparation of sins (Lv 16:1 ff.; 23:26 ff.; Nm 29:7). A deeper and permanent significance of this atonement was attained in the sacrifice of Christ on the cross, wherein He is both the Priest and the Victim of the sacrifice (cf. Rom 5:10; Eph 2:13; 1 Pt 2:24; Heb 9:28; 2 Cor 5:19). Cf. CCC 433, 578

Attention (uh-TEHN-shuhn): The focusing of one's mind on a specific person, object, or activity — either the substance itself or its moral quality. To possess incomplete attention when performing a sinful act may lessen the guilt of the sin; however, unwilled distractions are not sinful and, if occurring during the administration of the sacraments, do not negate the validity of the sacraments.

Attributes of God: See God, Attributes of

Attributes of the Church (A-trih-byööts uhv *th*uh TSHERTSH): Authority (by which are taught truths otherwise unknowable), infallibility (by which these teachings are expressed without error), and indefectibility (by which the Church retains authentic identity) are the three attributes of the Church. These attributes are ascribed to the work of the Holy Spirit in the Church. CCC 551-553, 869, 1108

Attrition (uh-TRIH-shuhn): Sorrow for sin resulting from the consideration of the horror of sin or from fear of being punished. Contrition, which is sorrow for sin based on the love of God, is superior to attrition. Yet, the latter is sufficient for the absolution of sin. CCC 1453

Audience, Papal (PAY-puhl AW-dee-ehns): A reception granted by the Pope to either an individual or a group of persons. General audiences, usually held each Wednesday, involve thousands of persons; semiprivate audiences are granted to small groups, and private audiences are normally bestowed upon Church and State leaders who have important matters to discuss with the Pontiff.

Auditor (AW-dih-ter): An official of a Church tribunal who is designated to gather evidence and take testimony in trials.

Augsburg, Diet of (DAI-eht uhv AWGS-berg): The assembly convened in 1530 in Augsburg, Bavaria, at which Emperor Charles V heard the Lutheran party argue that they be afforded equal standing with Catholics. Catholic respondents agreed with nine articles of the Augsburg Confession, agreed with reservations about another six articles, and rejected an additional thirteen articles. Emperor Charles refused to grant the Lutheran appeal. In the 1555 Diet ("Peace of Augsburg"), the Augsburg Confession and the Catholic Faith were both accepted as valid (see Augsburg, Peace of).

Augsburg, Peace of (PEES uhv AWGS-berg): The political resolution of the Catholic-Lutheran conflict within the German Empire stated at Augsburg, Bavaria, on September 25, 1555. The religion of the ruling prince determined the religion of the land. Only Catholics and the Protestants who had signed the Augsburg Confession of 1530 were affected.

Augustine, Rule of St. (RÖÖL uhv saynt aw-GUHS-tihn [AW-guh-steen]): A rule, almost certainly composed by St. Augustine of Hippo for a community of male religious, stressing the love of God and neighbor, common life, abstinence, and care for the sick. A variety of manuscript traditions makes reconstruction of the original rule difficult. The rule served as the basis for community life among many chapters of cathedral canons in the eleventh century. St. Dominic adopted it as the basis for his Order of Preachers in the thirteenth century. The Fourth Lateran Council considered it an approved rule.

Augustinian Fathers (aw-guhs-TIHN-ee-uhn FAH-therz): A union of monasteries following the Rule of St. Augustine, approved by Pope Alexander IV in 1256, lies at the origins of the Order of St. Augustine (O.S.A.) as it exists today. Along with the Dominicans, Franciscans, and Carmelites, the Augustinians were known as friars from medieval times. Education, parochial ministry, and missionary work are the areas on which they focus their apostolic activity.

Augustinians (aw-guhs-TIHN-ee-uhnz): In addition to referring to religious who follow the Rule of St. Augustine, this appellation also refers to theologians whose thought is shaped by the particular interpretations of St. Augustine's theology that developed in the Middle Ages by Alexander of Hales, St. Bonaventure, and Bl. John Duns Scotus.

Augustinism (aw-GUHS-tihn-ih-zuhm): The teachings of St. Augustine of Hippo (354-430), much of which are acknowledged as sound Catholic doctrine, especially on the following subjects: the fall of Adam and Eve, Original Sin, atonement, grace, and predestination.

Aumbry (AWM-bree) or Ambry (AM-bree): Wall cupboard used for the reservation of the holy oils and, prior to the development of the tabernacle, for the Blessed Sacrament as well.

Aurcole (AW-ree-ol): The gilt backdrop, not to be confused with the halo, which totally surrounds artistic representations of the Blessed Trinity, Jesus, and Mary. The aureole (Italian *mandorla*, "almond-shaped") denotes divinity and the glory attached to a person.

Auricular Confession (aw-RIHK-yöö-ler kuhn-FEH-shuhn): The acknowledging of one's sins to a priest for the purpose of being absolved and amending one's life. This practice probably began at the outset of the sixth century in the Celtic Church and was accepted by the entire Church by the end of that century. This form of the Sacrament of Penance remains the standard today. Mortal sins are to be confessed in kind and number, while it is strongly encouraged to confess venial sins. CCC 1455-1458

Auriesville (AW-reez-vihl): Near Amsterdam, New York, the site of the shrine of the North American Martyrs. In the seventeenth century, the Mohawk village of Ossernenon was located here. St. René Goupil was martyred here in 1642, and St. Isaac Jogues and others were held captive. It is the birthplace of Bl. Kateri Tekakwitha.

Aurifrisium (aw-rih-FREE-zee-øøm): A stiff piece of embroidery used to decorate the upper part of the amice, usually made of gold thread, but sometimes conforming to the liturgical color of the season. An amice decorated in this way is known as an "appareled" amice. See Apparel.

Aurora, Mass of the (MAS uhv *thee* uh-RO-ruh): On Christmas, the liturgy provides for three distinctive Masses: midnight, dawn, and morning. The Mass of the Aurora, or dawn, is the second of these.

Austerities (aw-STEHR-ih-teez): Practices of self-denial that foster Christian perfection. Fasting, flagellation, hair shirts, night vigils, and other forms of penances have been used for centuries to contribute to growth in holiness by inculcating a profound sense of sorrow for sin. Cf. CCC 1434-1439

Australia, Christianity in (krihs-tih-AN-ih-tee ihn aw-STRAYL-yuh): Christianity in the form of Anglicanism first came to Australia in the late eighteenth century. The first Catholic diocese was established in 1834.

Authentic: See Authenticity, Biblical

Authentication of Relics (aw-THEHN-tih-KAY-shuhn uhv REH-lihks): Ecclesiastical approval of relics for the veneration of the faithful. This process does not constitute a guarantee of the genuineness of relics, but a declaration that there is no evidence to the contrary.

Authenticity, Biblical (BIH-blih-kuhl aw-thehn-TIH-sih-tee): The reliability and trustworthiness of the manuscripts that form the basis of our biblical texts. Their authentication is determined in terms of their acceptance by Church authority, their exactness in expressing the words of the human writers, and their consistent acceptance and use in the Catholic Tradition over the centuries.

Authority (uh-THOR-ih-tee): An authority is one who holds a position of superiority to others with respect to some field or realm. This authority may be one of competence or expertise, or one of power and right. Thus a specialist in some field of knowledge is acknowledged to possess an authority with respect to this field. A person with the right and power of governance in a realm (e.g., the family, the State, the Church, an institution) is said to possess executive authority.

Authority, Civil (SIH-vuhl uh-THOR-rih-tee): The right and power to govern society in temporal affairs for the sake of the common good are possessed directly by the legitimate leaders of the State, according to the particular form of government in effect and consented to, at least implicitly, by the governed. Catholics are required to be obedient to legitimate civil authority, and to recognize that, ultimately, all authority exercised in the earthly realm comes from God. Civil authority is not absolute, but is limited to its sphere of competence and must be in accord with divine law. Parental, religious, and other forms of authority retain their scope within the family, the Church, and other legitimate institutions in society. CCC 1900-1904

Authority, Ecclesiastical (eh-klee-zee-AS-tih-kuhl uh-THOR-ih-tee): The authority exercised by the Church, and particularly by the Pope and the bishops, is the authority delegated to St. Peter by Jesus Christ. This authority extends to all those matters entrusted to the Apostles by Christ: teaching of the Faith, formulation of the liturgy and sacraments, guidance in morals, administration of discipline, etc. CCC 551-553

Authority of Papal Acts (uh-THAW-rih-tee uhv PAY-puhl AKTS): Papal encyclicals, decrees, and decisions — coming either expressly from the Pope or from offices of the curia with papal approval — should be obeyed by those in the Church to whom they are addressed. The most solemn authority attaches to those decisions that are explicitly rendered *ex cathedra* or infallibly. Normally, papal decisions constitute part of the ordinary Magisterium. In matters of faith, internal assent is required. CCC 1594, 2034

Authority of Scripture (uh-THOR-ih-tee uhv SKRIHP-tsher): Since "all that the inspired authors, or sacred writers, affirm should be regarded as affirmed by the Holy Spirit. . . , we must acknowledge that the books of Scripture firmly, faithfully and without error, teach that truth which God, for the sake of our salvation, wished to see confided to the Sacred Scriptures" (DV, n. 11). Together with Tradition, Scripture forms one deposit of the Word of God, which is entrusted to the Church and shapes its life according to God's design. It is read within a Tradition of liturgical practice, patristic exegesis, and magisterial interpretation. In this way, it serves as the basis for all Christian teaching, preaching, theological reflection, and pastoral care. Cf. CCC 106-107

Authority of Tradition (uh-THOR-ih-tee uhv truh-DIH-shuhn): The Church regards the Scriptures along with Tradition as constituting the supreme rule of faith. "Sacred Tradition, Sacred Scripture and the Magisterium of the Church . . . are so connected and associated that one of them cannot stand without the others. Working together, each in its own way under the action of the one Holy Spirit, they all contribute effectively to the salvation of souls" (DV, n. 10). Tradition functions primarily as the mode of transmission of the Word of God. Scripture and Tradition are like a single mirror in which the Church contemplates God. Cf. CCC 75-79

Authority, Parental: See Parenthood; Parents, Duties of

Authorized Version (AW-ther-aiz'd VER-zhuhn): Commonly known as the "King James Version," this revised version of previous English translations of the Bible was undertaken under King James I and was published in 1611. The revisers, who were professors of Hebrew and Greek at Oxford and Cambridge universities, were to take existing English versions of the Bible into account (especially, the Bishops' Bible, the Douai-Rheims, and the Geneva Bible). Although the words "appointed to be read in the churches" are found on the title page, this version was never officially authorized.

Autocephalous (aw-to-SEH-fuh-luhs): From the Greek "self-heading," term used primarily among Orthodox Christians to describe the autonomy enjoyed by a national church that can elect its own head (metropolitan or patriarch) without interference from another patriarch or national church.

Auto-da-fé (AU-to-duh-FAY): The term used in the Spanish Inquisition for the public pronouncement against one accused of a crime. It was used only in Church tribunals and included condemnations, pardons, and reconciliations.

Autoeroticism (aw-to-ehr-AH-tuh-sih-zuhm): A pattern of sexual self-stimulation, usually regarded as sinful except where there are extenuating circumstances (e.g., where voluntariness is impeded). Cf. CCC 2351-2352, 2354

Autonomous Religious House (aw-TAHN-uh-muhs rih-LIH-dzhuhs HAUS): A community of religious men or women with no superior higher than its own local superior.

Autonomy (aw-TAH-nuh-mee): The independence of the moral agent enabling him or her to perform actions with full knowledge, freedom, and consent. Immanuel Kant asserted that autonomy is essential to the human person and must be defended from obstacles. The Church recognizes the value of autonomy in promoting spiritual growth; yet, it is subordinate to other values, such as the love of God and others. Cf. CCC 1730-1742

Autos Sacramentales (AU-tos sah-kruh-mehn-TAH-lehz): Spanish morality plays, centered on the Eucharist and popular in the seventeenth and eighteenth centuries. Abuses led to the eventual suppression of such plays.

Auxiliary Bishop (awg-ZIHL-yer-ee BIH-shuhp): A bishop assigned to assist a diocesan bishop in the administrative and pastoral care of a diocese.

Avarice or Covetousness (A-ver-ihs or KUH-veh-tuhs-nehs): The capital sin, also called greed, which is an extreme desire for material goods and worldly honors. A person with this vice seeks material goods over the welfare of others and often offends against the poor and needy. CCC 1866

Ave Maria (AH-vay muh-REE-uh): The prayer said by Christians that repeats the greetings of the Archangel Gabriel and Elizabeth to the Virgin Mary. The latter half of the prayer is derived from the Church's Tradition, in order to entreat Mary as Protectress and Auxiliatrix at the hour of death. The *Ave Maria* has been a special focus for many musical composers; Franz Schubert's rendition is perhaps the best known. CCC 2676-2677

Avenir, L' (LAH-veh-NEER): (French: the future) A newspaper published by French Catholic liberals, beginning in 1831; its editorial policies, reflecting the thought of Felicité de Lamennais, Charles de Montalambert, and Jean-Baptiste Lacordaire, advanced the legitimate goals of the French Revolution, such as freedom of speech, democracy, and separation of Church and State.

Ave Regina Caelorum (AH-vay reh-DZHEE-nuh tshay-LO-røøm): One of the ancient antiphons ("Hail, Queen of Heaven") in honor of the Blessed Virgin, sung traditionally at Compline from the feast of the Purification to Holy Thursday.

Aversion (uh-VER-zhuhn): The revulsion for the truly "good," resulting from Original Sin and concupiscence; aversion is the opposite of attachment and desire; such a repulsion from the good is mysterious and difficult to explain.

Aviators (AY-vee-ay-terz): In 1920, the Holy See proclaimed Our Lady of Loreto as the patron of aviators.

Avignon Papacy (AH-veen-YON PAY-puh-see): A period, beginning in 1309 and lasting for seventy years, during which the papacy was located in Avignon, France, in an effort to reconcile feuds between French and Italian factions of the Church.

Azrael (AZ-ray-ehl): Angel of death in Jewish and Islamic tradition.

Azyme (A-zaim): (Greek: unleavened) Eucharistic bread made without yeast. Unleavened bread is used in the Jewish celebration of Passover, and is used by the Latin Rite Churches for the Eucharist.

Azymes (A-zaimz): A Jewish agricultural feast lasting seven days.

Azymites (AZ-ih-maitz): From the Greek meaning "the unleavened ones," derogatory term used by Eastern Christians after the Great Schism (1054) to refer to Latin Rite Christians because they used unleavened *(azyme)* bread in the liturgy as opposed to the Eastern tradition of leavened bread.

B

Baal (BAY-uhl): (Hebrew: master, husband) In reference to men, a term with the strictly literal meaning of a husband in the physical sense; also the owner or master of a place or household; frequently used in the O.T. of the Canaanite gods, with the meaning that a god is the *baal* of that particular place, especially applied to the gods of plant and animal fertility, more specifically of Hadad, the Amorite god of winter, rain, and storm. The Hebrew prophets, in particular Hosea, inveighed against the practice of syncretizing the cult of Yahweh with that of the local *baalim*, often employing word-play on the double meaning of *baal*, as both a master of the people and a husband with whom Israel had consorted, as would a prostitute. Both the prophet Elijah and King Josiah moved to level the high places where the worship of these deities was rooted.

Babel, Tower of (TAU-er uhv BA-behl): (Hebrew, *Babel;* Assyrian, *Babilu:* Gate of God) According to the account in Gn 11:1-9, a tower in the land of Shinar that the descendants of Noah began to build in order to reach heaven. As a punishment for their presumption in attempting this feat, God caused them to speak many languages; because they could no longer understand one another, they were prevented from completing the tower. CCC 57

Babylonian Captivity (ba-bih-LO-nee-uhn kap-TIH-vih-tee) or Babylonian Exile (ba-bih-LO-nee-uhn EHG-zail): Period when the inhabitants of Judah and Jerusalem were forced to leave their homes for the enforced exile in Babylonia, variously dated from 598 B.C. (the first deportation) or from 587 B.C. (the second forced migration) to 538 B.C. (when the Jewish people were allowed to return by order of King Cyrus). There had been an earlier deportation of the inhabitants of the Northern Kingdom to Assyria under Tiglath-Pileser III in the mid-eighth century B.C.

Babylon, Patriarch of (PAY-tree-ark uhv BA-bih-lahn): The archbishop who has jurisdiction over Catholics of the

Chaldean Rite; the Catholic Patriarch of Babylon resides in al Mawsil, Iraq.

Bachelor (BATSH-uh-ler): An unmarried or single man. According to the discipline of celibacy, only bachelors or widowers can be ordained to the priesthood in the Western Church, except those dispensed under the "Anglican Use" (see Anglo-Catholics). Cf. CCC 1579

Bad Faith (BAD FAYTH): One who willfully acts contrary to the dictates of conscience is said to act in bad faith (particularly when one refrains from becoming a Catholic even after becoming convinced that the full reality of the Church of Christ subsists in the Catholic Church).

Baha'i (buh-HAI): Originating in the teachings of Mirza Ali Muhammad (killed in 1850) and founded as a religious community by Mirza Husayn Ali (known as Baha'u'llah, "the glory of God"; d. 1892), Baha'i teaches the universal community of the human race and the unity of all religions. The worldwide headquarters of the religion are in Haifa, Israel, while the center for Baha'i in the U.S. is located in Wilmette, Illinois, the site of a large and distinctively designed temple. There are about twenty-five thousand local assemblies in the world. Baha'i religionists have been subjected to considerable persecution in Islamic countries.

Baldacchino (bahl-duh-KEE-no): 1. The canopy, composed of wood, metal, or stone, over the high altar protecting the Sacred Species from dust. Bernini designed the famous baldacchino in St. Peter's Basilica for Pope Urban VIII (1623-1644). 2. The covering protecting the Blessed Sacrament from dust, used during Eucharistic processions. 3. The canopy covering the *cathedra* (episcopal chair).

Balm or Balsam (BAHLM or BAHL-suhm): Thick, aromatic resin, prized for both its pleasant fragrance and assumed medicinal powers, derived from the terebinth or balsam tree. Mixed with olive oil, balm is one of the ingredients for chrism, blessed on Holy Thursday by the bishop for use in his diocese for the administration of the Sacraments of

Baptism, Confirmation, and Holy Orders. It was used in ancient times primarily for anointing kings and priests, with the symbolism of the good and healing presence of cultic and civil leaders within the community and the royal priesthood of all the baptized.

Baltimore (BAWL-tih-mor): The first diocese in the U.S., dating from the consecration, in 1790, of John Carroll as first bishop. Three plenary councils were held there (1852, 1866, 1884). The first American to be named a cardinal — James Gibbons — was Archbishop of Baltimore. In 1791, the Sulpicians established the first seminary in the U.S. in Baltimore.

Baltimore Catechism (BAWL-ti-mor KAT-eh-kih-zuhm): One of the most influential books in the history of catechetical efforts by the Catholic Church in the U.S., originally mandated in 1884 by the Third Plenary Council of bishops, meeting in Baltimore. The catechism, largely the work of the first Bishop of Peoria, John Lancaster Spalding, who wrote from drafts submitted by Msgr. Januarius de Concilio, a pastor in Jersey City, was given formal approbation by the Archbishop of Baltimore, James Cardinal Gibbons, on April 6, 1885, as the official text recommended for the religious instruction of Catholic children in the United States. It remained a standard text, undergoing many revisions, notably that of Bishop Edwin V. O'Hara of Kansas City, though it fell into disfavor in the 1960s as representing allegedly outdated pedagogy and theology, not representative of the postconciliar reforms.

Baltimore, Councils of (KAUN-sihlz uhv BAWL-tih-mor): Ten councils held in Baltimore, the premier see of the U.S.; seven were provincial councils, when the entire country was one province under the ecclesiastical jurisdiction of the Archbishop of Baltimore (1829, 1833, 1837, 1840, 1843, 1846, 1849), and three were plenary, including all the U.S. ecclesiastical provinces (1852, 1866, 1884). Although the Archbishop of Baltimore always presided, the real guiding spirit of the first four was Bishop John England of Charleston (1820-1840), who insisted on regular meetings of the hierarchy to foster harmony in their work of providing a structure for Catholic life in the young nation. The councils dealt with a variety of subjects crucial for the survival of Catholicism in the U.S.: the organization of dioceses, the recommendation of new sees and bishops, the promotion of priestly vocations, protection of Catholic life, and vigilance against anti-Catholic bigotry. The most influential was the Third Plenary Council, which mandated parochial schools, the famous *Baltimore Catechism*, and the creation of The Catholic University of America.

Bambino (bahm-BEE-no): (Italian: infant) Usually refers to representations of the Infant Jesus, particularly in Nativity scenes and celebrations.

Bankruptcy and Restitution (BANK-ruhpt-see and reh-stih-TÖÖ-shuhn): The moral obligations of a bankrupt person with respect to his creditors are fulfilled when he has met the legal requirements stipulated by the civil code for the payment of outstanding debts.

Banner (BAN-ner): A large, usually rectangular, piece of cloth depicting some religious figure or symbol. Banners can be affixed to the walls of churches or hung from pillars. They are also carried aloft in parades and religious processions.

Banneux, Apparitions of (ap-puh-RIH-shuhnz uhv bah-NØØ): The eight visions of Our Lady to Mariette Beco, a twelve-year-old girl, in Banneux, a tiny hamlet near Liège, Belgium, from January 16 to March 2, 1933. Mary appeared dressed in white with a blue sash and rosary over her right arm, identifying herself as the "Virgin of the Poor." Today, she is honored at over one hundred shrines dedicated to her under the title "Our Lady of the Poor, the Sick, and the Indifferent."

Banns (BANZ): The public proclamation, either verbally or in writing, of an intended marriage. The purpose of the banns is to discover the existence of impediments or other conditions that would result in an invalid marriage. Cf. 1625

Baptism, Conditional (kuhn-DIH-shuhn-uhl BAP-tih-zuhm): Baptism is administered conditionally when there is a doubt about the capacity of the person to be baptized, or about the fact or validity of a previous Baptism.

Baptism, Lay (LAY BAP-tih-zuhm): A Baptism administered in danger of death by an unordained (indeed, even a non-Christian) person when no priest or deacon is available. For validity, the person administering the sacrament must pour water while reciting the formula, "I baptize you, in the name of the Father, and of the Son, and of the Holy Spirit," all the while intending what the Church intends. The full liturgical rites should be supplied if the person baptized survives. CCC 1256, 1284

Baptism, Sacrament of (SA-kruh-mehnt uhv BAP-tih-zuhm): The sacrament in which, by pouring water upon a person, or immersing in water, and using the words "I baptize you in the name of the Father, and of the Son, and of the Holy Spirit," the one baptized is cleansed of Original Sin and (in the case of one who has reached the age of reason) of actual sins, is incorporated into Christ and made a member of His Body the Church; he or she is infused with sanctifying grace and receives the gifts of the Holy Spirit and the theological virtues of faith, hope, and charity. The ordinary minister of Baptism is a bishop, priest, or deacon; however, in an emergency anyone can baptize validly. A person must be baptized in order to receive any of the other sacraments effectively. CCC 1213-1284

Baptismal Certificate (bap-TIHZ-muhl ser-TIH-fih-kuht): A document, issued by the parish church in which a person was baptized, certifying that the person named was baptized in that church. The certificate states the date of the Baptism and the names of the parents and godparents of the baptized, and is signed by the one who administered the sacrament or the pastor. The back of the certificate usually has sections in which the subsequent sacramental history of the person can be recorded. An up-to-date baptismal certificate is required as part of the documentation for the reception of Orders, profession of vows, or for entry into matrimony.

Baptismal Font (bap-TIHZ-muhl FAHNT): Fixed basin or, more traditionally, pool with fountain of "living" or flowing water, used for the administration of Baptism. Cf. CCC 1238

Baptismal Name (bap-TIHZ-muhl NAYM): Traditionally a saint's name taken by an adult or given to an infant at the time of Baptism, and signifying the beginning of a new life in Christ. CCC 2156

Baptismal Robe (bap-TIHZ-muhl ROB): White garment given to the newly baptized, signifying from Roman civic tradition maturity *(candidatus)* and from scriptural references purity of new life in Christ. CCC 1243

Baptismal Vows or Promises (bap-TIHZ-muhl VAUZ or PRAH-mih-sehz): Renunciation of Satan and profession of Trinitarian faith expressed before Baptism or as a renewal of one's Baptism. CCC 1237, 1427; cf. 1254, 2340

Baptismal Water: See Baptismal Font

Baptism of Bells (BAP-tih-zuhm uhv BEHLZ): A popular name for the elaborate ceremony for the blessing of church bells.

Baptism of Blood (BAP-tih-zuhm uhv BLUHD): A person (even an infant) who dies for the Faith before being baptized is said to have received the "Baptism of blood," i.e., the removal of sin and the bestowal of sanctifying grace that are the effects of the Sacrament of Baptism. CCC 1258

Baptism of Children of Non-Catholics (BAP-tih-zuhm uhv CHIHL-drehn uhv NAHN-KATH-uh-lihks): Baptism of a non-Catholic child in danger of death, even without the consent of the parents, is legitimate when there is no chance that the child will survive to the age of reason. In ordinary circumstances, the consent of the child's parents or guardians must be secured, and rearing of the child in the Faith must be guaranteed. Cf. CCC 1246, 1256, 1261

Baptism of Desire (BAP-tih-zuhm uhv dee-ZAIR): A person (not an infant) who performs a perfect act of charity that at least implicitly includes the desire for Baptism by water is said to have received the "Baptism of desire." The implicit desire for baptism by water is thought to be included in a person's desire to do God's will: such a person would want to receive Baptism by water if he or she knew that this was God's will. Baptism of desire brings with it the grace of salvation, even for the non-Christian. But when faith becomes explicit, Baptism by water should nonetheless be sought. CCC 1258, 1260, 1281

Baptism of the Dead (BAP-tih-zuhm uhv *th*uh DEHD): The Catholic Church forbids the administration of Baptism to persons who are known to be dead. Where a doubt exists, Baptism can be administered conditionally. Baptism of the dead is practiced in the Mormon Church in a ceremony in which a living person stands proxy for the dead. Cf CCC 1246

Baptist (BAP-tihst) or Baptizer (BAP-tai-zer): Title used for St. John, who was the forerunner of Christ and who preached baptism for the forgiveness of sins. CCC 535, 720

Baptistery (BAP-tihs-tree): 1. Building, separate from the church proper, in which the baptismal font is located and the Sacrament of Baptism conferred. 2. Area within the church building where the font is located.

Baptists (BAP-tihsts): The loose union of independent evangelical Christian bodies, deriving from the seventeenth-century alliance between Mennonite Anabaptists and British Protestants who dissented, and adhering to Calvinism, with more than thirty million members worldwide. John Smyth (1554-1612) is considered to be the founder. Baptists stress Baptism by immersion of conscious adults and, therefore, oppose infant Baptism. They also emphasize the sufficiency of Scripture, justification by faith alone, and the independence of local churches; most reject double predestination and insist on human freedom to choose various possibilities. There are national (e.g., the U.S. Southern Baptist Convention) and international (e.g., the Baptist World Alliance) associations of Baptists that are strictly advisory. Cf. CCC 1252, 1282

Barefoot Friars (BEHR-foot FRAI-erz): Those religious priests and Brothers who, due to poverty and simplicity, go without shoes or socks. Today, many orders that are "discalced" (like the Discalced Carmelites and Franciscans) direct their members to wear sandals.

Barnabas (BAHR-nuh-buhs): (Aramaic: son of consolation) A Levite from Cyprus named Joseph who received the name of Barnabas (Acts 4:36-37) from the Apostles; the cousin of John Mark (Col 4:10), he was a leader in the Jerusalem Church; he introduced Paul to the Apostles and was their representative to the Church at Antioch (Acts 11:22 ff.). With Paul, Barnabas brought famine relief to Jerusalem (Acts 11:29-30); both were commissioned to preach the Gospel in regions not yet evangelized (Acts 13:1 ff.). The early patristic text of the Letter of Barnabas is attributed to him; Tertullian believed Barnabas to be the author of the Letter to the Hebrews.

Baroque Art (buh-ROK AHRT): Art chiefly characterized by the strong suggestion of movement and the resultant harmony between the environment and the building or the work of art, frequently employing sweeping imagination, with a strong sense of the immensity of the subject. Baroque architecture is markedly flamboyant; cherubs, sunbursts, and clouds are commonly employed as architectural details. As it emerged in the sixteenth century, the baroque represents a strong reaction to the earlier Gothic that called for the orderly, clear, and independent arrangement of figures; in the baroque, the parts are assembled so that no part or figure stands alone; rather, all the figures constitute one vast panorama.

Bartholomew (bahr-THAHL-uh-myöö): (Aramaic, *bar talmai;* Greek, *bartholomaios:* son of Tolmai) One of the Twelve Apostles, usually coming after Philip in Synoptic lists of the Apostles, thus leading some to think that he may be

Nathanael, brought to Jesus by Philip (Jn 1:45-51). Eusebius records that Bartholomew brought the Gospel to India; Jerome considered him the author of one of the apocryphal gospels.

Baruch, Book of (BØØK uhv bah-RØØK): A book of only five chapters attributed to Baruch, son of Neraiah, the secretary of the prophet Jeremiah; generally held today to be the work of three separate authors, though skillfully edited into one consistent work. Directed to the Jews exiled in Babylon, Baruch preaches to Israel that her people now languish in an alien land for having abandoned "the fountain of wisdom," i.e., the Torah. **Cf. CCC 120**

Base Communities (bays kuh-MYÖÖ-nih-teez): Concept and operational models envisioning relatively small groups of the faithful integrated for religious and secular life, with maximum potential for liturgical and sacramental participation, pastoral ministry, apostolic activity, personal and social development. Originating mainly in Latin America as *comunidades de base,* they contribute to the vitality of parishes and dioceses around the world, supported by Pope Paul VI in his letter *Evangelii Nuntiandi* if they are truly ecclesial in nature.

Basel, Council of (KAUN-sihl uhv BAH-zehl): The first of the three Councils of Florence, taking place in the Swiss city of Basel.

Basic Teachings of Catholic Religious Education (BAY-sihk TEE-tshihngs uhv KATH-uh-lihk rih-LIH-dzhuhs ehd-yöö-KAY-shuhn): The statement of the United States National Conference of Catholic Bishops that gives focus to catechetics. It was published in 1973 and includes doctrines that are to be taught. Three themes are paramount — prayer, participation in the Sacred Liturgy, and Sacred Scripture. Topics presented: God and salvation, the Trinity, the Church, sacraments, sin, morality, the Blessed Virgin Mary, eternal destiny. This publication also offers a list of the Ten Commandments, the Beatitudes, and the precepts of the Church.

Basil, Liturgy of St. (LIH-ter-dzhee uhv saynt BA-zihl): A Eucharistic liturgy, said to be edited by St. Basil the Great (330-379), and customary in the Church of Constantinople. The liturgy remains in use among Orthodox and Catholic Christians of the Byzantine Rite. Cf. CCC 1203

Basilian Fathers (buh-ZIHL-yuhn FAH-therz): The Congregation of St. Basil (C.S.B.) was founded in France in 1822. Members of the congregation serve in a wide variety of apostolates, but have tended to concentrate on education and evangelization. They are represented throughout the U.S. and Canada.

Basilian Order (buh-ZIHL-yuhn OR-der): The Order of St. Basil the Great (O.S.B.M.) traces its origins back to St. Basil himself. Today, its members work chiefly among Eastern Rite Catholics, particularly the Ukrainians, Ruthenians, Rumanians, Hungarians, and Croatians, for the U.S. and worldwide.

Basilian Rule (buh-ZIHL-yuhn RÖÖL): A rule of life composed by St. Basil the Great (329-379), which serves as the basis for monasticism in the Eastern Church. There are two forms, the shorter (consisting of fifty-five prescriptions) and the longer (consisting of three hundred thirteen prescriptions). The rule was revised by St. Theodore the Studite in the eighth century, and it continues to be used in this form. The Rule has an emphasis on obedience, with the requirement of manual work and set times for prayer. Opportunity is to be provided for schools for children, and there is to be provision for the care of the poor.

Basilica (buh-SIHL-ih-kuh): (Greek: royal hall) In ecclesiastical usage, a church of particular religious or historical importance, major (or patriarchal) churches in Rome and minor (honorary) churches abroad so designated by the Pope.

Basilidians (bah-zih-LIH-dee-uhnz): Followers of Basilides, second-century Alexandrian Gnostic who claimed to have been instructed by the Apostle Matthew. Cf. CCC 285

Bay Psalm Book (BAY SAHLM BØØK): First book published in the American colonies (1640), containing metrical translations of the hundred fifty Psalms and, in later editions, music for singing them.

B.C. (BEE SEE): The abbreviation for the English "Before Christ," it is used in the common system of dating by which years are marked as converging on the birth of Christ.

Beads (BEEDZ): Small, often round objects strung together for the purposes of assisting in prayer. Usually, the term refers to the fifteen decades of the Rosary, but other forms of prayer employ beads in various arrangements and enumerations. Cf. CCC 1674, 2708

Beatification (bee-A-tih-fih-KAY-shuhn): In the process for the canonization of a saint, this is the next-to-last step, the last being canonization itself. The act of beatification is performed by the Supreme Pontiff after a person's life, writings, and teachings have been examined and found to contain nothing contrary to the teaching of the Church, nor to the demands of Christian perfection. At this stage, the person's heroic virtues are said to be recognized and the Holy Father, with the aid of consultors from the Congregation for the Causes of Saints and especially the postulator of the person's Cause, declares the person Venerable, i.e., that the person may be venerated by the faithful. At this point, all that remains are the miracles. In cases of martyrs, sometimes the necessity of a miracle is waived by the Pope, who in any case may do so *ad libitum* if he so chooses for any person whose Cause has been introduced. However, the miracles are of great importance and must be of major proportions and proven to be an intervention of the supernatural order into the natural order whereby natural causes offer no plausible explanation. For beatification, one miracle is required, and for canonization, two. Once the required miracle has been performed through the intercession of the Venerable in question and recognized as such (i.e., unexplainable by human science or causes), the way is made clear for the beatification, whereby the Pope grants the newly elevated Blessed a Mass and Office of his or her own and a particular feast day to be celebrated in the places related to his or her life and in the religious order or diocese of origin. Sometimes the Blessed in question is of such popularity or of such particular importance to the whole Church that he or she is honored with a universal cult. Unlike the case with canonization, the Pope does not exercise his infallible authority when beatifying. He simply grants permission for public acknowledgment. This act is also a declaration that the person involved did practice virtue to a heroic degree or suffered a true Christian martyrdom. Among those Blessed held in honor native to the United States are Kateri Tekakwitha and Junípero Serra.

Beatific Vision (bee-uh-TIH-fihk VIH-zhuhn): The clear, immediate, intuitive knowledge of God, deriving from an act of the intellect, granted to those in heaven. On earth, believers know God through faith and reason; in heaven, faith will disappear and God will be known as He is. Then, the faithful will participate in the happiness of the Trinity. Jesus enjoyed the beatific vision on earth in His human nature; the angels also experience this reality. **CCC 163, 2548, 2550**

Beatitude (bee-A-tih-tööd): 1. Among Eastern Rite Christians, the term "beatitude" is an honorific, similar to "excellence" or "eminence" and used to honor patriarchs. 2. The Beatitudes (q.v.) are also the eight statements of Our Lord contained in the Gospel according to St. Matthew, delineating the qualities of one who aspires to blessedness. **CCC 1716**

Beatitude of Heaven (bee-A-tih-tööd uhv HEH-vuhn): The perfect happiness resulting from the direct vision of God ("light of glory"), which the blessed enjoy in heaven. This vision is unending and, therefore, completely satisfies the soul's desires. The beatitude of heaven consists in the attainment of God and other gifts (freedom from sickness, a glorified body, etc.). Gifts obtained on earth through nature and grace will be enhanced and remain in heaven. The degree of beatitude that each person experiences will be determined by one's "merit" and will differ accordingly. **CCC 2550**

Beatitudes (bee-A-tih-töödz): (Latin *beatus:* blessed, happy) Promises of eschatological blessing made by Jesus to His followers who embrace His teaching (Mt 5:3-12; Lk 6:20-23); as a literary form, the macarism (from the Greek *makarios,* blessed, happy) is found throughout the O.T. and Greek literature contemporary with Christ. The Beatitudes look to the arrival of the kingdom of God and the fulfillment of salvation; the inherent paradoxes, such as the comforting of mourners, force the listeners to redefine suffering within the global context of the Father's plan of salvation in His Son. CCC 1716-1717

Beatus or Beata (bay-AH-toos, -ah): (Latin: blessed one) Any holy person. Usually, it designates one who has been beatified.

Beauraing, Our Lady of (aur LAY-dee uhv bo-RAING): The title referring to Mary's thirty three apparitions at Beauraing, Belgium, to five children from November 29, 1932, to January 1, 1933. The youths saw Mary dressed in white with outstretched arms and wearing a crown of golden rays with her golden heart exposed. She exhorted the children to pray and to do penance — much as she had at Fátima. Many cures have been reported by those who have visited the shrine of Our Lady under this title.

Beautiful Gate (BYÖÖ-tih-fuhl GAYT): One of the entries of the Solomonic Temple as it was rebuilt in the time of King Herod, therefore contemporary with both Christ and the Apostles, called "beautiful" in Acts 3:2. Although archaeologists are not convinced of its exact identification and location, it is generally taken to be the same as the Corinthian Gate spoken of by Josephus, who locates it on the east side of the Temple. Rabbinic tradition holds that the Messiah will enter Jerusalem in triumph through this gate; it is thus of some significance that Christ did in fact enter the city on Palm Sunday from Bethany, east of Jerusalem, and in all likelihood through the gate spoken of by Josephus. There is today on the east side of the old city of Jerusalem a highly ornamented gate with Corinthian capitals that tradition holds to be the Beautiful Gate.

Beauty (BYÖÖ-tee): Often listed as one of the transcendentals, after unity, truth, and goodness, as universal qualities of all that exists. Beauty includes unity, truth, and goodness in the sense that it represents the harmony and inner perfection of a being. CCC 2500

Beda, The (*thuh* BAY-duh): Founded in 1852 and named for St. Bede of England, the Collegio Beda in Rome is a seminary that provides theological formation for former Anglicans who are studying for the Catholic priesthood and for delayed vocations.

Beelzebub (bee-EHL-zuh-buhb) or Beelzebul (-bøøl): (Hebrew, *báalzevuv:* god of insects) In Mt 12:24, called the "prince of demons," it is used to refer to Satan, or any demonic influence.

Befana (buh-FAH-nuh): (Italian: puppet or goblin) In Italian legend, an old woman (known as *La Befana)* who had refused hospitality to the Magi when they were traveling to visit the Christ Child. As her punishment, God decreed that she should have to perform good deeds on the feast of the Epiphany by delivering gifts to all the children of Italy. Epiphany is sometimes referred to by this title, and is also known as "the feast of children."

Beguines and Beghards (bay-GEENZ and buh-GAHRDZ): Groups of the laity given to extraordinary mortification and the development of personal spirituality linked with apostolic activities and the evangelical virtues; the female groups were called beguines; the male, beghards; their residences, beguinages. They flourished primarily in the Low Countries during the height of the medieval *Devotio Moderna*; after two centuries of faithful life, various heresies crept in and they were ultimately condemned by the Church, though several Belgian beguinages continue to witness to this form of spirituality.

Behaviorism (bee-HAY-vyøør-ih-zuhm): A theory affirming that all psychological activity can be explained in terms of observable behavior. Behaviorism is thus materialistic in its account of human nature, since it denies the spiritual character of the mind and the reality and immortality of the soul.

Being (BEE-ihng): Everything that exists is a being. In Christian thought, God is understood as the Source of all being, and all created reality participates in the being that comes from God and depends on God's action to continue in existence. Metaphysics is the branch of philosophy that is chiefly concerned with the study of being as such. **CCC 300**

Belfry (BEHL-free): An architectural structure designed to house and protect bells, usually those of a church. When it stands in the center of the church roof, as is typical of churches built in the American colonial style, it is also called a steeple. In churches built in the European style, one frequently sees two bell towers balancing the church façade. If there is only one, it usually stands to the side of the church; if freestanding, it is called a *campanile* (q.v.).

Belial (BEE-lee-uhl): From the Hebrew for "useless" or "dissolute," the term came to be used as a name for Satan (2 Cor 6:15).

Belief (buh-LEEF): An act of the mind assenting to a truth, or the truth itself to which assent is given can be termed "belief." In theology, the term refers especially to the act of faith by which the truths of revelation are accepted, and to the particular truths themselves. **CCC 1814**

Bell, Book, and Candle (BEHL BØØK and KAN-duhl): Three symbolic actions from the Middle Ages to signify that a major excommunication had been formalized: the church bell was tolled as at a funeral, symbolic of the spiritual death of the excommunicated party; the Book of Gospels was solemnly closed, to signify that the heart and ears of the excommunicant were similarly closed to the message contained therein; a candle was snuffed out, to symbolize that the faith was now extinguished for the former communicant.

Bells (BEHLZ): Used to call the faithful to worship, to announce the beginning of feasts and the deaths of the faithful, and, optionally during the liturgy, to signal the approach of the consecration and to accompany the showing of the consecrated Species to the faithful.

Bema (BEE-muh): In the Eastern Rite, the elevated portion of the church from which the Gospel is proclaimed and upon which the altar (and, in cathedrals, the bishop's chair) is located.

Benedicite (beh-nuh-DEE-tshee-tay): The *Benedicite,* or "Canticle of the Three Children" (Dn 3:57-90), is that song of praise intoned by the three young men Sidrach, Misach, and Abednego (Hananiah, Azariah, and Mishael in Hebrew) when they remained unharmed in the fiery furnace into which they had been thrown by order of King Nebuchadnezzar because they refused to adore him. The name comes from the Latin version of the canticle, which begins with the words *Benedicite, omnia opera Domini, Domino,* "All ye works of the Lord, bless the Lord." For centuries it has been chanted or recited in the Divine Office at Lauds, or Morning Prayer, on Sundays and solemnities. Because of the liturgical revision of Pope Paul VI, it is not recited every Sunday, but on the first and third Sundays of the four-week division of the Psalter for the Liturgy of the Hours, and always on feasts and solemnities.

Benedictines (beh-nuh-DIHK-tihnz): The religious order of both men and women following the Rule of St. Benedict of Nursia, which was compiled in the first half of the sixth century. The Rule emphasizes obedience to superiors, the importance of the balance between liturgical prayer and manual labor, and the essential value of community life. The Benedictine Rule is the foundation for monasticism in the Western Church.

Benediction (beh-nuh-DIHK-shuhn): 1. From the Latin word *benedicere,* benediction is the general term for any kind of blessing. Usually, a benediction is accompanied by extended hands and the Sign of the Cross over the one who is being blessed. 2. More commonly, it refers to the action whereby the congregation is blessed with the monstrance in the context of Exposition of the Blessed Sacrament (see Benediction of the Blessed Sacrament). **Cf. CCC 1378**

Benedictional (beh-nuh-DIHK-shuh-nuhl): A book of liturgical and devotional blessings of persons, places, and things, popular as a separate book in the Middle Ages, incorporated into the Roman Ritual after the Council of Trent, and now once again published as a separate book, *Ordo Benedictionum* in Latin and *Book of Blessings* in English.

Benediction, Apostolic (a-pah-STAH-lihk beh-nuh-DIHK-shuhn): A blessing imparted by the Pope or by one who has received the privilege of imparting such a blessing in his name.

Benediction of the Blessed Sacrament (beh-nuh-DIHK-shuhn uhv *th*uh BLEH-sehd SA-kruh-mehnt): Devotional celebration to honor the Real Presence of Christ in the Eucharist, in which a consecrated Host is placed in a monstrance and enthroned on the altar between lighted candles and incensed, during which hymns and prayers are sung and silent adoration is offered, concluding with the blessing of the people by a priest or deacon with the Eucharist and the singing of a hymn of praise. **CCC 1378**

Benediction with a Ciborium (beh-nuh-DIHK-shuhn with uh sih-BOR-ee-uhm): Form of benediction celebrated when the number of worshippers is small, during which the monstrance is not used but rather a veiled ciborium is exposed in the doorway of the tabernacle or even on the altar, and the people are blessed with the Eucharist in this vessel. **Cf. CCC 1378**

Benedict, The Rule of St. (*th*uh RÖÖL uhv saynt BLEH-nuh-dihkt): A monastic rule drawn up by St. Benedict of Nursia (c. 480-543) as the basis for a community of monks who gathered around him. St. Benedict consulted other monastic rules in developing his own. It is marked by common sense, balance, an emphasis on the following of Christ, the chanting of the Divine Office, stability, work, and the leadership of an elected abbot. The Rule of St. Benedict has been the most influential and widely used monastic rule in the West.

Benedictus (beh-neh-DIHK-tøøs): Also known as the "Canticle of Zechariah," it is the song of praise that Zechariah sang as soon as his lips were loosed at the circumcision of his son, St. John the Baptist, according to the Gospel of St. Luke (1:68-79). It has long been used by the Church at Morning Prayer in the Divine Office. Cf. CCC 1174-1178

Benefice (BEH-nuh-fihs): (Latin: favor or advantage) Formerly, an ecclesiastical office or post involving property and assured income.

Benefit of Clergy (BEH-nuh-fiht uhv KLER-dzhee): 1. In medieval times, the privilege of a priest or prelate to be tried for a crime in an ecclesiastical rather than civil court. 2. Today, usually applied to sacramental, as opposed to civil or common-law, marriage.

Benemerenti Medal (beh-nay-mer-EHN-tee MEH-duhl): (Latin: one who is well-deserving) A medal bestowed by the Pope, usually on the laity, in recognition of some meritorious service to the Church and society. First issued by Pope Pius VI (1775-1799), its design has changed over the years. This award is granted at the request of a diocesan bishop to the Vatican Secretariat of State.

Benignity (beh-NIHG-nuh-tee): One of the twelve fruits of the Holy Spirit enumerated by St. Paul (Gal 5:22), benignity (from *bonus ignis,* "good fire") is fervent love in doing good for others. CCC 736, 1832

Benjamin (BEHN-juh-mihn): A son of Jacob by Rachel (Gn 35:18) and the ancestor of one of the twelve tribes of Israel, Benjamin was the youngest son and was much beloved by his only full brother, Joseph. Benjamin played an important role in the story of Joseph.

Bequest for Masses (bee-KWEHST for MAS-ehz): A portion of a legacy designated in someone's will as reserved to supply stipends for the celebration of Masses for the repose of the soul of the deceased, his relatives, or others.

Berakoth (beh-ruh-KOTH): (Hebrew: blessings) Blessings beginning with the words "Blessed are you, Lord God, King of the ages" and recounting those gifts for which God is being thanked and praised. Such prayer formulas influenced the development of Christian worship, notably in the Eucharist and the Liturgy of the Hours. **Cf. CCC 1333**

Bestiaries (BEHS-tee-ehr-eez): Popular didactic accounts of the activities of both real and imaginary animals, usually with an allegorical or moral value given to the animal, often illustrated by way of illuminated capitals and marginal details depicting the animals discussed in the text; these in turn influenced the depiction of the animals in art and architecture, even into our own day, as seen in the gargoyles of the neo-Gothic style. One of the most popular subjects of medieval bestiaries was the unicorn.

Bethel (BEH-thuhl): (Hebrew: house of God) 1. An important Palestinian sanctuary where sacrifices could be offered (cf. Gn 28:10-22) until Jerusalem was designated as the sole place of sacrifice. 2. The term is also used by some Protestant denominations for a place of worship.

Bethlehem (BEHTH-luh-hehm): (Hebrew, *beth lechem: house of [the god] Lahm*, or house of bread) A town ten miles southwest of Jerusalem, in Judah, one of the oldest towns in Palestine, called Ephrathah to designate it as the birthplace of King David (1 Sm 17:12-15). It is the setting for most of the Book of Ruth, but it is prominent primarily as the birthplace of Jesus (Mt 2:1-16; Lk 2:4-15; Jn 7:42). The Church of the Nativity, built by Constantine (A.D. 330) surrounding some caves thought to have been the site of Jesus' birth, enlarged and further embellished by Justinian (A.D. 527-565), is one of the oldest Byzantine churches. In the underground cave is the altar of the Nativity; underneath the altar is a silver star set in the marble floor; in the center of the star is an opening that reveals the original stone floor; and around the opening is the declaration in Latin: "Here

Jesus Christ was born of the Virgin Mary." Cf. CCC 423, 565

Betrothal (bih-TRO-thuhl): In some legal systems, a legal act whereby a couple promise to marry each other at a future date. In Canon Law, there is provision for a betrothal or engagement ceremony with no legal obligation to marry eventually.

Betting (BEHT-ihng): A form of gambling in which someone lays down a sum of money or some other valuable as a wager on an athletic contest, race, or other event whose outcome cannot be predicted in advance. Like other forms of gambling, betting is not prohibited by Christian teaching, so long as it is done in moderation and does not jeopardize the livelihood and support of an individual or one's family. CCC 2413

Bible (BAI-buhl): The collection of books acknowledged by the Christian community as written by human authors under divine inspiration and as comprising, with Tradition, the indivisible source of revelation given by God for the salvation of humankind. The books of the Bible are grouped in two "testaments" representing the two great stages of the economy of salvation: the Old, or First, Testament (Genesis, Exodus, Leviticus, Numbers, Deuteronomy, Joshua, Judges, Ruth, 1 and 2 Samuel, 1 and 2 Kings, 1 and 2 Chronicles, Ezra, Nehemiah, Esther, Job, Psalms, Proverbs, Ecclesiastes, Song of Songs, Isaiah, Jeremiah, Lamentations, Ezekiel, Daniel, Hosea, Joel, Amos, Obadiah, Jonah, Micah, Nahum, Habakkuk, Zephaniah, Haggai, Zechariah, Malachi, Tobit, Judith, Wisdom, Sirach, Baruch, 1 and 2 Maccabees) and the New, or Second, Testament (Matthew, Mark, Luke, John, Acts, Romans, 1 and 2 Corinthians, Galatians, Ephesians, Philippians, Colossians, 1 and 2 Thessalonians, 1 and 2 Timothy, Titus, Philemon, Hebrews, James, 1 and 2 Peter, 1, 2, and 3 John, Jude, Revelation). The history of the selection of these books as constituting the canon of Sacred Scripture is complex, but it is believed by the Church to have taken place under the guidance of the Holy Spirit. Although the Bible is understood by the Church to be one book authored by God, the human authors and editors are recognized as exercising a true literary causality as instruments of the primary divine author. CCC 120; cf. 105-108

Bible, English Editions of the (IHN-glihsh eh-DIH-shuhnz uhv *th*uh BAI-buhl): The first complete English translation of the Bible dates from 1382 to 1384 and is associated with the work of John Wycliffe (1330-1384). Since the Council of Trent mandated the Latin Vulgate as "the authentic edition for public reading," all Catholic vernacular editions were based on this Latin text until the 1930s; English translations derived from the Vulgate include the Douay-Rheims (1582-1609), the Challoner Revision (1749-1763), the Confraternity Revision of the N.T. (1941), and the Knox Bible (1944-1950). Modern Catholic editions translated from the original languages include the Westminster Version (1935-1949), Kleist Lilly N.T. (1950-1954), Jerusalem Bible (1966, 1985), and the New American Bible (1952-1970, 1972, 1987). Important Protestant English translations are Tyndale's Bible (1535) and the Geneva Bible (1560), both largely supplanted by the Authorized Version or King James Bible (1611), which in turn led to the Revised Version (1881-1885) and the Revised Standard Version (1946-1952, 1990), published since 1966 in a Catholic edition. Other English translations include the New English Bible (1961-1970), now the Revised English Bible (1989); Today's English Version (1966-1979); and the New International Version (1973-1978).

Bible Reading (BAI-buhl REE-dihng): The spiritual exercise of reading the Scriptures as an aid to prayer and meditation. In monastic traditions, this meditative reading is called *lectio divina* and is regarded as especially beneficial for the development of a deep interior life. All Christians should read from the Bible daily, in order to draw guidance and inspiration from the Word of God. Cf. 1177, 2708

Bible Societies and Study Groups (BAI-buhl suh-SAI-eh-teez and STUH-dee grööps): Groups that generally meet informally for a discussion of the Scriptures and an attempt at relating their message to the daily lives of the participants, fairly common from the time of *Divino Afflante Spiritu,* the encyclical of Pope Pius XII, which first encouraged Catholics to become informed regarding the Scriptures, and further fostered by the Second Vatican Council in *Dei Verbum*.

Bible Studies, Catholic (KATH-uh-lihk BAI-buhl STUH-deez): The Second Vatican Council gave great impetus to Catholic Bible study and reading. Earlier in the twentieth century, Pope Pius XII, in his encyclical *Divino Afflante Spiritu* (1943), had encouraged renewed scholarly study of the Bible. In effect, this important encyclical constituted a kind of charter for Catholic biblical studies. Building on this renewal, the Council sought to stimulate study and reading of the Bible at all levels of the Church. The council taught that such reading and study are vital for an authentic Christian life, for in the Bible, God "meets His children with great love and speaks to them."

Bible Vigil (BAI-buhl VIH-dzhuhl): A paraliturgical service in which public readings from the Scriptures are combined with periods of prayer, singing, and silence, and often involving a sermon or reflection on the themes of the readings. Such vigils are particularly appropriate on the eve of a feast.

Biblia Pauperum (BIH-blee-uh PAU-peh-røøm) (Latin: Bible of the Poor) Popular illustrated books that sought to make Bible stories available to the poor and illiterate of the Late Middle Ages, especially popular as a didactic tool for demonstrating the N.T. fulfillment of the O.T. prophecies.

Biblical Chronology (BIH-blih-kuhl krah-NAH-luh-dzhee): Attempts to date the events and personalities of the Bible from scientific evidence.

Biblical Commission, Pontifical (pahn-TIH-fih-kuhl BIH-blih-kuhl kuh-MIH-shuhn): Established with full pontifical rights and privileges by Pope Leo XIII, with the issuance of his apostolic letter *Vigilantiae* on October 30, 1902, the Pontifical Biblical Commission (P.B.C., called by its official Latin title *Pontificia Commissio de Re Biblica)* has as its stated purpose the assurance "that Holy Writ should everywhere among us receive that more elaborate treatment which the times require and be preserved intact not only from any breath of error but also from all rash opinions." The P.B.C. comes under the direct authority and supervision of the Congregation for the Doctrine of the Faith. Aside from the Pontifical Biblical Institute, only the P.B.C. has the faculties from the Holy See to grant both the pontifical license and doctorate in Sacred Scripture (S.S.L. and S.S.D.), while the École Biblique of Jerusalem grants only the S.S.D.

Biblical Institute: See Pontifical Biblical Institute

Biblical Institute of Jerusalem: See École Biblique

Biblical Revival (BIH-blih-kuhl ree-VAI-vuhl): The renewal of the study, reading, and teaching of the Scriptures in the Catholic Church in the twentieth century and especially since the Second Vatican Council. The beginnings of this renewal are attributed to the French Dominican scholar Père M. J. Lagrange (1855-1938), who in 1890 founded a school for the study of the Bible in Jerusalem. Pope Pius XII confirmed and encouraged this renewal with his encyclical *Divino Afflante Spiritu,* issued in 1943. Today, Catholic biblical scholars are at the forefront of the fields of archaeology, Near Eastern languages, history, and interpretation.

Bigamy (BIH-guh-mee): The state of one who has married more than one spouse. It is forbidden by civil and Canon Law. Cf. CCC 1645, 2387

Bigot (BIH-guht): One who holds false or unreasonable religious and racial views, combined with prejudice and intolerance toward others who hold different views. Cf. CCC 1934-1938

Bilocation (bai-lo-KAY-shuhn): The simultaneous presence of the same substance in two distinct locations. This phenomenon does not imply that the substance is multiplied but rather that the substance's relations to other entities are increased. The Holy Eucharist is an example of bilocation as Christ's presence — unlimited, unlike other realities — exists at once throughout the world. Holy persons like Blessed Padre Pio (1887-1968) were said to manifest bilocation.

Bination (bai-NAY-shuhn): (From Latin: a pair) The act of a priest celebrating two Masses in a single day, permitted when pastoral necessity requires.

Binding and Loosing (BAIN-dihng and LÖÖ-sihng): From the commission of Christ to St. Peter and the other Apostles (Mt 16 and 18), "binding and loosing" refers to the power to forgive sins (the "power of the keys") that is handed on to the successors of the Apostles. **CCC 1444-1445**

Biretta (buh-REH-tuh): Square cap worn by clerics of the Latin rite, the color indicating the rank of the cleric and the number of ridges, in some cases, his academic degree.

Birth Control (BERTH kuhn-TROL): A deliberate, intentional act to prevent conception or birth, including contraception, sterilization, and abortion. There are many methods of birth control: the "pill," the intrauterine device, the diaphragm, foam, condom, "withdrawal," and abstinence. The Church has consistently condemned contraception because it ruptures the connection between the life-giving and love-giving dimensions of marital intercourse. Two of the best-known condemnations of contraception are *Casti Connubii* (Pope Pius XI, 1930) and *Humanae Vitae* (Pope Paul VI, 1968). If there are just reasons, a couple may use natural family planning to postpone conception. N.F.P. has many merits but especially that it is moral, safe, and effective; it is also a communications-builder for the couple. Many of the artificial methods (e.g., the "pill") can be abortifacient and fail on all four counts. **CCC 2366-2372**

Birth Control Pill (BERTH kuhn-TROL PIHL): One of a variety of anti-fertility drugs that suppress ovulation and thus prevent pregnancy. Birth control pills are a common form of contraception. Some of these are actually abortifacients.

Bisexual (bai-SEHK-shöö-uhl): One who can relate to members of both sexes as sexual partners.

Bishop (BIH-shuhp): (Greek *episcopos:* overseer) A successor of the Apostles, in the highest order of the threefold ministry, with the fullness of Christ's priesthood. He has the authority and power to administer all the sacraments, including ordination. CCC 1555-1561

Bishop, Auxiliary (awg-ZIHL-yer-ee BIH-shuhp): An assistant bishop, appointed by the Pope to aid the bishop who is the Ordinary of a diocese. Large dioceses can have more than one auxiliary, who sometimes serve as territorial vicars.

Bishop, Coadjutor (ko-uh-DZHÖÖ-ter BIH-shuhp): A bishop assigned by the Holy See to assist the residential bishop, often with special powers. Upon the death, retirement, or removal of the residential bishop, the coadjutor automatically becomes the residential bishop.

Bishop, Residential (reh-zih-DEHN-tshuhl BIH-shuhp): Another term for the Ordinary or bishop of a diocese.

Bishop, Suffragan (SUH-fruh-guhn BIH-shuhp): The residential bishop of a diocese that is part of an ecclesiastical province, where the primary bishop is known as the metropolitan archbishop.

Bishop, Titular (TIH-tshöö-ler BIH-shuhp): A nonresidential bishop who holds the title to a defunct see.

Bishop-Elect (BIH-shuhp eh-LEHKT): Prior to his consecration but after being named a bishop, one is called a bishop-elect.

Bishop of Rome (BIH-shuhp uhv ROM): As the first Bishop of Rome, St. Peter founded the see in A.D. 42, and the divinely appointed primacy of St. Peter has been entrusted to each successor who has taken his place. The Pope, as the Bishop of Rome, is considered "another Peter" and, therefore, the head of the College of Bishops. Agreement with the judgment of the Bishop of Rome has been a test of orthodoxy from the earliest years of the Church, attested to by such writers as St. Irenaeus (d. 200). Cf. CCC 881-883

Bishopric (BIH-shuhp-rihk): A bishop's see or diocese, the territory under his jurisdiction, or his office and authority as such.

Bishops, Appointment of (uh-POINT-mehnt uhv BIH-shuhps): The procedures according to which nominations and appointments of bishops are made. In the Western Church, the right to appoint a bishop is reserved to the Pope, although nominations may be submitted to him by various procedures of nomination (e.g., by vote of a cathedral chapter).

Bishops, Collegiality of (kuh-LEE-dzhee-AL-ih-tee uhv BIH-shuhps): The joint fellowship and authority enjoyed by all the bishops of the world in union with the Holy See. With the Pope at its head, the College of Bishops, as successors to the Apostles, exercises supreme authority over the Church in teaching, sanctifying, and leading. Vatican Council II gave renewed attention and emphasis to bishops' collegiality. **CCC 880-887**

Bishops, Jurisdiction of (dzhøø-rihs-DIHK-shuhn uhv BIH-shuhps): The ordinary jurisdiction exercised by a bishop over his diocese (except, as stipulated by law, exempt religious), subject to Canon Law and to the universal jurisdiction of the Pope. **CCC 879**

Bishops, Obligations of (ah-blih-GAY-shuhnz uhv BIH-shuhps): The primary obligation of a bishop is to guide the people of his diocese in all aspects of the living of the Christian Faith. Other obligations include care for the administration of the sacraments, maintenance of permanent residence in the diocese, the completion of periodic pastoral visitations, representation of the diocese to other dioceses and to the national conference of bishops, and the completion of the required *ad limina* visits to the Holy See. **CCC 894**

Bishops' Committee on the Liturgy [BCL] (BIH-shuhps kuh-MIH-tee awn *th*uh LIH-ter-dzhee [BEE SEE EHL]): Committee whose responsibility is to assist the National Conference of Catholic Bishops, diocesan Ordinaries, and liturgical commissions in fulfilling the directives of the Holy See in regard to the Sacred Liturgy.

Bishops in the Church, Decree on the Pastoral Office of: See Christus Dominus

Black (BLAK): As a liturgical color, one of the three options permitted for Masses for the dead.

Black Fast (BLAK FAST): Formerly in the Latin Rite, and still in the Eastern Rite (and among some monastic orders), a day of penance on which only one meal is permitted in the evening and meat, dairy products, and alcoholic beverages are forbidden.

Black Friars (BLAK FRAI-erz): Term used to designate the Order of Preachers or Dominicans, derived from their practice of wearing a black cloak (called the "cappa") over their white habit.

Black Legend (BLAK LEH-dzhuhnd): An anti-Spanish legend describing the conquest and government of the New World in wholly malevolent terms and portraying the Spaniards as a universally rapacious, greedy, and brutal lot who were motivated by nothing more than the quest for adventure, power, territory, and gold. While the historical truth of the harm suffered by Native Americans and their cultures at the hands of the conquistadors cannot be denied, the legend gives a completely one-sided account of these events, largely to exalt the rectitude and sobriety of English undertakings in the Americas. The legend ignores the civilizing and evangelizing accomplishments of the Spaniards. Ironically, Spanish colonization encouraged intermarriage with the Native American population, which still constitutes a major cultural and ethnic force in Latin American countries, whereas in countries settled by the English the Native Americans, after ferocious and unremitting warfare, were driven to the margins of society to a kind of internal exile.

Black Madonna (BLAK muh-DAH-nuh): Images of the Blessed Virgin painted in black or now turned black by age. The two most famous such Madonnas are the jeweled icon of Our Lady of Czestochowa in Poland and carved statue of Our Lady of Montserrat in Spain. Both images are the object of deep devotion and continual pilgrimages.

Black Mass (BLAK MAS): 1. Because the Mass of Christian Burial, or Requiem Mass, was for centuries always celebrated only in black vestments, it came to be called the "black Mass." 2. This term is also used for sacrilegious parodies of the Mass, celebrated to give honor and worship to the devil or simply to mock the Church and desecrate her sacraments.

Black Monks (BLAK MUHNKS): Title given to the Benedictine monks because of their black religious habits.

"Black Pope" (BLAK POP): A sobriquet for the Father General of the Society of Jesus, indicating both the supposed power and influence of the Jesuits and the color of their religious garb.

Blaise, Blessing of St. (BLEH-sihng uhv SAYNT BLAYZ): The traditional blessing of throats, conferred on the liturgical memorial of St. Blaise (February 3) by means of two crossed candles often tied with a bow. The blessing invokes the intercession of St. Blaise against infirmities of the throat.

Blasphemy (BLAS-fuh-mee): (Greek *blasphemia:* abusive language damaging to a person's reputation) Abusive, contemptuous, and irreverent language toward God. In the O.T. it is punishable by stoning and defiles the whole community (Lv 24:16); not limited to speech, as adultery, murder, stealing, and unbelief are also seen as blasphemous (2 Sm 12:14; Ps 10:3, 13; Nm 14:11; 16:30; Is 1:4; 5:24). In the N.T. the claim of Jesus to be the Messiah (Mt 26:64; Mk 14:61-62) and God's Son (Jn 8:49-59; 10:31-36) was taken as blasphemy; the attribution of His power and authority over demons as diabolical was considered a blasphemy against the Holy Spirit (Mt 12:31; Mk 3:28; Lk 12:10). In Catholic moral theology, blasphemy, which can be directly against God or indirectly against God by blaspheming the Church or the saints, is a sin against the virtue of religion; St. Thomas Aquinas terms it a sin against faith. CCC 2148

Blessed (BLEH-sehd): 1. Something that has been hallowed by a religious rite of blessing. 2. A title bestowed on a deceased person by the Holy See, indicating that the person excelled in virtue and is worthy of public veneration. CCC 1671-1672

Blessed Earth, Holy Ground (BLEHST ERTH, HO-lee GRAUND): A plot of land consecrated for use as a place of burial for Christians.

Blessed in Heaven (BLEH-sehd in HEH-vehn): The Church Triumphant, or those members of the communion of saints known as the blessed in heaven, are those who enjoy perfect union with God and the beatific vision. CCC 954, 1023

Blessed Sacrament (BLEH-sehd SA-kruh-mehnt): The term for the consecrated bread and wine when they become the Body and Blood of Christ. The Blessed Sacrament is perpetually reserved in Catholic churches in a prominent place, marked by a burning sanctuary lamp. CCC 1374-1381

Blessed Trinity (BLEH-sehd TRIH-nih-tee): The mystery of the three Persons — Father, Son, and Holy Spirit — in the one God, revealed to us by Christ, and the focus of all Christian life and worship. The Son proceeds from the Father by generation, while the Spirit proceeds from the Father and the Son through spiration. Each Person of the Blessed Trinity is equally God; in everything They do in the orders of creation and redemption, They act as one. Human destiny in Christ is to be drawn into the intimate communion of life and love They share with One Another.

Blessing (BLEH-sihng): Ritual in which the right hand is raised and usually the Sign of the Cross is made over the person or thing, invoking God's favor or intervention upon the one blessed; in some cases, such as the Nuptial Blessing, the arms of the priest remain outstretched; while the ritual contains over two hundred blessings, some are reserved to bishops or to members of some religious orders, as, for example, the erection of the Stations of the Cross. In the Scriptures, blessings express God's generosity, favor, and unshakable love for His children (Hebrew *beraka;* Greek *eulogia;* Latin *benedictio);* in the O.T., blessing is linked to reconciliation, fertility, and fruitfulness; inheritance is rooted in paternal blessing. In the N.T., Jesus blesses the food He multiplies (Mt 14:19; Mk 6:41; 8:7; Lk 9:16; Jn 6:1-15) and the bread and wine that will become the Eucharist (Mt 26:26; Mk 14:22). **CCC 1669-1672**

Blessing, Apostolic (a-pah-STAH-lihk BLEH-sihng): The benediction given by the Pope to the faithful at the end of Mass and other liturgical ceremonies, at papal audiences, and on other festive solemnities. Bishops may bestow this blessing, as may priests at their first solemn Mass and when they attend to the dying. A plenary indulgence under the usual conditions is attached to this benediction and may be gained by the faithful even when they listen to a radio transmission or television broadcast of the Holy Father's Mass.

Blessing, Last (last BLEH-sihng): The final blessing at the conclusion of the celebration of the Eucharist, occurring just after the postcommunion prayer and before the dismissal.

Blessing, Papal (PAY-puhl BLEH-sihng): A blessing conferred by the Pope himself or by someone who has been delegated by him. Sometimes the term is used to refer to an illuminated document bearing the picture of the Pope and attesting to the Pope's conferral of his blessing upon the person or persons named thereon. Such documents are suitable for framing and are a popular gift on the occasion of weddings, ordinations, and anniversaries.

Blessing of Fire: See Fire, Blessing of the

Blessings, Book of (BØØK uhv BLEH-sihngz): English translation of the Latin *Ordo Benedictionum,* the *editio typica* (or standard, official Latin edition) of that section of the

Roman Ritual containing the blessings of persons, places, and things, published by the Holy See in 1984 and reflecting the liturgical principles promulgated at the Second Vatican Council.

Bless Oneself (BLEHS wuhn-SEHLF): To make the Sign of the Cross on oneself. **CCC 2157**

Bliss (BLIHS): The state of perfect happiness of those who behold God face-to-face in the beatific vision. **CCC 2548**

Block Rosary (BLAHK RO-zuh-ree): The practice of regular gatherings of Catholics in a particular neighborhood for the sake of the communal recitation of the Rosary.

Blood, Baptism of: See Baptism of Blood

Blue (BLÖÖ): The color traditionally reserved for the Blessed Virgin Mary. Normally, blue is not used as a liturgical color except in Spain, which has a long-standing indult.

Blue Army, The (*thuh* BLÖÖ AHR-mee): The Blue Army of Our Lady of Fátima was founded in 1946 to perform the prayers commended during the Fátima apparitions, especially the Rosary for the conversion of Russia and for world peace. The society continues to offer such prayers and to engage in charitable and educational works.

Blue Laws (BLÖÖ LAWZ): Civil laws that seek to regulate public morality in regard to alcohol, sexual activity, gambling, and Sunday observance.

Boat (BOT): 1. Often employed in literature and art as a symbol of the Church, most likely because of the common employment of the Apostles as fishermen. 2. In particular, since Peter and his successors give the Church specific direction as would a helmsman, the Church is often called the boat or bark of Peter. 3. Because of its shape, the small liturgical vessel used for containing incense is called a boat. **CCC 845**

Boat Bearer (BOT BEHR-er): The altar server who carries the vessel containing incense (the "incense boat") at liturgical services in which incensation will take place. When — as is often the case — the thurifer carries both the thurible and boat, the boat bearer is dispensed with.

Bodily Defect (BAHD-ih-lee DEE-fehkt): Defects (like blindness or the lack of a finger) that would prevent the proper celebration of the Eucharist or some other function of the priest.

Body (BAH-dee): Along with the soul, the body goes to make up the composite that constitutes every human being. According to Christian teaching, the body is the temple of the Holy Spirit and, as such, must be treated with reverence and respect. Modesty in dress and action befits the Christian person.

Body and Soul (BAH-dee and SOL): Together, body and soul constitute the whole human being. The unity between body and soul is real and substantial, not just instrumental or functional. Personal identity subsists in body and soul together, not simply in the soul. Although the soul survives the death of the body, its being is incomplete until it is united with the resurrected body in glory. CCC 362-368

Body, Glorified (GLO-rih-faid BAH-dee): The immortal and incorruptible body (1 Cor 15:53) that each person will possess after the resurrection of the dead in glory. Cf. CCC 645

Body, Resurrection of the (reh-zer-REHK-shuhn uhv *th*uh BAH-dee): The eschatological restoration of the body to the soul of each human person, such that the risen body united to the soul passes into a completely new sphere of existence, totally different from the life as lived on earth, as promised by Christ (Mt 22:29-32; Lk 14:14; Jn 5:29, 6:39-40, 11:25); the Church as Christ's Body, over which He is Head, shares in an integral fashion in His resurrected life; doctrine preached by St. Paul and the early Church as a central mystery of the Christian Faith (1 Cor 15:20-21; Col 1:18). The prophets attest to belief in the corporate resurrection of God's People; God revives, raises up, and restores "dry bones" (Ez 37:1-14; cf. Hos 6:1) and raises up a dead Jerusalem (Is 51:17; 60:1). While the later O.T. does attest to individual resurrection in the context of a final judgment (Dn 7:13-27), where this new life will differ radically from the current life (Dn 12:2-3; 2 Mc 7:9-23; 14:46), the N.T. doctrine of bodily resurrection is firmly rooted in Christ's teaching on His own resurrection. **CCC 988-991**

Bollandists (BOL-luhn-dihsts): A small group of seventeenth-century Dutch Jesuits who discovered, sorted, and edited records of the lives of the ancient saints. Their project continues even today.

Bolshevism (BOL-shuh-vih-zuhm): (Russian *bolshe:* the greater, majority) The policies and practice of the communists who overtook the provisional government of the Russian Empire in 1917, five months after the Czar was overthrown. Because of its atheistic foundation, it was hostile to religion in general. In the more precise meaning, the Bolsheviks were the majority of the Russian Social Democratic Labor Party.

Bond of Marriage (BAHND uhv MEHR-ihdzh): The unique relationship between a man and a woman as husband and wife, coming into existence when consent is exchanged. See also Marriage. **CCC 1626**

Book of Common Prayer (BØØK uhv KAH-muhn PREHR): Liturgical book of the Church of England (and other churches of the Anglican Communion, e.g., the Episcopal Church in the United States), first issued in 1549 as a compilation and "reformation" of the medieval Roman Missal, Breviary, Ritual, and Benedictional.

Book of Hours: See Hours, Book of

Book of Life, The (*th*uh BØØK uhv LAIF): The names of the saved are known by God and thus are written in the Book of Life (Rv 20:15).

Books, Liturgical (lih-TER-dzhih-kuhl BØØKS): The Church's officially approved volumes, containing the texts and rituals of its ceremonies and rites.

"Born Catholic" (BORN KATH-uh-lihk): A popular term for a person who is born of Catholic parents and reared in the Faith from infancy.

Bowing (BAU-ihng): A liturgical gesture in which either just the head or the whole body from the waist is lowered in reverence to the Blessed Sacrament, the altar, the cross, or some person (e.g., a presiding bishop or the principal celebrant).

Boycott (BOI-kaht): The avoidance of business or other relations with some organization or institution in protest of its policies. Boycotting is a common form of moral and political protest.

Boys' Town (BOIZ TAUN): An institution founded on December 10, 1917, by Fr. Edward Flanagan, to care for abandoned, orphaned, and underprivileged boys. It is now an incorporated city near Omaha, Nebraska, and its work has spread beyond its place of foundation. Since the latter part of the 1960s it has been coeducational.

Branch Theory (BRANTSH THEER-ee): The opinion that three distinct churches — Anglican, Catholic, and Eastern Orthodox — comprise the "true church" founded by Jesus Christ. This theory, advocated especially by members of the Anglican Church, is opposed to the "oneness" of the Church and the decree *Apostolicae Curae* (September 13, 1896) of Pope Leo XIII, who wrote that the Anglican Church lacks valid orders.

Brasses (BRAS-ehz): Engraved sheets of brass used for funeral monuments or markers, usually representing the person buried in life-size scale as he would appear beneath the marker; they also give the person's name and important dates from his life, at times with an epitaph or verse descriptive of the person's achievements. The brass may be placed flush with the floor or attached to the top of an above-ground sepulcher. Brass plates attached at the end of burial niches are also called brasses. Though most common in the medieval period, they remained in use through the eighteenth century and have a modern adaptation in brass plaques.

Breach of Promise (BREETSH uhv PRAH-mihs): After the making of a contract, the refusal of one party to fulfill his or her part of the contract. The term refers especially to the refusal to enter into matrimony after a betrothal.

Bread (BREHD): As the staff of life, bread exists in a kind of transformed state, such that it combines basic elements, viz., flour, water and yeast (in non-Eucharistic bread of the Latin Rite), which are refashioned into a union difficult, if not impossible, to reverse; bread thus provides an excellent image to speak of Eucharistic unity (cf. 1 Cor 10:17) and is a sign of the new creation. At His last paschal meal, Christ took bread as the fruit of human work and raised it to a divine dignity by offering to the world His very Body and Blood under the species of bread and wine (Mt 26:26-29; Mk 14:22-25; Lk 22:14-20; 1 Cor 11:23-26). Ritual use of bread is common in the O.T.: Passover and the Feast of Unleavened Bread (Ex 12:8-20; 13:3-10); cereal offerings (Ex 29:2-25; Lv 2:4-16, 7:9; 1 Sm 10:3-8); the sustenance of Israel in the wilderness with bread from heaven (Ex 16:14-30). Cf. CCC 1333-1336

Bread, Blessed (BLEHST BREHD): The blessing of bread is associated with a variety of liturgical celebrations and saints' feast days throughout the Church. See also Pain Bénit.

Bread, Eucharistic (YÖÖ ker-IHS-tihk BREHD): The bread used for consecration in the Eucharist. In the Western Church, unleavened wafers are used. Leavened bread is used in all the Orthodox and Eastern Rite Churches (except for the Catholic Malabar Rite, the Armenian Rite, and the Maronite Rite).

Bread of Life (BREHD uhv LAIF): Title of Christ as He reveals Himself in Jn 6; specifically, He is the "Bread which is from heaven and gives life to the world" (Jn 6:33-35). He first feeds the crowd with loaves and fishes to establish His credentials as the provider of sustenance (Jn 6:1-15); then in metaphorical language He shows Himself to be the true manna sent from God in heaven (Jn 6:22-58). The manna, which is Christ, fulfills Israel's experience of receiving daily bread from God (Ex 16); the liturgy of the Eucharist, focused on the bread and wine, transformed into His Body and Blood, which become the spiritual food and drink of the faithful, draws the Church into the one Sacrifice and into His being sacrificed on Calvary. CCC 103, 1338, 1405, 2835

Breaking of Bread (BRAY-kihng uhv BREHD): In the Acts of the Apostles (Acts 2:42), expression used to designate the Eucharist, during which, at the Lord's command, bread is taken, blessed, broken, and distributed. CCC 1329

Breath (BREHTH): In the Bible, breath is the symbol of life or of the soul, and as such it can stand for a living being itself. CCC 691

Brethren of the Lord (BREH*TH*-rehn uhv *th*uh LORD): Kinsmen of Jesus, likely no closer than cousins, as suggested by the patristic writers, notably St. Jerome, who, for example, argues that James the brother of the Lord was likely James the son of Alphaeus (Mk 3:18), also identified with James the younger (Mk 15:40), the brother of Joses; both Joses and James are called "brothers" of Jesus (Mk 6:3) and their mother is Mary Clophas, sister of Mary, the Mother of Jesus; thus, both brothers have parents other than Joseph and Mary; their mother is likely Jesus' aunt, so they are His cousins. These brethren of the Lord are mentioned numerous times in the N.T. (Mt 12:46, 13:55; Mk 3:31, 6:3; Lk 8:19; Jn 2:12, 7:3, 20:17; Acts 1:14; 1 Cor 9:5; Gal 1:19); individual brethren are identified as James and Joses (Mk 6:3), Simon (Mt 13:55) and Judas (Mk 6:3). Confusion arises from the use of the Greek term *adelphos,* which can mean a brother or sister in blood, from the same parents, or as it appears to be used here with the meaning of one's extended family, i.e., one's cousins, as, in fact, it is used in the Greek O.T. (Gn 13:8,

29:12-15), where it probably reflects a holdover from the nomadic societal structure in which the leader of the tribe is called "father" and one's fellow tribesmen are called "brothers and sisters." The obvious consequence of the misunderstanding of this term to mean "blood brothers and sisters" would be the compromise of Mary's perpetual virginity. **CCC 500**

Breve (BRAY-vay): (Italian: short inscription) A papal brief (see Brief, Apostolic; also Brief, Papal).

Breviarium Romanum (breh-vee-AHR-ee-øøm ro-MAHN-øøm): (Latin: Roman Breviary) The book containing the Divine Office. It came to be called a breviary, or abridgement, because it was a shorter and more portable version of the choir books used for choral celebration of the Liturgy of the Hours in monasteries and cathedral chapters.

Breviary (BREE-vyuh-ree): (From Latin: abridgement) Term formerly, and still often popularly, used for the book containing the Liturgy of the Hours, or Divine Office, since the versions prepared for the friars and secular clergy represented an abridgement of the monastic offices. **Cf. CCC 1096, 1174-1178**

Bribery (BRAI-ber-ee): The offer and acceptance of a gift (usually, but not necessarily, monetary) in return for the performance of some favor by a person in a position of responsibility in some organization or institution. The presumption is that the individual offering the bribe would not otherwise obtain the desired favor without the influence or action of the person taking the bribe. Bribery is a sin against justice.

Bride of Christ (BRAID uhv KRAIST): Metaphorical title for the Church (occurs only in 2 Cor 11:2), bespeaking the intimate, "nuptial" union that Christ enjoys with the Church; it is as "one flesh" (Eph 5:31; cf. Gn 2:24), clearly defined elsewhere in the N.T.: as Christ is the "New Adam" of the New Creation (1 Cor 15:22; Rom 5:12-14; cf. Eph 2:15; Gal 6:15), the Church as the "New Eve" is taken from the side of the New Adam on the cross (Eph 2:15). Patristic writers develop this imagery, teaching that the New Eve was born from Christ's side during His three days in the tomb; His death is therefore a creative act (Jn 19:34; Eph 2:15), which the Fathers clarify in terms of sacramental life: The blood and water flowing from Christ's side are the sacramental signs of how He animates His Bride through the Sacraments of Baptism and Eucharist. CCC 796

Brief, Apostolic [Breve] (a-pah-STAH-lihk BREEF [BRAY-vay]): Concise papal letter, of less formality than a papal bull; though prepared and signed by the Secretary of State of the Holy See, it is authenticated with the stamped representation of the papal ring.

Brief, Papal (PAY-puhl BREEF): A papal document, less formal than a bull, but carrying the Pope's authority and the signature of the Cardinal Secretary of State or his delegate.

Brotherhood of Man (BRUH-_ther_-hood uhv MAN): According to the Christian Faith, all men and women are created equal, in being, dignity, and destiny, and are called to true brotherhood in Christ as adopted sons and daughters of the Father. This spiritual and supernatural brotherhood has as its natural basis the identical biological species of all human beings of all races. CCC 361, 1931

Brotherly Love (BRUH-_ther_-lee LUHV): Christ commands us to love all other human beings as our brothers and sisters, precisely because in Him all are united in one family of God. Cf. CCC 1789, 2054, 2212, 2219, 2231, 2269, 2302

Brothers (BRUH-_ther_z): The term designating the members of a religious community who are either not ordained and not intending to receive Holy Orders or those who are in the process of preparing for the sacrament.

Buddhism (BÖÖ-dih-zuhm): Western name given to a religious tradition that originated in India in the sixth century B.C. in the teaching of Gotama the Buddha. The doctrine preached by the Buddha is known as the Dharma. It presents an analysis of the human condition and the means by which suffering and mortality can be transcended. Central to the Dharma is the teaching of the Excellent Eightfold Path by which Nirvana, or enlightenment, is to be attained. A monastic movement is central to the practice of Buddhism, but all forms of Buddhism incorporate some type of lay membership. The two principal forms of Buddhism are Mahayana and Hinayana (Theravada). The religion spread into all of southeast Asia and then into China and Japan, and today shows signs of attracting a significant following in Western countries.

Bugia (böö-DZHEE-uh): A short candle with a small, straight handle. The name "bugia" derives from Bougie in Algeria, where candlewax was manufactured for export.

Bull, Apostolic or Papal (a-pah-STAH-lihk [PAY-puhl] BØØL): Common but unofficial name given to certain decrees issued by the Holy Father. The term "bull" comes from the Latin *bulla,* a seal affixed to the decrees.

Bulla Cenae (BØØ-luh TSHAY-nay): Latin term for a comprehensive list of excommunications in force. It was read yearly in the presence of the Pope and the cardinals on Holy Thursday. It was abrogated in 1869.

Bulla Cruciata (BØØ-luh kröö-SHAH-tuh): The grouping of papal documents mentioning the favors bestowed upon those Spaniards who resisted the Muslims during the Crusades. The favors were initiated in 1063 and apply even today to all persons on Spanish territory (even to countries once under Spain's dominion). One such privilege is the dispensation of all fasting and abstinence, except for a few days.

Bullarium (bøø-LAH-ree-øøm): Latin word for a collection of papal bulls or pronouncements of the Holy Father.

Burial, Christian (KRIHS-tshuhn BEHR-ee-uhl): The funeral rites of the Church, beginning with prayers at the wake and concluding with the Mass of Christian Burial and interment in the consecrated ground of a Catholic cemetery. CCC 1690, 2300

Burial, Ecclesiastical (eh-KLEE-zee-AS-tih-kuhl BEHR-ee-uhl): Interment with the rites of the Church, a right of the Christian faithful. The Church recommends burial of the bodies of the dead, but cremation is permissible if it does not involve reasons against Church teaching. Ecclesiastical burial is in order for catechumens; for unbaptized children whose parents intended to have them baptized before death; and even, in the absence of their own ministers, for baptized non-Catholics unless it would be considered against their will. CCC 1690, 2300

Burse (BERS): 1. A stiff cardboard pocket, bound on three sides and covered with material matching the Mass vestments, which provides an envelope or pouch for the corporal. Although not often used today, the burse is carried on top of the veiled chalice to and from the altar. 2. The leather case, used for Communion calls to the elderly and sick, containing the pyx that carries the Blessed Sacrament. 3. The fund, to which the faithful contribute, which provides for the education of seminarians.

Burse, Financial (fai-NAN-shuhl BERS): A special fund, usually endowed by a private benefactor and maintained by a diocese, religious institute, or private foundation, often with the express purpose of educating candidates for the priesthood. They vary in size and availability, of course, but sometimes have been of crucial importance in providing for the expenses of priestly education. Depending on the ownership of the burse, generally it is regulated as a "nonautonomous pious foundation," i.e., a special classification of temporal goods under Canons 1303-1310 of the 1983 Code of Canon Law.

Buskins (BUHS-kihnz): Ceremonial stockings, matching in color the vestments of the day, formerly prescribed for use by a bishop at Pontifical Mass.

Byzantine Art (BIH-zuhn-teen AHRT): Style of pictorial or architectural expression particular to the era of the Byzantine Empire and of the Eastern Rite that flourished within it, rich in color and design and, in its iconography, expressing in visual form the Church's doctrinal belief with orthodox integrity.

Byzantine Church (BIH-zuhn-teen TSHERTSH): In its primary sense, this term refers to the Orthodox Church under the leadership of the Patriarch of Constantinople (a city also known as Byzantium). The term is also often used as an umbrella term for all the Orthodox churches, as well as the various Eastern Rites in communion with the Bishop of Rome.

Byzantine Empire (BIH-zuhn-teen EHM-pair): The Eastern division of the Roman Empire after the division of the Empire into West and East became permanent in 395. Constantine had earlier made his capital at Byzantium in Asia Minor and renamed it Constantinople. With the fall of Rome in 476, the Byzantine emperors claimed power over the entire Roman world. Byzantine Christian culture reached its high point in the sixth and seventh centuries. The Empire collapsed with the conquest of Constantinople by the Turks in 1453.

Byzantine Rite: See Rite, Byzantine

Byzantine Rite, Catholics of the (KATH-uh-lihks uhv *thuh* BIH-zuhn-teen RAIT): Eastern Rite Christians, following the Byzantine Rite in their liturgy and customs, who are in communion with the Holy See.

C

Caeremoniale Episcoporum (tshehr-eh-mo-nee-AH-lay eh-PIHS-ko-POR-øøm): Latin title of the *Ceremonial of Bishops,* the book containing rubrics and directives that govern ceremonies celebrated or presided over by bishops of the Latin Rite.

Caeremonius (tshehr-eh-MO-nee-øøs): Latin term for the liturgical "master of ceremonies," who offers assistance and direction at celebrations, especially when a bishop presides.

Caesaropapism (SEE-zuh-ro-PAY-pih-zuhm): 1. Theory that Church and State should be under one ruler. 2. Exercise of complete authority over ecclesiastical affairs by a secular ruler. 3. Government in which Church is subordinate to State or a secular ruler.

Calatrava, Order of (OR-der uhv kah-lah-TRAH-vuh): Spain's oldest military order, founded in 1158, whose members were dedicated to living poverty, chastity, and obedience according to the Rule of St. Benedict. Approved by Pope Alexander III in 1164, the order flourished and eventually became an honorary order of noblemen. In 1219, an associated order of nuns was begun at Calatrava, and it exists even today.

Calefactory (kal-eh-FAK-to-ree): (From Latin: to warm) 1. In former times, the heated room of a monastery where the monks could warm themselves during breaks in the night offices. 2. In some monastic communities at present, a term to designate the recreation room. 3. A hollow globe of glass or silver, sometimes gold-plated, filled with warm water and used by the priest to warm his hands during liturgical functions.

Calendar (KA-luhn-der): In liturgical usage, the ordering of time so as to recall and celebrate annually the mysteries of redemption, as well as the memory of the Blessed Virgin and other saints (see Cycle of Church Calendar). Cf. CCC 1168-1173

California Missions (kal-ih-FOR-nyuh MIH-shuhnz): Founded by Bl. Junípero Serra (1713-1784) and his successor, Fermín de Lasuén (1785-1803), these missions were established by the Franciscans under the authority of the king of Spain for the evangelization and civilization of the Native Americans of the area. When the area came under the control of Mexico, the missions were secularized (1833) and sold; however, the mission sites were later returned to Church ownership and are now used for religious purposes.

Calling (KAWL-ihng): 1. A summons from God to a human being, inviting the person to embark upon a specially chosen work. The O.T. has numerous examples of the calling of prophets (Abraham — Gn 12 ff.; Isaiah — Is 6 ff.); in the N.T., Jesus called His Twelve by name (Mk 3:13). 2. The technical term used during the Protestant Reformation for ordained and non-ordained ministry. 3. In contemporary Catholic language, the vocation given to one by God, especially the call to the priesthood and consecrated life. Cf. CCC 941, 1578

Calumny (KAL-uhm-nee): The unjust and false revelation against another, either through spoken word or publication. Calumny differs from detraction, which is the unjust but true revelation of another's faults. Calumny demands retraction and the restitution of the other's honor. CCC 2477, 2479, 2507

Calvary (KAL-vuh-ree): The site, outside Jerusalem, where Jesus was crucified (Mt 27:33; Mk 15:22; Jn 19:17). The Aramaic *gulgata* ("skull") and the Latin *calvaria* refer to Calvary. In the fourth century, the Church of the Holy Sepulcher was built over this spot.

Calvinism (KAL-vih-nih-zuhm): A form of Protestantism based upon the thought of the French Protestant leader John Calvin (*Jean Chauvin* or *Caulvin*), who lived from 1509 until 1564. Calvinism accepts the Scriptures (except for the so-called "apocryphal" books) as the only source of divine revelation. It teaches that men and women cannot change their eternal destiny by anything they do (predestination), and that salvation comes solely through grace and has nothing to do with works.

Camauro (kuh-MAU-ro): The red velvet cap, trimmed in ermine or white fur, worn by the Pope in place of the biretta outside of liturgical functions. By the late eighteenth century, it was replaced by the white zucchetto, although Popes have worn it occasionally since that time.

Camera (KAH-meh-ruh): (Latin: vault; Italian: chamber) The word has similarly passed into ecclesiastical use with the meaning simply of a room, though usually reserved for a division of the Roman Curia, specifically the Apostolic Chamber.

Camerlengo, also Camerarius (kah-mehr-LEHN-go, kah-mehr-AH-ree-øøs): Cardinal chamberlain assigned to direct day-to-day operations of the Holy See in the period between the death of a Pope and the election of his successor; he calls the conclave for the election of a new Pope.

Camisia (kuh-MEE-see-uh): (Latin *camisa:* a loose-fitting shirt) 1. Another name for the alb. 2. A covering for the Book of the Gospels used at Mass.

Campanile (kahm-puh-NEE-lay): A freestanding bell tower; though usually associated with church architecture, it can also serve a totally secular purpose as a memorial bell tower. It is very typical of northern Italian church architecture, with the leaning tower of Pisa as an obvious example. Although it is not entirely freestanding, the Knights of Columbus Tower is not integral to the symmetrical façade of the Basilica of the National Shrine of the Immaculate Conception, Washington, D.C., and could be described as a campanile.

Cana (KAY-nuh): The village, whose Greek name *(kana)* has an uncertain origin, where Jesus changed water into wine (Jn 2:1-11); the home of Nathanael (Jn 21:2); and the site where Jesus healed the official's son (Jn 4:46-54). Traditional testimony suggests that Cana was four miles northeast of Nazareth; however, modern research claims that nine miles north-northwest is the more likely location.

Cana (or Pre-Cana) Conferences (KAY-nuh [PREE-KAY-nuh] KAHN-fer-ehn-sehz): (Also called Pre-Cana) Taking their name from the location of the wedding at which Our Lord performed His first miracle, these conferences are sessions sponsored by the Church to assist engaged couples in preparing for sacramental marriage.

Canada, The Church in (*th*uh TSHERTSH ihn KA-nuh-duh): First introduced into the area by the French in the sixteenth century, major missionary efforts were undertaken by the Jesuits in the seventeenth century. In the eighteenth century, the territory came under British rule, but the French-speaking Catholics were allowed to continue the practice of their Faith. In 1766, the first bishop was consecrated, although he was not permitted use of his title by the British; but this situation was changed in 1844. With large numbers of immigrants from Ireland, Scotland, and Ukraine, the Church experienced great growth, and in 1908 it was no longer a mission territory. Today the Latin Rite has sixteen metropolitan provinces, one archdiocese with no suffragans, and the Military Ordinariate. The Ukrainian Catholic Church has an archeparchy with four eparchates, and many other Eastern Rites are represented throughout the country.

Canadian Shrines (kuh-NAY-dee-uhn SHRAINZ): The devotion of the Catholic settlers in French Canada prompted the establishment of many shrines to saints of local significance or of importance to the settlers in their native regions. Except for the North American Martyrs' Shrine, near Midland, Ontario, all of the Catholic shrines in Canada are located in the Province of Quebec: Ste. Anne de Beaupré, Quebec City; St. Joseph's Oratory, Montreal; Hermitage of St. Anthony, La Bouchette; Our Lady of the Holy Rosary, Cap de la Madeleine; Ste. Anne de Micmacs, Restigouche; Chapel of Atonement, Pointe aux Trembles; Our Lady of Lourdes, Rigaud; and St. Benoît du Lac, near Magog.

Cancelli (kahn-TSHEH-lee): Originally, low decorated walls in Roman basilicas used to shield the singers from the view of the congregation while permitting them to see the altar; developing in the West into rood screens and, later, into Communion rails and in the East into the iconostasis.

Candle, Paschal (PAS-kuhl KAN-duhl): Large candle symbolizing the risen Christ, lighted at the beginning of the Easter Vigil, prominently displayed in the sanctuary throughout Eastertime and in the baptistery after Pentecost, used at baptisms and funerals; traditionally inscribed with a cross, the alpha and omega, as well as the numerals of the current year, and imbedded with grains of incense and five wax "nails."

Candlemas (KAN-duhl-muhs): Popular name given to the liturgical celebration of February 2, now designated "Presentation of the Lord," but previously "Purification of Mary," at which candles are blessed and carried in procession.

Candles (KAN-duhlz): Wax tapers, both portable and stationary, figure prominently in the liturgies and rites of the Western and Eastern Churches. Their function is ornamental in part, but the symbol of the lighted candle reminds the believer of the light of Christ. The foremost use is the paschal candle at Easter, which stands for the risen Christ. According to the rubrics of the Roman Rite, at least two lighted candles must be placed on or near the altar during Mass. Candles are also widely used as signs of prayer and honor when burning before the images of Our Lady and the saints. Cf. CCC 1154, 1189, 1243

Candlestick (KAN-duhl-stihk): A metal or wooden holder for candles, allowing them to be carried in procession or placed upon an altar or other flat surface. The basic design of the candlestick includes a base, a stem, a knob at the center of the stem, and, at the top of the stem, a receptacle into which is set a pricket (sharp point) or socket to hold the candle itself. Candlesticks are made of a variety of materials such as gold, silver-plated brass, bronze, and wood.

Canon (KA-nuhn): (Greek *kanon:* rule or measure) 1. A law of the Church or a doctrinal and disciplinary formula of a council or synod. The body of Church law is known as Canon Law. 2. The canon of Scripture comprises books of the Bible received in the Church as authentically inspired and normative for the Faith. 3. Formerly, the Eucharistic Prayer; the Roman Canon is the ancient anaphora now listed as Eucharistic Prayer I in the Missal. 4. A canon is also a member of a cathedral chapter, a body of priests who assist the bishop in celebrating the Liturgy of the Hours and in other ways as well. 5. The list of holy persons officially acknowledged as saints by the Church is known as the canon of saints. 6. Finally, a type of contrapuntal music in which each voice or instrument enters at different points, each beginning with the first bars of the melody and flowing in a manner that avoids dissonance. **CCC 120; cf. 828**

Canoness (KA-nuhn-ehs): 1. From the fourth century, a devout woman whose name was inscribed in the church's register ("canon"), designating her as a "canoness" (Latin *canonica*), who performed a special function in the church. 2. During the Middle Ages, an unvowed pious woman. 3. A vowed woman who lived according to a religious rule similar to that of St. Augustine.

Canonical Hours (ka-NAH-nih-kuhl AURZ): The sections of the Liturgy of the Hours, or Divine Office, prayed throughout the course of the day: Office of Readings (also called Vigils or Matins), Lauds, Prime (now suppressed), Terce, Sext, None, Vespers, and Compline.

Canonical Mission (ka-NAH-nih-kuhl MIH-shuhn): The official conferring of an ecclesiastical office on a candidate by a competent superior. Also, the mandate to teach theological disciplines in Catholic institutes of higher studies.

Canonical Possession (ka-NAH-nih-kuhl po-ZEH-shuhn): The official act whereby a person assumes a canonical office, distinct from the appointment to an office or the liturgical celebration associated with the assumption of an office.

Canonist (KA-nuhn-ihst): A person with a graduate degree in Canon Law; a Church lawyer.

Canonization (ka-nuhn-ih-ZAY-shuhn): The Church's official declaration, following beatification and an intensive exploration into one's sanctity and entire life, that a person is in heaven and worthy of public imitation and veneration. The Pope, who makes the formal declaration, can dispense from some usual procedures; two miracles are required for canonization but not in the case of martyrs. Seven honors are attached to canonization: (1) inscription in the catalog of saints and public veneration; (2) inclusion in the Church's public prayers; (3) dedication of churches in the saint's honor; (4) inclusion in the Mass and the Liturgy of the Hours; (5) day assigned in the liturgical calendar; (6) pictorial representation; (7) public veneration of relics. St. Ulrich of Augsburg was the first formally canonized saint (Pope John XV, 933). Cf. CCC 828

Canon Law (KA-nuhn LAW): The name given to the official body of laws by which the Church is governed. Present Church law originated in regulations, or canons, enacted by councils or synods. Gradually, collections of these canons were made. The first systematization of these collections was the work of a monk named Gratian who composed a *Concordance of Discordant Canons* or *Decree of Gratian* (as it was commonly known) in 1140. In 1234, the Dominican canonist St. Raymond of Peñafort completed a systematic arrangement that became known as the *Decretals of Gregory IX.* Pope St. Pius X, who recognized the need for a systematic arrangement of Church law, commissioned Pietro Cardinal Gasparri to accomplish this work and promulgated the Code of Canon Law in 1917. The current code – incorporating revisions required by the Second Vatican Council — was promulgated by Pope John Paul II in 1983.

Canon Law, Eastern (EES-tern KA-nuhn LAW): The official body of laws that governs the Eastern (or Oriental) Rites (or Churches), which are part of the universal Catholic Church.

Canon Law, History of (HIHS-to-ree uhv KA-nuhn LAW): The study of the development and refinement of the legal or canonical heritage of the Roman and Oriental Churches.

Canon Law, Interpretation of (ihn-TER-preh-TAY-shuhn uhv KA-nuhn LAW): According to Canon 16, authentic interpretation comes from the legislator, and that interpretation has the same authority as the law itself. Any divergence from the mind of the legislator is termed "nonauthentic." Canon 17 states that the laws are to be understood in accord with the proper meaning of the words (both in text and in context), and where it is unclear, in the light of parallel passages and in accord with the mind of the legislator.

Canon of Muratori (KA-nuhn uhv MÖÖ-ruh-TO-ree): The document, dating from the eighth century and composed of eighty-five lines, which is the oldest extant literature of the N.T. books. Discovered by Ludovico A. Muratori (1672-1750), the Canon of Muratori refers to the Gospels, the Acts of the Apostles, the Pauline and Johannine letters, the letters of St. Jude, and the Book of Revelation.

Canon of Scripture (KA-nuhn uhv SKRIHP-tsher): Authoritative list of writings that would become the Holy Bible. CCC 120

Canon of the Mass (KA-nuhn uhv *th*uh MAS): The Eucharistic Prayer of the Mass, during which bread and wine are changed into the Body, Blood, Soul, and Divinity of Jesus Christ. In the United States, in addition to the four Eucharistic Prayers that are "regular," there are those for children's liturgies, Masses of Reconciliation, and special occasions.

Canon Penitentiary (KA-nuhn PEH-nih-TEHN-tsher-ee): A priest member of a cathedral chapter whose special responsibility is the administration of the Sacrament of Penance.

Canons, Chapter of (TSHAP-ter uhv KA-nuhnz): A collegiate body of priests whose duties include the celebration of the solemn liturgical functions of a cathedral or collegiate church. Canons are appointed by the bishop and ordinarily reside at the cathedral. There are many chapters of canons in Europe and Latin America, but none in the United States.

Canons of the Apostles (KA-nuhnz uhv *the*e uh-PAH-suhlz) or Apostolic Canons (a-pah-STAH-lihk KA-nuhnz): A collection of eighty-five documents dealing with Church order and discipline. Though attributed to the Apostles, they were actually compiled toward the end of the fourth century by an Arian or Apollinarian author and are included in the larger collection of so-called *Apostolic Constitutions.* The canons are important for their list of acceptable books of the Bible, omitting Revelation while adding the two letters of Clement of Rome and the actual *Apostolic Constitutions* in which the canon itself is contained.

Canons Regular (KA-nuhnz REHG-yöö-ler): The communities of clergy, dating from the eleventh century and often following the rule of St. Augustine, which embraced a monastic form of life. The Order of Premonstratensians (Norbertines) is the largest such order existing today.

Canopy (KAN-uh-pee): Honorific covering meant to enhance the presence of a sacred place or person; e.g., fixed canopy over an altar or throne, portable canopy carried in procession over the Blessed Sacrament.

Canossa (kah-NO-suh): 1. City in Tuscany where Holy Roman Emperor Henry IV made a public act of obedience and submission to Pope St. Gregory VII. The Emperor had been excommunicated for insisting upon the right to appoint bishops, and the event in Canossa established the primacy of papal prerogatives. 2. As a result of this event, the phrase "going to Canossa" came to mean "doing penance."

Cantata, Sacred (SAY-krehd kahn-TAH-tuh): A musical composition on sacred themes, employing chorus, soloists, and organ, piano, or orchestral accompaniment; usually less elaborate than an oratorio (q.v.), it is not considered liturgical but may be performed in church with proper permission and under strict conditions.

Canticle (KAN-tih-kuhl): (From Latin *canere, cantare:* to sing) A sacred song or chant with a scriptural text (other than from the Psalms), used within the official liturgy of the Church. The three so-called "evangelical canticles" are the *Magnificat,* the *Benedictus,* and the *Nunc Dimittis,* all taken from St. Luke's Gospel and used at Evening Prayer (Vespers), Morning Prayer (Lauds), and Night Prayer (Compline) respectively. CCC 2619, 2641

Canticle of Canticles: See Song of Songs

Cantor (KAN-ter), also Precentor (pree-SEHN-ter): (Latin *cantor:* singer) The one who leads the congregation in singing the music within the liturgy in a prayerful way. In the Western Church, any qualified person may serve as a cantor, and there is no formal institution; in the Eastern Church, either a male or female may serve in this capacity, but only men may be admitted to the office of cantor (reader) by ordination.

Cap-de-la-Madeleine, Shrine of (SHRAIN uhv KAHP-duh-lah-MAH-duh-LEHN): The pilgrimage site, also called Our Lady of the Cape and Queen of the Most Holy Rosary, in Three Rivers, Quebec, Canada. The first church was built by Jesuit missionaries in 1659 to honor Our Lady; the present shrine (the oldest stone church in North America) was completed in 1714 and in 1964 was declared a minor basilica.

Capital Punishment (KA-pih-tuhl PUHN-ihsh-mehnt): The taking of life by the State of a person convicted of a serious crime. Pope John Paul II, in his encyclical letter *Evangelium Vitae* ("The Gospel of Life"), wrote: "There is a growing tendency, both in the Church and in civil society, to demand that it (capital punishment) be applied in a very limited way or even that it be abolished completely." Quoting the *Catechism of the Catholic Church,* the Pope wrote: " 'If bloodless means are sufficient to defend human lives against an aggressor and to protect public order and the safety of persons, public authority must limit itself to such means, because they better correspond to the concrete conditions of the common good and are more in conformity to the dignity of the human person.' " **CCC 2263-2267**

Capital Sins (KA-pih-tuhl SIHNZ), also Capital Vices or Deadly Sins (KA-pih-tuhl VAI-sehz, DEHD-lee SIHNZ): The "death-dealing" evils that are the causes of other sins and are sins in themselves. Original Sin brought about these seven sins (pride, envy, sloth, lust, greed, intemperance, anger). St. John (1 Jn 2:16) writes that the root of all sin is "the lust of the flesh and the lust of the eyes and the pride of life." (See each capital sin: anger, envy, etc.) **CCC 1866**

Capitulary (ka-PIH-tshöö-leh-ree): 1. The laws pertaining to a chapter or society attached to the cathedral or a religious community. 2. The collection of canons effective for a religious province.

Cappa (KAH-puh): (Latin, Italian: cape) 1. Another name for the liturgical cope. 2. A large mantle with shoulder cape worn by members of some religious orders over the habit or by prelates on solemn occasions.

Cappa Magna (KAH-puh MAHN-yuh): (Latin: large cape) A hooded cloak with a long train, worn by cardinals and bishops on certain occasions.

Cappa Pluvialis (KAH-puh plöö-vee-AHL-ihs) or Pluviale (plöö-vee-AH-lay): (From Latin: rain cape or cloak) The liturgical cope, which may be worn for ceremonies that do not require the chasuble; e.g., processions, solemn blessings, Liturgy of the Hours.

Captivity Epistles (kap-TIH-vih-tee ih-PIH-suhlz): The four Pauline letters (Philippians, Colossians, Ephesians, Philemon) that are thought to have been written when St. Paul was under house arrest in Rome. In these letters, he refers to his situation (Phil 1:7; Col 4:18; Eph 4:1; Phlm 9).

Cardinal (KAHR-dih-nuhl): (Latin: hinge; Late Latin: principal) 1. Highest-ranking prelate below the papacy itself, now nearly always a bishop or archbishop, appointed by the Pope to assist him as a member of the College of Cardinals (q.v.). 2. Distinctive red color of a cardinal's garments.

Cardinal Archbishop (KAHR-dih-nuhl artsh-BIH-shuhp): Cardinal who governs an archdiocese — not used as a canonical title.

Cardinal Legate (KAHR-dih-nuhl LEH-guht): One named by the Pope to represent him by performing an important task or ceremony. This cardinal is accorded the same privileges as the Pope and possesses the Pope's authority. The use of the cardinal legate has been restricted.

Cardinal Protector (KAHR-dih-nuhl pro-TEHK-ter): One who was named by the Pope or the Roman Curia to care for religious congregations and lay confraternities. Today, the cardinal protector is rarely used; however, many congregations and lay associations know members of the Curia to whom they can turn for assistance.

Cardinal Vicar (KAHR-dih-nuhl VIH-ker): Differing from the vicar general of Vatican City, the vicar general of the Diocese of Rome is a cardinal appointed by the Pope to care for the administrative and pastoral dimensions of the diocese.

Cardinal Virtues (KAR-dih-nuhl VER-tshööz): The "good habits" infused at Baptism that enable one to control his or her moral conduct according to grace and right reason. The cardinal virtues — prudence, justice, fortitude, and temperance — are the foundation of all other virtues except the theological virtues. **CCC 1805-1809**

Care of Souls (KEHR uhv SOLZ): A canonical-theological term that describes the pastoral authority of the Pope, residential bishops, and pastors. **Cf. CCC 857, 879, 881, 886, 1595-1596**

Caritas Internationalis (KAH-ree-tahs ihn-ter-NAHT-see-o-NAHL-ihs): The international conglomerate of national Catholic charity-relief organizations that provides monies and material assistance to the destitute harmed by droughts, earthquakes, floods, and other natural disasters.

Carmel, Mount (MAUNT KAHR-mehl): The site near Haifa that divides Israel into the Plains of Acro and Sharon and was associated with the lives of Elijah and Elisha (1 Kgs 18:19-46; 2 Kgs 2:25, 4:25). Mt. Carmel is an honored place for the Carmelite Order and is associated with Marian devotion, especially the Brown Scapular of Our Lady of Mt. Carmel.

Carnival (KAHR-nih-vuhl), also Carnivale (KAHR-nee-VAH-lay): (From Latin and Italian: "good-bye to meat"; *Mardi Gras,* or "Fat Tuesday," in French) The time of celebration and merrymaking before the Lenten fast begins on Ash Wednesday.

Carolingian Schools (kehr-o-LIHN-dzhuhn SKÖÖLZ): A series of Church-sponsored and State-supported schools established in Europe after the Carolingian Reform of the ninth century that laid the foundation for later intellectual renaissance.

Carthage, Councils of (KAUN-suhlz uhv KAHR-thehdzh): Series of ecclesiastical synods at Carthage between the third and sixth centuries. Those under St. Cyprian (mid-third century) undertook the issues of reconciling Christians who had capitulated during the persecution of Decius (250) and the rebaptism of heretics. The Council of Carthage in 412 condemned Pelagius. Boniface presided over the last councils in 525 and 534.

Cases of Conscience (KAY-sehz uhv KAHN-shehns): The actual or hypothetical situations proposed in Canon Law and moral theology to assist one in applying principles to concrete cases. Today, such issues as the morality of nuclear war and the provision of artificially directed nutrition and hydration are often used as cases of conscience.

Cassock (KA-suhk), also Soutane (söö-TAN): Close-fitting, ankle-length robe worn by the clergy and, in some places, by other liturgical ministers, with the color of cloth and/or buttons and piping denoting the rank of the cleric.

Castel Gandolfo (kah-STEHL gahn-DAWL-fo): The site of the Pope's summer residence, located in the Alban Hills about eighteen miles southeast of Rome. In 1629, Pope Urban VIII began to build this villa, which is considered "extraterritorial" (i.e., outside the Vatican State but completely under the governance of the Holy See).

Casuistry (KA-zhöö-ihs-tree): (From Latin *casus:* case) The framework in moral theology that applies moral principles to specific cases. Casuistry has been helpful because it takes the abstract and makes it "real" in a particular situation; however, it has its limitations. Casuistry cannot replace one's conscience in the decision-making process; furthermore, it must be aligned with the cardinal virtue of prudence.

Catacombs (KA-tuh-komz): (Latin *cata tumbas:* at the graves) Underground areas used for burial, with a network of galleries with wall-niches in which were placed the bodies of the dead. This form of burial was used extensively by Christians in the first centuries of the Church, and they were protected by Roman Law from being disturbed. Because the locations of these burial places were well known by the authorities, the stories of Christians hiding in the catacombs to escape persecution have no basis in fact. The tombs of martyrs developed into places of veneration, and the offering of the Holy Sacrifice of the Mass often took place in the catacombs. **Cf. CCC 1368**

Catafalque (KA-tuh-fawlk): 1. An elaborate stand on which the body of the deceased is placed for lying in state, as is customary for some dignitary, while people of lesser rank are usually accorded a simple bier. For a memorial Mass or service, when the body is not present, a mock coffin, covered with a pall, typically rests on a catafalque. 2. Another name for the *castrumdoloris,* the middle coffin of the three in which a deceased Pontiff is buried; it is that which is seen during his funeral Mass at St. Peter's in Rome. The word "catafalque" likely comes from the Late Latin *catafalicum,* a word for a "siege tower," probably not unlike a catapult; it is named for its physical resemblance, although the idea of the deceased besieging heaven from the catafalque is not totally absent from folk etymology.

Catechesis (ka-teh-KEE-sihs): (Greek *katekhein:* to resound) The use of written and spoken words, plus visual and audio aids, to pass down the Gospel of Christ. Catechesis was discussed in the Acts of the Apostles and by St. Paul as a handing down of that received from Jesus, in order to instruct others in the way of the Lord. Catechesis is based on Scripture and Tradition, as well as the liturgy, the wisdom of the saints, etc. It is a lifelong process of conversion. **CCC 4-7, 426, 983, 1095, 2688**

Catechetics (ka-teh-KEH-tihks): The study — drawing upon theology, biblical studies, and the social sciences — of the history, goals, and principles of handing down the Faith. It recognizes that catechesis is a lifelong process of conversion and employs varied visual and audio aids, along with solid catechisms.

Catechism (KA-teh-kih-zuhm): A book containing the truths of the Faith, especially an explanation of the Apostles' Creed, the Ten Commandments, the Seven Sacraments, and a discussion of prayers, often in question-and-answer form for the education of the faithful. Three catechisms are particularly well known: the *Roman Catechism,* issued by Pope St. Pius V in 1566; the *Baltimore Catechism,* produced in the United States toward the end of the nineteenth century; and the *Catechism of the Catholic Church,* commissioned by Pope John Paul II and published in 1992. **CCC 11-18**

Catechist (KA-teh-kihst): The title designating one who instructs another in the Faith. Pope John Paul II has stressed that the catechist — whether cleric, religious, or layperson — shares the Gospel by personal witness and by teaching the doctrines of the Church. **CCC 12, 428, 2663**

Catechumenate (KA-teh-KYÖÖ-meh-nayt): The Rite of Christian Initiation of Adults (q.v.) has introduced a new focus on the catechumenate, wherein the neophytes are gradually brought both liturgically and catechetically into Church membership. The catechumenate has its origin in the early Church. When a pagan sought conversion to Christianity, he or she was given basic instruction as an inquirer into the Faith. Since the catechumens were allowed to attend only the first part of the Mass, what is today called the Liturgy of the Word was then called the Mass of the Catechumens. With Baptism, they entered into full union with the Mystical Body and could rightly participate in the Eucharist or Mass of the Faithful. CCC 1230-1233, 1247-1248

Catechumen (KA-teh-KYÖÖ-mehn): (From Greek: instruction) A person preparing in a program (catechumenate) of instruction and spiritual formation for baptism and reception into the Church. The Church has a special relationship with catechumens. It invites them to lead the life of the Gospel, introduces them to the celebration of the sacred rites, and grants them various prerogatives that are proper to the faithful (one of which is the right to ecclesiastical burial). CCC 281, 1248-1249, 1253, 1259, 1281, 1537

Categorical Imperative (ka-tuh-GOR-ih-kuhl im-PEHR-uh-tihv): The principle, grounded in the work of Immanuel Kant (d. 1804), that the evaluation of one's ethical duty must agree with a general and universal norm, viz., that if the rule imposes a strict moral duty, one must decide whether others are obliged to act in the same fashion. Furthermore, one is to treat others as "ends" rather than means. The difficulty with Kant's categorical imperative is the lack of precision in deciding what specific moral norms are to be performed.

Cathari (KAH-tah-ree): A medieval heretical sect of Neo-Manicheans who rejected Baptism and marriage and preached an extreme form of poverty. Their influence was eliminated by the time of the Renaissance.

Cathedra (KAH-teh-drah): (From Greek and Latin: chair or throne) The chair from which a bishop presides and hence exercises his liturgical and spiritual authority in his cathedral church. (*Ex cathedra:* literally, "from the chair," to teach officially in virtue of one's authority.) **Cf. CCC 1184**

Cathedral (kuh-THEE-druhl): (Greek and Latin: *cathedra,* chair) The central church of the diocese and the bishop's official church, so called for the placement in the cathedral of the chair of the bishop who has jurisdiction over the diocese. Ordinarily, the cathedral is the site of the central liturgical activities of the bishop and his diocese. Here the bishop is consecrated and enthroned upon his *cathedra,* an ancient symbol of a man's teaching authority; diocesan synods are also ordinarily held in the cathedral. In his cathedral, the bishop most properly ordains, confirms, and blesses the sacred oils on Holy Thursday, celebrates the liturgy of the Sacred Triduum, and presides at pontifical Masses. Often bishops are interred in a cathedral crypt. The cathedral must be located in the diocese, usually in the see city in which the bishop exercises his authority. The papal *cathedra* is at St. John Lateran, the actual cathedral of Rome and mother church for all Catholic churches. The first cathedral established in the United States is Baltimore's Basilica of the Assumption, a masterpiece of the neoclassical style, designed by Benjamin Latrobe, also the architect of the U.S. Capitol.

Cathedraticum (kah-teh-DRAH-tih-køøm): A regular monetary tribute paid by parishes to the diocese as a sign of filial dependence, not to be confused with diocesan taxes enacted for the general support of a diocese.

Catholic (KATH-uh-lihk): (From Greek *katholikos:* universal) Term first used by St. Ignatius of Antioch in the second century and today referring to the members, the churches, the institutions, the hierarchy, the clergy, and the teachings of the Church founded by Jesus Christ and given to the Apostles. "Catholic" is often used to denote: (1) the entire Church; (2) the doctrines of the Church; (3) the Church before the Schism of 1054; (4) the Anglicans, Old Catholics, and others who claim a link to the Church founded by Our Lord; (5) individual Christians who adhere fully to the Faith. **CCC 830-838**

Catholic Action (KATH-uh-lihk AK-shuhn): The cooperation of the laity with the hierarchy of the Church for the work of sanctifying the world. In the period immediately preceding the Second Vatican Council, it had come to be known as the "lay apostolate," and although reference is made to Catholic Action in the documents *Apostolicam Actuositatem* and *Christus Dominus,* it is open to broad interpretation, with further pastoral and theological development in the Apostolic Exhortation *Christifideles Laici,* issued in January 1989.

Catholic Church (KATH-uh-lihk TSHERTSH): (From Greek *katholicos:* universal) The designation "Catholic" was given to the Church by St. Ignatius of Antioch (d. 107): "Wheresoever the bishop shall appear, there let the people be, even as where Jesus is, there is the Catholic Church" (Epistle to the Smyrnaeans, 8:2). Universal in place, scope, and time, the Catholic Church is no mere human invention, but the community called into being by Jesus Himself. The Pope, as Bishop of Rome, exercises the particular authority given to St. Peter by Jesus Himself (Mt 16:13-20; Mk 8:27-29; Lk 9:18-20) to guide the Catholic Church in the ways of the Holy Spirit and to teach the faithful infallibly, with divine truth, in matters of faith and morals. Catholic bishops, in union with the Holy See, are entrusted with the mission of the Apostles to be the Church's shepherds, leaders, and teachers. Priests and deacons, through the Sacrament of Holy Orders, assist the bishops in their work of offering sacrifice, teaching, and ministering to the People of God. Professed religious anticipate the *eschaton* (last time) in their vowed life of poverty, chastity, and obedience. All the baptized, the majority of whom are the laity, benefit from these ministries and strive, especially in their faithful sacramental lives, to participate more fully in the Mystical Body of Christ and to present again to the Father His Beloved Son. The Nicene Creed articulates what is implicit in Paul's Letter to the Ephesians as the four distinctive characteristics or marks of the Catholic Church: (1) *One:* though made up of many members, the Church, united to one Head, professes one Faith and shares one Baptism and one Communion with the Lord; (2) *Holy:* founded in God's grace, the Church subsists in Christ, and through Him is made holy; (3) *Catholic:* the Church is universal, embracing all in the household of God, not tied to any one culture, nation, or race; (4) *Apostolic:* the Church's doctrine is that of Christ as He entrusted it to the Apostles. **CCC 748-972**

Catholic Epistles (KATH-uh-lihk ih-PIH-suhlz): The N.T. letters written to the universal (hence, "catholic") Church rather than to a specific person or region (e.g., St. Paul's Letter to the Ephesians). The Catholic epistles are James; 1 and 2 Peter; 1, 2, and 3 John; Jude.

Catholic Foreign Mission Society of America (KATH-uh-lihk FOR-ehn MIH-shuhn SUH-sai-eh-tee uhv uh-MEHR-ih-kuh): The official name of the American religious community popularly known as Maryknoll, founded in 1911 by Fr. James Walsh and Fr. Thomas Price. In 1912, the community of the Maryknoll Sisters of St. Dominic was founded. Maryknoll trains missionaries for work throughout the world.

Catholic Household Blessings and Prayers (KATH-uh-lihk HAUS-hold BLEH-sihngs and PREHRZ): Companion volume to the ritual *Book of Blessings,* published by the National Conference of Catholic Bishops of the United States (1988), intended as a manual of prayers for use by families and individuals in the "domestic church" of the home, and thus the modern successor to the *Manual of Prayers* authorized by the U.S. Bishops at the Third Plenary Council of Baltimore (1888).

Catholic League for Religious and Civil Rights (KATH-uh-lihk LEEG for rih-LIH-dzhuhs and SIH-vuhl RAITS): Founded in 1973 by Jesuit Fr. Virgil Blum and numbering about thirty thousand members, the Catholic League works to defend the civil and religious rights of Catholics in the United States. Through educational programs, the League provides a forum for discussion of Catholic participation in the public life of the nation. The League also seeks to counter anti-Catholic propaganda and prejudice.

Catholicos (kah-THAL-ih-kos): (From Greek: universal) Title formerly designating Catholic bishops in specific episcopal sees on the eastern borders of the Roman Empire; today, the term is used to denote the heads of the Oriental Churches of Armenia, Assyria, and Georgia.

Catholic Press (KATH-uh-lihk PREHS): The press — encompassing all forms of print media — is fostered by the Church in order to form and influence public opinion in accordance with Catholic principles and teaching.

Catholic Press Association [C.P.A.] (KATH-uh-lihk PREHS a-SO-see-AY-shun [SEE PEE AY]): Organization of more than three hundred American and Canadian newspapers, magazines, and general publishers, with their staff members, founded in 1911.

Catholic Relief Services: See Relief Services, Catholic

Catholics in Statuary Hall (KATH-uh-lihks in STA-tshöö-ehr-ee HAWL): Thirteen Catholics honored with statues in the United States Capitol, Washington, D.C.: (1) Mother Joseph (1823-1902), Washington, a Sister of Charity of Providence, a missionary, educator, and builder; (2 and 3) Fr. Jacques Marquette, S.J. (1637-1675), Wisconsin, and Fr. Eusebio Kino, S.J. (1645-1711), Arizona, honored for their efforts at exploring the Midwest and Southwest in their missionary endeavors; (4) Bl. Junípero Serra, O.F.M. (1713-1784), California, noted for his establishment of numerous California missions, among them San Diego and San Francisco; (5) Bl. Damien de Veuster (1840-1889), Hawaii, a priest of the Sacred Hearts Congregation who ministered to the lepers of Molokai; (6) Charles Carroll of Carrollton (1737-1832), Maryland, the brother of the first Catholic bishop in the United States, John Carroll, and a signer of the Declaration of Independence; (7) Dr. John McLoughlin (1784-1857), Oregon, a physician, who mastered the Indian languages and became a trader in the vast Northwest territories; (8) Brigadier General James Shields (1806-1879), Illinois, who emigrated from Ireland, fought in the Mexican War and the Civil War, served briefly as governor of the Oregon Territory, and was elected to the U.S. Senate as the only man ever to represent three different states, Illinois, Minnesota, and Missouri; (9) Edward Douglass White (1845-1921), Louisiana, who was educated at Mt. St. Mary's College, Emmitsburg, Maryland, Jesuit College, New Orleans, and Georgetown College, Washington, D.C., and appointed Chief Justice of the Supreme Court by President Taft in 1910; (10) John E. Kenna (1848-1893), West Virginia, who fought in the Confederate Army and later represented West Virginia in both the U.S. House of Representatives and the U.S. Senate; (11) John Burke (1859-1937), North Dakota, who, as governor of North Dakota, rid the State of corrupt political control and was appointed Treasurer of the United States by President Wilson in 1913; (12) Dennis Chavez (1888-1962), New Mexico, a graduate of Georgetown University Law School, who championed the rights of Indians and Puerto Ricans; (13) Patrick Anthony McCarran (1876-1954), Nevada, who served as Chief Justice of the Nevada Supreme Court from 1917 to 1919 and was elected to the U.S. Senate in 1932.

Catholic Truth Society (KATH-uh-lihk TRÖÖTH suh-SAI-eh-tee): The organization founded in England in 1868 to foster understanding of the Faith. Four objectives mark the society's work: (1) to propagate inexpensive devotional works; (2) to help Catholics grasp the Faith more fully; (3) to aid non-Catholics in their knowledge of the Faith; (4) to circulate Catholic books.

Catholic University of America (KATH-uh-lihk yöö-nih-VER-sih-tee uhv uh-MEHR-ih-kuh): The Catholic university founded by the American bishops in 1889 and located in Washington, D.C.

Catholic Worker Movement (KATH-uh-lihk WER-ker MÖÖV-mehnt): Inspired by Peter Maurin and Dorothy Day and founded in 1933, this movement seeks to encourage Catholics to assist the poor by alleviating their distress through monetary gifts and voluntary service. It invokes Scripture as the mandate from God to eliminate sufferings and inequality based on race and poverty. The newspaper *The Catholic Worker* is the organ of the movement.

Catholic Youth Organization [C.Y.O] (KATH-uh-lihk YÖÖTH OR-guhn-ih-ZAY-shuhn [SEE WAI O]): A program, founded in 1930 by Bishop Bernard J. Sheil in Chicago, aimed at developing the spiritual, moral, mental, and physical welfare of Catholic youth. Currently, many American dioceses have their own C.Y.O. programs. Athletics are stressed by the C.Y.O. as a vehicle through which fair play and health are gained.

Cause (KAWZ): 1. Canonical term for any trial conducted before an ecclesiastical court. 2. More specifically, it generally refers to the process whereby a person is investigated with a view to being canonized a saint.

Causes, Four (FOR KAW-zehz): First explained by Aristotle, the four causes of everything (except God) are material, formal (both "intrinsic," making up the thing itself), efficient, and final (both "extrinsic," always other than the thing itself). These were adapted by St. Thomas Aquinas to explain the Faith, including God as the efficient and final causes of creation.

Cautiones (KAUT-see-O-nehz): Written or oral promises required of the Catholic party to a mixed marriage, intended to remove all dangers to the practice of the Faith, to baptize any children born to the marriage, and to rear them in the Catholic Faith. These promises are no longer required of the non-Catholic party.

Celebrant (SEHL-uh-bruhnt): Bishop, priest, or deacon who presides at a liturgical function.

Celebret (TSHEHL-eh-breht): (Latin: let him celebrate) 1. A document carried by priests traveling outside their home diocese, attesting to the fact that the bearer is an authentic priest, duly ordained, in good standing, and therefore able to celebrate Mass. 2. Since 1988, a permission granted by the Pontifical Commission Ecclesia Dei, and qualified by the terms of each specific document, authorizing the bearer to celebrate Mass according to the Missal of 1962.

Celestial Hierarchy (seh-LEHS-tshuhl HAI-er-ahr-kee): The ranking of the angels according to duty and perfection. Nine choirs comprise this grouping: seraphim, cherubim, thrones, dominations, powers, virtues, principalities, archangels, and angels (see Angels).

Celibacy (SEHL-ih-buh-see): The discipline of the Latin Church that forbids the ordination of married men. Celibacy is perfect continence and is meant to foster imitation of Christ, Who gave up all, including the right to marry and have children, to serve His Father. A married man may be ordained to the diaconate but generally cannot remarry if his wife dies. Jesus Himself (Mt 19:11-12) and St. Paul (1 Cor 7:32) encouraged celibacy, as did the Council of Elvira (306). The Eastern Church allows deacons and priests who are married before ordination to remain so; however, bishops are required to be celibate. CCC 915, 1579-1580, 1599

Cell (SEHL): (Latin *cella:* small room) 1. The small living quarters allotted to an individual monk, hermit, or other religious. 2. A small group of monks who live apart from their home monastery are thus said to constitute a cell. 3. In the early Church, a small chapel erected over a tomb. 4. Formerly small Vatican apartments (cells) assigned cardinals meeting in conclave to elect a new Pope. 5. In the context of politics or sociology, a basic unit of an organization; usually, a small, effective group established for a specific purpose — as, for example, a cell in Catholic Action may meet for the common goal of prayer, work, or study.

Cellarer (SEHL-er-er): The title of the monk in the ancient monastery who was responsible for the temporal goods of his community. Such a monk today is called the "procurator."

Celtic Cross (KEHL-tihk or SEHL-tihk KRAWS): Distinguished by the circle at the intersection of the crossbar and upright shaft, usually with a continuous weaving line intertwined with the circle and cross arms, serving as a double symbol of eternity and unity, both that of the Son with the Father and the Holy Spirit and that of the believer with the Trinity, the common theme of St. Patrick's preaching. The Celtic cross comes from Ireland, where it is still commonly found; similarly, it is often used to mark an object as having an association with Ireland.

Celtic Rite (KEHL-tihk or SEHL-tihk RAIT): Liturgical calendar and usages of the ancient churches of Ireland, England, and Wales, superseded over the centuries by the Roman Rite.

Cemetery (SEH-muh-tehr-ee): (From Greek: sleeping place or resting chamber) The field where the dead are buried, either a "Catholic" cemetery specially blessed or a secular one, in which case the individual grave of the Catholic to be buried must be blessed. **CCC 1686**

Cenacle (SEHN-uh-kuhl): (Latin *cenaculum:* dining room) The upper room (Mt 26:17-19, Mk 14:12-16, Lk 22:7-13) that the Apostles prepared for the Lord's celebration of His Last Supper, during which He instituted the Eucharist and the priesthood. The cenacle was also the site of Christ's resurrection appearance to the Apostles (Jn 20:19) and the descent of the Holy Spirit upon the Apostolic Church (Acts 1:13-14, 2:1-36). Given its great significance at the inception of the Church, the cenacle has been called the first Christian church. Tradition places the cenacle in the southwest quarter of Jerusalem. Early reverence for the spot prompted the Emperor Hadrian to order its destruction and replacement with a pagan temple. This desecration helps the modern archaeologist in confirming its location: Crusaders, using stone of the Herodian era, contemporary with the upper room's construction, built a chapel there. Today this chapel is a mosque, although the Islamic authorities allow the Patriarch of Jerusalem to celebrate Mass there once a year on Holy Thursday.

Cenobite (SEHN-o-bait): (Greek *koinobion: koinos,* common + *bios,* life) A member of a religious order living in community, rather than a hermit or anchorite living in solitude.

Censer (SEHN-ser): Liturgical implement in which incense is placed upon glowing coals to provide fragrant smoke for the celebration.

Censor of Books (SEHN-ser uhv BØØKS): A person appointed by ecclesiastical authority to read and give an opinion about books that require ecclesiastical permission for publication.

Censures (SEHN-shøørz): Sanctions imposed by the Church on baptized Roman Catholics eighteen years of age or older for committing certain serious offenses and for being or remaining obstinate therein: (1) *excommunication* — exclusion from the community of the faithful, barring a person from sacramental and other participation in the goods and offices of the community of the Church; (2) *suspension* — prohibition of a cleric to exercise orders; (3) *interdict* — deprivation of the sacraments and liturgical activities. The intended purposes of censures are to correct and punish offenders; to deter persons from committing sins that, more seriously and openly than others, threaten the common good of the Church and its members; and to provide for the making of reparation for harm done to the community of the Church. Censures may be incurred automatically (*ipso facto*) on the commission of certain offenses for which fixed penalties have been laid down in Church law (*latae sententiae*); or they may be inflicted by sentence of a judge (*ferendae sententiae*). Automatic excommunication is incurred for the offenses of abortion, apostasy, heresy, and schism. Obstinacy in crime — also called contumacy, disregard of a penalty, defiance of Church authority — is presumed by law in the commission of offenses for which automatic censures are decreed. The presence and degree of contumacy in other cases, for which judicial sentence is required, is subject to determination by a judge. Absolution can be obtained from any censure, provided the person repents and desists from obstinacy. Absolution may be reserved to the Pope, the bishop of a place, or the major superior of an exempt clerical religious institute. In danger of death, one can be absolved from all censures by any priest; in other cases, faculties to absolve from reserved censures can be exercised by competent authorities or given to other priests. The penal law of the Church is contained in Book VI of the Code of Canon Law.

Cerecloth (TSHEH-reh-klawth) or Chrismale (kriz-MAH-lay): A cloth, waxed on one side, formerly placed over the altar to absorb chrism left from the altar's consecration and to keep the Precious Blood (if spilled) from soaking into the altar stone.

Ceremonial of Bishops (seh-reh-MO-nee-uhl uhv BIH-shuhps): English translation (1989) of the *Caeremoniale Episcoporum* (1984-1985) containing rubrics and directives for the celebration of rites at which a bishop presides or is present.

Ceremonies, Master of: See Master of Ceremonies

Ceremony (SEHR-eh-mo-nee): Complex of signs, gestures, vesture, objects, and movements that surround and embellish the liturgy of the Church.

Certitude (SER-tih-tööd): A canonical term that refers to the adherence of the mind to a proposition without fear that its opposite will be true. Certitude is required by judges in canonical trials.

Chains of St. Peter (TSHAYNZ uhv SAYNT PEE-ter): Chains preserved in Rome at San Pietro in Vincoli, said to be those bound to the imprisoned St. Peter (Acts 12).

Chair (TSHEHR): In ancient times, the seat of authority to teach; hence bishops usually preached while seated and medieval scholars generally taught in the same posture. When the Pope teaches authoritatively, he is said to speak *ex cathedra,* or from the chair, denoting the teaching's nature as binding on the individual conscience. See also Cathedra. **CCC 1184**

Chair of St. Peter (TSHEHR uhv SAYNT PEE-ter): Throne dating from the sixth century, containing pieces of an earlier throne said to be that of St. Peter, presently ensconced (since the seventeenth century) in Bernini's "Altar of the Chair" in St. Peter's Basilica.

Chalcedon, Council of (KAUN-sihl uhv kal-SEE-duhn): The fourth ecumenical council (451) defining that Jesus Christ is one Son, one Person, with two complete and distinct natures: a divine nature consubstantial with the Father, a human nature consubstantial with us. This most significant Christological council brought to conclusion a quarter-century of fierce theological and ecclesiastical debate. Nestorianism held that Christ was two Persons (human and divine) united in an intimate but accidental fashion, something like God dwelling in a human. The Council of Ephesus, strongly influenced by the theology and terminology of St. Cyril of Alexandria, insisted on the unity of Christ but, to the dismay of Antiochene bishops, gave less attention to the reality and integrity of the humanity of Jesus. Representatives of Cyril and the Antiochenes came to an agreement in the Formula (or Symbol) of Reunion in 433, a forerunner of the definition of Chalcedon. Extremists on both sides were unhappy with the formula. After the death of Cyril (444), the aged and theologically inept Archimandrite Eutyches proposed an extreme Alexandrian position: That Christ was *from* two natures but *in* one nature. A more developed form of this Monophysitism held that the human nature of Jesus was transformed into His divine nature or was "swallowed up" by the divine nature. Opposition to Eutyches led to his condemnation and deposition, but with the support of Dioscorus, Patriarch of Alexandria, he persuaded Emperor Theodosius II to call a council at Ephesus in 449. Dioscorus manipulated the council, excluding opponents of Eutyches, refusing a hearing to the papal legates, and intimidating antagonistic bishops by sending in soldiers, monks, and a corps of stretcher bearers. The uproar caused Pope St. Leo to call it a *Latrocinium,* or Robber Synod. It reinstated Eutyches, deposed and exiled Flavian, Patriarch of Constantinople, and deposed other bishops opposed to Monophysitism. Remonstrances of the Pope were unheeded, but in 450 the emperor died and was succeeded by his sister Pulcheria and her consort Marcian. A council was convened in a suburb of Constantinople, Chalcedon, with more than five hundred bishops, including two papal representatives. The doctrinal letter, or *Tome,* of Pope Leo to Flavian in 459 was accepted ("Peter has spoken through the mouth of Leo"), and a formula of belief was elaborated. Rome refused to accept Canon 28 of this council, which gave the See of Constantinople patriarchal authority second only to Rome. Cf. CCC 247, 467

Chaldean Rite (kal-DEE-uhn RAIT): Also called the "East Syrian Rite." Liturgical calendar and usages originating in the primitive liturgies of Jerusalem and Antioch, used by Catholics chiefly in and from Iraq.

Chalice (TSHAL-ihs): (From Latin *calyx:* cup) The sacred vessel made of solid and worthy material, with nonporous cup portion, used for the celebration of Mass.

Chalice Veil (TSHAL-ihs VAYL), also Peplum (PEHP-luhm) and Sudarium (söö-DAH-ree-øøm): The cloth, of the same color and material as the chasuble (or just white), that is used to cover the chalice before the Presentation of the Gifts and after Holy Communion at Mass.

Chamberlain (TSHAYM-ber-luhn): Any one of the following Church officials: (1) The Cardinal Chamberlain, or *Camerlengo,* who administers the Holy See when the Pope dies, retires, or is impeded. (2) The Chamberlain of the College of Cardinals, who oversees the financial affairs of the College. (3) Formerly, Chamberlains of the Sword and Cape, laymen who attended the Pope during solemn ceremonies (office abolished by Pope Paul VI in 1968). (4) Papal Chamberlain, an honor given to priests that carries with it the title "Reverend Monsignor."

Chambre Ardente (SHAHM-bruh ar-DAWNT): 1. The commission, created by the French Parliament in 1547, which tried the Protestant Huguenots and followers of Calvinist Hugues Besançon. Meaning "burning room," the

Chambre Ardente's name came from either the severity it demonstrated to heretics or the fact that burning torches were used to light the room in which it met. 2. The court established by King Louis XIV to eradicate all witches and sorcerers.

Chancel (TSHAN-suhl): The area of the church that provides room for the altar and the assisting clergy. In some churches, the chancel, which today is less distinctive from the other sections of the church, also provides room for the choir.

Chancellor (TSHAN-sehl-ler): Notary of a diocese, who draws up written documents in the government of the diocese; takes care of, arranges, and indexes diocesan archives, records of dispensations, and ecclesiastical trials.

Chancery (TSHAN-ser-ee): A term commonly used in the United States and some other countries for the diocesan administrative offices, lately supplanted by "diocesan curia." 1. A branch of church administration that handles written documents used in the government of a diocese. 2. The administrative office of a diocese, a bishop's office.

Chancery, Papal or Apostolic (PAY-puhl [a-pah-STAH-lihk] TSHAN-ser-ree): Created in the eleventh century and abolished by Pope Paul VI in 1973, this office of the Holy See issued various documents and was custodian of the papal leaden seal. The Secretariat of State now performs such duties.

Chant (TSHANT): Type of sacred singing, either recitative in nature with a short two-to-six tones for an accentus, or melodic in one of three styles: syllabic, neumatic, or melismatic.

Chant, Ambrosian (am-BRO-zhuhn TSHANT): A simple chant in the iambic dimeter melodic scheme. The melodies were composed by St. Ambrose and his followers for use in the Ambrosian or Milanese Rite. These chants, though now mostly unused, were important in the evolution of the

Gregorian chant over the centuries. See also Ambrosian Hymnography.

Chant, Gregorian: See Gregorian Chant

Chantry (TSHAN-tree): 1. Endowment left for Masses for the dead. 2. Chapel where such Masses were said or chanted for the repose of the benefactor whose bequest built it and supported its clergy.

Chapel (TSHA-puhl): (From Latin: cape) 1. Originally the special room in which the cape of St. Martin of Tours was preserved. 2. From that usage, any small place of worship that may (but need not) house the relics or mementos of martyrs or saints.

Chapel of Ease (TSHA-puhl uhv EEZ): More convenient or accessible place of worship in a large territorial parish, but still under the jurisdiction of the pastor of the mother parish.

Chaplain (TSHAP-luhn): A canonical term that describes a priest to whom is entrusted the pastoral care of a special group of people, such as military personnel, migrants, hospital patients. Also, a priest or deacon who accompanies a bishop attending a liturgical celebration.

Chaplet (TSHAP-leht): (From French: wreath or crown) A set of beads strung together for counting prayers, sometimes used to describe the five-decade rosary *(rosarium:* Latin for rose garden) in honor of Our Lady.

Chapter (TSHAP-ter): General meeting of delegates of a religious order for elections and handling important affairs of the community. (Cf. Chapter, Conventual.)

Chapter, Cathedral (kuh-THEE-druhl TSHAP-ter): A body of priests who live together at the cathedral to assist the bishop in administrative duties and who perform certain liturgical functions, such as the recitation of the Liturgy of the Hours. Today more commonly found in Europe, the chapter is often composed of priests involved in administration.

Chapter, Conventual (kuhn-VEHN-tshöö-uhl TSHAP-ter): The gathering of vowed religious in a particular religious house in order to confess faults, consider the business of the community, elect superiors, and receive instruction. Communities may meet monthly, weekly, or daily for these chapters, which provide an important element in the growth of the community. Occasionally, an entire province (composed of numerous religious houses) will assemble for a large chapter.

Chapter House (TSHAP-ter HAUS): The section of a cathedral or religious house in which the cathedral or conventual chapter assembles. Most chapter houses are rectangular and consist of a large room with a single row of benches along the walls; the superior (abbot, bishop, or prior) sits on an elevated chair.

Chapter of Faults (TSHAP-ter uhv FAWLTS): A spiritual exercise practiced in certain religious communities wherein the members, presided over by the superior, publicly confess faults but not sins.

Character (KEHR-uhk-ter): (Latin: engraving instrument) 1. Those qualities that combine to make up the distinctive identity of an individual. 2. The permanent and unrepeatable spiritual quality imprinted upon the soul by the Sacraments of Baptism, Confirmation, and Holy Orders. **CCC 698, 1264, 1810**

Charismata (kehr-IHZ mah-tuh) or Charisms (KEHR-ih-zuhms): Our English word "charism" is from the Greek *charisma(ta)*, which refers to a "free gift." The term has both a nontechnical and a technical sense to it. At a nontechnical level, *charismata* refers to spiritual gifts in general (Rom 1:11, 5:15 ff., 11:29; 1 Cor 1:17), eternal life (Rom 6:23), or answers to prayers (2 Cor 1:11). *Charismata* are special gifts that, as service directed to the Lord, manifest the work of God through the Holy Spirit all for the common good of the body of believers, the Church. This "work of God" includes a myriad of behaviors, and especially a knowledge of God, as the following four texts make clear: Rom 12:6-8; 1 Cor 12:8-10, 12:28, 12:29-30. The gifts always point to the giver; their authentic use in the Church is a fulfillment of God's work initiated in the O.T. (e.g., prophetic discernment: 1 Kgs 22:28; gifts of the Spirit for the messianic age: Is 11:2; change of heart: Ez 36:26 ff.). CCC 688, 798-800, 809, 1508, 2003, 2024, 2684

Charismatic Renewal, Catholic (KATH-uh-lihk kehr-ihz-MA-tihk ree-NÖÖ-uhl): A movement within the Church emphasizing experience that has been termed "Baptism of the Holy Spirit," often accompanied by such gifts as healing and glossolalia. Although the gifts of the Holy Spirit are given to the Christian at the time of Baptism, those involved in the Catholic Charismatic Renewal seek to develop and use those gifts, often meeting in small groups to pray, sing, and give personal testimony about the activity of the Holy Spirit. This movement has the support of the Pope and bishops, and more recently those involved in the Catholic Charismatic Renewal have shown deep devotion to the Holy Eucharist and the Blessed Virgin Mary, with a strong obedience to the Holy Father.

Charity (TSHEHR-ih-tee): The supernatural virtue, infused by God and having Him as its motive and object, that flows from God and constantly seeks the good of others. St. Thomas Aquinas states that charity is the highest virtue and the source of all the other virtues. One who possesses charity loves God above all things and loves his neighbor with the love of God as he loves himself. CCC 1694, 1813, 1822-1829, 1841, 1844, 2013

Charity, Heroic Act of (hehr-O-ihk AKT uhv TSHEHR-ih-tee): The offering to God of all the merits of a good action or all the benefits gained after death for the souls in purgatory. To make this offering, in which one renounces all spiritual graces during life that would lessen punishments in purgatory, a person has to possess a firm resolve not to sin.

In St. John's Gospel, Jesus gives the foundation for the heroic act of charity: "If a man loves me, he will keep my word, and my Father will love him and we will come to him and make our home with him" (14:23). Cf. CCC 1394, 1472, 2011, 2026

Charity, Works of (WERKS uhv TSHEHR-ih-tee): These good actions, like the corporal works of mercy and other social deeds, are performed to assist others in need and not for profit or recognition. Works of charity illustrate the love of Christ, give glory to God, and represent the highest form of "active" work in the world. Cf. CCC 791, 1789, 1825, 1829, 1878, 1931-1932, 2447, 2462

Chartres, Cathedral of Notre Dame de (kuh-THEE-druhl uhv NO-truh DAHM duh SHAHRT-ruh): Located in Chartres, France, the famous "High Gothic" cathedral containing, among other treasures, a relic said to be Our Lady's veil and adorned with magnificent sculptures and stained-glass windows.

Chartreuse, The Great (*th*uh GRAYT shahr-TRØØZ): The great charter-house, the name by which the original foundation house of the Carthusian monks is called.

Chastity (TSHAS-tih-tee): The virtue that regulates one's sexual thoughts, desires, and actions. For the married person, chastity tempers the desire for legitimate marital acts for the good of the spouse and the family; for the unmarried person, chastity prohibits all willful sexual thoughts, desires, and actions. Primarily a natural virtue, chastity helps one to see the dignity of other persons as children of God and not as sexual objects. CCC 2337, 2341, 2344, 2346, 2348, 2394-2395

Chasuble (TSHAZ-yøø-buhl): From the Latin for "little house," the outer liturgical vestment worn by the celebrant at Mass, which, in its classical form, almost completely covered the wearer. Its color changes according to the feast or liturgical season.

Cherubikon (tsheh-RÖÖ-bih-kahn): In the Byzantine Rite, the "Hymn of the Cherubim" chanted prior to the "Great Entrance," or offertory procession, from the "table of preparation" to the altar.

Cherubim (TSHEHR-uh-bihm): The second of the nine choirs of angels. Ranking after the seraphim, the cherubim are known for their knowledge, symbolized God's glory in the O.T., and served as attendants of the Lord in the Book of Revelation (chps. 4-6). (See also Angels.)

Chevet (shuh-VAY): The east end of many Romanesque and Gothic churches, consisting of a single apse surrounded by an ambulatory connecting a number of apses or chapels, with the central chapel often dedicated to the Blessed Virgin Mary (known as a Lady Chapel).

Childermas (TSHIHL-der-mas): "Children's Mass," medieval English name for the feast of the Holy Innocents, December 28.

Child of Mary (TSHAILD uhv MEH-ree): One who belongs to a specific confraternity of Our Lady. In the thirteenth century, Bl. Peter de Honestis founded in Italy the oldest known Children of Mary sodality. The Vincentian Fathers and the Daughters of Charity, wishing to promote the Miraculous Medal, began a sodality of Mary in 1847.

Children, Duties of (DÖÖ-tees uhv TSHIHL-drehn): The responsibilities incumbent upon children, particularly those of loving and obeying God and respecting parents. The Fourth Commandment of the Decalogue states: "Honor your father and your mother." This commandment applies to children who have reached the age of reason and to "adult" children, too. Children who have reached adulthood must love their parents and especially care for them when they have become elderly and/or feeble. **CCC 2197, 2199, 2200, 2214-2220**

Children, Mass for (MAS for TSHIHL-drehn): In 1973 a special Directory for Masses with Children permitted various adaptations to be made in the Order of Mass, its readings and prayers, when children form the majority of the congregation.

Children's Communion (TSHIHL-drehnz kuh-MYÖÖN-yuhn): The practice allowing children who have reached the age of reason (usually seven years) to make their First Holy Communion. Pope St. Pius X originated this practice in his 1910 decree *Quam Singulari*.

Children's Crusade (TSHIHL-drehnz kröö-SAYD): An attempt, after the Fourth Crusade, to organize a crusade of children to retake the Christian shrines of the Holy Land. Although forty thousand participated, it was a failure.

Chiliasm (KIHL-ee-a-zuhm): (Greek *chilioi:* one thousand) Same as "millennialism," or beliefs having to do with the thousand-year reign of Christ (cf. Rv 20:4 f.). Premillennialists believe the reign will occur before the Second Coming; postmillennialists hold that the reign will happen after Jesus' coming, while amillennialists contend that the thousand years is symbolic of the period from Christ's earthly life to His return in glory.

Chinese Rites: See Rites, Chinese

Chi-Rho (KEE-ro): The abbreviation and term used to designate "Christ" that employs the first two letters in the Greek Christos, the "Chi" ("X") and the "Rho" ("P"), often with the "X" superimposed on the stem of the "P."

Chirograph (KEE-ro-graf): Literally, "written by hand"; in ecclesiastical use, it refers specifically to a letter written by the Pope in his own hand to a dignitary of the Church or a State regarding a significant concern shared by the Holy See.

Chirotony (Kee-RAH-tuh-nee): The term (Greek: laying on of hands) that refers to the Sacrament of Holy Orders in the Eastern Church.

Chivalry (SHIH-vuhl-ree): A body of customs guiding the actions of men in the Middle Ages. It advanced knighthood and also emphasized the importance of such Christian virtues as charity, fortitude, and modesty. Chivalry encouraged men to show loyalty to civil society in times of war and peace and to defend the Church when necessary.

Choir (KWAIR): (Latin *chorus:* singers, from Greek *choros:* a group of singers or dancers) 1. A group of singers at liturgical services that either leads the congregation in singing or sings music to which the congregation listens. 2. That part of the church building in which the choir is located. 3. The stalls in which members of religious orders chant the Divine Office. 4. A synonym for an order of angels. Cf. CCC 1143

Chrism (KRIH-zuhm): Mixture of olive or other vegetable oil and balsam (or balm), consecrated by a bishop, for use in liturgical anointings at Baptism, Confirmation, Holy Orders, the blessing of an altar, and, in former days, the coronation of a king. Cf. CCC 1183, 1241, 1289, 1291, 1294, 1297, 1312, 1574

Chrismal (KRIHZ-muhl), or Chrismatory (KHRIZ-muh-taw-ree): Small cylindrical metal jar or container where the holy oils are kept (oil stocks); formerly also designating the cloth wrapped around relics or covering a newly consecrated altar, an early pyx for the Blessed Sacrament, and the white-hooded robes of the newly baptized.

Chrismarium (krihz-MAH-ree-øøm): 1. Formerly the area of the church reserved for the conferral of Confirmation (during which the candidate is anointed with chrism). 2. A jar used to store chrism and other holy oils.

Chrismation (krihz-MAY-shuhn): In the Eastern Rite, the term used for the sacrament called Confirmation in the West, the anointing of the newly baptized with chrism. Cf. CCC 695, 1113, 1289

Christ (KRAIST): The kingdom of God would come about, in Jewish thinking, through the Messiah, God's anointed one, rendered in Greek as *Christos*. Throughout much of Israel's history, it seems that the Messiah was seen as a king or political figure. Even the famous oracles in Isaiah had their original setting in the imminent expectation of a king. The Church, in reading the Scriptures, perceived a deeper meaning in these prophecies (Is 7:14, 9:6, 11:1-4) and saw them admirably fulfilled in the Person of Jesus, Whose message of love would ultimately enable the wolf to be the guest of the lamb (Is 11:6), thus bringing about the total harmony that the kingdom of God is destined to be. The Servant Songs of Isaiah in chapters 42 and 49-53 also note the essential place of suffering in the establishment of God's reign in people's hearts. Once more, the Church found these prophecies fulfilled in the passion, death, and resurrection of Christ. **CCC 436-440, 453, 486, 629, 690, 695, 727, 745, 783, 1289**

Christ of the Andes (KRAIST uhv *the*e AN-deez): The statue of Jesus, located on the border between Argentina and Chile atop a mountain fourteen thousand feet above sea level, commemorating the peaceful resolution of a conflict between these countries in the nineteenth century.

Christ, Supreme Order of (söö-PREEM OR-der uhv KRAIST): Of the five pontifical orders of knighthood, this is the highest. It was founded in 1318 as the "Militia of Jesus Christ" for the defense of Portugal against the invasion of the Moors, given approval in 1319 by Pope John XXII. In the sixteenth century it was divided into two branches, with the religious branch under the Pope and the civil branch under the Portuguese sovereign. After a time of disuse, it was restored and reorganized by Pope St. Pius X in 1905, and in 1966 Pope Paul VI decreed that the Supreme Order of Christ would be bestowed only upon Christian heads of State.

Christendom: See Christianity

Christening: See Baptism, Sacrament of

Christian (KRIHS-tshuhn): The designation of a believer in Christ. Christians appear not to have used this term of themselves until the second century. Earlier they preferred to think and speak of themselves as "brothers," "disciples," "believers," etc. For the first two centuries the forms *Christiani* and *Chrestiani* were used interchangeably. The word occurs in the N.T. only in Acts 11:26, 26:28, and 1 Pt 4:16. The term is thought to have originated with outsiders. Opinions vary as to who precisely coined the name. The following have been suggested: (1) the Roman police in Antioch; (2) the Roman people in the city of Rome; (3) unknown pagan origin. In areas of Christian culture, the word is employed at times without any reference to faith but rather with the sense of something morally or ethically laudable, e.g., "the Christian thing to do." **CCC 83, 1289**

Christian Brothers (KRIHS-tshuhn BRUH-*th*erz): A title that can refer to two separate congregations of religious Brothers devoted to the teaching apostolate: (1) the Brothers of the Christian Schools founded by St. John Baptist de la Salle in Rheims, France, in 1680; (2) the Irish Christian Brothers, founded by Edmund Rice in Waterford, Ireland, in 1802 and modeled on the La Salle Brothers. Both communities are well represented in the United States.

Christian Democrats (KRIHS-tshuhn DEH-muh-crats): A political party with its strength in the countries of Western Europe, promoting human dignity, democratic participation in government, religious liberty, the strengthening of the family, workers' rights, and economic cooperation. It defends the right of private property and encourages governmental involvement in programs for social welfare. Generally, Christian Democrats are viewed as the moderate center between political extremes.

Christian Doctrine (KRIHS-tshuhn DAHK-truhn): Those teachings that are considered applicable to all Christians for leading a Christian life. By Christian doctrine, the whole person — body, mind, and soul — is developed according to the norms of reason and revelation with the help of God's grace, in order to prepare the Christian for a happy and useful life here and for eternal happiness in the life to come. The Catholic Church understands Christian doctrine broadly as including the child's first learning of simple prayers, catechism, elementary religion courses, and more advanced theology. More specifically, it comprises the early instructions given by the Apostles to the first generation of Christian believers. CCC 5, 11, 186, 427, 2179

Christian Doctrine, Confraternity of: See Confraternity of Christian Doctrine

Christian Education, Declaration on: See Gravissimum Educationis

Christian Family Movement (KRIHS-tshuhn FA-mih-lee MÖÖV-mehnt): Organized in 1950, this movement intended to apply Catholic Action by reforming society and the family. C.F.M. was composed entirely of laity; by 1960, thirty thousand couples belonged to it in the United States and other countries.

Christian Philosophy (KRIHS-tshuhn fih-LAH-suh-fee): This term has come to designate chiefly the practice of philosophy in the light of Christian Revelation, a practice that was championed chiefly in the works of the Catholic philosopher Étienne Gilson (1884-1978). In this sense, Christian philosophy is identical with neither pure philosophy (whose principles derive solely from reasoning about the structures of the world as these can be known by experience, generalization, and analysis), nor with dogmatic theology (whose principles are derived from Revelation, but whose methodology involves the use of philosophical ideas).

Christian Science (KRIHS-tshuhn SAI-ehns): Popular name for the beliefs of the Church of Christ Scientist, based in Boston, Massachusetts, this is a system of philosophy and therapy developed by Mary Baker Eddy (1821-1910), who maintained that Scripture teaches that such things as disease, pain, and sin are merely illusionary and will disappear when confronted with spiritual truth. According to this teaching, healing is achieved not through medicine but through correct thought. Christian Science is based upon the belief that the material world is unreal and that man's true nature is solely spiritual; this teaching is outlined and developed in

Mrs. Eddy's book *Science and Health,* published originally in 1875.

Christian Socialism (KRIHS-tshuhn SO-shuhl-ih-zuhm): The movement seeking to imbue society, economics, and politics with Christian values, prevalent in the nineteenth and twentieth centuries, and emphasizing harmony among diverse groups. It teaches that man must have justice in society and advocates a "middle ground" between socialism and capitalism, asserting that property belongs both to the State and to the individual.

Christianity (krihs-tshee-A-nih-tee): Broadly understood as the religion derived from the teachings of Jesus Christ as professed historically by Roman Catholics, Orthodox, and Protestants. Comprising faith in the person of Jesus as Messiah, the spiritual life He inspired, and adherence to the moral dictates He advanced, Christianity has influenced the arts and sciences, government and society for nearly two thousand years. Christian humanism, in particular, looks to the mystery of Christ's Incarnation and promotes the great dignity of the human person that the Second Person of the Trinity so values by His having shared our humanity in His earthly life and that He has now glorified in heaven. In the West, typically Christian values are joined to their historical antecedents in Judaism to produce what is called the Judaeo-Christian ethic. The Apostles continued, expanded, and spread the teachings of Christ throughout the world: the hierarchical order was established, with the bishops as successors to the Apostles and the presbyterate for the continued administration of the seven sacraments instituted by Christ. With organization and growth, there followed the logical consequences of Christian thought, notably its effect on the family and society, especially the Christian condemnation of slavery, the dignity accorded the human person, and the exercise of civil authority. **CCC 108**

Christmas (KRIHS-muhs): Our current English term can be traced back to at least A.D. 1123 and in one of the Old English spellings appears as *Christes maesse*, which by A.D. 1568 clearly meant "Mass of Christ," i.e., the celebration of

His birth. By the sixth century the annual feast day was almost universally celebrated on the twenty-fifth of December (the exception still to this day being the Church of Armenia). Speculation about the correct birth date originates in the early third century when Clement of Alexandria suggested May 20. The date of December 25 is marked for Christmas in the Philocalian Calendar, which represents Roman practice in the year 336 *(natus Christus in Betleem Judeae)*. Scholars speculate that the selection of December 25 was aimed at replacing the pagan winter festival dedicated to the "Sun of Righteousness" *(Natalis Solis Invicti)*. In the Eastern part of the Church, the feast of the Epiphany, which celebrated Christ's Baptism, was celebrated on January 6 and was later connected to the Nativity (in the fourth century). By the sixth century most of the East had adopted the December 25 date.

Christology (krihs-TAHL-uh-dzhee): The study of the Person of Jesus, particularly in the mystical union of His divine and human natures. Since the patristic age, serious Christological studies have taken place, with various aspects being defined by the ecumenical councils of Nicaea, Constantinople, Ephesus, and Chalcedon, all based upon the N.T. teaching that Christ is fully human and fully divine. These conciliar definitions have come in response to various heresies that have denied the fullness of His humanity (such as Docetism) or His divinity (such as Arianism) or have exaggerated the distinctiveness of His two natures (as in Nestorianism) or have given the natures a false unity (as in Monophysitism). CCC 456-478

Christophers (KRIHS-tuh-ferz): (Greek: Christ-bearers) The name of adherents of the movement founded in 1946 by Fr. James Keller, M.M. The Christophers' motto is: "It's better to light one candle than to curse the darkness." By sponsoring radio and television programs and by publishing their monthly *Christopher News Notes,* the Christophers have spread the Gospel to millions.

Christus Dominus (KRIHS-tøøs DO-mee-nøøs): The Decree on the Pastoral Office of Bishops in the Church, which was issued on October 28, 1965. This Decree deals with the various roles of bishops in the universal Church, in their own dioceses, and in their cooperation with one another. It states that the Pope and the bishops in communion with him are the successors to St. Peter and the other Apostles, and are to carry out the mandate from Christ "to teach all peoples, to sanctify men in truth, and to give them spiritual nourishment." The importance of the collegiality of bishops is stressed, giving encouragement to establish national episcopal conferences, which are to "formulate a program for the common good of the Church." Cf. CCC 857, 879, 881, 886

Chronicler (KRAH-nihk-ler): The unknown author of 1 and 2 Chronicles, who many speculate was a Levite. Scripture scholar W. F. Albright believed Ezra to be the Chronicler.

Chronicles, First and Second Books of (FERST and SEHK-uhnd BØØKS uhv KRAH-nih-kuhlz): Originally a single work, this O.T. text was first divided into two scrolls in the Septuagint. This became necessary because the Greek version required more space than the original Hebrew, which typically did not write in the vowels. The title of these books in Greek is *Paraleipomena* — "things left over" or "things omitted." It was Jerome who proposed the title "Chronicle of the Whole of Sacred History," whence the present English designation of the books as "Chronicles." These books present a narrative that runs from the creation to the return from the Exile under Cyrus. Paralleling the account found in Genesis through 2 Kings, Chronicles reworks history in order to make a religious statement. The clear goal of the work is to foster regard for the Law and to assert the blessings that accrue from adherence to it.

Chronista (kro-NIHS-tuh): The priest or deacon (or in necessity, a layman) who chants or reads the part of the narrator in the reading of the Passion on Palm Sunday and Good Friday.

Chronology, Biblical: See Biblical Chronology

Church (TSHERTSH): Our English word is related to the Scots *kirk,* the German *kirche,* and the Dutch *kerk,* all of which are derived from the late Greek *kyriakon,* meaning "the Lord's (house)." The classical Greek *ekklesia* meant "assembly of citizens" and implied a democratic equality among its members who met for legislative and other deliberations. In the Greek O.T. (LXX), *ekklesia* represents the Hebrew *kahal,* meaning the "religious assembly" (Dt 23; 1 Kgs 8; Ps 22). In the N.T. the term *ekklesia* always refers to a group of people: (1) those Christians in a region or city (e.g., Acts 14:23 ff.; 1 Cor 1:2; 2 Cor 1:1); (2) those gathered in a particular house (Rom 16:5; 1 Cor 16:19); (3) all Christians gathered in the Church (Mt 16:18; Eph 1:22). The Church is a mystery that, prior to Jesus, was hidden in the people of Israel and, since Jesus, has been revealed, in successive generations of believers (Eph 1:9 ff.; Rom 16:25 f.). The mystery is this: A sinful people possess an initial taste of salvation within a divine-human institution in which revelation from God, forgiveness, and grace through the work of Christ at the cross and the Father at the resurrection are like leaven working to transform what is broken and to free what is in bondage. The N.T. witness may be summarized thus: The Church is created by God, is the Body of Christ, Who is her Head (cf. Ephesians and Colossians), and is indwelt and empowered by the Holy Spirit (Eph 1:3, 22, especially 14; 2:22; 1 Cor 3:16). Jesus entrusted His teachings to the Apostles, chosen by means of the Holy Spirit (Acts 1:2), and to their successors (1 Tm 4:14; 2 Tm 1:6). The Holy Spirit guides the Church (Jn 16:13) and helps her guard the deposit of sound doctrine (2 Tm 1:13 ff.), which includes her authentic role of teaching in the name of Christ. The Church's existence is drawn from the Person of Christ (Eph 2:16-18), is born of one Baptism (Eph 4:5), is fed with one Bread (1 Cor 10:17), and is a single people (Gal 3:28). The Church is a gathering of sinners who are somehow being made holy and perfect because of Christ's love for her (Eph 5:26-27). The Church's perfect model and witness to Christ's Gospel in terms of faith, hope, and love is Mary, the Mother of God. She not only participated in the mysteries of salvation (e.g., Incarnation) and witnessed the Church's birth at Calvary (e.g.,

Jn 19:25) and Pentecost (Acts 1:14); she pondered and cherished these events and understood them (Lk 2:51). At the Second Vatican Council the doctrine of the Church received much attention, particularly in *Lumen Gentium*. In this constitution, the Council affirmed that the Church is in the first place that assembly of people, united in Christ, that is called into existence by God Himself (n. 2). Stating a position with regard to some past and present controversies, the Council said that "the society furnished with hierarchical organs and the Mystical Body of Christ, the visible society and the spiritual community, the earthly Church and the Church endowed with heavenly riches, are not to be thought of as two realities. On the contrary, they form one complex reality that comes together from a human and a divine element" (LG, n. 8). An image of the Church much favored by the Council was that of "People of God," evoking a dynamic and communitarian understanding of the Church. CCC 748-975, 2030-2051

Church and State (TSHERTSH and STAYT): The relationship between these two entities, which has undergone many changes over the centuries. The Church believes that each was created by God for particular ends; both involve some of the same members. The State may remain separated from the Church but must permit freedom to worship. Each may actually assist the other in fulfilling goals. CCC 748-972

Church, Dogmatic Constitution on the: See Lumen Gentium

Church, Early (ER-lee TSHERTSH): The period from Pentecost Sunday (c. A.D. 30) through Constantine's Edict of Milan (313). Church historians divide this era as follows: the "Apostolic Age" (30-180), noted for the work and impact of the Twelve Apostles upon their successors, especially regarding the development of the Creed and Church doctrines, along with the flowering of her hierarchical structures; the "Sub-Apostolic Church" (180-313), known for the growth of and persecution against the Church, connected with the theological activity of the Alexandrian and Antiochean schools. CCC 124, 642, 763, 766-767, 1185

Church History (TSHERTSH HIH-stuh-ree): The study of the development of Christianity from the time of Christ to the present. While the Church possesses a divine element, the existence of her human dimension means that the Church's role in time and culture may be discussed. St. Luke's Acts of the Apostles is the earliest "work" of Church history. St. Eusebius of Caesarea (d. 339) is the patron of this discipline. Scholars often divide the Church's history into three parts: Apostolic Age to Charlemagne (30-800); Middle Ages through the Protestant Reformation (800-1563); Counter-Reformation through the end of the Second Vatican Council (1563-1965).

Church in the Modern World, Pastoral Constitution on the: See Gaudium et Spes

Church Militant, Suffering, Triumphant: See Communion of the Saints

Church Property: See Goods, Temporal

Churching of Women (TSHERTSH-ihng uhv WIH-mehn): Name formerly used to designate the rite for invoking God's blessing upon a woman after childbirth, now entitled "Thanksgiving after the Birth of a Child."

Churchyard (TSHERTSH-yahrd): Literally, the property surrounding a church. The term is more common in rural communities, where the churchyard, which could be more expansive than in urban areas, would be used for the parish cemetery. The term is almost obsolete today, but it can be a significant concern where State laws exempt such land from real estate taxes.

Ciborium (sih-BOR-ee-uhm): 1. Chalice-shaped vessel with cover used for the reservation of the Blessed Sacrament in the tabernacle. 2. In the Middle Ages, term sometimes applied to the "sacrament tower" in which the Blessed Sacrament was reserved, and from that usage to the vessel itself.

Cilicium: See Hair Shirt

Cincture (SIHNK-tsher): A cord, either white or the liturgical color of the day, used to gather the alb at the waist.

Circumcillions (ser-kuhm-SIHL-yuhns): During the fourth century, a schismatic church developed in the Roman provinces of Africa and Numidia (present-day Tunisia and eastern Algeria). Called the "Donatist Church" after its founder, Bishop Donatus, this sect, which espoused a rigorist doctrine and enforced the rebaptism of lapsed Catholics, perdured into the fifth century. The Circumcillions (Latin, *circumcilliones*) were a fanatical movement on the fringe of the Donatist Church. They considered themselves to be the true heirs of the early Christians and willingly sought martyrdom in the defense of their faith, against Catholics as well as pagans. Their fanatical enthusiasm was exploited by the leaders of the Donatist Church, who used them to resist the imperial troops seeking to restore the Catholic bishops in the area. Some authors have tried to portray the Circumcillions as an agrarian reform movement, but the wealthy status of most of the Donatist leaders makes this thesis doubtful.

Circumcision (ser-kuhm-SIH-zhuhn): Cutting off the foreskin of the penis, an ancient practice signifying membership in the House of Israel. Symbolically, circumcision refers to the rending of all that is not in keeping with God and His commandments. The Council of Jerusalem (Acts 15:28 ff.) decided that circumcision was not necessary for Gentile converts. St. Paul argues that authentic circumcision is a spiritual entity (e.g., Rom 2:28 ff.; Gal 6:13). CCC 527, 1150

Circumincession (ser-kuhm-ihn-SEH-shuhn) or Divine Perichoresis (dih-VAIN peh-rih-ko-REE-sihs): The term for the mystery of the Godhead and the reality of the compenetration of each Divine Person of the Blessed Trinity with One Another. When, for example, the Father acts, the Son and the Holy Spirit are also present. They can never be separated from One Another even though each Person is distinct from the Others. St. Gregory Nazianzen used this term in referring to the two natures in the Divine Person of Jesus Christ. Cf. CCC 253-260

Citation (sai-TAY-shuhn): The formal and mandatory notification of a party that he or she is the subject of an ecclesiastical court proceeding (cf. Canon 1507).

City of God (SIH-tee uhv GAHD): One of the most important works (written 412-427) of St. Augustine, this theological book treats the differences between the City of Man and the City of God.

Civil Allegiance (SIH-vuhl uh-LEE-dzhuhns): The responsibility of citizens, including Christians, to be loyal to their country and to obey laws. Civil allegiance is an act of charity and justice; it involves defending one's country against unjust aggression, demonstrating respect for governmental officials, and paying taxes. One must not obey laws if they are in violation of the autonomy of the Church or morality. CCC 2234-2246

Civil Law (SIH-vuhl LAW): The body of laws of secular governments: nations, states, cities, etc. The term also refers to legal systems of certain countries that are based on Roman Law. Cf. CCC 1897-1917

Civil Marriage (SIH-vuhl MEHR-ihdzh): Stable union of a man and a woman according to the norms of secular governments and witnessed by an official of the State. Cf. CCC 1650-1651

Civory (SIH-vuh-ree): The canopy, or baldacchino, over the main altar of a church, representing the protection of heaven over the sacred action of the Mass.

Clandestinity (klan-deh-STIH-nih-tee): The exchange of marriage vows secretly, without the presence of an official witness. Clandestine marriages were common from the fourteenth century until the Council of Trent, which abolished them. Cf. CCC 1631

Clapper (KLAP-er), also Clepper and Crotalum (KLEHP-er, KRO-tuh-luhm): Wooden instrument designed to produce noise by means of wood striking wood as a substitute for bells from the *Gloria* of Holy Thursday until the Easter Vigil.

Clementine Instruction (KLEH-mehn-tain ihn-STRUHK-shuhn): Rubrics published by Pope Clement XII in 1731 for Forty Hours Devotion, superseded by the post-Vatican II instruction on Worship of the Eucharist Outside of Mass (1973).

Clergy (KLER-dzhee): A canonical classification for members of the Church in Holy Orders, and thus pertaining only to males. Also, a term used for a religious minister of any Christian or non-Christian denomination of either sex. **Cf. CCC 934, 1174**

Clergy, Byzantine (BIH-zuhn-teen KLER-dzhee): Catholic bishops, priests, and deacons, in full communion with the See of Rome, who observe the liturgical usages of the Byzantine Rite and the canonical prescriptions proper to the revised Code of Canons of the Eastern Churches (1991).

Cleric (KLEH-rihk): In Canon Law, a man who is a member of the clergy. **Cf. CCC 934, 1174**

Clerical Dress: See Dress, Clerical

Clericalism (KLEHR-ih-kuhl-ih-zuhm): 1. An attitude that seems to imply that clergy are somehow superior to laity. 2. A term generally used in a derogatory sense to mean action, influence, and interference by the Church and the clergy in matters with which they allegedly should not be concerned. Anticlericalism is a reaction of antipathy, hostility, distrust, and opposition to the Church and clergy arising from real and/or alleged faults of the clergy, overextension of the role of the laity, or for other reasons.

Clerical Obligations (KLEHR-ih-kuhl ah-blih-GAY-shuhnz): Special obligations or responsibilities that bind members of the clergy because of their state (cf. cc. 273-289).

Clerical Privilege (KLEHR-ih-kuhl PRIHV-lehdzh): Privileges enjoyed by clerics in the realm of secular society and found in Canon Law prior to Vatican II.

Clerks Regular (KLERKS REHG-yöö-ler): (Old English: clerks) Priests engaged primarily in the active ministry of the diocesan clergy, such as parish work or teaching, as distinct from the more restricted life of the monastic orders. They are called regular (from the Latin *regula*, meaning "rule") because they follow the rule of their founder or the rule established by a spiritual writer from within the Catholic Tradition.

Clinical Baptism (KLIHN-ih-kuhl BAP-tih-zuhm): A term, no longer in general usage, to describe the Baptism given to a person in some urgent necessity, such as danger of death; now more commonly called "emergency Baptism." Cf. CCC 1256

Cloister (KLOIS-ter), also Close (KLOS): (Latin *claustrum:* bar or bolt; from *claudere:* to close) The term for limited access to particular monastic communities that willingly embrace the contemplative life and thereby separate themselves from life in the world. A cloistered religious has limited opportunity to leave his or her cloister; similarly, outsiders are restricted in entering the cloister. Frequently, cloistered monasteries are surrounded with high walls to preserve the privacy of the enclosure and to keep outsiders at a distance. Cloister can also refer to this physical enclosure: in architecture, cloister is often restricted to the covered passageway around the open courtyard or quadrangle (technically called the garth) at the center of such an enclosed monastery.

Clothing (KLO-thihng): Ceremony by which a candidate for religious life is received into the novitiate and invested with the habit of the Order or Congregation.

Cluny (KLÖÖ-nee): Founded in 910, this Benedictine abbey, named after the south-central French village in which it was built, was the center of spiritual renewal and was marked by profound prayer and adherence to the Rule of St. Benedict.

Religious houses similar to Cluny sprang up in England, Germany, Italy, and Spain. The influence of this abbey, which existed until 1790, waned in the twelfth century.

Coadjutor Bishop: See Bishop, Coadjutor

Coat-of-Arms (KOT-uhv-AHRMZ): A pictorial representation of what originally was a shield marked with personal insignia, following heraldic traditions and rules, representing either an individual or some entity. Ecclesiastical coats-of-arms are regulated by the Vatican Secretariat of State.

Co-Consecrators (ko-KAHN-suh-kray-terz): Those bishops, at least two in number, who join the principal consecrator in ordaining (consecrating) a priest to the episcopacy.

Code (KOD): A digest of rules or regulations, such as the Code of Canon Law (q.v.).

Code of Canon Law (KOD uhv KAN-uhn LAW): The book containing the universal and fundamental laws of the Roman Catholic Church, revised and newly promulgated in 1983.

Codex (KO-dehks): Forerunner of modern books, a tome composed of cut and stacked papyrus rolls. Existing codices in Greek and Latin, dating from the fourth and fifth centuries and containing texts of Holy Scripture, include *Codex Alexandrinus, Codex Vaticanus, Codex Sinaiticus,* and *Codex Bezea.*

Codex, Canonical (ka-NAH-nih-kuhl KO-dehks): Technical term for a unified body of ecclesiastical laws, like the *Codex Iuris Canonici* of 1917, its revision of 1983, and the Eastern Code of Canon Law promulgated in 1990 (cf. Canon Law).

Coenobites (SEH-no-baits), also Coenobium (tshay-NO-bee-uhm): (From Greek *koinon:* common) 1. The ecclesiastical term for a group of monks who live their religious life in community. The individual in such a community is called a coenobite or cenobite, a term used in the early Church for monks. While Isidore of Seville reflects a knowledge of the Greek etymology, he also relates this term to the Latin *cena* (meal), since the coenobites, as distinct from hermits and anchorites, would share their meals in common (Isid. Sev., *Etym.* VII:13, 2; XII:13, 2; XV:3, 7; 4, 6). St. Pachomius (d. 346), author of the earliest rule for coenobites, is honored as the "Founder of Monasticism." 2. *Coenobium* is also the Latin name for the monastery where the coenobites live their community life. 3. The specific name for the monastery church, as distinct from the other buildings.

Collateral (kuh-LA-ter-uhl): A term, in Canon Law pertaining to consanguinity, that refers to blood relations outside the direct line but of the indirect line of descent, such as siblings, cousins, aunts, and uncles.

Collation (ko-LAY-shuhn): (Latin *collatus,* brought together) 1. The light meal taken on a fast day in place of lunch or dinner. Its name likely derives from the *collationes,* selections from the Fathers of the Church usually read at mealtimes in monastic communities. In religious houses, a collation can also refer to light refreshments provided in the afternoon or evening, outside of Lent or Advent. 2. In Canon Law, the act of appointment of a new person to an ecclesiastical office or benefice.

Collect (KAH-lehkt): Also known (in the English-language liturgical books) as the "Opening Prayer," a formal prayer, usually addressed to the Father, through the Son, in the Holy Spirit, by which the introductory rites are brought to a close and the assembly is prepared for the Liturgy of the Word.

Collection, Offertory: See Offertory Collection

Collection of Masses of the Blessed Virgin Mary (kuh-LEHK-shun of MAS-uhz uhv *th*uh BLEH-suhd VER-dzhin MEH-ree): A compilation of over forty Mass formularies honoring Mary under a variety of titles, arranged according to the liturgical year, promulgated in Latin in 1986, and in a definitive English translation in 1992.

Collections, Canonical (ka-NAH-nih-kuhl kuh-LEHK-shuhnz): Unofficial compilations of the laws, or canons, of local church synods and councils that took place prior to the twelfth century.

Collectivism (kuh-LEHK-tih-vih-zuhm): A socialist view of society in which the individual is subordinate to the whole. This is contrary to Catholic social doctrine, which teaches that the person is not to be seen simply as a member of a collective, and that society is to be ordered in such a way as to develop the dignity of the individual.

College (KAH-lehdzh): In the Church, an organized group of persons having a common purpose and recognized by Canon Law.

College of Cardinals, Sacred (SAY-krehd KAH-lehdzh uhv KAHR-dih-nuhlz): The group, serving as consultors to the Holy Father and members of the conclave that elects the new Pope, comprised of: (1) the bishops who are titulars of the suffragan sees of Rome and Eastern patriarchs; (2) priests who are titulars of certain presbyteral churches in the Diocese of Rome; (3) deacons who are titulars of various diaconal churches in Rome. Pope John XXIII decreed in 1961 that to be a cardinal, one had to be a bishop (although the Pope can dispense with this requirement). Before this time, a layman could be promoted to the cardinalate.

College of Consultors (KAH-lehdzh uhv kuhn-SUHL-terz): One of three official colleges recognized in Canon Law. A stable body prescribed by Canon Law to assist a bishop in the administration and governance of a diocese.

Collegiality (kuh-lee-dzhee-AL-ih-tee): A term in use especially since the Second Vatican Council to describe the authority exercised by the College of Bishops. The bishops of the Church, in union with and subordinate to the Pope — who has full, supreme, and universal power over the Church that he can always exercise independently — have supreme teaching and pastoral authority over the whole Church. In addition to their proper authority of office for the good of the faithful in their respective dioceses or other jurisdictions, the bishops have authority to act for the good of the universal Church. This collegial authority is exercised in a solemn manner in an ecumenical council and can also be exercised in other ways sanctioned by the Pope. Doctrine on collegiality was set forth by the Second Vatican Council in *Lumen Gentium* (the Dogmatic Constitution on the Church). By extension, the concept of collegiality is applied to other forms of participation and co-responsibility by members of a community. CCC 877, 880-885

Collegiate Church (kuh-LEE-dzhiht TSHERTSH): A church staffed and served by priests known as canons (q.v.).

Collegiate Tribunal (kuh-LEE-dzhiht trai-BYÖÖ-nuhl): A panel of three or five judges assigned to hear a case in an ecclesiastical tribunal.

Collegium Cultorum Martyrum (ko-LAY-dzhee-øøm køøl-TO-røøm MAHR-tih-røøm): An association founded in 1897 to spread devotion to the saints through addresses, remembrances, and research.

Colors, Liturgical (lih-TER-dzhih-kuhl KUH-lerz): In the Latin Rite, white, red, green, violet (and optionally, gold, black, and rose) vestments are used according to the feast, season, or event being celebrated, as determined by the norms of the *General Instruction of the Roman Missal*.

Colossians (kuh-LAH-shuhnz): Colossae was a city in the northwest region of Asia Minor called Phrygia, whose other principal cities were Laodicea and Hierapolis. Paul brought the Gospel to the first two cities on his second (Acts 16:6) and third (Acts 18:23) missionary journeys. The Church in Colossae may have been founded by Epaphras (Col 1:7), who was a native (Col 4:12). There were faulty teachings about the direct effect that spiritual beings known as "principalities and powers" (2:15) were thought to have on the destiny of humans. In addition, Jewish and non-Jewish cultic practices were being combined through syncretism (2:16,

21). Given the cultural context of the Church's Gentile and Jewish population, it is highly likely that belief in the "principalities" and widespread use of unacceptable cultic and liturgical rituals were combined with the biblical traditions about angelic mediation of divine revelation (e.g., Dn 10:21; 12:1). The author of Colossians addresses these problems, which ensued from such a combination. Long-standing tradition accepts the Pauline authorship of the epistle. Current opinion is divided on this question because of differences in style, vocabulary, and theology between this work and uncontested Pauline writings. Objections to Pauline authorship are intriguing but unconvincing, given the quantitative lack of historical data currently available. Pauline authenticity should not be rejected. Traditional dates should be followed, placing the time of writing sometime during Paul's Roman house arrest, ca. A.D. 62-63.

Commandments of God (kuh-MAND-mehnts uhv GAHD): The Decalogue, the "Ten Words" given by God to Moses on Mt. Sinai, directs the faithful to observe true worship and morality, thereby attaining the authentic fulfillment and union with God meant by Him. The Ten Commandments have been said to be the "minimal" requirement for the God-loving person, but the Two Great Commandments given by Jesus (i.e., to love God fully and one's neighbor as oneself) are viewed as the "fullness" of the divinely instituted covenant. CCC 2052-2550

Commandments of the Church (kuh-MAND-mehnts uhv *th*uh TSHERTSH): Often called the "precepts of the Church," these commandments emerged during the Middle Ages and have been hailed by Cardinal Gasparri as "of very great significance for the general spiritual life of the faithful." The seven precepts are: (1) to attend Mass on Sundays and Holy Days of Obligation; (2) to receive the Sacrament of Penance once a year in the case of serious (mortal) sin; (3) to receive Holy Communion at least once a year during the Easter Season; (4) to contribute to the support of the Church; (5) to fast and abstain on the appointed days; (6) to obey Church discipline regarding the Sacrament of Matrimony;

(7) to join the missionary spirit of the Church (this especially regarding those who have been confirmed). These precepts aim at fulfilling the "minimum expectations." The Church encourages her children to surpass the minimum and to strive for spiritual perfection. **CCC 2041-2043**

Commemoration (kuh-MEH-mo-RAY-shuhn): 1. In Mass, the practice, now suppressed, of observing more than one feast on a particular day by adding an additional "Collect" to that of the proper feast. 2. In the Liturgy of the Hours, a simple observance of a saint's day whose proper office was not celebrated, by which an antiphon and the saint's Collect replace those of Morning Prayer (Lauds) and Evening Prayer (Vespers). **Cf. CCC 1173**

Commemoration of the Living and the Dead (kuh-meh-mo-RAY-shuhn uhv _th_uh LIH-vihng and _th_uh DEHD): 1. In Eucharistic Prayer I (Roman Canon), the brief pauses for intercessory prayer during which priest and people silently remember those for whom they wish to pray. 2. Similar intercessions, though without the formal pauses, found in all of the Church's Eucharistic Prayers.

Commendation of the Soul (kah-mehn-DAY-shuhn uhv _th_uh SOL): Special prayers found in the Rite of Pastoral Care for the Sick to be offered with and for a dying person when the moment of death seems near. **CCC 690, 1020**

Commentaries, Biblical (BIH-blih-kuhl KAH-mehn-tehr-eez): Books or series of books written to explain the Scriptures, generally studies intended for the average educated reader; strictly speaking, not the works of biblical criticism, which are properly the domain of the trained exegete. In the Jewish corpus, one finds classes of commentaries among the rabbinical writings such as _haggadah, halakhah,_ and _midrash._ In the Catholic Tradition, we distinguish among the patristic (such as Origen, Jerome, Augustine, Ambrose, and Theodoret of Cyr), the medieval (Rabanus Maurus, Bernard of Clairvaux, and Peter Comestor), and the modern (the first of which has to be the Jesuit Cornelius à Lapide).

Commissariat of the Holy Land (kah-mih-SEH-ree-at uhv *th*uh HO-lee LAND): Special jurisdiction in the Order of Friars Minor for collecting alms for support of the Holy Places in Palestine (of which the Franciscans have had custody since 1342) and staffing of missions in the Middle East.

Commissary (KAH-mih-seh-ree): One who possesses delegated jurisdiction, who may be one of four types: (1) An apostolic commissary, appointed by the Pope, is an administrator or judge in a particular case. (2) The commissary of the Holy Land, a Franciscan priest, collects monies to be used for the Holy Places of Palestine. (3) A provincial commissary acts as the superior of a province of Franciscan Conventuals and Franciscan Friars Minor where there are too few religious to form an independent province. (4) A simple commissary, a priest, has jurisdiction from the bishop.

Commissions, Ecclesiastical (eh-klee-zee-AS-tih-kuhl kuh-MIH-shuhnz): 1. In the wide sense, any distinct bodies to which is assigned a specific task or duty by Church authorities. 2. In the strict sense, special groups to gather information established by the Holy See.

Commixture, Liturgical (lih-TER-dzhih-kuhl kuh-MIHKS-tsher): The dropping of a particle of the consecrated Bread into the chalice prior to Holy Communion.

Common Life (KAH-muhn LAIF): Phrase describing religious life as sharing a common ideal and apostolic goal, as well as a common table, dwelling, and fund, under a common rule and superior. Cf. CCC 925-927

Common of the Saints (KAH-muhn uhv *th*uh SAYNTS): Body of prayer formularies and texts in the Roman Missal and the Liturgy of the Hours in which can be found the Masses and Offices for saints not having their own prescribed texts.

Common Prayer, Book of: See Book of Common Prayer

Common Teaching of Theologians (KAH-muhn TEE-tshihng uhv thee-uh-LO-dzhunz): Classical theological note used to characterize opinions enjoying almost universal acceptance, but held with less certitude than those characterized as theological conclusions.

Communicatio Idiomatum (kuh-möö-nih-KAHT-see-o ih-dee-O-mah-tøøm): (Latin: communication of properties) A linguistic rule for predications about Christ according to which divine and human attributes may be interchangeably ascribed to the divine or human natures in Him by reason of their unity in the one divine Person. Church Fathers such as Cyril of Alexandria (d. 444) propounded the rule in order to counter the sharp disjunction between the two natures in Christ, characteristic of the Nestorian heresy. The rule found its way into normative Christian Tradition by its inclusion in Pope St. Leo's Tome (449). Since there is one hypostasis, or Person possessing both natures, properties of either nature refer to that one hypostasis. Thus it is proper to say both that "Jesus Christ is God" and "Jesus Christ is man." Although it is inappropriate, according to this rule, to distinguish things predicated of Christ, still we do distinguish the basis upon which they are predicated: What belongs to the divine nature is predicated of Christ in His divine nature, and what belongs to the human nature is predicated of Christ in His human nature. CCC 466; cf. 461-478

Communicatio in Sacris (kuh-möö-nih-KAHT-see-o ihn SAH-krihs): The reception of sacraments of the Church by nonmembers or the reception of sacraments in non-Catholic churches by Catholics.

Communications, Decree on the Means of Social: See Inter Mirifica

Communion, Holy (HO-lee kuh-MYÖÖN-yuhn): The Body, Blood, Soul, and Divinity of Jesus Christ received under the forms of bread and wine. CCC 1244, 1355, 1385-1390, 1415

Communion of the Mass (kuh-MYÖÖN-yuhn uhv *th*uh MAS): The section of the Mass from the praying of the Our Father through the concluding Prayer after Holy Communion. The Communion of the Mass has been called the "culmination" of the liturgy and the "climax" of the faithful's participation. The intimacy between Christ and His Bride the Church is especially evident during this part of the Mass.

Communion, Spiritual (SPIHR-ih-tshöö-uhl kuh-MYÖÖN-yuhn): The pious act of expressing a desire to receive Christ in Holy Communion when unable to do so in a sacramental manner for various reasons (e.g., unavailability of the Eucharist, failure to observe the Eucharistic fast, lack of the state of grace).

Communione e Liberazione (ko-möö-nee-O-nay eh lee-behr-AHT-zee-o-nay): (Italian: Fellowship and Liberation) A movement of laypeople, particularly the young, founded in 1958 by Monsignor Luigi Giussani, a professor of philosophy at the Catholic University of Milan, in order to help its members restore Catholic values to secular society. This fast-growing organization stresses fidelity to Christ and the Church, recognizing that Christ's presence is most evident in the solidarity of believers, and that a true relationship with Christ entails three essentials: Scripture, the sacraments, and the teaching authority of the Church. Since, according to Monsignor Giussani, contemporary society ignores God and religion, the followers of *Communione e Liberazione* are encouraged to bring their Christian convictions to the workplace, school, home, and politics, thus functioning as the leaven of the Gospel. While some members live together in community, others are free to continue a life of work, home, and family. The movement has enjoyed the backing of Pope John Paul II.

Communion of the Saints (kuh-MYÖÖN-yuhn uhv *th*uh SAYNTS): Affirmed by the Second Council of Nicaea, the Council of Florence, and the Council of Trent, the ninth article of the Apostles' Creed states that a spiritual union exists among the saints in heaven, the souls in purgatory, and the faithful living on earth (traditionally referred to as respectively the Church triumphant, suffering, and militant); this communion of the saints is described by the Second Vatican Council as "the living communion which exists between us and our brothers who are in the glory of heaven or who are yet being purified after their death. . ." (LG, n. 51). CCC 946-962

Communism (KAHM-yöö-nih-zuhm): The political and philosophical system championed by Karl Marx (1818-1883), advocating the sharing of goods, the State as owner of all property, the economy as the foundation of society, the State as sole ruler of all elements of society, and the rejection of God and faith in Him. Pope Pius XI, in his 1937 encyclical *Divini Redemptoris*, condemned Communism and cautioned Catholics not to associate with Communists in political or social affairs.

Community (kuh-MYOO-nih-tee): A gathering of individuals who share the same beliefs and who are subject to the same authority. In Catholic usage, all those followers of Christ who are joined to Him through justifying and sanctifying grace. This finds particular expression in those local communities that comprise dioceses, parishes, religious orders, and individual religious houses. CCC 751-752, 832-835

Comparative Religion (kuhm-PEHR-uh-tihv reh-LIH-dzhuhn): The study of the similarities and differences among the major world religions that exist today, and also among the various primitive or ancient religions. Such study considers the various understandings of a Supreme Being, sacred writings, religious practices, beliefs, etc. While such study is encouraged by the Catholic Church, it should not be used to attempt to disprove the unique revelation of the Christian Faith, nor is it to be used to attempt to prove that Christianity simply evolved from existing religious systems.

Competence (KAHM-peh-tehns): Jurisdiction over a case or the ability of a tribunal to hear a case.

Complaint of Nullity (kuhm-PLAYNT uhv NUHL-ih-tee): A complaint or charge that the final decision or sentence in a canonical court case suffers from a substantial defect that makes it null or invalid.

Compline or Complin (KAHM-plihn): (From Latin: completion) The Night Prayer of the Church that completes the daily *cursus* (course) of the Liturgy of the Hours (Divine Office).

Compostela, Pilgrimage of (PIHL-grih-muhdzh uhv kahm-po-STEH-luh): Santiago de Compostela in Spain is the site of the medieval shrine of St. James the Greater, to which pilgrims have traveled from as early as the eighth century. Typically, the pilgrims to this shrine, which have included Pope John Paul II, identify themselves with a seashell or some portrayal of one; often the shell may hang from their pilgrim's staff, or it may be worn on their clothing, especially on the front of their hat, as in the typical portrayal of the saint himself.

Concelebration (kahn-sehl-eh-BRAY-shuhn): Mass offered by more than one bishop or priest, in which all "concelebrants" are vested and recite together the core parts of the Eucharistic Prayer as a way of manifesting the unity of the priesthood.

Conciliar Theory (kahn-SIH-lee-er THEE-uh-ree), also Conciliar Movement (kahn-SIH-lee-er MÖÖV-mehnt): Theory or belief, condemned but recurring, that the Pope is subject to the authority of an ecumenical council.

Conclave (KAHN-klayv): (Latin *con:* with + *clavis:* key) The enclosed meeting of the cardinals of the Church for the purpose of electing a Pope. This practice dates from 1274, when Pope Gregory X ordered papal elections to be held in conclave so that there would be no outside interference and also to hasten the process, since a vacancy in the papacy had existed for nearly three years before his own election.

Concomitance (kuhn-KAH-mih-tehns): The state in which an object is associated with and simultaneously present to another object. When the Body of Christ is substantially present under the Eucharistic Species of bread, the Blood, Soul, and Divinity of Christ are also present — by virtue of concomitance — because Jesus cannot be divided; His whole Self is present. CCC 1374, 1377

Concordance (kuhn-KOR-duhns): (Latin *concordans:* putting things in harmony) Research tool that lists in alphabetical order the principal words of an author or of an individual book; it gives the word in its immediate context and the exact location of the word. For classical authors and books of the Bible, this is done by citing the source by book, chapter, and verse. In a biblical concordance, for "beginning," one finds the context: "In the beginning God created. . ." with the location: Genesis 1:1. As translations of the Bible differ one from the other, so do biblical concordances, and an individual concordance is useful only insofar as it lists the words of a particular translation or text. Concordances exist for all the major English translations of the Bible, as for the Vulgate and Septuagint and the original Hebrew and Greek texts. Most of these concordances are also available on computer disks. Biblical concordances, in whatever form, are useful for research and especially so for clerics in their homily preparation.

Concordat (kuhn-KOR-dat): A treaty between the Holy See and a secular government.

Concordat of Worms (kuhn-KOR-daht uhv WERMZ): Treaty of 1122 between the Holy See and the Holy Roman Emperor over the appointment of bishops. By it, German bishops were to be elected in the presence of the emperor.

Concord, Formula of (FOR-myöö-luh uhv KAHN kord): A document drafted in 1547 by a number of Lutheran theologians, giving definitive expression to Lutheran belief. It dealt with doctrinal controversies with Catholicism on one hand and with Calvinism on the other. In 1580 it was combined with other creeds and Lutheran documents to comprise the Book of Concord, but it did not gain the acceptance or authority within Lutheranism of the more influential Augsburg Confession.

Concupiscence (kuhn-KYÖÖ-pih-sehns): The inclination to sin arising from the disobedience of Adam and Eve. All persons, except Jesus and Mary, possess concupiscence, which specifically refers to the desire for bodily pleasure. Concupiscence is not evil *per se* but does lead to sin when its impulses are not checked. CCC 376, 400, 405, 2514-2527

Concursus (kahn-KØØR-søøs): 1. The activity, called "divine operation," by which God as the First Cause relates to His creatures as secondary causes. Everything that God made depends upon Him for its existence and preservation. 2. The examination in which one seeking an ecclesiastical office competes with others. Cf. CCC 238-239

Condign Merit (kuhn-DAIN MEHR-iht): The favor bestowed by God upon one who has performed a morally good action, to which one has a "right" based on a promise from God. The reward is in proportion to the act. To benefit, one must be in the state of grace and be free in performing the action.

Conditional Administration of the Sacraments (kuhn-DIHSH-uh-nuhl ad-mih-nih-STRAY-shuhn uhv *th*uh SA-kruh-mehnts): The celebration of a sacramental rite when a doubt is present about whether or not a sacrament has been received already or whether one is capable of receiving the sacrament. If unsure that a person in danger of death has been baptized, the minister of the sacrament would preface the formula with, "If you are not already baptized. . . ." If uncertain about the physical state of someone to be anointed, the priest says, "If you are alive. . . ."

Conferences, Clergy (KLER-dzhee KAHN-fer-ehn-sehz): Gatherings of bishops, priests, and deacons for the purposes of continuing education, spiritual reflection, or consultation.

Conferences, Episcopal (ih-PIHS-kuh-puhl KAHN-fer-ehn-sehz): A body or grouping of all bishops of a given territory with statutes approved by the Holy See to foster Catholic unity in that area.

Confession (kuhn-FEH-shuhn): Admission by telling something that was not known to another. In the Catholic context, confession occurs in the Sacrament of Penance, in which one reveals one's sins to a priest who grants absolution when there is true repentance. Catholics are to confess once a year when in serious sin. Mortal sins are to be confessed in kind and number. One is to receive the Sacrament of Penance, if baptized in infancy, before receiving Holy Communion for the first time. The Church strongly urges that Catholics go to confession often in order to grow in sanctity; venial sins, while not, strictly speaking, necessary to confess, should be confessed in order to receive the grace of the sacrament and the pardon of God. **CCC 1455-1458**

Confessional (kuhn-FEH-shuh-nuhl): Place designated for celebrating the Sacrament of Penance; since the sixteenth century, most commonly a boxlike structure providing a confessor's chair and a penitent's kneeler with a screen for anonymity, or now a "reconciliation room" in which the penitent has the option of confessing face-to-face or anonymously.

Confession of a Martyr (kuhn-FEH-shuhn uhv uh MAHR-ter), also Confessio (kon-FEH-see-o): The Latin *confessio* has three meanings (cf. Augustine's *Confessions,* 1:1) — the admission of sin, the proclamation of praise, and the profession of faith. Originally, the tomb of a martyr, particularly one in the catacombs, was called the confession of a martyr, since it was in these precious relics that one saw a witness to God's glory and a witness to the Faith in a death suffered for the Lord. Today it refers to the crypt where the remains of a martyr are kept beneath the main altar of a church. In the style of the basilicas and many of the major churches in Rome, the crypt is entered from above by a grand staircase, at the top of which is a low railing with a gate in the middle. Since the crypt is not always accessible, there is usually a *prie-dieu* with the text of the Nicene Creed provided (as is, for example, the case at St. Peter's Basilica in Rome); thus the modern pilgrim is provided the opportunity of realizing again the ancient act of the *confessio,* whereby he makes a profession of faith and proclaims the glory of the Lord present in the Eucharist immediately above the crypt, or *confessio.*

Confessor (kuhn-FEH-ser): (From Latin: to declare openly) 1. One who bears witness publicly to the Faith. 2. A priest who has canonical faculties to hear confessions.

Confirmation Name (kahn-fer-MAY-shuhn NAYM): Name that may be chosen by one to be confirmed, properly that of a patron saint on which to model one's life.

Confirmation, Sacrament of (SA-kruh-mehnt uhv kahn-fer-MAY-shuhn): Sacrament instituted by Christ in promising to send the Holy Spirit (Jn 14:15-21) and attested to in the early Church (Acts 8, 19), in which the celebrant (in the Latin Rite, a bishop or priest delegated by him) invokes the gift of the Holy Spirit upon a baptized person and anoints the candidate with holy chrism. **CCC 1285-1314**

Confiteor (kon-FEE-tay-or): (Latin: I confess) The name popularly given to the penitential prayer that begins with these words, a prayer that, among other options, may be used in the penitential rite of the Mass.

Confraternity (kahn-fruh-TER-nih-tee): Term used in the 1917 Code of Canon Law for voluntary associations of the clergy or laity established under Church authority. Now known as "Associations of the Faithful."

Confraternity of Christian Doctrine (kahn-fruh-TER-nih-tee uhv KRIHS-tshuhn DAHK-trihn): One of the numerous societies that appeared around the time of the Council of Trent (1545-1563), with the purpose of providing religious education in Milan for children and adults who had never received formal catechesis in a Church-sponsored program. Further impetus was given to the movement by both the Council itself and the Catechism of the Council of Trent, approved by St. Pius V in 1566. By decree of St. Pius X, *Acerbo nimis* in 1905, the establishment of the Confraternity of Christian Doctrine (CCD) was mandated for every diocese and parish of the Catholic Church to provide education in the Faith (cf. Christian Doctrine) for the young, converts, and those otherwise unable to benefit from the parochial school system. Usually this is accomplished by way of instructions given to the student during the weekend or on a weeknight. Some parishes have adopted a variation of the CCD program as their Faith Formation Program (F.F.P.). Since CCD is conducted on the parish level under the immediate supervision of the local pastor, it comes under the authority of the Vatican Congregation of the Clergy. Nationally, it is supervised by the Department of Education, U. S. Conference of Catholic Bishops in Washington, D.C.

Congregation (kahn-gruh-GAY-shuhn): 1. The people joined together to form a parish. 2. Unofficial term for a group of men and women joined in a religious community or institute of consecrated life. 3. An administrative department of the Roman Curia.

Congregationalism (kahn-gruh-GAY-shuhn-uhl-ih-zuhm): A form of Protestantism that believes that each local group of believers is independent and autonomous. Church government is based upon the principle of democracy, and no individual has a claim to any right to teach or govern except that which is delegated by the congregation.

Congregational Singing: See Singing, Congregational

Congresses, Eucharistic (yoo-ker-IHS-tihk KAHN-grehs-ehz): Assemblies of the Catholic faithful intended to show and foster greater devotion to the Lord in the Eucharist. Devotion is shown by the public celebration of the Mass, reception of Holy Communion by properly disposed Catholics in attendance, and periods of exposition with Benediction of the Blessed Sacrament. Devotion is promoted by way of lectures and discussions conducted during the congress. Since the first formal Eucharistic congress held at Lille, France, in 1881, there have been over forty international congresses, including two in the United States, at Chicago in 1926 and at Philadelphia in 1976.

Congruism (KAHN-gröö-ih-zuhm): (Latin *congruitas:* suitability, fitness) A theory, developed in the sixteenth century by certain Jesuits, that holds that God bestows grace with man's cooperation and also in accordance with the fitness of a particular grace to the specific condition of the one receiving it. As the grace is suitable to the interior disposition and external circumstance of an individual, it becomes effective by a free consent of the will. Cf. CCC 2006-2011

Consanguinity (kahn-san-GWIHN-ih-tee): The blood relationship between persons. Also, a diriment impediment to marriage within certain degrees. Cf. CCC 2388

Conscience (KAHN-shuhns): The "inner core" of the human person that identifies morally good and evil choices in accord with right reason and the teachings of the Church. From the Greek *synderesis* and the Latin *conscientia,* conscience was for St. Paul an awareness of the difference between good and evil. St. Thomas Aquinas wrote that conscience is the judgment of practical reason by which is known what is morally correct and the actions to be performed in a situation. CCC 1776-1802

Consecration (kahn-seh-KRAY-shuhn): (From Latin: to set apart for a sacred purpose) 1. Any formal designation of a person, place, or thing for the service of God. 2. The Words of Institution in the Eucharistic Prayer, by which bread and wine are transubstantiated into the Body and Blood of Christ. Cf. CCC 438, 534, 901, 931-933, 1294, 1297, 1352, 1535, 1538, 1548, 1556-1559, 1672

Consecration Cross (kahn-seh-KRAY-shuhn KRAWS): The painted or sculptured cross attached at each of the places where the bishop anoints with chrism the walls in the formal consecration of a church, making the Sign of the Cross on the inside walls of the church in twelve places, symbolic of both the twelve tribes of Israel and the Twelve Apostles, since the Church is the New Israel and is apostolic in her origin and life. Church law forbids the removal of these crosses; it is traditional on the anniversary of the church's consecration that a lighted candle be burnt before each of the twelve crosses. Cf. CCC 1293-1294

Consent, Marital (MA-rih-tuhl kuhn-SEHNT): The action, either verbally or through other signs, whereby a man and a woman give themselves to each other for the purpose of establishing marriage. CCC 1621, 1623, 1625-1632, 1639, 1662

Consequentialism (kahn-suh-KWEHN-shuhl-ih-zuhm): The moral theory, aligned with proportionalism and utilitarianism, that holds that the preferable action is one that brings about the best consequences. The preferred result, rather than the objective truth and intentionality, is the focus in consequentialism. Traditional moral theology holds that consequences are important in determining the rightness of an act, but so are the intrinsic morality of the act and the agent's intention. CCC 1753

Consistory (kuhn-SIHS-tuh-ree): A special meeting of the Pope with all the cardinals to conduct very important Church business. Also, meetings to elect the Pope and proclaim new cardinals.

Consortium Perfectae Caritatis (kon-SORT-see-øøm pehr-FEHK-tay kah-ree-TAH-tihs): An association formed in 1971 to assist women religious in developing religious life in accordance with those principles set forth by the Second Vatican Council in *Perfectae Caritatis* and other related documents. It is based upon the fundamental belief that the true renewal of religious life comes from faithful obedience to the teaching of the Catholic Church. Since 1992, this group has been replaced by a papally approved association known as the Council of Major Superiors of Women Religious.

Constance, Council of (KAUN-sihl uhv KAHN-stuhns): The sixteenth ecumenical council, held between 1414 and 1417, at which the Western Schism was resolved.

Constancy (KAHN-stuhn-see): The virtue enabling one to persevere in suffering without surrendering to despair and apathy. Trials and distress are able to be withstood when one prays for patience and courage and receives the sacraments often. Cf. CCC 1808, 2733

Constantine, Donation of (do-NAY-shuhn uhv KAHN-stuhn-teen): A document, dating from the late eighth century, purporting to reproduce a legal text in which the Emperor Constantine recognized the superior dignity of the Pope in the spiritual order and conferred upon him privileges in the temporal realm. Incorporated into various influential collections, this document was universally accepted as genuine until the fifteenth century, when it was proved by Lorenzo Valla to have been a forgery.

Constantinople, Councils of (KAUN-sihlz uhv KAHN-stan-tih-NO-puhl): As political and social forces of the fourth and fifth centuries forced Rome into eclipse, Constantinople, the "Rome of the East," began to be considered the *caput mundi*, "head of the world." Thus from 381 to 869 four ecumenical councils were convoked in this city on the Bosphorus, the capital of the Byzantine Empire: the first (381), which was the second ecumenical council after Nicaea, condemned the Arian heresy and reaffirmed the teaching of its predecessor; the second (553) condemned the Nestorian heresy; the third (681) reasserted the Christological clarifications of the Council of Chalcedon; the fourth (869) condemned Photius and his followers.

Constantinople, Patriarch of (PAY-tree-ahrk uhv KAHN-stan-tih-NO-puhl): "Patriarch" is a title of honor rendered to a bishop of a see with special dignity, usually due to its historic connection to one of the Apostles. The traditional patriarchates were listed by the Council of Nicaea (325) as Rome, Alexandria, and Antioch, with the Council of Chalcedon (451) adding Jerusalem and Constantinople. This last one was so honored because of its claim to be the "new Rome," established by Constantine I in 330 at Byzantium on the Bosphorus. Because of this prominence, the Bishop or Patriarch of Constantinople began to presume prerogatives similar to those traditionally reserved to the Bishop (or Patriarch) of Rome, the Pope, thus leading to tensions. These tensions reached tragic proportions at the time of the Great Schism in 1054. Recent Popes and patriarchs, beginning with Paul VI and Athenagoras in 1965, have sought to minimize differences, to stress the vast areas of common agreement in an effort to effect corporate reunion.

Constantinople, Rite of: See Rite of Constantinople

Constitution (kahn-stih-TÖÖ-shuhn): 1. The highest and most authoritative form of a papal pronouncement. 2. The organizational rule of a body within the Church, such as a religious community.

Constitutional Clergy (kahn-stih-TÖÖ-shuh-nuhl KLER-dzhee): The priests, called the "juring" clergy, who took the oath pledging their belief in and cooperation with the efforts of the National Assembly of France during the French Revolution, especially in 1790. Those who refused to take the oath, termed the "nonjuring" clergy (i.e., the Sulpicians who fled to Baltimore, Maryland, and began St. Mary's Seminary in 1791), were scorned and persecuted. The oath was condemned by Pope Pius VI and revoked in 1801.

Consubstantial (kahn-suhb-STAN-shuhl): The term used by the Council of Nicaea in A.D. 325 to teach that the Three Persons of the Blessed Trinity, while distinct and separate, share one and the same substance. **CCC 248, 253, 689, 2789**

Consubstantiation (kahn-suhb-stan-see-AY-shuhn): Also known as "impanation," theory espoused by the followers of Martin Luther at the time of the Protestant Reformation, asserting the coexistence of the substance of bread and wine with the Body and Blood of Christ in the Eucharist. It was rejected by the Church at the Council of Trent with the definition of the Catholic doctrine of transubstantiation. **Cf. CCC 1376**

Consultors (kuhn-SUHL-terz): Specialists or experts who assist authority figures in the Church, such as bishops or members of Roman congregations.

Consummation (kahn-suh-MAY-shuhn): The first act of integral sexual intercourse that takes place between a man and a woman after marital consent has been exchanged. Cf. CCC 1640, 2366

Contemplative Life (kuhn-TEHM-pluh-tihv LAIF): Term meaning the "way of life that seeks God by prayers and mortification." Traditionally, two dimensions of the Christian vocation are delineated by the Church and the spiritual writers: the "active" life (e.g., performing the corporal works of mercy) and the "contemplative" (e.g., praying and sacrificing for oneself and for the world). The "vowed" religious life — a kind of contemplative life — offers a higher degree of perfection than the active life. Cf. CCC 920-921

Contentious Trials (kuhn-TEHN-shuhs TRAILZ): Canonical trials for the vindication of rights of persons or the declaration of juridic facts, such as a marital nullity trial.

Continence (KAHN-tih-nehns): (Latin *continentia,* restraint) The self-restraint to be exercised in the area of sexual pleasure. The absence of sexual activity for those who are unmarried, or by mutual agreement between husband and wife within marriage. Cf. CCC 1650, 1832, 2340, 2349-2350, 2370, 2520

Contraception (kahn-truh-SEP-shuhn): Anything done to prevent conception in sexual intercourse. Direct contraception is against the order of nature. Indirect contraception — as a secondary effect of medical treatment or other action having a necessary purpose — is permissible under the principle of double effect (q.v.). Practicing periodic continence is not contraception because it does not directly interfere with the order of nature. CCC 2370, 2399

Contraceptives (kahn-truh-SEHP-tihvz): Mechanical devices or chemical agents that directly interfere with the conception of human life.

Contract (KAHN-trakt): An agreement between two or more persons concerning certain actions and having definite legal consequences. Cf. CCC 2213, 2410

Contrition (kuhn-TRIH-shuhn): (From Latin *contritio*: crushing or grinding) A feeling of remorse or repentance for sins that have been committed, with a trust in God's mercy and a determination not to sin again. CCC 1451-1454

Contumacy (kuhn-TÖÖ-muh-see): Deliberate disregard for ecclesiastical authority. In Canon Law, it refers to (1) those who refuse to respond to the citation of a judge, or (2) those who refuse to desist from criminal behavior after canonical warnings.

Contumely (kuhn-TÖÖM-uh-lee): The unjust ridiculing of another, contrary to justice and charity, by way of gestures and insults. Contumely inclines others to anger and contempt. The Christian responds to contumely with patience and silence (Rom 12:19).

Convalidation (kahn-val-ih-DAY-shuhn): The act of making valid, according to the norms of Canon Law, a marital consent that has been exchanged invalidly.

Convent (KAHN-vehnt): The building or group of buildings in which a religious community lives. Convent, meaning an "assembly of people," is usually applied to the residence of religious Sisters in the United States.

Conventual Mass (kuhn-VEHN-tshöö-uhl MAS): The name of the daily Mass offered publicly in churches where professed religious either live or publicly celebrate the Liturgy of the Hours. "Conventual" refers to the various aspects of communal living in religious life.

Conversion (kuhn-VER-zhuhn): A turning away from someone or something and a turning toward another person or thing. 1. In the Christian context, an embracing of Jesus Christ and a disavowal of whatever keeps one from God. Both Old and New Testaments emphasize the necessity of conversion. Each conversion, according to St. Thomas Aquinas, consists of preparation, merit, and glory. 2. The process by which an individual leaves one religious affiliation for another. CCC 160, 545, 981, 1036, 1422-1423, 1428, 1430-1433, 1435, 1797, 2608-2609

Convert (KAHN-vert): 1. A person whose beliefs and convictions have changed from one position to another. 2. A person, in the religious context, who now embraces virtue after having been involved in sin. *Metanoia* (Greek, "conversion") means an interior change in the person. 3. One who accepts a new religious affiliation, while renouncing former ties.

Cope (KOP): The vestment worn by clergy at Benediction, processions, and solemn celebrations of the Liturgy of the Hours. The cope, extending to the floor, is fastened around the neck by a clasp. A hood shaped like a shield is usually on the back of the cope.

Copt (KAHPT): A member of the Orthodox or Catholic Coptic Rite, centered in Egypt and the Near East, under patriarchs who reside in Alexandria. The Catholic Copts date back to the resumption of communion with the Holy See in 1741.

Coptic Rite (KAHP-tihk RAIT): An Alexandrian Rite employing the liturgies of St. Basil, St. Mark, St. Cyril, and St. Gregory Nazianzen in Coptic translation. This rite is used both by Orthodox and Catholic Copts. Cf. CCC 1203, 2678

Coram Cardinale (KO-rahm kahr-dee-NAH-lay) or Episcopo (ay-PIHS-ko-po): (Latin: before a cardinal or bishop) A term used to describe those liturgical ceremonies done in the presence of a prelate.

Corinthians, First Epistle to the (FERST ih-PIH-suhl töö *th*uh kuh-RIHN-thee-uhnz): What is now called 1 Corinthians is the first of two surviving letters written to the Church Paul founded on his second missionary journey and first visit to Corinth (Acts 18:1-18) ca. A.D. 50-51. He lived with Aquila and Priscilla for about eighteen months before eventually continuing on his missionary journey. He wrote 1 Corinthians from Ephesus (16:8), accompanied by

Sosthenes (1.1) and three representatives of the Corinthian Church (Stephanus, Fortunatus, and Achaicus, 16:17-18). In this work, Paul deals with divisions in the Christian community at Corinth, as well as reports he has received about incest, the use of pagan courts, and fornication. He likewise addresses matters such as marriage, celibacy, and virginity. St. Paul confronts problems surfacing in the worship life of the Church at Corinth and finally sets forth authentic teaching on the resurrection of the dead. This epistle is universally accepted as coming from Paul, probably written around A.D. 54.

Corinthians, Second Epistle to the (SEHK-uhnd ih-PIH-suhl töö *th*uh kuh-RIHN-thee-uhnz): In the past two centuries scholars have noted the contrasts in tone and subject matter between 2 Cor 1-9 and 10-13; these and other considerations have led some to suggest that these two sections were once individual letters, later combined into their current canonical form. We shall consider the letter in its current form for the sake of conciseness. In 2 Cor 1-9, Paul encourages the Corinthians from his heart and in love to continue their repentance from various maladies that have recently infected the community; in doing so, he also defends his apostolic authority over and care for them (1:12—7:16). He exhorts them to be generous in their donations to the Church at Jerusalem (8-9). In Chs. 10-13, Paul rejects charges against his apostolic authority and pastoral integrity, counter-challenging his adversaries (10-11). His personal integrity is grounded in his suffering for the Gospel (11:21—12:13). Put in the form of a question, the central issue both Paul and the Corinthians were struggling with is: "What is an apostle?" Paul's authentication of his ministry is in terms of service to the Gospel of God's great reconciling love through Christ (5:11-19). The "credential" of an apostle is ultimately an act of God. The mystery of Christ's death and resurrection must be present and witnessed to in that apostolic ministry (4:10-12). As with 1 Corinthians, scholars of all persuasions accept 2 Corinthians as from Paul. If we date 1 Corinthians around A.D. 54, then the earliest we can date 2 Corinthians would be sometime after this, perhaps during the summer or fall of A.D. 55.

Cornette (kor-NEHT): The extensive, spreading white head-gear, not often worn today, that originated in fourteenth-century France and was worn by some men and women religious.

Corona (kuh-RO-nuh): 1. Band of hair left after shaving the crown of a male religious's head for monastic tonsure, rarely seen today. 2. Circle of candles hung over the altar in the early Church. 3. Franciscan Crown (cf. Crown, Franciscan).

Coronation of the Blessed Virgin Mary (kaw-ro-NAY-shuhn uhv *th*uh BLEH-sehd VER-dzhihn MEH-ree): 1. Commemorated in the fifth of the Glorious Mysteries of the Rosary, the belief that following her Assumption, Mary was crowned by Christ the King as Queen of Heaven and Earth (or the Angels and Saints). 2. Any painting or image depicting this event.

Coronation of the Pope (kor-o-NAY-shuhn uhv *th*uh POP): Ceremony, in use until 1978, in which the newly elected Pope received the papal tiara as a sign of supreme jurisdiction over all earthly powers; replaced now by a rite called "installation as supreme pastor," in which the new Pope receives the pallium, the vesture of a metropolitan archbishop, signifying spiritual jurisdiction and the unity of the world-wide episcopate with the See of Rome.

Corporal (KOR-puh-ruhl): (From Latin: body) Square piece of linen cloth used during Mass, so called because in the pre-Vatican II rite, the Host (Body of Christ) rested directly upon it.

Corporal Works of Mercy (KOR-puh-ruhl WERKS uhv MER-see): Charitable actions that show reverence for the human body and respect it as the temple of the Holy Spirit. Six works are listed in Matthew's Gospel (25:34-40): feeding the hungry, giving drink to the thirsty, clothing the naked, sheltering the homeless, visiting the sick, and visiting prisoners. The seventh work, burying the dead, was a later addition. **CCC 2447**

Corpus Christi (KOR-pøøs KRIHS-tee): (Latin: Body of Christ) Feast honoring the Real Presence of Christ in the Eucharist, traditionally kept on the Thursday following Trinity Sunday, now frequently transferred to the following Sunday and, since the calendar reform of the Second Vatican Council, kept also as the feast of the Precious Blood and thus entitled *Corpus et Sanguis Domini* (the Body and Blood of the Lord).

Corpus Iuris Canonici (KOR-pøøs YÖÖ-rihs kah-NO-nee-tshee): (Latin: Body of Canon Law) Since 1580, term refers to the composite of the five most important collections of Canon Law of the late medieval period.

Cor Unum (KOR ÖÖ-nuhm): (Latin: one heart) The organization founded by Pope Paul VI in 1971, in order to provide information and coordination for Catholic relief efforts throughout the world.

Cosmology (kahz-MAHL-uh-dzhee): (Greek *kosmos,* world + *logia:* science) The philosophy of the nature and principles of the universe.

Costume, Clerical (KLEHR-ih-kuhl KAHS-tööm): The dress worn by the clergy within and outside liturgical ceremonies. The cassock *(soutane),* worn by diocesan priests as street dress before the French Revolution, is generally worn today by priests only on church grounds. Cassocks differ in color and ornamentation for bishops, priests, and monsignors. The most common clerical dress in the United States is the Roman collar and black suit (cf. Dress, Clerical).

Cotta (KAH-tuh): Italian word for the liturgical parament known in English as a surplice, referring especially to a surplice that is somewhat abbreviated in length and at the sleeves.

Council (KAUN-sihl): A formal meeting of Church leaders, called by the appropriate bishop, to deliberate, clarify, study, and enact decrees pertaining to the life and belief of the Church. There are various levels: a *diocesan council* is referred to as a *synod,* and is a meeting of a bishop, representative clergy, religious, and laity, in which matters of diocesan Church discipline and procedure are discussed. *A provincial council* is an assembly of the metropolitan archbishop with his suffragan bishops, while *a plenary council* summons all the bishops of a given nation. The highest convocation of all is an *ecumenical council* (cf. Councils, Ecumenical), in which all the bishops of the world meet in union with the Bishop of Rome. Cf. CCC 9, 192, 250, 884, 887, 891

Council of Major Superiors of Women Religious in the United States (KAUN-sihl uhv MAY-dzher söö-PIH-ree-erz uhv WIH-mehn rih-LIH-dzhuhs ihn *th*ee yöö-NAI-tehd STAYTS): In 1992, the Holy See approved a second organization for women religious; it takes its place alongside the Leadership Conference of Women Religious. Both are of equal canonical standing. The CMSR is committed to the fostering of traditional forms of religious life and represents over ten thousand American Sisters.

Councils, Ecumenical (eh-kyöö-MEH-nih-kuhl KAUN-sihlz): The most solemn and official assembly of all bishops of the world (thus "ecumenical," or universal) that, when summoned by the Bishop of Rome, constitutes the highest teaching authority in the Church. These meetings are usually convoked at pivotal, critical moments in the life of the Church and are charged with discussing and then articulating formal statements on doctrine or discipline. At times throughout Church history, secular rulers, theologians, superiors of religious orders, and most recently, representatives of other creeds are also invited to attend. Catholics recognize twenty-one ecumenical councils, listed as follows, with the Orthodox Churches accepting only the first seven: (1) Nicaea I, 325, condemned Arianism and declared the Son "consubstantial" with the Father; (2) Constantinople I, 381, condemned Macedonians and declared the Holy Spirit consubstantial with Father and Son; (3) Ephesus, 431, condemned Nestorians and Pelagians and declared the divine maternity of the Blessed Mother; (4) Chalcedon, 451, condemned Monophysitism; (5) Constantinople II, 553, condemned the Three Chapters; (6) Constantinople III, 680, condemned Monothelitism and censured Honorius; (7)

Nicaea II, 787, condemned iconoclasm; (8) Constantinople IV, 869, ended the Greek schism and deposed Photius; (9) Lateran I, 1123, issued decrees on simony, celibacy, and lay investiture, and confirmed the Concordat of Worms; (10) Lateran II, 1139, ended the papal schism and enacted reforms; (11) Lateran III, 1179, condemned the Albigenses and Waldenses and regulated papal elections; (12) Lateran IV, 1215, planned a crusade, enacted decrees on annual Communion, repeated the condemnation of the Albigenses, and enacted reforms; (13) Lyons I, 1245, deposed Frederick II and planned a crusade; (14) Lyons II, 1274, reunited the Church with the Greeks and enacted disciplinary reforms; (15) Vienne, 1311-1312, abolished the Knights Templar and enacted reforms; (16) Constance, 1414-1418, ended the Great Schism and condemned Huss; (17) Basel, Ferrara, Florence, 1431-1445, effected union of Greeks and enacted reforms; (18) Lateran V, 1512-1517, treated of the Neo-Aristotelians and enacted reforms; (19) Trent, 1545-1563, condemned Protestantism and enacted reforms; (20) Vatican I, 1869-1870, condemned errors and defined papal infallibility; (21) Vatican II, opened by Pope John XXIII, October 11, 1962, until the close of the first session on December 8, 1962. After Pope John's death it was reconvened by Pope Paul VI in three additional sessions: September 29 to December 4, 1963; September 14 to November 21, 1964; September 14 to its solemn closing on December 8, 1965. It promulgated sixteen documents. Cf. CCC 9, 192, 250, 884, 887, 891

Counseling, Pastoral (PAS-ter-uhl KAUN-seh-lihng): The interaction between a cleric or other Christian and some individual living within some difficult situation or problem. It deals not only with practical realities, but also incorporates the spiritual dimension of the individual.

Counsels, Evangelical: See Evangelical Counsels

Counter-Reformation (KAUN-ter-reh-for-MAY-shuhn): Movements for Church renewal emphasizing deeper personal holiness, works of the apostolate, and exercise of charity were developing in a number of places prior to the Reformation;

they took on a new urgency because of the challenge to Catholicism. These intensified movements are usually called the Counter-Reformation. Five dimensions of this movement are worthy of special consideration: 1. *New vitality in religious life.* One aspect of this is the formation of new religious communities: e.g., Theatines, Barnabites, Ursuline Nuns, and especially the Jesuits. Older orders were renewed, sometimes leading to new branches of a religious family; e.g., Capuchins, Discalced Carmelites. 2. *Work of the Council of Trent* (1545-1563). The teaching of the Church was proposed authoritatively in doctrinal decrees on the role of Sacred Scripture, Original Sin, Justification, and Sacraments. Reform decrees aided the renewal of Church life. Of special importance was the decree establishing the seminary system. 3. *Development of the spiritual life.* A true vitality of Catholicism involves a deep interior union with Christ. The Church was strengthened by the lives of heroic men and women who were later canonized; e.g., Teresa of Ávila, John of the Cross, Catherine de Ricci, Ignatius Loyola. Confraternities encouraged more frequent reception of the sacraments. The Rosary and other forms of popular devotion developed. 4. *Flourishing of theology.* Especially in Spain and Italy, theology, both scholastic and positive, developed and prepared trained Church leaders. 5. *Growth of missionary spirit.* There was a new interest in missionary activity in the New World, Africa, and Asia, as well as in the areas previously Catholic but now dominated by Protestants. This movement, characteristic of the century or so after the beginning of the Reformation, had a significant effect in later centuries.

Courts, Ecclesiastical (eh-klee-zee-AS-tih-kuhl KORTS): Tribunals or Church entities that administer justice according to Canon Law.

Covenant (KUH-veh-nuhnt): A solemn promise, fortified by an oath, concerning future action. The oath might be expressed in words or in a symbolic action. In the rhetoric of the Near East, covenants were spoken of as oaths and stipulations. Diverse situations of secular life were regulated by covenants, e.g., international relations. In the O.T. the usual (but not the only) word for covenant is *b'rith*. The religious covenants spoken of in the O.T. may be divided into two classes: those in which God is bound, as for example, the covenant struck by Abraham (Gn 15); and covenants in which Israel is bound, e.g., Jos 24. In the N.T. the notion of covenant surfaces preeminently in the account of the Last Supper (Mk 14:24), where the meaning of Christ's sacrifice is defined as the "new covenant." Both the Sinai covenant and the covenant in Christ's blood brought into being a people of God and called for complete surrender to God in response to His love. Cf. CCC 73, 346, 577, 610-613, 709, 1091, 1116, 1129, 1222, 1339, 1365, 2060-2063

Cowl (KAUL): 1. Hood worn by monks and other religious. 2. Long-hooded robe worn by monastic men and women during the chanting of the Office.

Creation (kree-AY-shuhn): The activity of God by which He brought all things into existence. Creation is said to be *ex nihilo* ("out of nothing"), because there was no preexisting material from which things were made. **CCC 282-289**

Creationism (kree-AY-shuhn-ih-zuhm): 1. Belief that all things are created by God, and that the reality of the universe cannot be explained by science alone. 2. The doctrine that teaches that each human soul is created directly by God at the moment of conception. 3. Especially among certain Protestant Fundamentalists, the rejection of the theory of evolution in any form. **CCC 282-289**

Creator (kree-AY-ter): The title referring to God as Maker of all from nothing. He alone directs and preserves the universe. **CCC 279, 320-324**

Creature (KREE-tcher): Anything in the realm of being except for God. **CCC 293, 327**

Crèche (KREHSH): (Old French: manger) Used more specifically for the manger in which Christ was born in Bethlehem. Tradition holds that this very manger is today preserved as a relic at the Basilica of St. Mary Major in Rome, although the authenticity of that crèche cannot be proven.

Crèche is also used for any representation of the Nativity, with figures of the significant participants: Jesus, Mary, and Joseph, the ox and the donkey, and the shepherds with their sheep. On the Epiphany, the figures of the "three kings" and their camels are added.

Credence (KREE-dehns): Small side table in the sanctuary used to hold the chalice, cruets, lavabo bowl, and other liturgical implements when they are not being used at the altar.

Creed (KREED): Popular term for the profession of faith, from the first Latin word of the formula (*Credo,* "I believe"). The word is generally used with another specifying which profession is meant (e.g., Nicene, Apostles', Athanasian). **CCC 14, 184, 187-188, 197**

Creed, Athanasian (A-thuh-NAY-zhuhn KREED): A statement of the Church's truths, dating to the fourth or fifth century, which, although not written by St. Athanasius, mirrors his teaching on the Trinity and Incarnation. Little is treated besides these two dogmas and the penalties incurred by those who do not accept them. St. Ambrose may have written or revised this creed.

Cremation (kree-MAY-shuhn): The disposal of a dead body by burning it. Cremation is now permitted by the Church when certain criteria are met. **CCC 2301**

Crib: See Crèche

Crimen (KREE-mehn): (Latin: crime) Generally, a diriment impediment to marriage that arises when one brings about the death of his own spouse or that of another, either directly or by cooperation, in order to marry.

Criticism, Biblical (BIH-blih-kuhl KRIH-tih-sih-zuhm): The study of Sacred Scripture employing scientific tools like "form criticism" and "literary criticism." Modern Popes such as Pope Leo and Pope Pius XII have stressed the importance of using exegetical techniques, always within certain parameters set by the Magisterium, remembering that the Church alone can give the authentic interpretation of a passage.

Crosier (KRO-zher): Pastoral staff, modeled on a shepherd's crook, conferred upon bishops and abbots at their installation as a sign of their pastoral care of souls.

Cross (KRAWS): The instrument composed of wood on which Christ suffered and died to redeem humanity. Far from a mere object, the cross represents the anguish and pain that followers of Jesus must endure if they are to be faithful to their vocation as Christians. Crosses are often used atop churches and buildings associated with a spiritual motive. CCC 555, 561, 617, 813, 1364-1366, 1505, 1741, 1939, 1992, 2305

Cross, Processional (pro-SEH-shuhn-uhl KRAWS): A cross bearing the image of the Crucified One, carried in processions and generally placed in the sanctuary in a prominent place during the celebration of the Sacred Liturgy, most especially during the Holy Sacrifice of the Mass, which represents the mystery of the Lord's Paschal Mystery.

Cross, Relics of the True (REH-lihks uhv *th*uh TRÖÖ KRAWS): Fragments of the Holy Cross, generally the size of a sliver, authenticated by an accompanying document and bound into a container that has been sealed with red wax and stamped with the signet ring of the authenticating prelate.

Cross, Veneration of the (veh-neh-RAY-shuhn uhv *th*uh KRAWS): 1. Showing reverence to the authenticated relics of the Holy Cross. 2. Ceremony in the Good Friday liturgy during which the congregation reverences a cross individually by genuflecting before it or kissing it, or communally by paying silent homage to it.

Crown, Episcopal (ih-PIHS-kuh-puhl KRAUN): Miter of a bishop in the Eastern Church, fashioned as a royal crown and adorned with embroidery and sometimes with precious jewels and small icons.

Crown, Franciscan (fran-SIHS-kuhn KRAUN): Rosary of seven decades, said to be given by Our Lady to a Franciscan novice, and used for meditation upon the "seven joys of Mary" (Annunciation, Visitation, Birth of the Lord, Adoration of the Magi, Finding in the Temple, Resurrection, Assumption-Coronation).

Crown of Thorns (KRAUN uhv THORNZ): The wreath of briars or "thorns" (Greek: *akanthai)* used to punish and humiliate Jesus during His sacred passion (Mt 27:29; Mk 15:17; Jn 19:2). This instrument of torture, fashioned from a plant with thorns growing near Jerusalem, was used for convicted criminals and was shaped as a ringlet or helmet and placed on the accused's head. Some traditions indicate that Our Lord's Crown of Thorns has survived to this day.

Crucifix (KRÖÖ-sih-fihks): A cross with a reproduction of Christ's body, used in public and private devotions in the Western Church. Most Protestants use a cross without the corpus. The Eastern Church employs an icon with the representation of Jesus. Crucifixes are sometimes worn about the neck.

Crucifixion (kröö-sih-FIHK-shuhn): An ancient form of punishment, probably begun by the Persians, meant to shame the victim and to discourage rebellion. One's hands and feet were nailed or tied to a cross; the victim was naked and could not take care of his bodily needs. Jesus' crucifixion has been made the subject of many works of art. He was crucified by the Romans, who, along with the Carthaginians, often employed this means of torture. **Cf. CCC 512**

Cruet (KRÖÖ-eht): Vessel, usually glass or ceramic, used to hold wine or water for the celebration of Mass.

Crusade, Children's: See Children's Crusade

Crusades (kröö-SAYDZ): Those expansive military expeditions that Western Europe undertook between 1096 and 1270 for the purpose of driving the Muslims ("the Infidel") from, or keeping them out of, Palestine, the Holy Land. The name comes from the cross, embroidered, on the garments worn and pennants carried by the participants. These initiatives lasted almost two centuries, and, since proclaimed by the Pope and commissioned to rescue the holiest shrines of Christendom, were looked upon as holy causes. However, although many of the participants were indeed inspired by such a lofty motive, others entered for more political, economic, adventuresome, or selfish motives. Because they lasted so long and involved hundreds of thousands of people from every country and background, the crusades, while ultimately failing to make Palestine a Christian kingdom, did have profound cultural effects on both Europe and the Mideast. Commerce and travel were encouraged, religious zeal promoted, the papacy was viewed as the center of a stable Europe, Eastern views and products entered the Western scene, and a sense of freedom prevailed in the continent. Negative effects, such as a widening of the cleavage between East and West, and the scandal caused by the excesses of these ventures, cannot be overlooked. Although somewhat difficult to number, since many of them overlap, scholars generally list eight major crusades. The First Crusade (1095-1101), proclaimed by Pope Urban II, ended with the Christian forces entering Jerusalem. Pope Eugene III commissioned St. Bernard to preach the Second Crusade (1145-1148), calling for recapture of Edessa from Islam, but it ended in failure. The Third Crusade (1188-1192), sparked by Pope Gregory VIII, ended when the Emperor Frederick Barbarossa, Philip Augustus of France, and Richard the Lion-Hearted agreed upon a truce with Saladin. Pope Innocent III ended up excommunicating the leaders of the Fourth Crusade (1207-1214) when they abandoned the drive. Sometimes the fifth one (1217-1221) is called the "Children's Crusade," in which perhaps forty thousand children, mostly from France and Germany, boarded ships in the hopes of arriving in the Holy Land to help the cause and ended up in Muslim slave markets. This Fifth Crusade also included a military scheme to recapture Jerusalem, not by way of Syria but through Egypt, which failed. Jerusalem was opened to Christians as a result of the Sixth Crusade (1228-1229), led by Frederick II, who signed a treaty with the Sultan. St. Louis of France led both the Seventh Crusade (1248-1254), which had been commissioned by Pope Innocent IV, and, along with Charles Anjou, the Eighth Crusade (1267-1270), both of which ended disastrously with the loss of the last Christian bastions.

Crypt (KRIHPT): (Latin *crypta*, Greek *krypte:* vault, hidden cave) An underground vault or cave, often beneath churches, used as a burial place and sometimes for religious services.

Cubiculum (kyöö-BIHK-yöö oo-luhm): (Latin: bedroom) Burial chamber, located on both sides of a catacomb's galleries and hewn from tufa rock, which served as the resting place for the deceased.

Culpability (kuhl-puh-BIH-lih-tee): Blameworthy conduct that is considered serious enough to apply ecclesiastical penalties. Cf. CCC 2352, 2485

Cult (KUHLT), also Cultus (KØØL-tøøs): In ecclesiastical tradition, the devotion or honor accorded to deceased persons because of their virtuous lives. Cf. CCC 1378, 1566

Cult, Disparity of (dih-SPEHR-ih-tee uhv KUHLT): A diriment impediment to marriage that arises from the union of a baptized person and a non-baptized person. CCC 1633-1637

Cult of the Martyrs (KUHLT uhv *th*uh MAR-terz): Devotion to those who died witnessing to the Faith in the early Church, forerunner to veneration of the saints.

Cura Animarum (KYÖÖ-ruh AH-nih-MAH-røøm): (Latin: care of souls) Pastoral ministry of bishops and priests. Cf. CCC 857, 879, 881, 886, 1595-1596

Curate (KYØØ-reht): A term more commonly used in Canada and Great Britain to refer to an associate pastor of a parish.

Curator (KYØØ-ray-ter): A person appointed by an ecclesiastical judge to act as guardian for a party to an ecclesiastical trial.

Curia, Diocesan (dai-AH-seh-zuhn KYØØ-ree-uh): The administrative department of a diocese, comprising chancery and all institutions, offices, and departments involved in the administrative governance of a diocese.

Curia, Roman (RO-muhn KYØØ-ree-uh): The entire body of administrative and judicial agencies that assist the Pope in the governance of the Church. It consists of congregations, tribunals, councils, committees, offices, and tribunals.

Cursillo (køør-SEE-yo): The renewal movement, begun in 1949 by Spanish laymen, that strives to restore the world to Christ by encouraging Christians first to change their own hearts and then to support others who are disciples of Jesus. From the Spanish word meaning "little course," the *cursillo* is divided into: pre-*cursillo* (preparation); *cursillo* (the course itself); post-*cursillo* ("follow-up"). Those who take part are called *cursillistas* who meet after the *cursillo* in small groups called *ultreyas*.

Cursing (KER-sihng): The calling down of evil on another, which offends against charity and may be scandalous in the presence of children. Although common in the O.T., cursing is infrequent in the N.T. Christ exhorts His Apostles to return a blessing for a curse. St. Paul wrote that Jesus Himself became a "curse" in order to remove the curse of sin from humanity.

Cursing Psalms: See Imprecatory Psalms

Custom (KUHS-tuhm): A constant manner of doing something, with roots in human behavior rather than in legislative act.

Custos (KØØS-tos): (Latin: guardian) 1. A minor official entrusted with limited duties. 2. Also used by the Franciscan Order as a title for local superiors.

Cycle of Church Calendar (SAI-kuhl uhv TSHERTSH KA-luhn-der): Early Christians followed the Roman calendar of Julius Caesar with a seven-day week and divisions into months. Sunday, regarded by the earliest Christians as the first day of the week and the Sabbath day, was designated the center of each seven-day period. Christian feasts were developed, many of which coincided with Jewish feasts and all of which were set around the high point of the liturgical year, the Resurrection. The second center of the calendar, the Christmas cycle, began as a response to the pagan imperial feast *Sol Invictus,* the Unconquered Sun. Later, the periods of Advent and Lent were instituted. Over the ages, other feasts celebrating the life of Christ, His Mother, and the saints spread throughout the calendar cycle. **Cf. CCC 1168-1173**

Cycle of Readings (SAI-kuhl uhv REE-dihngz): The assignment of Scripture readings for a particular Sunday or weekday. There is a three-year cycle of Scripture readings for Sundays, a two-year cycle for weekdays, and a one-year cycle for saints' days.

D

Dalmatic (dal-MA-tihk): This vestment, which draws its name from its place of origin, Dalmatia, is today the proper liturgical vestment of the deacon at Mass, worn over all the other vestments, i.e., the amice, alb, cincture, and stole. For solemn Masses, it is also worn under the chasuble by a bishop to signify his possession of the fullness of Orders. As was the case with most vestments, the dalmatic was originally a garment used in secular society that gradually fell out of use, was retained in the Church, and became proper to the clergy.

Dance, Liturgical (lih-TER-dzhih-kuhl DANS): The practice of having dance or rhythmic bodily movements as part of the liturgy. Beginning to appear during the years after the general liturgical reform of Vatican II, it has occurred in various dioceses of the United States, as well as in other countries, although without the approbation of the Holy See. A document on inculturation from the Congregation for Divine Worship and the Discipline of the Sacraments in 1994, however, did note the possibility for such activity in cultures where dance has a sacred rather than a merely social or romantic connotation, or even sexual overtones; obviously, that is not the case for the developed Western world.

Daniel (DAN-yehl): One of the four "major" prophets of the O.T., whose Hebrew name means "God is my judge" and who lived six centuries before Christ. He was exiled to Babylon from his royal family and was given wisdom and the gift of interpreting dreams. He was loved by King Nebuchadnezzar, who changed Daniel's name to Belteshazzar; however, the king later threw him into the lions' den. But Daniel was saved by God's power.

Daniel, Book of (BØØK uhv DAN-yehl): The O.T. work, dating from 166-165 B.C., is divided into two parts: five stories concerning Daniel plus one involving Shadrach, Meshach, and Abednego (Chs. 1-6); and four visions granted to Daniel (Chs. 7-14). Written in Hebrew and Aramaic, this book reminds all that God will support those who — like Daniel — remain faithful to Him.

Dark Ages (DAHRK AYDZH-uhz): The period following the collapse of the Roman Empire up to the "Middle Ages." Though this era from the middle of the fifth century to the eleventh century had many upheavals caused by the onslaught of the barbarians, figures like Pope St. Gregory the Great preserved the patrimony of Western civilization, thereby enabling much advance in art and education to occur.

Dark Night of the Senses (DAHRK NAIT uhv *th*uh SEHN-sehz): The spiritual period in which God draws one from meditation to contemplation in order that one may grow in Christian perfection. During this initial stage of perfection, one cannot rely on his senses for contact with God and may feel repulsed by prayer and experience temptations against faith and even illness. St. John of the Cross (1542-1591) deals with this stage in *The Dark Night* and stresses that, through this period, God is inviting one to the deeper prayer of contemplation.

Dark Night of the Soul (DAHRK NAIT uhv *th*uh SOL): The purification by which God draws one to Himself and to a deeper sanctity. This period is marked by a purging of self-love and a feeling of abandonment by God; one cannot "see" Him as before. The Dark Night is a transitory prelude to "mystical marriage" and occurs only for those who have attained contemplation. St. John of the Cross (1542-1591), in his *Dark Night,* writes extensively about this spiritual cleansing.

David (DAY-vihd): (Hebrew: prince, beloved) The second king of Israel and Judah, succeeding Saul and followed by David's son Solomon. Jesus, the promised Messiah, was born of David's line.

Day Hours (DAY AU-erz): In liturgical usage the word "Hour" refers to any section of the daily cycle of prayer, known in its totality — officially since Vatican II — as "the Liturgy of the Hours," and formerly as "the Divine Office."

Technically, the term "day hours" is best suited to what is now called Daytime Prayer, which may (but need not) be celebrated in three sections: midmorning (officially, Terce, or the "third" hour, about 9:00 A.M.); midday (Sext, the "sixth" hour, noon); and midafternoon (None, the "ninth" hour, about 3:00 P.M.). Only one of these "Hours" is obligatory for priests and religious working in an active apostolate. Contemplatives are expected to keep the traditional observance. Cf. CCC 1174-1178

Day of Atonement: See Atonement, Day of

Day of Indiction (DAY uhv ihn-DIHK-shuhn): In the Byzantine Rite, September 1, the beginning of the liturgical year. The beginning of Advent is December 10.

Day of the Lord (DAY uhv *thuh* LAWRD): As an O.T. expression that may have its origins in the language of ancient Israelite holy war, the "Day of Yahweh" was understood to be the occasion on which Yahweh would defeat His enemies in combat. This is the case in texts like Ez 30:4, where the Day of the Lord is the day when "a sword shall come upon Egypt." It followed that because Yahweh's enemies were also Israel's enemies among the nations, their defeat should be an occasion for Israel to rejoice. The expression "Day of Yahweh" first appears in the book of Amos, a prophet of the eighth century B.C. The prophet warns, "Woe to those who yearn for the day of the Lord! Why would you have the day of the Lord? It is darkness, and not light" (Am 5:18). The woe is addressed to complacent Israel, which believed that the Day of the Lord would mean punishment only for Israel's enemies. Instead, for idolatrous and unjust Israel the Day of the Lord would be "gloom with no brightness in it" (Am 5:20). Accustomed to being Yahweh's chosen instrument, the agent by which Yahweh's victory was gained, and accustomed to enjoying the spoils of victory, Israel could instead expect to be the object of Yahweh's punitive judgment. In other O.T. texts, the Day of the Lord is spoken of as a past event, so that it would be more appropriate to speak of days of the Lord, moments of divine vengeance and vindication. Ez 13 speaks out against the prophets of peace, who did not build "a wall for the house of Israel that would stand in battle in the day of the Lord" (Ez 13:6), referring to the fall of Jerusalem in 587 B.C.; Lam 2:12 speaks of this time as the day of the Lord's blazing wrath. The Day of the Lord is the dominant theme of the book of the prophet Zephaniah, from which the hymn *Dies Irae* draws its inspiration: "A day of wrath is that day, a day of distress and anguish, a day of ruin and devastation, a day of darkness and gloom, a day of clouds and thick darkness, a day of trumpet blasts and a battle cry" (Zep 1:15). That day will be "the day of the wrath of the Lord" (Zep 1:18), a manifestation of Yahweh's positive judgment against corrupt Jerusalem. In post-exilic prophecy, the Day of the Lord acquired an apocalyptic tone, as in Mal 4:5, which promises the return of the prophet Elijah "before the great and terrible day of the Lord comes." There, as well as in the book of the prophet Joel, the Day of the Lord is the day of God's definitive judgment against the wicked and on behalf of the faithful, who are urged to prepare themselves by penance (cf. Jl 2). The apocalyptic tone of the expression "Day of the Lord" in post-exilic O.T. prophecy was transformed when the expression entered the N.T. vocabulary as the "Day of the Lord Jesus Christ." In the letters of Paul, the "Day of Christ" is the *parousia*, the glorious eschatological return of Christ. The Day of the Lord will come unexpectedly (cf. 1 Thes 5:1-11) so that believers must ready themselves by remaining vigilant, faithful, pure, and blameless (cf. Phil 1:10), prepared for the advent of the eschatological Judge and Savior. In the Apocalypse of John, the seer's inaugural vision takes place "on the Lord's Day." This is the *kyriake*, the day on which Christians gathered for worship. This combines the Christian liturgical meaning of the Lord's Day as the occasion when believers gather for the Eucharistic celebration with the O.T. prophetic sense of the Day of the Lord as the moment of God's eschatological advent as righteous Judge. **CCC 2174-2188**

Days of Prayer (DAYZ uhv PREHR): At these times, once called rogation days and ember days, the Church continues the custom of publicly thanking the Lord and prays to Him for the needs of all, especially for the productivity of the earth and for human labor. The general norms for the Calendar of the Liturgical Year promulgated in 1969 leave the time and manner of the celebration of these days to national episcopal conferences. The American Conference of Bishops in 1971 left the determination of such days to the local bishops, and since then they seem to have fallen into disuse.

Deacon, Permanent (PER-muh-nehnt DEE-kuhn): A man who is ordained to the order of deacon and who will remain such. The restored diaconate is open to single and married men who assist priests in the administrative and pastoral care of souls. CCC 1571

Deacon, Transitional (tran-ZIH-shuh-nuhl DEE-kuhn): A man who has been ordained to the diaconate but who ultimately will be ordained to the priesthood. CCC 1571

Deaconess (DEE-kuhn-ehs): A woman who served the early Church as a servant in a variety of duties. Often deaconesses were widows. While there was a liturgical rite connected with their institution, there is no evidence that deaconesses were ordained. The Council of Nicaea (325) stated that deaconesses were laypersons and not ordained. These servants helped catechumens during the Baptism immersion rite, read the Scriptures to the community, and distributed Holy Communion to other deaconesses when a priest was not available.

Deacons, First Seven (FERST SEH-vehn DEE-kuhnz): Those seven men of the Jerusalem Christian community ordained to help the Apostles distribute provisions to the widows of the Greek-speaking Jews. Acts 6:1-6 is seen as the institution of the Order of Deacon; the passage uses the Greek *diakonein* to designate the "serving" function of deacons.

Dead Sea Scrolls (DEHD SEE SKROLZ): Manuscripts and fragments of manuscripts written chiefly in Hebrew and Aramaic, found in the vicinity of Khirbet Qumran (some seven or eight miles south of Jericho) near the Dead Sea from 1947 onward. These works are thought to be the remains of an extensive library of a community of Essenes (q.v.) living in this area from ca. 125 B.C. to ca. A.D. 66-70 (with an interruption of about thirty or forty years). The script of these manuscripts has been identified as typical of the first century B.C. and the first century A.D. This dating of the works is supported as well by archaeological data. The manuscripts were enclosed in jars, as manuscripts in ancient times were often stored. Nearly every book of the O.T. is represented in the finds at Qumran. A variety of other works as well has been found, e.g., a commentary on Hb 1-2; a curious book on The War of the Sons of Light against the Sons of Darkness; and The Manual of Discipline, a rule book dealing with the government of the group, the scrutiny and admission of candidates, rules of conduct, and various ritual regulations. The correspondence between the Qumran community (as revealed in the scrolls) and Christianity are interesting but do not postulate a contact between the two. For that matter, the differences between the two ought not to be minimized.

Dean (DEEN): 1. A canonical position held by a priest who holds limited authority over the common pastoral activities of a certain area of a diocese. 2. "First among equals" guiding the College of Cardinals, assisted by a sub-dean.

Deanery (DEEN-er-ee): A section of a diocese made up of parishes and other ecclesiastical institutions within the area under the limited authority of a dean.

Death (DEHTH): The separation of soul and body in which the soul assumes a novel relation to the body. Death is a result of Original Sin and is the inevitable result of bodily life. Yet Christ has redeemed death and has made it a passage into the new life of eternal glory. **CCC 1006-1014**

Deborah, Song of (SAWNG uhv DEHB-ruh): Canticle celebrating the victory inspired by Deborah (ca. 1125 B.C.), a *nebiah* (prophetess) and wife of Lappidoth, who accompanied Barak and the Israelites in battle with the Canaanites under Sisera and Jabin, their king. Making up the fifth chapter of the Book of Judges, it is likely the oldest extant Hebrew literary composition, going back to the period of the Judges, though probably not the work of Deborah herself. Because of her noble work on behalf of the nation, Deborah is called the "Mother of Israel" (Jgs 5:7).

Decade (DEH-kuhd): In Roman Catholic usage, a section of the Rosary of Our Lady, consisting of one Our Father, ten Hail Marys, and one Glory Be. These prayers are recited while meditating upon the "mystery" assigned to that decade. Although the particular subjects for meditation have varied over the centuries, the most common schema traditionally in use consists of fifteen decades and corresponding mysteries for the complete Rosary (five joyful, five sorrowful, five glorious mysteries), while the more commonly seen and used Rosary consists of five decades and is sometimes referred to as a "chaplet." The rosaries and chaplets of some religious orders and those recited in honor of various saints may vary in the number of decades prescribed or may change the number of prayers to more or less than a decade.

Decalogue (DEHK-uh-lawg): (Greek: ten sayings) The Ten Commandments (Ex 20). Christ told His disciples that He intended to fulfill these precepts of the Law (cf. Mt 5:18). See Commandments of God. CCC 2052-2527

Decision (dee-SIH-zhun): Judgment or pronouncement on a cause or suit, given by a Church tribunal or official with judicial authority, with the force of law for concerned parties.

Declaration (deh-kluh-RAY-shuhn): In the ecclesiastical and canonical sense, an expositive pronouncement about some matter of importance to Catholics, but not a law.

De Condigno (day kawn-DEEN-yo): (Latin: from worthiness) The merit one receives when the reward is equal to the action. The reward is "in justice" because it was promised on the basis of the specific act.

De Congruo (day KAHN-gröö-o): (Latin: from suitability) The merit one gains when no reward was promised yet one is appropriate for the action performed. This reward is "in

245

charity" because it comes from the giver's generosity and is not strictly deserved.

Decorations, Pontifical (pahn-TIH-fih-kuhl deh-ko-RAY-shuhnz): Awards presented by the Holy See to those who are notable for remarkable service to the Church or society. These honors may be a title, a cross, or a medal, and are given either in Rome or in one's diocese.

Decree (duh-KREE): Generic term for an official pronouncement of a Church court or a decision, clarification, or administrative declaration of one in ecclesiastical authority.

Decretal (duh-KREE-tuhl): Papal letter issued in response to a question.

Decretalist (duh-KREE-tuhl-ihst): A specialist who commented on one of the three books of papal letters or decretals found in the *Corpus Iuris Canonici.*

Decretals (duh-KREE-tuhlz): Papal letters issued in response to a question. Historically, in reference to the collections included in the *Corpus Iuris Canonici,* it refers to the Decretals of Gregory IX, Boniface VIII, and Clement V.

Decretals, False (FAHLS duh-KREE-tuhlz): A collection of papal decrees composed in A.D. 850. They contained genuine texts interspersed with forgeries.

Decretist (duh-KREE-tihst): A canonical scholar who composed a commentary on the *Decree of Gratian.*

Decretum Gratiani (deh-KRAY-tøøm GRAHT-see-AH-nee): Latin title of the *Concordance of Discordant Canons* or *Decree of Gratian,* as it is commonly known. It is the first systematic collection of the laws of the Catholic Church, dated from 1140.

Dedication of a Church (deh-dih-KAY-shuhn uhv uh TSHERTSH): The term formerly denoted a simple blessing of a church as opposed to the more solemn "consecration," but the revised Vatican II rite makes no such distinction. The prayers of the Mass of Dedication celebrate the church building as an image of the universal Church built of the living stones of God's baptized people, and so it is not surprising that the liturgical rite dedicating the building evokes in many ways the rite for baptizing Christians. The church is also, of course, the place of intercessory prayer, proclamation of the living Word, and celebration of the Eucharistic Sacrifice — the very dwelling-place of God among His people — and the rite manifests these realities as well. The liturgical book for the dedication of a church provides auxiliary rites for the blessing and laying of a cornerstone, the dedication of a church already in use, the blessing of a new altar, and a simple blessing for a place that will be used for worship only temporarily. Cf. CCC 1672

Defect, Irregularity of (IHR-rehg-yöö-LEHR-ih-tee uhv DEE-fehkt): A perpetual impediment or barrier to either the reception of Holy Orders or the exercise of orders already received.

Defect of Form (DEE-fehkt uhv FORM): Canonical term for a marriage between a Catholic and a non-Catholic or one between two Catholics that was celebrated before a non-Catholic minister or a civil official without a dispensation. Cf. CCC 1630-1631

Defender of the Bond (duh-FEHN-der uhv *th*uh BAHND): An official of an ecclesiastical court whose duties include the defense of the marriage bond in marriage nullity cases and the defense of the Sacrament of Holy Orders in cases alleging nullity of orders. Cf. CCC 1629

Defender of the Faith (duh-FEHN-der uhv *th*uh FAYTH): An honorary title given to persons for their writings or other actions in defense of the Faith. The three recipients have been King Henry VIII, King James V of Scotland, and the author G. K. Chesterton.

Defensor Ecclesiae (deh-FEHN-sor eh-KLAY-zee-ay): The "defender of the Church" who was appointed by a territorial ruler to conduct the Church's temporal affairs.

Definition, Papal (PAY-puhl DEH-fuh-NIH-shuhn): The infallible decision binding on all the faithful by the Pope concerning a matter of faith and morals. This definition may be made solemnly by the Pontiff as universal teacher *(ex cathedra)* or by an ecumenical council convened and approved by the Pope. All papal definitions are rooted at least implicitly in either Scripture or Tradition. CCC 891

Definitors (duh-FIH-nih-terz): Designated members of the general or provincial governing councils of some religious orders. Normally, definitors exercise an authority equal to and in conjunction with that exercised by the major superior, at least for the duration of the general or provincial chapters at which they have been elected or appointed. During the interval between chapters — which usually constitutes their term in office — the definitors join with other elected councilors and with the major superior to form the governing council at the general or provincial level. The office of definitor does not play a role in the governance of local communities (i.e., in the conventual council).

Defrocking (dee-FRAHK-ihng): Common but incorrect term referring to the reduction of a cleric to the lay state. More correctly, it refers to the penalty of deprivation of the right to wear clerical dress.

Degradation (DEH-gruh-DAY-shuhn): The term formerly used for the process whereby a cleric was reduced to the lay state against his will. The term has been replaced by "dismissal" in the new code.

Deification (dee-ih-fih-KAY-shuhn): A major theological theme of the Eastern Churches regarding salvation. By uniting God to mankind in Himself, Jesus, God the Son Incarnate, made it possible for all humanity to be redeemed from enslavement to sin and death, and to be raised up to share in God's eternal life and glory. Literally, we become partakers of the divine nature (2 Pt 1:4) by living life in Christ through prayer, meditation, fasting, good works, the sacraments, and God's grace acting in us. Also called *Theosis.* **Cf. CCC 460, 1692, 1996**

Deipara (day-EE-pah-ruh): This Latin translation (from *Deus,* God, and *parire,* to bring forth, to bear) of the Greek *Theotokos* (literally, God-bearing) was conferred as a title on the Blessed Virgin Mary at the Council of Ephesus in the year 431. Cf. CCC 495

Deisis (day-EE-sihs): (Greek: prayer or entreaty) Prayers of petition in the liturgy of the Byzantine Rite. Also, in Byzantine art, the depiction of Christ as Judge, together with Mary, His Mother, and St. John the Baptist.

Deism (DEE-ih-zuhm): (From Latin *Deus:* God) A philosophical view that holds that God exists, and that He created the universe and its laws; however, after the initial act of creation God is thought not to intervene in history. Within this system, there is no place for revelation or miracles, which would be viewed as a failure in God's creative work. **Cf. CCC 421**

Dei Verbum (DAY-ee VEHR-bøøm): The Dogmatic Constitution on Divine Revelation promulgated by Vatican Council II on November 18, 1965. This succinct document of twenty-six paragraphs was no doubt intended to complement the Dogmatic Constitution on Catholic Faith of Vatican Council I, *Dei Filius.* The new statement carefully incorporates a number of scholarly agreements on the nature of Divine Revelation and its transmission that had developed since *Dei Filius* was issued in 1870. The fundamental revelation was of God Himself and of the mystery of His will (n. 2). It is composed of deeds and words, which are intimately bound up with one another, and have to do with mankind's access to the Father, through Christ, the Word made Flesh, in the Holy Spirit. God's revelation in Christ is not the first time He revealed Himself to His people, but it is "the new and definitive covenant [that] will never pass away and no new public revelation is to be expected before the glorious manifestation of Our Lord, Jesus Christ" (n. 4). This definitive revelation was faithfully transmitted by Christ to the Apostles, and by them to others either by their preaching or in written form. Thus there were born the twin sources of Revelation: Sacred Scripture and Sacred Tradition (n. 7). To them is added a third component, the Magisterium, "at the divine command and with the help of the Holy Spirit" (n. 10). "It is clear therefore that in the supremely wise arrangement of God, Sacred Scripture, Sacred Tradition and the Magisterium of the Church are so connected and associated that one of them cannot stand without the others" (n. 10). In its discussion of inspiration, *Dei Verbum* sums up the previous doctrine of Trent and Vatican I (n. 11). It then adds an important clarification: ". . . we must acknowledge that the books of Scripture, firmly, faithfully, and without error, teach that truth *(veritatem)* which God, for the sake of our salvation, wished to see confided to the Sacred Scriptures" (n. 11). *Dei Verbum* acknowledges the fact that God made use of human means of communication when He inspired human authors, as well as literary forms: "Due attention must be paid to the customary and characteristic patterns of perception, speech, and narrative that prevailed at the age of the sacred writer" (n. 12). Regarding the O.T., *Dei Verbum* affirms that it was designed to "prepare for and declare in prophecy the coming of Christ. . ." (n. 15). Addressing the question of the authorship of the N.T., *Dei Verbum* accepts the consensus of contemporary N.T. scholars, which speaks of a three-part development of the composition: the N.T. faithfully hands on "what Jesus . . . really did and taught. The sacred authors . . . selected certain of the many elements which had been handed on, either orally or already in written form . . . always in such a fashion that they have preserved for us the honest truth about Jesus" (n. 19). Finally, *Dei Verbum* strongly encourages ongoing study of the Sacred Scriptures, especially by priests, whose responsibility, together with that of the bishops, is to preach the Word. Cf. CCC 80-84, 101-141

Delator (deh-LAH-tor): The person, appointed by the pagan ruler during the period of the early Church, who accused anyone suspected of being a Christian. This denouncer often abetted the authorities in capturing and martyring the believers.

Delegation (dehl-uh-GAY-shuhn): The canonical act whereby one with ordinary power of governance shares it with another person capable in law.

Delict (deh-LIHKT): The canonical term for a crime as set forth in the Code of Canon law.

Deluge (DEHL-yöödzh): The great flood as recorded in Gn 6:5—9:17, from which Noah, his family, and the pairs of animals and birds were preserved in the ark. In Christian theology, baptismal symbolism is seen in the deluge. **Cf. CCC 701, 1094, 1219**

Demiurge (DEH-mee-erdzh): (Greek *demiurgos:* craftsman, maker, fashioner) The fourth-century B.C. philosopher Plato used this term in his treatise on the beginning and nature of the world, called the *Timaeus.* In his cosmology (i.e., how the world was created as an explanation of why it is the way it is), Plato affixed the term "demiurge" to a divine Being who created or fashioned the visible or material universe. This term was applied to the God of the O.T. by various Greek-speaking Jewish communities before and after the birth of Christ. It appears only once in the N.T. at Heb 11:10, where it refers to God the Creator. Second-century Gnostic Christianity made much use of the term, applying it to the God of the O.T. because this divine Being was the Creator of the material universe (e.g., Genesis 1). The Gnostics devalued material reality, viewing it as *intrinsically* evil; any force or power that creates material existence (e.g., the God of the O.T. and women giving birth) must be intrinsically inferior or of a status less than the Supreme Being. This unfortunate understanding of God and creation can lead to anti-Semitism and other forms of fear and hate. After a number of heated exchanges between various orthodox and Gnostic theologians, the universal Church rejected this teaching about God and creation.

Demon (DEE-muhn): (Greek: *daimon*) In classical Greek culture, spiritual beings of an order lower than gods and goddesses. By the sixth century B.C., it was widely believed that demons held influence over spheres of ancient Near Eastern politics, economy, religious rituals, and other practices. This conviction led to the understanding that many of these beings were in collaboration with the forces of evil. In the O.T., such a belief, if not widespread, is found with modifications necessary for a theocentric point of view (Gn 6:1-4; Lv 16:6-10; Is 34:14; Jb 6:4; Ps 91:5). The N.T. perpetuates and assumes the O.T. view and clarifies that these beings are antagonistic toward believers and indeed toward all human life (Mt 8:31; Mk 5:8-13; Rv 18:2). The N.T. witness is that the demonic kingdom is hierarchical, led by "principalities" *(arche)* followed by "authorities" *(exousia),* evil angels (Rom 8:38), and the "powers" *(dynamis).* According to the N.T., their powers are not limited to the spiritual realm; and it is as spiritual forces that they can cause mental illness, physical disease, blindness, epilepticlike illness, etc. Perhaps John's Gospel is the clearest on this point: Satan, the prince of this world, the father of lies who was a murderer from the beginning (Jn 8:44), leads this massive rebellion of spiritual beings against God, His love, Son, and plan for creation (e.g., Jn 13:27 ff.). Exorcisms performed by Jesus (Mt 8:28-34; Mk 1:23-27; Lk 8:26-39; Mt 12:22-32; Mk 3:22-27; Lk 11:14-26) demonstrate the power of God's kingdom over Satan at several levels of reality. First and foremost, the exorcisms express God's compassionate mercy, love, and irrevocable commitment to those oppressed at the deepest level of existence (i.e., spiritual) where only God can reach. Second, when physical healing is involved, they demonstrate that the kingdom of God is indeed more powerful than the kingdom of evil. Third, the kingdom of God is the specific "power sphere" through which God reconciles all of creation back to Himself. All these powerful beings hostile to God have been defeated in Christ (1 Pt 3:22; Col 2:15). **CCC 391-395**

Demoniac (deh-MO-nee-ak): The English word "demoniac" is from the Greek participle *daimonidzomenos,* which functions as a noun and means "one-who-is-demonized" or someone "possessed" by a demon. Such a belief is consistent with pre-technological cultures, which make very little distinction between nature and the supernatural. Demonic possession does not seem to be widespread within the pre-Christian Jewish tradition. The Greek term occurs only once in the Jewish historian Josephus (*Antiquities* VIII.ii.5), and there is no formal corresponding term in rabbinic literature. It occurs only thirteen times in the N.T. (Mt 4:24; 8:16, 28, 33; 9:32; 12:22; 15:22; Mk 1:32; 5:15-16, 18; Lk 8:35, 36; Jn 10:21). Possession by a demon apparently caused mental illness (Mk 1:15; Lk 8:35) and physical illnesses (Mt 4:24; 8:16; Mk 1:32), such as dumbness and blindness (Mt 9:32; 12:22). In popular understanding the term "demoniac" is usually associated with that part of the Gospel narrative known as the "Gerasene Demoniac" (Mt 8:28-34; Mk 5:1-20); that story makes dramatically clear that the kingdom of God is present in the Person of Jesus and that such a presence has complete power over the kingdom of Satan, of darkness, and of death, personified in the possessed man (in a graveyard, no less). Jesus does come to destroy the kingdom of darkness once and for all at the cross. The exorcism He performs by the word of His mouth is simply a foretaste of the effects that His work on the cross and the Father's work in the Resurrection will have on all who become God's friends. In short, God's kingdom liberates humanity from the clutches of the demonic and frees people to become what they were intended to be: children of God as brothers and sisters of Jesus. Cf. CCC 517, 550, 1673

Denunciation (dee-nuhn-see-AY-shuhn): The act of reporting to ecclesiastical authority an offense by a priest or religious; e.g., the fact that a priest solicited a person in confession for sexual favors.

Deontological Ethics (dee-ahn-to-LAH-dzhih-kuhl EH-thihks): (From Greek *deon:* duty) The study of the obligations that are mandatory for one striving to live a moral life. The system that values many exceptionless moral norms as always binding, regardless of circumstances. Catholic theologians have criticized deontological ethics because of its lack of emphasis on prudence and the connection between man's actions and the authentic goods that result. Cf. CCC 1750-1754

Deposing Power, Papal (PAY-puhl dee-PO-zihng PAU-er): The Pope's right to declare that subjects of a secular ruler no longer owe him allegiance. Used rarely since the Middle Ages.

Deposition (DEH-po-ZIH-shuhn): A canonically recognized statement of evidence or testimony accepted by a court.

Deposition, Bull of (BØØL uhv DEH-po-ZIH-shuhn): The papal decree (1570) by which Elizabeth I of England was excommunicated and her Catholic subjects absolved from allegiance to her.

Deposit of Faith (dee-PAH-ziht uhv FAYTH): The body of saving truth, entrusted by Christ to the Apostles and handed on by them to the Church to be preserved and proclaimed. In this sense, the term is very nearly coextensive with "objective revelation," in that it embraces the whole of Christ's teaching as embodied in Revelation and Tradition. But the metaphor of "deposit" highlights particular features of the apostolic teaching. It suggests that this teaching is like an inexhaustible treasure, one that consistently rewards reflection and study with new insights and deeper penetration into the mystery of the divine economy of salvation. Although our understanding of this teaching can develop, it can never be augmented in its substance. Thus, the teaching is a divine trust, something not to be tampered with, altered, or, as it were, "devalued." This feature of the apostolic teaching has also been expressed in the traditional conviction that Revelation, properly so-called, was complete with the death of the last Apostle. The treasure of saving truth — in itself nothing other than Christ Himself — contains the definitive revelation of God's inner life and of His intentions in our regard. There can be no more complete revelation than that imparted by the very Word of God, the Son Who is the perfect image of the Father and Who sends the illumining Spirit into the Church. The position of the Church with respect to the Deposit of Faith is thus something like that of a trustee: charged to preserve a living tradition with fidelity, she must nonetheless proclaim it in new historical circumstances in such a way that its efficacy and richness are undiminished. Although the term "Deposit of Faith" entered official Catholic teaching only with the Council of Trent, its substance is well-attested in the Scriptures and the Fathers. Cf. CCC 84-87, 97

De Profundis (day pro-FØØN-dihs): Psalm 130, characterized as a "gradual" and "penitential" psalm, which begs God for deliverance from sin. Viewed as a prayer for the faithful departed, the opening words of Psalm 130 are *De profundis* ("Out of the depths").

Derogation (dehr-oh-GAY-shun): The partial revocation of a law, as opposed to the abrogation or total abolition of a law (c. 20). Dispensation differs from derogation principally in the fact that the latter affects the law itself that is thereby partially revoked, while the former affects the persons bound by the law, from whose obligation some of them are in particular cases totally or partially released.

Desecration of a Church (DEH-seh-KRAY-shuhn uhv uh TSHERTSH): The new *Ceremonial of Bishops* notes that "crimes committed in a church affect and do injury to the entire Christian community, which the church building in a sense symbolizes and represents." Without specifying particular acts, the *Ceremonial* refers to crimes that do grave dishonor to sacred mysteries (especially to the Eucharistic Species), crimes that are committed to show contempt for the Church, or crimes that are "serious offenses against the dignity of the person or of society" (1070). The diocesan bishop is to decide if such a crime has taken place, and he himself, if possible, is to preside at the "rite of penitential reparation" before any Mass or other sacramental rite (except Penance) may be celebrated.

Desire, Baptism of (BAP-tih-zuhm uhv dee-ZAIR): The act of perfect contrition along with the desire for Baptism of water. Baptism of desire is the equivalent of Baptism of water, even though the former does not impart the indelible character. One who possesses Baptism of desire is required to be baptized with water when possible. CCC 1258-1259

Despair (dih-SPEHR): The deliberate and willful abandoning of hope in God and trust in His providence. It offends against hope as well as faith and charity. To despair is an implicit denial of God's goodness and intervention in creation. This vice cripples one's willingness to love God and to serve Him and others, paralyzing any desire to better a given situation. Despair is not the same as fear and anxiety, which may result from illness, trauma, etc. CCC 2091

Detachment (dih-TATSH-mehnt): In each person's vocation to holiness, that virtue which frees an individual from any inordinate attachment to another person, object, or state of mind. True detachment is not simply a lack of care, but rather it is a liberation from any excessive affection that would hinder one's love and worship of God. CCC 2544-2550

Determinism (dee-TEHR-mihn-isum): Determinism is a name employed by writers, especially since J. Stuart Mill, to denote the philosophical theory that holds — in opposition to the doctrine of free will — that all man's volitions are invariably determined by preexisting circumstances, usually rooted in biology or psychology. The theory is fatalistic, giving too much sway to admittedly important factors in human affairs without giving sufficient attention to man's capacity to master these elements; it is destructive of ethics, as well as of the notion of sin and the fundamental Christian belief that we can merit both reward and punishment.

Detraction (dih-TRAK-shuhn): The revealing of embarrassing truths about another through words or actions, often done with the intention of destroying another's reputation. Detraction is immoral even if not done to injure another. To reveal the faults of another when there is sufficient reason (e.g., for the common good) is not detraction.

Deuterocanonical Books (DÖÖ-tehr-o-ka-NAH-nih-kuhl BØØKS): The phrase designates those books that are found in the LXX (Septuagint), the early Greek version of the O.T., but are not included in the Hebrew O.T. They are 1 and 2 Maccabees, Tobit, Judith, Sirach, Wisdom, Baruch, and additional parts of Daniel and Esther. Although it is sometimes asserted that there was a definition of the Jewish canon of Scripture at the synod of Jamnia (ca. A.D. 100) that definitely excluded the deuterocanonicals from the roster of inspired books, too little is known of the activities of this gathering to say with certainty. Back in the third century, Origen defended the right of Christians to use the deuterocanonical books, even though these were disapproved of by the Jews. The Reformers seemed loath to put these books on a par with the rest of Scripture, but the Council of Trent on April 8, 1546, listed all the books of the O.T., including the deuterocanonicals, and declared that they were being accepted by the Council Fathers "with equal devotion and reverence." The reformed churches refer to the deuterocanonicals as "apocrypha." There is some sentiment among Protestants today for conceding the spiritual value of these books. The expression "deuterocanonical" derives from Sixtus of Siena (1528-1569), who used the word to designate those books of Scripture whose placement in the canon of Scripture was at some time challenged.

Deuteronomy (döö-tehr-AHN-uh-mee): The fifth book of the O.T. It is cast in the form of a farewell address given by Moses. Its content is a mixed bag of materials: a tally of events from the time the Hebrews left Sinai until their arrival in the area east of the Jordan, followed by an exhortation to observe commands and statutes, then a throwback to the Sinai period as the message received by Moses as that time is now communicated to the people (5:29—6:3). There follows a call for loyalty, obedience, and thanksgiving as the people are about to set foot in Canaan. Next comes a rundown of individual legal regulations — rules for worship, the Year of Release, the indenture of debtors, feasts, the responsibilities of kings, priests, and prophets. The appointment of Joshua as leader is given, and the book concludes with an account of Moses' demise on Mt. Nebo (Ch. 34). It is quite possible that many of the texts of Deuteronomy are in fact what they appear to be: liturgical and legal treatises intended to be read to large groupings of people in Israel. The Deuteronomist (literary) source is one of the four widely accepted sources of the Pentateuch. It is to be found exclusively in this book. Traces of the other three sources (Yahwist, Elohist, and Priestly) as found in this book are insignificant. In the original Hebrew no name is given to the book. It was referred to with the words of the opening clause. The term "Deuteronomy" stems from the Septuagint, the early Greek translation, with the word occurring in Dt 17:18 of that version. Perhaps the strongest impact the book had was on the centralization of the cult of Israel at the place determined by God.

Development of Doctrine (dee-VEHL-uhp-mehnt uhv DAHK-truhn): The belief that the Church's understanding of revealed truth develops throughout the centuries. The truths of the Faith remain the same; however, the grasp of these truths can change and grow, thanks to the grace of God manifested in the devotion of the faithful, the research of theologians, and the wisdom of the saints. Nothing can be added to or subtracted from Divine Revelation, but the mysteries do become clearer over the years. **Cf. CCC 94**

Development of Peoples (dee-VEHL-uhp-mehnt uhv PEE-puhlz): The notion that society must meet the needs of all peoples if they are to attain the fulfillment intended by God. The Church continues to proclaim the dignity of man; she has championed the rights of all, especially in the "labor" encyclicals since 1891. **CCC 1908**

Devil (DEH-vuhl): The created essence — truly existing and not a mere "personification of evil" — that was created good but freely chose to be constituted in evil by way of a definitive choice. Scripture and Tradition are clear that the devil (also called "Satan" or "Beelzebub") works contrary to God and His eternal will. **CCC 391, 395**

Devil and Evil Spirits (DEH-vuhl and EE-vuhl SPIH-rihts): Those fallen angels who, after being created by God and endowed with grace, succumbed to the sin of pride and so turned away from God's love. Although they no longer have supernatural grace, the fallen angels retain the powers of spiritual beings, and use these to impede the fulfillment of God's plan for creation. However, their power is limited, and they cannot change the divine will of God. The devil, or Satan, is the leader of the evil spirits. **CCC 391-395**

Devil's Advocate (DEH-vuhlz AD-vo-kuht): Former term denoting the official of the Congregation for the Causes of Saints whose purpose was to present material militating against one's beatification and/or canonization. The devil's advocate is no longer used, his duties now fulfilled by other officials of the process. (Cf. Advocatus Diaboli.)

Devolution (DEH-vo-LÖÖ-shuhn): 1. The act whereby the right to appoint someone to ecclesiastical office passes from a lower body or person to a higher authority. 2. Regarding canonical trials, a sentence or decision presumed to stand as is unless overturned by higher authority.

Devotion (dee-VO-shuhn): 1. The desire to dedicate oneself to God's service. Prayer seeks to animate one to abandon himself fully to God's will — which is the core of sanctity. 2. Consolation experienced at times during prayer; a reverent manner of praying. **CCC 24, 1674-1676**

Devotions, Private (PRAI-vuht dee-VO-shunz): Pious practices beyond participation in various acts of the liturgy, often called "popular devotions." *Sacrosanctum Concilium* (n. 13) says: "Popular devotions of the Christian people, provided they conform to the laws and norms of the Church, are to be highly recommended, especially where they are ordered by the Apostolic See. Devotions proper to individual churches also have a special dignity. . . . Such devotions should be so drawn up that they harmonize with the liturgical seasons, accord with the Sacred Liturgy, are in some way derived from it, and lead the people to it, since in fact the liturgy by its very nature is far superior to any of them." Devotions of a liturgical type include Exposition of the Blessed Sacrament and recitation of prayer in the Liturgy of the Hours. Examples of paraliturgical devotions are a Bible service or vigil, the *Angelus*, Rosary, and Stations of the Cross, each with a strong scriptural basis. **CCC 1674-1676**

Diabolical Possession (dai-uh-BAHL-ih-kuhl po-ZEH-shuhn): Condition that occurs when an evil spirit is said to possess and control the personality and body of a person. A number of instances of this are recorded in the four Gospels and Acts (e.g., Mt 8:16; Mk 1:34; Lk 7:21; Acts 5:16). These and other accounts in Sacred Scripture show the power that both the demonic and sin have on the human condition. The reign of evil overcomes human freedom at the psychological, physical, and social levels. The witness of Sacred Scripture that human shortcomings are indeed connected to sin and in some cases to demonic activity only serves to heighten one's awareness of the need for a savior, a deliverer, a redeemer. The Son of God's mission to redeem includes "set[ting] at liberty those who are captive." This theme from Isaiah, on which Jesus draws to describe His own commission from God, is key to understanding that the kingdom of God has the power to overcome diabolical possession. Unlike illustrations in popular films such as *The Exorcist,* God's power over demonic forces is not relative but absolute, not a struggle but a *fait accompli* in Christ's death and resurrection. The Church provides for exorcisms but only after specific conditions have been met, only under competent ecclesiastical authorities (i.e., under the supervision of the local bishop). See also Demoniac. **Cf. CCC 1673**

Diaconate (dee-AK-uh-nit): The state of being a deacon. (See Deacon, Permanent; also Deacon, Transitional.)

Diakonikon (dee-a-KO-nih-kahn): The place, usually a table, in or near the sanctuary in Byzantine churches, attended to by the deacon, on which may be placed vestments, sacred vessels, books, or other items utilized in the celebration of liturgical services. Architecturally, the diakonikon often is balanced with the Proskomide, or Table of Preparation, on the opposite side of the sanctuary. It is not essential to the sanctuary appointments and thus may even be absent in some churches.

Dialogue Mass (DAI-uh-lawg MAS): The revised Roman Missal, promulgated in 1970, fulfilled the mandate of Vatican II's Constitution on the Sacred Liturgy (*Sacrosanctum*

Concilium) that the faithful's participation in the liturgy was to be "full, active and conscious." This participation was to manifest itself particularly by the people singing or saying (whether in Latin or the vernacular) those parts of the liturgy pertaining to them, and responding to the greetings, invitations, invocations, and verses pronounced by priest, deacon, lector, or cantor. In Masses celebrated according to the former rite ("Tridentine"), however, it was sufficient for the server to make the responses in the name of the people and common practice for the choir alone to sing the chants that were really meant to be sung by all. From Pope St. Pius X (1903-1914) on, numerous instructions from the Holy See urged "congregational participation" in the Mass. Those Masses at which this request was fulfilled were called "dialogue Masses," a term obviously rendered obsolete by the normative Mass promulgated after Vatican II. **Cf. CCC 1071, 1140-1144, 1157-1158**

Diaspora (dee-AS-po-ruh): (Greek: exile) The name given first to the Jews, and then to any nation or large national group, dispersed throughout foreign lands. In the case of the Jews in biblical times, they were divided into two classes. Those who lived in the Eastern lands of Babylonia, Persia, etc., were referred to as the Aramaic Diaspora, or Dispersion. Those who lived in the lands surrounding the Mediterranean, such as Egypt, Greece, and its islands, Italy, or Asia Minor, were called the Diaspora of the Greeks (cf. 2 Mc 1:1; Jn 7:35).

Diatesseron (dee-uh-TEH-suh-rahn): A harmony of the Gospels drawn up by Tatian ca. A.D. 170. There are no extant complete manuscripts of the Diatesseron, save for a single fragment in Greek (fourteen lines that give an account of Joseph of Arimathea's request for the body of Jesus). All the other witnesses are secondary or tertiary. Still under discussion is the question of the language in which the Diatesseron was originally written and the question of its place of origin. Some scholars have judged that the work was originally drawn up in Greek and subsequently put into Syriac. Others seem to believe that it was composed by Tatian in his native tongue, Syriac. There is also the opinion of F. C. Burkitt, according to which the Diatesseron began as a Gospel harmony compiled in Latin at Rome, a Greek copy of which came to the attention of Tatian, who forthwith put it into Syriac. The Diatesseron enjoyed a wide circulation in the Syriac-speaking churches. Until the fifth century it served as the standard Gospel text in those churches.

Dicastery (dai-KAS-tuh-ree): (Greek *dikasterion:* court of law) A court or body with authority to judge.

Didache, The (*th*uh DIH-duh-kay): (Greek: teaching) A short but important early Christian work by an unknown author, written probably in Syria around A.D. 60 and presenting in sixteen chapters a summary of Christian moral teaching framed in terms of the two ways of life and death (Chs. 1-6), instructions concerning liturgical practice (Chs. 7-10), and a set of disciplinary norms (Chs. 11-15). The final chapter contains a prophecy of the approaching end of the world and mentions the Antichrist. Perhaps the chief interest of the work lies in the picture it presents of the life of the early Christian community, for example: Baptism by immersion, station fasts on Wednesday and Friday, thrice-daily recitation of the Lord's Prayer, and confession of sins before prayer in church. Two primitive Eucharistic Prayers are also included. The disciplinary instructions reflect a still-developing Church order in which prophets continue to play an important role; bishops and deacons, though not the presbyterate, are mentioned as well. Although the *Didache* was known to the Fathers of the Church and exercised considerable influence on early Church orders (such as the *Didascalia* and the *Apostolic Constitutions*), modern acquaintance with the complete text dates only from 1873 when a manuscript (dating from 1056) was discovered in a monastery in Constantinople.

Didascalia Apostolorum (dee-duh-SKAHL-yuh uh-pahs-to-LO-røøm): (Latin, from Greek: The Teaching of the Apostles) Attributed to the Apostles, this book nevertheless seems to have been written in the first part of the third century, probably by a convert from Judaism who also from the text seems to have been a physician. The work is modeled on the *Didache,* but the format is unmethodical. Christian living and government are first treated, with a section on penitents that is more lenient than other ancient documents on readmitting sinners back to communion. The Liturgy is described as hierarchical and eastward in orientation, and of great importance, and therefore not to be neglected for work or amusements. Fasting is enjoined on Wednesdays and Fridays, as well as a week before Easter. The duties and roles of husbands and wives, widows, deacons, deaconesses, presbyters, and bishops are spelled out as members of the local church, as well as a concern for catechumens, the persecuted, and the imprisoned.

Dies Irae (DEE-ayz EE-ray): (Latin: Day of Wrath) Sequence of the Requiem Mass, this piece is now used only as a hymn for the Divine Office on All Souls Day and the thirty-fourth week in "ordinary time." It is a fifty seven-line poem divided into nineteen three-line stanzas. Authorship of the *Dies Irae* has been the subject of historians' search over the centuries. It has been translated into almost every language and has been set to music by some of the greatest composers of all time. The Gregorian chant melody of it has also been used as a primary or secondary theme of master composers throughout the ages.

Diet of Augsburg: See Augsburg, Diet of

Diffinitor: See Definitors

Dignitatis Humanae (dihn-yee-TAH-tihs höö-MAH-nay): The Declaration by the Fathers of the Second Vatican Council on Religious Freedom. It states "that the human person has a right to religious freedom. Freedom of this kind means that all men should be immune from coercion on the part of individuals, social groups, and every human power, so that, within due limits, nobody is forced to act against his convictions in religious matters in public or in private, alone or in association with others." This right is based upon the dignity of the human person as revealed by reason and by Holy Scripture. **CCC 2104-2109**

Dimissorials (dih-mih-SOR-ee-uhlz): Official letters that the proper bishop or religious superior of a candidate for diaconate or priesthood presents to another bishop who will ordain the candidate.

Diocesan Administrator (dai-AH-suh-suhn ad-MIHN-ih-stray-ter): A bishop or priest elected by a diocesan college of consultors to administer the day-to-day affairs of a diocese during the period following the death, resignation, or removal of a diocesan bishop and the assumption of authority by a new bishop (cc. 409, 421, 424).

Diocesan Clergy (dai-AH-suh-suhn KLEHR-dzhee): Clerics, either deacons or priests, who are attached to a diocese with the diocesan residential bishop as their proper superior.

Diocesan Pastoral Council (dai-AH-suh-suhn PAS-ter-uhl KAUN-sihl), also Archdiocesan (ARCH-dai-AH-suh-suhn): A purely consultative body of the faithful made up of clergy, religious, and laity, established to assist the bishop or archbishop by advising him on pastoral matters of the diocese or archdiocese.

Diocesan Right (dai-AH-suh-suhn RAIT): The authority of a bishop over a type of religious institute having its principal headquarters in his diocese.

Diocese (DAI-o-seez): A territorial division of the Church comprised of all the Catholics living in a specific geographic area under the pastoral care and authority of a residential bishop. **CCC 833**

Diptychs (DIHP-tihks): A set of two tablets, hinged in the center, containing the names of the living and the dead, once read by the deacon during the Canon of the Divine Liturgy. At present, any memorial listing.

Direct Line (dih-REHKT LAIN): The type of blood relationship that exists between and among persons directly descended one from another, as grandparent, parent, child.

Directorium (dih-rehk-TOR-ee-uhm) or Ordo (OR-do): Technical term referring to the booklet published annually for a diocese or archdiocese or group of dioceses prescribing the dates of liturgical seasons and movable feasts with rank and liturgical colors required. These texts also summarize liturgical legislation concerning fasting and list the names of deceased priests in a given diocese or archdiocese.

Diriment Impediment: See Impediment, Diriment

Discalced (dihs-KALST): (Latin: unshod) The term denoting the male and female religious congregations that spurn shoes in favor of sandals. The Discalced Carmelites are especially noted for this practice, which began in the West with St. Francis of Assisi and St. Clare.

Discernment of Spirits (dih-SERN-mehnt uhv SPIH-rihts): Ability to distinguish between spirits, mentioned by St. Paul in 1 Cor 12:10 as a gift of the Holy Spirit, enabling one to choose the right path morally and spiritually.

Disciple (dih-SAI-puhl): (Latin: *discipulus*, student) The general term for any student or follower of a particular teacher. In the N.T., the disciples are understood more specifically as the seventy-two who received instruction from Jesus (Lk 10:1-24). They, in turn, were to share this privileged knowledge with others as teachers of the faith. Tradition correctly or incorrectly identifies St. John as the "Beloved Disciple" singled out in Jn 13:23 as "the disciple whom Jesus loved." After Our Lord's Ascension, the Apostles added to the number of disciples, with one hundred twenty gathered at Jerusalem in Acts 1:15. Consistent with the etymology of the term "apostle" (from the Greek *apostolos,* one sent out on a mission), the Apostles were distinguished in the early Church from the disciples: each Apostle had a singular mission, while the disciples were to go out only in pairs with the specific charge of preparing for the coming of Christ (Mk 6:7). These two ranks of Apostles and disciples are often compared to the O.T. offices of priests and levites and to the N.T. bishops and presbyters. In modern usage, the term "disciple" is generally applied to all the baptized. CCC 562, 915, 1693, 1816, 1823, 1986, 2262, 2347, 2427, 2466, 2612

Disciplina Arcani (dih-shih-PLEE-nuh ahr-KAH-nee): (Latin: Discipline of the Secret) The practice of the early Christians, in an era of persecution, of not discussing their beliefs freely and openly, but only revealing them gradually to catechumens as they were prepared by instruction for the sacraments of Christian initiation. This would hold especially for the most sacred of mysteries, the Eucharist. Whether some influence of the mystery religions of the time is seen in this practice is disputed by scholars. Allusions to the practice are seen in many of the Fathers, both Eastern and Western. By the sixth century this custom had disappeared with the widespread Christianization of many areas and the collapse of the Roman Empire.

Discipline (DIH-sih-plihn): 1. The small whip used by some ascetics to mortify themselves and to repair for their sins. Its use has greatly diminished today. 2. The way of life to which all are called by the Church as disciples of Christ.

Discrimination (dih-skrih-mih-NAY-shuhn): 1. The act of choosing one thing or person over another, as part of the process of human development. 2. A prejudice, or bias, against individuals or groups of people, usually on the basis of race, religion, social conditions, or gender. CCC 1935, 2358, 2433

Diskos (DIHS-kos): A rimmed and circular tray with a stand or foot, used in the Eastern Liturgy as the paten is used in the West.

Dismissal (dihs-MIHS-suhl): The canonical penalty whereby a member of a religious institute is involuntarily released from the institute or a cleric is involuntarily separated from the clerical state.

Disparity of Worship: See Cult, Disparity of

Dispensation (dihs-pehn-SAY-shuhn): The relaxation of the obligations or effect of an ecclesiastical law. Dispensation can only be granted by competent authority.

Dissent (dih-SENT): In theological language, dissent refers to the rejection of authentic Church teaching in matters of faith and morals. Such dissent cannot be justified according to Catholic teaching, whether the position in question has been proposed by the extraordinary Magisterium (a solemn definition by a Pope or ecumenical council) or by the ordinary Magisterium (i.e., the constant teaching of Popes and bishops). Persistent and radical theological dissent places one outside the bounds of communion with the Catholic Church.

Dissident (DIHS-ih-dihnt): One who dissents from Church teaching.

Dissidio (dih-SIHD-ee-o): (Italian: division) The separation between the Holy See and Italy's government from 1870 to 1929. The *Risorgimento,* championed by proponents of Italian unification, completely disrupted the temporal authority enjoyed by the Pontiff since the eighth century. Pope Pius IX, who was confined to Vatican City, warned Catholics not to cooperate with the Italian government. Later Pope St. Pius X encouraged Catholic participation in society. The *dissidio* was officially ended with the Lateran Agreement and Concordat of 1929.

Dissolution of Marriage (dih-so-LÖÖ-shuhn uhv MEH-rehdzh): A canonical act whereby a valid and/or sacramental marriage is declared to exist no longer. Dissolution takes place in cases of nonsacramental unions and sacramental but nonconsummated unions. **Cf. CCC 1640**

Divination (dih-vih-NAY-shuhn): The practice of acquiring information other than by the ordinary ways of knowing. It encompasses the use of crystal balls, horoscopes, ouija boards, and tarot cards. All such endeavors are gravely wrong because they indicate a mistrust of God and His providence. CCC 2115-2117, 2138

Divine Comedy (dih-VAIN KAH-muh-dee): The title of an allegory, written in 1321 by Dante Alighieri, which continues to be recognized as one of the premier Christian literary works. The *Divine Comedy* was written in Italian and is based in part on the Fathers of the Church and such eminent Doctors of the Church as St. Bernard and St. Thomas Aquinas. Dante's masterpiece is divided into three parts: *Inferno* (Hell), *Purgatorio* (Purgatory), and *Paradiso* (Heaven).

Divine Office (dih-VAIN AW-fihs): The former name for the official, public (although often recited privately), daily liturgical prayer by which the Church sanctifies the hours of the day. Hence, the Vatican II revision of this prayer is entitled the Liturgy of the Hours, although the title page of the official books still bears the designation "The Divine Office: revised by decree of the Second Vatican Ecumenical Council." *Officium* was the common Latin word for public services of prayer, and indeed "office" is still more or less commonly used among the Churches of the Reformation to describe their non-Eucharistic worship services. (Cf. Liturgy of the Hours, Breviary.) Cf. CCC 1174-1178

Divine Praises (dih-VAIN PRAY-zehz): Spoken or sung at the conclusion of Benediction, this litany recitation of the names of the Holy Trinity, Holy Family, and Blessed Mother is traced back to the eighteenth-century Jesuit Luigi Felici, who promoted them as reparation for public blasphemy.

Divine Revelation, Dogmatic Constitution on: See Dei Verbum

Divinity of Christ (dih-VIH-nuh-tee uhv KRAIST): Sacred Scripture clearly and repeatedly proclaims the divinity of Christ at many levels and in many voices. Even in those places where there is no explicit reference to this reality, it is either assumed or implied (e.g., Mk 3:1-6). From the perspective of Christ's preexistence, we see that He was with God from the beginning and was God (Jn 1:1). Jesus' use of

"I AM" (Jn 8:58) is normally taken as a direct reference to God's words to Moses (Ex 3:14), thus implying His divinity; Christ is supreme above all things and prior to all things — in this instance, priority implying superiority (Jn 1; Col 1:16-17). In Christ's relationship to the Father we see His divinity with ease and certainty — at His Baptism a voice from heaven (God) called Him "Son," thus indicating Jesus' divine status (Mt 3:17; Mk 1:11; Lk 3:22); Jesus is the Father's only begotten Son (Jn 1:14), not by adoption but by nature (Heb 1:3); Jesus was with the Father from the beginning (Jn 1:1), reveals the Father (Jn 1:18), is in the Father as the Father is in Him (Jn 14:11), in unity (Jn 10:30). The Church's faith in Christ expresses a clear conviction about Christ's divinity — from Peter's confession at Caesarea Philippi (Mt 16:16), including the centurion's confession at Jesus' death, preserved and proclaimed in the Gospel (Mk 15:39), to the post-resurrection confession of Thomas (Jn 20:28), to name only a few. In a special way Jesus' authority to forgive sins, which in Judaism was restricted to God alone, shows not only His divinity but also something about divinity — His compassionate and loving nature as the King of kings, Whose kingdom arrives in force and power for the reconciliation and re-creation of a world scarred by the forces of sin and death. CCC 209, 455, 464-469, 484, 515, 653, 663, 1374, 1413

Divino Afflante Spiritu (dee-VEE-no ah-FLAHN-tay SPEE-ree-töö): On September 30, 1943, Pope Pius XII issued an encyclical that draws its title from the first three words of the document, *Divino Afflante Spiritu* (DAS). This document was to provide guidance to Catholic biblical scholars for whom the use and abuse, the advantages and limits of historical and linguistic methods in biblical research had become a pressing issue. The atmosphere into which this document was inserted was less stressful than that of fifty years earlier, when Pope Leo XIII issued the encyclical *Providentissimus Deus,* also intended as guidance for Catholic scholars and professors of Sacred Scripture who were using scientific (historical archaeology, ethnography, etc.) and linguistic approaches to the analysis of Sacred Scripture. DAS encourages the careful study of the original languages in which Sacred Scripture was written, in order to study and determine which of the surviving manuscripts of Sacred Scripture are closest to the "autographs" that did not survive (this is called "lower criticism" or "textual criticism"). One cannot study the manuscripts without competent knowledge of the language in which they are written. In addition, DAS warned against excessive application of the sciences mentioned above, especially when the rash application of these methods led to questioning and, in some instances, outright rejection of essential elements of the Faith. Much of the teaching found in DAS is reaffirmed in *Dei Verbum* (Dogmatic Constitution on Divine Revelation), issued at the Second Vatican Council. The Catholic scholar must master the technical details of Sacred Scripture and also test the yield of that research against the witness of the whole of Sacred Scripture, the teachings of the Fathers, the Councils, the liturgies (East and West), and the lives of the saints. CCC 112-119

Divorce (dih-VORS): A legal act by a competent civil authority that severs a bond of marriage. In the Catholic Church divorce is not acknowledged to give the right to remarriage. CCC 1650-1651, 1664, 2382-2386, 2400

Divorce from Bed and Board (dih-VORS fruhm BEHD and BORD): Term used in the 1917 code to describe the separation of spouses, permitted by Church authorities.

Docetism (DO-suh-tih-zuhm): (From Greek *dokeo:* to seem) The heresy denying the hypostatic union, asserting that Christ merely "appeared" in a human body and therefore only seemed to die. The second-century Gnostics articulated docetism. CCC 465

Doctor (DAHK-ter): Historically, an accomplished teacher. Properly, the highest academic degree to be earned in any field of study.

Doctor Angelicus (DAHK-tor ahn-DZHEHL-ih-køøs): (Latin: Angelic Doctor) Title given to St. Thomas Aquinas (1225?-1274), who is the author of some of the most learned theological works of all time, including the *Summa Theologiae.*

Doctor Communis (DAHK-tor ko-MÖÖ-nihs): (Latin: Common Doctor) Title applied to St. Thomas Aquinas (1225?-1274) in appreciation of his writings, which transcend cultures and centuries. His is the only theological work that has been recommended by an ecumenical council — the Second Vatican Council.

Doctor Gratiae (DAHK-tor GRAHT-see-ay): (Latin: Doctor of Grace) Title given to St. Augustine of Hippo (354-430) in commemoration of his study of the theology of grace in refuting the various Pelagian errors of his day.

Doctor Marianus (DAHK-tor MAH-ree-AH-nøøs): (Latin: Marian Doctor) Title given to St. Anselm of Canterbury (1033-1109) in memory of his esteemed writings on the Blessed Virgin Mary. St. Anselm, also considered the "Father of Scholasticism," wrote remarkable treatises on the Incarnation and Our Lady's perpetual virginity.

Doctor Mellifluus (DAHK-tor meh-LIHF-löö-uhs): (Latin: Honeysweet Doctor) Title conferred on St. Bernard of Clairvaux (1090-1153) in remembrance of his "sweet" or beautiful writings. The works of this saint, who is often considered the last Father of the Church, are many and varied, including treatises on the Infant Jesus, Our Lady, and a commentary on the Song of Songs.

Doctor Seraphicus (DAHK-tor sehr-AHF-fih-køøs): (Latin: Seraphic Doctor) Title used for the Franciscan St. Bonaventure (1218-1274), referring to the vision experienced by St. Francis of Assisi in which seraphim held aloft the crucified Jesus. St. Bonaventure treated the hypostatic union and the sacred humanity of Jesus Christ in his works and is thus called "Seraphic."

Doctor Subtilis (DAHK-tor søøb-TEE-lihs): (Latin: Subtle Doctor) Title conferred on Bl. John Duns Scotus (1270-1308) in honor of his attention to detail in his masterful theological works. It was this Franciscan priest who helped unlock the riddle of the mystery of the Immaculate Conception, later defined by Pope Pius IX in 1854.

Doctor Universalis (DAHK-tor ÖÖ-nee-vehr-SAH-lihs):
(Latin: Universal Doctor) Title granted to St. Albert the Great (1206-1280), the Dominican theologian, teacher of St. Thomas Aquinas, and Archbishop of Cologne, Germany, known for the breadth of his theological and philosophical treatises.

Doctrine of the Catholic Church (DAHK-trihn uhv *th*uh KATH-uh-lihk TSHERTSH): A generic phrase for the teachings of the Church regarding faith and morals, given by her Founder, Jesus Christ, to the Apostles for the salvation of all. "Doctrine" means the contents of Divine Revelation, as well as each specific tenet of the Faith. There are various levels of doctrine (e.g., *de fide definita* and "common teaching"). **CCC 5, 9-11**

Documentary Process (dah-kyöö-MEHN-tuh-ree PRAH-sehs): The judicial process used to demonstrate marriage nullity based on certain and authentic documents. Used in cases of undispensed impediments.

Dogma (DAWG-muh): A teaching of the Church, held as revealed by God and therefore binding on the faithful, that is revealed implicitly or explicitly either by solemn definition or by the Church's ordinary Magisterium. **CCC 88-90**

Dogmatic Theology (dawg-MA-tihk thee-AHL-uh-dzhee): The systematic treatment of theology that considers each article of faith and the entire deposit of the Faith. Also called "systematic" theology, dogmatic theology seeks to show that the dogmas of the Church are true and compatible with reason.

Dolor or Dolour (DOH-lohr): Often used as a synonym for "sorrow," especially in reference to the Blessed Virgin Mary's association with the Passion of Christ. (See also Sorrows of the Blessed Virgin Mary.)

Dom (DAHM): A title used before the names of monks of certain monasteries.

Domestic Prelate (duh-MEHS-tihk PREH-luht): An honorary title conferred upon a priest with the right to be called "monsignor." Known as "Honorary Prelate to His Holiness" since 1968.

Domicile (DAH-mih-sail): The place where a person lives for an indefinite period of time. Ecclesiastical laws generally bind a person based on his or her domicile.

Dominations (dah-mih-NAY-shuhnz): The name of the first order (also known as dominions) within the second hierarchy of the nine choirs of angels that directs the other two orders within this second hierarchy, the powers and the virtues.

Dominic, St. (SAYNT DAH-mih-nihk): Priest-founder (1170-1221) of the Order of Preachers (Dominicans), originally organized to fight against the Albigensian heresy; his memory is kept in the liturgy on August 8.

Dominicans (duh-MIH-nih-kuhnz), also Order of Preachers (OR-der uhv PREE-tsherz): Members of the Dominican Order, formally known as the Order of Preachers, a mendicant Order founded by St. Dominic in 1215 for the special purpose of preaching and teaching.

Dominions: See Dominations

Donation of Constantine: See Constantine, Donation of

Donatism (DO-nuh-tih-zuhm): A North African rigorist movement that takes its name from Donatus, who became the schismatic Bishop of Carthage in A.D. 313. Donatists insisted that sacraments administered by unworthy ministers were invalid. St. Augustine worked for fifteen years to refute Donatism. He argued the Catholic doctrine that the efficacy of the sacraments depends not on the worthiness of the ministers but on the power of Christ, Who is their true and ultimate minister. **CCC 1127-1128**

Doorkeeper: See Porter

Dormition of the Blessed Virgin Mary (dawr-MIH-shuhn uhv *th*uh BLEH-sehd VER-dzhihn MEH-ree): The falling asleep of Our Lady, a feast celebrated in the East on August 15 (when the West celebrates her Assumption) and considered one of the twelve great feasts of the East. Originally all Christians spoke of death as falling asleep (cf. Thes 4:14) until the general resurrection when all would be reunited, soul and body, to enjoy eternal happiness. From the fifth century on, legend told of Our Lady's death surrounded by the Apostles, when her soul was taken into heaven, only to be followed by their keeping vigil at the grave and witnessing the Assumption of her body as well. The fanciful aspects of these legends notwithstanding, they bear witness to the truth of early belief of the faithful in Our Lady's being taken to heaven, soul and body. This feast was observed in the East as early as the sixth century and spread throughout the whole of the East. It was adopted in Rome during the seventh century, when Pope Sergius I (687-701) ordered a solemn procession for the feast. The Western emphasis has always been on the glorification of Our Lady rather than on her dormition or her death, although when Pope Pius XII solemnly defined her Assumption, he left open the question as to whether she died or was taken bodily into heaven alive. **Cf. CCC 966**

Dossal (DAH-suhl), also Dorsal (DOR-suhl): The suspended backdrop for the crucifix over the altar, often made of tapestry or rich cloth, extending the length of the altar. Today, liturgical banners often replace the dossal.

Douay Bible (DÖÖ-ay BAI-buhl): The English Catholic translation (also called Douai or Doway) of the Scriptures begun in Douai, Belgium, by members of the English College there and later continued in Rheims (Reims). The translation was published in 1609. A convert from Presbyterianism, Richard Challoner, revised the Douai-Reims translation in 1749-1750.

Double (DUH-buhl): Name once given in the Missal for the highest rank of feasts in the liturgical calendar. There were ordinary doubles, major doubles, and doubles of the second and first class. The new terminology is simplified to memorials, feasts, and solemnities.

Double Effect, Principle of (PRIHN-sih-puhl uhv DUH-buhl ee-FEHKT): Actions sometimes have two effects closely related to each other, one good, the other bad. A difficult moral question can arise: Is it permissible to perform an action from which two such results follow? It is permissible if: the action is good in itself and directly productive of the good effect; the circumstances are good; the intention of the person is good; and the reason for the action is proportional to the seriousness of the indirect bad effect. Example: a pregnant woman undergoing medical or surgical treatment for a pathological condition, with the indirect and secondary effect of the treatment being possible loss of the child. Cf. CCC 2263

Doubt of Law (DAUT uhv LAW): An objective uncertainty about the meaning of a law that arises when the text of a law is so obscure or confusing that it cannot be understood.

Dove (DUHV): In Christian iconography, the dove symbolizes the Holy Spirit. The chief basis for this symbolism is the scriptural assertion that the Holy Spirit descended upon Jesus "like a dove" immediately after His baptism by John (Mt 3:16; Mk 1:10; Lk 3:22; Jn 1:32). CCC 535, 701

Doxology (dahk-SAHL-uh-dzhee): (Greek *doxologia*, from *doxa:* glory + *logos:* word) Giving praise or glory to God in the liturgy. Traditionally, the *Gloria* at Mass has been called the greater doxology, while the prayer "Glory be to the Father . . ." is known as the lesser doxology. CCC 1003, 2641, 2855-2856

Dream (DREEM): 1. The result of subconscious activity during sleep. 2. Within the Judeo-Christian tradition, dreams are included in the scriptural accounts of God's dealings with certain individuals, revealing some course of action to be taken or to make clear some divine purpose; however, it would be sinful to seek to know or foretell the future through the guidance of dreams.

Dress, Clerical (KLEHR-ih-kuhl DREHS): Traditionally, Church law has held that clerics should dress in a distinctive and appropriate manner. The present law states that "clerics are to wear suitable ecclesiastical garb in accord with the norms issued by the conference of bishops and in accord with legitimate local custom" (Can. 284). The manner with which legislation has been observed throughout history has varied from country to country. The Councils of Baltimore II and III issued legislation applicable to the United States. Clerics were to wear cassocks or religious habits in the church and rectory and a black suit with a Roman collar outside. Clerics were forbidden to wear beards and elaborate hairstyles. The 1917 code contained the provision about wearing suitable and distinctive garb. It also prohibited the wearing of rings, except when allowed by law (bishops, abbots, vicars apostolic, and those with doctorates in theology or Canon Law from pontifical universities). There were several penalties set for laying aside clerical dress. After Vatican II, there were significant changes in the norms for clerical dress. In those countries where the wearing of the cassock and religious habit on the streets was the norm, clerics were allowed for the first time to wear black or gray suits with the Roman collar. The appropriate garb for permanent deacons is another matter. The general law leaves this matter up to the episcopal conferences. In the United States, permanent deacons have been encouraged to wear lay dress, although no specific prohibition has been made from their wearing clerical garb.

Dualism (DÖÖ-uhl-ih-zuhm): 1. Various theories asserting that two distinct elements, the spiritual and the material, comprise the human person. Most dualistic positions (e.g., Cartesianism) hold that the connection between these two realities is loose, as opposed to Thomism, which contends that matter and spirit are unified in humans. 2. The philosophy or religious belief that good and evil are distinct principles that fight each other. Some adherents of this theory believe that the spiritual is good while the material is evil; hence, one's material body "traps" one's good spirit. The Church believes that the human body is a great good created by God. Cf. CCC 285

Duel (DÖÖ-uhl): A fight to the death (or at least to maim the other) by two persons using weapons at an agreed-upon location and time, in order to defend one's honor or to win the hand of a woman. The Church has consistently rejected dueling as cold-blooded murder; however, many, especially gunfighters and politicians, have ignored the caution.

Due Process (DÖÖ PRAH-sehs): That aspect of a legal system that is established to protect the rights of individuals, especially individuals accused of wrongdoing. Includes arbitration, conciliation, administrative recourse, judicial recourse, and appeal.

Dulia (DÖÖ-lee-uh): (Latin from Greek *douleia:* service) Term used in the Church to describe the kind of honor given to angels and saints. **Cf. CCC 1090, 1192, 2131-2132**

Duplication: See Bination

Duties (DÖÖ-teez): The responsibilities, designating the "minimal" requirements of Catholics, which seek to inculcate the desire for spiritual growth, imposed by the Church on her members. Some of these moral and religious duties are to obey the Ten Commandments, to observe the Church's law concerning marriage, to receive Holy Communion at least once a year during the Easter season, etc. **CCC 578, 848, 888, 907, 1141, 1163, 1932-1933, 2037, 2052-2527, 2784**

Duties of Parents (DÖÖ-tees uhv PEHR-uhnts): Broadly speaking, the obligations of parents to provide for the physical, emotional, and psychological welfare of their children. In Canon Law, these duties are described as the physical, social, cultural, moral, and religious nurture or upbringing of children (cf. Can. 1136). **CCC 2221-2231**

Dying, Prayers for the (PREHRZ for *th*uh DAI-ihng): Prayers for the commendation of the soul (not the Last Rites or Extreme Unction, as the Sacrament of Anointing the Sick used to be called) consisted in the Asperges, the Litany of the Saints, prayers, the Kyrie, and various aspirations, as well as the Apostolic Blessing. In the current rite, much of the same material has been retained but greatly enriched with psalms and other biblical selections, and with more texts optional. The Apostolic Blessing for the dying is not mentioned in the new rite. Cf. CCC 1020, 2299

E

Early Church: See Church, Early

Easter (EES-ter): The feast of the Resurrection of Christ derives its name from Eastre, the goddess of Spring, according to St. Bede the Venerable, but others think that the term comes from a misunderstanding of *Hebdomada Alba* ("White Weeks") when *alba* ("white") was mistranslated into the High German word for dawn, when the risen Lord was seen by the holy women. In any event, this festival is the high point of the Christian year, as it celebrates the central mystery of Christ: His triumph over death and the cross in His resurrection, which in the Synoptic Gospels is associated with the Jewish Passover. **CCC 640, 677, 731, 793, 1096, 1164, 1169-1170, 1225, 1340, 1362-1366, 1403, 1449, 1680-1683**

Easter Controversy (EES-ter KAHN-truh-ver-see): A series of disputes concerning the date of the celebration of Easter, which had been based variously upon the date of Passover, the fourteenth day of Nisan in the lunar calendar, and the date determined by the Roman calendar. The date was made uniform in the Western Church by the ninth century, using the Roman calendar. **CCC 1170**

Easter Duty (EES-ter DÖÖ-tee): Also known as Paschal Precept, the obligation of Catholics to receive the Eucharist at least once a year between Easter and Trinity Sunday (cf. Can. 920). **CCC 1389, 2042**

Easter Season (EES-ter SEE-zuhn): This joyous season in the liturgical year extends fifty days from Easter Sunday to Pentecost. On the fortieth day of the Easter Season, the Ascension of the Lord is celebrated, and nine days from the Ascension to the Vigil of Pentecost are an intensive preparation for the coming of the Holy Spirit. **CCC 1095-1096, 1168-1169**

Easter Water (EES-ter WAH-ter): The holy water blessed during the celebration of the Easter Vigil is used for Christian Initiation on that night, for the renewal of baptismal promises at the Masses of Easter Day, and for Baptism throughout the Easter Season. The revised *Book of Blessings* encourages pastors to continue the practice of blessing homes during this season as well, and the Easter Water with its powerful reminder of the baptismal covenant and ecclesial communion is most fittingly used for this blessing as well. By popular custom among many ethnic groups, and worthy of revival or introduction throughout the Church, is the practice of taking the Easter Water home from the Vigil celebration to be used for personal prayer and devotion in the setting of "the domestic church" of the household. Cf. CCC 1217-1222

Eastern Churches (EES-tern TSHERTSH-ehz): That division or group of four Churches tracing their origin to the original four patriarchates of Jerusalem, Antioch, Alexandria, and Constantinople (Byzantium), and distinct from the Western Church of Rome, the fifth original patriarchate. To the Antiochene Church belong the West Syrians, Maronites, and Malankarese, as well as the Chaldeans (Iraqi and Malabarese) and Armenians. To the Alexandrian Church belong Coptic and Geez Ethiopians. The largest of the Eastern Churches is the Byzantine, among whom are Greeks, Bulgarians, Georgians, Italo-Albanians, Syrians (Melkite and Arab), Russians, Ruthenians, Ukrainians, Rumanians, Croatians, Yugoslavs, Estonians, Hungarians, and Serbs. All of the Eastern Churches, Orthodox and Catholic, have communities and jurisdictions permanently established in the United States. The Eastern Schism in 1054 separated Constantinople from Rome and marked a major break in Christian unity that persists to our own time. Earlier schisms involving the Nestorians, Armenians, Coptics, and Syrian Jacobite Churches have also contributed to the scandal of Christian disunity. There have been major reunions of Eastern Orthodox Churches with the Church of Rome in centuries past, chief of these being the Union of Brest-Litovsk in 1596 among the Ukrainians and the Union of Uzhorod in 1646 among the Ruthenians. These and other reunions have earned in the eyes of Orthodox the pejorative term "Uniates" for Eastern Catholics. The Orthodox view the reunions as a submission, or surrender, to Latinism, a sacrifice of one's patrimony and native religious heritage for an artificial unity. Nonetheless, Eastern Catholics and Orthodox share a common tradition that includes for Roman Catholics as well a valid sacramental system, orthodox moral teachings, a deep devotion to the Mother of God, and the indelible stamp of the genius of the Eastern Fathers of the Church: Ignatius, Ephrem, Athanasius, Cyril of Jerusalem, Cyril of Alexandria, Gregory of Nyssa, Basil, Gregory Nazianzus, John Chrysostom, and John Damascene. Christian theology and monasticism began in the East before being adopted and modified in the West. For nine hundred years every ecumenical council took place in the East. Prayers borrowed from the Eastern liturgies — the Kyrie, the *Gloria*, the Nicene Creed, and others — are still in use today in the Roman liturgy. The Eastern Churches are rich in symbolism, mysticism, and a deep sense of the transcendence of God. The Eastern Churches are organized under a system of collegiality. Local autonomy is emphasized, with the role of the local bishop stressed. The Church is seen as a theophany, i.e., the manifestation of the eternal in time, an unfolding of the divine life through the deifying transformation of humanity in worship and sacrament. Life in the Eastern Churches is spoken of in terms of glory, light, vision, union, and transfiguration. The decree of the Second Vatican Council on the Eastern Churches emphasizes their equality with the Church of the West and enjoins Eastern Catholics to know and preserve their unique heritage while urging Westerners to become familiar with and to respect the rites, discipline, doctrine, history, and characteristics of Easterners. Cf. CCC 247, 838

Eastern Churches, Decree on the Catholic: See *Orientalium Ecclesiarum*

Eastern Monasticism (EES-tern muh-NA-stih-sih-zuhm): Christian monasticism originated in the East in early third-century Egypt when St. Antony (A.D. 251-356) sold all his possessions and went into the desert to follow Christ more perfectly. When he attracted followers, he organized them into a community of hermits under a rule (later formulated as the Rule of St. Pachomius). The Eastern models were imitated in the West by John Cassian and St. Martin of Tours. While Western monasticism came eventually to be shaped by St. Benedict's adaptation of Eastern models, in the East it was the Rule of St. Basil the Great (mid-fourth century) that had the widest influence. Eastern monasticism evolved into two principal forms: cenobitic (large communities living under one roof) and idiorhythmic (groups of individuals living in separate quarters and coming together for meals and prayer). Monasticism flourished in the Byzantine world, spreading from Greece to Russia and the Slavic countries. Despite persecution, monasticism remained a powerful force throughout the Communist period and has now emerged as an important source of Christian renewal in Eastern Europe.

Eastern Rites: See Rites, Byzantine, etc.

Eastern Studies, Pontifical Institute of (pahn-TIH-fih-kuhl IHN-stih-tööt uhv EES-tern STUH-deez): Founded in 1917 near the Basilica of St. Mary Major in Rome by Pope Benedict XV, this house of studies specializes in disciplines particular to the Catholic and Orthodox Eastern Churches. The Society of Jesus directs the institute in affiliation with the Gregorian University.

Ebionites (EH-bee-o-naits): Jewish converts to Christianity who believed that Christians were still bound by the law of the O.T. They were absorbed by Gnostics by the fourth century. **Cf. CCC 1963-1968**

Ecce Homo (EH-tshay HO-mo): (Latin: "Behold the man") Words used by Pontius Pilate when he displayed Christ to the Jewish populace after having had Him scourged and crowned with thorns (Jn 19:5).

Ecclesia (eh-KLAY-zee-uh): The Latin transliteration of the Greek word *ekklesia,* referring in the N.T. to the Church, either local (e.g., Acts 5:11) or universal (e.g., Acts 9:31). The use of the term in this sense seems to originate chiefly with the Septuagint translation of the Hebrew term *kahal* (referring to the gathering of God's people for the purpose of worship) by means of the Greek word *ekklesia*. CCC 751-752

Ecclesiam Suam (eh-KLAY-zee-ahm SÖÖ-ahm): The first encyclical letter to be written by Pope Paul VI. Its purpose was to share "three thoughts" about the Church with the bishops then meeting for the Second Vatican Council. These three points are: (1) that the Church should be more aware of her origin, nature, mission, and destiny; (2) that the Church should lead her members to a greater perfection in living the Christian life; (3) that the Church should seek to present the Gospel to the world in new and more effective ways.

Ecclesiastes, Book of (BØØK uhv eh-KLEE-zee-AS-teez): A sapiential book of the O.T., also known as Qoheleth (meaning "member of the religious assembly"), written in the third century B.C. and accepted as canonical by both Jews and Christians. The book emphasizes the vanity of merely human desires and achievements. Wisdom consists in moderate pursuit of the good things of this world.

Ecclesiastic (eh-KLEE-zee-A-stihk): An informal term used to describe a cleric or member of the clergy. Cf. CCC 934

Ecclesiastical (eh-KLEE-zee-A-stih-kuhl): A term describing something or someone pertaining to or connected with the Church.

Ecclesiastical Law (eh-KLEE-zee-A-stih-kuhl LAW): Church or Canon Law that is enacted by competent Church authority, as opposed to divine or natural law. Ecclesiastical law includes disciplinary, liturgical, procedural, and penal laws. Cf. CCC 2037-2043

Ecclesiastical Regions (eh-KLEE-zee-A-stih-kuhl REE-dzhuhnz): Groupings of neighboring ecclesiastical provinces for purposes of fostering common pastoral action. They are created by the Holy See but have no preeminent see as with provinces.

Ecclesiastical Titles (eh-KLEE-zee-A-stih-kuhl TAI-tuhlz): The following titles are the standard forms for referring to ecclesiastical persons in the English language: The Pope: His Holiness, Pope N. (with number); (in speaking: Your Holiness); Cardinals: His Eminence, N. Cardinal N. (in speaking: Your Eminence); Archbishops and Bishops: His Excellency, The Most Reverend N. N., [Arch]Bishop of N. (in speaking: Your Excellency); Abbots: The Very Reverend Abbot N. N. (in speaking: Father Abbot); Monsignori: The Reverend Monsignor N. N. (in speaking: Monsignor); Priests: The Reverend [Father] N. N. (in speaking: Father); Abbess or Superior of Religious Women: [Reverend] Mother N. N. (in speaking: Sister or Mother). (See also Appendix IV.)

Ecclesiasticus: See Sirach

Ecclesiology (eh-KLEE-zee-AHL-uh-dzhee): The study of the Church's nature, mission, and structures as revealed in Scripture, apostolic writings, conciliar documents, etc. Cf. CCC 751-780

École Biblique (ay-KOL bih-BLEEK): An institute for advanced biblical studies conducted by the French Dominicans in Jerusalem. Founded in 1890 by Fr. Marie-Joseph Lagrange, O.P., the school is noted for its publication of a series of scholarly studies of the Bible, for its immensely popular *Jerusalem Bible*, and for its quarterly journal, the *Revue Biblique*.

Economic Affairs, Prefecture of (PREE-fehk-tsher uhv eh-kuh-NAH-mihk uh-FEHRZ): A commission of the Vatican, established by Pope Paul VI in 1967. The membership of this prefecture is comprised of at least five cardinals who oversee the finances, investments, and properties of the Holy See.

Economics (eh-kuh-NAH-mihks): The branch of the social sciences devoted to the study of commerce, goods, services, spending, labor, and output. The Church encourages governments and individuals to work for a deeper understanding of the economy and for material prosperity that aims at advancing the social welfare of all peoples. **Cf. CCC 2420-2436**

Economy, Divine (dih-VAIN ee-KAH-nuh-mee): The fulfillment of God's plan of salvation, fully developed in His divine mind from eternity, and fully revealed in Jesus Christ. Before the Incarnation it was known only obscurely, but after the ascension of Christ and the coming of the Holy Spirit at Pentecost, it is the substance of that apostolic preaching which is preserved in its integrity for each generation. **CCC 56, 66, 122, 260, 489, 705**

Ecstasy (EHK-stuh-see): The state of "standing outside oneself," or the elevation of the soul above the senses, which is the effect of the Holy Spirit giving a person in prayer an experience of union with God. In Sacred Scripture ecstasy accompanies the communication of God's Word to the prophets, and in the N.T., both St. Peter and St. Paul are said to have gone into ecstasy while praying (Acts 10:10; 22:17). In Christian mysticism, ecstasy is a temporary state that accompanies contemplative prayer; it is an intense, though passing, awareness of the soul's union with God, which may be either pleasant (as when sensory awareness is gently suspended) or painful (as when the soul is suddenly "seized away" from its senses). A person in ecstasy is usually radiant in the face and unaware of anything around him (including things touching him). Ecstasy is a by-product of prayer, whose object is not to produce an experience but to progress in the love of God. Deliberate attempts to produce ecstasy (as in Transcendental Meditation) are not consistent with Christian prayer, and they may be both psychologically and spiritually dangerous.

Ecthesis (ehk-THEE-sihs): (Greek, *ekthesis:* a statement of faith) The formula issued in A.D. 638 asserting that the two natures of Christ were united in a single will. Although it was accepted by the Councils held in Constantinople in 638 and 639, it was subsequently condemned by Pope Severinus (638-640) and Pope John IV (640-642) as being heretical.

Ecumenical Councils: See Councils, Ecumenical

Ecumenical Theology (ehk-yöö-MEH-nih-kuhl thee-AHL-uh-dzhee): (Greek-Latin, from Greek *oikoumene:* inhabited world) Term referring to a variety of approaches to the theology and relationship among the various Christian Churches and denominations. This can be thematic (the study of those doctrinal disagreements that have divided Christians), procedural (reflecting the diversity of Christian traditions), or a combination of both. Its purpose is to pursue a dialogue, with the hope of achieving institutional unity among Christians. CCC 816-822, 855, 1271, 1636

Ecumenism (ehk-yöö-MEH-nihzm): The movement of Christians and their churches toward the unity willed by Christ. The Second Vatican Council called the movement "those activities and enterprises which, according to various needs of the Church and opportune occasions, are started and organized for the fostering of unity among Christians" (Decree on Ecumenism, n. 4). Spiritual ecumenism, i.e., mutual prayer for unity, is the heart of the movement. The movement also involves scholarly and pew-level efforts for the development of mutual understanding and better interfaith relations in general, and collaboration by the churches and their members in the social area. CCC 816, 819-822

Ecumenism, Decree on: See Unitatis Redintegratio

Eden, Garden of (GAHR-dehn uhv EE-dehn): The beautiful place of happiness that Adam and Eve inhabited before the Fall. Meaning "prairie" or "steppe," Eden has not been definitively located by modern scholars.

Edict of Milan (EE-dihkt uhv mih-LAHN): An agreement reached in A.D. 313 between the Roman co-emperors Constantine I and Licinius, according to which Christianity was permitted to exist as one of the sects tolerated within the Empire. In effect, this agreement brought official Roman persecution of Christians to an end.

Edict of Nantes (EE-dihkt uhv NAHNT): An agreement between the French Huguenots and the monarchy in 1598, restoring the rights of Catholic clergy and guaranteeing freedom of worship to the Huguenots.

Edict of Restitution (EE-dihkt uhv reh-stih-TÖÖ-shuhn): A decree issued in 1629 by the Holy Roman Emperor Ferdinand II, providing for the restitution of all church property confiscated during the Reformation, the proscription of all Protestants except Lutherans of the Augsburg Confession, and the reaffirmation of the principle of *cuius regio, eius religio* (local option on religion).

Edification, Christian (KRIHS-tshuhn eh-dih-fih-KAY-shuhn): Edification, or upbuilding, draws on the Pauline metaphor of the Church as the temple of the Holy Spirit (1 Cor 13:16), an edifice of living stones (Eph 4:1-6, 25-32). Each member of the Church contributes to the edification of other members through example, mutual support, and instruction. Cf. CCC 791, 798-801, 872, 951, 2045

Editio Typica (eh-DIHT-see-o TIH-pee-kuh): Latin term for the official version or original, authoritative, and legally binding text of an ecclesiastical document.

Efficacious Grace (eh-fih-KAY-shuhs GRAYS): The actual grace given by God in which the individual freely consents; hence, the desired result is achieved. Báñez and the Dominicans contended that the efficacy of the grace depended on the grace *per se,* while Molina and the Jesuits asserted that efficacious grace is granted in accord with the receptivity of the recipient; however, both agreed that the act of the will was not necessary. CCC 2000

Eileton (ay-LEH-tahn): In the Byzantine Rite, a piece of linen spread out on a consecrated altar beneath the chalice and the paten. It is now generally replaced by the Antimension (q.v.), but its name is retained by the outer wrapping of the Antimension.

Ejaculation (ee-JAK-yöö-LAY-shuhn): A short prayer, usually a phrase or brief sentence, prayed frequently from memory. When the Psalter became less known by laypersons, prayers such as the Our Father, Hail Mary, and ejaculations took their place as the staple of the way to fulfill the injunction to "pray always." Early examples include: "Have mercy on me, God; Forgive me my sins, Lord," "My Lord and my God," "My Jesus, mercy." The revised edition of the *Enchiridion* (Handbook) *of Indulgences* (Latin, third edition, 1986; English translation, 1969), which replaced the *Raccolta*, contains many examples of ejaculations. **Cf. CCC 2625, 2766**

Ekphonese (ehk-FOH-nuh-see): In Eastern churches, the elevating of the priest's voice at the end of certain prayers, or the parts of these prayers that are said aloud.

Ektene (ehk-TEH-nay): A litany. There are two Ektenes recited during the celebration of the Divine Liturgy in the Byzantine Rite.

Elect (eh-LEHKT): According to the Bible, those chosen before all time by God to live with Him in holiness and blamelessness. The eternal decree of God receives historical expression in the election of Abraham and reaches its definitive manifestation in the person of Christ and in the Church. Divine election itself flows from the eternal divine plan to reconcile all things for the glory of God. The elect participate in this plan and are drawn into its realization. **Cf. CCC 1031, 1045, 1344, 1994**

Election, Canonical (ka-NAH-nih-kuhl eh-LEHK-shuhn): A means of providing for ecclesiastical offices or positions, whereby certain qualified people cast votes for a candidate. Most elections take place in the context of religious institutes; however, there are provisions in Canon Law for certain other elections, the most important one being the election of a Pope.

Election, Papal (PAY-puhl eh-LEHK-shuhn): Regulated by Canon Law and other directives from the Holy See, this process involves electing a new Pope. Those cardinals under age eighty are locked in "conclave" and vote by way of secret ballot. To be elected, the candidate must receive two-thirds plus one vote and must accept the office.

Eleemosynary Office (eh-leh-MOH-sih-ner-ee AW-fihs): An office in the Vatican that assists in minor charitable projects carried on by the Holy See. Through this office the popular papal blessings are administered.

Elevation at Mass (eh-leh-VAY-shuhn at MAS): The present Order of Mass states that at the beginning of the institution narrative, the priest takes the bread, "raising it a little above the altar," and that after the words "This is my body which will be given up for you," he "shows the consecrated host to the people, places it on the paten, and genuflects in adoration." He does the same with the chalice. Before the doxology at the end of the Eucharistic Prayer the priest "takes the chalice and the paten with the host and, lifting them up, sings or says, 'Through him, with him, in him. . . .' " The 2000 revised edition of the *Institutio Generalis (General Instruction of the Roman Missal)* states that "depending on local custom [the server] also rings the bell at the showing of both the host and the chalice" (n. 150). In addition, the 2000 revision of the *General Instruction* states that one of the places where incense may be used is "at the showing of the Eucharistic Bread and chalice after the consecration" (n. 276). Cf. CCC 948

Elizabethan Settlement (ee-LIH-zuh-BEE-thuhn SEH-tuhl-mehnt): A series of legislative provisions enacted under Elizabeth I of England (sixteenth century), solidifying the position of the Anglican Church.

Elkesaites (EHL-kuh-saits): A second-century heretical group of Jewish Christians whose name derives from the Book of Elkesai. Like other such groups, the Elkesaites regarded Jesus as merely one of the prophets. Frequent purification by water baths and washings seems to have been a central ritual.

Elne, Council of (KAUN-sihl uhv EHLN): The "Truce of God" was proclaimed by a canon of this council held southwest of Marseilles in 1027. It prohibited hostile engagements between Saturday night and Monday morning.

Elvira, Council of (KAUN-sihl uhv ehl-VAI-ruh): The earliest Spanish ecclesiastical council recorded (A.D. 304).

Ember Days (EHM-ber DAYZ): These were the Wednesdays, Fridays, and Saturdays of four weeks of the year on which fast and abstinence were required for the universal Church in preconciliar custom and liturgical legislation. Their origins are difficult to define precisely. Controverted matters include whether there were three or four originally and whether they originally corresponded with the four seasons of the calendar. The 1969 *General Norms for the Liturgical Year and the Calendar* describes Ember Days as days on which "the practice of the Church is to offer prayers to the Lord for the needs of all people, especially for the productivity of the earth and for human labor, and to give him public thanks" (n. 45). The local conference of bishops is to determine the "time and plan of their celebration" (n. 46). "On each day of these celebrations the Mass should be one of the votive Masses for various needs and occasions that is best suited to the intentions of the petitioners" (n. 47).

Emblems of Saints (EHM-blehmz uhv SAYNTS): In Christian iconography, a system of symbols by which to depict and recognize particular saints through distinctive emblems. In the first place, Christ Himself is associated with such symbols as the fish, the instruments of His passion (cross, nails, crown of thorns), and so on. Perhaps the most common emblem of Mary is the *fleur-de-lis,* while the lily or carpenter tools are associated with St. Joseph. The four Evangelists are known by symbols: St. Matthew by a winged man, St. Mark by a winged lion, St. Luke by an ox, and St. John by an eagle. There are many other such emblems.

Embolism (EHM-bo-lih-zuhm): At the celebration of the Eucharist, the rites introducing the reception of Communion include the recitation of the Lord's Prayer, the embolism, the doxology, the sign of peace, and the Lamb of God. The embolism derives from and offers a fuller development of some part of the Our Father. An important Roman example of the embolism, the *Libera,* may well date from the time of St. Gregory the Great; in it the Apostles Andrew, Peter, and Paul are asked to intercede for the present congregation, along with "the blessed and glorious ever-virgin Mary, Mother of God," so that the faithful may enjoy peace as they come to share in the Eucharist. Many Eastern Rites add similar extensions of the Lord's Prayer. Liturgical tradition attests to the use of a variety of tests at this point. The present *General Instruction of the Roman Missal* notes that the embolism beginning with "Deliver us . . ." is said by the priest with the congregation participating in the concluding doxology, "For the kingdom, the power, and the glory are yours. . . ." "The embolism, developing the last petition of the Lord's Prayer, begs on behalf of the entire community of the faithful deliverance from the power of evil" (n. 81).

Eminence (EH-mih-nehns): This is the proper form of address afforded to cardinals of the Roman Church. The only exception to this is the Grand Master of the Knights of St. John of Jerusalem, who is also addressed as "Eminence." Once used to address German ecclesiastical prince-electors, the title was first bestowed on cardinals by Pope Urban VIII in a 1630 decree.

Emmanuel or Immanuel (ec-MAN yöo-ehl): Hebrew for "God [is] with us" or "[may] God [be] with us" (Is 7:14, 8:8). In Matthew's Gospel, the name is given to Christ and is traditionally construed as a prediction of the virgin birth of Jesus (Mt 1:23). **CCC 744**

Empire, Holy Roman (HO-lee RO-muhn EHM-pair): The Empire in the West, dating from the coronation of Charlemagne by Pope St. Leo III on Christmas Day in 800 and enduring until the defeat of Francis II by Napoleon in 1806. During its thousand-year existence, the Empire was comprised of territories of varying extent and was led by emperors of fluctuating influence. Not all the emperors were actually crowned by the Pope. After 1440, the emperors were members of the Hapsburg dynasty and increasingly concerned themselves with German affairs.

Enchiridion (ehn-kih-RIH-dee-ahn): (From Greek *encheiridion:* in hand or close at hand) A reference manual divided according to subject matter. Of particular noteworthiness are: (1) the *Enchiridion of Indulgences,* a listing of all the indulgences granted by the Church to the faithful for certain prayers, devotions, pious practices, and charitable works; (2) the *Enchiridion of Symbols, Definitions, and Declarations Concerning Faith and Morals,* a compilation of ecclesiastical symbols, creeds, and papal declarations; (3) the *"Enchiridion Patristicum,"* a collection of the most important sayings of the Church Fathers, especially St. Augustine.

Enclosure (ehn-KLO-zher): Also known as cloister, it is the practice of setting aside part of a religious house for the sole use of its residents, ensuring privacy in prayer and study (Can. 667). Though enclosures vary in degree from one religious enclave to another, their purpose is to protect a community's way of life. Withdrawn from the world, cloistered nuns and other religious carry out their special vocation of prayer, work, and study.

Encratism (EHN-kruh-tih-zuhm) or Encratites (EHN-kruh-taits): (Latin *encratita* from Greek *enkrates:* self-discipline) An early movement of ascetic Christian sects demanding that their followers not eat meat, drink wine, or — in some cases — marry. The Encratites wrote many "gospels" and "acts" that are apocryphal (i.e., not divinely inspired).

Encyclical (ehn-SIHK-lih-kuhl): The highest form of papal teaching document, generally addressed to all the bishops and/or to all the faithful.

Encyclical Epistle or Letter: See Encyclical

Encyclicals, Social (SO-shuhl ehn-SIHK-lih-kuhlz): Apostolic letters from the Popes, beginning with *Rerum Novarum* of Pope Leo XIII in 1891, which have addressed the social ills of the day and various components of the economy: poverty, fair wages, capitalism, socialism, just working conditions, relations with labor management, inequalities, etc. The Church has great concern that families, workers, employers, and society as a whole will benefit in the current complex economic situation.

Encyclopedists (en-sai-klo-PEE-dihsts): The writers of the French Encyclopedia (1751-1765), containing the "advanced" ideas of the Enlightenment Period, contributing to the secularization of European Christian culture.

End (EHND): In philosophical and theological terms, that for which something exists or is done, or that for which an agent acts or an action occurs. The ultimate end of a thing or action is the final good that it is intended to achieve.

End Justifying the Means (EHND JUHS-tih-fai-ihng *th*uh MEENZ): Unacceptable ethical principle stating that evil means may be used to produce good effects. Cf. CCC 1753, 1759

End of Man (EHND uhv MAN): The goal of the human person, i.e., the encounter with God in heaven (beatific vision), which will last forever. Only by faithfully accepting God's will can one eventually enjoy this reality, which is the "new creation" referred to by Scripture. CCC 260, 356, 1024

End of the World (EHND uhv *th*uh WERLD): The final reality whereby the earth will pass away. The time and method by which this will occur is unknown; however, the certainty of the Last Judgment and the fact that Christ will continue to reign forever is verified in the Scriptures and Tradition. CCC 682, 686, 865, 1042, 1048, 1059

Endowment (ehn-DAU-mehnt): A gift of property, usually cash or securities, but including land, made to an official Church institution.

Ends of the Mass (EHNDZ uhv *th*uh MAS): Each Mass, regardless of specific intention, has four purposes: adoration, contrition, petition, and thanksgiving.

Energumen (ehn-er-GÖÖ-mehn): A demoniac; one possessed by evil spirits. Cf. CCC 550, 1673

English Martyrs (IHNG-lihsh MAHR-ters): About four hundred martyrs of England and Wales who gave their lives rather than deny their faith during the reigns of Henry VIII (1509-1547), Elizabeth I (1558-1603), James I (1604-1635), Charles I (1625-1649), and Charles II (1660-1685). Most were executed for treason, for their refusal to accept the conferral of the headship of the Church upon the British monarch and the proscription of the celebration of Mass. The most famous canonized martyrs are St. John Fisher and St. Thomas More. Many have been beatified, and some are under consideration for canonization.

Enkolpion (ehn-KOL-pee-ahn): (Greek: on the breast) A medallion suspended on a chain around the neck of a Byzantine Rite bishop, having on it an icon of the Blessed Virgin or of Christ.

Enlightenment, The Age of (*thee* AYDZH uhv ehn-LAI-tehn-mehnt): A broad intellectual movement that emerged in the eighteenth century and transformed Western culture and thought. A rejection of the role of tradition or authority and an exaltation of human reason are perhaps the most characteristic of the many strands that went together to make the Enlightenment. The Enlightenment movement was perceived to be in conflict with Christianity because many of its chief figures espoused the view that the central tenets of religion could be derived through rational reflection without the aid of revelation. Individualism in social life and autonomy in moral existence were other influential tenets of the movement.

Entelechy (ehn-TEHL-uh-kee): (Greek: actuality) In Aristotelian philosophy, a term used to describe the soul, as giving purpose and direction to the body. It is complete actuality, as distinguished from potentiality.

Enthronement of the Sacred Heart (ehn-THRON-mehnt uhv *th*uh SAY-krehd HAHRT): A ceremony in which an image of the Sacred Heart of Jesus is enshrined in the home. Fr. Mateo Crawley-Boevey initiated this practice, often employing hymns and prayers, which was approved by Pope

St. Pius X in 1907 and introduced in the United States in 1913.

Enthusiasm, Catholic (KATH-uh-lihk ehn-THÖÖ-zee-a-zuhm): A variety of movements in the history of the Church stressing the experience and activity of the Holy Spirit in the believer's life. When subject to lawful ecclesiastical authority, it has been the occasion of renewal in the Church.

Entrance Antiphon/Song (EIIN-trchns AN-rih-fahn/ SAWNG): Formerly known simply as the "Introit," the Vatican II Missal restores this chant to its more ancient title and form. Now called the *antiphona ad introitum* (entrance antiphon or song), it is clearly seen as a refrain to the psalm that accompanies the entrance of the celebrant and his ministers. In the Missal (Sacramentary) and people's participation booklets, only the antiphon (or refrain) itself is given, the complete psalm being found in a separate publication for the cantor called the *Roman Gradual* or its abridgment, the *Simple Gradual.*

Envy (EHN-vee): One of the seven capital sins characterized by pain and misery when one sees another prosper. Envy is a sin against charity and justice that makes some believe that by another's success, they themselves are losing something. CCC 2538-2540, 2553-2554

Eparch (EH-pahrk): A bishop enjoying canonical jurisdiction is called in the Byzantine Rite an eparch (diocesan bishop); his area of jurisdiction is called an eparchy (diocese).

Eparchy (EH-pahr-kee): This Byzantine term describes the portion of jurisdiction or territory over which a bishop or episcopal substitute has charge. The equivalent term in the Roman Rite is "diocese." The resident bishop is called an eparch.

Ephesians, Epistle to the (ih-PIH-suhl to *th*ee eh-FEE-zhuhnz): A letter to the Church at Ephesus, or more generally to the churches of Asia Minor, written by St. Paul (in the early A.D. 60s) or, more likely, by one of his disciples or associates (and dating from sometime in the second half of the first century). The letter contains a masterful summary of Paul's teaching about Christ: The divine plan that all things will be reconciled to the Father in Christ (1:10), hidden in God prior to creation (1:4), has now been revealed to the Apostles and prophets (3:5) and accomplished through Christ's death and resurrection.

Ephesus, Council of (KAUN-suhl uhv EH-feh-suhs): The third ecumenical council (A.D. 431), convened by Emperor Theodosius II in response to the Nestorian and Pelagian heresies.

Ephesus, Robber Council of (RAH-ber KAUN-suhl uhv EH-feh-suhs): A council convened by Emperor Theodosius in A.D. 451 but not attended by the Pope. The heretical bishop Dioscorus seized control and forced through several Nestorian decrees. The council was later repudiated by the Council of Chalcedon.

Epiclesis (eh-puh-KLEE-sihs): The calling down of the Holy Spirit upon the Holy Gifts after the Consecration in the Eastern Liturgy and before the Consecration in the Roman Rite. **CCC 1105-1106, 1109, 1353**

Epieikeia (EH-pee-ai-KAI-yuh): (Greek: reasonableness) Interpretation of law that presumes it is not applicable in a case of hardship (e.g., a mother missing Sunday Mass to care for a sick child).

Epigonation (eh-pee-go-NAHT-ee-ahn): In the Eastern Church, a diamond-shaped board covered with cloth and adorned with a cross, worn by ecclesiastics as a sign of dignity. The epigonation is worn by pastors and priests of higher rank. It symbolizes the sword of power.

Epimanikia (eh-pee-mah-nee-KEE-uh): In the Eastern Church, a pair of stiff embroidered cuffs, laced on one side, worn by the priest over the sleeves of the sticharion.

Epiphany (eh-PIH-fuh-nee): (From Greek *epiphaneia:* manifestation) 1. A term that refers principally to the feast occurring on January 6 (or on the Sunday falling closest to this date) and commemorating the manifestation of Christ to the whole world as represented by the Magi from the East (Mt 2:1-12). 2. In the Eastern Churches, the feast is associated chiefly with the manifestation of Christ at His Baptism in the Jordan. CCC 528, 1171

Episcopacy (ih-PIHS-kuh-puh-see): A term for the office of bishop. CCC 1536, 1554

Episcopalians (ih-pihs-kuh-PAY-lee-uhnz): Members of the Episcopal Church in the United States (formerly the Protestant Episcopal Church). This church is associated with the worldwide Anglican Communion stemming from the establishment of the Church of England during the reigns of Henry VIII (1509-1547) and Elizabeth I (1558-1603). The modifier "episcopal" distinguishes American Anglicans from Protestant denominations whose polity does not include bishops. The Episcopal Church in America dates from the General Convention of Philadelphia in 1789, which recognized Samuel Seabury as first bishop. In doctrine, the church accepts the Nicene-Constantinopolitan Creed and a modified version of the Thirty-Nine Articles. There exists a wide latitude of expression in matters of liturgy and theology. The Book of Common Prayer is the basis of worship. Governance is by a triennial general convention composed of the House of Bishops and the House of Deputies. The General Convention elects the Presiding Bishop, who is the chief officer of the church. Local dioceses are headed by bishops.

Episcopalism (ih-PIHS-kuh-puhl-ih-zuhm): An ecclesiological theory holding that supreme authority within the Church resides within the body of bishops independent of the Holy See. Expressed in such movements as conciliarism in the Middle Ages, as well as in Gallicanism in seventeenth-century France, this theory should be clearly distinguished from the doctrine of episcopal collegiality propounded at the Second Vatican Council. According to the Council, the College of Bishops exercises its authority as a group only when acting in union with the Pope as head.

Episcopal Vicar (ih-PIHS-kuh-puhl VIH-ker): A priest appointed by a bishop to exercise certain powers, similar to those of a vicar general but over a specific group of people or the people in a specific region.

Episcopate (ih-PIHS-kuh-puht): 1. Office, dignity, and sacramental powers bestowed on a bishop at ordination (cf. Episcopacy). 2. The body of bishops collectively. **CCC 857, 869, 883-885**

Epistle (ih-PIH-suhl): A type of letter, addressed to the general public and concerned with matters of common interest. While some of the books of the N.T. are clearly of an epistolary nature, it is difficult to apply the distinction rigidly. For this reason, the terms "letter" and "epistle" tend to be used interchangeably to designate the correspondence of Paul, Peter, John, and other inspired authors.

Epitaphion (eh-pee-TAH-fee-ahn): A representation of the Tomb of Christ, richly decorated and covered with flowers, solemnly venerated on Friday and Saturday of Holy Week in the Churches of the East.

Epitrachelion (eh-pee-truh-KEE-lee-ahn): In the Byzantine Rite, a stole sewn down along the middle with an opening on top for the head. The epitrachelion is part of the holy vestments of the priest, corresponding to the priestly stole of the Roman Rite. Normally, it is decorated with seven crosses, three on each side of the double band and one at the back of the neck, to symbolize the seven sacraments. The priest is required to wear the epitrachelion when administering any sacrament. It is the distinguishing vestment of a priest.

Equality (ee-KWAHL-uh-tee): The sameness in dignity that human beings enjoy because they are made in God's image. Each person has access to Christ's grace and forgiveness; however, not all will take advantage of these gifts. Equality does not entail sameness in function. For instance, man and woman are equal in God's sight but only men are called to Holy Orders because of the express will of Jesus. By virtue of complementarity, men and women have their distinctive but complementary roles in the Church. **CCC 369, 872, 1934-1935**

Equivocation (ee-kwih-vo-KAY-shun): 1. Use of words, phrases, or gestures having more than one meaning, in order to conceal information a questioner has no strict right to know — a form of mental reservation, permissible in some cases. 2. A lie, i.e., statement of untruth, intrinsically wrong. A lie told in joking, evident as such, is not wrong. **Cf. CCC 2471**

Erastianism (eh-RAS-tee-uhn-ih-zuhm): A sixteenth-century heresy developed by a Zwinglian, Thomas Erastus, that held that the State was the lawful superior of the Church. **CCC 2107-2109**

Error (EHR-er): From the Latin for losing one's way, a mistake, or blunder, not always culpable or sinful. **Cf. CCC 250, 1707, 1714**

Error and Marriage (EHR-er and MEHR-ehdzh): A mistaken judgment in the context of marriage that, if objective, can invalidate the marriage. Error can be about the person whom one is marrying, about a significant and unique quality of the person, or about the essential properties of marriage.

Error, Common (KAH-muhn EHR-er): The false belief existing among an identifiable community, such as a parish, that one lacking power of governance or faculties exercised an act of jurisdiction validly. The most common example is the false belief that a priest had power to hear confessions when in fact he did not, in which case confessions were still valid.

Eschatology (ehs-kuh-TAH-luh-dzhee): Christian doctrines and theology concerning the "end-times" or "last things" (*eschatos* in Greek), including the Second Coming of Christ *(parousia)*, death, the intermediate state (the condition of those who die before the general resurrection), the general resurrection, judgment, heaven, hell, purgatory, and so on. The end-times refer to the consummation of the divine plan of salvation, both for individuals and for the entire human race and cosmos. This consummation will mark the end of the world as we know it. According to the Scriptures, this final period has already begun with the birth of Christ, but it continues to unfold in the period after Christ's death and resurrection until He comes again. **CCC 676, 1186, 2771, 2776**

Espousal (eh-SPAU-zuhl): A promise of marriage, more popularly termed "engagement." In times past, such a promise to marry was the equivalent of a binding contract to marry. The promise to marry, however, does not carry with it the exercise of any rights of marriage, such as sexual intercourse. Use of the rights of marriage is gained only subsequent to the actual sacramental celebration of the contract of marriage.

Espousals of the Blessed Virgin: See Spouses of the Blessed Virgin Mary

Essence (EH-suhnts): The nature of a particular object, in contrast to its existence. The essence is the "whatness" of the object.

Essenes (eh-SEENZ): A Jewish ascetic group that lived a highly structured communal life in the desert near the Dead Sea from the second century B.C. to the second century A.D. Until the mid-twentieth century, little was known about the group beyond the information provided by Philo, Josephus, and Pliny the Elder. Our present knowledge of the Essenes stems from the discovery of a large collection of scrolls at Qumran (the Dead Sea Scrolls), which apparently represents a portion of their library. A three-year novitiate was required of those who sought to join the community. They practiced a form of Pharisaic Judaism, but pursued an austere regimen not unlike that associated with strict monastic orders in the Christian era.

Established Church (eh-STA-blihshd TSHERTSH): A Church recognized by law and supported by civil government as the official religious body of a nation, usually receiving some form of financial support.

Esther, Book of (BØØK uhv EHS-ter): This book of the O.T. tells of the events commemorated in the Jewish festival of Purim when Queen Esther saved her people from destruction in the time of Ahasuerus (Xerxes), king of Persia (485-465 B.C.). The Jewish heroine foiled the plot devised by Haman, a court official, to exterminate all the Jews. In turn, he and his accomplices were executed, and the Jews still in captivity in Persia were spared.

Eternity (ee-TER-nih-tee): 1. The reality defined as: (a) everlasting, continuing infinitely (e.g., the human soul); (b) timeless, having no boundaries of past and future. 2. In the Christian context, eternity is perfect everlasting life, viz., unending union with God. CCC 33, 488, 679

Ethics (EH-thihks): The systematic reflection on human goodness and righteousness along with human fulfillment and the role of the human person in decision-making. It analyzes the end of human existence, studies human acts, and defines the qualities that make one "complete." Ethics encourages one to live in freedom from outside pressures and to develop a truly upright character. Other realities like the social, political, economic, and medical fields also have an ethical component.

Ethics, Situation (sih-tshöö-AY-shuhn EH-thihks): The moral system, condemned by Pope Pius XII in 1952, that rejects moral norms and considers only circumstances and the agent's intention when determining the morality of a human act. Situation ethics fails to acknowledge normative principles of morality, the inherent nature of objects, the binding moral obligations that all encounter, and the limitation of "self" and the supposed good intention of the agent. American Joseph Fletcher was a chief proponent of situation ethics.

Ethiopian Church (ee-thee-O-pee-uhn TSHERTSH): One of the ancient Eastern Churches, having its roots in the Church of Alexandria. It did not accept the pronouncements of the Council of Chalcedon or any subsequent ecumenical councils; together with the Alexandrian Church, it was considered part of the Coptic (or Egyptian) Church. In 1959 it ended its dependence on the See of Alexandria and elected its own patriarch (Abuna). Through missionary efforts in the nineteenth and twentieth centuries, many Ethiopian Christians were reunited with the Holy See under the jurisdiction of the Catholic Archbishop of Addis Ababa.

Eucharist (YÖÖ-kuh-rihst): (From Greek *eucharistia:* thanksgiving) The sacrament of the Body, Blood, Soul, and Divinity of Jesus Christ really, truly, and substantially present under the appearances of bread and wine. The Eucharist was instituted by Jesus at the Last Supper. The bread and wine are changed by transubstantiation (q.v.). The Holy Eucharist is the primary act of worship of the Catholic Church in which Christ perpetuates the sacrifice of the cross; the Church, in turn, offers herself with Jesus to the Father in the unity of the Holy Spirit. The Blessed Sacrament is to be adored with the same worship due God. CCC 1373-1381

Eucharist, Celebration of the (sehl-uh-BRAY-shuhn uhv *th*uh YÖÖ-kuh-rihst): The Church's action, known as the "Holy Sacrifice of the Mass," the "Eucharistic Liturgy," etc., by which the Sacrifice of Christ on Calvary is made present now. A validly ordained priest using proper matter and form and possessing the correct intention offers the same sacrifice (although in an "unbloody" manner) that Jesus offered to His Father in the Holy Spirit on Good Friday. CCC 1345-1355

Eucharistic Devotions (yöö-kuh-RIHS-tihk dee-VO-shuhnz): The postconciliar ritual and instruction regarding *Holy Communion and Worship of the Eucharist Outside Mass* (1973) appropriately places Eucharistic devotions in the context of instructions about the relationship between Eucharistic worship outside Mass and the celebration of the Eucharist, the purposes of Eucharistic reservation (the administration of Viaticum and adoration), and the forms of worship of the Eucharist. It asserts that "the Eucharistic sacrifice is the source and culmination of the whole Christian life" and that the cult of Eucharistic devotion "should be in harmony with the sacred liturgy in some sense, take their origin from the liturgy, and lead people back to the liturgy" (n. 79). Four forms of Eucharistic devotions derive from reserving the sacrament: exposition, benediction, processions, and congresses.

Eucharistic Congress: See Congresses, Eucharistic

Eucharistic Prayer (yöö-kuh-RIHS-tihk PREHRZ): The central rite of the Mass, which combines *anaphora* (Greek: elevation, lifting up); *oratio oblationis* (Latin: prayer of offering); *illatio* (Latin: contribution or sacrifice); *canon* (from Greek: rule or norm); *prex precis* (Latin: prayer of request); and *canon actionis* (Latin: rule of the action). Earliest evidence of the outline of the Eucharistic prayer (not the text itself) comes from the *Apostolic Tradition* of Hippolytus (d. 215). The fourth and fifth centuries saw important developments in both East and West toward establishing these texts, which formed the center of the Eucharistic celebration during which the bread and wine are changed into the Body and Blood of Christ. The structure of the prayer includes: thanksgiving, acclamation, epiclesis, narrative of the institution and consecration, anamnesis, offering, intercessions, and final doxology. CCC 1353-1354

Euchites (YÖÖ-kaits): A fourth-century mendicant community (also called Messalians or "men of prayer"), originating in Mesopotamia, who strove to live literally the Sermon on the Mount. They were eventually opposed by St. Basil the Great and St. Epiphanius and condemned by the Council of Ephesus (A.D. 431).

Euchologion (yöö-ko-LO-dzhee-ahn): The liturgical book of the Eastern Church containing the text and rubrics of the Liturgies of Sts. John Chrysostom and Basil the Great, and that of Lent. It also contains the permanent portions of the Office as well as the sacramental rites.

Eugenics (yöö-DZHEHN-ihks): (From Greek *eugenes,* well-born) Science of heredity and environment for the physical and mental improvement of offspring. Extreme eugenics is untenable in practice because it advocates immoral means: compulsory breeding, sterilization of the unfit, abortion, and unacceptable methods of birth regulation. **CCC 2268**

Eulogia (yöö-lo-DZHEE-uh): (Greek: praise) Unconsecrated bread used in an ancient practice still common in the Byzantine Church but discarded in the West. The unconsecrated bread is given to those too young or those not in the state of grace who were unable to receive Holy Communion at the Eucharistic celebration.

Eunomianism (yöö-NO-mee-uh-nihzm): An extreme type of Arianism formulated by Eunomius in the fourth century, which stressed that the Son is not only of a different essence from the Father, but that the Son is not strictly God. It is known also as Anomoeism (Greek *anomoios,* unlike) because it teaches that the Son is unlike the Father. Cf. **CCC 242, 248, 467**

Eusebians (yöö-SEE-bee-uhnz): People who took their name from Eusebius of Nicomedia (d. 342), who converted them from paganism to Arian Christianity. Although Eusebius accepted the anti-Arian creed of the Council of Nicaea (325), he refused to recognize the Council's excommunication of Arius, who had appealed personally to Eusebius for help. That same year, the Emperor Constantine deposed and banished Eusebius, presumably for his support of Arius. Within two years, however, the two were reconciled, and Eusebius became the emperor's primary ecclesiastical adviser. In fact, it was Eusebius who administered Constantine's deathbed Baptism. Constantine's heir, Constantius II, appointed Eusebius as Bishop of Constantinople.

Euthanasia, Active (AK-tihv YÖÖ-thuh-NAY-zhuh): (From Greek: easy death) The deliberate killing of a dying, disabled, or chronically ill person in order to end his or her suffering. Active euthanasia is the exploitation of the sick and dying and the murder of innocent human life, hence always immoral. Many today support active and passive euthanasia as being the "merciful" response to human suffering; yet euthanasia is still the usurping of the power of God, Who alone gives and takes life. CCC 2276-2279, 2324

Euthanasia, Passive (PA-sihv YÖÖ-thuh-NAY-zhuh): The deliberate killing of another by refusing to administer life-saving measures that are "ordinary" (i.e., non-risky, not excessively expensive or burdensome). To deny food and water is to be guilty of passive euthanasia. Euthanasia — passive or active — is the direct killing of another, which is always immoral, regardless of whether or not it is portrayed as being the "compassionate" thing to do. CCC 2276-2279, 2324

Eutychianism (yöö-TIHK-ee-uhn-ih-zuhm): A heresy similar to Monophysitism, which held that Christ had but one nature.

Evangeliarum (ay-VAHN-dzheh-lee-AH-røøm): Gospel book containing the four Gospels in their complete form or a book with the Gospel pericopes for Mass for each day of the year. The 1969 *Ordo Missae,* Order of Mass, envisions the use of two ceremonial books of readings at the Eucharist, one for the first and second readings (a Lectionary) and the other for the Gospels (the Gospel Book), the latter receiving the honor of being carried in procession by the deacon, placed on the altar at the entrance rite, and carried in procession with candles and incense to the lectern for proclamation.

Evangelical Counsels (ee-van-DZHEHL-ih-kuhl KAUN-suhlz): A theological term for poverty, chastity, and obedience, taken as vows or promises by members of institutes of consecrated life. CCC 903, 914-916, 918, 920, 925, 929, 931, 944, 1973-1974, 1986, 2053, 2103

Evangelical United Brethren (ee-van-DZHEHL-ih-kuhl yöö-NAI-tehd BREHTH-rehn): Broadly Methodist in doctrine, discipline, and polity, the Evangelical United Brethren Church merged in 1968 with the Methodist Church to form a single denomination as the United Methodist Church. The

Evangelical United Brethren Church was itself the outcome of a merger in 1946 joining two closely related groups, the United Brethren in Christ and the Evangelical Church. The United Brethren in Christ emerged in 1800 from the preaching activities of William Otterbein (1726-1813) and Martin Boehm (1725-1812) among the Germans of Pennsylvania, Maryland, and Virginia, while the Evangelical Church similarly grew in 1807 from the preaching of the formerly Lutheran Jacob Albright (1759-1808) among Germans in Pennsylvania. The Church of the United Brethren in Christ broke from this group because it opposed the constitutional changes of 1889 and continues as an independent denomination with nearly twenty thousand members. Some congregations of the Evangelical United Brethren Church rejected merger with the Methodist Church in 1968 and established the Evangelical Church in North America. But at that time seven hundred fifty thousand Evangelical United Brethren swelled the ranks forming the new United Methodist Church to make it, with about ten million members, the largest Methodist body in America.

Evangelion (eh-vahn-GEHL-ee-ahn): (Greek: good news) The proclamation of the "good news" at liturgy, or a text of the Gospels.

Evangelist (ee-VAN-dzhuh-lihst): (Greek *euangelistos:* one who announces good news) 1. Originally referring to one who proclaimed the Gospel in the Apostolic Age of the Church, it is most commonly used in reference to the four men whose names are associated with the Gospels of Matthew, Mark, Luke, and John. In Eph 4:11-12, the office of evangelist is listed with the Apostles and prophets for the purpose of "building up the body of Christ." 2. In current Protestant usage especially, any preacher of the Gospel.

Evangelization (ee-van-dzhuh-lih-ZAY-shuhn): (From Greek *euangelion:* good news) All those activities by which every member of the Church proclaims and presents to the world the saving message of the Gospel of Jesus Christ. **CCC 429, 848-856, 905, 927-933, 1072, 1122, 2044, 2225, 2472**

Evangelization of Peoples, Congregation for the (kahn-greh-GAY-shuhn for *thee* eh-van-dzhuh-lih-ZAY-shuhn uhv PEE-puhlz): Founded in 1622, and originally called the Congregation for the Propagation of the Faith, it is responsible for the coordination and direction of all missionary activities throughout the world, except for that which comes within the responsibility of the Congregation for the Eastern Churches.

Eve (EEV): The name of the first woman (Gn 3:20), who was called "the mother of all the living." She and Adam lost the happiness of the Garden of Eden through Original Sin. It was Mary who reversed Eve's disobedience by her obedience (St. Irenaeus). CCC 375, 399, 404, 411, 417, 489, 494, 726, 2618, 2853

Evil (EE-vuhl): The antithesis of good; whatever is harmful or contrary to what is moral or religious. Because God is perfectly good, He is never the direct cause of any evil; however, He sometimes permits occurrences that are evil as a matter of course in the universe, or in the exercise of man's free will. CCC 309-314, 401, 403, 407, 412, 549

Evolution (eh-vo-LOO-shuhn): A process of orderly change from a simple state to one of more complexity. Although this concept is applied to a variety of academic disciplines, it is most commonly used as a theory to explain the biological changes in organisms. To hold that such a process underlies the emergence of existing species and organisms is not contrary to the Catholic understanding of creation, provided that any theory of evolution does not deny that God brought all things into existence, and that He creates each individual soul. Cf. CCC 283-284

Exaltation of the Cross (ehks-awl-TAY-shuhn uhv *th*uh KRAWS): The liturgical festival of the Exaltation (now translated as the "triumph") of the Holy Cross on September 14 can be traced to two historical occurrences in the city of Jerusalem. The first was the dedication of the Constantinian basilica of the Holy Sepulchre on this date in the fourth century. The other event was the recovery of the True Cross from the Persians in the seventh century, which event prompted the declaration of this special feast. In the present form of the Roman Calendar, this day ranks as a feast, i.e., second in prominence in the ordering of liturgical days and seasons.

Examen (ehg-ZA-mehn): The daily examination of conscience done to root out sin and to "put on the Lord Jesus Christ." This discipline is crucial for one who desires sanctity. Cf. CCC 1435

Examination of Bishops (ehg-zam-uh-NAY-shuhn uhv BIH-shuhps): The section in the Rite of Ordination of a Bishop in which the bishop-elect answers specific questions directed at him by the principal consecrating bishop. He promises to be a faithful bishop by proclaiming the Gospel of Christ, upholding the teachings of the Church, obeying the Pope, building up the Church, sustaining the People of God, showing kindness to all, seeking out the lost, and praying constantly for all — until the end of his life.

Examination of Conscience (ehg-zam-uh-NAY-shuhn uhv KAHN-shehnts): The deliberate act of evaluating one's thoughts, desires, words, and actions with the purpose of amending one's life. Usually, the examination is performed before receiving the Sacrament of Penance, during the day (e.g., "particular examen," which focuses on a predominant fault, a virtue that should be obtained or a duty connected with one's vocation), or before retiring at night (e.g., "general examen," which considers the entire day and how one failed against God, self, and others). CCC 1385, 1427-1429, 1435, 1454, 1456, 1482, 1779

Examiners, Synodal (SIH-nuh-duhl ehg-ZAM-ih-nerz): Priests appointed by the bishop during a synod to conduct examinations of candidates for pastorates and Holy Orders. Mandatory in the 1917 Code of Canon Law, they are optional under the present code (Can. 469).

Exarch (EHG-zahrk): (Greek: guide) In the ancient Byzantine Empire, an exarch was the governor of an outlying province. In the Byzantine Church, this term came to be applied to the patriarch, and later to an archbishop, bishop, or other clergyman serving in the place of a bishop but without the power to ordain priests. Today this title is given to a priest who is not a bishop but who heads a church. The area of an exarch's jurisdiction is termed an "exarchate."

Excardination (ehks-kahr-dih-NAY shuhn): The canonical term for the act of officially separating a cleric from the diocese to which he is attached.

Ex Cathedra (ehks KATH-uh-druh): (Latin: from the throne) Term describing the most solemn and authoritative infallible statements of the Church. The First Vatican Council (1869-1870) declared that the Pope may teach infallibly when he speaks: (1) as the Supreme Pastor; (2) in virtue of his apostolic authority as St. Peter's successor; (3) in matters of faith and morals; (4) so as to bind the universal Church. **CCC 891**

Excellency, Your (yøør EHK-suh-lehn-see): The proper form of address in the Roman Church for bishops and archbishops, as well as ambassadors from other countries to and accredited by the Holy See. Over the course of time, "Your Lordship" and "Your Grace" have also been used, though less commonly.

Exclaustration (ehks-klaw-STRAY-shuhn): Canonical term for the act whereby a religious, with proper permission, lives outside his or her religious community while remaining a member.

Excommunication (ehks-kuh-myoo-nuh-KAY-shuhn): Canonical penalty whereby a Catholic is excluded from the Church. It can be incurred automatically for certain offenses or imposed by competent authority. **CCC 1463**

Exegesis (ehks-uh-DZHEE-zihs): (Greek: to bring out) Interpreting Sacred Scripture by using the various rules of hermeneutics (i.e., methodologies employing language, literary, and other skills). Exegesis, practiced from ancient times, is needed when a passage is unclear so as to understand — as much as possible — the original meaning of the sacred text. On the other hand, "exposition" is the determining of the passage's meaning for contemporary times. CCC 116, 119

Exegete (EHKS-uh-dzheet): One who practices "exegesis" (i.e., the interpretation of Sacred Scripture). Cf. Exegesis. CCC 119

Exemption (ehg-ZEHMP-shuhn): A privilege held by certain religious institutes whereby they are removed from the authority of the local bishop in matters of internal discipline and placed under the authority of the Holy See.

Exercises, Spiritual (SPIHR-ih-tshöö-uhl EHK-ser-saiz-ehz): A treatise of spiritual theology and practice composed by St. Ignatius Loyola (1491-1556), in order to guide souls in deepening the Christian life. Normally, one undertakes to practice the exercises over a period of thirty days of spiritual retreat under the guidance of a director. The four sets of exercises presented by St. Ignatius can then be distributed over a four-week period: consideration, first, of sin and its consequences *(deformata reformare);* second, the reign of Christ *(reformata conformare);* then, consideration of the "Two Standards," the passion of Christ *(conformata confirmare)* and the risen Christ *(confirmata transformare).* The mainstay of these exercises is the practice of meditation, keyed to these moments of spiritual development, and the recommendation of various ascetical rules for life. The first draft of this treatise dated from shortly after St. Ignatius' conversion, but he revised and amplified the text throughout his life. This work of mature and distilled practical wisdom has won a wide readership and the status of a spiritual classic.

Existence (ehg-ZIHS-tehnts): The state of being, as distinct from simply the capacity for being; corresponding to *esse* (*that* something is) rather than *essentia* (*what* something is).

Existence of God: See God

Existentialism (ehgz-uh-STEHN-shuhl-ih-zuhm): A philosophical system that emphasizes the existence and experience of the individual over more abstract concepts of reality.

Exodus (EHGZ-uh-duhs): The second book of the O.T., so named because it centers on the departure of the Jewish slaves from their captivity in Egypt. It tells the story of how the Jews came to be a nation and happened, after forty nomadic years, to occupy the territory, promised long before to Abraham, that they still claim as their own. The great hero of the book is Moses, whose life story is told in such great detail as to contrast sharply with the brevity of the narrative about the many centuries the Jews suffered in servitude in Egypt. Moses is traditionally regarded as the author of the book, and there can be no doubt that oral traditions from him and about him influenced the written narrative that we have. The book and the wisdom that it embodies had great political importance for the Jews. They kept alive as a unifying force the story of their oppression at the hands of the Egyptians; it nourished their conviction that they were God's chosen people, and that God had supported them both by sending plagues upon their enemies and by providentially feeding and guiding them in the desert. From the religious point of view, Exodus explained the origin of the great feast of Passover, the importance of monotheism, and the folly of the idolatrous and licentious religious practices of their pagan neighbors. The giving of the Ten Commandments in the desert has made a lasting impact on the moral education of many nations in the world. The Sabbath law showed both economic wisdom in its insistence on six days of labor and revealed a humane spirit in equally insisting on a strict day of rest. Other penal legislation, which may seem to us overly severe, was no doubt necessary for a people recently emancipated from slavery. From the covenant given after the Exodus grew the notion that a people is wisely governed when it recognizes its responsibility to the higher Power Who made the universe. A covenant (pact or treaty) had been made between God and Abraham, progenitor of the Jewish people: Its external sign was the rite of circumcision; its promised blessing was the multiplication of his offspring. It was broadened to include all the Jewish people through the revelation made to Moses: The external sign of God's special favor to them was the annual immolation of the paschal lamb at Passover; the promised blessing was the earthly prosperity of Israel. Christianity introduced the notion that people of all nationalities and races are beloved to God; all are offered a new covenant, for Christ established a theocracy embracing all men and women, promising to all who observed it the transcendental reward of everlasting life and happiness.

Ex Opere Operantis (ehks O-per-ay o-per-AHN-tis): (Latin: by the work of the doer) Term in sacramental theology meaning that the effectiveness of sacraments depends on the moral rectitude of the minister or participant. When it first evolved in the thirteenth century, this term was applied to rites of the O.T. in contrast with those of the N.T. **Cf. CCC 1128**

Ex Opere Operato (ehks O-per-ay o-per-AH-to): (Latin: by the work done) Term in sacramental theology meaning that sacraments are effective by means of the sacramental rite itself and not because of the worthiness of the minister or participant. **CCC 1128**

Exorcism (EHK-sor-sih-zuhm): Expelling of demons from persons or things. Known in the ancient world especially in Egypt or Mesopotamia (third century), exorcisms were performed by Jesus on those possessed (e.g., Mk 5:1-20). The Sacrament of Baptism contains an exorcism performed on the catechumen so as to usher in the reign of Christ into the heart of the individual.

Exorcist (EHK-sor-sihst): Until 1972, one of the traditional minor orders; in the present practice of the Church, a bishop may grant permission to certain priests in his diocese to perform exorcisms. According to the Code of Canon Law (Can. 1172), this specific permission is required for legitimacy, and the exorcist must be a priest "endowed with piety, knowledge, prudence, and integrity of life." **CCC 517, 550, 1237, 1673**

Experts (EHKS-perts): Persons with special knowledge in a particular field or science who may be called to testify in a canonical trial in order to assist the judge in establishing the truth.

Expiatory Penalty (EHKS-pee-uh-tor-ee PEH-nuhl-tee): A type of canonical penalty imposed for the commission of certain crimes. Unlike censures or medicinal penalties, expiatory penalties (formerly called vindictive penalties) seek more to punish the offender.

Exposition of the Blessed Sacrament (ehks-po-ZIH-shuhn uhv *thuh* BLEH-sehd SA-kruh-mehnt): The ceremony in which a priest or deacon removes the Sacred Host from the tabernacle and places It on the altar for adoration by the faithful. It is private when the Eucharist remains in the ciborium and the door of the tabernacle stays open. Solemn (public) exposition takes place when a large Host in the lunette of the monstrance is positioned for all adorers to see. Private or solemn adoration ceremonies have Scripture readings, hymns, prayers, and some time for silent adoration, followed by the blessing with the monstrance. The purpose of exposition is to highlight the presence of Christ in the Eucharist. The ceremony was introduced in the Middle Ages through the influence of the Feast of Corpus Christi in the thirteenth century. Some religious monasteries, convents, and other pious groups practice Eucharistic adoration for various periods of time.

Exsequatur (ehg-say-KWAH-tøør): (Latin: Let him act) The medieval practice whereby certain civil authorities claimed the right to approve ecclesiastical decrees before publication.

External Forum (ehks-TER-nuhl FOR-uhm): The public ordering of the Church as a society or the manner in which the powers of governance and judicial powers are exercised.

Extraordinary Form (ehk-STROR-duh-nehr-ee FORM): The manner of exchanging marriage vows without the presence of a sacred minister. The form is used under specific circumstances when no priest or deacon is available (cc. 1116 and 1117).

Extraordinary Medical Treatments (ehk-STROR-duh-nehr-ee MEH-dih-kuhl TREET-mehnts): Forms of life-sustaining care that are not usually required but could be if the common good demanded (e.g., a country's president is ill and could be helped by extraordinary treatments). Extraordinary care is either: (1) very painful; (2) excessively expensive; (3) doubtfully beneficial; or (4) extremely burdensome to the patient or to those responsible for him. CCC 2278-2279

Extreme Unction, Sacrament of: See Pastoral Care of the Sick

Exultet, also Exsultet (ehgs-UHL-teht): With the restoration of the rites of Holy Week effected by Pope Pius XII in 1956, this ancient hymn of praise of the risen Christ was reintroduced into the Easter Vigil Liturgy as it calls the entire Church — in heaven and on earth — and the whole world, including all creation, to rejoice in the Resurrection of the Lord. It is traditionally chanted by a deacon or, in his absence, by a priest but may also be sung by a layperson if a sacred minister lacks the musical ability to do justice to the piece.

Ezekiel (eh-ZEE-kee-uhl): One of the four major prophets (638?-568? B.C.), who lived in Jerusalem and exercised his priesthood through the religious revival under Josiah (640-610). But in his later years he beheld such moral corruption in Judah that the prophet warned of a coming fall of the nation. When Nebuchadnezzar attacked Jerusalem, Ezekiel was taken prisoner and exiled in 597. Thus his prophetical mission was to the exiles, extending from 592 to 570. He never ceased to teach the exiles that the catastrophe had come from a just God Who was punishing the nation and its citizens for their sins. Nevertheless, he retained his faith in the mercy and fidelity of the Lord and consoled the repentant with the hope of restoration from their exile. Much of his message is faithfully recorded in the forty-eight chapters of his book. An extrovert, he taught not merely by abstract words but also with parables, thought-provoking visions, dramatically symbolic actions. He defended the justice of God and pilloried the sins of princes and citizens alike. His love of his people did not blind him to their flagrant sins. Jerusalem had been an unfruitful vine (15:1-8), an ungrateful child (16:1-4), an unfaithful spouse, a harlot who paid her patrons (16:15-34), comparable to Sodom and Samaria.

Ezra (EHZ-ruh): The Vulgate contains two biblical books under the name of Ezra, but modern authorities list the second of these under the name of Nehemiah. Both men returned from the exile after the first return of the sixth century, Ezra in 458 B.C. (or 428 or 398) and Nehemiah in 445 B.C. Nehemiah was a civil governor; Ezra, a priest and scribe. To follow the history, it is wise to read Ezra 1-6 before Nehemiah 1-13 and Ezra 7-10 after. The Jews were certainly grateful to have been liberated from their slavery and to be permitted to return to their homeland, but this was made into a province of the Persian empire. Prophets such as Ezekiel had convinced the repatriates that God had punished the infidelity of their forefathers; thus they were ready for reform. The Temple had been rebuilt toward the end of the preceding century, and priests such as Ezra were filled with zeal. Ezra was insistent that the religious renewal was to begin with devout Jewish families: non-Jewish wives were expelled, and further mixed marriages were strongly disapproved. The survivors in Samaria had profited from the downfall of Jerusalem, resenting the returnees; this explains the hostility shown by Ezra toward the Samaritans. No attempt was made to restore the monarchy, but the priests grew more and more influential, so that they even became political authorities.

F

Fabric (FAB-rihk): The buildings, possessions, and funds of any church or institution.

Faculties (FAK-uhl-teez): Permission required for a minister to exercise specific powers of Holy Orders; *e.g.*, to hear confessions, preach, or witness marriages. Cf. CCC 1313, 1463, 1495

Faculty, Canonical (ka-NAH-nih-kuhl FAK-uhl-tee): 1. An educational institution or department of an educational institution officially erected or recognized by the Holy See. 2. Power granted to a person by law or competent authority to perform certain juridical or canonical acts. Cf. CCC 1313, 1463, 1495

Faculty, Ecclesiastical (eh-klee-zee-AS-tih-kuhl FAK-uhl-tee): Another term for canonical faculty.

Faculty, Pontifical (pahn-TIH-fih-kuhl FAK-uhl-tee): An institution of higher learning officially erected or recognized by the Holy See and governed by its special regulations.

Faith (FAYTH): The acceptance of the word of another, trusting in that person's authority or right to be believed; in theological terminology, faith means specifically the assent given to a truth, as in the subjective acts and disposition by which doctrine is believed *(fides qua creditur);* faith can also be defined as the objective body of saving truth as contained in the Scriptures, creeds, and Magisterium of the Church, especially as exercised by the Pope and Church Councils *(fides quae creditur).* Faith is the first of the three theological virtues; with hope and love, faith brings about the life of sanctifying grace in the human person. By faith, one adheres in intellect to the truth revealed by God because of God's authority rather than the evidence given; thus faith has God as its primary object and secondarily the various truths about Him that are taught in the Church. While faith is a disposition of the intellect, it also involves an act of the will, which is moved by the grace of God to believe, so that one responds to the revealing God in faithful obedience and trust. CCC 13-18, 23, 84-95, 150-159, 170, 178, 182, 206, 1236, 1253-1255, 1813-1816

Faith, Mysteries of (MIHS-ter-eez uhv FAYTH): Those truths of the Christian Faith that are not able to be discovered and comprehended fully by the human mind but yet are known because God has revealed them. These are termed "mysteries," not because they are in need of a solution, but because they involve such a depth of truth that they demand continual reflection, inquiry, and contemplation. CCC 158, 234, 647, 2558

Faith, Rule of (RÖÖL uhv FAYTH): Norm or standard of religious belief. Catholic doctrine holds that belief must be professed in the divinely revealed truths of the Bible and Tradition as interpreted and proposed by the Magisterium of the Church. Cf. CCC 84-95, 173-175

Faithful [Christifideles] (FAYTH-fuhl [KREES-tee-fee-DAY-lehz]): Broadly understood, all the baptized who have been instructed and admitted to communion within the Church; more strictly, the faithful are baptized Catholics in full communion with the See of Rome (Can. 204), who make together the same Profession of Faith and thus enjoy a right to the sacraments and to the worship of God according to one's own liturgical rite. Incorporated into the Church through Baptism, the faithful are constituted as the People of God; sharing in Christ's priestly, prophetic, and royal office, they are called to exercise the mission given by God to the Church of working for the salvation of souls. The faithful are thus obliged to lead a holy life; to promote the growth of the Church, her continual sanctification, and the spread of the Gospel; to obey legitimate ecclesial authority; to provide for the needs of the Church; and to promote social justice. Significant for the Church's treatment of the lay faithful are the 1988 apostolic exhortation of Pope John Paul II *Christifideles Laici* and the constitutions of Vatican II, *Lumen Gentium* and *Gaudium et Spes*. Cf. CCC 655, 737, 796, 873-945

Faithful, Prayer of the: See Prayer of the Faithful

Faith Healing (FAYTH HEEL-ihng): The attempt to take authority over an illness and cast it out by invoking the name of Jesus Christ, with success of healing considered dependent on the faith present in the one to be cured, and with failure sometimes blamed on insufficient faith. Though a recent movement in Christianity, faith healing of the past century has obviously taken its impetus from the miracles of healing performed by Jesus in the Gospels and those of the early Church (Acts 5:15-16). Exercise of the charisma of divine healing has been found throughout the history of the Church, but the Church has viewed such miraculous cures as primarily dependent on the will of God.

Falda (FAWL-duh): (Italian: train) A white silk train formerly worn by the Pope over his rochet on certain solemn occasions. The length of it necessitated four monsignori holding it up whenever the Pope walked in it. It is now in disuse.

Faldstool (FAWLD-stööl): In preconciliar liturgies, this backless stool made of gilt metal or wood was used by a bishop who was not an Ordinary of a diocese or by an Ordinary in the presence of a prelate of higher rank. The stool's frame was in an X shape with a seat of leather or cloth stretching across its upper extremities. It was often used by bishops and cardinals in a variety of liturgical settings and seasons.

Fall of Man (FAWL uhv MAN): The reality occurring as a result of Original Sin. Through the sin of Adam and Eve, man's intellect became clouded and his will weakened. He was subjected to illness and death. However, the "happy fault" of the Fall is that the Son of God would become incarnate to suffer, die, and rise for the salvation of the human race. **CCC 55, 70, 215, 289, 385, 390, 410**

Families, Rights of (RAITS uhv FAM-uh-leez): The privileges that parents and children enjoy as a unit. The Church constantly calls for the respect of the rights of families to live in peace and freedom, to be able to train their children in the "ways of God" by teaching morality, and to be able to worship God without outside pressure. Cf. CCC 1908, 2209-2211, 2229-2230

Fan: See Flabellum

Fanon (FA-nuhn): (Latin *fano,* a piece of cloth) A short cape consisting of white silk striped with gold and with a narrow stripe of red bordering each gold stripe. Proper only to the Roman Pontiff, it was worn over the chasuble, under the pallium.

Fascism (FA-shih-zuhm): (Latin *fasces:* bundle of iron rods symbolic of political unity) State absolutism in which one person or a small group holds dictatorial power, suppresses by force all opposition, and controls industry, trade, and business with a strong emphasis on aggressive nationalism and racial superiority. Condemned in 1931 by Pope Pius XI as an "ideology that clearly resolves itself into a true, pagan worship of the state," Italian Fascism flourished under Benito Mussolini, who governed Italy from 1922 to 1943. Nazism was the German form of this government, as exercised by Adolf Hitler in his rule of Germany from 1933 to 1945.

Fast (FAST): Ascetic practice, limited in duration, undertaken as a means of mortification or penance for one's spiritual welfare as a way of affirming the human need for a dependence on God; thus, one stops what is otherwise self-controlled and waits upon God to meet one's needs. With food understood as a gift from God (Dt 8:3; Mt 6:11; Lk 11:3), fasting is the willingness to face one's own weakness, frailty, and need not only for the provision of nourishment but also for the Provider Himself, Who in the N.T. reveals Himself as nourishment itself: "I am the Bread of Life. He who comes to me will never be hungry; he who believes in me will never thirst" (Jn 6:35). The life of Jesus reflects constantly His dependence on God, Who is forever faithful and promises action. Moses fasted (Ex 34:28), as did Elijah (1 Kgs 19:8); Jesus, too, inaugurated by a forty-day fast (Mt 4:2) His Messianic mission as a sign of complete surrender to His loving Father. Not only a physical expression of our need for God, fasting is a path that can lead us to the reality of God's kingdom. CCC 1434, 1438, 1969, 2043

Fast, Eucharistic (yöö-kuh-RIHS-tihk FAST): The one-hour period before receiving the Holy Eucharist in which one abstains from food and drink (except water and medicine) in order to prepare for reception of the Body and Blood of Christ. CCC 1387

Fasting (FAST-ihng): The practice of limiting the intake of food and water so as to imitate the suffering Christ during His passion and throughout His earthly life. The Church requires fasting (i.e., two small meals and one larger meal, with no eating between meals, and abstinence from meat) on Ash Wednesday and Good Friday. All Christians are called to fast and to consider Jesus, Mary, and the saints as examples of mortification. CCC 1434, 1438, 1969, 2043

Fatalia Legis (fah-TAH-lee-uh LAY-dzhihs): Latin term for the time limits set by Canon Law for the performance of certain judicial or procedural acts in canonical trials.

Father (FAH-ther): 1. A form of address to God, after the example of Jesus Christ, Who taught His disciples to pray, "Our Father. . . ." 2. The familiar title for priests because of their role as pastors of the faithful. It was used in the early Church for those who gave special witness to the Faith, and was then extended to all bishops because of their spiritual authority and care. By the fourth century, it was used by monks among themselves, and during the nineteenth century it came to be used for all priests in English-speaking countries. CCC 198, 232-260, 2735-2736

Fathers of the Church, Apostolic Fathers (FAH-therz uhv *th*uh TSHERTSH; a-pah-STAH-lihk FAH-therz): Title given to writers of the early Church, many of whom were also bishops; originally, a mark of respect accorded only to heads of churches as indicative of their responsibility for discipline and doctrine within the family of the Church as the human father is in his family; later extended more broadly to those notable for the orthodoxy of their doctrine, who by their writing, preaching, and holy lives defended the Faith. There are four marks required of the Fathers of the Church: antiquity, orthodoxy, personal holiness, and Church approval. Johannes Quasten, the foremost scholar of patrology in the twentieth century, dates the end of the patristic period in the East with the death of John Damascene in 749 and in the West with the death of Isidore of Seville in 636; he divides the patristic era into four periods: (1) Apostolic Fathers, from the time of the Apostles through the end of the second century: Clement of Rome, Ignatius of Antioch, Polycarp, and the authors of the *Didache,* the *Shepherd of Hermas,* and the *Epistle of Barnabas*; (2) Schools of Alexandria and Antioch, through A.D. 315: Clement and Cyril of Alexandria, Eusebius; (3) Golden Age, from the Council of Nicaea (325) through the Council of Chalcedon (451): Basil and Gregory of Nyssa, Athanasius, Gregory Nazianzen, John Chrysostom, Ambrose, Jerome, and Augustine; (4) Decline, ending ca. 750: Pope Gregory the Great stands out at the end of the patristic period. **CCC 11, 688**

Fátima, Apparitions of (a-puh-RIH-shunz uhv FAH-tih-muh): The visions of Mary witnessed by three shepherd children — Lucia, Jacinta, and Francisco — between May and October 1917 near Fátima, Portugal. Our Lady requested prayer (especially the Rosary) and penance for the conversion of sinners. Every Pope since Pope Pius XI in 1930 has encouraged devotion to Our Lady of Fátima. Pope John Paul II visited the shrine on May 13, 1982, the sixty-fifth anniversary of Our Lady's first appearance, in order to thank her for preserving him from death exactly one year earlier during the attack on his life.

Favor of the Law (FAY-ver uhv *th*uh LAW): Canonical term that indicates that a certain juridic or canonical act is presumed to be valid unless the contrary is proven.

Fear (FEER): A strong emotion or trepidation of the mind caused by the threat of grave danger or evil. In Canon Law, fear may invalidate marriage if it is the reason for the marriage having taken place. **CCC 1041, 1453, 1765, 1772, 2144, 2217**

Fear of God (FEER uhv GAHD): The experience and knowledge of God as utterly holy, totally other, incomprehensible, absolute, almighty, all-powerful, and all-knowing; in religious language, this concept is best described by the term "reverence," which comes from the Latin *revereor,* meaning "I fear, stand in awe." The priest, who comes into intimate contact with the divine daily, is thus addressed as "Reverend," literally one who is to be feared. So, too, in archaic English God may be described as "awe-ful"; because He wields a "terrible, swift sword." God in His absolute majesty and kingship inspires this reverent fear in the hearts of the faithful as they come to know the *mysterium tremendum* that God is; this genuine reverence in turn expresses itself in acts of worship by the faithful. Biblical examples of the fear of God include the overwhelming presence of God as shown in the portents of lightning flashes, peals of thunder, and dense clouds (Ex 19:16); in contrast with His gentle yet overwhelming voice heard by Elijah, who failed to see God in a mighty wind, an earthquake, or fire (1 Kgs 19:9-13); Gideon's response to the fire (Jgs 6:11-24); Isaiah's response to God's call (Is 6:1-8); the disciples' reaction to the sight of Christ walking on water (Mt 14:25-26); and Simon's response to Christ after a massive catch of fish (Lk 5:1-11). In Is 11:2, fear of the Lord is one of the seven qualities of the prophesied Messiah and is thus appropriated by the Church as one of the seven gifts of the Holy Spirit; similarly, fear of the Lord is often a response to a decisive moment in salvation history, when the person who is genuinely in fear of the Lord is reassured by divine agency (God Himself, Christ, or an angel of the Lord) with such statements as "Fear not, God has sent me," "It is I," and "You have found favor with God." In the N.T., such a knowledge of God, together with His will for a way of life, often called the way of wisdom or of peace, is usually associated with the Holy Spirit, as in Acts 9:31, where the fear of the Lord brings the consolation of the Holy Spirit, and in Eph 5:17-21, where being filled with the Holy Spirit is a consequence of subordination in "reverence for Christ." **CCC 1041, 1303, 1831, 2144, 2217**

Feasts of the Church (FEESTS uhv *th*uh TSHERTSH): 1. Technically, liturgical days of lesser rank than a solemnity and higher rank than a memorial. 2. In popular usage among the faithful, all liturgical days on which the Church commemorates a mystery of Our Lord or Our Lady or the life of a saint. Cf. CCC 1169, 1172-1173, 2043, 2174, 2180, 2187-2188, 2193

Febronianism (feh-BRO-nee-uhn-ih-zuhm): An eighteenth-century heretical movement claiming that Scripture taught that the State and not the Pope was the arbiter in matters of Church discipline.

Fee: See Stipend

Feminism, Christian (KRIHS-tshuhn FEH-mih-nih-zuhm): A system of thought that seeks the same social, political, and economic rights for women as those exercised by men. Authentic Christian feminism advocates these rights within the scriptural and traditional understanding of the differences between men and women as created by God, whereas radical feminism seeks to obliterate these differences by viewing them as being artificially imposed by a "patriarchal" understanding of society. Cf. CCC 369

Ferendae Sententiae (fer-EHN-day sehn-TEHNT-see-ay): Latin term for a canonical penalty that must be imposed or applied by a judge or other competent ecclesiastical authority but cannot be imposed automatically (Can. 1356).

Feria (FEHR-ee-uh): Originally the Latin term for feast, *feria* has come to signify a day with no proper feast in today's common ecclesiastical usage. The prior usage was to repeat Sunday's Mass readings on such a day, but since the 1969 Lectionary there are readings for every day of the year. Today's equivalent for *feria* is simply weekday.

Ferraiolone (fehr-ee-uh-LO-nay): A cloak worn by clerics over the cassock or choir dress on solemn extraliturgical occasions, formerly obligatory at papal audiences, but now optional.

Festival of Lights: See Hanukkah

Fetishism (FEH-tihsh-ih-zuhm): 1. An attraction — irrational and either conscious or unconscious — to a person or object that is often sexual in nature. 2. Superstitious belief in and reverence for the magical power of a material object. Voodoo uses fetishes in order to harm others. Cf. CCC 2111, 2115-2117, 2138

Feudalism (FYÖÖ-duhl-ih zuhm): Social, economic, and political system of class distinctions that flourished in Europe during the Middle Ages. In this organization of society, the landed nobility exercised the highest authority and enjoyed the greatest wealth and power. They in turn were served by vassals of the lower nobility, while subservient to both ranks was the great mass of serfs who performed the menial labor of farming, crafts, and the military. As the lord provided protection and sustenance for his serfs, so the serfs owed their masters work, respect, and obedience. The medieval Church was feudal in that the clergy was divided into higher and lower classes, with the bishops viewed as lords, free to award benefices to the lower clerics; this system, in turn, led to such abuses as simony, the buying and selling of ecclesiastical offices, and lay investiture. These abuses in many ways helped to provoke the Protestant Reformation; they were, in turn, resolved by the actions of the Catholic Counter-Reformation of the late sixteenth century.

Fides (FEE-dayz): Located in Rome, this news agency of the Holy See's Congregation for the Evangelization of Peoples provides information on the Church's missionary activity throughout the world.

Filioque (fee-lee-O-kway): (Latin: and from the Son) Term inserted into the Nicene Creed by the Council of Toledo (A.D. 589) to declare the twofold procession of the Third Person of the Trinity, the Holy Spirit, from both the Father and the Son. The clear definition of the procession of the Holy Spirit had been a source of controversy since the fourth century because the Eastern Church preferred to speak of the procession "through the Son." The presence or absence of the word in the Creed became a source of mounting tension between East and West, proving a major cause of the

Great Schism of A.D. 1054. Within the Catholic Church it remained an obstacle to unity, especially from the Eastern perspective; it was settled at the Council of Florence (1438-1445), when the Eastern Catholics accepted the dual procession with the understanding that the principle of single progression, explicit in the Greek concept of "through the Son," did not exclude the progression implicit in the Latin *filioque*. **CCC 246-248**

Final Perseverance (FAI-nuhl per-suh-VEER-ehnts): The assistance, granted by God, to be preserved in the state of grace until one's death, which is often a particularly trying period. This grace counters sloth *(acedia)* and despair. **CCC 2016, 2849, 2863**

Finance Council (FAI-nants KAUN-suhl): A group of at least three laypersons who assist a pastor or bishop with advice in managing financial matters of a parish or diocese. Mandated by Canon Law (cc. 492, 493).

Finance Officer (FAI-nants AW-fih-ser): A position mandated by the Code of Canon Law to administer the financial affairs of a diocese under the authority of the bishop (Can. 494).

Finding of the Cross (FAIN-dihng uhv *th*uh KRAWS): Celebrated in the liturgy on September 14 as the Triumph (or Exaltation) of the Cross. Tradition holds that in A.D. 326 St. Helena, mother of the Emperor Constantine, found the actual cross of Christ at the site in Jerusalem long revered as Calvary. Here Constantine built the Church of the Holy Sepulcher.

Fire, Blessing of the (BLEH-sihng uhv *th*uh FAIR): The opening rite of the Easter Vigil. The rite prior to Vatican II specified the lighting of "a new fire, struck from flint," but the Vatican II rite simply calls for the blessing of a fire (outdoors if possible, since the Latin term actually indicates a rather sizeable fire) that may already have been kindled before the arrival of the celebrant and ministers. The celebrant begins by reminding the assembly that "this is the passover of the Lord," observed by the Church throughout the world, as on this night she calls her children together "in vigil and in prayer." The fire is blessed, and then from it the Easter Candle is lighted, and from this in turn, eventually, the candles of the people and the altar tapers as well. **CCC 696, 1147, 1189**

Firstborn (FERST-bawrn): 1. In Hebrew thought, the eldest son and the privileges and blessings that are his by right. 2. In general, a figurative state designating a special quality or relationship. **Cf. CCC 2188**

First Communion (FERST kuh-MYÖÖN-yuhn): The initial act of receiving the Holy Eucharist. Pope St. Pius X (1903-1914) determined that children who reached the "age of reason" (usually around seven) should be granted this privilege. In the Latin Rite, sacramental confession must precede First Holy Communion. **CCC 1244, 1457**

First Friday Devotions (FERST FRAI-day dee-VO-shuhnz): Derived from revelations made by Christ to St. Margaret Mary Alacoque (1647-1690), the practice of receiving Holy Communion on nine consecutive First Fridays in reparation to "the Heart that has loved men so and is loved so little in return" (Christ to Margaret Mary). Among the graces Christ is said to have promised to those faithful to this devotion are: final perseverance in the Catholic Faith, reception of the last sacraments, death in the state of grace, the consolation of the love of Christ's Sacred Heart at the time of death. Related rites centered on devotion to the Sacred Heart are First Friday Holy Hour, including exposition of the Blessed Sacrament, the Litany of the Sacred Heart, the Act of Consecration of the Human Race, and Benediction.

Firstfruits (FERST-FRÖÖTS): Sacred to Yahweh, the first products of man: animals, fleece, trees, grain, wine, oil, and "whatsoever was sown in the field," by the law of Moses to be offered to the Lord (Ex 23:19, 34:26; cf. Lv 19:24, 23:9-11, Nm 18:12, Dt 26:1-2). In Ez 44:30, it is further specified that the firstfruits are the proper domain of the priests. The firstfruits of Yahweh is a metaphor for Israel (Jer 2:3);

similarly, the Church, as the New Israel, is described as the firstfruits of God (Jas 1:18, Rv 14:4), while other Christians are called firstfruits because they were the first to be converted (Rom 16:5, 1 Cor 16:15), and all Christians are said to possess the firstfruits of the Holy Spirit (Rom 8:23). As the first to rise to new life, Christ is described by St. Paul as the "first fruits of those who have fallen asleep" (1 Cor 15:20). CCC 528, 655, 972, 1832

First Saturday Devotion (FERST SA-ter-day dee-VO-shuhn): The practice of receiving Holy Communion on five consecutive first Saturdays, receiving the Sacrament of Penance within an octave before or after this reception, reciting five decades of the Rosary, and making a fifteen-minute meditation on one of these mysteries. Originating with St. John Eudes (1601-1680) and Ven. John J. Olier (1608-1657), and popularized by the 1917 Fátima apparitions, this devotion's dominant theme is reparation to Christ through Mary, His Blessed Mother.

First Vatican Council: See Vatican Council I

Fiscal Procurator (FIHS-kuhl PRAH-kyöö-ray-ter): An unofficial term for the finance officer of an ecclesiastical institution or religious community.

Fish (FIHSH): Symbol of Christ in Christian art as early as the fifth century, derived from the Greek word for fish, *ichthus,* which provides an acrostic for the name and titles of Jesus in Greek: *Iesous Christos Theou Uios Soter,* Jesus Christ, God's Son, the Savior. The tracing of the form of a fish was used in the early Church as a secret way of revealing one's identity as a Christian to other believers. Fish are also used as a symbol of the Christian faithful with reference to the miraculous catch of fish (Lk 5); similarly, they serve as a symbol of the Apostles, who by their missionary work were designated as "fishers of men" (Lk 5:10; cf. Mt 7:10; Mk 6:41; Jn 21:9-13).

Fisherman's Ring (FIHSH-er-muhnz RIHNG): The signet ring placed upon the finger of a new Pope but not subsequently worn. It carries a depiction of St. Peter in a boat fishing, with the name of the Pontiff encircling the engraving. The ring is used to seal papal briefs and is ceremonially broken upon the death of the Pope.

Fistula (FIHS-tshöö-luh): A liturgical "straw," or tube, for drinking the Precious Blood used during the Middle Ages. Its usage continued into the modern period at solemn Papal Masses. Even with the reintroduction of Communion under both species after Vatican II, it was one of the methods recommended that seems never to have caught on.

Five Wounds (FAIV WÖÖNDZ): The marks on Christ's body (on His hands, feet, and side), which have been the focus of a special devotion by the faithful since the Middle Ages.

Flabellum (fluh-BEH-luhm): (Latin. fan) Flabella (the plural form) are long-handled fans used until recently in the liturgy to keep away insects from the Sacred Species. At one time part of the solemn procession of the Pontiff at Papal Masses, these instruments were constructed of leather upholstered in red velvet with gold embroidery and white ostrich feathers.

Flag: See Papal Flag

Flagellation (fla-dzhuh-LAY-shuhn): (Latin *flagellum:* whip) In imitation of the scourging of Jesus (Mt 27:27-31; Mk 15:16-20; Jn 19:2), some ascetics have willingly subjected themselves to a similar beating, usually self-imposed, but also inflicted by others with the individual's consent. Flagellation is considered an extreme form of ascetical piety and is generally discouraged by spiritual writers and Church authority. Flagellant movements, such as the Brotherhood of Flagellants, have consistently met with papal prohibition. In the fourteenth century, the Flagellants organized religious ceremonies and set forth their own heretical doctrines, which were condemned by Pope Clement VI in 1349.

Flat Hat (FLAT HAT): The hat worn by ecclesiastics when the cassock is worn outdoors. Made of beaver fur or felt, it has a round crown with a three-inch-wide brim. The Pope's flat hat is red with an elaborate red-and-gold band, while cardinals have a black hat with red-and-gold cord around the crown. Bishops wear a green-and-gold cord, and simple priests use black hats with black cords. This *cappello Romano*, or Roman hat, was obligatory dress until 1966.

Flectamus Genua (flehk-TAH-møøs DZHEHN-öö-uh): (Latin: Let us kneel) Spoken invitation usually offered by a deacon or an assistant minister. The appropriate response to this invitation is for the congregation to kneel in silence for a few moments. Dating to its earliest known use by Egyptian monks at the recitation of the Divine Office, this expression later came to be spoken or sung by a deacon after the reading of each intention at the celebration of the Lord's Passion on Good Friday.

Flock (FLAHK): Image of the Church derived from the N.T. image of Christ as the Good Shepherd (Jn 10). While the term "flock" is not often used explicitly, it is certainly implicit whenever sheep are mentioned as symbols of the faithful; Jesus compares Israel to "lost sheep" (Mt 10:6; cf. Is 53:6) without a shepherd (Mt 9:36); the image of a flock is also implicit in the parables about sheep (Mt 12:11-12; 18:12; 25:32-33). The theme of the Good Shepherd Who gives His life for His sheep (Jn 10:11; cf. Heb 13:20) develops imagery already present in the O.T. (cf. Ex 20:24; Ps 23:1). CCC 754, 764, 861, 881, 893, 1548, 1575, 1586

Florence, Council of (KAUN-suhl uhv FLOR-ehnts): The seventeenth ecumenical council, held in the fifteenth century. Famous for its decree reuniting certain Eastern, or Oriental, Churches with Rome.

Florida Pascua (FLO-ree-duh PAHS-kwuh): A Spanish phrase meaning "flowery Easter," referring to the time of the year in which the paschal feast occurs.

Focolare Movement (fo-ko-LAH-ray MÖÖV-mehnt): (Italian *fuoco:* hearth) An association of Catholic men and women, formally approved by the Church, established for the personal spiritual benefits of a more intensive prayer life among the membership and the realization of spiritual good through the everyday service of work for the social welfare of many, as the members strive to realize the prayer of Jesus "that they all may be one" (Jn 17:21). The movement is named for the aim of bringing all the human family together around one central hearth; it was begun by Chiara Lubich in 1943 in Trent, Italy.

Font: See Holy Water Font

Fontes (FON-tehz): (Latin: founts) The sources or background documents upon which each of the canons of the Code of Canon Law is based.

Footpace: See Predella

Forgiveness of Sin (for-GIHV-nehs uhv SIHN): Catholics believe that sins are forgiven by God through the mediation of Christ in view of the repentance of the sinner and by means of the Sacrament of Penance. (Cf. Penance.) CCC 430-431, 523, 536, 545, 602-618, 615, 981-982, 987, 1433-1434, 1437, 1443, 1452, 1496, 1708, 1741

Form (FORM): 1. In classical philosophy, the essence or distinctive nature of a thing. 2. In sacramental theology, the words and signs that contribute to the validity of the sacrament.

Form, Canonical (ka-NAH-nih-kuhl FORM): Technical term for the external formalities that accompany the exchange of marital consent. Canonical form consists of this exchange in the presence of a duly delegated sacred minister and two witnesses. Cf. CCC 1631

Form Criticism (FORM KRIH-tih-sih-zuhm): Method of biblical analysis of a single literary unit that seeks to establish the literary history of the text from its earliest existence to its final form in the Scriptures. There are two principal methods employed in this analysis: tradition-history, which seeks to trace the history of the literary unit from its oral stage to its written form; and literary criticism, which seeks to isolate any literary elements, grammatical constructions, words, or phrases that come from a later redactor, or editor, and are therefore extraneous to the original pericope. What emerges, then, in rough form is the unit as it likely originated in its oral form before a history of literary development had begun to mold it into its final written form.

Fortitude (FOR-tih-tööd): The cardinal virtue and gift of the Holy Spirit that enables one to attain good even when suffering and effort are needed. It grants the strength to overcome all obstacles in living the Gospel and to avoid temptations. CCC 712, 1303, 1805, 1808, 1831, 2846

Forty Hours Devotion (FOR-tee AURS dee-VO-shuhn): A time of forty semicontinuous hours of adoration of the Blessed Sacrament in a monstrance. This devotion may be carried out in a parish church or a chapel. As best we know, this devotion developed in sixteenth-century Europe. Both St. Anthony Zaccaria and St. Philip Neri strongly encouraged and promoted this Eucharistic devotion. St. Charles Borromeo was also known to have endorsed the practice and commended it to his flock in Milan. By the end of the sixteenth century, a plenary indulgence was granted to those who participated in Forty Hours — so rapid was its spread among the faithful. The 1973 *Instruction on Holy Communion and Worship of the Eucharist Outside Mass* does not specifically mention Forty Hours Devotion. However, the document does recommend that there be Exposition of the Blessed Sacrament for an extended period (perhaps forty hours) once a year in every parish.

Fortune-telling (FOR-tshuhn-TEHL-ihng): The predicting of one's destiny, contrary to the First Commandment, by using cards, crystal balls, etc. This practice is not only superstitious but also illustrates a lack of trust in God, Who alone knows the future and gives the grace to accept it. Cf. CCC 2115-2117

Forum (FOR-uhm): Canonical term meaning "the place where a judgment or other canonical act takes place." (See also External Forum and Internal Forum.)

Foundation Masses (faun-DAY-shuhn MA-suhz): Masses celebrated for the intentions of donors who bequeath an amount of money to an ecclesiastical institution.

Four Causes: See Causes, Four

Fraction (FRAK-shuhn): The *General Instruction of the Roman Missal* (2000) calls this the "gesture of Christ at the Last Supper, which in apostolic times gave the entire Eucharistic action its name" (n. 83). Strong ecclesiological understandings are attached to this rite, as derived from the injunction of St. Paul in 1 Cor 10:16b-17: "The bread which we break, is it not a participation in the body of Christ? Because there is one bread, we who are many are one body, for we all partake of the one bread." This rite was a necessary preparation for the reception of the Holy Eucharist and took some time when the number of communicants was large. The *General Instruction* states that the *Agnus Dei* is sung or said aloud during the fraction rite. The priest then breaks off a small particle of the Host and places It in the chalice. This custom goes all the way back to Rome, when Pope St. Innocent wrote of such a practice to Bishop Decentius of Gubbio in A.D. 416. This practice emphasized the unity that exists between the Pope and the various *tituli* (parish churches) in the city and is referred to as the *fermentum*. Cf. CCC 1329, 1342-1343

Franciscan (fran-SIHS-kuhn): A follower of the Rule of St. Francis of Assisi (d. 1226) as a professed religious, with an emphasis on simple communal life, giving particular attention to living in the spirit of poverty. Franciscans include both men and women religious, and laypeople can adapt the Franciscan charism to their lives as "tertiaries," or Secular Franciscans.

Franciscan Controversy (fran-SIHS-kuhn KAHN-truh-ver-see): A dispute in the thirteenth and fourteenth centuries within the Franciscan Order, concerning what constituted an authentic observance of the vow of poverty. The controversy centered on whether or not it was appropriate for there to be corporate ownership of property by the Order for the carrying out of its ministries. After lengthy debate, a papal decision indicated that Christian perfection did not require a complete renunciation, and so corporate ownership of property was allowed. However, those who had argued against ownership subsequently gave rise to a reformed Franciscan group known as the "Observants," which was approved by the Church in 1415. Cf. CCC 544, 786, 852, 915, 2544-2545

Franciscan Crown (fran-SIHS-kuhn KRAUN): Seven-decade rosary used to commemorate the seven joys of the Blessed Virgin: Annunciation, Visitation, Nativity of Jesus, Finding Jesus in the Temple, Apparition of the Risen Jesus to Mary, Assumption, and Coronation. Introduced in 1422, the beads originally had seven Our Fathers and seventy Hail Marys. Two Hail Marys were added to complete the number seventy-two (thought to be the number of years in Mary's life). One Our Father, Hail Mary, and Glory Be are said for the intention of the Pope.

Frankfort, Council of (KAUN-suhl uhv FRAHNK-fert): A local council convened by Charlemagne in A.D. 794 with papal approval, in order to enact general reforms in Church discipline.

Frankincense (FRANK-ihn-sehnts): (Old English: pure, unadulterated incense) A gumlike resin that whitens upon exposure to the air; when burnt, it produces a sweet and pleasant aroma. It was frequently used in religious rituals (Ex 30:34-38) and for offerings at the Temple (Is 43:23; 66:3; Jer 17:26; 41:5); it was also placed beside the bread of presence (Lv 24:7). Frankincense was offered to the Infant Christ on Epiphany by the Magi (Mt 2:11) as an acknowledgment of His future priestly role.

Fraternal Correction (fruh-TER-nuhl kuh-REHK-shuhn): The pointing out of another's faults, done in charity and without hatred, so as to encourage one to grow in love of God and neighbor. Fraternal correction, if done imprudently, can lead another to anger; if done properly, it can spur one on to practice charity more deeply. CCC 1435, 1829

Fraud (FRAWD): A deliberate act of deception whereby one person hides a significant fact from another in order to achieve a given end. In Canon Law, fraud about a significant aspect of a person can invalidate a marriage (Can. 1098). CCC 1916, 2286, 2409, 2534

Freedom (FREE-duhm): The capacity, free of pressures, to "self-determine" one's actions. The Church has emphasized the necessity of a person's freedom and has worked for the protection of that freedom. People can reject God's grace and gift of eternal life. True freedom recognizes the place of God in life and responds to His invitation to live free from sin and darkness. CCC 33, 154, 160, 180, 311, 387, 396-450, 908, 1700, 1707, 1714, 1730-1748, 1828, 1884, 1993, 2008

Freedom, Religious: See Liberty, Religious; Dignitatis Humanae

Freemasonry (FREE MAY-suhn-ree): An international secret fraternity whose present organization dates from the first part of the eighteenth century. It borrows symbolism from architecture and the mason's craft, which is communicated to its members through various "degrees." It proposes itself to be the means of conciliation among men, but at times, and in some places, it has shown itself to be hostile to the Catholic Church. From as early as 1738, Catholics have been forbidden to join Masonic Lodges, and this has been reaffirmed as recently as 1983 by the Congregation for the Doctrine of the Faith.

Free Will (FREE WIHL): The faculty or capability of making a reasonable choice among several alternatives. Freedom of will underlies the possibility and fact of moral responsibility. CCC 1704-1705, 1711, 1730-1731, 1853

Friar (FRAI-er): (Latin *frater,* French *frère,* Middle English *fryer:* brother) A member of one of the mendicant orders founded since the thirteenth century; the term distinguishes the mendicants' itinerant apostolic character, exercised broadly under the jurisdiction of a superior general, from the older monastic orders' allegiance to a single monastery formalized by their vow of stability. The most significant orders of friars are the Dominicans, Franciscans, and Carmelites.

Friary (FRAI-er-ee): The residence of members of a mendicant order of friars, though it is usually applied only to a Franciscan house; Dominicans and Carmelites call their houses priories.

Friendship (FREHND-shihp): The relationship between God and humans or between two humans that invokes closeness, companionship, and helpfulness. Christ emphasized the necessity of friendship when He laid down His life for His disciples. He called His Apostles to friendship with Himself and with others. Many friendships throughout the centuries, such as those of St. Francis and St. Clare or St. John of the Cross and St. Teresa of Ávila, illustrate the importance and beauty of such relationships. CCC 55, 277, 355, 374, 384, 396, 1023, 1030, 1395, 1468, 1829, 1939, 2665, 2709

Friends of God (FREHNDZ uhv GAHD): (German *Gottesfreunde)* An informal fellowship of religious and laity that originated in fourteenth-century Switzerland and spread through Germany and the Netherlands with the purpose of cultivating a personal union with God and a strong devotional life under the influence of such Dominican mystics as Meister Eckhart, Johannes Tauler, and Henry Suso. With other such groups, they are generally regarded as forerunners of the Reformation.

Fruits of the Holy Spirit (FRÖÖTS uhv *th*uh HO-lee SPIH-riht): The virtues put into action through the inspiration of the Holy Spirit. St. Paul names them: love, joy, peace, patience, kindness, goodness, faith, gentleness, and self-control (Gal 5:22-23). He contrasts the Christian freedom realized through these fruits with slavery (Gal 5:1, 13); he also characterizes the fruits as directly antagonistic to a life lived under the power of the flesh, as a consequence of fallen human nature (Gal 5:13-21). For these fruits to be realized, the fallen nature, or "flesh," must be crucified, i.e., it must undergo a death linked to Christ's death on the cross (Rom 6:5); with the death of the flesh, God fashions a new creation (2 Cor 5:17; Eph 2:15, 4:24), such that one anticipates the reality of resurrected life at an early stage (Gal 6:15). CCC 1832

Fruits of the Mass (FRÖÖTS uhv *th*uh MAS): Those spiritual and temporal blessings that result from the celebration of the Holy Sacrifice of the Mass. The general fruits are shared by all the faithful, living and departed; the special fruits are applied to the priest who celebrates it, to those for whose intention it is offered, and to all those who participate in its celebration. Cf. CCC 1391-1401

Fundamental Articles (FUHN-duh-MEHN-tuhl AHR-tih-kuhlz): A series of doctrinal statements, originating within conservative American Protestantism in the early twentieth century, that reaffirmed the fundamental beliefs that were basic to the theology of the Reformation, in opposition to the growth of modernism and liberalism that had taken place in some mainline Protestant denominations during the nineteenth century. These statements were printed in twelve pamphlets under the title "The Fundamentals: A Testimony of the Truth," which gave rise to the term "fundamentalist."

Fundamental Option (FUHN-duh-MEHN-tuhl AHP-shuhn): The orientation of one's life either to God by obedience or against Him through disobedience. Catholic Tradition acknowledges that one free and deliberate act with knowledge renders one at odds with God. A prevalent theory today asserts that one act cannot change one's "orientation" to God — no matter how grave — unless the action comes from the person's "center." The Church has cautioned against this vague position. Cf. CCC 1730-1748

Fundamental Theology (FUHN-duh-MEHN-tuhl thee-AHL-uh-dzhee): The branch of theology that establishes the sources and the reasons for the Christian Faith. It is so named because it deals with those doctrines that form the foundation of the Faith.

Funeral Mass (FYÖÖ-ner-uhl MAS): In the *Order of Christian Funerals,* Funeral Mass is the official name for the second and principal service associated with the death of a Catholic. It follows a Wake Service or Vigil for the deceased and precedes the Rite of Committal at graveside. Formerly, the Funeral Mass and all Masses for the dead were called "Requiems." This designation derived from the first word of the Latin chant that opened the Mass: *Requiem aeternam dona eis, Domine* . . . ("Eternal rest grant unto them, O Lord"). The Funeral Mass begins with the greeting of the body and mourners at the door of the church, the sprinkling of the casket with holy water as a reminder of Baptism, and the placement of the pall on the casket as a reminder of the white garment of Baptism. The procession goes forward, and Mass continues with the Liturgy of the Word and the Liturgy of the Eucharist as usual. At the end of Mass, after a moment of silence, the Song of Farewell is sung and the body is honored with holy water and incense. The Prayer of Commendation and invitation to join the procession to the grave brings the Funeral Mass to a close. **CCC 1680-1690**

G

Gabbatha (GA-buh-thuh): (Aramaic: pathway, stone pavement) The place where Jesus was put on trial by Pontius Pilate (Jn 19:13). It is described by John as just outside the Praetorium, the barracks for Pilate's official guard where Pilate often found accommodations when in Jerusalem. Some archaeologists identify the Antonian fortress built by Herod as the site of the paved court, now occupied by the Basilica of the Ecce Homo, which takes its name from the Latin words spoken by Pilate in putting Jesus on trial: "Behold the Man."

Gabriel (GAY-bree-uhl): (Hebrew: God is my hero, my warrior) One of the three named angels in the O.T. (Dn 8:16; 9:21), the others being Michael and Raphael. In the Lucan infancy narrative of the N.T., Gabriel announces the birth of John the Baptist to Zechariah (Lk 1:19) and the birth of Jesus to Mary (Lk 1:26); since he appears elsewhere only in the apocalyptic visions of Daniel (Dn 8:16-26; 9:21-27), Gabriel's announcement of these N.T. births brings a strong sense of eschatological fulfillment. Cf. CCC 148, 332, 335, 430, 490, 722, 2676

Galatians, Epistle to the (ih-PIH-suhl töö thuh guh-LAY-shuhnz): Addressed to the converts of St. Paul's first missionary journey (Acts 13:4—14:28; 16:6), this letter was meant to counter the false preaching by the Judaizers to the Galatians, mostly Gentiles (Acts 13), that circumcision and the Mosaic Law were necessary for salvation and that redemption by Christ was insufficient. Paul's opponents maintained that every believer in Christ, who as the Jewish Messiah remained Himself a faithful Jew, must similarly first become a full Jew according to the demands of the law and the cult. Therefore, they held that Paul's preaching about the law, circumcision, and the freedom that comes from Baptism in Christ is a false gospel preached by a pseudo-Apostle. Paul countered these arguments with the instruction that when the Galatians first heard the Gospel he preached (Gal 3:2-5), they received the Holy Spirit (Gal 3:3-4; 4:6) and thus became sons and daughters of God, the true offspring of Abraham in faith (Gal 3:26-28), so that, as with Abraham, they enjoyed a proper relationship with God by reason of justification from God, now linked to faith in Christ and the effects of His cross, and not by their own efforts 'at fulfillment of the Jewish law (Gal 1:4; 2:15-16). The Galatians could rightly expect their inheritance of the kingdom of God as the gift of faith and a consequence of their reception of the Holy Spirit, not because of the "works of the law" (Gal 3:29; 5:5; 6:8, 16-18). Paul also taught the dogma of the Trinity (Gal 4:6) and the authority of the Apostles (Gal 1:9). It is considered substantially Paul's own work, in the form we now possess, probably written while Paul was on his way to Ephesus.

Galilee (GAL-uh-lee): (Hebrew: ring, circle, district) Northernmost region of ancient Palestine, the focal point in the N.T. for most of the life and ministry of Jesus (Mt 4:23; Mk 1:39; Lk 4:14; Jn 7:9), ruled at that time by Herod Antipas. Isaiah calls the area "Galilee of the nations" (Is 9:1), meaning "region of the Gentiles," with reference to the ethnic and cultural mix of its population at the crossroads of so many trade routes. The area was bounded by the Mediterranean on the west, the Jordan River and Sea of Galilee on the east, the Plain of Esdraelon on the south, and the present-day Nahr el-Qasimeyeh on the north.

Galileo Affair (gahl-ih-LAY-o uh-FEHR): The early seventeenth-century case having to do with the Italian physicist and astronomer Galileo Galilei, who was a supporter of the Copernican theory. Because of the heliocentric nature of the theory, it seemed to contradict certain aspects of Holy Scripture as it was then understood. Because this could be disturbing to the faithful, the Church prohibited Galileo from teaching this theory until his hypothesis could be harmonized with Scripture. Contrary to subsequent popular belief, this case did not involve papal infallibility or any doctrine whatsoever, but was simply a disciplinary prohibition from teaching as true something that was, at that time, merely opinion, yet had implications regarding matters of faith.

Gallicanism (GAL-lih-kuhn-ih-zuhm): A complex schismatic movement in France that held that the French Church was autonomous from papal authority.

Gallican Liturgies (GAL-ih-kuhn LIH-ter-dzheez): Unlike other ecclesiastical centers in the West (e.g., Rome and Milan) that spawned distinctive Western liturgical rites, what have come to be termed the "Gallican liturgies" actually had no organizing center. Thus to speak of Gallican liturgies is to speak in a general way about rites emanating from and in use in Gaul between approximately the fifth and eighth centuries. Indirect references to local Gallican liturgical practices are found in the sermons of Caesarius of Arles (d. 542), the writings of Gregory of Tours (d. 594), and in the Merovingian Councils. The seventh-century *Explanation of the Gallican Liturgy* by Pseudo-Germanus of Paris attests to a strong Eastern influence on Gallican liturgy and contains the first example in the West of an allegorical interpretation of the liturgy. Another locale that spawned what has been termed a "Gallican liturgy" is Ireland, where in all likelihood an old Gallican rite was mixed with Celtic customs. It is generally asserted that forms of private prayer, devotions, the cult of the saints, and the confession of sins point at least indirectly to Celtic influence.

Gallican Psalter (GAL-ih-kuhn SAWL-ter): A revision of the Vulgate psalter translated into Latin by St. Jerome in A.D. 346, the Gallican Psalter is so called because it was introduced into Church use primarily in Gaul (now modern France) by St. Gregory of Tours in the sixth century. In the ninth century, it was established as the official psalter of the Church by the Emperor Charlemagne.

Gambling (GAM-blihng): The playing of games of chance, which is morally neutral. However, gambling may be easily abused and often is associated with other moral evils like alcohol and drug abuse, neglect of supporting one's family, organized crime, and sexual promiscuity. Cf. CCC 2413

Garden of Eden: See Eden, Garden of

Gaudete Sunday (gau-DAY-tay SUHN-day): In the preconciliar division of the liturgical year, this term referred to the Third Sunday of Advent. It derived this designation from the first word of the Introit at Mass: "Rejoice in the Lord always; again I will say, rejoice. . . . The Lord is at hand" (Phil 4:4-5). The rejoicing comes from the fact that Advent is half over and Christmas is soon to follow. This Sunday is further set apart by the custom of wearing rose vesture. In the postconciliar reform of the liturgy, the Introit (now entrance antiphon) is the same as it was in the preconciliar era. However, the term "Gaudete Sunday" is missing from the *General Norms for the Liturgical Year and the Calendar*. In the present Lectionary, the second reading for the Third Sunday of Advent "C" Cycle is Phil 4:4-7, the text from which we derive the term "Gaudete." And, fittingly enough, the Church in the postconciliar era has not withdrawn the option of using rose-colored vesture. The *General Instruction of the Roman Missal* indicates such in n. 308f.

Gaudium et Spes (GAU-dee-øøm eht SPEHZ): (Latin: joy and hope) Pastoral Constitution on the Church in the Modern World, promulgated as the last of the sixteen documents of the Second Vatican Council, on December 7, 1965; it is also the longest, providing a more pastoral complement to the highly dogmatic *Lumen Gentium* and a final exhortation of the Council to the faithful regarding the Council's hopes and intentions. The document is evenly divided into two parts: the condition of the modern world and the state of humanity in relation to one another and to the world in which they live (nn. 11-45) and the application of this analysis to various moral issues, especially as they relate to marriage, contraception, the family, education, war and peace, and the economy (nn. 47-90). GS presents a summary of the most traditional biblical and magisterial pronouncements on the Christian understanding of anthropology, with a frank treatment of atheism and secularism as popular distractions from the Christian Gospel and the Christian humanism that results from it. The document concludes with the positive encouragement of the Council Fathers: "Let there be unity in what is necessary, freedom in what is doubtful and charity in everything" (n. 92). The message of GS has been further developed in *Populorum Progressio* (1968), *Evangelii Nuntiandi* (1976), *Christifideles Laici* (1988), and *Centesimus Annus* (1991).

Geez, Ge'ez, or Gheez (gee-EHZ): The liturgical language of the Ethiopian Rite. It was once the vernacular of the Ethiopian nation but now is a dead language.

Gehenna (guh-HEHN-uh): A valley south-southwest of Jerusalem, mentioned seven times in the N.T., that was known as the location of the human sacrifices to Molech (cf. 2 Kgs 23:10). Some believe Gehenna (Hebrew, *ge-hinnom* from the Aramaic, *ge-hinnam*, "valley of the Son of Hinnom") to be the name of the Jebusite owner of the valley. In the N.T., the name is used figuratively to mean hell. **CCC 1034**

Genealogy of Christ (dzhee-nee-AHL-uh-dzhee uhv KRAIST): In the ancient Near East the genealogy represents the principal way of recording lineages of persons, families, tribes, or nations. The O.T. contains approximately two dozen lists, each varying in historical value. Genealogies secured personal rights and privileges in the clan or tribe and represented (often the only) written record of membership. Genealogies are an important source of historical information because they contain historical data not found in other sources (inscriptions, ancient monuments, manuscripts, etc.). Given the above, it is important to note that genealogies do more than record genetic and social or economic pedigree — they also contain "stories" about families, tribes, clans, or nations with the assumptions, underlying beliefs, and values of the recorder and his social setting that can be detected by noting what materials (names of people or of places, specific events recalled, etc.) were used to tell the story or connect the generations. After the Babylonian exile (587 B.C.), genealogies rose in importance within Judaism because they provided a proof for priestly descent and so helped to determine inclusion in and exclusion from the priesthood. The two genealogies of Jesus in Mt 1:1-17 and Lk 3:23-38 should be viewed in light of the literary, social, and especially religious intent the Gospel writers had in mind. The two lists represent two very different ways of communicating not only Jesus' lineage but the revelation of His divine Person and the role He has relative to God's self-disclosure for the coming of His kingdom and His plan of salvation for the world. Comparing similarities and differences helps detect what the authors intended to communicate. *Similarities:* In both Gospels Jesus' lineage is traced on Joseph's side, the legal father upon whom Jewish Law conferred complete legal paternity and all the rights of natural paternity. Both genealogies make clear Jesus' Davidic descent (Mt 1:1, 6, 17; Lk 3:31). *Differences:* Matthew begins the list of ancestors from Abraham (Mt 1:1—2:17) while Luke traces Jesus' ancestors back to "Adam, the Son of God" (Lk 3:38). Matthew lists forty-two names divided or organized into three units of fourteen names, omits names from David's royal line between Joram and Uzziah, and counts Jechoniah twice (Mt 1:11-12). Luke lists fifty-six names for the period corresponding to Matthew and an additional twenty for the period of Adam. Why the differences? Matthew's interest in addressing the Gospel to a Jewish Christian listener or reader helps explain the significance of Abraham, the Father of Israel and the first to receive the promises of God in the form of the covenant that was "signed" by circumcision. For Matthew, in the person of Jesus we find fulfilled all of the O.T. hopes, anticipations, and prophecies about God's promises of friendship, love, and salvation to Abraham (the Father of Israel) and David (the great king of Israel). The birth of Jesus at the conclusion of three groups of fourteen generations might suggest that God's sovereign plan of salvation is both carefully planned and indeed sovereign regardless of how many "family skeletons" are hidden in the "closet" (Mt 1:18-25). With Luke, the emphasis is on the universal scope of God's plan of salvation through the Gospel that Jesus brings in Himself, His teachings, and His actions. In both instances there are aspects of salvation history central to the history of Judaism that reach their fullest possible expression in the life, teaching, and person of Jesus and the Church that embodies His message.

General (DZHEHN-er-uhl): A common term denoting the highest superior of a religious institute under the authority of the Pope, as in "superior general."

General Absolution (DZHEHN-er-uhl ab-so-LÖÖ-shuhn):
The practice of giving sacramental absolution to a number of penitents without their previous individual confession in extreme cases, such as danger of death and grave need. The postconciliar revision of the rites for the Sacrament of Penance offers a "Rite for Reconciliation of Several Penitents with General Confession and Absolution" (Ch. 3, nn. 60-66), containing additions to the "Rite of Reconciliation of Several Penitents with Individual Absolution" (Ch. 2, nn. 48-59). The rite for General Confession and Absolution provides two formulas for sacramental absolution, the one a rather expanded form proper to this rite and the other taken from the other rites (i.e., for individuals). Some indications as to what constitutes "grave necessity" for the use of general absolution are given in the Rite of Penance itself (nn. 31-34), in the Code of Canon Law (cc. 961-963), and the decree from the Congregation for the Doctrine of the Faith, *Normae pastorales circa absolutionem sacramentalem generali modo impertiendam* of June 16, 1972 (*AAS* 64 [1972] 510-514). CCC 1483-1484

General Chapter (DZHEHN-er-uhl TSHAP-ter): The primary legislative body of a religious institute having the supreme authority of an institute according to its constitutions. General chapters take place on a regular basis and are made up of representatives of the institute.

General Confession (DZHEHN-er-uhl kuhn-FEH-shuhn):
1. The repetition of some or all of a penitent's previous confessions, either because some previous confessions were invalid or in preparation for some important step, such as marriage or the reception of Holy Orders. 2. Under certain emergency circumstances, the confession associated with the granting of general absolution, but only with the intention of making a private confession of any grave sins at the earliest opportunity. CCC 1483-1484

General Instruction of the Roman Missal: See Roman Missal, General Instruction of the

General Intercessions: See Prayer of the Faithful

General Judgment: See Judgment, General

Genesis (DZHEHN-uh-sihs): This first book of the O.T. sketches the Jewish view of the origin of the world, of mankind, and of the Jewish people. Traditionally thought to be the work of Moses, it is today considered to be a compilation made by a redactor who formed a patchwork of four different sources, all of whom lived some centuries after Moses. Of the fifty chapters, the first eleven are devoted to what is called primeval history. In Ch. 1, the creation of the world is artistically presented as having been accomplished on the six working days of the Jewish week. Light is created on the first day, the sky on the second, the dry land and the plants on the third. On the fourth day, the sun, moon, and stars are made; on the fifth the animals in the sea and the sky; and on the sixth day the earth is commanded to bring forth the animals that inhabit it, and God makes man in His own image. Ch. 2 presents a more detailed description of the making of man and woman and their primitive happy state. It was their disobedience that brought the origin of evil and the fall of our race, depicted in Ch. 3. Adam is shown (Chs. 4 and 5) to have ten generations of offspring before the Flood, eight of them in his own lifetime; only Noah and Shem (who survived the Flood) were born after Adam died. This flood is shown to have covered the entire land and to have exterminated all life, except that saved by Noah in the ark. After the Flood, there are eight generations leading to Abraham, from whom the Jewish nation took its origin. Chs. 11-25 cover the life of Abraham. Born in southern Mesopotamia, he is called by God with the promise that he will be the founder of a great nation in which all the nations of the earth will be blessed. His was a seminomadic life, taking him north from Ur to Haran, then southward through the Holy Land to Egypt and back to Hebron. In Ch. 14, we find him in Jerusalem, in significant contact with the mysterious priest Melchizedek. In Ch. 17, the promise is repeated, and the rite of circumcision is mandated. Since his wife Sarah was barren, Abraham's first son was by her maid, Hagar. But when Isaac was born (Ch. 21), Sarah's jealousy brought the expulsion of Hagar and her son Ishmael. The great testing of Abraham's faith came when God asked him (Ch. 22) to sacrifice Isaac, but then mercifully accepted a substitution. The significant events in the life of Isaac and his son Jacob are told in Chs. 24-36. Isaac is a mild, even bland, figure, who returned to Mesopotamia to take a wife, Rebekah, by whom he had the twin sons Esau and Jacob. When Isaac was old, by a ruse (Ch. 27) Jacob obtained the blessing intended for the firstborn. As his father had done, Jacob also went back to Mesopotamia to take a bride (Ch. 29), but was first deceived into taking Leah, the elder sister of his intended, Rachel. God renewed the great promise to Jacob and it was he, renamed Israel, who fathered the men who were the ancestors of the twelve tribes of Israel: Reuben, Simeon, Levi, Judah, Dan, Naphtali, Gad, Asher, Issachar, Zebulun, Joseph, and Benjamin. The final fourteen chapters (Chs. 37-50) focus on Joseph. Envied and sold by his brothers, he yet attained high position in Egypt. When a famine came, Jacob and his remaining sons had to go to Egypt for food. There Joseph magnanimously welcomed them, and during his lifetime they prospered. It was in Egypt that they multiplied into clans and tribes, and although they became slaves of the Egyptians for many centuries, the children of Abraham did indeed become a great nation.

Genocide (DZHEHN-uh-said): The killing of innocent persons, usually based on race, so as to achieve a political purpose such as the elimination of those considered "undesirables." The Second Vatican Council clearly condemned genocide and related crimes against human life. **CCC 2313**

Gentile (DZHEHN-tail): (Latin *gentiles*) 1. Originally meaning simply "people," the term came to be used by the Jews to denote non-Jews. 2. Similarly used by Latter Day Saints to denote non-Mormons.

Genuflection (dzhehn-yöö-FLEHK-shuhn): This act of bending the right knee to the floor and rising up again has had a number of meanings associated with it, from an act of penitence and supplication (e.g., before one's master), to an act of veneration in front of a person of prominence (e.g., emperor or bishop) or a holy object (e.g., altar, relics, especially those of the True Cross), to an act of reverence before the exposed or reserved Sacrament in church. The post-conciliar liturgical books indicate that "three genuflections are made [by the priest-celebrant] during Mass: after the showing of the Eucharistic Bread, after the showing of the chalice, and before Communion" (*General Instruction of the Roman Missal,* n. 274) and that "genuflection in the presence of the Blessed Sacrament, whether reserved in the tabernacle or exposed for public adoration, is on one knee" (*General Instruction on Holy Communion and the Worship of the Eucharist Outside Mass,* n. 84). Cf. CCC 1378

Georgian Byzantine Rite (DZHOR-dzhuhn BIH-zuhn-teen RAIT): The Church of Georgia (an area between Russia and Turkey) was founded in the fourth century by the preaching of St. Nino (also known as St. Christiana) to the royal family of the realm, which adopted the Christian religion for their land. The Georgian Church, avoiding Monophysitism, flourished particularly in the eleventh through the thirteenth centuries, although it ended up in schism from the Church, as did the Orthodox Churches. In the nineteenth century, it was absorbed by the Russian Orthodox Church, although at the same time some of its members were attracted to Catholicism, returning to full communion with Rome. Some of these adopted the Latin Rite, and others the Byzantine.

Gethsemane (geth-SEHM-uh-nee): (Greek, from either Aramaic or Hebrew: oil press) The place on the Mount of Olives where Jesus prayed after the Last Supper and where He was handed over to the temple guard (Mt 26:36; Mk 14:32). The Gospels refer to a "place" called Gethsemane, the name implying a location somewhere on the Mount of Olives. Luke does not mention Gethsemane but does record "Mount of Olives" (22:39). The Gospel of John records that Jesus went to a "garden" on the Mount of Olives (probably on its western slopes across from the Kidron Valley). The current location of Gethsemane contains very few olive trees (by some counts, no more than eight, none of which is older than nine hundred years) and is in an enclosed grove. It is one of several sites that various traditions claim to be authentic. None of the traditions can be traced back beyond the fourth century. The current location, if not the correct one, is undoubtedly very near the original. Cf. CCC 612

Ghibellines: See Guelfs and Ghibellines

Ghost, Holy: See Holy Spirit

Gift of Tongues (GIHFT uhv TUHNGZ): One of the gifts of the Holy Spirit described by St. Luke (Acts 2:4, 18; 19:6) and referred to thirty-five times in the N.T. This gift *(glossolalia)* enables one to speak so as to be understood (as at Pentecost) and also in a manner incomprehensible to the hearers. It is meant to praise God (1 Cor 14:2 ff.) and to communicate the "mind of God" to the listeners. Mentioned in early N.T. documents, this gift is subordinate to charity (1 Cor 14:1) in building up the Mystical Body of Christ (1 Cor 14:5). CCC 2003

Gifts of the Holy Spirit, The Seven (*thuh* SEH-vehn GIHFTS uhv *thuh* HO-lee SPIH-riht): From Is 11:2, the seven gifts are: wisdom *(sapientia)*, understanding *(intellectus)*, knowledge *(scientia)*, fortitude or courage *(fortitudo)*, counsel *(consilium)*, piety or love *(pietas)*, and fear of the Lord *(timor Domini)*. These gifts are given by Christ to His followers to assist them in following the promptings of the Holy Spirit. CCC 1266, 1303, 1785, 1830-1831, 2217

Gifts, Preternatural (pree-ter-NA-tsher-uhl GIHFTS): The unique blessings given to Adam and Eve, beyond fallen human nature as we now know it, which were lost through Original Sin but are now able to be exercised to some degree because of Christ's death and resurrection. These gifts are: immortality, freedom from suffering, acute knowledge, and the right ordering of the passions and emotions.

Gifts, Supernatural (söö-per-NA-tsher-uhl GIHFTS): Spiritual blessings, superior to those of the human condition, that, when infused, enable one to live by God's grace. These gifts are, among others, the theological virtues (faith, hope, charity) and the seven gifts of the Holy Spirit (wisdom, understanding, counsel, fortitude, knowledge, piety, and fear of the Lord). Cf. CCC 1812-1831

Girdle: See Cincture

Glagolithic Alphabet (gla-guh-LIH-thihk AL-fuh-beht): The ancient Slavonic alphabet devised by St. Cyril in the ninth century and still used by the Roman Rite in Dalmatia (now called Croatia). It is a version of the Cyrillic alphabet but has round or flowing letters, rather than the block letters employed by the latter.

Gloria in Excelsis Deo (GLO-ree-uh ihn ehg-SHEHL-sees DAY-o): The first words of the Latin version of the hymn "Glory to God in the highest," presently used at Masses on Sundays outside of Advent and Lent, on solemnities and feasts *(General Instruction of the Roman Missal,* n. 53). These first words of the hymn derive from the angels' song at the birth of Jesus (Lk 2:14). The text is highly Christocentric, but also addresses God the Father. In early Christian literature this hymn is described as among the "nonbiblical psalms" *(psalmoi idiotikoi)* used in liturgy *(Phos hilaron* is another), modeled after N.T. hymns. The *"Gloria"* was used originally in the Liturgy of the Hours in the East and was assigned to Morning Prayer in the West, probably by St. Hilary (d. 367); St. Cesarius of Arles (d. 542) notes its use at Morning Prayer. It was moved to the Eucharist in the sixth century, when it was first used at the Papal Mass of Christmas Day. It was later extended to Masses for Sundays and feasts of martyrs, but at first this occurred only when a bishop presided at these Masses. According to *Ordo Romanus II* (a seventh-century Roman Ordo), a priest could sing it but at first only at Easter. Cf. CCC 333

Gloria Patri (GLO-ree-uh PAH-tree): The doxology "Glory be to the Father and to the Son and to the Holy Spirit, as it was in the beginning is now and ever shall be world without end" is customarily added to the end of the psalms at the Liturgy of the Hours and to the entrance and Communion verses at Mass. The original text of the doxology was, "Glory be to the Father, through the Son, in the Holy Spirit"; but this text was changed at the height of the Arian controversy, lest it appear to diminish Christ's divinity. (Such was not the case, however, for the ending to the collects retained the important mediatorial role "we ask this through Christ. . . .") Important ecclesiological connotations derive from the earlier doxology worded "in the Holy Spirit," since this referred both to the Third Person of the Trinity and to the Church assembled to voice their praise in that same Spirit. The *General Instruction of the Liturgy of the Hours* (1971) states that "this is a fitting conclusion endorsed by Tradition, and it gives to Old Testament prayer [specifically the Psalms] a note of praise and a Christological and Trinitarian sense" (n. 123). The directives to the present *Graduale Romanum (Simple Gradual,* 1967) for Mass state that the verses for the entrance and Communion antiphons conclude with the *Gloria Patri* and the *Sicut erat* (n. 15).

Glorified Body (GLOR-ih-faid BAH-dee): Humanity's definitive state in eternity. The risen Christ calls humanity to the glory of His resurrection, a theological premise that presupposes that, like Christ, all of His brothers and sisters will be transformed physically. The ascension of Christ, "now raised from the dead, the first fruits of those who have fallen asleep" (1 Cor 15:20), demands similar corporal fulfillment for His brothers and sisters (cf. 1 Cor 15:21-23). It is humanly unknowable how the physical body will be glorified or spiritualized; this is the mystery of which St. Paul writes: "all of us are to be changed, in an instant, in the twinkling of an eye, at the last trumpet. For the trumpet will sound and the dead will be raised imperishable, and we shall be changed. When the perishable puts on the imperishable, and the mortal puts on immortality" (1 Cor 15:51-53). It is Catholic doctrine that resurrected bodies will have four essential qualities: (1) *impassibility* — freedom from all pain, suffering, or other physical defects; (2) *clarity* — the brightness of glory and splendor that overflows from the beatific vision and transforms all bodies; (3) *subtlety* — the true nature of the body, docile in a spiritual manner; (4) *agility* — that quality of the body, as a perfect instrument of the soul, whereby the glorified body will exist in harmony with and have access to the wonders of creation. **CCC 997**

Glory (GLOR-ee): Most frequently used to translate the Hebrew *kabod*; when referring to God it describes His "weightiness" or the imposing nature of His appearance, which in the O.T. was conceived of as light and fire. It has been developed further to include the self-revelation of God in nature and in history, especially in the Person of Jesus Christ. In Holy Scripture, mankind is enjoined to "give glory to God," which is to recognize the weight and claims of God's revelation, and to live according to His truth. CCC 210, 257, 434, 824, 1204, 2059, 2639

Glossator (GLAH-say-ter): A medieval scholar of theology or Canon Law who wrote explanatory notes in the margins of primary texts.

Glossolalia (glahs-ah-LAY-lee-uh): (From Latin: singing difficult words) 1. "Gift of tongues" to the disciples at Pentecost (Acts 2:4, 6-11). 2. Speaking in tongues: the practice of ecstatic speech among pentecostal or charismatic Christians (1 Cor 14:2). CCC 2003

Gloves, Episcopal (ih-PIHS-kuh-puhl GLUHVZ): Normal preconciliar episcopal liturgical vesture for Pontifical Mass and at certain Low Masses included the wearing of gloves, either white or the liturgical color of the day. During a pontifical Mass, except for the *Requiem,* gloves were worn from the beginning of Mass to the Offertory. The 1968 instruction *Pontificalis ritus* ("On the simplification of pontifical rites and insignia") states that the use of gloves ("which may be white on all occasions") is left to the bishop's discretion (n. 15).

Gluttony (GLUH-tuh-nee): Excessive desire and/or use of food and drink, in opposition to the cardinal virtue of temperance. Gluttony also includes the excessive craving for exquisite food and drink, along with a fastidiousness about such. CCC 1866

Gnosis (NO-sihs): (Greek: knowledge) In the N.T., *gnosis* can refer to "knowledge," which is an attribute of God (Rom 11:33) or of humans (1 Cor 8:1, 7, 11), or that which is embodied in the law (Rom 2:20). The term also refers to a class of knowledge about and from God that is specific to Christianity; we might call it "revelation," which we cannot know or come to know by reason alone. This is especially the case in terms of knowledge about the nature and character of God and how such knowledge directly affects and strengthens one's life (e.g., Wis 2:13; 14:22; 2 Cor 6:6, 10:5; 2 Pt 1:5). This kind of knowledge enlightens the intellect and originates from God (not the human: 2 Cor 4:6, 11:6; 1 Cor 1:5). Divine "enlightenment" of the intellect enables it to grasp the profound depths of the Faith, God's wisdom, God's will and intent for the unfolding of His majestic plan of salvation in Christ (Eph 1:9, 18). Hence this type of "gnosis" is "charismatic," in that it is a gift guided by the Holy Spirit and is grounded in love; as such, it illuminates the knower with a light that radically alters the believer's interior life and self-awareness by means of a more intimate knowledge of God. In Christian Tradition after the N.T. period, various sectarian movements (e.g., Valentinians, Manicheans, Mandeans) developed heterodox interpretations of "revelation," "illumination," and "gnosis." Differences among these groups notwithstanding, they shared specific assumptions and orientations that collectively are called Gnosticism. The characteristic features of Gnostic thought are: (1) *Cosmological Dualism.* Spirit and matter are diametrically opposed to each other; spirit is in essence morally good, while matter (i.e., our bodies, creation, etc.) is in essence morally evil (as distinct from being essentially good but under the domination of sin and death). (2) *Secret Gnosis.* The written words of Jesus in the N.T. are for the commoners and virtually worthless for "true salvation"; the words and teachings of Jesus were actually transmitted orally, in secret, and only to the Twelve Apostles (Jesus' inner circle of "true disciples"); this "secret teaching" was in turn transmitted orally through a line of the spiritually gifted. (3) *Gnostic Liberation.* This "gnosis" liberates the soul. Salvation occurs by or through enlightenment, and not by means of God's action. Cf. CCC 36-49, 285

Gnosticism: See Gnosis

God (GAHD): The one perfect Spirit, absolute and infinite, the Creator of all things. He is unchangeable and eternal, distinct from His creation, and by His will all things exist. CCC 198-747

God, Attributes of (A-trih-byööts uhv GAHD): Essential characteristics or various aspects under which God is viewed in His perfection. God does not have *separate* attributes because God is one, but our finite minds are not capable of grasping God in His unity. Therefore, we can think of Him in terms of various attributes such as simplicity, immutability, infinity, eternity, omnipotence, and omniscience. (Cf. Analogy.) Catholic teaching concerning the attributes distinguishes itself from the view of some that God is so transcendent that we cannot speak of Him at all. CCC 62, 205, 208, 210-211, 214-217, 218-221, 230, 233, 238-240, 257, 268-278, 312, 315, 339, 342, 370, 385, 993, 1352, 1723, 1955, 2052, 2112, 2465, 2575, 2577, 2779-2785, 2794-2796, 2802

Godparents (GAHD-pehr-uhnts): Those who act as sponsors for persons who are to be baptized. Historically, they have assumed a certain amount of responsibility for the Catholic nurture of the person baptized. CCC 1255, 1311

God, Presence of (PREH-zehnts uhv GAHD): Manifestation of the Creator in human life. *Lumen Gentium* teaches that "God shows to men, in a vivid way, his presence and his face in the lives of those companions of ours in the human condition who are more perfectly transformed into the image of Christ" (LG 50).

God-spell (GAHD-spehl): (Greek *euangelion:* good news; Anglo-Saxon *god-spel:* good tidings) The origin of the modern English word "Gospel." The musical play *Godspell* was so named for its attempt to present anew and in a popular fashion the abiding message of the Gospels.

Golden Bull (GOL-dehn BØØL): 1. A kind of papal decree, such as the bull of Pope Leo X proclaiming King Henry

VIII *Fidei Defensor* (Defender of the Faith), often sealed with a leaden seal. 2. The decree of 1356, remaining in effect until 1806, which regulated the election of the kings of Germany and the Holy Roman Empire.

Golden Legend (GOL-dehn LEH-dzhuhnd): The account of the lives of Jesus, Mary, and the saints authored by the Dominican Archbishop of Genoa, Jacobus de Varagine (1228?-1298). After the Middle Ages, the Golden Legend's contents were scorned as being uncritical.

Golden Rose (GOL-dehn ROZ): The ornament composed of gems and gold, with an inner container of balsam and musk, bearing a likeness to a spray of roses, that is blessed by the Pope on the Fourth Sunday of Lent (Laetare Sunday) and is given to an individual, community, or institution known for outstanding service to the Holy See. The origin of the Golden Rose is unknown but was referred to by Pope St. Leo IX in 1049 as an ancient practice.

Good Faith Solution (GØØD FAYTH suh-LÖÖ-shuhn): An unofficial process of the internal forum for reconciling invalidly married Catholics to the Church when an annulment is not obtainable. Cf. CCC 1649-1651, 1665

Good Friday (GØØD FRAI-day): Day commemorating the passion and death of Christ for the salvation of the world. The present afternoon liturgy on Good Friday is called the "Celebration of the Lord's Passion" and consists of the Liturgy of the Word, Veneration of the Cross, and Holy Communion.

Good Shepherd (GØØD SHEHP-erd): The image that Jesus used to describe Himself in Jn 10:11-18. He "lays down His life for his sheep" (v. 11) and knows them intimately (vv. 14-15). The O.T. also uses the imagery of a shepherd and sheep. God is the kind Shepherd Who ever cares for His flock (Gn 49:24; Ps 23:1-4; Ps 80:1) — in marked contrast to false shepherds who worry only about their own gain (Ez 34). (See also Flock.) Cf. CCC 160, 754

Goodness (GØØD-nehs): Term describing God and all that He has made. He is without limit and is perfect. His creatures, especially humans, participate in His goodness and therefore are good themselves (although they are limited and not perfect). One may increase in goodness by exercising free will to grow closer to Christ by frequenting the sacraments and performing charitable works. Satan, too, was made good but, like the other fallen angels, he deliberately chose to be constituted in evil. CCC 1, 214, 284, 293, 295, 299, 302, 308, 339, 353, 759, 970, 1333, 1359

Goods, Temporal (TEHM-per-uhl GØØDZ): Canonical term for property belonging to an official Church entity such as a parish, diocese, or religious institute.

Goods of Marriage (GØØDZ uhv MEHR-ehdzh): Three blessings first enumerated by St. Augustine in a work on marriage: children, faithful companionship, and permanence. CCC 1643, 2333, 2363

Gospel (GAH-spuhl): (Anglo-Saxon *god-spel,* translating the Greek *euangelion:* good news) 1. The message of salvation in Jesus Christ, the fulfillment of O.T. expectations about God's sovereign salvific actions in history. 2. Communication of the message, which came to mean each of the accounts of the four Evangelists who recorded the life, passion, death, resurrection, and words of Jesus Christ (viz., Matthew, Mark, Luke, John). CCC 76-79, 125-127, 139, 514

Gospel, The Fifth (*th*uh FIHFTH GAH-spuhl): 1. The letters of Paul, as "the Fifth Evangelist," are sometimes seen as constituting a fifth Gospel. Since his letters antedate the written composition of the Synoptics and John, the Pauline letters might more correctly be termed the "first" or "archetypal" Gospel. 2. The title of Fifth Gospel has also been applied to the Holy Land.

Gospel, The Last (*th*uh LAST GAll-spuhl): The Prologue of St. John's Gospel (1:1-18), which, being a summary of the entire Gospel and of the mystery of the Incarnation, has from earliest times been regarded with great respect and love.

St. Augustine repeats the saying of a contemporary of his who had remarked that this pericope of the Gospel of St. John should be written in gold letters and placed in a prominent place in every church. Indeed, it was often copied by the faithful and carried about on their person as a sacramental. Just as blessings were and are imparted through the use of some sacramental or other — a cross, a relic, an icon — so blessings were imparted using the words of the Prologue. The Dominican Rite was among the first to prescribe it for the priest privately after Mass (in their Ordinarium of 1256), and eventually the custom arose here and there of reciting it right after Mass. In 1558 the Jesuits voted at their General Chapter to use in their Missal either this text or that of Lk 11:27: "Blessed is the womb that bore you!" By the time the Missal of Pope St. Pius V was published after the Council of Trent in 1570, it had become a regular appendage at Low Mass. Again, this pericope was regarded as a form of blessing. Around the time of the Second Vatican Council its use was discontinued; however, because of its special place in the Gospel writings, it should be used by Christians everywhere in order to ponder the great things God has done for us and for their own spiritual growth and edification.

Grace (GRAYS): (Latin *gratia:* favor) The supernatural gift from God to assist persons in achieving eternal salvation. It is an undeserved gift, to which individuals have no right or claim, but which rather comes simply from the benevolent nature of God. CCC 1996-2005

Grace, Actual: See Actual Grace

Grace, Efficacious: See Efficacious Grace

Grace, Habitual: See Habitual Grace

Grace, Sanctifying: See Sanctifying Grace

Grace at Meals (GRAYS at MEELZ): The custom of offering a prayer of thanksgiving and blessing before and after food and drink are taken at meals. This custom is frequently emphasized as an important family ritual to carry over the spirit of the day's liturgical prayer, especially at morning and evening, as well as to acknowledge God in a prayer of blessing for His providence in offering sustenance for His creatures. The practice derives largely from the important Jewish domestic ritual custom of offering special prayers at meals, especially the weekly Sabbath meal and the annual seder. To offer a "blessing" is to acknowledge God as the source of all blessings. Attitudes of praise, glory, and thanksgiving are denoted in the Hebrew word *berakah* ("to bless").

Gradine (GRAY-deen or grah-DEEN): A ledge or shelf above and behind the altar proper (when affixed to the wall) for cross, candles, flowers, etc. In former liturgical legislation and theory, it was stressed that gradines were not part of the altar, nor necessary; with the possibility of altars facing the people, they have all but disappeared.

Gradual (GRA-dzhöö-uhl): A term denoting the psalmody sung (most often responsorially) between readings at the celebration of the Eucharist, derived from the Latin *gradus* ("step"), indicating that the reader would sing this chant from the step of the ambo. St. Augustine refers to "the psalm which we have just heard sung and to which we responded in song" *(Enarr. in ps. 119);* often he made it the subject of his homily. At times the chant was sung by a deacon, a practice that St. Gregory the Great ended because it led to the abuse of selecting deacons only for the quality of their voices. Its later evolution often saw it reduced to a few verses of the psalm with very elaborate musical notation sung by a soloist. In this case, the congregation was unable to participate in singing and could only reflect on what it heard sung. In the present *Ordo Missae* the preferred usage for the psalm that follows the First Reading at Mass is the Responsorial Psalm. However, the terms *Graduale Simplex* ("Simple Gradual") and *Graduale Romanum* ("Roman Gradual") are used as the titles of the books containing the Gregorian chant settings for the texts of the Mass propers of the revised liturgy.

Graduale Romanum (grah-döö-AH-lay ro-MAH-nøøm): The liturgical book containing Gregorian chant notation and Latin text of the proper chants sung at Mass (e.g., Introit,

Responsorial Psalm, and Alleluia). The book is distinguished from the *Liber Usualis,* which contained all the chants at Mass plus the musical notation and texts for much of the Divine Office. The postconciliar *Graduale Romanum* is an adaptation of its predecessor in accord with the directives of *Sacrosanctum Concilium* (SC), the Constitution on the Sacred Liturgy, n. 114. It eliminates Mass propers no longer in use (e.g., the season of Septuagesima, octave of Pentecost), transfers the texts of those saints whose feast days were changed, and adds new chants for new Mass propers. A shortened version "for use in smaller churches" has been published in accord with SC 117 under the title *Graduale Simplex.*

Gradual Psalms (GRAD-dzhyöö-uhl SAHMZ): (Latin *gradus:* step) Those psalms sung or recited by Jewish pilgrims as they made their way (or went step by step) to Jerusalem to celebrate the major festivals. Also called pilgrimage psalms, they include Pss 119-133.

Graffito (grah-FEE-to): (Italian, from Greek *graphein:* to write) One of the handmade inscriptions (graffiti) found in caves and catacombs, helping to date a particular site. An important graffito was discovered under the main altar of St. Peter's Basilica in Rome that read *Petros eni* ("Peter within"), signifying that St. Peter was indeed buried at this spot.

Grail Movement, The (*th*uh GRAYL MÖÖV-mehnt): An international movement founded in the Netherlands in 1921 by Jacques van Cinneken, S.J., for Catholic laywomen, both married and single, active in religious education, Christian formation, community development, social action, medical services, and various cultural programs, for the spreading of Christian values throughout society.

Grail, The Holy (*th*uh HO-lee GRAYL): The chalice used by Jesus during the Last Supper, which has been the subject of many legends and books. The earliest known story is *Perceval (Le Conte de Graal)* by Chrétien de Troyes in the twelfth century.

Gravissimum Educationis (grah-VEE-see-møøm eh-döö-KAH-tsee-O-nihs): Declaration of the Second Vatican Council concerning Christian education. It teaches that all Christians have a right to a Christian education; that parents have the primary duty and right to teach their children; and it gives a warning against a State monopoly of education, stating that there should be Catholic schools on every academic level, used and supported by all the faithful. Cf. CCC 1653, 2206, 2221, 2223, 2376

Greater Double (GRAY-ter DUH-buhl): In preconciliar liturgical legislation, this was one of the terms used to designate the priority of a given liturgical feast. Feasts were graded (in descending order): doubles of the first class, doubles of the second class, greater doubles, doubles, and simples. Sometimes feasts of the greater double or higher rank were known as "red letter days" because their titles were printed in red in the calendar. Examples of greater doubles: Commemoration of the Baptism of Our Lord (January 13; now celebrated as a feast on the Sunday or day following Epiphany when celebrated on Sunday); St. Peter's Chair at Rome (January 18, now celebrated as a feast on February 22); Conversion of St. Paul (January 25, now celebrated as a feast on the same day); the Commemoration of St. Paul (June 30, now eliminated); and St. Ignatius Loyola (July 31, commemorated as a memorial on the same day).

Greca (GREH-kuh): (Italian: Greek) The modern overcoat worn since the nineteenth century in particular, but not solely, by the Roman clergy. It is a double-breasted woolen coat worn over the cassock and reaching to the ankles. The Pope often wears a white *greca*, while all others wear black. It is called *greca* because in the minds of some of those who first saw it worn, it resembled the Greek or Byzantine rason (also spelled rhason), which is also an overcoat worn over the cassock.

Greek Church (GREEK TSHERTSH): The Catholic Church of Greece, which is part of the Byzantine Rite. The Greek Church shares the Byzantine Rite with a host of other churches, especially those located in Eastern Europe and near the Mediterranean Sea. The term may also apply to the Orthodox Church in Greece, not in communion with the See of Rome.

Greek Church, United (yöö-NAI-tehd GREEK TSHERTSH): A term sometimes used to describe all Byzantine Rite Catholics, although it is applied only because the original liturgical language of that rite was Greek. It is really an incorrect term, since not all Byzantine Catholics are of Greek ethnicity. The more correct term is "Eastern Catholics."

Greek Corporal (GREEK KAWR-puh-ruhl): A modification of the usual square of white linen material placed on the altar for Mass, on which are placed the chalice and paten. The Greek corporal contains the relics of a saint and in the preconciliar liturgy supplied for the relics placed in the altar stone. Hence, Mass could be celebrated in a place other than a church and not on an altar, provided that a Greek corporal was used.

Greek Fathers (GREEK FAH-therz): Bishops of the early Church who wrote fundamental theological works in Greek.

Gregorian Calendar (greh-GOR-ee-uhn KAL-chn der): A system of reckoning the days of the year more in conjunction with the seasons and decreed by Pope Gregory XIII in 1582. It replaced the Julian calendar, which was determined to be ten days out of step with the seasons.

Gregorian Chant (greh-GOR-ee-uhn TSHANT): A plain chant with more individuality and characteristic expression than other early chants (such as Ambrosian). These chants appear to have been compiled and arranged by Pope St. Gregory the Great (540-604), whence the name "Gregorian." After Vatican Council II and the introduction of the vernacular into the liturgy, Gregorian chant was put aside by most Church musicians. In 1974, however, a publication, "Letter to Bishops on the Minimum Repertoire of Plain Chant," was sent to all bishops and heads of religious congregations throughout the world. This letter spoke of *"Jubi-*

late Deo," which contains basic chants that should be taught to all the faithful, a copy of which was also sent to the bishops and religious leaders.

Gregorian Masses (greh-GOR-ee-uhn MA-sehz): A set of thirty Masses said on thirty consecutive days for the deceased. Because of the difficulties of doing this in a parish with the many requests for Requiem Masses, Gregorian Masses are often taken by a monastery or a house of religious priests. Pious belief attributes a special efficacy to this series of Masses, named after Pope St. Gregory the Great, who began the custom.

Gregorian Modes (greh-GOR-ee-uhn MODZ): The eight musical scales used in Gregorian chant, divided into authentic and plagal groups. Only one accidental occurs in the Gregorian modes, the half-tone lowering of the seventh note of the scale to "B-flat."

Gregorian Reform (greh-GOR-ee-uhn reh-FAWRM): An eleventh-century reform movement aimed at correcting moral abuses within the Church and those elements connected with feudal society that weakened her independence. It was named for its most significant leader, Pope St. Gregory VII (Hildebrand), although it took definite shape earlier, at least after the election of Pope St. Leo IX (1049-1054). The earlier reformer Popes concentrated on two persistent problems: simony (paying for spiritual favors, including election to ecclesiastical office) and the neglect of clerical celibacy. Other serious problems included the interference of secular rulers in the elections of bishops and Popes and the investiture of clerics by laymen. Often those chosen in this way were unworthy. Nicholas II, in a synod of 1059, took a significant step toward achieving freedom in papal elections. This led to the twelfth-century practice of election of Popes by the cardinals.

Gregorian Sacramentary (greh-GOR-ee-uhn sa-kruh-MEHN-tuh-ree): The Sacramentary was the book containing the prayers and texts that priests and bishops needed to celebrate different liturgical rites (e.g., the Mass and other sacraments); it did not contain the Scripture readings or chants. The Gregorian is one of three (Leonine, Gelasian, Gregorian) that figure prominently in the development of the Roman liturgy through the Carolingian era. The Gregorian is known from a copy sent by Pope Hadrian I to Charlemagne around 788. Known as the *Hadrianum,* this text was likely compiled at Rome around 630; it contains approximately eighty prayers attributed to St. Gregory the Great himself (590-604). To the *Hadrianum* was added a supplement (termed *Hucusque* because of its first word) attributed to St. Benedict of Anianne (formerly ascribed to Alcuin) that completed what was lacking in the original text to make it serviceable for the whole Church year. A second type of Gregorian sacramentary is entitled *Paduensis,* a papal sacramentary that was adapted for use by priests; it is dated 670-680. A third type is entitled the *Tridentinum,* the central part of which closely paralleled the *Hadrianum,* and is dated before the reign of Pope Sergius 1 (687-701).

Gremial (GREH-mee-uhl): An episcopal liturgical veil (or "apron") made of silk in the variety of liturgical colors, formerly used at pontifical Masses to cover the bishop's knees while he was seated. The rubrics called for the placing of the miter on the bishop's head after the gremial was put in place.

Grille (GRIHL): 1. The wooden or metal grating prescribed by C.I.C. (Can. 964, 2) that must be permanently fixed in the confessional between the penitent and the confessor when confession is not made face-to-face but anonymously. This latter has been and remains an important right of the penitent when confessing his sins to a priest. The requirement is emphasized by the above-mentioned canon, which makes it a precept that a traditional confessional with a grille separating the confessor and the penitent can be found in every church or oratory where confessions are heard. 2. The so-called grille, usually constructed of wrought iron or bronze, to be found in monasteries of religious women, or nuns, of strictly enclosed orders, referred to as papal enclosures or cloisters. It is usually found in the parlors of these monasteries where the families of the nuns and other guests may visit them. The grille usually takes the place of a wall and goes from the ceiling to about three or four feet from the floor. 3. A grille is also to be found in the chapel between the sanctuary and the nuns' choir.

Guadalupe, Our Lady of (aur LAY-dee uhv gwah-duh-LÖÖ-pay): On December 12, 1531, the Blessed Virgin appeared at Tepeyac, Mexico, to Juan Diego and requested that a church building be erected there. Juan Diego presented himself to the local bishop wearing a cloak on which an image of the Virgin had been inexplicably imprinted. Two years later, a church was erected there, and in 1555 a feast was established in honor of the church's patroness, Our Lady of Guadalupe. By 1746 the Virgin of Guadalupe was the patroness of New Spain; in 1910 she was declared the patroness of Latin America, and in 1946 Pope Pius XII declared her to be the patroness of all the Americas. In 1988 the liturgical celebration of Our Lady of Guadalupe on December 12 was raised to the status of a feast in all dioceses in the United States.

Guardian (GAHR-dee-uhn): A person appointed to safeguard the rights of one unable to do so in the course of a canonical trial. Also called a curator (Can. 1479).

Guardian Angels (GAHR-dee-uhn AYN-dzhehlz): Those created heavenly spirits whose job is to assist those to whom they have been commended. Guardian angels intercede for, guide to holiness, and protect from harm those entrusted to them. The guardian angels are commemorated in the liturgical calendar on October 2. **CCC 336**

Guards, Papal: See Swiss Guards

Guelfs and Ghibellines (GWEHLFS and GIHB-eh-leens): Rival medieval factions or houses that represented papal and imperial concerns. The German word *Welf* refers to the Saxons who allied themselves with the papacy; the Italian form of their name is *Guelfo*. The Hohenstaufens of Swabia had a rallying cry, *Weibelungen*, after a castle at Weibelung, and the Italian form came to be *Ghibellino*. Welf VI joined an alliance with the papacy in 1162, but the emergence of two distinct parties belongs more fully to the reign of Frederick

II (1218-1250). The imperial, or Ghibelline, cause under the grandson of Frederick Barbarossa ignited a furious struggle with the papal, or Guelf, allies, with Italy torn apart by this feud. By the year 1300, however, the Guelf allies had largely won. At that point, Ghibelline and Guelf represented only lingering local and familial frictions.

Guilds (GIHLDZ): Associations organized in Europe in the Middle Ages by merchants and craftsmen for the promotion of individual initiative, special skills, social standing, and religious life of their members. Guilds declined during the eighteenth and nineteenth centuries, although they are generally regarded as the forerunners of labor unions and religious social action groups.

Guilt (GIHLT): (From Anglo-Saxon *gylt:* sin or offense) The condition of an individual who has committed some moral wrong and is liable to receiving punishment as a consequence of wrongdoing. Cf. CCC 1784, 1801, 2290

Gyrovagi (DZHAI-ro-vah-dzhee): Wandering monks who either are not attached to a monastic community or never reside in their proper community. This has always been regarded by Church authorities as an abuse.

H

Habakkuk, Book of (BØØK uhv huh-BAHK-uhk): The brief O.T. book whose author relates the plan of King Nebuchadnezzar to attack Jerusalem (598 B.C.). Like Job, Habakkuk struggles with the question of why the Lord permits His children to suffer. God answers this seventh-century prophet by revealing that the Chosen People will learn patience through this necessary chastisement.

Habit (HA-biht): (Latin *habitus,* possession) 1. An acquired function of the body or mind that, through repetition, enables certain performances to be done more easily and efficiently. A good habit is a virtue, and a bad habit is a vice. 2. Also, the special garb worn by religious (see Habit, Religious).

Habit, Religious (rih-LIH-dzhuhs HA-biht): The distinctive clothing worn by members of institutes of religious life and required by Church law as a sign of public witness to the evangelical counsels.

Habitual Grace (huh-BIHT-tshöö-uhl GRAYS): The infused gifts of the Holy Spirit that make one a friend of God. This grace is called "sanctifying" grace and carries with it the three theological virtues (faith, hope, charity), the seven gifts of the Holy Spirit (wisdom, understanding, counsel, fortitude, knowledge, piety, fear of the Lord), the four cardinal virtues (prudence, justice, fortitude, temperance), and the twelve fruits of the Holy Spirit (charity, joy, peace, patience, kindness, goodness, long-suffering, humility, fidelity, modesty, continence, chastity). Habitual grace enables one to live as a true disciple of Christ, whatever the cost. CCC 2000, 2024

Haceldama: See Akeldama

Haggai, Book of [also Aggai or Aggaeus] (bøøk uhv ha-GAI): This O.T. book takes its name from the purported author, the minor prophet Haggai, whose name is derived from the Hebrew *hag* (feast). Post-exilic, probably written ca. 520 B.C., the book is unusual in the prophetic corpus in that it is written in the third person. It contains five oracular utterances, concerned primarily with the building of the Second Temple and the survival of the promise of the messianic dynasty in the person of Zerubbabel.

Hagia (Hahg-EE-uh): The name of the consecrated species in the Byzantine liturgy, from the Greek for "holy things."

Hagiography (hag-ee-AH-gruh-fee): (Greek *hagios:* holy + *graphein:* to write) The writing of the lives of the saints or books about the saints. Sources for investigation include martyrologies, liturgical texts, calendars, legends, and biographies. From the seventeenth century, the Bollandists have been primarily responsible for this investigation.

Hail Mary (HAYL MEHR-ee): This popular prayer of Christian devotion is composed of two texts from the Scriptures — the angelic greeting to Mary in Lk 1:28, "The Lord is with you," and her cousin Elizabeth's greeting to her in Lk 1:42, "Blessed are you among women and blessed is the fruit of your womb!" — plus a section composed in light of the growing popular devotion to Mary as the *Theotokos,* "Holy Mary, Mother of God, pray for us sinners, now and at the hour of our death." St. Peter Damian (d. 1072) is the first to testify that the *Ave Maria* had become a favorite prayer of the people. From the Synod Statutes of Paris around 1210, episcopal directives express the desire that the faithful should learn the *Ave Maria,* in addition to the Lord's Prayer and the Creed. **CCC 2673-2682**

Hair Shirt (HEHR SHERT): Worn by Christians for mortification, this rough undergarment has been all but abandoned today in favor of other penances representative of a shift in values and perceptions of asceticism.

Halo: See Aureole

Hampton Court Conference (HAMP-tuhn KORT KAHN-fuh-rens): A conference at Hampton Palace in London (1604) between representatives of the Anglican Church and the Puritan factions to settle differences.

Hanukkah [also Chanukah] (HAH-nuh-kuh): (Hebrew: dedication) The Jewish feast recalling the rededication of the Temple by Judas Maccabeus in 165 B.C., Hanukkah is also called the "Feast of Lights"; it is celebrated for eight days and involves the lighting of the "menorah" (the eight-branched candelabrum).

Happiness (HA-pee-nehs): The fulfillment toward which all are impelled. For Christians, true contentment is attainable only in heaven by virtue of the beatific vision. Even on earth, happiness is possible to some degree by accepting God's will and living continually in sanctifying grace. CCC 27, 30, 33, 384, 1028, 1035, 1718-1719, 1723, 1818, 2546, 2548

Harmony, Biblical (BIH-blih-kuhl HAHR-muh-nee): An attempt at integrating the four Gospels in such a way that a single narrative is produced, with the verses of all four Gospels arranged in chronological order. In recognition of the distinctive theological perspectives and characteristics peculiar to each of the Evangelists, most biblicists today reject the attempt at a biblical harmony, which otherwise imposes an artificial reordering of the biblical texts at odds with the original intentions of the inspired writers.

Hasmonaeans (haz-muh-NEE-uhnz): (Hebrew *Hashmoni:* descendants of Hashmon) Members of the Jewish family (beginning with the Maccabees) whose lineage can be traced back to 135 B.C. and who contributed the high priests and monarchs who ruled prior to the birth of Christ. The Hasmonaeans, according to first-century Jewish historian Josephus, produced Mattathias, who led the revolt against Antiochus in 168 B.C. (cf. 1 Mc 2:1-70). Later, they were crushed by Pompey around 68 B.C.

Hatred (HAY-trehd): An extreme loathing that often seeks revenge. All Christians are called to cast aside hatred and to love as Christ does. Sin must be "hated" and scorned completely; however, no person may rightly hate another. CCC 395, 1033, 1765, 1933, 2094, 2148, 2262, 2302-2303, 2539

Hearse (HERS): (From Latin *hirpex* via French *herse:* harrow) 1. A metal or wooden framework placed over the bier or coffin at funeral services. Since numerous prickets were placed throughout it to hold burning tapers and this bore a resemblance to the spikes of a harrow, the name "hearse" was given to the whole structure. 2. Any receptacle in which the coffin was placed for transportation, as in our modern understanding of the word, whether a carriage as originally used and sometimes still used in some cultures, or the modern motorized vehicle. 3. In Church parlance, the type of candelabrum used since the seventh century for the Holy Week service of Tenebrae (q.v.), during which the candles are extinguished ceremonially, one by one. This hearse is a triangular candlestick on which, historically, there have been from seven to twenty-four candles of unbleached wax. The usual number nowadays, where Tenebrae has been revived (as it fell into disuse after the Second Vatican Council), is fifteen. The Tenebrae hearse is laden with symbolic meaning. The triangle itself represents the Blessed Trinity. The highest candle (sometimes, incorrectly, bleached) represents Christ. The rest of the candles represent the Twelve Apostles.

Heart of Mary, Immaculate (ih-MAK-yöö-luht HAHRT uhv MEHR-ee): Both Pope Leo XIII and Pope St. Pius X called St. John Eudes (d. 1680) the "father, teacher, and first apostle" of devotion to the hearts of Jesus and Mary. By 1643, there was a public celebration in honor of the Immaculate Heart of Mary in the diocese of Autun; Pope Pius VII extended the celebration to any diocese requesting it. The liturgical text to be used was slightly modified from that of Our Lady of the Snows (August 5). The Missal of 1914 assigned the Mass to an appendix, but Pope Pius XII raised it to the rank of "double" (q.v.) in 1942 (the year he had consecrated to the Immaculate Heart of Mary) and assigned it to the octave of the Assumption, August 22. The 1969 reform of the calendar changed the status of the celebration to an optional memorial to be celebrated on the day following the feast of the Sacred Heart, the Saturday after the Second Sunday after Pentecost. In *Marialis Cultus,* the Apostolic Exhortation on Devotion to Mary, Pope Paul VI cited devotion to the Immaculate Heart of Mary as one example of contemporary devotions to Mary (n. 8). Pope John Paul II develops the theme of the unity of Mary's heart with her Son's in *Redemptor Hominis,* "Redeemer of Man" (n. 22).

Heaven (HEH-vehn): (Hebrew: *shamayim;* Greek: *ouranos)* 1. In biblical cosmology, either the physical sky or the spiritual "abode" of God. 2. For Christians, the state of those who, having attained salvation, are in glory with God and enjoy the beatific vision. 3. The phrase "kingdom of heaven" refers to the order or kingdom of God (q.v.), grace, salvation. CCC 326, 1024-1026, 2794-2795, 2802

Hebdomadarius (hehb-doh-muh-DEHR-ee-uhs) or **Hebdomadary** (hehb-DAH-muh-deh-ree): (Latin, from Greek *hebdomas:* week) Title generally given in a religious community bound to the common celebration of the hours to the leader who changes weekly (hence the name) in rotation with others in the community. The *General Norms of the Liturgy of the Hours* state that "in the absence of a priest or deacon, the one who presides at the office is only one among equals and does not enter the sanctuary or greet or bless the people" (n. 258).

Hebrew Catholic (HEE-broo KATH-uh-lihk): An individual of Jewish descent who is a member of the Catholic Church through Baptism. This term is preferable to "Jewish convert" since there are those who are of Jewish descent but who have had no formal relationship to Judaism. "Jewish convert" might also be misunderstood to mean one who had converted to Judaism.

Hebrew Feasts (HEE-broo FEESTS): The Jewish calendar is a lunar calendar; i.e., it is based on the revolution of the moon about the earth. Since Jewish feasts must be kept in their proper season, the calendar is adjusted every few years to the cycle of the sun. The Bible records only four original Hebrew names of the months. The Hebrew names were dropped, however, and all twelve months now have names of Babylonian origin, established after the Babylonian Exile. *Rosh Hashanah* (literally, "Head of the Year") takes place during the first two days of the month of Tishri (September-

October). Frequently it is called the Feast of the New Year. It emphasizes spirituality, morality, and holiness and is not tied to national historic events (cf. Nm 29:1). *Yom Kippur* (Day of Atonement) takes place at the end of the ten days of repentance that Rosh Hashanah inaugurates. The entire day is given to fasting, prayer, and contemplation (cf. Nm 29:7), emphasizing the same things as Rosh Hashanah. *Sukkot* (Feast of Tabernacles) is celebrated on the fifteenth of the month of Tishri and lasts for seven days. As with Passover and Shavuot, it is associated with both agriculture and history (cf. Lv 23:16, 34; Dt 16). *Hanukkah* (Feast of Dedication or Lights) is celebrated for eight days in the month of Kislev (November-December). It commemorates the victory of Judah Maccabee and his men over the Seleucids during the second century before Christ. Though not biblical in origin, it is a historical feast. *Purim* (Feast of Lots), falling on the fourteenth day of Adar (March), is a biblical festival based on the story in the Book of Esther. Jews of Persia were saved from being destroyed by Haman through the efforts of Mordecai and Queen Esther. *Passover (Pesach)* is celebrated in the month of Nisan (March-April) and is one of the three pilgrimage festivals named in the Bible (the other two being Shavuot and Sukkot). It is the celebration of the Jewish people's deliverance from Egyptian slavery through the intervention of God (cf. Lv 23:5-6). *Shavuot* (Feast of Pentecost) comes in the May-June months and commemorates God's giving of the Torah (Ten Commandments) to Moses on Mt. Sinai. **Cf. CCC 1096**

Hebrew Language (HEE-bröö LAN-gwehdzh): The language, spoken in the Palestinian area until the fourth century, that, with Aramaic, forms the Northwest Semitic language group. Most of the O.T. was written in Hebrew (except for some parts of Daniel and Ezra), which differs drastically from modern Hebrew.

Hebrew Poetry: See Psalms, Book of

Hebrews, Epistle to the (ih-PIH-suhl töö *th*uh HEE-brööz): The letter "to the Hebrews" is "a word of exhortation" (13:22), most likely addressed to Christian converts from Judaism. The recipients of the letter are not recent converts (5:12) and have undergone some persecution (10:32-44), which has not ceased (12:3-13, 13:3). Scholars do not agree as to the exact purpose of the letter. The believers are encouraged and exhorted to hold fast to their confession of faith (4:14-16), not to "drift away" from the message of salvation (2:1), and not to avoid community worship (10:25). They are urged to push on and not lose their enthusiasm for the Faith (10:23-25, 32-39). Much of the teaching illustrates how superior and potent is the work of salvation effected by Christ, the High Priest, which is contrasted to what was revealed in the past. Jesus, the exalted One (1:3), is the culmination of God's prophetic Word to humanity (1:1 ff.). Christ, Son of God and High Priest (3:1), has passed into heaven (4:14) and is far superior to the angels and even the greatest High Priest of old — Melchizedek (7:3). He, therefore, is supreme ruler of the House of God (3:6), the Author of salvation (2:10), the Great Shepherd (13:20). Christ proclaims and brings salvation (2:3) and is the cause of salvation for those who obey Him (5:9), which salvation He will dispense at His Second Coming (9:28). He saves from sins by cleansing (11:3) and bringing about the remission of sins (8:12, 9:14, 10:18), which renews and sanctifies the soul (2:11). The Church in Alexandria, from the second century on, accepted Hebrews as an authentic letter from Paul. Origen and a few others had serious doubts about its Pauline origins. In the Latin West, Tertullian and others doubted its Pauline authorship from the beginning. By the fourth century and on through to the Reformation, both East and West accepted the letter as being from Paul. Names that have been proposed as alternatives include Apollos, Barnabas, Prisca, Aquila, Silas, and Jude. The latest date for the letter is ca. A.D. 95 or 96, the traditional dating of 1 Clement, which mentions Hebrews in Ch. 36.

Hedge Schools (HEHDZH SKÖÖLZ): The means of providing Catholic education for Irish children during the eighteenth century. Because of the decree of King William III, issued in 1695, that outlawed the use of private homes and buildings to teach the Faith, teachers and pupils would congregate under the hedges near the roads. The law was relaxed in 1760.

Hedonism (HEE-duhn-nih-zuhm): The belief that one is only truly fulfilled when he possesses as many sensual and material pleasures as possible, regardless of their morality. The Church has always taught that this system excludes the necessary virtues of self-denial, charity, and patience.

Hegoumenos (heh-GÖÖ-meh-nos) or Hegumen (heh-GYÖÖ-muhn): The title of the superior in an Eastern monastery, similar to a Latin Rite abbot, who rules for life, assisted by a council. (Cf. Archimandrite.)

Hell (HEHL): The place or state that Satan and the fallen angels inhabit, along with those who have knowingly and willingly rejected God for all eternity. It is a condition of sense pain and separation from God that will never end. The N.T. speaks of fire and darkness related to hell, but its precise nature is unknown. **CCC 1033-1037, 1861**

Hellenism (HEHL-eh-nih-zuhm): General term used to describe a wide variety of Greek practices and influences that helped shape the identity and activity of the early Greek Church.

Henotikon (heh-NO-tee-kahn): Document issued by Emperor Zeno in 482 that states Trinitarian and Christological doctrines, attempting to mollify the Monophysites. The Henotikon accepted the Nicene Creed as interpreted by the Councils of Constantinople (381) and Ephesus (431), but not the interpretation of the Council of Chalcedon (451). The Monophysites were not satisfied, and the Magisterium also opposed the document.

Heortology (heh-or-TAHL-uh-dzhee): The study of the history, development, and theology of the feasts and seasons of the liturgical year.

Heptateuch (HEHP-tah-töök): (Greek: seven books) The first seven O.T. books from Genesis to Judges. Modern experts no longer believe that there is an underlying unity between the Pentateuch (the first five O.T. books) and Joshua and Judges. St. Ambrose used this term, but not in the same way as the early scholars.

Heresy (HEHR-uh-see): (From Greek *heresis:* faction) The deliberate post-baptismal denial or doubt by a Catholic of any truth that must be believed as part of Divine Revelation (cf. Can. 751). Heresy, if formal, is the deliberate resistance to God's authority, punishable by automatic excommunication (cf. Can. 1364). St. Paul warned strongly against those guilty of heresy. **CCC 465, 817, 2089**

Heretic (HEHR-eh-tihk): A baptized and professed person who knowingly, willingly, and culpably refuses to accept the teaching authority of the Church, thereby making himself a "formal" heretic. A "material" heretic denies that the Church has a teaching authority and consequently denies her teachings as well.

Herm, also Herma (HERM, HER-mah): A bust of a saint containing a reliquary of the saint whose likeness it represents.

Hermeneutics (her-meh-NOO-tihks): (Greek *hermeneuein:* to interpret) The methodological interpretation of the Bible, an attempt at determining the true sense of Scripture texts according to the principles of exegesis. In Catholic teaching, the Magisterium enjoys a privileged position in exercising the role of hermeneutics and thereby communicates to the Church the intended truth. In the Protestant traditions, the individual believer is encouraged to interpret Scripture on his own, while Catholics have the corporate assurance of exegesis provided by the Holy See, specifically through the guidance of the Pontifical Biblical Commission. Cf. **CCC 116**

Hermesianism (hehr-MEE-zhuhn-ih-zuhm): The philosophical and theological position of Georg Hermes (1775-1831) that attempted to blend elements of Catholicism and Enlightenment philosophy. Hermes held Kantian epistemology but not Kant's theory that God's existence could not be proved by reason. He also embraced semi-rationalistic positions regarding the relationship of faith to reason. Hermesianism was condemned by Pope Gregory XVI (*Dum acerbissimas,* 1835) and the First Vatican Council (1869-1870).

Hermit (HER-miht): (Greek *heremites:* one who dwells in the desert) A religious ascetic who lives a solitary life for the contemplation of God through silence, penance, and prayer. CCC 920-921

Heroic Act of Charity (hih-RO-ihk AKT uyv TSHEHR-ih-tee): Completely unselfish offering to God of one's good works and merits for the benefit of the souls in purgatory rather than for oneself. It is not a vow and so revocable at will.

Heroic Virtue (hih-RO-ihk VER-tshöö): The exemplary practice of the four cardinal virtues and three theological virtues sought in persons considered for sainthood. CCC 828

Hesperinos (heh-spehr-EE-nos): (From Greek: pertaining to the evening) The Byzantine liturgical office of Vespers.

Hesychasm (HEH-zih-ka-zuhm): (From Greek: tranquillity, silence, or condition of rest) A method of interior prayer of the spirit characterized by a conscious and constant attitude and awareness of the presence of God, a style of uninterrupted prayer as regular as the beating of the heart or breathing. This method of prayer is a part of the patrimony of the Eastern Church and is of great antiquity. It was transmitted by Eastern monks from master to disciple by word of mouth, by example, and by spiritual direction, and was only committed to paper at the beginning of the eleventh century in a treatise attributed to Symeon the New Theologian. Some Western writers have fixed their attention on the external technique of this prayer, and some have criticized it as a form of spiritual yoga or rationalist asceticism with no correlation to contemplation in its authentic sense.

There is a certain physical aspect involved: procedures in the control of breathing, bodily posture, and the rhythm of prayer. However, this external discipline is only an aid to concentration. The whole of one's attention must be given to the text of the short prayer "O Lord Jesus Christ, Son of God" (as the person breathes in deeply), "have mercy on me, a sinner" (as the person exhales). This prayer, continually repeated at each drawing of breath, becomes to the practitioner, as it were, second nature. Far from rendering the interior life mechanical, it has the opposite effect, of freeing it and turning it toward contemplation by constantly driving away from the region of the heart all contagion of sin and every external thought or image; and this by the power of the Most Holy Name of Jesus. Thus this particular style of spiritual prayer makes the heart ready for the indwelling of grace by constantly guarding its interior disposition This constant remembrance and perpetual prayer in the name of Jesus is meant to produce in the practitioner the habit of loving God perfectly and without hindrance. CCC 2717

Hesychasts (HEH-zih-kasts): Practitioners of hesychasm, usually applied to monks of the Eastern Church who lead a life of contemplation.

Heterodoxy (HEH-ter-o-dahk-see): False doctrine, teaching, or belief; a departure from true faith.

Hexaemeron (hehks-AHM-uh-ruhn): (Greek *hexaemeron:* six days) 1. The narrative of the six days of creation recorded in the first chapter of Genesis. 2. Also, the title of a poetic account of creation by St. Ambrose.

Hexapla (HEHK-suh-pluh): (Greek; sixfold) The O.T. edition by Origen, completed in Caesarea around 245, consisting of the Hebrew O.T., a Greek transliteration of the Hebrew, and the four Greek translations by Aquila, Symmochus, Theodotian, and the Septuagint. Origen's *Hexapla* actually included a seventh translation of the O.T. Portions of this massive volume were circulated, but the entire work was probably never reproduced.

Hexapteryga (HEHK-sap-TEHR-ih-guh): The fan, also called "ripidion," representing a six-winged angel and used to ventilate the Eucharistic Species after the Consecration in the Byzantine Rite.

Hexateuch (HEHKS-uh-töök): (Greek: six books) The term given by Julius Wellhausen to the first six O.T. books. Wellhausen and others thought that the *Hexateuch,* which included Genesis to Joshua, came from the same literary sources; today, however, scholars separate Joshua from the Pentateuch.

Hierarch (HAI-er-ahrk): A term sometimes used to designate any member of the episcopacy but more commonly used to designate bishops of the Eastern, or Oriental, Churches.

Hierarchy (HAI-rahr-kee): (Greek *hierarchia:* holy rule) That body of clergy which gives spiritual care to the faithful, governs the Church, and guides the Church's mission in the world. The hierarchy of order consists of the Pope, bishops, priests, and deacons, who carry out the sacramental, teaching, and pastoral ministry of the Church; the hierarchy of jurisdiction consists of the Pope and bishops, who give pastoral governance to the faithful. **CCC 871-876, 1569, 1571**

Hieratikon (hai-er-AH-tee-kahn): The prayer book of a priest in the Byzantine Rite. It contains the texts of the usual liturgical services, except for the Divine Liturgy (Mass) itself, which is found in a book called the *Leitourgikon.*

Hierodeacon (HAI-ro-dee-kuhn): In the Byzantine Church, the title of a monk who has been ordained a deacon.

Hieromonk (HAI-ro-muhnk): A monk invested with the priesthood in the Eastern Church.

Hierurgia (hai-uh-røør-DZHEE-uh): (From the Greek: acting as a priest or performing some holy service) This rather inclusive designation may include the administration of the sacraments, the celebration of Mass, or the imparting of a simple blessing.

High Priest (HAI PREEST): 1. In the Temple of Jerusalem, one who presided over the Great Council, the Sanhedrin, and the Temple ceremonies. He alone offered the sacrifice of the Day of Atonement and was able to enter the Holy of Holies. Ex 28 details the vesture and institution of the high priest, an office that after 37 B.C. became largely political. 2. A title used for Jesus Christ, Who is the One Mediator with His Father. CCC 540, 662, 784, 1137, 1187; cf. 433

Hirmos (HIHR-mos): In the Byzantine Rite, an ancient troparion that has become the model from which others have derived their rhythm and melody. The opposite of the *Idiomelon.* (Cf. also Canon.)

History, Church (TSHERTSH HIH-stuh-ree): Ecclesiastical history is the theological discipline that studies "the growth in time and space of the Church founded by Christ" (Hubert Jedin). This study applies all the methods of secular historical scholarship, but in such a way as to subordinate these tools to the light of faith. For in this light, the Church is confessed to be a divine-human reality, an extension of the Incarnation itself, a mystery of the communion of human beings in Christ across time and culture. As a visible society with a past and a history, the Church is naturally subject to historical study. But this visible, social, historical institution is also the mystical body of Christ. In the light of faith, the Church's history is the history of the realization of salvation, the fulfillment of the divine plan from Pentecost to the Parousia. As a visible institution, the Church is subject to historical observation. Historical explanations can be offered for development, for her engagement in the events of world and religious history, and for the role of her leaders and membership. Nonetheless, such observation and explanation are understood not to be exhaustive. The presence of the Holy Spirit directing the Church on her way through time can never be the object of complete historical observation and explanation. In a sense, the first exercise in ecclesiastical history occurs within the canon of Scripture in the Acts of the Apostles. But Eusebius of Caesarea

(c. 260-c. 340) is generally regarded as the father of Church history. His *Ecclesiastical History* is the chief source of knowledge of Church history from apostolic times to his own day. Church history has continued to be the object of vigorous scholarship and investigation.

Hogan Schism (HO-guhn SIH-zuhm): A nineteenth-century schismatic movement led by Fr. William Hogan in Philadelphia.

Holiness (HO-lee-nehs): Sanctity attained by self-dedication to God, separation from worldly values, and conformity to Christ, bringing about a profound transformation, allowing for participation in the life of the Blessed Trinity. CCC 375, 405, 2013-2014, 2028, 2813; cf. 459, 492, 564, 670, 824-828, 867, 1030, 1475, 1709, 1986, 2015, 2030, 2045, 2809

Holiness Churches (HO-lee-nehs TSHERTSH-ehz): A group of "perfectionist" sects that stress Christian perfection, or holiness, as a "second blessing" or work of grace instantaneously accomplished subsequent to justification. Most of the Holiness groups in the United States have their roots in Methodism, and often are Pentecostal in belief and practice.

Holiness, Mark of the Church (HO-lee-nehs, MAHRK uhv *th*uh TSHERTSH): One of the four marks or properties of the Church, along with oneness, catholicity, and apostolicity. This holiness arises from her constitution as a communion of faithful members under the Headship of Jesus Christ. CCC 823-829

Holocaust (HO-luh-kawst): 1. The burnt offering in the Mosaic Law (Lv 1:3), presented as a sacrifice under the Old Covenant for the sins of the people. 2. During the Second World War, the systematic mass killing of Jews and others by the Nazis. Cf. CCC 2583

Holy (HO-lee): Of God, sacred. Something that has been hallowed by a religious rite of blessing. An attribute of God.

Holy Alliance (HO-lee uh-LAI-uhnts): A laudable but eventually unsuccessful treaty signed by Austria, Russia, and Prussia in 1815, by which signatory nations would settle future disputes according to Christian principles.

Holy Communion (HO-lee kuh-MYÖÖN-yuhn): The sacrament of the Body, Blood, Soul, and Divinity of Jesus Christ, usually received during the Mass, bringing about "communion" or a profound union with God. To receive the Holy Eucharist worthily, one must be a practicing Catholic who has been catechized about the Eucharist, be free from mortal sin, and have fasted from food and drink (except water and medicine) for one hour. Holy Communion at the hour of one's death is called *Viaticum* (q.v.). **CCC 1331, 1355, 1384; cf. 1244, 1385-1390, 1411, 1415, 1650, 2120**

Holy Days (HO-lee DAYZ): Also called days of precept, holy days are feasts of such importance in the liturgical calendar that attendance at Mass is required. The Code of Canon Law (cc. 1246-1248) discusses these, rightly beginning with Sunday, describing it as "the day on which the paschal mystery is celebrated in light of the apostolic tradition and is to be observed as the foremost day of obligation in the universal Church" (Can. 1246). It then lists the following to be observed: Christmas; Epiphany; Ascension; Corpus Christi; Mary, Mother of God; Immaculate Conception; Assumption; St. Joseph; Sts. Peter and Paul; and All Saints. This list is the same as that given in the 1917 code, with the feast of the Circumcision eliminated in favor of the restored title for January 1, Mary, Mother of God. The present code then states that "the conference of bishops can abolish certain holy days of obligation or transfer them to a Sunday with the prior approval of the Holy See" (Can. 1246). The United States bishops decided not to make the feasts of St. Joseph and Sts. Peter and Paul days of precept and transferred the Solemnities of the Epiphany and Corpus Christi to a Sunday. **CCC 2177; cf. 2042, 2180, 2185**

Holy (or Royal) Doors (HO-lee [ROI-uhl] DORZ): The double door in the center of the iconostasis. It only opens for a bishop, a priest, or the deacon during the most solemn part of the celebration of the Divine Liturgy.

Holy Family (HO-lee FAM-ih-lee): This term refers to the community of Jesus, the Blessed Virgin Mary, and her chaste spouse, Joseph. Christian reflection on the life of this holiest of families revolves around the virtues of faith, hope, charity, chastity, and loving obedience that characterized their common life at Nazareth. The Feast of the Holy Family is celebrated on the Sunday that falls within the Octave of Christmas or, if no Sunday occurs within the Octave, on December 30. Cf. CCC 1655

Holy Father (HO-lee FAH-ther): A title of the Pope that is the commonly shortened translation of the Latin title *Beatissimus Pater,* the Most Blessed Father. It refers to his position as the spiritual father of all the Christian faithful.

Holy Hour (HO-lee AUR): An uninterrupted hour of prayer and meditation in the presence of the Blessed Sacrament, which may be exposed on the altar or reserved in the tabernacle. During His agony in the Garden of Gethsemane, Our Lord asked the Apostle Peter: "Could you not watch one hour with me?" (Mt 26:40). As a result, the content of our prayer and meditation during a Holy Hour is usually Our Lord's passion. A Holy Hour is an affirmation of our faith in the Real Presence of Christ in the Holy Eucharist. Parishes, then, are well advised to offer the faithful regular opportunities to adore the Eucharistic Lord.

Holy House of Loreto: See Loreto, Holy House of

Holy Name of Jesus (HO-lee NAYM uhv DZHEE-zuhs): A feast in the Roman Rite that used to fall on the first Sunday after the Octave of Christmas, i.e., between January 1 and the Feast of the Epiphany on January 6. If there was no Sunday between these two dates, the feast was observed on January 2. First celebrated in Germany, Belgium, England, and Scotland, this feast was observed universally at the behest of Pope Innocent XIII (1721-1724). However, Pope Paul VI suppressed the feast when he reformed the Roman Calendar following Vatican II. Although it is no longer celebrated as a feast, the idea behind it is ever valid. Since we love and respect the name of Jesus, it is right and proper that we pay honor and homage to it. The spirit of this is captured by St. Paul: "At the name of Jesus every knee should bow, in heaven and on earth and under the earth, and every tongue confess that Jesus Christ is Lord, to the glory of God the Father" (Phil 2:10-11). Cf. CCC 2145-2146, 2668, 2750

Holy Office, Congregation of the (kahn-greh-GAY-shuhn uhv *th*uh HO-lee AW-fihs): Former name for what is now known as the Congregation for the Doctrine of the Faith.

Holy of Holies, The (*th*uh HO-lee uhv HO-leez): The inner sanctuary of the Temple, shaped like a cube and containing the Ark of the Covenant, access to which was reserved for the high priest on rare occasions.

Holy Oils (HO-lee OILZ): Oil is frequently mentioned in the O.T. in connection with the commissioning of priests, prophets, and kings. Jesus' title as Messiah (*Christos* in Greek) specifically means "the Anointed One." In the N.T., Christ sends His Apostles to anoint the sick, while the Epistle of James advises the sick to call for the presbyters of the Church to anoint them. Oil has long signified healing and being set apart for special work and responsibilities. Not surprisingly, then, oil has been used in the Church's sacramental rites from the earliest days. Three oils are traditionally used: holy chrism (usually a mixture of pure olive oil with balsam or perfume), oil of catechumens, and oil of the sick. They are consecrated or blessed by the bishop during the Chrism Mass of Holy Thursday. Chrism is used in the Sacraments of Baptism, Confirmation, and Holy Orders. The oils are kept in vessels called "stocks" and are stored in an "aumbry," often a kind of wall safe in the sanctuary. Cf. CCC 695, 1183, 1237, 1241, 1289, 1293-1294

Holy Places (HO-lee PLAY-sehz): Those sites in the Holy Land, Palestine, or modern Israel associated with the life and ministry of Our Lord. In many cases, we must rely on tradition for the location of these places that are so important for the faith and reverence of Christian believers. The Holy Places would include the Basilica of the Annunciation in Nazareth and the Basilica of the Nativity in Bethlehem. In Jerusalem, the Cenacle (Upper Room), the Basilica of the Ecce Homo (once thought to be the site of Pilate's Praetorium), the Via Dolorosa (the original Way of the Cross to Calvary), and Calvary itself together with the tomb of Jesus, both contained within the Church of the Holy Sepulcher. Across from the city, on the Mount of Olives, are the Church of the Dominus Flevit, where Our Lord was said to have wept over the city of Jerusalem, Gethsemane (the Church of All Nations), and the Sanctuary of the Ascension, where it is also thought Christ taught the Our Father. Also included among the Holy Places are the site of the Temple, the Church of the Dormition of Our Lady, and the Sanctuary of her Assumption. The Crusades, of course, were waged largely to regain control of these Holy Places from the Muslims. Since the thirteenth century, care of the Holy Places has been entrusted to the Order of Friars Minor (Franciscans).

Holy Roman Empire (HO-lee RO-muhn EHM-pair): Some date the beginning of this political entity to Christmas, A.D. 800, when Pope Leo crowned Charlemagne as "Emperor ruling the Roman Empire," thus restoring the imperial dignity to the West. More properly, the "Roman Empire" may be said to have been effectively established by Otto I (ruled 936-973). It was not called "Holy" until the reign of Frederick I Barbarossa (ruled 1152-1190). Never a unitary State in the modern sense, it was a federation of kingdoms, duchies, principalities, and free cities, over which the emperor exercised loose authority. The office of emperor was in theory elective, but from the thirteenth century until the end of the empire, it was held by the Hapsburgs of Austria, with one exception. After the sixteenth century, the title of emperor was largely honorific. At its greatest extent the Holy Roman Empire included modern Germany, Austria, Switzerland, the Low Countries, and parts of Italy, France, Czechoslovakia, Yugoslavia, and Poland. The existence of the empire continued to remind Europe of the dream of political unity that had been lost with the collapse of the Roman Empire. In the eighteenth century, the French philosopher Voltaire remarked that it was "neither Holy, nor Roman, nor an Empire." In 1386 Napoleon I abolished the empire. The Hapsburg emperors of Austria continued to regard themselves as the heirs of the Holy Roman Emperors until the collapse of that monarchy in 1918.

Holy Saturday (HO-lee SA-ter-day): The Saturday of Holy Week. The Roman Missal notes that, according to a most ancient tradition, the sacraments are not celebrated on this day (the exception, of course, being the Sacrament of Penance and emergency ministrations of Anointing or Viaticum). On this day, the Church keeps vigil at the tomb of Our Savior. In the cathedral church of the diocese and many parish churches, the Office of Readings and Morning Prayer are celebrated. Midday Prayer and Vespers are also celebrated, since the Easter Vigil cannot begin until after sundown. Up to the Easter Vigil, preparatory rites may be celebrated with the catechumens. Wherever possible, the paschal fast is prolonged until the vigil. **CCC 624**

Holy See (HO-lee SEE): Often called the "Apostolic See," this is the residence of the Pope and center of the administrative offices of the Church. The Holy See has its headquarters in Vatican City and is composed of a host of departments. Over one hundred twenty nations have formal diplomatic relations with the Holy See, whose mission is to carry on the spiritual and moral authority as exercised by the Sovereign Pontiff.

Holy Sepulcher in Jerusalem, The (*th*uh HO-lee SEH-pøøl-ker in dzheh-RÖÖ-suh-lehm): The Church historian Eusebius has recorded the intention and work of Constantine, who initiated and completed the first Church of the Holy Sepulcher in Jerusalem, dedicated in 335. The site, originally used for earlier Jewish burials, had been covered over by Hadrian's temple of Venus, built upon the imperial construction of the pagan Jerusalem, Aelia Capitolina (A.D. 135). The temple was destroyed by Constantine in 326, thus revealing the tomb of Christ, along with the True Cross and other relics of the Lord's death. Immediately, the emperor instructed Bishop Macarius of Jerusalem to erect a magnificent structure to enshrine the sites of the Lord's death and resurrection. The present-day building is the product of centuries of destruction and rebuilding, from the invasions of Persians and Muslims to accidental fires. The Holy Sepulcher proper is housed within the small shrine built in 1810, under the rotunda of the main church. The entire structure of the Basilica of the Holy Sepulcher is a hodgepodge of architectural styles, fragments from previous monuments, buildings, and shrines, much of which is under constant restoration and reconstruction. The architectural disharmony is echoed by that of the various Christian Churches that control sections of the church. The church is divided among various Christian Churches, primarily the Latins, Greeks, Armenians, Copts, and Syrian Jacobites. Another site, known as Gordon's Calvary, was declared to be the true location of the Lord's crucifixion by Otto Thenius in 1849. It is today a popular tourist site, offering a recently constructed rendering of an artist's imagined sepulcher. Various Protestant communions hold this to be the true Calvary, even though there is no archaeological evidence at all to support this view.

Holy Sepulcher, Knights of the (NAITS uhv *th*uh HO-lee SEH-pøøl-ker): The Equestrian Order of the Most Holy Sepulcher of Jerusalem, founded during the First Crusade in 1099, receiving papal approval in 1122, with the original purposes of defending the universal Church, defending the city of Jerusalem, guarding the Basilica of the Holy Sepulcher, ensuring the safety of pilgrims, and fighting the Muslims. The Knights were driven out of Jerusalem in 1244, and after many transformations, were reestablished in 1847 by Pope Pius IX as an honorary, ceremonial, and charitable order.

Holy Souls: See Purgatory

Holy Spirit (HO-lee SPIH-riht): The Third Person of the Blessed Trinity, often called the "Advocate," the "Consoler," the "Paraclete," and the "Sanctifier," Who is coeternal, coequal, consubstantial with and distinct from the Father and the Son. He proceeds from both the Father and the Son by "spiration." Scripture and Tradition mention much about the Holy Spirit's role in grace and the gifts, virtues, and fruits. CCC 683-747

Holy Spirit, Sins Against the (SIHNZ uh-GEHNST *th*uh HO-lee SPIH-riht): 1. The disobedience to God, considered especially offensive to the Third Person, that are sins against faith and may possibly result in hatred of God and even a pact with Satan. The six traditional sins are: (a) presumption of God's mercy; (b) despair; (c) resisting the known truth; (d) envy of another's spiritual good; (e) obstinacy in sin; (f) final impenitence. 2. The offense against the Paraclete referred to by Our Lord in the Gospels as the "sin against the Holy Spirit." Many authors have offered an interpretation as to what this sin is. The standard view is that the "unpardonable sin" against the Consoler is final impenitence, often caused by despair or presumption. Other writers have suggested that the unforgivable sin is *any* sin that one refuses to turn over to God for forgiveness. Cf. CCC 1864

Holy Thursday (HO-lee THERZ-day): Thursday of Holy Week. In the morning, the Chrism Mass is celebrated at the diocesan cathedral (unless pastoral necessity requires that it be celebrated at another time and place). This Mass is concelebrated by the bishop and his presbyterate as a sign of their unity in the priestly service of God's people. At this Mass, the bishop and his priests renew their ordination commitment. Later on in the day, the evening Mass of the Lord's Supper is offered. At this time, a solemn reception in the church of the oils blessed previously by the bishop at the cathedral may take place. The evening Mass commemorates the institution of the Holy Eucharist, the institution of the ministerial priesthood, and the precept of Christian charity (as symbolized in the washing of the feet). The homily should illumine these mysteries. The *mandatum*, or foot washing, may follow. Enough Hosts are consecrated at this Mass to provide for the people's reception of Holy Communion on Good Friday. At the conclusion of the Evening Mass, the Blessed Sacrament is borne in procession to the place of repose for solemn adoration up until midnight. Priests are forbidden to offer Mass without a congregation on Holy Thursday. Cf. CCC 532, 1297

Holy Water (HO-lee WAH-ter): Water blessed at the Easter Vigil for the Baptism of catechumens and infants that night. It is then used at the Rite of Blessing and sprinkling with holy water and for Baptisms during the Easter Season. Formerly, this water was used from Easter to the following Holy Week. Now, water is blessed each time Baptism is celebrated. Holy water is a sacramental and may be used in the blessing of religious articles, homes, automobiles, and other items. A priest or deacon is lawfully permitted to bless holy water. Cf. CCC 694, 1214, 1217

Holy Water Font (HO-lee WAH-ter FAHNT): Receptacle at the entrance to churches containing holy water, so that upon entering and leaving, the faithful can dip their fingers into the font and bless themselves, recalling their Baptism. Cf. CCC 1185

Holy Week, Liturgy of: See Triduum, Paschal

Holy Year (HO-lee YEER): By custom, declared every twenty-five years by the reigning Supreme Pontiff. The Pope may grant a plenary indulgence for those who make a pilgrimage to one of the patriarchal basilicas of Rome. In 1974, Pope Paul VI issued *Apostolorum limina,* announcing that 1975 would be a holy year. That holy year was dedicated to reconciliation and occasioned the appearance of two Eucharistic Prayers for Reconciliation and a formula for the Mass of Reconciliation. Apart from every twenty-fifth year, the Holy Father may decree the observance of another holy year. The last such one was called by Pope John Paul II in 1983. He wished that the period from the Solemnity of the Annunciation in 1983 through Easter in 1984 be given over to a commemoration of the redemption. This coincided with the 1983 Synod on Reconciliation and Penance. The most recent holy year, in 2000, was proclaimed by Pope John Paul II as the Great Jubilee of the two-thousandth anniversary of the Lord's Birth. Cf. CCC 2449

Homiletics (hah-muh-LEH-tihks): That branch of theology that deals with the art and science of the preparation and delivery of sermons, homilies, and other instructions in the Faith.

Homily (HAH-muh-lee): A form of preaching consisting of an address or sermon given by an ordained minister (bishop, priest, deacon) after the Gospel at Mass and intended as an explanation or application of the Gospel passage. CCC 132, 1154, 1346

Homoousios and Homoiousios (ho-mo-ÖÖ see os and ho-MOI-öö-see-os): The former (Greek for "consubstantial") is the term accepted at the Council of Nicaea (A.D. 325) and incorporated into the Nicene Creed to affirm the full divinity of the Son, as He shares the divine substance of His Father. By the 360s, *homoousios* was also applied to the Holy Spirit. Before Nicaea, some theologians had preferred the term *homoiousios* ("of like substance"). But the Council concluded that the expression allowed for too much distinction of Persons in the Godhead and settled instead for "of the same substance." CCC 465; cf. 242, 248, 253, 262, 467, 685

Homosexuality (ho-mo-sehk-shöö-AL-ih-tee): Condition of a person whose sexual orientation is toward persons of the same rather than the opposite sex. The condition is not sinful in itself, but homosexual acts are seriously sinful; subjective responsibility for such acts, however, may be conditioned and diminished by compulsion and related factors. CCC 2357-2359

Hood (HØØD): A conical, flexible, and brimless headdress that, when worn, covers the entire head except for the face. It is either a separate garment or part of a cloak. Today, the hood is usually associated with orders made up of contemplatives, monks as well as nuns and/or mendicants.

Hope (HOP): The supernaturally infused virtue, having God as its object and motive, that gives assurance of salvation based on the merits of Jesus Christ. Hope enables one to carry the cross of Christ and to battle amid the world's temptations, confident that those who remain faithful will live forever with God. In the past, hope was thought to be oriented only to the next life; however, now it is viewed as also having significance for this world and encourages those who possess it to care for the disadvantaged, thereby giving them assuredness in their struggles. **CCC 1813, 1817-1821**

Horologion (haw-ruh-LO-dzhee-ahn): (Greek: book of hours) Eastern Church term for a psalter that closely parallels the Roman Breviary and contains the ordinary portions of the Church year.

Hosanna (ho-ZAH-nuh): A Hebrew imperative meaning "Grant your salvation!" (cf. Ps 118:25). In time, the term came to be used as a form of exultant greeting and acclaim, as in Our Lord's triumphal entry into Jerusalem on Palm Sunday (Mt 21:9; Mk 11:10; Jn 12:13). Isidore of Seville explains its liturgical use as having the understood object of "your people" or "the whole world" *(Etymologeia,* VI:19, 22-23). It is used in this sense in the *Sanctus* at Mass (both in Latin and in the vernacular) and in the traditional Palm Sunday hymn *Pueri Hebraeorum.* **CCC 559**

Hosea (ho-ZAY-uh): Prophet of the O.T. book by that name, whose activity was a continuation of the work of Amos and directed to the people of the Northern Kingdom. It extended over a long period in the eighth century, probably ending before the fall of Samaria in 721 B.C. Israel enjoyed prosperity in the eighth century, but much of its wealth was gained by social injustice and was spent on frivolous pleasures. True religion was forgotten, with many of the Jews embracing the licentious worship of Baal. Many of the priests had become corrupt, negligent, and avaricious. The external rites were carried on, but with no inner spirit of love. Hosea himself was a married man, and he envisioned the Lord as the husband of Israel. Since his own wife had been unfaithful to him, he found it easy to empathize with the Lord, forsaken by His Chosen People, and much of the writing employs this comparison. In so doing, he anticipated the theology of Jesus and the beloved disciple. Hosea makes it clear that God does expect fidelity of His people, that He is grievously offended by their sins, but that He is ever ready to forgive them and receive them back.

Host (HOST): (Latin *hostia:* victim) 1. Originally referring to any victim used in sacrifice to a divinity (pagan god), but used by the Church to refer specifically to a sacrifice to the one, true God. Christ is the spotless Victim or Host. 2. The bread that is used at the Holy Sacrifice of the Mass, the unbloody reenactment of the bloody Sacrifice of the Cross on Calvary. Strictly speaking, however, this bread is only the Host after the consecration and in view of its consummation at Holy Communion. **CCC 1378, 1992**

Hosts: See Sabaoth

Hours: See Canonical Hours

Hours, Book of (BØØK uhv AU-erz): Devotional books used by laypeople who could not participate (for various reasons) in the celebration of the Liturgy of the Hours. Such books became popular in the thirteenth century and usually were commissioned by wealthy people. The artistic quality of the books was very high, and the Blessed Virgin Mary was especially honored through their artwork.

Hours, Little (LIH-tuhl AU-erz): The four lesser sections of the Divine Office that took their names from the times of the day at which they were recited. Originally Prime, Terce, Sext, and None, they have been replaced by one "hour" called Daytime Prayer in the revised Liturgy of the Hours. **Cf. CCC 1174-1178**

Huguenots (HYÖÖ-guh-nahts): French Calvinists of the sixteenth and seventeenth centuries who opposed a central monarchy and supported local autonomy. The persecution of the Huguenots was brought about both by religious and political motives, and many of them fled from France to settle in North America, South Africa, the Netherlands, and England.

Human Acts (HYÖÖ-muhn AKTS): The performance of certain behavior done with deliberation, knowledge, and free consent. Nonhuman acts are spontaneous and lacking in knowledge, deliberation, or free consent; hence, the agent has no control. On the other hand, human acts are controlled by the individual and are expressive of the doer's nature. When acting humanly, one moves toward a "good" or what is perceived as such. If in fact one does authentic good, that person becomes more fully who he or she was meant to be and participates in the goodness of God. CCC 1709, 1731, 1744-1745, 1749-1761, 1782, 1805, 1813, 1853, 1954, 2008, 2085, 2106, 2157

Humanae Vitae (höö-MAH-nay VEE-tay): (Latin: "Of Human Life") An encyclical issued by Pope Paul VI on July 29, 1968, which reiterated the Church's teaching that each act of marital intercourse must be open to the transmission of new life. Much uproar ensued after the publication of this letter. However, several theologians, priests, and laity who at one time dissented from this authoritative teaching have come to recognize the wisdom of the Church and since changed their positions. Cf. CCC 2370, 2399

Human Dignity (HYÖÖ-muhn DIHG-nih-tee): The inherent worth of each human person. Humans are made in God's image and likeness; they alone — of all God's creatures on earth — have an immortal soul. Pope John Paul II has made human dignity one of his favorite themes. CCC 27, 306-308, 357, 1700, 1706, 1738, 1930, 2339, 2393

Humani Generis (höö-MAH-nee DZHAY-neh-rihs): (Latin: "Of the Human Race") An encyclical issued in 1950 by Pope Pius XII as an assessment of twentieth-century Catholic theology. While encouraging modern exegesis, it stresses the importance of interpreting the Scriptures within the context of traditional Catholic teaching, and cautions against compromising the integrity of Catholic doctrine in an attempt to harmonize it with modern thought. Cf. CCC 116, 297

Humanism (HYÖÖ-muh-nih-zuhm): Movement begun in the fourteenth and fifteenth centuries to justify the Renaissance, advocating an intellectual approach to antiquity devoid of religious belief. Humanism has periodically made comebacks in post-Jansenist France (1700s) and in the works of Marx and Lenin (1800s), in which the goal was to eliminate all "dehumanizing" elements by exalting man's power, often not considering God as the guarantor of one's destiny. Christian humanism recognizes Christ as the Way to a truly human life, and its Model.

Humanitarianism (hyöö-MAN-ih-TEHR-ee-uhn-ih-zuhm): 1. In popular usage, altruism. 2. In philosophy, a system of thought, separated from traditional Christianity in the sixteenth and seventeenth centuries and continuing to exist as a contemporary ethical system that makes human welfare and happiness the exclusive goal of all human effort, with no reference to God or His revelation. Pope John Paul II, in his encyclical *Redemptor Hominis,* maintains that humanitarianism actually defeats its own goal by ignoring the essential role God has in the well-being of mankind. Cf. CCC 360, 775-776, 1045

Human Life International (HYÖÖ-muhn LAIF ihn-ter-NA-shuh-nuhl): Founded by Fr. Paul Marx, O.S.B., in 1981 for the purposes of protecting the unborn, elderly, and handicapped; strengthening family life; encouraging chastity; and promoting the practice of natural family planning.

Humeral Veil (HYÖÖ-mer-uhl VAYL): A scarflike liturgical garment about eight or nine feet in length and approximately two or three feet in width, worn over the shoulders. It is used most often in conjunction with the cope. The humeral veil is worn out of reverence when sacred objects are carried in procession or when the faithful are blessed with them. It is used to hold the monstrance at Benediction or procession of the Blessed Sacrament. The minister covers his hands with the ends of the veil so that it, not his hands, touches the monstrance. The color of the humeral veil can be white, silver, or gold.

Humiliati (öö-mihl-ee-AH-tee): An order of penitents founded in the twelfth century, dedicated to mortification and care for the poor. Originally intended to adhere to the Rule of St. Benedict, the Humiliati were suppressed in 1571; some of the members attempted to assassinate St. Charles Borromeo, the reigning Cardinal-Archbishop of Milan, in 1569.

Humility (hyöö-MIHL-ih-tee): The supernatural virtue by which one attains the correct perception of one's relationship with God. Man himself was made in original justice and then fell; now, he has been redeemed in Christ. The attitude of humility is: "I am good only because of God's mercy." Humility counters pride and seeks to serve God and others, as Mary did. **CCC 2546; cf. 2559, 2631, 2713**

Hylics (HAI-lihks): One of the dualistic branches of Gnosticism, holding that matter is superior to the spirit. The Hylics were also called "materials."

Hymn (HIHM): A song of praise or petition to God or the saints. **Cf. CCC 1156-1158**

Hymnal (HIHM-nuhl): A book containing hymn texts, usually with music.

Hymnody (HIHM-nuh-dee): Religious lyric poetry. Hymnody may be either liturgical or nonliturgical, depending on how it should be used.

Hymnology (hihm-NAHL-uh-dzhee): Historical study of the origins and development of various hymn styles.

Hyperdulia (hai-per-DÖÖ-lee-uh): Extended praise or respect reserved for the Blessed Mother. **CCC 971**

Hypnosis (hihp-NO-sihs): A mental state resembling sleep, induced by suggestion, in which the subject does the bidding of the hypnotist. Hypnotism is permissible under certain conditions: the existence of a serious reason (e.g., for anesthetic or therapeutic purposes) and the competence and integrity of the hypnotist. Hypnotism should not be practiced for the sake of amusement. Experiments indicate that, contrary to popular opinion, hypnotized subjects may be induced to perform immoral acts that normally they would not do.

Hypostasis (hai-PAH-stuh-sihs): Greek philosophical term that can refer to the nature of something, or to a particular instance of that nature. During the Christological and Trinitarian controversies (third and fourth centuries), the second meaning of the term prevailed in doctrinal usage. The term came to acquire a meaning roughly synonymous with that of the Latin word *persona:* an individual of a rational nature. In the Council of Constantinople (A.D. 381), the doctrine of the Trinity was formulated as "three *hypostases* in one *ousia* (substance)." Later, the expression "hypostatic union" (q.v.) was used to refer to the unity of the divine and human natures in the one divine Person *(hypostasis)* of Jesus Christ. CCC 252, 466, 468

Hypostatic Union (hai-po-STA-tihk YÖÖN-yuhn): The substantial unity of the divine and human natures in the one Person *(hypostasis)* of Jesus Christ. This doctrine was proclaimed at the Council of Chalcedon (A.D. 451), ruling out both Nestorianism (which denied the real unity of the natures of Christ) and Monophysitism (which denied the real distinction of the human and divine natures of Christ). CCC 466, 468

Hyssop (HIH-suhp): A caper plant indigenous to the Near East, used by the elders of Israel, at Moses' command, for sprinkling the blood of the Passover lamb on the lintels of Hebrew households (Ex 12:22). Its sprigs, bound into a bunch, were used by the ancient Hebrews for other rituals of purificatory sprinkling. Since its pungent leaves have a medicinal property, hyssop was considered symbolic of healing.

I

ICEL [International Committee (Commission) on English in the Liturgy] (AI-sehl [ihn-ter-NA-shun-uhl kuh-MIH-tee (kuh-MIH-shun) awn IHNG-lihsh ihn *th*uh LIH-ter-dzhee]): Based in Washington, D.C., this commission came into existence at the close of Vatican II for the purpose of translating liturgical texts into English. Translations by ICEL are submitted for critique and approval to the national conferences of bishops in countries where English is spoken. The conferences must then present their approved texts to the Holy See for confirmation. In recent years, ICEL's work has come up for considerable criticism from various episcopal conferences, scholars, and the Holy See itself.

Icon or Ikon (AI-kahn): A representation of Our Lord, the Virgin Mary, or a saint, painted on a wall, a partition, or a wooden panel. The icons of Eastern Churches take the place of statues in the Western Church. **CCC 1161**

Iconoclastic Controversy (ai-kahn-uh-KLAS-tihk KAHN-truh-ver-see): (Greek *eikon:* image + *klaein:* to break) Controversy that rejected the veneration of sacred images as superstitious. There were two phases of iconoclasm in the East between A.D. 726 and 842. Believing that icons fostered idolatry and hindered the conversion of Muslims and Jews, Emperor Leo III, in 726, ordered their destruction; his edict was countered by bitter opposition, especially among the monks. St. John Damascene wrote a defense of icons; in the West, Pope Gregory III condemned iconoclasm in 731. Leo's successor, Constantine V, continued his father's policy, even convening the Synod of Hieria in 753 to secure the condemnation of images. After the death of Leo IV, who had not pursued the matter, the Empress Irene reversed the earlier iconoclastic policies. With the cooperation of Pope Hadrian I, she was instrumental in convening the Second Council of Nicaea in 787, which condemned the Synod of Hieria; Nicaea II advanced the principle that veneration accorded to an image actually passes to that which it represents. The second phase of iconoclasm began in 814, when Emperor Leo V ordered the destruction of icons and the persecution of those who opposed him. Leo's policies were maintained until the restoration of the veneration of images by the Empress Theodora in 842 with a feast in their honor, observed in the Eastern Church as the Feast of Orthodoxy. Cf. CCC 1159, 1161-1162, 1192, 2131, 2705

Iconostasis (ai-kahn-AH-stuh-sihs): 1. Properly speaking, any support for an icon. 2. Generally, the screen covered with icons that separates the sanctuary from the rest of the church in the Eastern Church.

Ideology (ih-dee-AHL-uh-dzhee): (Greek *idea* + *logia:* voicing ideas) A set of ideas, whether true or false, that influences individuals, a certain group, or a whole society, motivating them to some action.

Idiomelon (ih-dee-O-meh-lahn): (Greek: proper melody) In the liturgy of the Eastern Church, a troparion that is sung on a melody that belongs to it alone; the opposite of the hirmos (q.v.).

Idioms, Communication of: See Communicatio Idiomatum

Idol (AI-duhl): (Greek *eidolon:* phantom; Latin *idolum,* image, picture) 1. Any created thing that is accorded honor owed only to God, its Creator. 2. More strictly, an object — usually an animal figure or the representation of a deity — that is worshipped in place of God. CCC 2112-2114; cf. 1723, 2129, 2289, 2424

Idolatry (ai-DAHL-uh-tree): The practice of giving the worship due God to another person or object. Idolatry is a manifest disregard for the responsibility that all have to adore God alone. In general, the prophetic condemnation of idolatry centers on the reversal of the creation of humanity by God in His image and likeness; when a human being fashions an idol, the god is made in the image and likeness of the human maker. CCC 2112-2114; cf. 1723, 1852, 2097, 2129, 2138, 2289, 2424

Ignorance (IHG-ner-uhnts): The absence of knowledge of a subject on the part of one who is presumed to have such knowledge. It is applied in various places in Canon Law. CCC 1735, 1790-1791, 1793, 1859-1860, 2087, 2409

IHS (AI AYTSH EHS): A monogram for the name of Jesus, using the first three letters of the word written in Greek. As a sign for the Holy Name, it was popular with the Dominicans, Franciscans, and Jesuits.

Illegitimacy (ih-leh-DZHIH-tih-muh-see): A legal and canonical category that refers to the status of children born out of wedlock. In the new code there are no effects of illegitimacy.

Illuminative Way (ih-LOO-mih-nuh-tihv WAY): The second stage of the spiritual life in which one concentrates on responding to the gifts of the Holy Spirit so as to follow Christ. One may attain this level by cooperating with the "ordinary" movements of grace (receiving the Holy Eucharist, frequenting the Sacrament of Penance, doing acts of charity, etc.).

Image of God [also Imago Dei] (IH-mudzh uhv GAHD [ee-MAH-go DAY-ee]): The reflection that every person has of God by virtue of being made by the Creator with a human body and an immortal soul (which has a rational intellect, a will, and a memory). Christ has come to enable man to see what an authentic exercise of human dignity really is. CCC 225, 356-361, 705, 1701-1702, 2713, 2809

Images (IH-mudzh-ehz): Artistic representation of Christ, the Blessed Virgin Mary, angels, saints, or other sacred subjects for the veneration or instruction of the faithful, or for decorative purposes. (Cf. Iconoclastic Controversy.) CCC 1159-1162

Imitation of Christ (ih-mih-TAY-shuhn uhv KRAIST): The famous spiritual work traditionally ascribed to Thomas à Kempis (d. 1471), which teaches Christians how to attain perfection by imitating Jesus. The volume has four parts: the first two are devoted to general comments about the spiritual life, while the third is about the necessary inner life of the soul, and the last about the splendor of the Holy Eucharist.

Immaculate Conception (ih-MA-kyöö-luht kuhn-SEHP-shuhn): Doctrine affirming that "the Blessed Virgin Mary was preserved, in the first instant of her conception, by a singular grace and privilege of God omnipotent and because of the merits of Jesus Christ the Savior of the human race, free from all stain of Original Sin," as stated by Blessed Pius IX in his declaration of the dogma, December 8, 1854. Thus, Mary was conceived in the state of perfect justice, free from Original Sin and its consequences, in virtue of the redemption achieved by Christ on the cross. In this sense, the privilege of the Immaculate Conception was the anticipated fruit of Christ's saving passion, death, and resurrection. It was only fitting that she who was to bear the Savior of the world should herself be preserved by Him from sin and its consequences and so be the first to benefit from what He would obtain for the whole human race. **CCC 490-493, 2177**

Immaculate Conception, Basilica of the National Shrine of the (buh-SIHL-ih-kuh uhv *th*uh NA-shuh-nuhl SHRAIN uhv *th*ee ih-MA-kyöö-luht kuhn-SEHP-shuhn): The bishops of the United States in 1847 petitioned Pope Pius IX to declare the Blessed Mother the patroness of the United States under her title of the Immaculate Conception. With the approval of the Holy See, plans were then made to erect a monumental church, to be called the National Shrine of the Immaculate Conception, in the nation's capital, Washington, D.C., on the campus of The Catholic University of America. The cornerstone was laid in 1920; with the completion of the external structure, the National Shrine was formally dedicated on November 20, 1959. The shrine is built in an eclectic fashion, combining elements of both neo-Byzantine and Romanesque design. Covering 77,500 square feet, it is the largest Catholic church in the U.S., raised to the rank of a basilica by Pope John Paul II, who in 1979 addressed women religious during a service there. Regularly, the bishops' conference uses the shrine for Mass during their annual meeting in Washington. The Archdiocese of the Military Services routinely uses the shrine in place of a cathedral of their own. The National Shrine has many outstanding features: the Knights' Tower, the elaborate mosaics of the exterior dome, various shrines dedicated to Our Lady as she is venerated in different cultures, the crypt church with its exquisitely carved altar, the mammoth marble pillars that support the baldacchino, the seven-foot statue of Mary Immaculate by sculptor George Snowden that surmounts the baldacchino, and the forbidding mosaic of "Christ in Majesty," designed by John Rosen. The papal crown of Pope Paul VI and the stole worn by Pope John XXIII at the opening of the Second Vatican Council are reverently displayed in the crypt.

Immanence (IHM-muh-nuhnts): 1. The philosophic use of the word refers to: (a) an activity when it produces its effect from within; or (b) an entity when its being within something else contributes to the existence of that thing. 2. In theology, the absolute immanence of God in the universe would be pantheism, and the absolute independence of God from the universe would be deism; the Christian doctrine of immanence teaches that God is present in His creation but is not part of it. **CCC 239**

Immanuel: See Emmanuel

Immensae Caritatis (ee-MEHN-say kah-ree-TAH-tihs): (Latin: "Of Immense Love") An instruction of the Sacred Congregation for the Discipline of the Sacraments on January 29, 1973, which allowed for extraordinary ministers of the Holy Eucharist without requiring the diocesan bishop to apply for indults. There are three conditions that must obtain for extraordinary ministers to be used: (1) absence of a priest, deacon, or acolyte; (2) the incapacity of the ordinary ministers of Holy Communion due to illness or some other apostolic endeavor; (3) so large a number of communicants that without such ministers the Mass would be unduly prolonged. According to Can. 230, those who are not ordinary ministers of the Holy Eucharist may distribute the Holy Eucharist either during or outside Mass. Further, they may distribute the Body of Christ or the Precious Blood.

Immersion, Baptism by (BAP-tih-zuhm bai ih-MER-shuhn): A method of baptizing whereby the whole person is submerged in water three times while the Trinitarian formula is pronounced. In the Rite of Baptism, immersion is indicated as the first way to baptize. In point of fact, however, the vast majority of Catholics (adults and infants) are baptized by infusion. For immersion, the candidate steps down or into a pool of water at waist height. Patristic catecheses noted the rich symbolism of Baptism by immersion, connected the washing away of Original Sin with rising from the tomb of death, and connected entering the Church with emerging from the womb with life.

Immortality of the Soul (ih-mor-TA-lih-tee uhv *th*uh SOL): The belief that the soul (i.e., the animating principle of the human person) exists forever after the moment of conception. Eternal life is a long-cherished belief in many religions. Scripture and the Magisterium have always taught that the soul will endure; hence, all are called to care for their souls by practicing virtue and avoiding vice. **CCC 366, 382**

Immovability of Pastors (ih-möö-vuh-BIHL-ih-tee uhv PAS-terz): A status of certain pastors found in the 1917 code whereby they could not be removed without permission of the Holy See. This status was dropped in the new code.

Immovable Feasts (ih-MÖÖ-vuh-buhl FEESTS): Liturgical observances that are assigned to a specific date (month and day) and do not change annually. These include: January 1, Solemnity of Mary the Mother of God; February 2, Feast of the Presentation of Our Lord; March 19, Solemnity of St. Joseph; November 30, Feast of St. Andrew, Apostle.

Immunity (ihm-MYÖÖ-nih-tee): An exemption from some form of responsibility or from the obligations of certain laws. **Cf. CCC 491, 1008, 2108**

Immutability (ih-myöö-tuh-BIHL-ih-tee): The term, meaning "unchangeableness," that refers to God, Who can never experience any alteration because He is immaterial and perfect. **CCC 202; cf. 212-213**

Impeccability (ihm-pehk-uh-BIHL-ih-tee): Not merely the absence of sins committed by a person, but also the impossibility of sinning, which Jesus enjoyed because of His divinity. Though Mary enjoyed complete freedom from Original Sin (because of the Immaculate Conception) and was in fact personally sinless, she, like the first Eve, was not impeccable. The saints in heaven also are impeccable because they experience the beatific vision.

Impediment (ihm PEH-dih-mehnt): A barrier that arises out of a person's condition or something he or she has done that prevents the valid reception of the Sacraments of Matrimony or Holy Orders. CCC 1577-1580, 1625, 1635

Impediment, Diriment (DEER-uh-mehnt ihm-PEH-dih-mehnt): A condition of a person specified in Canon Law preventing a valid marriage. There are twelve diriment impediments (cc. 1083-1094).

Impediments, Hindering (HIHN-der-ihng ihm-PEH-dih-mehnts): Impediments or barriers found in the 1917 code that rendered a marriage illicit or illegal but not invalid.

Imperfections (ihm-per-FEHK-shuhnz): Deficiencies in one's character that, although not serious, are obstacles to attaining Christian perfection. The Sacrament of Penance, fraternal correction, prayer, and acts of humility and penance are salutary helps in overcoming these weaknesses.

Imposition of Hands (ihm-po-ZIH-shuhn uhv HANDZ): An ancient symbol adopted by the Catholic Church from apostolic days to convey power, blessing, or consecration. In the O.T., the laying on of hands carried with it a sacrificial connotation (Nm 8:10 ff.). It also imparted blessing (Gn 48:14). In the N.T., Our Lord imposed hands to cure the sick (Mk 6:5; Lk 4:40). The Apostles imposed hands to confer authority and powers, and this gesture was soon acknowledged as the means of ordaining and conferring Church office. There is also a laying on of hands by the priest in the Sacrament of the Anointing of the Sick. At the epiclesis in the canon of the Mass, the priest places his hands over the Eucharistic gifts. In the Sacrament of Penance, the priest extends his hand forward when imparting absolution. CCC 699, 1150, 1288, 1504, 1538, 1556, 1558, 1573

Impotence (IHM-po-tehnts): The incapacity or inability of a man or a woman to complete the act of sexual intercourse. Impotence is a diriment impediment to marriage (Can. 1084).

Imprecatory Psalms (IHM-preh-kuh-to-ree SAHMZ): Psalms that give expression to an extreme vindictiveness, also called the cursing psalms; they speak vividly of the retribution that is exacted for evil that is done. Such psalms should be read as the ardent statement of the human writer seeking God's punishment of evildoers, while still faithful to the inspired intention of God to thwart those who oppose His will (Pss 7, 35, 69, 109, 137).

Imprimatur (ihm-prih-MAH-tøør): (Latin: Let it be printed) A canonical term for the permission needed to publish certain kinds of religious books.

Improperia (ihm-pro-PEHR-ee-uh): A series of reproofs imagined to be addressed by Our Savior from the cross to an ungrateful people. Beginning in the seventh century, the reproaches have been chanted on Good Friday during the Veneration of the Cross. They are retained in the current rite but are optional. Correctly understood, these are not anti-Semitic but are reminders to all of the need for repentance and conversion.

Impurity (ihm-PYØØR-ih-tee): The entertaining of illicit sexual thoughts, desires, words, or actions. In order to overcome these, one must practice virtue as exemplified in the life of the Most Holy Virgin; pornography and other lewd attractions must be avoided. Frequenting the sacraments, especially Penance and Holy Eucharist, is a beneficial practice. Cf. CCC 2331-2357, 2517-2533

Imputability (ihm-pyöö-tuh-BIHL-ih-tee): A canonical term for the moral responsibility of a person for an act that he or she has performed. CCC 1735, 1860, 2125, 2355

In Articulo Mortis (IHN ahr-TIH-köö-lo MOR-tihs): A term referring to the state of a person "on the brink of death." References to this condition are found in the rites for the sacraments and in the Canon Law of the Church. Examples of where this clause is found: sacramental absolution, anointing, Baptism, celibacy dispensations, censures and remissions, Confirmation, powers of dispensation, reception of the Holy Eucharist, laicization, religious profession, suspension of penalty, Viaticum, and the power of penalized clerics in such situations. CCC 1512, 1528

Incardination (ihn-kahr-dih-NAY-shuhn): The canonical act whereby a cleric is formally attached to a diocese or religious community and subject to its superiors.

Incarnation, The (*the*e ihn-kahr-NAY-shuhn): The central mystery of Christianity, the doctrine that in the union of the divine nature of the Second Person of the Holy Trinity with human nature, the Son of God assumed our humanity, body and soul, and was born of the Virgin Mary, to dwell in our midst in order to accomplish the work of our redemption. CCC 461-463

Incense (IHN-sehnts): Granulated or powdered aromatic resin, obtained from various plants and trees in Eastern or tropical countries. When sprinkled on glowing coals in a vessel called a censer (thurible), the incense becomes a fragrant cloud of smoke to symbolize prayer rising to God (Ps 141:2, Rv 8:3-5), honoring sacred persons and things in liturgical worship. The use of incense comes into the Church from both pagan worship and Judaism. Generally speaking, incense is used with greater frequency in the East than in the West. Incense may be used at several points in the celebration of the Mass. It may also be used at Morning and Evening Prayer. Incense is used whenever there is Benediction of the Blessed Sacrament, during processions with the Blessed Sacrament, at funeral Masses, and when churches are dedicated. CCC 1154

Incest (IHN-sehst): Sexual intercourse with relatives by blood or marriage, a sin of impurity and a grave violation of the natural reverence due to loved ones. Other sins of impurity (desire, etc.) concerning relatives participate in the nature of incest. CCC 2356, 2388

Inculturation (ihn-kuhl-tsher-AY-shuhn): The appropriate adaptation of Catholic liturgy and institutions to the culture, language, and customs of an indigenous or local people among whom the Gospel is first proclaimed. CCC 854, 1232, 2684

Indefectibility (ihn-dee-fehk-tuh-BIHL-ih-tee): The quality of the Church, based upon the promise of Christ Himself, Who said that "the powers of death shall not prevail against it" (Mt 16:18), assuring that it perpetually will be the Church instituted by Jesus Christ, and that it is unchangeable in its teaching and in all those essentials mandated by Our Lord. Indefectibility does not exclude the possibility of change in nonessential matters, nor does it preclude the failure and dissolution of individual parishes or even of whole dioceses. Cf. CCC 1108

Index of Forbidden Books (IHN-dehks uhv for-BIHD-ehn BØØKS): An official list of books and writings that Catholics were forbidden to read or possess. Established in 1557, it was abolished in 1966.

Indifferentism (ihn-DIH-frehn-tih-zuhm): 1. The refusal to give God the worship and glory that He deserves because of sloth or neglect. 2. The notion that all religions are the same and that one is as good as another. This theory contradicts the Church's teaching that she alone possesses the "fullness of truth" and was the only Church to be founded by Jesus Christ. One has an obligation to follow one's correctly formed conscience concerning which religion to adopt. CCC 1634, 2094, 2128

Indissolubility (ihn-dih-sahl-yöö-BIHL-ih-tee): The quality of the marriage bond indicating that it cannot be dissolved or terminated. CCC 1610-1611, 1615, 1643-1645, 1647, 2364

Individualism (ihn-dih-VIH-dzhöö-uhl-ih-zuhm): A system of thought that places the desires, rights, and well-being of individuals on a higher level than those of society. All institutions and social organizations are measured by their effect upon the interests, welfare, and destiny of individuals, and it holds that the good of the community consists of the sum of those things that are good for the individuals who compose it. CCC 2425, 2792

Indulgences (ihn-DUHL-dzhehn-sehz): The remission — either partial or full — of temporal punishment for sins and the resulting satisfaction owed to God. Both the Sacrament of Penance and a perfect act of contrition bestow indulgences. They may be gained for oneself or for those in purgatory. CCC 1471-1479

Indult (IHN-duhlt): A special permission given by the Holy See whereby the obligations of an ecclesiastical law can be waived for a person or group of persons.

Indwelling of the Holy Spirit (IHN-dwehl-lihng uhv *th*uh HO-lee SPIH-riht): The presence of the Holy Spirit, which implies the indwelling of the Holy Trinity within a person, as a manifestation of the love of God. Cf. CCC 2781

Inerrancy (ihn-EHR-uhn-see): The absence of error, usually applied to the Bible as the revealed Word of God, which teaches "firmly, faithfully and without error . . . that truth which God, for the sake of our salvation, wished to see confided to the Sacred Scriptures" (DV, n. 11). CCC 107

Infallibilists (ihn-FAL-ih-buhl-ihsts): Those bishops, under the leadership of Edward Cardinal Manning of Westminster, who wanted the First Vatican Council to proclaim solemnly that the Pope, when teaching *ex cathedra* in matters of faith and morals, is infallible due to the special grace that is his as a successor of St. Peter (cf. Infallibility).

Infallibility (ihn-FAL-lih-BIHL-uh-tee): The inability to err in teaching the truth. In theology, it refers to: (1) the Church, in that she preserves and teaches the deposit of truth as revealed by Christ; (2) the Roman Pontiff, when he teaches *ex cathedra* in matters of faith or morals, and indicates that the doctrine is to be believed by all the faithful; (3) the College of Bishops, when speaking in union with the Pope in matters of faith and morals, agreeing that a doctrine must be held by the universal Church, and the doctrine is promulgated by the Pontiff. **CCC 889-891, 2035, 2051**

Infamy (IHN-fuh-mee): A canonical penalty found in the 1917 code but dropped from the new code. Infamy resulted in various deprivations such as inability to participate in worship services, to assume ecclesiastical positions or titles, or to perform ministerial acts.

Infant Jesus of Prague (IHN-fuhnt DZHEE-zuhs uhv PRAHG): Eighteen-inch-high wooden statue of the Child Jesus in Bohemia that has figured in devotion to the Holy Childhood and Kingship of Christ since the seventeenth century. Of uncertain origin, the statue was presented by Princess Polixena to the Carmelites of Our Lady of Victory Church, Prague, in 1628. **Cf. CCC 527-530**

Infidel (IHN-fih-dehl): Unfaithful one. Although used formerly in reference to one who did not believe in the Christian Faith, now it is used more commonly for those who have no faith, i.e., atheists and agnostics.

Infinite (IHN-fih-niht): Having no limitations or bounds, most basically applied to the being of God, in that His existence and attributes are beyond the comprehension of human intellect. **Cf. CCC 41, 43, 48, 202, 251, 256**

Infused Virtues (ihn-FYÖÖZD VER-tshööz): Those virtues of faith, hope, and love that are imparted to the soul by God's sanctifying grace and are not acquired by any human effort other than having the willingness to receive them. **CCC 1812-1829**

Infusion: See Baptism, Sacrament

Inopportunists (IHN-ah-per-TÖÖN-ihsts): The minority number of bishops at the First Vatican Council who felt that it would be untimely for the Council to proclaim solemnly the doctrine of the infallibility of the Pope. When the doctrine was promulgated in *Pastor Aeternus,* the Inopportunists submitted and accepted the decree.

In Petto (ihn-PEH-toh): A term that means "in the breast" referring to papal appointments that are not made public, but known to the Holy Father alone.

Inquisition (ihn-kwih-ZIH-shuhn): The special court established by the Church in the thirteenth century for the purpose of curbing heresies and punishing heretics, particularly those of the Albigensian sect, whose beliefs and practices were disruptive of faith and social order. The task of the members of the Inquisition was to seek repentance from those involved in heresy. If they did not reform, they were then handed over to the civil government. It was the secular law that could prescribe death, since heresy was considered to be an act of anarchy and treason.

Inquisition, Spanish (SPA-nihsh ihn-kwih-ZIH-shuhn): The court established by Pope Sixtus IV in 1478 at the request of the Spanish monarchy for the purpose of preserving religious unity and doctrinal orthodoxy throughout Spain and its colonies. At first dealing primarily with those Jews and Muslims who had been baptized, it was broadened to include any suspected heretics, becoming an agency of both Church and kingdom. Although the brutality and injustice of the Spanish Inquisition have been exaggerated, there were excesses, condemned at the time by Pope Sixtus IV.

I.N.R.I. (Al EHN AHR AI): An abbreviation for the inscription above the head of Christ when He died on the cross at Calvary. These letters stand for "Jesus of Nazareth, King of the Jews" in Latin, words that were ordered to be placed at the top of the cross by Pontius Pilate, the Roman procurator. This is recorded in the Gospels (Mt 27:37; Mk 15:26; Lk 23:38; Jn 19:19-22). The inscription was offered in three languages: Latin, Hebrew, and Greek.

Insemination, Artificial: See Artificial Insemination

In Sin (ihn SIHN): Condition of a person considered spiritually dead because he or she lacks sanctifying grace, the principle of supernatural life, action, and merit. Such grace and new spiritual life can be regained through penance.

Inspiration of Scripture (ihn-spih-RAY-shuhn uhv SKRIHP-tsher): (Latin *inspirare:* to breathe into; cf. Greek *theopneustos:* God-breathed) The influence that God exercises over human writers to communicate through them His divine revelation; as the N.T. attests, "All scripture is inspired by God" (2 Tm 3:16; cf. 2 Pt 1:19-21, 3:15-16; Jn 20:31). The O.T. is the initial witness for the inspiration of Scripture (2 Sm 23:2; Dt 31:19; Mal 4:4); all language that is inspired is properly called prophetic because it communicates to humanity the very mind of God. *Dei Verbum,* a dogmatic constitution of the Second Vatican Council and fully reflecting the consistent teaching of the Church, makes clear that the human writers were true authors, in full command of their faculties and literary skills, while at the same time instruments of God as the original and divine Author. They wrote everything and only that which God wanted to communicate; thus, the Scriptures "firmly, faithfully and without error, teach that truth which God, for the sake of our salvation, wished to see confided to the Sacred Scriptures" (DV, n. 11). CCC 76, 81, 105-108, 111, 135-136, 2008

Installation (ihn-stuh-LAY-shuhn): 1. Canonically, the assumption of an ecclesiastical office by a designated individual. 2. Commonly, the ceremony whereby a bishop assumes his duties.

Institute on Religious Life (IHN-stih-tööt awn rih-LIH-dzhuhs LAIF): Founded in 1974 in Chicago for the promotion of vocations to the religious life and the priesthood, and to help all members of Christ's Body attain holiness in their various states in life, in accordance with the teachings of the Church.

Institute, Religious (rih-LIH-dzhuhs IHN-stih-tööt): A type of institute or organization of consecrated life. It is distinguished from others because its members take public vows of poverty, chastity, and obedience. Cf. CCC 914-927, 931-933

Institute, Secular (SEHK-yöö-ler IHN-stih-tööt): An institute of consecrated life made up of laypersons and/or clerics who live in the world and strive for the perfection of charity and the sanctification of the world. Members of secular institutes profess the evangelical counsels of poverty, chastity, and obedience, not by means of public vows but by some other bond determined by the institute's own law. Lay members retain their marital or single status and their occupation in life. Clerical members remain incardinated in their dioceses. In short, they are organizations of people who consecrate their lives in a special way to God through the life and work of the institute. Members are required to fulfill a period of probation before making temporary profession into the institute. When the period of temporary profession is completed, they may make permanent profession or incorporation into the institute. An indult from the Holy See is required to leave the institute. Although secular institutes have existed in the Church since the sixteenth century, they were only officially recognized by the Holy See in 1947. Although no provision was made for secular institutes in the 1917 Code of Canon Law, they were nevertheless covered by the apostolic constitution *Provida Mater Ecclesiae*, issued by Pope Pius XII. Legislation on secular institutes has been included in the revised code (cf. cc. 710-730). CCC 928-933

Instruction, Canonical (ka-NAH-nih-kuhl ihn-STRUHK-shuhn): 1. An official document clarifying or elaborating on the method of applying a Church law (Can. 34). 2. The process in a canonical trial wherein evidence and other information are gathered.

Intellect (IHN-teh-lehkt): The power of knowing reality in a nonmaterial way, as distinguished from knowing simply through the senses or imagination, thus giving the ability to reason and to understand.

Intention (ihn-TEHN-tshuhn): 1. An act of the human will for the achievement of some purpose or objective, e.g., in prayer. 2. In sacramental theology, the necessary disposition and purpose required for both the administration and reception of a sacrament. CCC 1750-1753

Intercession (ihn-ter-SEH-shuhn): A form of the prayer of petition made to God on behalf of others, whether living or departed. CCC 1096, 1354, 1509, 2634-2636, 2734, 2770

Intercommunion (ihn-ter-kuh-MYÖÖN-yuhn): An agreement between two churches that allows their respective members to receive Holy Communion in either church. Although there is some intercommunion between certain Protestant denominations, there are no other Christian bodies with whom the Catholic Church has reciprocal intercommunion. Cf. CCC 1398-1401

Interdict (IHN-ter-dihkt): 1. In the 1917 C.I.C., a canonical penalty that prohibited the use of sacred things either by groups of people or in specific places; e.g., the closing of a church to sacred services. 2. In the new code, a canonical penalty applied to individuals, prohibiting them from taking part in services or receiving sacraments or sacramentals.

Inter Mirifica (IHN-tehr mih-RIH-fih-kuh): The Decree on the Means of Social Communication, issued by the Second Vatican Council, outlining the opportunities and responsibilities presented to the Church in the use of the media for the propagation of the Gospel.

Internal Forum (ihn-TER-nuhl FO-ruhm): The place of judging or dispensing that remains totally confidential and not recorded in public records of the Church, e.g., sacramental confession.

International Committee (or Commission) on English in the Liturgy, Inc.: See ICEL

International Theological Commission [I.T.C.] (ihn-ter-NA-shuh-nuhl thee-uh-LAH-dzhih-kuhl kuh-MIH-shuhn [AI TEE SEE]): Provisionally established in 1969 and given definite status in 1982, the commission that has the task of studying important doctrinal problems and offering the results to the Congregation for the Doctrine of the Faith. It is made up of thirty members, appointed by the Pope for terms of five years.

Internuncio (ihn-ter-NØØN-see-o): A special legate of the Pope sent as a temporary representative to attend to matters of lesser importance. The term is no longer used.

Interpretation of Law (ihn-TER-pruh-TAY-shuhn uhv LAW): An official and authentic statement as to the meaning of a Church law.

Interpretation, Scriptural (SKRIHP-tsher-uhl ihn-TER-pruh-TAY-shuhn): Hermeneutics (from Greek *hermeneuein,* to explain), the theological science that attempts to give a clear explanation of biblical texts, taking into account the historical background of the human writer and the literary genre of the text, read in the context of the whole of Sacred Scripture, while remaining faithful to the Magisterium of the Church in determining the divine truth intended by God as the divine Author of Scripture. Whether one examines the spiritual sense of the passage or the more straightforward meaning derived from the literary-historical methods of criticism, the meaning or interpretation must agree with the factual features of the text. The interpretation must further be faithful to the use of the passage in the Sacred Liturgy and by the Fathers and Doctors of the Church, who enjoy an especially significant place in biblical interpretation. The Fathers taught four basic ways of interpreting Scripture: *littera,* which corresponds to modern literary criticism;

tropologica, the moral or homiletic interpretation; *allegoria*, the symbolic, figurative interpretation, and *anagogia*, the mystical, which often attempts to draw a spiritual, rather than literal, interpretation from the text. CCC 115-119

Interregnum (ihn-ter-REHG-nuhm): That period of time between the death of a sovereign and the assumption of rule by a successor. When referring to the time following the death of a Pope and the election of a successor, it is more commonly known as *sede vacante* ("while the See is vacant").

Interstices (ihn-TER-stuh-seez): (Latin *inter:* between + *stare:* stand) The periods of time that must elapse between the reception of different ministries or orders by the same person leading to ordination to the priesthood, which may be shortened by a bishop only for exceptional reasons.

Intinction (ihn-TIHNIK-shuhn): A way of distributing the Holy Eucharist under both species. The *General Instruction of the Roman Missal* requires that the one distributing Holy Communion dip a particle of Eucharistic Bread (or a small Host) "into the chalice, and showing it, says: The Body and Blood of Christ. The communicant responds: Amen, and receives the Sacrament in the mouth from the priest . . . and returns to his or her place" (n. 287). The 1970 instruction *Sacramentali Communione* gives preference to drinking from the chalice if Holy Communion is received under both forms. However, intinction remains a perennially valid way of distributing and receiving Holy Communion because "[it] is more likely to obviate the practical difficulties and to ensure the reverence due the sacrament more effectively." The same document goes on to say that intinction makes it "easier and safer" for all the faithful to receive Holy Communion. Intinction also "preserves the truth present in a more complete sign" (in contradistinction to the Eucharistic Bread only).

Introduction, Biblical (BIH-blih-kuhl ihn-tro-DUHK-shuhn): Courses designed to introduce the student to each book of Sacred Scripture under the topics of time and place of composition, content and structure, purpose, authenticity, intended audience, literary form, literary sources, and manuscript tradition. The Oratorian Richard Simon (d. 1712) is the most prominent Catholic originator of the "Introduction" method, which can be divided into two classes: (1) the scientific study of the circumstances in which each book was composed, the literary and historical data underlying a given book of Sacred Scripture, and (2) the systematic study of the history of the canon and transmission of texts, called textual criticism. In an address entitled "Biblical Interpretation in Crisis," given in New York on January 27, 1988, Joseph Cardinal Ratzinger, Prefect of the Sacred Congregation for the Doctrine of the Faith, criticized some for the misuse of historical-critical exegesis, e.g., unfounded hypotheses and the exegesis of putative sources rather than the extant text itself; he also criticized some of the philosophical presuppositions underlying it, particularly those of Bultmann and Dibelius. At the same time, he rejected fundamentalism or overliteralism as alternatives.

Introit (IHN-tro-iht, -troit): In use before Vatican II, the entrance prayer of the Mass, consisting of an antiphon, psalm verse, Glory Be, and the antiphon repeated. Normally, these would be sung by a schola, choir, or soloist at High Mass and recited by the celebrant at all Masses after he finished the prayers at the foot of the altar. Following Vatican II, the Missal restored the Introit to its more ancient title and form, called *antiphona ad introitum* (entrance antiphon or song). Only the antiphon now appears in the Missal; the full psalm is in a separate book for the cantor called the Roman Gradual.

Investiture (ihn-VEHS-tih-tshøør): The process whereby a superior turned the control of real property over to a subordinate.

Invitatory (ihn-VAI-tuh-tor-ee): The verse or psalm that begins the Liturgy of the Hours on a given day. The *General Instruction on the Liturgy of the Hours* stipulates that the Office begin with the invitatory (n. 34). The verse reads, *Domine, labia mea aperies: Et os meum annuntiabit laudem tuam* ("Lord, open my lips: And my mouth shall proclaim your praise"), followed by Psalm 95 (94). Sometimes another verse is added as a response to Psalm 95. Other psalms that may be used are Psalms 100 (99), 66 (67), or 24.

In Vitro Fertilization (IHN VEE-tro fer-tihl-ih-ZAY-shuhn): The process of using artificial means to conceive a child, which separates the life-giving and love-giving dimensions of marital intercourse. Child-bearing is relegated to a laboratory experiment. *In vitro* ("in glass") fertilization separates a child from his or her parents at the moment of conception. Usually, the sperm is obtained through masturbation; furthermore, many eggs and sperm are united in the laboratory. If any of these new human beings are "deformed" because of health defects, they are immediately destroyed. The Church has roundly condemned *in vitro* fertilization. **Cf. CCC 2376-2379**

Irenicism (ih-REH-nih-sih-zuhm): (From Greek *eirene:* peace) The promotion of peace and conciliation among individuals and churches in matters of theological dispute, with an emphasis on areas of agreement and convergence rather than on divisive issues.

Irregularity, Canonical (ka-NAH-nih-kuhl ih-rehg-yöö-LA-rih-tee): A circumstance rooted in a person or something he has done that constitutes a barrier or impediment to receiving Holy Orders, or, if Orders have been received, from exercising them (cc. 1041, 1044-48).

Irremovability of Pastors (ihr-ree-moov-uh-BIHL-ih-tee uhv PAS-terz): The canonical status of certain pastors under the 1917 code and prior to it, whereby certain pastors could not be removed, except with permission of the Holy See.

Isaac (AI-zuhk): (Hebrew: He [God] laughs) The son born to Abraham and Sarah in their old age (Gn 21:1-3) in fulfillment of the promise made by God that Abraham would become the father of many nations.

Isaiah (ai-ZAY-uh): A major prophet of the eighth century B.C. who devoted himself to calling the kings and people of his time to reform in a time of moral and religious decline. The prophetic book bearing his name has many foreshadowings of the coming Messiah. The prophet himself is considered the author of most of the first thirty-nine chapters under his name, but later chapters, including the "Servant songs" (see Servant of Yahweh), are considered by experts to have been appended by an imitator ("Deutero-Isaiah") during the Babylonian Exile. The whole work, however, is nonetheless considered inspired and canonical.

Islam (IHZ-lahm): The religion of the Muslims, founded by their prophet, Muhammad, in A.D. 622 as a monotheistic religion in which God is known as Allah. Their scriptures, called the Koran (from Arabic *Qur'an:* reading), are considered to be God's final revelation to the world. Islam has "Five Pillars" outlined by the Koran: (1) belief in Allah and His prophet, Muhammad; (2) prayers to be offered at five certain times each day, facing in the direction of their holy city, Mecca; (3) alms to be given often; (4) fasting to be observed; (5) the requirement that all Muslims go to Mecca on pilgrimage. **Cf. CCC 841**

Israel (IHZ-ray-ehl): 1. The name given to Jacob after wrestling with the angel (Gn 32:28). 2. The Hebrew nation, as the descendants of Jacob 3. The Northern Kingdom, made up of ten tribes of Israel that broke with the Southern Kingdom of Judah (1 Kgs 11:31). 4. The name of the modern Jewish State, which came into existence on May 15, 1948, with the partition of Palestine by the United Nations. **Cf. CCC 60, 62-64, 201, 203-204, 209, 212, 214, 218-219, 228, 287-288, 401, 431, 436, 528-529, 535, 587-591, 594, 673-674, 708-710, 759-762, 781, 839, 1093, 1539, 1611-1612, 1965, 2085**

Itala Vetus (EE-tah-luh VAY-tøøs): (Latin: old Italian) A translation of the Bible into Latin predating the Vulgate translation.

Itinerarium (ai-tih-nuh-RAH-ree-uhm): Prayer in the Breviary for one who is about to make a journey.

Iuspatronatus (YØØS-pah-tro-NAH-tøøs): The ancient right of landowners to make appointments to ecclesiastical offices. This right has long been abolished (cf. Advowson).

J

Jacob (DZHAY-kuhb): (Hebrew *ya'aqob:* seizing by the heel, a supplanter) Son of Isaac and Rebecca whose name was changed to Israel after wrestling with an angel (Gn 32:29). The twelve tribes of Israel are descended from him through his twelve sons.

Jacobins (DZHAK-uh-bihns): Originally the name given to French Dominicans, from their first house in Paris on the Rue St.-Jacques. When this house was acquired by a radical group during the French Revolution, the term came to be applied to anyone holding revolutionary ideas.

Jacobite Church (DZHAK-uh-bait TSHERTSH): The name given to the Syrian Monophysite Church, which did not accept the teaching affirmed by the Council of Chalcedon (A.D. 451) that there are two natures united in the one divine Person of Jesus Christ. The term is taken from the name of Jacob Baradaeus, who had formed them into the national Church of Syria in the sixth century.

Jahweh: See Yahweh

James, Epistle of (ih-PIH-suhl uhv DZHAYMZ): This letter is the first of the Catholic Epistles (with 1 and 2 Peter, 1 through 3 John, and Jude), classified as such because in the West these letters were *accepted* by *all* the Churches ("canonical"); in the East they were taken as *addressed* to *all* the Churches — hence their universal acceptance. The fact that this epistle is written in elegant Greek style, coupled with the letter's distinctive emphasis on an authentic faith of single-mindedness and humble devotion to God through action (e.g., 1:22-25; 2:15-16; 5:3-6), suggests that the author was familiar with Hellenistic Judaism. The author draws from practical biblical wisdom, as well as from teachings of Jesus (Jas 1:2/Mt 5:12; Jas 1:5/Mt 7:7; Jas 1:22, 2:14/Mt 7:26; Jas 4:11/Mt 7:1), to encourage and exhort Greek-speaking Jewish Christians who suffered under various trying circumstances. The letter teaches in general rather than in specific terms, applying wisdom rooted in an active faith in the living God to problems arising from persecution. Who is James? The tone of authority throughout the epistle, the reference to "servant" (1:1), and the address to "the twelve tribes in the Diaspora" suggest someone of authority, perhaps James "the brother of the Lord" (Gal 1:19; Mt 13:55; Mk 6:3) and leader of the early Church in Jerusalem (Acts 12:17; 15:13; 1 Cor 15:7; Gal 2:9, 12), who was later known as James the Just (Eusebius, *Ecclesiastical History,* 2.23, 4). There is very little evidence in the letter that helps us fix a date with certainty. If the date is prior to A.D. 70, then the letter could have originated in Jerusalem; if the date is after that, then it could have originated in Antioch or Alexandria.

James, Liturgy of St. (LIH-ter-dzhee uhv SAYNT DZHAYMZ): The liturgy belonging to the city of Jerusalem, where St. James the Apostle was bishop. The texts of the Mass are strikingly similar to the *Catecheses,* probably written by St. Cyril of Jerusalem. The Liturgy of St. James spread outside Jerusalem but was suppressed in the twelfth century.

James the Greater, St. (SAYNT DZHAYMZ *th*uh GRAY-ter): James and his brother John, sons of Zebedee, were called by Jesus from their livelihood as fishermen to become "fishers of men" as Apostles. By reason of their impetuous temper, James and John are identified in Mk 3:17 as the Sons of Thunder (Boanerges). In keeping with their personality traits, James and John are shown guilty of blind ambition in seeking prominence in the Lord's kingdom (Mt 20:20-28; Mk 11:35-45). With John and Peter, James was a privileged witness to the raising of the daughter of Jairus (Mt 9:18-26; Mk 6:35-43; Lk 8:41-56), Our Lord's Transfiguration (Mt 17:1-13; Mk 9:2-13; Lk 9:28-36), and the agony in the garden at Gethsemane (Mt 26:36-46; Mk 14:32-42; Lk 22:40-46). Herod Agrippa ordered his beheading in A.D. 44. He is called "the greater" not by reason of any ecclesiastical prominence but merely to distinguish him from the other Apostle of the same name, who was likely smaller or younger.

Jansenism (DZHAN-suhn-ih-zuhm): The teaching of Cornelis Jansen, Bishop of Ypres, who believed in predestination and denied the free will of man in either accepting or rejecting God's grace. Jansenism was condemned as heretical by Pope Innocent X in 1653, and recondemned by Pope Alexander VII in 1656, when Jansenists claimed that their beliefs had been misunderstood. Later developments in Jansenism contained a general disregard for papal teaching concerning the sacraments and authority within the Church, leading to another condemnation by Pope Pius VI in 1794.

Januarius, Miracle of St. (MIHR-ih-kuhl uhv SAYNT DZHAN-yöö-EHR-ee-uhs): A vial of dried blood, alleged to be that of the martyr St. Januarius, liquefies on several feast days every year or nearly every year in the place where it is kept in the Cathedral of Naples. The liquefaction has been photographed and is judged by investigators to be genuine. The Church, however, has never rendered an official confirmation of the "miracle."

Jehovah (dzheh-HO-vuh): The English equivalent of the Hebrew *Adonai* ("my Lord") used out of fear and reverence for the Holy Name of Yahweh. "Jehovah" uses the consonants YHWH and the vowels of *Adonai* (a, o, a). Scholars today maintain that Jehovah is a false derivation.

Jehovah's Witnesses (dzheh-HO-vuhz WIHT-nuh-sehz): A sect founded by Charles T. Russell (1852-1916), who believed that the end of the world was near, except for those who were his followers, the "elect of Jehovah." Upon the death of Russell, leadership was taken over by J. R. "Judge" Rutherford, with his theological views supplanting those of Russell. The Witnesses deny the Holy Trinity and the divinity of Jesus Christ, and so are not a Christian denomination. They are politically inactive and pacifists, and have as little contact with non-Witnesses as possible, except in their efforts to convert others to their religion.

Jeremiah, Book of (BØØK uhv dzheh-reh-MAI-uh): While Manasseh (the king said to have killed Isaiah) reigned in Judah (698-642 B.C.), this great prophet was born of a priestly family in Anathoth, a few miles north of Jerusalem. During the long reign of Manasseh, the people seem to have forgotten the Torah. In 628 B.C., during the reign of the pious Josiah, who had inaugurated a national religious reform, Jeremiah was called to spread a renewed religious spirit. The dusty Torah was found in the Temple, solemnly read to the people, and the covenant reaffirmed. When Josiah died in battle at Megiddo in 609, it seems that the renewal died with him. Like most of the prophets of the time, Jeremiah became politically involved. Like most prophets of all times, he had reason to complain that no one, king or citizens, would listen to him. Once safely dead, he was extolled as a great man. Scorned, beaten, imprisoned, exiled from his own land, he ended his life perhaps martyred at the hands of Jews in Egypt. In his book, he reveals his own personality better than any other writer in the O.T. has done. He is among the most candid of men, deeply convinced of God's unalterable love for the Jewish people, yet sadly aware of their frequent grievous sins. No O.T. writer teaches so effectively the justice of God to all sinners, and no other is so emphatic about the bright possibility of repentance and salvation.

Jerusalem (dzheh-RÖÖ-suh-lehm): The "Holy City," located on the crest of some Palestinian mountains, which served as the religious and political center of Judaism, the site of the Temple and the home of the Benjaminite tribe. Its inhabitants were known as Jebusites. Symbolically, Jerusalem became the capital of belief in and fidelity to Yahweh.

Jerusalem, Council of (KAUN-sihl uhv dzheh-RÖÖ-suh-lehm): A meeting of certain Apostles in about the year 50 in Jerusalem to discuss which Jewish traditions the Greek converts needed to adopt before converting to Christianity.

Jerusalem, Patriarchate of (pay-tree-AHR-kuht uhv dzheh-RÖÖ-suh-lehm): The original sees that received the title of patriarchate because of their apostolic foundation and civil importance were Rome, Antioch, and Alexandria. When Constantinople became the capital of the empire, it was raised to this rank. The Council of Chalcedon in 451 raised Jerusalem to patriarchal rank because of the sacred nature of the city. Today it is the seat of several patriarchs of Eastern Catholic, Eastern Orthodox, and Ancient Oriental Churches. It is also the seat of a Latin patriarch. The Latin patriarchate was established during the Crusades in 1099, lapsed into a titular see, and was restored as a residential see in 1847.

Jesse Window (DZHEH-see WIHN-do): Used to illustrate the human genealogy of Christ, this stained-glass window depicts Jesus at the top of a tree; the lower branches show some of His biblical ancestors. Jesse, King David's father, is shown at the root of the tree, symbolically representing the foundation of his family (1 Sm 16:18-22; Is 11:1).

Jesuit (dzheh-ZHOO-iht): A member of the Society of Jesus, a religious order of men founded by St. Ignatius Loyola in 1534.

Jesuit Reductions (dzheh-ZHOO-iht ree-DUHK-shuhnz): Semiautonomous settlements of South American Indians founded and directed by Jesuit missionaries in the eighteenth century.

Jesuit Relations (dzheh-ZHOO-iht ree-LAY-shuhnz): A collection of narratives and reports written by Jesuit missionaries in North America in the seventeenth century to their superiors in France.

Jesus (DZHEE-zuhs): Name of the Savior, in Christian usage (derived from Aramaic-Hebrew Yeshua [Joshua]), meaning "Yahweh is salvation." (See also Christ.) CCC 436-440, 453, 486, 629, 690, 695, 727, 745, 783, 1289

Jesus Prayer (DZHEE-zuhs PREHR): Prayer form dating back to the fifth century: "Lord Jesus Christ, Son of God, have mercy on me (a sinner)."

Jewish Canon of Scriptures (DZHOO-ihsh KA-nuhn uhv SKRIHP-tshers): The Hebrews' canon of the O.T. (Masoretic Text) was settled by the rabbis around A.D. 100 at the Council of Jamnia. It contains twenty-four books and is divided into three categories: (1) the Law (Torah) in the five books of Moses (Genesis, Exodus, Leviticus, Numbers, Deuteronomy); (2) the Prophets: Joshua, Judges, 1 and 2 Samuel, 1 and 2 Kings, Isaiah, Jeremiah, Ezekiel, Hosea, Joel, Amos, Obadiah, Jonah, Micah, Nahum, Habakkuk, Zephaniah, Haggai, Zechariah, and Malachi; (3) The Writings: 1 and 2 Chronicles, Ezra, Nehemiah, Job, Psalms, Proverbs, Ecclesiastes, Song of Songs, Ruth, Esther, Daniel. The Protestant canon of the O.T., which is arranged in thirty-nine separate books, is the same as the Hebrew canon. The difference in number is due to the Protestant consideration of the minor prophets as twelve books and Samuel, Kings, Chronicles, and Ezra-Nehemiah as two each. The Catholic canon of the O.T., which was finalized by the Council of Trent (1546), includes the books contained in the Alexandrian canon. The Hebrew canon rejected these books and accepted only those books in the Palestinian canon. Therefore, the Catholic O.T. canon includes more books than the Jewish O.T. canon. These books are the books of Tobit, Judith, Wisdom, Sirach (Ecclesiasticus), 1 and 2 Maccabees, Baruch, Daniel (Ch. 3:24-90; Chs. 13-14), and parts of Esther. Today Protestants generally do not put these books into their Bibles, or if they do, they put them at the end of the Bible under the name "Apocrypha." (Cf. Bible.)

Jews (DZHÖÖZ): (Hebrew *yehudi,* citizen of the tribe of Judah) Those who are descended from the tribe of Judah, or who profess the religion of Judaism. **CCC 60, 762**

Jews for Jesus (DZHÖÖZ for DZHEE-zuhs): 1. Jews who especially emphasize their conversion as their personal acceptance of Christ as the Messiah and fulfillment of O.T. prophecy; many still preserve their Jewish customs, practicing what might be called a baptized Judaism. The El Shaddai (Hebrew: The Lord) Congregation, a Protestant group of Jewish converts, especially celebrates the abiding Jewishness of its members. 2. The first followers of Jesus were, like Him, adherents of Judaism. Similarly, the first converts to Christianity on Pentecost (Acts 2:5) were in Jerusalem specifically to fulfill the Jewish observance of going up to the city for their holy days. Initially, the Christians viewed themselves as Jews who had accepted Jesus Christ as their Messiah; it was the decision of Jewish authorities that they had in fact distanced themselves from true Judaism and should as a consequence be excluded from the Temple liturgy and synagogue activities (Acts 4:5, 5:26). In time, Gentiles joined the ranks of the first generation of Christians with significant repercussions for typically Jewish practices, most obviously circumcision and dietary laws. The Council of Jerusalem (Acts 15:1-22) decided in favor of participation in the Church by all believers in Christ, Jews and Gentiles alike, regardless of prior affiliation.

Job, Book of (BØØK uhv DZHOB): Suffering in the world, especially the suffering of the innocent, has been a classic religious problem. In this sapiential book, the problem is presented, not abstractly, but in a very concrete and intensified form. The book should not be classified as history; it is rather a philosophical discussion offered in a personalized and novelized form. Job is presented as being a very just and holy man, having all the earthly blessings Jews were led to expect from the faithful observance of their covenant with God. In short order, he lost all these and was reduced to the most miserable state imaginable. Naturally, he wondered why, and so began his dialogue with his few remaining friends. Religious people have always seen moral guilt as being at the base of human misery. Often the accusing finger is pointed at the suffering individual himself; this was the reaction of Job's friends. Sometimes, when this fails, the source is sought in the sins of the parents, in the corrupt structures of society, or in evil spirits. Irreligious people, on the other hand, find in these misfortunes the best proof that there is no God; they conclude that the forces ruling the universe are fundamentally amoral or impotent. The Book of Job touches all these explanations. The initial narrative establishes the role of the evil spirit: Satan is shown as being permitted by God to afflict Job. Job's friends belabor the supposed factor of his own guilt. When Job steadfastly continues to protest his innocence, they accuse him of pride and self-righteousness. The high point of the book is Job's dialogue with God. God does not explain things to Job's satisfaction, but He does bring Job to realize his own intellectual limitations. He is led to perceive that at this stage of religious development, he

425

must not expect a satisfying answer. When, in humility, he accepts this, his former blessings are restored to him many times over; the author, living on that theological plateau, could conceive of no other happy ending. Like most dramatic treatments of the topic, the question is more effectively presented than the answer. It is not until the N.T. presents the problem in its most excruciating form, with the crucifixion of Jesus, that we have a more satisfying reply. Human history is not meant to end here on earth, but it embraces an infinitely larger perspective. It is the consoling message of the beatitudes that God's justice is displayed very imperfectly in time, but perfectly in eternity. We may and should strive to bring about God's dominion here and now, but we should not expect perfect success in that endeavor.

Jocists (DZHAHK-ihsts): The popular name of the Catholic association of factory workers known as the *Jeunesse Ouvrière Chrétienne* (J.O.C.) founded by Joseph (later Cardinal) Cardijn in Brussels after World War I, inspired by the principles enunciated in the encyclical *Rerum Novarum,* issued by Pope Leo XIII. It endeavors to assist in the Christian formation of an active and socially aware laity within the Church.

Joel (DZHO-ehl): (Hebrew: Yahweh is God) The O.T. prophet whose book bearing his name gives no information about his person — a "minor prophet," probably a Judean.

Joel, Book of (BØØK uhv DZHO-ehl): As happens so often, we know nothing of the life of this minor prophet. Scholars rely on rather scanty evidence to place it in the fourth century B.C. The usual prophetic themes are sounded in the short book. Priests and people are called to return to the Lord in a sincere spirit. If that is done, the nations that are afflicting Israel will be destroyed, God's people will be exalted, and the Lord's day will come. The prophet knew that the Jewish people were familiar with plagues of locusts; such an experience offered writers a realistic basis to express their sentiments toward their rapacious oppressors from abroad. Those who had lived through the devastation brought by the locusts could rely on this experience to validate their hope that God would similarly deliver them from their human predators.

John, Epistles of, First, Second, Third (ih-PIH-suhlz uhv DZHAHN, FERST, SEH-kuhnd, THERD): All three letters serve a single purpose: to open us up to the concrete struggles within the Johannine Church of the late first century. According to 1 Jn 2:19, it appears that there was a schism in the Church that John had founded. This first letter is written to believers who stayed in the main Church ("the faithful") and encourages them not to follow the error of those who have left. In 1 Jn 4:2, we learn of the necessity of confessing not just that Jesus is God, but that He is God come *in the flesh.* The opponents appear to have denied Christ's humanity, perhaps because of an overspiritualized view of His divinity. Such a view could have easily been rooted in Platonic philosophy or other Hellenistic influences that viewed the body as necessarily unspiritual or morally evil. When read in reverse order, 3 John seems to be a cover letter for a messenger bringing either written or oral communication from the Elder to the community in question. The point of the letter is to encourage hospitality and a warm reception. In 2 John, we infer that the original problems were not rectified, thus the need to encourage positive relationships. This letter was probably a cover letter for 1 John, which is not in the traditional form of an ancient letter. In 1 John, we read about the substantial doctrinal matters at the heart of the problems. This letter is a remarkable expression of the intricate and inseparable links between orthodoxy and orthopraxis in the early Church. That is, it not only teaches the truth but also how to live it. Tradition attributes authorship of 1, 2, and 3 John to "John," the author of the Fourth Gospel. Current scholarly opinion supports the proposition that 1 John was written as an interpretive guide for the Fourth Gospel by the same author who "finalized" its narrative; 2 and 3 John were clearly written by the same person, but it is not certain whether or not their author was that of 1 John. It would be prudent to follow Tradition. If the Gospel was written around A.D. 90, then the epistles are sometime after that, perhaps between A.D. 92 and 100 or later.

John the Baptist, or Baptizer, St. (SAYNT DZHAHN *th*uh BAP-tihst, or BAP-tai-zer): The forerunner of Jesus, son of Zechariah and Elizabeth, who imitated Elijah in dress and style of life. Some experts believe him to be associated with the Qumran community. John's message was one of repentance in anticipation of the Messiah. John, who is commemorated by the Church on June 24 (birth) and August 29 (beheading), was martyred by Herod Antipas (Mt 14:3-12). (Cf. Nativity.) **CCC 523, 720**

John, The Gospel of *(th*uh GAH-spuhl uhv DZHAHN): Traditionally known as "the Fourth Gospel" because of its place in the canon, this Gospel is distinct from the other three Gospels because of its overall structure and thematic expression. When set against either the texts of the O.T. or their first-century A.D. interpretations within Judaism, many of Jesus' discourses, as well as their accompanying circumstances, convey deep religious, theological, and spiritual meaning. The use of such key images as "light," "darkness," "truth," "lies," "love," "hate," "from above," "from below," "sign," and "glory" unlock the worldview of the human author, while expressing the deeper meaning of salvation from the Divine Author. The Gospel is written to lead the believer to a deeper and fuller knowledge of the Father's plan of salvation revealed through Jesus Christ. The narrative begins with hymnlike material focusing on Jesus as the Word, or Logos, Who became flesh. As the Logos, Jesus is active in creating the world (Jn 1:1-4; cf. Gn 1-2 and Prv 8:22-30, 9:1-9 for the background to this text). But Jesus is also the "language of God," in that both His words and His life communicate God's message of salvation. His words and deeds reveal the Person and mind of the Father above. Jesus' mission is to descend, reveal the Father, die and enter His own glory, return to heaven (14:25-31), and send the Paraclete (e.g., 15:26-27; 16:4-24). Jesus' death is *the* moment of glory, at which point love reigns supreme over all evil, now defeated. Those who witness Jesus' words, works, and signs either come into belief (become children of God; cf. 2:11, 3:2, 4:54; 6:2, 14, 26, etc.) or remain in unbelief. Other key themes include rebirth from above (1:13; 3:3, 5, etc.) and belief that Jesus is the Christ, the Son of God, and is the only

Source of eternal life (6:35, 7:38, 11:25-26, 12:44; 14:1, 12; 16:9, etc.). The use of double meanings (e.g., the Greek word *pneuma* = breath or spirit), irony, symbolism, and the narrator's asides all suggest that the Gospel was intended for those Churches that came to faith through the oral preaching and teaching that preceded this Gospel. Due to the high degree of thematic and structural unity of the Gospel and for other reasons, we can say that the narrative of the Gospel is from the hand of a single author (with the exception, perhaps, of Ch. 21). In spite of certain historical questions concerning the identity of the author called "John," the early Church of the first few centuries defended the Gospel's apostolic origins. The position has been upheld by the witness of the universal Church throughout the centuries. While the historical problems remain, the authenticity of its apostolic character is secure. The narrative was probably written between A.D. 90 and 125.

Joinder of Issues (DZHOIN-der uhv IH-shööz): A procedural act in a canonical trial at which the terms of the question to be decided are determined by the judge.

Jonah, Book of (BØØK uhv DZHO-nuh): Modern exegetes regard this book not as a historical narrative but as a didactic short story about a reluctant prophet of the same name. The author is anonymous and does not appear in the story. Once upon a time, Jonah was called to take up a prophetic role in Nineveh, the capital of Judah's fierce enemy, Assyria. He ran away, taking a ship to escape so hopeless a task. Thrown overboard by his shipmates, he was swallowed by a great fish, but after praying to God for three days and three nights he was disgorged. He went to Nineveh, preached his message of repentance and divine justice, and the entire city was speedily converted. The book no doubt has its religious value: One should not shrink from an apostolic task, even when there seem to be insuperable difficulties. Older commentators and preachers assumed the historicity of the story, partly because it was divinely inspired and partly because Jesus used Jonah in the whale as a type of His own resurrection from the grave. On second thought, neither premise justifies the conclusion drawn therefrom. Inspired parables can be a fictional vehicle for conveying a truth, and fictional characters can serve as very striking types or antitypes.

Jonah, Sign of (SAIN uhv DZHO-nuh): In Mk 8:11-12, the Pharisees' demand that Jesus produce a sign from heaven to lend credibility to His claims is met with Jesus' reply that "no sign will be given to this generation." In Mt 12:38-42, 16:1-4, and Lk 11:29-32, Jesus responds to the demand for a sign by declaring that no sign will be given "except the sign of Jonah." The sign-of-Jonah episode is drawn from the Q document (q.v), the sayings source common to Matthew and Luke. Although the "men of Nineveh" and the "queen of the south" are mentioned in different order in Mt 12:41-42 and Lk 11:31-32, the wording of the sign-of-Jonah episode in Matthew and Luke is virtually identical. The principal difference between the Matthean and Lucan versions lies in the additional material found in Mt 12:40: "As Jonah was three days and three nights in the belly of the whale, so will the Son of man be three days and three nights in the heart of the earth." For Q and for Luke, the sense of the sign of Jonah is found in Lk 11:32 (parallel to Mt 12:41): "The men of Nineveh will arise with the men of this generation and condemn them; for they repented at the preaching of Jonah, and behold, something greater than Jonah is here." The sign of Jonah, the prophet come to pagan Nineveh from afar, was his preaching, which led the Ninevites to repentance and conversion. The sign of Jesus, the one "greater than Jonah," is Jesus' own preaching, a sign that "this generation" failed to recognize. To the material found in Q, Matthew adds an allegorization of Jon 2:1 to indicate that Jesus' death and resurrection, together with His preaching, constitutes the "sign of Jonah." This is so despite the fact that the preaching of the biblical Jonah makes no reference to that prophet's sojourn in the belly of the fish. Jonah's announcement is quite brief: "Yet forty days, and Nineveh shall be overthrown!" (Jon 3:4). The order of Lk 11:31-32, the queen of the south rising in condemnation followed by the men of Nineveh rising in condemnation, is more likely to represent the original order of Q than the order found in Mt 12:41-42. Because the mention of the queen of the south seems not to fit into the explanation of the sign of Jonah, Matthew mentions the men of Nineveh first and the queen of the south only subsequently. The later mention in Mt 16:4 of the sign of Jonah is brief and without explanation, clearly because the explanation offered in Mt 12:40-42 is presupposed.

Joseph, St. (SAYNT DZHO-sehf): The name "Joseph" is from the Hebrew *yosep* and can be translated as "let God add (or gather)." The N.T. figure in Mt 1-2 and Lk 1-2 is the spouse of Mary and the adoptive father of Jesus. A "just man" (Mt 1:19), from the House of David (Mt 1:19 ff.; Lk 2:4 ff.), he appears to have been a carpenter (Greek: *tekton* — Mt 13:55), as was Jesus (Mk 6:3). If Luke's infancy Gospel is narrated from Mary's experience and point of view, Matthew's Gospel narrates the major events from a distinctly Josephine perspective. It is Joseph who received revelation from an angel concerning the virgin birth of Jesus (Mt 1:20-25) and the escape to and return from Egypt (Mt 2:13-15, 19-23). Joseph witnessed the birth of Jesus (Lk 2:16), His circumcision (Lk 2:22), and, along with Mary, experienced the stress of searching for Jesus while He was in the Temple (2:41-52). Outside of the infancy narratives, Joseph is mentioned at Lk 4:22, Mt 13:55, and Mk 6:3. Joseph assumes varying degrees of importance under different aspects of Christian life. In the noncanonical *Protoevangelium of James,* he is described as being very old when he married Mary — and thus becomes the model of holiness and asceticism during the years after the persecutions, which coincided with the rise of monasticism and the development and ascendancy of the ascetical way of life. During the fourth through the seventh centuries, in Eastern Christianity, the apocryphal document *History of Joseph the Carpenter* was very popular and either stimulated or grew out of a strong veneration of Joseph. In the Western Church St. Bernardine of Siena and John Gerson (fifteenth century) established the theological implications for Joseph's role as foster father of Jesus. This theological development found its way into the liturgical tradition with the introduction of St. Joseph's feast day on March 19, 1479, in the Roman Calendar. After this point, St. Joseph's importance in the devotional life of the Church developed even further, the highlights of which are as follows. Formal liturgical devotion to St. Joseph became popularized through the work of St. Thérèse and St. Francis de Sales. Pope Clement XI created a special office of the hours for St. Joseph's feast day (in 1714); Benedict XIII established St. Joseph's name in the Litany of the Saints; St. Joseph was declared patron of the universal Church in 1870 by Pius IX. Between 1914 and 1955 his feast day was the third Wednesday after Easter. In 1955 the feast day of St. Joseph (the Worker) was transferred to the first of May, which ceased to be obligatory in 1969. Pope Leo XIII wrote an encyclical *(Quamquam pluries,* 1889), in which St. Joseph's preeminent sanctity was proclaimed. **CCC 437, 497, 532, 1014, 1846, 2177**

Josephism (DZHO-seh-fih-zuhm): The theory, put forth by Emperor Joseph II of Austria-Hungary in the eighteenth century, that the Church was subject to the State as its legitimate superior.

Joshua, Book of (BØØK uhv DZHAH-shöö-uh): A military man of the tribe of Benjamin and companion of Moses during the Exodus, Joshua succeeded him as leader of the Jewish people. The Book of Joshua tells of the conquest of Canaan (1-12) and the division of the occupied territory (13-21). Like the books of the Pentateuch, it seems to be a composite derived from many sources, but scholars have not yet come to agreement about their identity. That there was a Jewish military conquest of Canaan during the thirteenth century B.C. is historically certain. It has not yet been established that it was as extensive as biblical records indicate or that Joshua deserves credit for it. Some scholars believe that there were numerous Israelites already living in Palestine before the more reasonable date for the Mosaic exodus. Readers brought up in the Christian ethic will not be edified by the bloody and vindictive spirit shown in the book. Ours is not an age to glorify swashbuckling military heroes, even if we grudgingly admit that we owe our freedom and prosperity to them. The Jews were rightly convinced that God wished them to have this land; this conviction led them to believe they could justly take it by force. It is possible that the author has used hyperbole in recording the completeness of their triumph.

Joy (DZHOI): One of the twelve fruits of the Holy Spirit: the pleasure experienced by one who knows Christ as the ultimate happiness. Joy is a kind of completion to happiness when one becomes a disciple of Jesus; this pleasure will be most intense and perfect in heaven. CCC 736, 1846

Joys of the Blessed Virgin Mary: See Seven Joys of the Blessed Virgin

Jube: See Grille

Jubilee (DZHÖÖ-bih-lee): Derived from a reference in Lv 25:8-55 to a "jubilee" year. Leviticus says it is every fiftieth year (Lv 25:10). The jubilee was a special year of remission from guilt and sin and the return of lands to their original owners. The year began on the Day of Atonement, the tenth day of Tishri. The Catholic Church uses this term to refer to a "holy year" every twenty-fifth year. It is also used in reference to an extraordinary year of jubilee declared by the Holy Father. When a jubilee year is called, the bishop and his cathedral are the major focal points for celebration. When it is centered in Rome, the right inside door of St. Peter's, which is usually bricked closed, lies open, allowing for pilgrims to walk through and be the recipients of the graces of the jubilee year.

Judaism (DZHÖÖ-duh-ih-zuhm): The faith and practice of the Jewish people, expressing belief in one God, Who reveals Himself through the Law, the prophets, and the events of history. It is based upon the covenant that God made with the Jews, that He is their God and they are His people. Modern Judaism has come to be divided into Orthodox, Conservative, and Reform branches, and although each is based upon the Torah and the Talmud, they represent a wide theological spectrum.

Judaizers (DZHÖÖ-duh-ai-zers): A group or groups of early Jewish converts to Christianity for whom we have very little clear data. These people held that in order to become fully Christian, all Gentile converts to Christianity must first become full and legal Jews. This question prompted the first

Church council, the so-called Council of Jerusalem, circa A.D. 50, a summary account of which can be found in Acts 15. The Church's final decision included reference to restricted dietary practices and the inclusion of a general moral code based on the traditional teachings from the O.T. Torah. There is a second witness to the Judaizers in Paul's letter to the Galatians. At 2:14, we read the term *ioudaidzein,* which occurs only there in the N.T. and which literally means "to Judaize." In this context, Paul rebukes Peter for his "double-mindedness" concerning his relationship with Gentile- and Jewish-Christians on dietary and other purity laws. It is clear from the use of this term in the Greek O.T. (LXX) that it refers to those non-Jews who live as the Jews live (e.g., Est 8:17; but cf. also Plutarch's *Cicero* 7.6; Josephus's *Jewish Wars* II.xvii.10; xviii.2).

Jude, Epistle of (ih-PIH-suhl uhv DZHÖÖD): This letter is designated as a "catholic" epistle because it is addressed not to an individual or local church but to the universal (i.e., "catholic") Church (vv. 1-2). The author challenges the authenticity of certain teachers who held the position that living in Christ meant that no law, Jewish or other, was binding on the Christian, least of all moral law. By identifying himself with the Jerusalem Church, and as one of the "brethren [cousins] of the Lord," Jude is claiming apostolic authority for teachings used to challenge the dissenters from orthodoxy. He appeals to the Deposit of the Faith (v. 3) and to the Apostles (v. 17). The appeal to the Faith (vv. 3, 20-23) is critical for Jude's argument, as is reference to the fulfillment of judgment against those who reject God's commands. The debate on the pseudonymous nature of the document is not closed. There is no internal evidence that helps determine an exact date for its composition. The letter is quoted in 2 Pt, which most would concede is dependent on Jude. If 2 Pt is dated circa A.D. 100, then Jude would have been written at least before then. Most scholars estimate the date of composition to be circa A.D. 90. The author identifies himself as "Jude, servant of Jesus Christ and brother of James" (v. 1). Tradition identifies this person with Judas, one of the "brethren" of Jesus (Mt 13:55; Mk 6:3). Scholarly opinion holds that "Jude" is a pseudonym for a later first-century author who is familiar with the Jerusalem Church and its teachings.

Judges (DZHUH-dzhehz): An ecclesiastical office held by clerics or certain laypersons who are authorized by Canon Law to render decisions in canonical trials.

Judges, Book of (BØØK uhv DZHUH-dzhehz): This book follows that of Joshua and covers the same period of Jewish history, up to the establishment of the monarchy by Saul (1051 B.C.). Throughout the book the Israelites are settled in villages, united only in a religious way, worshipping the one God. They were not troubled by the great powers to the East (Mesopotamia) or to the West (Egypt). There were, however, intermittent periods of oppression by neighboring tribes; when these came, God sent brave and talented leaders to vindicate the just claims of His people. From this judicial function (which they enforced militarily), the "judges" are so called. The judges are Othniel, Ehud, Deborah and Barak, Gideon, Abimelech, Jephthah, Samson, Shamgar, Tola, Jair, Ibzan, Elon, and Abdon. For didactic moral purposes (later imitated by the prophets), Israel's setbacks are uniformly ascribed to their sin in abandoning Yahweh and following Canaanite gods. But after their repentance, the judge appears and his victory restores peace and happiness. A more mundane explanation would emphasize the disunity of the Jewish people and their rudimentary civilization at that time. Recently liberated from slavery, they did not have the discipline or the skills to establish control over the land they wished to occupy.

Judges, Synodal (SIHN-ah-duhl or sih-NO-duhl DZHUH-dzhehz): Ecclesiastical judges appointed by the bishop during a diocesan synod.

Judgment, General (DZHEH-ner-uhl DZHUHDZH-mehnt): The judgment given by God at the end of the world, occurring after Christ's Second Coming. Each human body will rise; those who have merited eternal life will possess a glorified body, while those condemned to hell will have bodies that are corrupt. **CCC 677-679, 1021, 1038**

Judgment, Liturgical (lih-TER-dzhih-kuhl DZHUHDZH-mehnt): One of the three judgments used to determine the appropriateness of any musical piece for use during a liturgical celebration. The liturgical judgment is multifaceted and includes a determination that must be made regarding structural and textual requirements, role differentiation, and the parts to be played by various individuals or groups such as congregation, cantor, choir, and instrumentalists. This judgment must be made by a competent liturgist and may not be based on personal preferences but on legitimate liturgical regulations.

Judgment, Musical (MYÖÖ-zih-kuhl DZHUHDZH-mehnt): The first of the three decisions used in determining the appropriateness of a musical work for use in the sacred liturgy. A competent musician makes his judgment on the basis of sound musicality. In order for a selection to be used, it must also pass the other two judgments: the liturgical and the pastoral.

Judgment, Particular (pahr-TIHK-yöö-ler DZHUHDZH-mehnt): The judgment rendered by God at one's death. The deceased will then go to heaven, purgatory, or hell. When the General Judgment occurs, body and soul will be reunited. CCC 1021-1022

Judgment, Pastoral (PAS-ter-uhl DZHUHDZH-mehnt): One of the three judgments used to determine the appropriateness of any musical piece for use in a liturgical celebration. It is the judgment made for a particular group of worshippers, in a particular place, age, and culture. This judgment presupposes a sensitivity to liturgy and a pastoral concern for the group gathered for prayer. A musical composition that is deemed acceptable in the pastoral judgment must then be judged as to appropriateness by virtue of the liturgical and musical judgments. These must be made by individuals with competency in those fields. Only after the selection has approval in each area is it to be used in the liturgy.

Judgment, Triple (TRIH-puhl DZHUHDZH-mehnt): The threefold judgment used to determine the appropriateness of any musical piece for a liturgical celebration. It includes the musical, liturgical, and pastoral judgments. The triple judgment was introduced in the 1972 document of the Bishops' Committee on the Liturgy, "Music in Catholic Worship." (Cf. Music in Catholic Worship; Judgment, Musical; Judgment, Liturgical; Judgment, Pastoral.)

Judica Psalm (YÖÖ-dih-kuh SAHM): (Latin *judica:* give judgment or sentence) Psalm 43 (42), with its versicle, "I will go to the altar of God," is recited at the beginning of the Mass of St. Pius V (the so-called "Tridentine Mass") during the Prayers at the Foot of the Altar, but that rite has been replaced by the Penitential Rite in the revised liturgy.

Judith, Book of (BØØK uhv DZHÖÖ-dihth): The O.T. work that relates how God saved His people by using a Jewish heroine, whose name means "Jewess." The book's author is unknown; it was probably written at the end of the second or the beginning of the first century B.C. Judith prays for deliverance (9:2-14) and eventually beheads the evil Assyrian general Holofernes.

Juridic Person (dzhøø-RIH-dihk PER-suhn): An aggregate of persons or things treated by the law as if it were a person with defined rights and obligations, as in a civil corporation.

Jurisdiction (dzhøør-ihs-DIHK-shuhn): The power of governance in the Church ordinarily exercised by clerics in legislative, judicial, or executive fashion.

Jurisprudence (DZHØØR-ihs-PRÖÖ-dehns): The legal science whereby the law is applied to specific cases. In Canon Law, jurisprudence is an indicator as to the correct meaning and application of the law.

Jus Patronatus: See Iuspatronatus

Justice (DZHUHS-tihs): 1. The giving to another of what is due him. Justice is extolled in the Scriptures and by the Magisterium. Commutative justice regards actions between individuals; distributive justice regulates actions between groups and persons. Social justice concerns the rights and duties that society and individuals have toward each other, while original justice was the state that Adam and Eve enjoyed before the Fall. 2. Used in some Bible translations as a synonym for "holiness" or "righteousness." CCC 375, 1807, 2411

Justification (dzhuhs-tih-fih-KAY-shuhn): The process by which a sinner is made "righteous" in the sight of God. This occurs when one accepts the free and unearned gift of faith and responds to it by acts of charity (i.e., good works performed out of love of God and neighbor). CCC 1987, 1991-1992

Just War Theory (DZHUHST WOR THEE-uh-ree): The parameters used to measure whether or not a war is ethically just. There are varieties of this theory. Catholic discussion of a just war derives from the natural law and contends that it is always morally evil to kill innocent human life. Hence, a country may enter a war if it or its allies are unjustly attacked, provided the war is a last resort and undertaken to repel the attack. Just means, just intention, and a just end all have to be present; only those military means absolutely necessary can be employed, and the war must be declared by legitimate authority. Furthermore, no civilian populations can be targeted, nor can there be any side effects so evil as to outweigh the benefit of engaging in the war. Today, many contend that the advent of nuclear weapons makes any consideration of a just war obsolete; however, the Magisterium has not condemned the possession of nuclear weapons if they are meant to be a deterrent against unjust aggression. CCC 2309

K

Kanan: See Canon

Kantism, also Kantianism (KANT-ih-zuhm [KANT-ee-uhn-ih-zuhm]): The philosophy based upon the thought of Immanuel Kant (1724-1804), who held that experience, or the content of knowledge, comes from sense perception, but that its form is determined by *a priori* categories of the mind. Kant also presupposed such things as the existence of God and of immortality, although he thought that they could not be proved. Kantism has been found useful by some Protestant theologians, but it cannot be harmonized with Catholic theology.

Kathisma (kuh-TIHZ-muh): When the Book of Psalms is divided into twenty sections, as it is in the Byzantine Rite, each section is called a kathisma. Each kathisma is further separated into three segments, concluding with the Glory Be. Psalm 119 is its own kathisma because of its length (176 verses). The other nineteen range in length from six to fifteen psalms, all depending on the length of the psalms.

Katholikon (kuh-TOL-ee-kahn): The main church of a Byzantine Rite bishop or monastic community. Its counterpart in the Western Church is the cathedral.

Katholikos (kuh-TOL-ee-kos): A Greek term literally meaning "universal." In some Eastern Churches, it refers to a patriarch because of the wide or universal jurisdiction a patriarch possesses.

Kenosis (keh-NO-sihs): (Greek: emptying) Christ's emptying of Himself in His free renunciation of His right to divine status, "the form of God," by reason of the Incarnation, particularly as celebrated in the kenotic hymn of Phil 2:6-11, where it is said that Christ "emptied himself" taking the form of a slave, born in the likeness of man, i.e., a full and real humanity, totally integrated with His divinity. In Gnostic circles, it was popular to depict the crucified Christ in the position of *kenosis,* viz., with His hands raised above His head to bespeak total and utter dependence upon the Father from Whom He had descended to earth. Cf. CCC 461-463

Kerygma (keh-RIHG-muh): (Greek: proclamation, preaching) The proclamation of the good news of what God has done and is doing in the Person of Jesus Christ; as such, distinct from the instruction, or *didache,* that followed upon the apostolic *kerygma* and occupied much of the life of the early Church. Given the inner unity between the words of Scripture and the events and Person they proclaim, the language of the *kerygma* of God's salvific activity in the Person of Jesus Christ is itself a divine self-expression or epiphany. Cf. CCC 6, 174, 900, 2044

Keys (Power of the): See Power of the Keys

Kingdom of Christ (KIHNG-duhm uhv KRAIST): The N.T. depicts the kingdom of Christ as the Father's gift to the Son, to be enjoyed as the great eschatological banquet (Lk 22:29-30) in Paradise (Lk 23:40-42), marked especially by the forgiveness of sins (Jn 18:28, 19:30); there the righteous, conformed to Christ, will shine like the sun in their Father's kingdom (Mt 13:26-43), with all things reconciled to Him (1 Cor 15:28). Thus, the kingdom of Christ is the same as the kingdom of God, though totally transcendent and eschatological; it is made up of all whom Christ has gained, that they might enjoy the eternal reward appropriate to the righteous. Cf. CCC 553, 671, 680, 763

Kingdom of God (KIHNG-duhm uhv GAHD): God's sovereign lordship or rule over salvation history, leading to the eschatological goal of eternal life with God. From the Lord's Prayer, it might be said that the kingdom of God exists where God's will is now being done: "The time is fulfilled, and the kingdom of God is at hand" (Mk 1:15; cf. Mt 4:17). The dual nature of the kingdom as both eschatological and "at hand" is aptly described by Karl Rahner as the "already-not-yet." The miracles of Jesus, like His Sermon on the Mount, confirm that the kingdom has already arrived on earth (Mt 5:1-12; 12:28; Lk 6:20-23; 11:20); yet, this kingdom does not originate in this world, as it is otherworldly, not controlled by human will, everlasting (Lk 1:33), eternal (2 Pt 1:11), heavenly (2 Tm 4:18), and a manifestation of Jesus (2 Tm 4:1); the kingdom is the site for the Messianic banquet (Mt 8:11; 22:1-10; 26:29; Mk 14:25; Lk 13:29). Both the present and future aspects of the kingdom are characteristic of the kingdom parables (Mt 13; 18:23-25; 20:1-16; 25:1-13; Mk 4; Lk 8:4-18; 13:18-21). **CCC 1720, 2819**

King James Version (KIHNG DZHAYMZ VER-zhuhn): An English Protestant translation of the Scriptures first published in 1611, with the authority of King James I of England, who called for the translation at the Hampton Court Conference in 1604. Fifty-four biblical scholars, including professors of Hebrew and classics from Oxford and Cambridge, worked from 1607 to 1610 on the King James Bible (as it is generally called in England), recognized today for the graceful and dignified translation, which serves still as a model of elegant English prose, comparable in literary style to the contemporary Catholic Douai-Rheims English translation of the Bible. The preface of the King James acknowledges that it is mainly a revision of the Bishops' Bible of 1572, rather than a fresh translation; the King James is commonly called the Authorized Version in recognition of its authoritative nature for most Protestant denominations.

Kings, First and Second Books of (FERST and SEH-kuhnd BØØKS uhv KIHNGZ): The two historical books of the O.T. that immediately follow upon 1 and 2 Samuel; in the Latin Vulgate, and in translations made from it, these four books are listed as 1-4 Kings. Written, with a decided influence by the Deuteronomistic history, probably by several authors, who display a distinctive bias for the Southern Kingdom (as revealed in their condemnation of every king of Israel for maintaining the separate shrines of Dan and Bethel in competition with the one Temple in Jerusalem), with a final redaction in the late sixth century, 1 and 2 Kings cover a span of four hundred years. In 1 Kings, the history of David, begun in 1 and 2 Samuel, is completed. There follows the monarchy of Solomon and the history of the kings of Judah and Israel up to Ahab. In 2 Kings, both kingdoms are treated up to the fall of Samaria in 721 B.C., then with the focus exclusively on Judah till the fall of Jerusalem, its capital city, in 587 B.C. The Books of Kings record primarily God's plan for His Chosen People from the true worship of Yahweh in Solomon's Temple, through their disintegration in the time of exile, to the preparation of the pious remnant, *anawim,* who would remain faithful to their covenant with God. The kings themselves are evaluated on the basis of the fidelity of the people under their kingship and their own efforts to remove the pagan shrines, as final holdovers from their Canaanite ancestors. Of all the kings, only the southern kings David, Solomon, Hezekiah, and Josiah are viewed positively and praised for their achievements.

Kingship of Christ (KIHNG-shihp uhv KRAIST): Doctrine formally declared by Pope Pius XI, in 1925 in his encyclical *Quas Primas,* that Jesus Christ is King (cf. Mt 21:9; Mk 11:10; Lk 1:33) both by birthright as the Son of God and by right as Redeemer. As early as the Annunciation, God's plan of salvation is revealed to Mary that she is to give birth to God's divine Son (Lk 1:26-38), thus linked to God's promise to give the Child the throne of David, His royal ancestor. For the individual believer, Christ's kingship will be realized as the fulfillment of His pledge of everlasting life and peace (Mt 16:28) in the *eschaton,* i.e., at the end of history (Mt 13:41), thus outside of human history, and conclusive of that history at one and the same time. Hence, the kingship of Christ signifies His rule, reign, and dominion, whereby He grants salvation, justice, and mercy to the righteous and judges the unrighteous with the same justice and mercy. Cf. CCC 783, 786, 908, 2105

Kinonikon (kih-NON-ih-kahn): (Greek: moving) In the Byzantine Rite, the troparion of the Communion of the priest; there is a major kinonikon for each of several major feasts.

Kiss, Liturgical Use of the (lih-TER-dzhih-kuhl YÖÖS uhv *th*uh KIHS): Liturgical tradition attests to two usages: a reverential gesture as prescribed in the rubrics (toward objects such as the Gospel Book and altar) and as one way of exchanging the sign of peace before Communion. In the 1964 instruction *Inter Oecumenici,* on the orderly carrying out of the Liturgy Constitution, the Sacred Congregation of Rites states that in the interest of simplifying the rites (in accord with *Sacrosanctum Concilium,* the Constitution on the Sacred Liturgy, n. 34) the kissing of the hand or of objects (such as the cruets at the presentation of the gifts) shall be omitted (n. 36d) and that the celebrant kisses the altar only at the beginning of Mass and at the end of Mass. The 1967 instruction *Tres abhinc annos* of the same Congregation (the second instruction "on the orderly carrying out of the Liturgy Constitution") states that the celebrant kisses the altar only at the beginning and at the end of Mass (n. 85). The 2000 *General Instruction of the Roman Missal* directs the celebrant (n. 123) and deacon (n. 173) to kiss the altar at the beginning and at the end of Mass (nn. 169 and 186). It also directs the deacon (or whoever else proclaims the Gospel, the celebrant or an assisting or concelebrating priest) to kiss the Gospel Book at the end of the proclamation of the Gospel, saying (inaudibly), "May the words of the gospel wipe away our sins" (n. 175). The 1984 *Caeremoniale Episcoporum,* the *Ceremonial of Bishops,* states that at the conclusion of the Gospel's proclamation, the deacon "carries the *Book of the Gospels* to the bishop to kiss, or he may kiss it himself" (n. 52). The *General Instruction of the Roman Missal* also states that "according to traditional liturgical practice, the altar and the *Book of the Gospels* are kissed as a sign of veneration. The Conference of Bishops may substitute some other sign of reverence, with the consent of the Holy See" (n. 273). The present order for the celebration of Mass contains no explicit reference to the way the gesture of peace is to be shared prior to Communion. It states that after speaking the words "The peace of the Lord be with you always," and the people's response ("And also with you"), "then the priest may add: 'Let us offer each other the sign of peace [Latin, *Offerte vobis pacem*].'" The priest may give the sign of peace to the ministers, always remaining within the sanctuary, lest the celebration be disrupted. He should do likewise if, for a good reason he wishes to offer the sign of peace to a few of the faithful. All, in accordance with the decisions of the Conference of

Bishops, make a sign to one another that expresses peace, communion and charity" (n. 154).

Knights of Columbus (NAITS uhv kuh-LUHM-buhs): The Catholic laymen's fraternal organization begun in 1882 by Fr. Michael McGivney in New Haven, Connecticut. It serves the Church by promoting unity among Catholic laymen, resulting in the performing of charitable works like contributing to causes to assist the mentally retarded and financially supporting the Holy See.

Knights of Malta, or Hospitalers (NAITS uhv MAHL-tuh [HAHS-pih-ta-lerz]): Common name of the sovereign Military Hospitaler Order of St. John of Jerusalem, of Rhodes, and of Malta, and the oldest religious order of chivalry. Begun during the First Crusade in 1070, it had as its purpose the protection and care of pilgrims in the Holy Land. It received papal approval in 1113, and when it was expelled by the Muslims, its members retreated finally to Malta, where they were the temporal rulers until the Napoleonic invasion in 1798. It is a religious order recognized not only by the Holy See but also under international law as a sovereign entity. At one time its membership was restricted to members of the nobility, but there is a more recent category of Knights and Dames for persons not of the noble classes.

Knights, Orders of (OR-derz uhv NAITS): Originating in the Middle Ages, a knight was a man who was raised to an honorable military rank by the monarch, or other qualified person, after serving an apprenticeship as a page or squire and pledging himself to the principles of chivalry. The most worthy of these knights were sometimes organized into orders, and some even made religious vows.

Knights, Papal (PAY-puhl NAITS): Pontifical Orders of Knighthood are: The Supreme Order of Christ, The Order of the Golden Spur, The Order of Pius IX, The Order of St. Gregory the Great, and The Order of Pope St. Sylvester. Membership in these orders is granted by the Supreme Pontiff to honor certain individuals, most often those who have rendered some meritorious service to the Church or society.

Knock, Our Lady of (AUR LAY-dee uhv NAHK): The apparition of Our Lady, St. Joseph, the Lamb of God, and St. John the Evangelist on August 21, 1877, in Knock, Ireland. In 1880, the vision was repeated twice. Knock has become a shrine for millions of visitors, including Pope John Paul II in 1979.

Knowledge (NAU-lchdzh): The internal representation of that external information and experience that has been acquired through the act of the mind. Growing in knowledge is part of the practice of the Christian Faith, since it is used to make judgments that can bring the individual closer to God. CCC 23, 31-38, 40, 50, 74, 94, 158, 186, 261, 286, 356, 396, 428-429, 471-474, 851, 1734, 1792, 2197, 2500, 2614, 2708, 2715, 2822

Know-Nothingism (NO-NUH-thing-ih-zuhm): A nineteenth-century political movement in the United States that sought to reduce the influence of any foreign peoples, religions, or ideas in the country.

Knox Version of the Bible (NAHKS VER-zhuhn uhv *thuh* BAI-buhl): At the request of the Catholic hierarchy of England and Wales, Msgr. Ronald Knox, a distinguished biblical scholar and linguist, undertook in 1939 a translation of the Bible from Jerome's Vulgate. His stated aim was to express the Bible "in timeless English" in a style that was "accurate, intelligible, idiomatic, readable." With the imprimatur of Cardinal Griffin, the Knox Version of the Bible was published in 1949. At times too free in style and given to personal idiosyncrasy, the Knox Version has never been especially popular as an English translation; its great importance, however, lies in the impetus it gave to later translations, such as the Revised Standard Version and the Jerusalem Bible.

Koimesis (KOI-meh-sihs): (Greek: falling asleep) Death in general, as applied in Byzantine usage; in particular, it refers to the Dormition, or Assumption, of the Mother of God, observed on August 15. The *koimesis* of St. Anne, the mother of Mary, is celebrated on July 25. **Cf. CCC 966**

Koinonia (koi-no-NEE-uh): (Greek: community, fellowship, association) Term favored by St. Luke for the fellowship of believers who worshipped together and held all their possessions in common (Acts 2:42-47); it is also used of fellowship with God (1 Jn 1:3, 6), with the Son (1 Cor 1:9), and with the Holy Spirit (2 Cor 13:13; Phil 2:1). In Pauline use, *koinonia* denotes the intimate union of the believer with Christ and the community that exists among all the faithful themselves (Rom 15:26; 2 Cor 6:14); similarly, the early Church saw the communion of the saints as a *koinonia* stronger than death (cf. Phil 1:5). This sense of association naturally leads to participation, as in our sharing in Christ's sufferings (Phil 3:10), in the Body and Blood of Christ (1 Cor 10:16), in the Holy Spirit (2 Cor 13:13), and participation in the Faith, even to the point of giving one's life (Phlm 3:10). CCC 948

Kontakion (kon-TAHK-ee-ahn): A troparion containing a summary of the subject of a feast. There is a proper kontakion for every feast in the Byzantine Rite.

Koran (ko-RAN): (Arabic *Qur'an:* book, reading, recitation; from *quar'a:* to read) The sacred writings of Islam, thought by Muslims to be the revelations and commands from Allah given to the prophet Muhammad by the archangel Gabriel.

Ku Klux Klan (KÖÖ KLUHKS KLAN): (Greek *kyklos,* circle) A secret society founded in the southern United States after the Civil War to maintain white supremacy and, through terroristic methods, to prevent the newly freed slaves from exercising their legal rights. Its activity expanded to include opposition to Jews, Catholics, and members of various other ethnic and religious groups.

Kulturkampf (køøl-TØØR-kahmpf): A nationalist movement in Germany that began in the nineteenth century and sought to reduce and eliminate the influence of foreign elements. It was particularly concerned with undermining the influence of Catholicism.

Kyriale (kih-ree-AH-lay): A book of some Gregorian chants. It predates Vatican II and is no longer used today. Some of these chants can now be found in *Jubilate Deo*.

Kyrie Eleison (KIHR-ee-ay ay-LAY-ee-son): The last vestige of Greek in the Order of Mass in the Latin Rite. Its literal translation is "Lord, have mercy." In the West, this phrase has been used as a response to a litany of intercessions (Prayer of the Faithful) and as part of the Penitential Rite of the Mass. **Cf. CCC 2613**

L

Labarum (lah-BAH-røøm): Military standard of the Christian Roman emperors, first used by Constantine after his victory in the battle at the Milvian Bridge in 312 as a sign of his conversion to Christianity. Described by Eusebius, in his *Vita Constantini,* as a long, gilded spear, with a crossbar giving it the shape of a cross; on the top of the spear was a wreath of gold and precious stones, within which the first two letters of the name of Christ in Greek were placed, the *chi* (X) intersecting the *rho* (P); hanging from the crossbar was a banner of imperial purple, inscribed in Latin, *In hoc signo vinces,* "In this sign, you shall conquer."

Labor (LAY-ber): The activity by which one develops his human gifts and earns a livelihood. The worker contributes to the commonweal and also expands his capacity for accepting challenge. Laborers are to be treated fairly by being given a just wage (for themselves and their families) for adequate work, medical attention, housing, etc. In turn, the worker owes his employer sound production and efficiency. Cf. CCC 378, 901, 1368, 1609, 1914, 1940, 2427-2428, 2431, 2434

Laborem Exercens (lah-BOR-chm EHK-zehr-tshehnz): The encyclical letter "On Human Work," issued by Pope John Paul II in 1981, stressing the value of exercising one's human dignity through work. Work contributes to society's welfare and to that of the individual. Governments and persons must do all they can to ensure that no one becomes just a "cog" in the wheel of production. Fair wages and decent working conditions are mandatory. Cf. CCC 378, 901, 1368, 1609, 1914, 1940, 2427-2428, 2431, 2434

Lady Chapel (LAY-dee TSHAP-uhl): A chapel dedicated to the Blessed Virgin Mary. This name has been used especially in England and France.

Lady Day (LAY-dee DAY): Another name for the Solemnity of the Annunciation, celebrated on March 25.

Laetare Medal (lay-TAH-ray MEH-duhl): The gold medal presented by the University of Notre Dame since 1883 on Laetare Sunday (Fourth Sunday of Lent) to an American Catholic noted for remarkable service to the Church and society. The founder of the university, Fr. Edward Sorin, C.S.C., suggested that such an award be given.

Laetare Sunday: See Gaudete Sunday

Laicism (LAY-ih-sih-zuhm:) An idea that gained prominence in the nineteenth century, calling for a minimizing of the role of the clergy in both ecclesiastical and civil affairs, and making all temporal and almost all spiritual matters the responsibility of the laity. It was a form of anticlericalism and secularism, opposed to any influence by the Church upon political or cultural matters. For these reasons, it was condemned in 1864 by Pope Pius IX in the *Syllabus of Errors*. Cf. CCC 897-913

Laicization (lay-ih-sih-ZAY-shuhn): The canonical process whereby a cleric is returned to the lay state, after which he lacks the ability to exercise Sacred Orders, except in emergency situations.

Laic Laws (LAY-ihk LAWZ): A series of laws enacted in France between 1875 and 1907, reflecting the anticlerical feelings of those in civil power at the time, with the goal of not only separating Church and State but even causing animosity between them. Their purported good was to take power from the clergy and give it to the people. The Laic Laws culminated in the Law of Separation in 1905, which led to the virtual secularization of French life.

Laity (LAY-ih-tee): All who have received Baptism but who are not in Holy Orders or in some religious state of life approved by the Church. CCC 864, 897-913, 2442

Laity, Institutions on (ihn-stih-TÖÖ-shuhnz awn LAY-ih-tee): Various organizations and groupings of laypersons in the Church with a variety of purposes that essentially serve the Church as a whole. (Cf. Associations of the Christian Faithful.) **Cf. CCC 928-933**

Lamb [Eucharist] (LAM): From "Lamb of God" (q.v.), the name given to the larger portion of the Bread of Offering in the Byzantine Rite. It is detached by the priest for Consecration. The Lamb is inscribed with the Greek lettering "IC," "XC," "NI," "KA" (an abbreviation for "Jesus Christ conquers").

Lambeth Conference (LAM-behth KAHN-fer-ehns): The gathering of the bishops of the Anglican Communion, first convoked in 1865 and subsequently taking place approximately every ten years, for the discussion of various topics of interest to the member churches. Although its decisions are not binding on the churches of the communion, they do carry some weight as being representative of the views of all the Anglican diocesan bishops.

Lamb of God (LAM uhv GAHD): A liturgical title for Christ recited three times before the distribution of the Eucharist at Mass; the priest then elevates the consecrated Host before the people and says: "This is the Lamb of God who takes away the sins of the world" (Jn 1:29). The Latin text further emphasizes the symbolism of the Lamb with the commendation *Beati qui ad cenam agni vocati sunt,* "Blessed are those called to the banquet of the Lamb" (Rv 19:9). The Scriptures provide ample background to this image; in the O.T., God commands the sacrifice of a lamb in preparation for the Exodus (Ex 12:5), the basis for the liturgical ceremony in celebrating the Passover and an archetype for the messianic lamb; Jeremiah described his experience of persecution as a lamb led to slaughter (Jer 11:19); the same image is used by Isaiah in speaking of the Suffering Servant (Is 53:7), a text explained by the Apostle Philip as fulfilled in the actions and Person of Christ. In the N.T., the title is applied directly to Jesus by John the Baptist (Jn 1:29-34); Jesus is the Lamb (1 Pt 1:19; Rv 5:6) without blemish or sin (Jn 8:46; 1 Jn 3:5; Heb 9:14); He brings deliverance by His Blood (Heb 9:12-15; 1 Pt 1:18; Rv 5:9), building up the redeemed by helping them to avoid sin (Jn 1:29; 1 Pt 1:15; 1 Jn 3:5-9), forming a consecrated nation of the royal priesthood (1 Pt 2:9; Rv 5:9). As a symbol in Christian art, the lamb, often depicted as reclining on a book with seven seals (cf. Rv 5:1-6), always refers to Christ. Cf. 523, 536, 602, 608, 613, 719, 757, 796, 1137, 1329, 1364, 1602, 1612, 1642, 2159, 2618, 2642

Lamentations, Book of (BØØK uhv la-mehn-TAY-shuhnz): Five poems, written in the style of a dirge or elegy, that tradition ascribes to Jeremiah, to whose prophecy the Septuagint and Vulgate attach them, though they are likely the work of his disciples. They provide an answer for the believing Jews to the complaints of those whose faith had weakened with the fall of Jerusalem (586 B.C.); they declare that God has not abandoned His Chosen People nor His covenant; infidelity to the covenant is the cause for the punishment of the people with Jerusalem's fall. The Catholic liturgy appropriates these poems in the Office of Tenebrae, celebrated during Holy Week to express the mourning of Christians over the suffering and death of the Messiah.

Lamp (LAMP): 1. The symbol representing God's Word, the lamp portrays knowledge, one of the seven gifts of the Holy Spirit. 2. The object, mandated by Canon Law, that reminds believers of the Real Presence of Christ in the Blessed Sacrament. Used in the sanctuary since the thirteenth century, the lamp also provided light during the liturgy in the early Church. Cf. CCC 141

Lamp-Lighting (LAMP LAI-tihng): The practice of lamp-lighting at Vespers or Evening Prayer harks back to the Jewish ritual of lighting lamps at the beginning of the Sabbath. In her fourth-century diary reflecting liturgical practice in Jerusalem, Egeria observes that Vespers was celebrated in the late afternoon and that lights were kindled from the lamp that always burned in the grotto of the Anastasis (the Sanctuary of the Resurrection). The revival of such a practice today seems entirely appropriate. The theme of light is present in many Vespers antiphons, psalms, and prayers. Cf. CCC 1243

Lance, Holy (HO-lee LANS): A liturgical knife, double-edged like the tip of a spear, recalling the lance of the Crucifixion. It is used by the priest to separate the Lamb or Seal from the Bread of Offering in the Eastern Churches.

Languages, Biblical (BIH-blih-kuhl LANG-weh-dzhehz): Hebrew, Aramaic, and Greek are the original languages in which the Scriptures were composed. Most of the O.T. was written in Hebrew, a Northwest Semitic dialect of Canaanite (Is 9:18), also called the language of Judah (2 Kgs 18:26). Hebrew remained the spoken language of Israel through the sixth century B.C., being gradually supplanted by Aramaic, a Hebrew dialect, probably first spoken by the Aramaeans of northern Syria whose scribes were valued by the Assyrians during the Exile, hence the importance of their dialect after that time. Aramaic was used for the writing of Gn 31:47; Ezr 4:8—6:18, 7:12-26; Jer 10:10-11; Dn 2:4—7:28. Some of the late books of the O.T., such as Wisdom and 1 and 2 Maccabees, have been transmitted only in Greek; the entirety of the O.T. was translated into Greek by Jews of the Diaspora living in Alexandria, Egypt, in the second century B.C. and is called the Septuagint. The original language of the N.T. was Koine Greek, a simplified form of Attic Greek, spread with the conquests of Alexander the Great and common in the Near East after 325 B.C.; the Greek of the Septuagint and N.T. is unique in its adaptation of the secular language to religious use.

Languages of the Church (LANG-weh-dzhehz uhv *th*uh TSHERTSH): Languages in which the Church's liturgy is celebrated. These include Geez, Syriac, Greek, Arabic, and Old Slavonic in the Eastern Churches. In the West, there is, of course, Latin and the various vernaculars. The Eastern Rites have always had the vernacular. The term may also refer to the languages spoken by the faithful who belong to the Church.

Lappet (LAP-et): One of the two cloths that hangs from the back of a miter. (See Miter.)

Lapsed (LAPST): (Latin *lapsi:* those who have slipped away) A term used as early as the time of Cyprian of Carthage (d.

258) to refer to those Christian converts who had abandoned the Christian Faith and practice and returned to their pagan beliefs. The controversy in Cyprian's time centered on the question of whether or not the lapsed had in fact abandoned the Faith or did so only for the sake of appearance, so as not to commit a crime against the State. Cyprian writes of three classifications of *lapsi: thurificati*, those who offered incense at pagan ceremonies; *sacrificati*, those who participated in the pagan sacrifices; and *libellati*, those who obtained legal documents stating that they had conformed to the required pagan practices. More frequently in modern usage, a lapsed Catholic is understood to be one who has consciously abandoned the Catholic Faith, specifically by absenting oneself from the sacramental life of the Church, which is most clearly observable in the failure to make the Easter duty. Penalties incurred by the lapsed are treated in the Code of Canon Law, cc. 1364-1369.

La Salette, Our Lady of (AUR LAY-dee uhv LAH sah-LEHT): The apparition of Our Lady to two children in La Salette, France, on September 19, 1846. Mary told Melanie Calvat and Maximin Giraud that prayer, penance, and humility were needed and that a terrible disaster would strike if persons did not repent of their sins. All of the Popes since Pope St. Pius X have approved of this apparition.

Last Day: See Judgment, General

Last Sacraments (LAST SA-kruh-mehnts): Usually refers to the Sacraments of Penance, Anointing of the Sick, and Viaticum. It may also refer to Confirmation, when it is known that this sacrament had not been received already. These may be administered to those who are dying or are in imminent danger of death. The manner in which they may be celebrated — along with appendices and supplements, a continuous rite, and emergency situations — is found in the *Pastoral Care of the Sick*. CCC 1517

Last Supper (LAST SUH-per): Traditional name given to the Passover meal that Christ ate in the upper room in Jerusalem with His Apostles the night that began His passion (Mt

26:20-29; Mk 14:17-25; Lk 22:15-20; 1 Cor 11:22); the site of this meal is also called the Cenacle, from the Latin *cena*, meal, in recognition of the Last Supper that was eaten here. During this meal, Christ instituted the Sacraments of the Eucharist and the priesthood, both foreshadowing the sacrificial act of the crucifixion to occur the next day. He also gave here the discourses, preserved uniquely in John's Gospel, on His relationship to God the Father (Jn 16:22-33) and the love of God that marks His followers (Jn 14:23). In Jewish tradition, all meals were sacred, with sacred ties established among the participants and with God, Who is blessed and praised for His bounty, which sustains those gathered at the table, in turn expressive of God's providential care and faithfulness to His covenantal love and promise to care for Israel. In a similar way, the Eucharist brings Christians into a deeper union with Christ and with one another: It intensifies their life with God by nourishing them and is a sign of the eternal life toward which the believer is led. While the Eucharist does repeat the historical event of the Last Supper, it also brings the participants into a present relationship with Christ and anticipates their future glory, with all three dimensions necessarily present at once in the sacrament. CCC 612, 1166, 1323, 1329, 1337, 1350, 1366, 1403, 1412, 2816

Last Things: See Eschatology

Latae Sententiae (LAH-tay sehn-TEHN-see-ay): The Latin term for the automatic imposition of a canonical penalty that occurs as soon as a canonical offense is committed. Cf. CCC 1463

Lateran (LA-ter-uhn): Name of a prominent Roman family whose Lateran Palace was taken over by the Emperor Nero, with the execution of Plautinus Lateranus in the first century A.D., and then given to Pope Miltiades by the Emperor Constantine in A.D. 312; it then served as the main papal residence until it was destroyed by fire in 1308. Adjacent to the Lateran Palace, Pope Sylvester dedicated the Lateran Basilica to the Savior on November 9, 324, designating it the cathedral of the Bishop of Rome, making it the "Mother and Head" of all the churches in the world; restored in the tenth century, it was dedicated to St. John the Baptist and so is known as St. John Lateran.

Lateran Church (LA-ter-uhn TSHERTSH): The Pope's cathedral or principal church in Rome. The Emperor Constantine gave what was once a royal palace and basilica to Pope Miltiades upon Constantine's conversion to the Faith (A.D. 313). Its name is derived from Plautinus Lateranus, a Roman senator whom the Emperor Nero had executed. The Lateran Church is known as the head and mother of all churches. It is dedicated under the title of the Most Holy Savior, *Sanctissimi Redemptoris,* and that of St. John the Baptist. In fact, it is better known under the title of St. John Lateran. The feast that celebrates the dedication of St. John Lateran falls on November 9 in the liturgical calendar.

Lateran Councils (LA-ter-uhn KAUN-suhlz): Councils convened at the Lateran Palace and Basilica by the Bishop of Rome. Four were local Roman synods: the first, convened in A.D. 313, condemned the Donatists; the second, in 649, curbed the Monothelite heresy; the third, in 769, repudiated iconoclasm; the fourth, in 1059, established the procedures governing papal elections. The ninth through twelfth ecumenical councils were held at the Lateran: Lateran I, 1123, the first general council in the West, decided questions of Church discipline, particularly the legislation of clerical celibacy; Lateran II, 1139, resolved the schism created by the antipope Anacletus; Lateran III, 1179, condemned the Albigensians and Waldensians and introduced further reforms of papal elections; Lateran IV, 1215, also called the "Great Council," reformed Catholic life, in particular mandating the Easter duty.

Lateran Palace (LA-ter-uhn PAL-uhs): A former residence of the Popes near the Basilica of St. John Lateran. It came into the possession of the Popes through the donation of Emperor Constantine, who wanted the Pope to have a residence befitting his dignity. Following the Avignon papacy, the Vicar of Christ began to stay more and more at the private residence on the Vatican Hill. The Lateran Palace then came to be used by the cardinal vicar whom the Pope appointed to govern the Diocese in his name. Today, the Lateran Palace is the residence not only of the Cardinal Vicar of Rome but also the Roman chancery. It is known as *il Vicariato,* the Vicariate.

Lateran Treaty (LA-ter-uhn TREE-tee): Concordat between the Holy See and the Italian government, signed on February 11, 1929, which established Vatican City as an independent State and Catholicism as the official religion of Italy. The Holy See renounced all claim to the Papal States, for which Italy agreed to pay financial compensation. The concordat has since been modified, with many of the Church's privileges being abrogated, including the end of mandatory Catholic instruction in State schools and the end of government salaries paid to Catholic clergy.

Latin (LA-tihn): In ancient times Latin was the language of the inhabitants of the Italian province of Latium, whose capital is Rome. With the increased influence and power achieved by the Romans and their subsequent colonization of most of the then-known world, the Latin language also spread along with Roman customs and laws. The Latin language was gradually adopted by Christians in the early Church as more and more Latin-speaking peoples were converted to the Faith. Curiously enough, this took place first in northern Africa, which in the first several centuries of the Church's existence was one of the most fruitful and influential Christian communities even before most of Europe was converted to Christianity. Though Greek remained the official language of the Roman Church until about the third century, when some of the first official documents and epistles from the Popes appeared in Latin, even in the second century the Scriptures and other documents for the faithful were being translated into Latin. By the fourth century, St. Jerome (342-420) had translated the entire Bible into this, the then "vulgar" language of the people, which is why this particular translation, the official translation of the Church, is still known as the "Vulgate." Up to this time, Greek was not only the official language of the Church but the language used by the upper classes and in learned circles, just as French was to become in modern times the language of the court and diplomacy. By the middle of the fourth century, the liturgy was also celebrated in Latin. Since then, up to our own day, Latin has been the official language of the Latin Rite of the Church. Even though today the vernacular tongues may be used regularly in the liturgy, the Second Vatican Council, responsible in part for the introduction of the vernacular into official worship, nevertheless refers to Latin as the official language of the Latin, or Roman, Church and the liturgy of the Latin Rite. Indeed, the Council even encourages its wide use by both the clergy and the faithful (cf. *Sacrosanctum Concilium.* nn. 36, 100; *Musicam Sacram* of March 5, 1967, by the Sacred Congregation of Rites, n. 41). Likewise, in regard to the laws of the Church, the Code of Canon Law, even today the only official version of the same is that to be found in Latin as promulgated in the Acts of the Holy See, the *Acta Apostolicae Sedis.* As a language, of course, Latin has seen some variations in style and usage, as with any other language, through the passage of time. Because of the great influence of the Roman Empire first, and then of the Church, for centuries the Latin language became the principal tongue spoken in the Western world and so it continued to develop, not as a dead language but as a living language, influenced by political, philosophical, theological, pastoral, and other practical requirements of the passing ages. Church Latin has its own flavor as well, which has been influenced, of course, by the mind-set that comes along as a natural development of the following of the Faith. Only in recent times, especially the last two hundred years, has Latin somewhat gone into practical disuse throughout the modern scholarly world. However, Latin retains its importance, not only because of its inherent beauty and usefulness (something that has always made it most appropriate for philosophy as well as for theology), but also because of its perpetual influence on most Western languages, even those not considered strictly Romance languages such as Italian, Spanish, French, Portuguese, and Romanian. In recent times the Popes have affirmed the necessity and importance of the Latin language for the Latin Church, as well as for the world's culture. Pope John XXIII wrote an encyclical on the matter, *Veterum Sapientia,* and Pope Paul VI established an association headquartered in the

Vatican, "Latinitas," for the promotion of Latin studies. Several voluminous Latin dictionaries incorporating modern technological and scientific language have also been published.

Latin Mass (LA-tihn MAS): The Eucharistic Sacrifice celebrated in the official language of the Roman Catholic Church. Contrary to what some erroneously think, Vatican II did not abolish Latin. Obviously, the vernacular is used predominantly in most places where Mass is offered in the Latin Rite; however, use of Latin is permissible at any time, in accord with the pastoral judgment of the celebrant. A Latin Mass (according to the present normative text) should not be confused with a Mass according to the Missal of Pope Pius V. In 1984 John Paul II granted an indult and authorized the use of the Mass according to the Tridentine Rite when certain conditions have been met. In 1988, he promulgated *Ecclesia Dei* and set up a commission bearing the same name to carry out its implementation.

Latin Rite (LA-tihn RAIT): The portion of the Catholic Church that follows the disciplines and teachings of the Diocese of Rome, especially regarding the liturgy. This rite is called "Latin" because that has been its official language since the fourth century. Most of the world's Catholics belong to the Latin Rite, which is headed by the Pope, the Bishop of Rome. Cf. CCC 1203

Latria (LAH-tree-uh): Greek-rooted Latin term that refers to that form of praise due to God alone. Cf. CCC 2135

Lauds (LAWDZ): The traditional name for the Office of Morning Prayer of the Liturgy of the Hours, from the (still current) Latin title *Ad Laudes Matutinas* ("for morning praises"), the morning counterpart to Vespers (or, in the current English usage, Evening Prayer), with which it is considered by Vatican II's Constitution on the Sacred Liturgy (*Sacrosanctum Concilium*) to be a "hinge" hour. In its present Latin Rite form, Lauds begins with the Invitatory verse (a "call to worship" antiphon) and Psalm 95 (several similar psalms are offered as alternatives), if it is the first Office of the day. If the Office of Readings (formerly "Matins" and in monastic communities "Vigils") precedes Lauds immediately, Lauds begins simply with the morning hymn. If a brief period of time intervenes between the Office of Readings and Lauds, the verse and response that commonly open the Offices are used: "O God, come to my assistance; O Lord, make haste to help me." After the morning hymn, Lauds continues with one psalm (referring in some way to the morning hour or the sanctification of the day), an O.T. canticle, and a "praise psalm." A brief Scripture reading follows (in communal celebrations a longer passage may be substituted and even followed by a homily), silent reflection, and a responsory, then the Gospel Canticle of Zechariah (the *Benedictus*) with its antiphon. A series of intercessions for the sanctification of the day's labors follows, concluding with the Lord's Prayer, a collect, blessing, and dismissal. **Cf. CCC 1174-1178**

Lavabo (lah-VAH-bo): (From Latin: I will wash) 1. The ceremonial washing of the hands by the celebrant at Mass at the conclusion of the Offertory, or Preparation of the Gifts. In the Tridentine Mass, the priest recited part of Psalm 26, which says: "I will wash my hands in innocence, and go about thy altar, O Lord." The lavabo symbolizes the need for the priest to be purified before offering the sacred mysteries *in persona Christi*. 2. The dish into which the poured water drops. 3. The sink in the sacristy.

L'Avenir: See Avenir, L'

Law (LAW): An ordinance of right reason, instituted by one in charge of the community, for the common good, and publicly promulgated. **CCC 1952; cf. 1904, 2196, 2425, 2541**

Law and Gospel (LAW and GAHS-puhl): The Christian mission demands a balanced integration of both Law and Gospel; the law of the O.T. has yielded to the new covenant of redemption, the Gospel, or Good News of salvation proclaimed in the Person of Jesus Christ, realized in His redeeming grace. In Jesus, the Torah is fulfilled, the benefit of which is made available to all incorporated into His death and resurrection; this is the Law of Life, the dynamic force that introduces the New Creation. The Gospel thus announces the fulfillment of Law in Christ, such that the Mosaic Law alone does not suffice for a full relationship with God (Rom 2:15, 3:20, 28; Gal 2:16, 3:2, 5:10); nor does physical circumcision, the surest sign of the old Law, guarantee contact with God (Rom 2:28, 3:1; Gal 2:3, 7; 5:6). While the Law does remain holy and good and an expression of God's will (Rom 2:27; 7:12, 16), of itself it cannot transform, renew, or sanctify, but it does teach (Rom 3:20, 28; Gal 2:16, 3:11). The Gospel is more compelling than the Law, for it is a compulsion of love; in this respect, the Sermon on the Mount (Mt 5:3-12) provides the best foundation for the relationship of Law to Gospel: Jesus fulfills the Law and teaches God's will in the Good News of His salvific life, death, and resurrection. CCC 1965-1971; cf. 459, 1972

Law, Canon: See Canon Law

Law, Universal (yöö-nih-VER-suhl LAW): Church law that binds the entire Church or all persons in the Church belonging to a group for whom the law was made. Cf. CCC 1904, 1952, 1965-1971, 2196, 2425, 2541

Laxism (LAKS-ih-zuhm): A system, arising in the seventeenth century within moral theology, which taught that if any doubt could be raised concerning the morality of some action, one would be free to ignore the law without sinning. Laxism was condemned by Pope Alexander VII in 1665 and again in 1666; in 1679, Pope Innocent XI condemned sixty-five propositions drawn from the Laxist system. Cf. CCC 1791-1793

Lay Baptism (LAY BAP-tih-zuhm): The administration of the Sacrament of Baptism by a layperson when a sacred minister is not available or is impeded. CCC 903

Lay Minister of Baptism (LAY MIH-nih-ster uhv BAP-tih-zuhm): The minister of solemn Baptism is a bishop, priest, or deacon, but in cases of emergency anyone, including a non-Catholic, can validly baptize. The lay minister pours water on the forehead of the person being baptized and says the words of the form ("I baptize you in the name of the Father and of the Son and of the Holy Spirit") while the water is flowing. Water used in solemn Baptism is blessed during the rite. CCC 903

Lay Minister of Marriage (LAY MIH-nih-ster uhv MEHR-ehdzh): A layperson who, with the proper permission of ecclesiastical superiors, acts as the official witness at the marriage of Catholics. Cf. CCC 1623

Lay People, Decree on the Apostolate of: See Apostolicam Actuositatem

Lay Reader (LAY REED-er): A layperson (man or woman) who has been trained and is competent to proclaim the Word of God (Sacred Scripture, except the Gospel) during liturgical celebrations. In addition, he or she may read the Psalm and announce the intentions of the Prayer of the Faithful. This person has not been installed formally in the ministry of lector. In *Ministeria quaedam,* the installation of readers is reserved to men. Those installed in this ministry now are almost always candidates for Holy Orders. Lay readers, however, are found nearly always in parishes and exercise "specific duties which he alone ought to perform, even though ordained ministers may be present" *(General Instruction of the Roman Missal,* n. 99). CCC 903

Lay Trusteeism (LAY truhs-TEE-ih-zuhm): The attempt by members of the laity to assume the prerogatives of the diocesan bishop to regulate all parochial affairs, even that of appointing and removing pastors. This first arose in 1776 in St. Peter's Church, New York City, and continued to be a problem in several parishes in this country until the mid-nineteenth century. In 1822, Pope Pius VII issued the brief *Non Sine Magno,* reaffirming the discipline that church property comes under the jurisdiction of the hierarchy, dismissing any claims to the right of patronage by the laity.

Leader of Song: See Song, Leader of

Leadership Conference of Women Religious (LEE-der-shihp KAHN-fer-ehns uhv WIH-muhn rih-LIH-dzhuhs): The association, approved by the Congregation for Religious and Secular Institutes in 1962, comprised of the major superiors of female religious institutes in the United States. The conference has a counterpart since 1992 in the Council of Major Superiors of Women Religious in the United States, committed to a more traditional approach to religious life.

Leadership, Pastoral (PAS-ter-uhl LEE-der-shihp): The guidance offered by a minister of the Church in exercising his pastoral office of inspiring all the faithful to contribute to the expansion of the Mystical Body of Christ. All pastoral leadership is to be performed in union with the Pope and the bishops. CCC 93, 816, 895, 899, 939, 1140, 1575, 2033, 2594, 2690

League for Religious and Civil Rights, Catholic: See Catholic League for Religious and Civil Rights

Lectern (LEHK-tern): The stand from which the Scriptures are proclaimed at Mass or the Liturgy of the Hours. Usually, it is a desk supported on a column of metal or wood, attached to a base. In liturgical documents, the lectern is frequently referred to as the ambo. The *General Instruction of the Roman Missal* stipulates that the readings, Responsorial Psalm, and *Exsultet* should all be proclaimed from the lectern. The homily and General Intercessions may also be offered at the lectern (n. 309). CCC 1184

Lectionary (LEHK-shuh-neh-ree): The liturgical book containing the Scripture readings for Mass. Whereas the Lectionary contains all of the readings assigned to a weekday or Sunday Mass, the Book of the Gospels contains only the Gospel text for Sunday Masses. CCC 1154

Lector: See Lay Reader

Legate (LEH-guht): An officially appointed representative or ambassador of the Pope. Legates may be appointed to act as papal representatives to secular nations, to the Catholic

Church in a particular place, for a specific event, or for other reasons determined by the Pope. Very often they hold the position of nuncio, pronuncio, or apostolic delegate, and are then generally titular archbishops.

Legate a Latere (LEH-guht ah LAH-tehr-ay): The special representative of the Pope, sent as his alter ego to perform a special diplomatic mission or to represent the Pope at a special function.

Legend, Golden: See Golden Legend

Legion of Decency (LEE-dzhuhn uhv DEE-sehn-see): Established in 1934 by the Catholic bishops in America for the purpose of promoting high moral standards in films and to encourage all Catholics to be discriminating in their viewing of films. Now part of the Department of Communication of the United States Catholic Conference, it assists individuals in selecting films suitable for viewing through a system of rating classifications.

Legitimation (leh-dzhih-ti-MAY-shuhn): The canonical means by which a child, born out of wedlock, is determined by the law to be legitimate. This happens when the parents marry or by canonical rescript (Can. 1139).

Lent (LEHNT): (From Middle English *lenten;* Anglo-Saxon *lencten:* spring) The forty-day liturgical season of fasting, prayer, and almsgiving in preparation for Easter. In the first three centuries, Lent lasted only two or three days. Later, it grew to three or four weeks. The number forty is first detected in the Canons of Nicaea (A.D. 325), probably to recall Our Lord's forty days in the desert before His public ministry. In the East and West and throughout the centuries, the length of the fast has varied. An important dimension of the Lenten observance was the celebration of Mass by the Holy Father at what are called station churches. The present sacramentary recalls this custom and "strongly encourages the chief shepherd of the diocese to gather his people in this way." The Lenten Liturgy also highlights the present restoration of the Scrutiny Masses on the third, fourth, and fifth

Sundays of the season for the catechumens (now called the "elect"), who will be initiated at the Easter Vigil. CCC 540, 1095, 1438

Leopoldine Association (lay-o-POL-deen uh-so-see-AY-shuhn): A missionary aid association founded in Austria in 1829 to channel resources to the developing Church in the United States.

Lepanto, Battle of (BAT-uhl uhv leh-PAHN-to): Military battle that took place in 1571 between Christian and Turkish forces, marking the decline of the Muslim military forces in Europe.

Leper (LEH-per): A person afflicted with leprosy, a dread disease mentioned in both the O.T. (Lv 13:8, 14:2; 2 Kgs 5:1, 6; 2 Chr 26:21) and the N.T. (Mt 26:6; Mk 1:40; Lk 5:13, 17:12) and subject to strict segregation by Jewish law. Jesus cured the condition often (cf. Lk 7:22), but many are convinced that it was an affliction other than the European malady (curable and only mildly infectious) now known as Hansen's disease. Cf. CCC 2616

Leper Window (LEH-per WIHN-do): A window covered with bars or shutters, situated in the lower section of a church's chancel wall, enabling lepers (who had to remain outside) to attend Mass and receive alms. The leper window is no longer used.

Lesson (LEH-suhn): A less common designation than "reading" for a proclaimed selection from the Sacred Scripture in the Liturgy. It could refer to any pericope before the Gospel or could just refer to the O.T. selection alone. At the Office of Readings in the Liturgy of the Hours, two readings are given — one from Scripture and the other from a Patristic source, liturgical commentary, or teaching document of the Church.

Levirate Marriage (LEH-vuh-ruht MERH-ehdzh): (Latin *levir*: brother-in-law) Marriage entered into by a widow and a brother of her dead husband to perpetuate the dead man's name through offspring and to prevent the loss of family possessions within the tribal structure. While Lv 20:21 appears to forbid such a marriage, three O.T. texts do speak of the practice (Gn 28; Dt 25:5-10; Ru 4). While the N.T. refers to the law (Mt 22:23-33; Mk 12:18-27; Lk 20:27-40), it appears not to have been a practice at that time.

Leviticus (leh-VIH-tih-køøs): The third book of the Pentateuch, it deals with the ritual law and liturgical duties of the Levites, hereditary priests of the tribe of Levi. Most likely redacted by members of the priestly class after the exile, in the fifth century B.C., it stresses the importance of liturgical service, especially the Temple sacrificial holocausts, the seasonal celebration of feasts and fasts, the sanctity of the priesthood, and the holiness of God; it records the consecration of Aaron and his sons as the first priestly class of the Israelites; it mandates the kosher food laws.

Liberalism (LIH-ber-uhl-ih-zuhm): Originally referred to the wide diversity of study that would be proper for a well-educated freeman, but since the eighteenth century it has become more narrow in its meaning, now including such ideas as indifferentism in religion and the subjectivity of truth, and so creating a false opposition between individual conscience and the authority of the Magisterium. Liberalism has appeared in various forms and under different names, and its doctrines have been condemned by several Popes.

Liberals, Catholic (KATH-uh-lihk LIH-ber-uhlz): 1. Several nineteenth-century French intellectuals who attempted to reconcile the progressive ideals of the French Revolution with the teaching of the Catholic Church. 2. Now often used to characterize Catholics who espouse moral libertarianism and anticlerical sentiments.

Liberation Theology (lih-ber-AY-shuhn thee-AHL-uh-dzhee): A contemporary theological movement growing out of the Church in Latin America, emphasizing the Christian commitment to the poor. It has gained a pluralistic outlook, growing beyond its roots in Latin America; in its analysis of the causes of poverty, it often divides society into economic classes, advocates violence as being necessary for change, and speaks of "sinful structures" within society. At the direction of Pope John Paul II, the Congregation for the Doctrine of the Faith undertook a study of Liberation Theology, which was published in two documents: the first, in 1984, under the title *Instruction on Certain Aspects of the Theology of Liberation;* and the second, in 1986, under the title *Instruction on Christian Freedom and Liberation.* In these documents serious reservations are expressed about several aspects of the movement, including its acceptance of certain elements of Marxist class analysis and its narrow understanding of the meaning of liberation. **Cf. CCC 2124**

Liber Pontificalis (LEE-behr pahn-tih-fee-KAHL-ihs): The Latin title of "the papal book," containing biographies of the Popes through Martin V (1431). For the first four centuries, these biographies are very sketchy. In later centuries, though, especially the eighth and ninth, the biographies of some Popes were so extensive that each could constitute a volume in itself.

Liberty, Religious (rih-LIH-dzhuhs LIH-ber-tee): The doctrine that it is morally permissible for nations and states to permit individuals to worship and practice their religious beliefs in good conscience when these do not harm the common good. Because religion is itself a basic human good, practicing religion is not to be restrained by the State or society; only when religious practices or beliefs cause clear and express harm to states can it be limited or curbed. The doctrine of religious liberty differs from that of religious freedom, which holds that all religions are essentially the same and therefore the State should be indifferent toward them. The doctrine of religious liberty, articulated by the Second Vatican Council's *Dignitatis Humanae* (Declaration on Religious Liberty), holds that not all religions have the same value, but that does not mean that some can be deliberately hindered if they cause no harm. Religious liberty holds that states have an interest in promoting religion because sound religion is an aid to the State. Religious liberty is based on the doctrine that individuals have an obligation in conscience to search for the truth, and an aspect of this search is the quest for religious truth. Because they have this obligation, they must have the liberty to pursue those truths. The doctrine of religious liberty holds that individuals who sincerely pursue religious truths in accord with the dictates of conscience must be permitted to do so. The Declaration on Religious Liberty, however, did hold that this liberty for the pursuit of religious truth must give special place to the teachings of the Catholic Church. CCC 1907, 2107-2109, 2211

Liber Usualis (LEE-behr öö-zhöö-AHL-ihs): Book containing chants for the Ordinary and Propers of the Mass, along with those used in the Liturgy of the Hours. Even though the chants were used before the Second Vatican Council, those chants for the Ordinary of the Mass are still usable today. The book is edited by the Benedictine Monks of Solesmes.

Licentiate (lai-SEHN-tshuht): The first graduate-level degree offered by pontifical faculties. Comparable to a master's degree in secular institutes of higher learning.

Licit (LIH-siht): A canonical term describing an act that has taken place in full accord with the norms of law. Cf. CCC 1903, 2274, 2275, 2312

Lie (LAI): Any action, expression, or word that deliberately, with free consent, expresses falsity and is done to deceive another who has the right to know the truth. Lying can be gravely or venially wrong. It is not immoral to withhold truth from one who has no right to know it. CCC 215, 392, 1954, 2482-2486, 2847

Life (LAIF): The creation of God that enables one to grow and develop. Life has always been considered by the Church to be a great good. To kill innocent human life is always immoral; however, nonhuman life can be taken with good reason (e.g., to kill animals for food). Cf. CCC 1, 68, 364, 2258, 2263-2267, 2270-2275, 2304, 2319, 2321-2322, 2559-2583

Life in Outer Space (LAIF ihn AU-ter SPAYS): A hypothesis often raised in contradiction to religion. Whether rational life exists on other bodies in the universe besides earth is a question for scientific investigation to settle. The possibility can be granted without prejudice to the body of revealed truth.

Life, Sanctity of: See Sanctity of Life

Life, Spiritual (SPIHR-ih-tshöö-uhl LAIF): The relationship with God that is attained by Baptism and strengthened through the reception of the sacraments, prayer, mortification, and charitable works. As a Christian, one is called to spiritual perfection, which is conformity to Christ — the center of the spiritual life. Cf. CCC 89, 131, 168, 375, 505, 628, 683, 694, 1071-1072, 1131, 1374, 1392, 1997, 2014, 2188, 2687, 2697

Ligamen (lih-GAH-mehn): A Latin term meaning "tie" or "bond," referring to the bond of marriage in canonical language.

Light (LAIT): Symbol of Christ, Who, as the Light of the World, illuminates the hearts and minds of the baptized, replacing the darkness of sin and death with the knowledge of God and life; His light further transforms the faithful into beacons pointing to Christ, symbolized by the baptismal candle given to the newly baptized and by the paschal candle, which, in the liturgy of the Easter Vigil, represents Christ risen from the darkness of the tomb and from which the individual candles of the faithful are lighted. CCC 26, 89, 141, 157, 214, 234, 242, 257, 280, 285-286, 298, 529, 697, 736, 748, 1027, 1147, 1189, 1202, 1216, 1243, 1695, 1707, 1785, 2105, 2466, 2665, 2715, 2730

Lily (LIH-lee): Symbol in Christian art for chastity, by reason of its pure white color and vessellike blossom, which is seen as a natural "vessel of devotion." The iris, a blue variant of the lily, has the same significance, especially as a symbol of the Blessed Virgin Mary; a stylized form of the lily is the *fleur-de-lis.* Other saints revered for their purity of life and often depicted holding a lily include St. Joseph, St. Anthony of Padua, St. Catherine of Siena, and St. Gertrude.

Limbo (LIHM-bo): (Latin *limbus:* edge) The state granted to those who deserve neither heaven nor hell. Theologians have used this term to denote the place where the just of the pre-Christian era dwelt before Jesus opened heaven and the place where unbaptized children go. The Church has not defined limbo in the latter sense. **CCC 1261**

Litany (LIH-tuh-nee): A prayer in the form of responsive petition; e.g., "St. Joseph, pray for us." Examples are the litanies of Loreto (Litany of the Blessed Mother), the Holy Name, All Saints, the Sacred Heart, the Precious Blood, St. Joseph, and Litany for the Dying. **CCC 1154, 1177**

Literal Sense of Scripture (LIH-ter-uhl SEHNS uhv SKRIHP-tsher): (Latin *sensus litteralis*: word-for-word interpretation) The sense understood and intended by the human writer of Scripture, as distinct from the moral or allegorical senses; mainly this sense is determined by the literary and historical criticism of the biblical texts. The literal sense can be explicit, as in the interpretation of Jn 1:14: "The Word became flesh," that Jesus Christ became human; or it can be implicit, from this same text, that the Son of God, as human, had a human soul, with intellect and will, and the sexual identity of a male. **CCC 115-116**

Literary Criticism (LIH-ter-ehr-ee KRIH-tih-sih-zuhm): The critical, analytical study of a literary composition with a view to its authorship, historical milieu, purpose, and literary form and structure. This criticism is employed particularly with regard to the Scriptures in raising philosophical questions about the nature of the text, as distinct from the interpretation of the text. Two basic modes of analysis proceed from this inquiry: (1) *Text-centered (semiotic) interpretation:* The text constitutes a closed system of signals that are decoded as having meaning only with reference to each other. (2) *Audience-centered interpretation:* The text's meaning is determined by the relationship between it and the reader or hearer of the text; thus, the context of the author and the audience is critical in determining the text's meaning.

Literary Qualities of the Bible (LIH-ter-ehr-ee KWAHL-ih-teez uhv *th*uh BAI-buhl): The reflection of the human writers of Scripture by way of poetry, history, biography, prophecy, parables, epics, and wisdom sayings. Not a diminishing of the divine authorship of Scripture, but rather, as St. Jerome has said, the divine intention given human expression. The O.T. shows three literary genres: *torah* (law), *nebiim* (prophets), and *ketubim* (writings). Similarly, the N.T. shows three literary forms: Gospel (history), epistles (essay or teaching), and revelation (the prophetic or apocalyptic).

Little Office of the Blessed Virgin Mary (LIH-tuhL AW-fihs uhv *th*uh BLEH-sehd VER-dzhihn MEH-ree): A devotion to Our Lady consisting of hymns, antiphons, psalms, and collects arranged according to a single day's cycle of "canonical hours" on the model of the Divine Office. Since the advent of the new Liturgy of the Hours, the Little Office of the Blessed Virgin Mary has been preserved almost in its entirety through the use of a Saturday memorial of the B.V.M. during Ordinary Time. Still, a new and somewhat expanded edition of the Little Office was published as recently as 1986 in England and 1988 in the United States. This edition suffices for those who are not bound to pray the Liturgy of the Hours or those who may find the Liturgy of the Hours too expensive to purchase or too daunting to use.

Liturgical Art (lih-TER-dzhih-kuhl AHRT): According to the section entitled "Arrangement and Decoration of Churches" in the *General Instruction of the Roman Missal,* the principal furnishings are, in order of importance, the altar, the chair, the lectern, the tabernacle, and images. These are "signs and symbols of heavenly realities" and therefore "should be truly worthy and beautiful" (n. 288). *Sacrosanctum Concilium* advised a "noble beauty" (n. 124) as far as style goes. This would seem to be the guiding principle in creating or finding a crucifix for the church, a statue or image of Our Lady, and a statue or image of the church's patron saint. In addition, images or depictions of the life of Christ, the mysteries of the Faith, and the lives of the saints are judged to be appropriate also. How this is done will depend on many factors. What is clear, however, is that the edifice and those objects of liturgical art in it are for the purpose of giving glory to Almighty God. (Cf. also Sacred Art and Furnishings.) **CCC 1159-1162, 1192**

Liturgical Books (lih-TER-dzhih-kuhl BØØKS): Those volumes used in official celebrations of the Church's public worship. Liturgical books in the vernacular are always translations or adaptations of the *editiones typicae* (official, standard versions of the Latin originals). The translations would always be under the supervision of a national conference of bishops or an international one appointed by conferences of bishops that share the same language. Numbered among the liturgical books would be the following: Sacramentary (translation of the Roman Missal), Lectionary, Book of the Gospels, Liturgy of the Hours; Rituals for Baptism, the Rite of Christian Initiation of Adults, Confirmation, Holy Communion, Worship of the Eucharist Outside Mass, Rites of Penance, Marriage, Pastoral Care of the Sick, Anointing, and Viaticum; the Order of Christian Funerals, the Roman Pontifical, and Book of Blessings. The *Ceremonial of Bishops* and *Raccolta* (prayers and litanies for popular devotions) may be considered among the liturgical books as well.

Liturgical Commission (lih-TER-dzhih-kuhl kuh-MIH-shuhn): Authorized by *Sacrosanctum Concilium,* the Constitution on the Sacred Liturgy, for the purpose of regulating "pastoral liturgical action throughout [a] territory, and to promote studies and necessary experiments whenever there is question of adaptations to be proposed to the Holy See" (n. 44). By taking advantage of the expertise available in liturgical science and related disciplines, a liturgical commission should also insure correct catechesis about the *Ordo Missae,* the Order of Mass, and should offer advice on music, art, and the construction of churches. A diocesan liturgical commission is distinguished from a national liturgical commission not only in jurisdiction but also in relationship to the Concilium on the implementation of the reformed liturgy.

Liturgical Judgment: See Judgment, Liturgical

Liturgical Law (lih-TER-dzhih-kuhl LAW): Church law pertaining to the rites and ceremonies of the liturgy including the Mass, sacraments, and sacramentals. It is contained in the liturgical books.

Liturgical Life (lih-TER-dzhih-kuhl LAIF): A desire expressed in the Church's official liturgical documents that the liturgy be closely linked to the concrete lives of, and be present among, those who participate in the Liturgical Movement. *Sacrosanctum Concilium,* Pius Parsch's five-volume work *The Church's Year of Grace,* and Virgil Michel's editorials in *Orate Fratres* are especially noteworthy in that they advocate a close relationship between worship and life. This expression also distinguishes the liturgical aspect of the Christian vocation from other related aspects, e.g., apostolic life, communal life, and pastoral life. **Cf. CCC 1072**

Liturgical Movement (lih-TER-dzhih-kuhl MÖÖV-mehnt): Influential figures, significant events, important publications, and strategic places in the organic and providential development of the Church's liturgy for the last one hundred years and more. Prosper Guéranger, Dom Lambert Beauduin, Odo Casel, Virgil Michel, Josef Jungmann, Pius Parsch, Pope St. Pius X, the Council Fathers of Vatican II and their *periti* (experts) would all have to be numbered among the influential figures. The revival of Gregorian chant, the frequent reception of Holy Communion, and the Dialogue Mass would surely be counted among the significant events. *The Mystery of Christian Worship* and *Orate Fratres* (now *Worship)* would be considered important publications for the advancement of liturgical ideas. Malines, Belgium, Maria Laach in Germany and Collegeville, Minnesota, would be regarded as strategic places where liturgical initiatives arose. Some of the work of the Liturgical Movement informed and inspired the liturgical changes authorized by Vatican II. The work of the Liturgical Movement continues today among those who have a sincere desire to serve the Church at prayer.

Liturgical Music Today: See Music, Liturgical

Liturgy (LIH-ter-dzhee): (Latin *liturgia* from Greek *leitourgia:* public service) The public worship of the Church, including the rites and ceremonies of the Mass and sacraments. CCC 1066-1070; cf. 1071-1209

Liturgy, Bishops' Committee on the: See Bishops' Committee on the Liturgy

Liturgy, Children's (TSHIHL-drehnz LIH-ter-dzhee): The correct designation is really "Mass with Children." It is found in the *Directory for Masses with Children,* published in 1974 by the Sacred Congregation for Divine Worship. Since the Mass is for all people, irrespective of age, nationality, and background, it cannot properly be called a Children's Mass. However, the Church has provided for adaptations in the liturgy when there is a large number of children who participate. Suitable adaptations in the liturgy make it possible for children to be introduced to the richness of the Eucharistic Sacrifice, so that in time they can join the regular congregation. In the meantime, a Lectionary for Masses with Children and Eucharistic Prayers for Masses with Children allow children the opportunity to experience the saving mysteries of our Faith in a modified form — all the while never diluting or mitigating the treasures found in the Mass. Cf. CCC 1204-1206

Liturgy, Constitution on the Sacred: See Sacrosanctum Concilium

Liturgy, Divine (dih-VAIN LIH-ter-dzhee): The title of the Holy Sacrifice of the Mass in the Eastern (Oriental) Catholic Churches. Cf. CCC 1386, 1389

Liturgy of the Hours (LIH-ter-dzhee uhv *th*ee AU-erz): The official cycle of the Church's daily prayer. It was formerly called the Divine Office (a title by which it still frequently goes). The renewal of the Liturgy of the Hours at Vatican II called for the public celebration of the Hours whenever possible. Whether recited privately or publicly, though, the Liturgy of the Hours has the following structure: Morning Prayer (Lauds), Midday Prayer (Terce, Sext, or None), Evening

Prayer (Vespers), Night Prayer (Compline), and the Office of Readings. The First Hour (Prime), while suppressed for the universal Church, continues to be observed in contemplative monastic communities. Among the Midday Hours, there is an obligation to pray one of them. Contemplative communities should recite all of these, however. The Liturgy of the Hours consists of hymns, antiphons, psalms, selections from Sacred Scripture, readings from the Church Fathers, commentaries on the Scriptures and the Christian life, writings of the saints, and standard Catholic prayers. It is arranged according to a four-week cycle called a Psalter. Usually, the Liturgy of the Hours is available in a four-volume set (three volumes in England and Ireland). There is a one-volume set, too, which is an abbreviated edition. CCC 1174-1178; cf. 1096, 1173, 1437, 2691

Liturgy Planning Sheet (LIH-ter-dzhee PLAN-ihng SHEET): A "sheet" indicating the music selected for a particular liturgy, along with the chosen options from the Sacramentary and the assigned readings in the Lectionary for the purpose of insuring a reverent and devout celebration. The *General Instruction of the Roman Missal* maintains that "harmonious planning and carrying out of the rites will help dispose the faithful spiritually to take part in the Eucharist" (n. 352).

Lives of the Saints (LAIVS uhv *th*uh SAYNTS): A collection of biographies of canonized saints that is meant to inspire the reader to practice the virtues of the saints. While *Butler's Lives of the Saints* is most popular today in the English-speaking world, there are many compendiums of stories and facts about the saints.

Local Ordinary (LO-kuhl AWR-dih-neh-ree): An ecclesiastical office of authority over people in a specific territory. The term includes residential bishops and those who have certain powers of a bishop in law, such as vicars general and vicars episcopal.

Loci Theologici (LO-tshee tay-o-LO-dzhee-tshee): (Latin: theological places, sources, or topics) Sources for theological study, introduced by the Dominican Melchior Cano (1509-1560) in his *De Locis Theologicis* (1563), as seven prime, or proper, bases (Scripture, Tradition, the Magisterium, the Councils, papal teaching, writings of the Fathers and Doctors of the Church, and other theologians) and three secondary bases (human reason, philosophy, and history). The topics proper to theological discussion include the nature and existence of God, the Trinity, creation, grace, Christology, anthropology, and ecclesiology.

Logic (LAH-dzhihk): (Greek *logos:* word, thought) The branch of philosophy having to do with the study of correct reasoning and methods of proper argumentation.

Logos (LO-gos): (Greek: word, speech, reason) Most commonly identified with the title given to Jesus in John's Gospel, though not exclusive to that Gospel; *logos* translates the Hebrew: *dabar,* the spoken word, understood as a distinct reality with its own power or dynamism. In the N.T., however, the term reflects more the influence of Hellenistic philosophy: St. Paul uses *logos* as interchangeable with *sophia,* wisdom (1 Cor 1:24); thus, the *Logos* is the Wisdom of God made manifest in the Son. As a name for the Second Person of the Trinity, the Incarnate Word, the term receives new meaning in the light of the life, death, and resurrection of Jesus Christ. In the prologue of St. John's Gospel (Jn 1:1-18), the *Logos* is presented as eternal, distinct from God the Father, yet truly God Who became Man, the God-Man, Jesus of Nazareth; thus, Jesus is God's Word (Jn 3:34, 8:47). Although He speaks of "my word" (Jn 5:24; 8:43, 51; 12:47-50; 14:23; 15:20), He actually speaks the *Logos* of the Father (Jn 8:55; 14:24; 17:6) and, in so doing, becomes the very *Logos* of the Father spoken into the world. **Cf. CCC 813**

Lollards (LAH-lahrdz): Derisive term for a heretical sect, fifteenth-century followers of John Wycliff, who were anticlerical and proponents of individual interpretation of the Bible.

Longanimity (lawng-guh-NIH-mih-tee): The good habit, related to the virtue of hope, that grants perseverance in the midst of trials. One with longanimity is blessed with "equanimity" (i.e., a balance and positive attitude in confronting obstacles). **Cf. CCC 1832**

Lord (LORD): Title used of God in the O.T. as a translation of the Hebrew *Adonai,* which is generally substituted in reading the Hebrew Bible as a reverent avoidance of the unspeakable Name. The vowels of *Adonai* are often written under the consonants of YHWH, so that the name Jehovah can also be derived from this combination. The Greek translation of this title, *Kyrios,* is used of God in the Septuagint and is applied to Christ in the N.T., as in Rom 10:9, "Jesus is Lord." As Jesus speaks of the Father as "Lord of heaven and earth" (Mt 11:25; Lk 10:21; Acts 17:24), so too Jesus Himself is addressed as Lord (Mk 7:28); after the resurrection, Christ was especially given this title of universal sovereignty (Jn 20:28; 21:7). This attribution of Lordship to Jesus meant that He was King over all mankind (Rom 14:9), including His enemies (Col 2:10, 15) and even over death (1 Cor 15:24; 1 Pt 3:22). The Lordship of Christ expresses His connection to the Davidic line, but more importantly His divine status as absolute Lord over the forces of darkness and death (Phil 2:10); He is Lord of the Church not by force but by love (Col 3:18; Eph 1:20; 4:15-16; 5:21-33). As Lord, Christ breaks the stranglehold of sin, death, and evil: He further transforms the New Creation, which awaits His "coming again in glory" (1 Cor 16:22; Rv 22:20), because in Him salvation is realized (Jn 10:11). Centered and rooted in Him, humanity witnesses to Christ's Lordship over His Church. **CCC 446-451**

Lord's Prayer (LORDZ PREHR): The prayer, taught by Jesus, which is often called the "Our Father," and is used during the Liturgy and recited daily by the faithful throughout the world. The text of the Our Father is found in Mt 6:9-13. **CCC 2759-2865**

Lord's Supper (LORDZ SUH-per): Another name for the Last Supper, generally favored by Protestants (Mt 26:26-29; Mk 14:22-25; Lk 22:18; Jn 13:4; 1 Cor 11:23). It also may refer to Holy Thursday, the day of the Last Supper. In non-Catholic usage, too, it is commonly applied to a ritual reenactment of the Lord's Supper, as in a Communion service. Cf. CCC 832, 1166, 1329

Loreto, Holy House of (HO-lee HAUS uhv lo-REH-to): A very important Marian shrine located in a small city near the Adriatic coast of central Italy. Inside the basilica church there are relics from the house where Mary is said to have conceived the eternal Word of God in her womb upon receiving the Archangel Gabriel's message (Lk 1:26-38). For this reason, Our Lady of Loreto is the patroness of homes. Under the same title, she is also the patroness of aviators and air travelers, since pious lore recounts the transferral of the house from the Holy Land by angels. She was proclaimed such by Pope Benedict XV (1914-1922).

Loreto, Litany of (LIH-tuh-nee uhv lo-REH-to): Name for the most popular litany of the Blessed Virgin Mary.

L'Osservatore Romano (lo-SER-vah-TO-ray ro-MAH-no): The daily newspaper in Italian, begun in 1861, issued by the Holy See containing the official news and announcements from the Vatican, along with current events and editorials reflecting the opinions of the Holy See. There are weekly editions published in other languages, including English.

Los-Von-Rom Movement (LOS-FAHN-ROM MÖÖV-mehnt): A nineteenth-century anti-Catholic movement founded in Bavaria that attempted to use racial and ethnic arguments to draw German Catholics away from loyalty to Rome.

Lourdes, Apparitions of (ap-puh-RIH-shuhnz uhv LÖÖRD): Eighteen appearances of Our Lady to Bernadette Soubirous between February 11 and July 16, 1858, in the rock cave of Massabielle along the River Gave, near Lourdes, France. In the final vision, the Blessed Mother revealed her identity with the words "I am the Immaculate Conception"; in 1854, the Church had defined as dogma the Immaculate Conception of the Blessed Virgin Mary. She instructed Bernadette to drink from a spring, which began to flow from the place of the apparitions; this spring of natural water has effected thousands of miraculous cures through the patronage of the Blessed Mother, as verified by the medical bureau established at Lourdes. With Church approbation of Lourdes as a place of pilgrimage in 1862 and the completion of the Basilica of the Holy Rosary in 1901, Lourdes has become one of the most popular sites of pilgrimage, primarily for the physical healings that are reported to occur either after bathing in the waters of the spring or during the blessing with the Blessed Sacrament in ceremonies at the Basilica. St. Bernadette was canonized on December 8, 1933; the memorial of Our Lady of Lourdes is observed on February 11.

Love (LUHV): A devotion to a person or object that has been categorized by Greek philosophy into four types: *storge* (one loves persons and things close to him); *philia* (the love of friends); *eros* (sexual love and that of a spiritual nature); *agape* (a self-giving to one in need). Christian charity is love, but not all love is true charity. **CCC 1822-1829**

Love of God (LUHV uhv GAHD): The greatest Christian virtue, enabling one to respond to God as He does to us: with charity. We are commanded to love God because of all He has done for us, especially for the charity of Christ shown in His death and resurrection. To love God makes loving our neighbors possible. **Cf. CCC 1011, 1599, 1824, 2055, 2063, 2083, 2086, 2093, 2615, 2633, 2658, 2709, 2712, 2738, 2742, 2792**

Love of Neighbor (LUHV uhv NAY-ber): Charity, i.e., desiring the true good of others. (In the Christian context, the true good is eternal life.) Because of one's love for God, he or she can then love others. This mandate means that one is called to love enemies as well as friends. One grows in fraternal charity especially through the reception of the sacraments, viz., the Holy Eucharist. **Cf. CCC 459, 533, 1337, 1822-1825, 1844, 1878, 2055, 2067, 2069, 2104, 2196, 2443-2445, 2608, 2793, 2843-2844**

Low Sunday (LO SUHN-day): The first Sunday after Easter, so called in contrast to the High Feast of Easter. This day was called *Dominica in Albis*, or Sunday in White Robes, because the newly baptized in the early Church wore white robes as a sign of their putting on Christ in Baptism from Easter until the Sunday after. Low Sunday is now called the Second Sunday of Easter.

Ludwig Mission Association (LØØD-vihg MIH-shuhn uh-so-see-AY-shuhn): Mission support organization founded in Germany in 1838 to assist religious communities working in the United States, as well as the Franciscans working at the shrines of the Holy Land.

Luke, The Gospel of *(th*uh GAHS-puhl uhv LÖÖK): Gospel attributed to St. Luke, who was probably a Greek from Antioch; he was a disciple of St. Paul, who calls him "the beloved physician" (Col 4:14) and knew him as a Gentile convert and missionary. Notable for the characteristics typical of classical historical methods and writing, the Gospel of Luke, intended primarily for Gentile converts to Christianity, makes use of material from Mark and gives the tradition of St. Paul's teaching, with a special place for the role of Mary in her Son's ministry. The Gospel of Luke is completed in the Acts of the Apostles, the two written between A.D. 70 and 85; together they articulate the unified and systematic account of God's decisive acts in salvation history, with the fulfillment of His promises to Israel in the life of Jesus and the life of the Church. The two are further composed in ways to make obvious the parallels to be drawn between events in the life of Jesus and those in the lives of figures prominent in the early Church. In particular, the journey of Jesus to Jerusalem, as detailed in the Gospel, is paralleled by the Church's mission to all nations, as preached by Paul in his journey to Rome and recounted in Acts, with particular emphasis on Jesus as the Son of God and the Son of Man, with universal salvation for all of humanity as realized by Christ through His death and resurrection.

Lumen Gentium (LÖÖ-mehn DZHEHN-see-øøm): The Dogmatic Constitution on the Church, issued November 21, 1964, as the third major document of the Second Vatican Council; as a dogmatic constitution, it is distinguished from *Gaudium et Spes,* the Pastoral Constitution on the Church in the Modern World. LG has as its declared purpose to explain the Church's nature as "a sign and instrument . . . of communion with God and of unity among all men" (n. 1), and to define the Church's universal mission as the sacrament of human salvation: "This is the sole Church of Christ which in the creed we profess to be one, holy, catholic and apostolic. . . . This Church, constituted and organized as a society in the present world, subsists in the Catholic Church, which is governed by the successor of Peter and by the bishops in communion with him" (n. 8). The major points of the constitution are shown in its chapter headings: (1) The Mystery of the Church; (2) The People of God; (3) The Hierarchy; (4) The Laity; (5) The Call to Holiness; (6) Religious; (7) The Pilgrim Church; (8) Our Lady. Added to LG at the order of Pope Paul VI is the unique Explanatory Note, which clarifies the meaning of episcopal collegiality such that bishops individually or collegially have no authority without explicit dependence on and in full communion with the Bishop of Rome. In this regard, too, LG treats of papal infallibility by repeating the criteria of *Pastor Aeternus* of Vatican Council I and maintains that the papal Magisterium, even though not taught solemnly, or *ex cathedra,* deserves a "loyal submission of the will and intellect" (n. 25).

Luna, also Lunette (LÖÖ-nuh, löö-NEHT): (From Latin: moon) Sacred vessel composed of two pieces of metal in the shape of a crescent. Between the two pieces of metal, the Sacred Host is placed for use in the monstrance during Exposition of the Blessed Sacrament and Benediction.

L'Univers: See Univers, L'

Lust (LUHST): The inordinate desire for sexual pleasures that inclines one to perceive others as mere objects solely for personal gratification. Reception of the Holy Eucharist, devotion to Mary, and self-denial are strong helps against lust. **CCC 1866, 2351; cf. 377, 1607, 2259, 2534, 2536, 2541, 2552**

Lustral: See Holy Water

Lutheran-Catholic Dialogue (LÖÖ-ther-uhn KATH-uh-lihk DAI-uh-lawg): Official conversations on the national and international levels between representatives of the Lutheran Church and the Catholic Church, begun shortly after the close of the Second Vatican Council, seeking a mutual doctrinal understanding through discussions of such topics as the Nicene Creed, Baptism, the Eucharist, Ministry, the Papacy, the Blessed Virgin Mary, and the Saints.

Lutheranism (LÖÖ-ther-uh-nih-zuhm): The belief and practice of those Protestants who follow the teaching of Martin Luther (1483-1546). Lutheranism emphasizes the primacy of Scripture over all other sources of doctrinal authority, justification by faith alone, and the centrality of Christ's role as Savior and Mediator. Beginning as a series of State churches, it was unified on an international level with the establishment of the World Lutheran Federation in 1947.

Lyons, Councils of (KAUN-sihlz uhv lee-ON): The thirteenth and fourteenth ecumenical councils held in Lyons, France (1245 and 1274).

Lyons, Rite of (RAIT uhv lee-ON): A variation of the Roman Rite with the addition of many more ministers at the altar and exquisite ceremonial. It began in Rome and passed through Aachen, where Charlemagne adapted papal liturgies to his own chapel. It showed up in Lyons at the beginning of the ninth century.

M

Maccabees, First and Second Books of (FERST and SEH-kuhnd BØØKS uhv MAK-uh-beez): The two canonical books of this name (also the apocryphal Third and Fourth Maccabees) relate Israel's resistance to Gentile domination and opposition to the influence of Hellenism. In fact, the Greek word for Judaism occurs for the first time in 2 Maccabees. Their title is derived from Maccabaeus, the name assumed by Judas, son of Mattathias, protagonist of the account and leader of the Jewish insurrection (165-161 B.C.) against Antiochus Epiphanes. Their significance lies in the great insight into contemporary religious beliefs that it provides, particularly belief in an afterlife and physical resurrection. Such ideas are new in Jewish thought, found only in texts of the last two centuries of the pre-Christian era. Written in Greek, 1 Maccabees and 2 Maccabees were likely the work of authors of the final quarter of the second century B.C.

Macedonianism (ma-suh-DO-nee-uhn-ih-zuhm): Broad term for a wide variety of Trinitarian heresies in the ancient Church, including denial of the divinity of the Holy Spirit, which were condemned by the Council of Constantinople in A.D. 381. Cf. CCC 253-255, 263

Madonna (muh-DAH-nuh): (Italian: my lady) Popular title of the Blessed Virgin Mary; when applied to her, it means the same as the French *Notre Dame* ("Our Lady"). The title is more Western in orientation than Eastern. Depictions of the Madonna in painting or sculpture are almost always with the Christ Child; even Eastern iconography shows Mother and Child. The Madonna is a favorite image on Christmas cards.

Magdalen (MAG-duh-lehn): 1. A reformed prostitute — from popular tradition about St. Mary Magdalene (q.v.). 2. Earlier designation of any penitent public sinner who wished to enter a religious community. These "magdalens" wore a distinctive habit (penitential in color) and usually lived separately from the other Sisters in a cloister. Today, this distinction is no longer operative.

Magi (MAY-dzhai): The Greek word *magoi* at Mt 2:1-18 refers to "wise men" who are said to be from "the East" (2:1), which could refer to Arabia, Mesopotamia, or somewhere else east of Palestine. The fact that they were guided by the star (2:2) suggests they were learned in astrology or the science of navigation and time calculation by means of stellar configurations. It was Origen who first proposed that there were three *magi* because of the three gifts offered to the Christ Child (2:11). Tertullian is the first to suggest that they were kings *(fere reges* ["almost kings"], cf. *Adv. Judaeam,* 9, and *Adv. Marcionem.,* iii. 13). On the basis of the implied reference to Ps 72:10, many speculated that they were royalty; by the sixth century it was a common assumption. The N.T. is silent concerning their number and relationship to royalty. By the Middle Ages, these "three kings" are not only named (Caspar, Melchior, Balthasar), they are venerated as saints. A favorite theme in art dating from the late second century is the Magi adoring the Christ Child. The fact that learned men, perhaps even of royal blood, come to worship the "King of the Jews" expressed the universal mission of Christianity — the Gospel, or good news from God, is not just for the Jews but for all the nations of the world. **Cf. CCC 528**

Magic (MA-dzhihk): Various superstitious or occult practices that aim at controlling one's destiny by invoking "hidden powers." "White" magic involves calling upon spiritual beings to grant favors; "black" magic concerns communicating with such beings to harm another person. The Church has condemned magic as being distrustful of God's goodness and concern for His children. **CCC 2115-2117**

Magisterium of the Church (MA-dzhih-STEHR-ee-uhm uhv *th*uh TSHERTSH): The Church's teaching authority, instituted by Christ and guided by the Holy Spirit, which seeks to safeguard and explain the truths of the faith. The Magisterium is exercised in two ways: *extraordinary,* when the Pope and ecumenical councils infallibly define a truth of faith or morals that is necessary for one's salvation and that has been constantly taught and held by the Church; *ordinary,* when the Church infallibly defines truths of the Faith: (1) taught universally and without dissent, (2) which must be taught or the Magisterium would be failing in its duty, (3) connected with a grave matter of faith or morals, and (4) which is taught authoritatively. Not everything taught by the Magisterium is done so infallibly; however, the exercise of the Magisterium is faithful to Christ and what He taught. CCC 77, 85-88, 95, 888-892, 2032-2036

Magnanimity (mag-nuh-NIHM-ih-tee): The virtue enabling one to perform outstanding, morally good actions not for recognition but for love of God and neighbor. Prudence directs magnanimity, which supports the cardinal virtue of fortitude. Only those who perform the other virtues regularly are usually able to be magnanimous. Cf. CCC 1832

Magnificat (mahg-NIH-fih-kaht): Mary's response ("My soul magnifies the Lord") to Elizabeth upon visiting her after the Annunciation. The *Magnificat* (Luke 1:46-55) is often compared to Hannah's Canticle (1 Sm 2:1-10). Mary serves as a model of how all Christians are called to accept the will of God joyfully. Cf. CCC 2097, 2619

Major Orders (MAY-dzher OR-derz): The sacred orders of subdeacon, deacon, and priest. Prior to 1972, orders were divided into major and minor orders. Diaconate and priesthood were considered sacramental.

Major Superior (MAY-dzher söö-PEER-ee-er): The member of a religious institute who has authority over all members of a given territory or province or some similar form of grouping. Also, abbots and superiors of entire institutes.

Makarisms (MA-kuh-rih-zuhmz): The name for the Beatitudes (Mt 5:3-11; Lk 6:20-22) in the Eastern Churches, from the first word of each verse in Greek: *makarios* (blessed).

Malabar Rites (MAL-uh-bahr RAITS): A controversy similar to the Chinese-rites question arose in the sixteenth-century Jesuit Province of Malabar, whence the name. The great missionary Robert de Nobili, in converting Hindus to Christianity, tried to adopt as many of their customs as possible so that new Christians would not feel estranged from their culture. In this era of inculturation, that strategy seems obvious, but at his time it was a revolutionary approach. Although De Nobili took only those customs he considered to be civil (not religious), nonetheless the Dominicans and Franciscans felt that these practices would still carry Hindu significance and that many converts would see no difference between their former religion and their new faith. The case was referred to Rome, which upheld De Nobili in 1623, but later in 1712 most of these adaptations were forbidden, as indeed were the parallel Chinese rites of Matteo Ricci, another great Jesuit missionary in the Orient.

Malachi, Book of (BØØK uhv MAL-uh-kai): The last book of the O.T. and part of the prophetic literature. It is helpful to read this book against the background of Ezra 7-10 and Nehemiah 1-13. During the Persian period, after the rebuilding of the Temple, the priests began to be negligent about offering sacrifices and instructing the people. The returned exiles entered into marriage with unbelievers; their own diluted faith resulted in failure to pay tithes, particularly in times of plagues and famines. This book was produced by a genuine religious reformer, probably a Jewish priest, who thought it prudent to remain anonymous. The first verse introduces "the word of the Lord through my messenger *(malaki)*" and makes of it a proper name. The author has a high sense of the responsibility of priests for religious education (2:6-9) and for reverence in liturgical worship (1:12-13). He is confident that God will send His messenger to purge the people (3:1-5); in N.T. times, John the Baptist strove to fulfill this role. Malachi looks forward (1:11) to a universal and pure sacrifice, to be offered at all times and in all places; the verse is often quoted as having been fulfilled in the Sacrifice of the Mass.

Malta, Knights of: See Knights of Malta, or Hospitalers

Mammon (MA-muhn): The N.T. Greek word *mamonas* occurs at Lk 16:9, 11, 13 and Mt 6:24. This word was borrowed from Aramaic and refers to material wealth and prosperity, especially property (Lk 16:9, 11). The word can be used to personify wealth (Mt 6:24; Lk 16:13) as a master at enmity with God. Cf. CCC 2113, 2424

Man (MAN): The term for the human person, male or female, made by God and endowed with a body and an immortal soul with understanding, will, and memory. Man is higher than the animals, plants, and inanimate objects because of his rational soul; yet he is lower than the angels because their intellects and wills were not debilitated by Original Sin as were man's. The Church teaches the unity of soul and body in man, in opposition to the *materialists* (who deny the soul) and the *dualists* or *angelists* (who discredit the body as a prison of the soul or as a mere appendage). CCC 311, 327, 355, 358, 362-365, 374, 383, 396, 1605, 1704, 2203, 2331, 2334

Mandatum (mahn-DAH-tøøm): The ceremonial washing of the feet of twelve men at the Evening Mass of the Lord's Supper on Holy Thursday. This action recalls the example of Our Lord, Who washed the feet of His Apostles at the Last Supper. The term is derived from the Latin *mandatum novum,* or "new commandment," that Jesus instituted at the Last Supper, recorded in Jn 13:34. In monasteries, there was once the custom of the abbot washing the feet of all the monks once every year. In some patristic literature, foot-washing symbolizes reconciliation.

Mandyas (mahn-DEE-ahs): The monk's full-length vesture in the Byzantine Church, differing in color and symbolism from the lower clergy's simple black cloak to the ornate vestments of the archimandrite (q.v.) and the bishop.

Manichaeism (man-ih-KEE-ih-zuhm): A religious and ethical doctrine propounded by Mani (216-277), or Manes (Latin form: Manichaeus), which taught an absolute dualism concerning God. Thus it held that there are two equal, eternal principles: one of good, light, and spirit; the other of darkness, matter, evil. It has affinities with a number of other religious and philosophical systems: Gnosticism (liberation of the soul from matter through enlightenment); Marcionism (distinction of the God of the O.T. from the Father of Our Lord Jesus Christ); Mandeanism (dualism with Persian roots); and even Buddhism (concern for escape from the present world). Manichaeism found a fertile field in those areas influenced by those forms of neo-Platonic thought that considered matter as "tainted." Mani argued that he was proposing a superior, universal religion whose previous messengers (Buddha, Zoroaster, Jesus) were concerned with only a part of the world and whose message was falsified, since it was not put into writing. Based on this belief in two fundamental principles of reality, the devout Manichee rejects anything that would link him to matter. He therefore should practice extreme asceticism, refrain from menial work (since it disturbs the fragments of light present in all visible things), and practice absolute sexual continence. Since in practice these demands are not fulfilled by most, a distinction is made between the *elect* and the *hearers.* The hearers serve the elect and hope in a future life to be born in the body of an elect and thus attain salvation. Part of the success of Manichaeism was due to its adaptation to the prevailing religious culture in which it was preached. Thus in the Near East and Egypt, it was clothed in Christian imagery; in Persia, in the vocabulary of Zoroastrianism; in India, in Buddhist terms. It had a highly developed form of church organization and was found in many parts of the Roman Empire, especially in the eastern part. Opposition from Roman civil authorities limited the influence of these ideas, especially from the fifth century in the West, and somewhat later in the East. Pockets of Manichaeist or Neo-Manichaeist thought were found in the Balkans in the medieval period. Groups with similar ideas — Albigensians or Cathari — were found in Western Europe in the twelfth to fourteenth centuries. It is not certain whether they have historical or only ideological links with the Manichaeans.

Manifestation of Conscience (ma-nih-feh-STAY-shuhn uhv KAHN-shehns): The disclosing of one's inner "core," often to a priest in the Sacrament of Penance, enabling one to receive spiritual direction. One is not to be coerced into sharing his conscience with another; however, it is a great vehicle for spiritual development.

Maniple (MA-nih-puhl): A small, narrow vestment formerly worn over the left forearm of the celebrant at Mass. Originally, it was a folded napkin but eventually took on greater ornamentation and symbolic meaning. It is no longer used, except when the so-called Tridentine Mass is celebrated.

Manna (MA-nuh): (Hebrew *man hu.* what is this?) The nourishment given to the Israelites by God in the desert (e.g., Ex 16:4-35; Dt 8:3-15). The exact composition of manna is unknown; however, this edible entity is a symbol of and a forerunner to the nourishment *par excellence* of the Holy Eucharist. **CCC 1094, 1334**

Mantelletta (mahn-tuh-LEH-tuh): (Italian: small cloak) A knee-length sleeveless garment of either purple or scarlet color (indicating ecclesiastical rank and season of the Church year) worn by prelates over the rochet (q.v.) when in choir dress. In 1969, Pope Paul VI abolished the mantelletta for all but selected monsignori living in Rome. Also excepted from this papal regulation are canons who belong to patriarchal basilicas. The canons of St. Peter's wear a purple mantelletta, while the canons of St. Mary Major wear gray.

Mantellone (mahn-tuh-LO-nay): A full-length sleeveless purple robe with long false sleeves hanging from the shoulders. Until 1969, the mantellone was worn by papal chamberlains, who were known as *monsignori di mantellone.*

Mantum (MAHN-tøøm): (From Spanish *manto:* cloak) A great cope worn by the Pope on selected occasions. Very long and wide, in color it is red, white, or rose (for Laetare Sunday).

Manual of Prayers (MAN-yöö-uhl uhv PREHRZ): A prayer book concise enough to be carried by hand (Latin *manus).*

Manual of Prayers of the Council of Baltimore (MAN-yöö-uhl uhv PREHRZ uhv *th*uh KAUN-sihl uhv BAWL-tih-

mor): Companion volume to the *Baltimore Catechism,* mandated by the same Plenary Council (Baltimore) of the United States' Bishops and reprinted numerous times between the end of the nineteenth century and a final printing in the early 1950s. Deploring what they termed "a lamentable lack of knowledge of the Church's official prayer as contained in the Missal and Breviary," and regretting the multiplication of devotional manuals "of questionable theological and literary quality," the far-sighted prelates gathered at Baltimore wanted the emerging Catholic Church in the United States not only to know what to believe (the Catechism) but how to pray (the Manual). A survey of its contents shows how astute the compilers of the Baltimore *Manual of Prayers* were. In addition to the simple "Mass Devotions" common to the devotional manuals of the time, this official manual contained the Ordinary of the Mass in Latin and English and, in a supplement, the proper texts (including the Scripture readings) for every Sunday and holy day of the year. In addition to devotional "morning and evening prayers," the entire Offices of Prime and Compline were excerpted from the Breviary and translated into English, along with Vespers in Latin and English for all Sundays and feast days (with an extensive collection of the classic Office hymns in Latin and English). The sacramental rites are given in full, together with a wide selection of litanies and indulgenced prayers. A helpful summary of Catholic belief and a solid guide to Christian life made the manual one of the most complete and helpful books ever sponsored by the national episcopate. Judging from the number of copies still extant (and frequently found in private homes and used-book stores), the manual was extremely popular, used as Sunday school prizes and Confirmation and wedding gifts. All subsequent and additional devotional books *(Blessed Be God, Key of Heaven,* etc.) were derived from this manual and took their translations from it but generally were not able to match the scope or quality of its presentation. The 1988 *Catholic Household Blessings and Prayers* is a modern attempt on the part of the United States' bishops to provide a compendium of prayer similar to the manual published so long ago by their predecessors.

Manuterge (MAN-yuh-terdzh): (From Latin *manus:* hand + *tergere* to dry or wipe) 1. the white linen or cotton towel used by the priest during Mass to dry his hands at the lavabo of the Preparation of the Gifts. 2. The towel in the sacristy used by priests to dry their hands when they wash before celebrating Mass or distributing Holy Communion.

Mappula (MAH-pøø-luh): (Latin: small napkin) A linen gremial used in the Dominican Rite of the Mass, probably for the purpose of preventing the soiling of the vestments worn by the priest. The mappula was placed on the lap of the priest while seated during Mass. The priest then placed his hands on the mappula. Since the Dominican Rite is no longer in use, the mappula is not used either.

Marburg, Colloquy of (KAHL-o-kwee uhv MAHR-berg): Sixteenth-century attempt to achieve Protestant unity on matters of doctrine, led by Luther and Zwingli.

Margarita (mahr-guh-REE-tuh): Meaning "pearl," the smaller particles of the Holy Eucharist distributed at Holy Communion in the Byzantine Rite.

Marialis Cultus (mah-ree-AHL-ihs KØØL-tøøs): The apostolic exhortation, issued by Pope Paul VI on February 2, 1974, meant to foster devotion to Our Lady as envisioned by the Second Vatican Council. She is the "most excellent exemplar" of union with Christ her Son. The document urges the faithful to pray especially the Rosary and the *Angelus* — prayers deeply grounded in the Gospels. Cf. CCC 971, 2678, 2708

Marian Year (MEHR-ee-uhn YEER): The dedication of a specific year, by way of prayers, indulgences, colloquiums, etc., in honor of the Mother of God. Pope Pius XII so proclaimed 1954 in acknowledging the one-hundredth anniversary of the defining of the dogma of the Immaculate Conception *(Fulgens Corona).* In *Redemptoris Mater,* Pope John Paul II announced the Marian Year 1987-1988 as a preparation for the inaugurating of Christianity's third millennium.

Mariology (mehr-ee-AHL-uh-dzhee): The study of the Blessed Virgin Mary in theology, which began in the sixteenth century. *Lumen Gentium,* from the Second Vatican Council, presents Mary in biblical, ecclesial, ecumenical, and patristic terms.

Maritain, Jacques (ZHAHK mah-rih-TAN): The most influential Catholic philosopher (1882-1973) of the twentieth century, who spent the last thirteen years of his life with the Little Brothers of Jesus of Charles de Foucauld.

Mark, Gospel of (GAHS-puhl uhv MAHRK): This Gospel is the shortest and generally thought of as the earliest of the four Gospels, at least as far as final editions go. It has a precise focus, the revelation of God's kingdom that comes to us through Jesus Christ, the Son of God (Mk 1:1). Jesus' identity, ministry, and purpose, as well as the response of the disciples, all relate to this central theme of God's kingdom, which is found in Jesus' preaching: "The time is fulfilled, and the kingdom of God is at hand. Repent and believe in the gospel" (1:15). God's kingdom arrives in power and might; it overtakes and breaks Satan's stronghold on "the world." Jesus uses the parables as an effective form of communicating various aspects of God's kingdom. Jesus is the parable of God's kingdom — He casts out demons, heals, forgives sins, and is crucified and raised to resurrected life, all of which are signals that the age of salvation that the Jews awaited for centuries was "at hand." Jesus' titles illustrate His role in the coming of God's kingdom; the term "Christ" occurs throughout Mark (1:1, 34; 8:29; 14:61; 15:32) and must be understood in terms of its O.T. use, which was mainly for royal leaders who were anointed either to save Israel from an enemy or to restore the Davidic rule (e.g., 2 Sm 7:12-14). Jesus is God's anointed in the sense that He fulfills the Davidic rule but in a totally just, righteous, and everlasting fashion, by bringing salvation, the power of God over sin, Satan, and even death. Mark's Gospel is a "saving action" Gospel, with more of Jesus' acts of power over the powers of darkness (e.g., exorcisms, healings, forgiveness of sins), all of which illustrate that the age of salvation (i.e., of being freed from the grasp sin has over the individual) is in fact present. The Gospel is written to draw out what this "age of salvation" means for the follower of Christ (discipleship). *Major themes:* The key theme is the Person of Jesus, what He does and says. Jesus, Son of God, brings the kingdom of God in divine power and might through forgiveness of sins (2:10-12); dominion over the Sabbath (2:28; 3:1-5); authority over demons (1:28, 34; 3:11); knowledge of the kingdom secrets (2:8; 8:17; 12:15), etc. The earliest explicit evidence that "Mark" wrote this Gospel is a reference to the remarks of Papias of Hierapolis (early second century) quoted by Eusebius *(Ecclesiastical History,* 3.39, 15). The widespread affirmation that "Mark" wrote this Gospel is probably behind the title of the Gospel "According to Mark," which did not originate with the narrative. Scholars do not agree as to the exact historical identity of "Mark" (Acts 12:12, 25; 15:37, 39; Col 4:10; 2 Tm 4:11; Phlm 24; 1 Pt 5:13). Thus, although the indirect evidence and traditional attestation point to Mark as the author of this Gospel, we are not yet certain of exactly who this person was. Tradition identifies this Mark as "Peter's interpreter," and situates this Gospel in Rome after Peter's death, circa A.D. 64-67.

Marks of the Church (MAHRKS uhv *th*uh TSHERTSH): The qualities of the Catholic Church, identifying her as being founded by Christ and belonging to Him as His instrument of salvation to the world. According to the Nicene, or Nicaean, Creed (381), the Church is "one," i.e., there is a bond present uniting all members under the Pope; "holy," i.e., the Church in all facets (sacraments, teachings, governance) is united to Christ and, therefore, "holy"; "catholic," i.e., there is a universality in the Church that makes her available to persons of every time and place; "apostolic," i.e., coming from the Apostolic Age, she remains faithful to what was handed down from Jesus to the Apostles. CCC 811-865

Maronites (MEHR-uh-naits): An Eastern Catholic Church in communion with Rome, having its origin in Syria, although most now live in Lebanon. It takes its name from St. Maron (d. 443), whose followers were opponents of the Monophysite heresy. The first Maronite patriarch was elected in 685, and in 1215 the Maronite patriarch participated in the Fourth Lateran Council, subsequently receiving the pallium from Pope Innocent III. Although the Maronite liturgy has been somewhat Latinized, the use of Syriac has been retained. The patriarch resides in Beirut but has jurisdiction over dioceses in Lebanon, Syria, Egypt, Australia, Brazil, and the United States. Cf. CCC 1203

Marriage Encounter (MEHR-ehdzh ehn-KAUN-ter): A movement, founded in Spain in 1958, that assists husbands and wives to deepen their relationship within the context of the Sacrament of Matrimony. The movement was brought to the United States in 1968 and continues to develop through its weekend conferences, using counseling, prayer, private reflection, interpersonal dialogue, and the Mass.

Marriage, Sacrament of (SA-kruh-mehnt uhv MEHR-ehdzh): The institution of marriage as recognized by the Church to be sacramental if between a baptized male and female. CCC 1601-1666

Martyr (MAHR-ter): (From Greek *martyria:* witness) One who gives up his or her life rather than deny Christ and the Gospel. A martyr strives for conformity to Christ and is willing to part with his or her earthly life rather than reject God. The Church's history is dotted with the heroism of martyrs. St. Augustine contended that martyrs are made not by the suffering endured but by the motive compelling them to relinquish their lives. CCC 957, 1173, 2113, 2473-2474

Martyrology (mahr-ter-AHL-uh-dzhee): A listing of all known Christian martyrs, not to be confused with the accounts of the suffering and martyrdom of individual saints. The first examples are actually calendars, onto which saints' names are inscribed. The Roman Martyrology dates from the fourth century, and the Carthaginian Martyrology dates from the sixth century. The first martyrology proper, called the Hieronymian Martyrology, is attributed to St. Jerome. Beginning in the ninth century, a new martyrology added short descriptions of the life of each martyr, as well as names from Sacred Scripture, the writings of the Fathers, and Church history to fill out dates on which some martyrs died.

The Roman Martyrology of the sixteenth century is derived from one such ninth-century example. In some monasteries, the martyrology used to be read at Prime before that hour was suppressed. In some monasteries and religious houses today, the martyrology is read before or after the main meal in common. A revised edition was released in 2001, to coincide with the advent of the millennium.

Marxism (MAHRK-sih-zuhm): Socialist movement resulting from the writings of Karl Marx (1818-1883). Its politico-economic theories and atheistic ideology enveloped half the world for over seven decades in the twentieth century. The movement considers reality in "materialistic" terms, rejects religion, and regards man as a mere economic cog in the wheel of production. Marx loathed capitalism and private property. The philosophy today is considered by most to be in serious error and obsolete, as witnessed by its fall in Eastern Europe. (Cf. Communism.)

Mary (MEHR-ee): (Greek form of O.T. Miriam [q.v.]) Name of several women mentioned in the N.T.: (1) Mary, Blessed Virgin, Mother of God (q.v.); (2) Mary Magdalene (q.v.); (3) the sister of Lazarus and Martha in Bethany (cf. Lk 10:42; Jn 11:5, 12:3); (4) the mother of John Mark (Acts 12:12); (5) a Christian woman of Rome (Acts 16:6), et al.

Mary, Blessed Virgin (BLEH-suhd VER-dzhin MEHR-ee): (Greek form of *Miryam,* possibly from Hebrew for "rebellion") Young woman of Nazareth in Galilee, betrothed to a righteous carpenter named Joseph and visited by the angel Gabriel, who announced that she had been chosen by God to be the Mother of His only-begotten Son, to be named Jesus, who would become the Christ, or Messiah, Savior of the world. She visited her cousin Elizabeth (mother of John the Baptist [q.v.]), sang the *Magnificat* (q.v.), gave birth in Bethlehem of Judea, fled Herod's wrath to Egypt with her husband, but returned to nurture Jesus until He began His mission (cf. Mt 1:16—2:23; Lk 1:26—2:52). She occasioned her Son's first miracle at Cana (cf. Jn 2:1-12), followed Him during His mission (cf. Mt 12:46; Mk 3:3), was with Him at His crucifixion and death on Calvary (Jn 19:25-26), and was with the Apostles in the upper room after His resurrection and at Pentecost (Acts 1:14 ff.). Catholics believe she was immaculately conceived and assumed bodily into heaven (cf. Assumption, Immaculate Conception), according her hyperdulia (i.e., veneration greater than for other saints [q.v.]) as Christ-bearer and Mother of God (cf. Deipara, Theotokos).

Mary, Feasts of (FEESTS uhv MEHR-ee): The most ancient of the Marian feasts are thought to be Byzantine in origin. They demonstrate how the early Christological controversies influenced devotion to Mary. They are: Feast of the Presentation of Our Lord (February 2 — sometimes referred to as the "Purification of Mary"); Solemnity of the Annunciation (March 25); Solemnity of the Assumption (August 15); Feast of the Birth of Mary (September 8). These celebrations came to the Roman liturgy through the Gelasian Sacramentary. The oldest Marian feast in the West is the Solemnity of Mary, Mother of God (January 1). Other Marian feasts of later origin include the Immaculate Conception (December 8) and the Visitation (May 31). Yet other Marian feasts are observed as well: Queenship of Mary (August 22), Our Lady of Sorrows (September 15), Our Lady of the Rosary (October 7), as well as the optional memorials of Our Lady of Lourdes (February 11), Our Lady of Mt. Carmel (July 16), the Dedication of the Basilica of St. Mary Major (August 5), the Presentation of Mary (November 21), and the Immaculate Heart of Mary, on the Saturday after the Second Sunday after Pentecost. CCC 1172, 1370, 2043, 2177

Mary, Saturday Office of (SA-ter-day AW-fihs uhv MEHR-ee): Tracing its origins to the Middle Ages, this practice went along with the use of the Mass Proper in honor of the Blessed Virgin Mary on Saturday, when no other obligatory commemoration was observed. The present reform of the Liturgy of the Hours makes the Saturday Office of Mary optional under the title of "Memorial of the Blessed Virgin on Saturday."

Maryknoll: See Catholic Foreign Mission Society of America

Mary Magdalene, St. (SAYNT MEHR-ee MAG-duh-lehn): Woman from Magdala in Galilee, relieved of seven demons (Lk 3:2), who followed Jesus, was with Him at the cross (cf. Mt 27:56; Mk 15:40; Jn 19:25), and to whom Jesus appeared first after the Resurrection (Jn 20:1-18).

Marymas (MEHR-ee-muhs): Technically, any feast of Mary. Usually, though, Marymas refers to the feast of the Annunciation (March 25). It is so named because of its direct relation to December 25, the Feast of Christmas. The two feasts, therefore, are united in the use of "mas" (for "Mass").

Masonry: See Freemasonry

Mass (MAS): (French *Messe,* Vernacular Latin *Messa,* thought to derive from the Latin dismissal *Ite, missa est:* Go, it is sent) Eucharistic liturgy, sacrifice, and meal (with formulae from the Last Supper), including the Liturgy of the Word and Liturgy of the Eucharist (q.v.); unbloody re-presentation of Jesus' sacrifice at Calvary, and principal celebration of the Church's public worship. (Cf. Eucharist, Liturgy.) **CCC 1330, 1345-1355, 1363**

Mass for the Dead: See Requiem

Mass for the People (MAS fawr *th*uh PEE-puhl): On Sundays and certain feasts throughout the year, pastors are required to offer Mass for the faithful entrusted to their care. If they cannot offer the Mass on these days, they must do so at a later date or provide that another priest offer the Mass.

Mass of the Catechumens (MAS uhv *th*uh ka-tch-KYÖÖ-mehno): Until Pope Paul VI revised the rites of the Western Church, the first part of the Mass was known as the Mass of the Catechumens and included everything from the entrance antiphon (or Introit) through the sermon. At the conclusion of the sermon, the catechumens (adults preparing for Baptism) were dismissed. Now, we refer to the first part of the Mass as the Liturgy of the Word, with the catechumens still being dismissed at this point in the Mass. **CCC 1349**

Master of Ceremonies (MAS-ter uhv SEHR-eh-mo-neez): The assistant at the altar, usually a priest wearing cassock and surplice, who coordinates a liturgical celebration by guiding the celebrant in correctly following the rubrics.

Master of Novices (MAS-ter uhv NAH-vih-sehz): A finally professed member of a religious institute who is placed in charge of those novices preparing to make vows, helping them to discern their vocations and forming them in the character of the religious life within that particular community.

Master of the Sacred Palace (MAS-ter uhv *th*uh SAY-krehd PAL-uhs): The canonist and theologian of the Holy Father who resides in Vatican City and advises the Pope and Roman Curia on theological matters. Dominican priests hold this office because the first Master was St. Dominic himself.

Master of the Sentences (MAS-ter uhv *th*uh SEHN-tehn-sehz): Peter Lombard (c. 1100-1160), so named as author of the "Sentences," which was used as the principal theological text during the Middle Ages before St. Thomas Aquinas's *Summa Theologiae.*

Mater et Magistra (MAH-tehr eht mah-DZHIHS-truh): The encyclical of Pope John XXIII issued in 1961, whose title means "Mother and Teacher," explained the issues of human rights, justice, peace, and development of society and contended that because the individual is the basis of all social activities, the individual must be served by society and have his or her legitimate needs met. The dignity of man, deriving from having been created by God, must be protected.

Materialism (muh-TEER-ee-uhl-ih-zuhm): The philosophical belief that only tangible matter (i.e., that which can be touched or seen) exists in the universe. First proposed by the "older Epicureans," materialism has undergone a transformation throughout the ages. Contemporary science now holds that factors other than matter (e.g., gravitational and magnetic fields) are prevalent in the universe. Hence, matter is thought to be one of the modes in which energy expresses itself. Cf. CCC 285, 2124

Matins (MA-tihns): (From Latin *tempora matutina:* morning hours) Originally, the morning hours of Lauds *(Laudes matutinae).* Later on, it referred to the preceding hour of Vigils, sung around midnight. These vigils eventually were incorporated into monastic practice and evolved into the hour of the Divine Office known as Matins. Matins has the following structure: Psalm 95 (94) (the invitatory); hymn; Psalms; readings from Sacred Scripture; commentaries on Sacred Scripture (or, on feast days, an appropriate reading); Responsories; Canticle on solemn feasts.

Matrimonial Court (ma-trih-MO-nee-uhl KORT): The marriage tribunal that explores and judges the validity of a marriage bond. The court grants decrees of nullity if there was an impediment, a defect in consent, or a lack of fulfillment of essential matrimonial requirements. The tribunal also judges unions that were not sacramental or consummated. Cf. CCC 1629

Matrimony: See Marriage, Sacrament of

Matthew, Gospel of St. (GAHS-puhl uhv saynt MA-thyöo): St. Matthew was unquestionably one of the Twelve Apostles, his name occurring in all four lists of the N.T. Prior to his calling, he had been a tax collector named Levi (cf. Mt 9:9-13 with Lk 5:27-32). It is the unanimous tradition of Christian antiquity that he was the author of the first of the four Gospels. In the latter half of the twentieth century, this ascription has been challenged by a solid phalanx of Catholic commentators. The problem is compounded by the fact, admitted by conservative commentators as well, that we do not have a single fragment of the Aramaic original writing that antiquity ascribed to him. The trend of contemporary opinion is that the Gospel "of St. Matthew" was written after and dependent upon the Gospel of St. Mark. If this is true, it is highly unlikely that one of the Twelve Apostles would have taken his material from Mark, who had not been an Apostle. Certainly no one who is aware of the evidence could convincingly maintain that modern scholars have in hand a literal Greek translation of St. Matthew's original Aramaic work. Clearly, its O.T. citations are from the Septuagint. Even the most skillful scholars find great difficulty in trying to retranslate this Greek into Aramaic. The parallel narratives in St. Mark are much more vivid and lifelike. At best, an informed conservative scholar would have to admit that the "translator" of Matthew has permitted himself considerable freedom. On the other hand, contemporary exegetical fashions seem to treat too lightly the massive fact of the unanimous testimony of all those who were closer to the event itself. No one ascribes the book to anyone but St. Matthew. We have no reason to believe that their intelligence was less than ours; we know their access to written and oral sources was much greater than ours. Moreover, one must not ignore the forest while scrutinizing the trees: The strong Semitic flavor of the first Gospel is inescapable. It is clearly an apologetical work directed to the Jews, aimed at showing them that the teaching of Jesus is a genuine reform of their own venerable and beloved religion. It is incredible to think that it was first written after the collapse of Palestinian Judaism and yet fails to play the trump card of such an apologetic, the fall of Jerusalem in A.D. 70. The suggestion that it was written in Antioch, the home of Christianity's liberation from the Law, is baseless. When we have properly dated the Epistle to the Galatians (before the Council of Jerusalem, in A.D. 49), we will better understand what evangelical support St. Paul's adversaries were able to exploit. It could have been none other than the Gospel that teaches that no jot or tittle of the Law was meant to pass. Only the priority of such a Gospel would explain how these Galatians (and Corinthians) could be presumed to know without explanation who Cephas (Peter) was.

Matthias, St. (SAYNT muh-THAI-uhs): (From Hebrew *Mattathias:* gift of Yahweh) The name of the disciple chosen to replace Judas Iscariot as one of the Twelve; he may have been a disciple of Christ from the beginning of His public ministry (Acts 1:15-21).

Maundy Thursday (MAWN-dee THERZ-day): A name for the Thursday of Holy Week, the anniversary of the Last Supper when Christ instituted the Holy Sacrifice of the Mass and the priesthood. This name is derived from the Latin *mandatum novum*, the "new commandment" given by Christ when He washed the Apostles' feet, that we should "love one another" (Jn 13:34).

Maurists (MAUR-ihsts): Members of the French Congregation of Benedictines (O.S.B.), founded by St. Maur in 1618 but dissolved as a consequence of the anticlericalism of the French Revolution. Maurists are especially associated with hagiography by reason of their research in the lives of the saints. Their work survives the demise of their order in the continued publication of the *Acta Sanctorum*. From their ranks came Montfaucon and Mabillon, the founders of Greek and Latin paleography.

Means of Social Communications, Decree on the: See Inter Mirifica

Medals, Religious (rih-LIH-dzhuhs MEH-duhls): Metal, plastic, or wooden objects depicting Jesus, Mary, angels, or saints, which are often worn about the neck and blessed (thereby making them "sacramentals"). Religious medals date from the early Church; they are meant to lead to deeper prayer and are signs of one's commitment to Christ and the Church. Cf. CCC 1667-1672

Mediator (MEE-dee-AY-ter): One who speaks or acts on behalf of another. Jesus Christ is the one and only mediator between God and man (1 Tim 2:5); Jesus has achieved reconciliation with God for man by His redemptive work. As the one Mediator, He can elect to share His role in salvation, as He has done with His Mother by making her "mediatrix" (q.v.), and with others to a lesser degree. CCC 65-73, 456-460, 480, 618, 667, 771, 846, 956, 969-970, 1369, 1544, 1546, 2574, 2593, 2674

Mediatrix of All Graces (mee-dee-AY-trihks uhv AWL GRAY-sehz): The doctrine that it is through Mary that all the graces of Christ are dispensed to the faithful. Because of Jesus' mediatorship, Mary is given the responsibility to share in His saving work as Redeemer. The Second Vatican Council called Mary "Advocate, Auxiliatrix, Adjutrix, and Mediatrix" because of her maternal solicitude for the brothers and sisters of her Son. CCC 969

Meditation (meh-dih-TAY-shuhn): Prayer that employs discursive reflection, enabling one to grow in sanctity. Meditation is the connecting of mind, heart, and soul in communicating with God and is a response to His invitation to offer oneself totally to Him. It uses images about God and events from the life of Jesus for meditational material. Contemplation is the highest level of meditation. CCC 2705-2708; cf. 94-95, 2186, 2699, 2723

Meekness (MEEK-nehs): A virtue related to temperance, controlling anger and keeping one from losing one's temper on account of insignificant or trivial matters. It is the virtue that enables one to accept and tolerate the ordinary adversities of life with equanimity, balance, and good humor. CCC 716, 1716

Megalynarion (may-guh-lih-NAH-ree-ahn): In the Byzantine Rite, the troparion of the Ninth Ode of the Canon of certain feasts. The Ninth Ode always corresponds to the *Magnificat* (in Greek, *Megalynei*). (Cf. Canon.)

Meletian Schism (muh-LEE-shuhn SIH-zuhm): A fourth-century power struggle for control of the Church of Alexandria involving many prominent Eastern Fathers.

Melkite (Melchite) Rite (MEHL-kait RAIT): The division within the Eastern Church, composed of Arabic-speaking Catholics of Egypt, Palestine, and Syria, that descended from those who agreed with the condemnation of Monophysitism (i.e., that Christ had only one nature) at the Council of Chalcedon (451). Although part of the Great Schism (ninth to eleventh centuries), the Melkites were reunited to Rome in the eighteenth century.

Membership in the Church (MEHM-ber-shihp in *th*uh TSHERTSH): Full communion with the Church through Baptism or profession of faith and adherence to the Church's discipline and teaching.

Memento (meh-MEHN-to): (Latin: remember) Two parts of the Roman Canon (Eucharistic Prayer I), in which the priest makes a remembrance of the living *(Memento, Domine . . . "Remember, O Lord")* and of the deceased *(Memento etiam, Domine . . . "Remember, also, O Lord").* From this there derives the custom of using the word "memento" to describe an intention in prayer. The Roman Canon also contains remembrances for Church officials and for the congregation. The three other anaphoras also include mementos for the living, the dead, the Church, and the world.

Memorare (meh-mo-RAH-ray): A prayer attributed to St. Bernard of Clairvaux (1090-1153) and made popular from the early seventeenth century on by a French priest, Claude Bernard. The prayer honors the Blessed Virgin Mary and takes its name from the first word: "Remember, O most gracious Virgin Mary, that never was it known that anyone who fled to thy protection, implored thy help, or sought thy intercession was left unaided. Inspired by this confidence, I fly unto thee, O Virgin of virgins, my Mother. To thee do I come, before thee I stand, sinful and sorrowful. O Mother of the Word Incarnate, despise not my petitions (in my necessity) but in thy mercy (clemency) hear and answer me. Amen."

Memoria (meh-MO-ree-uh): (Latin: memory, memorial, or remembrance) The lowest kind of feast that was found in the old liturgical calendar. In the current liturgical calendar, there are two kinds of memorials: obligatory and optional. As its name suggests, the obligatory memorial must be celebrated. The optional memorial, on the other hand, is celebrated at the discretion of the priest celebrant.

Menaion (meh-NAY-uhn): (From Greek: month or monthly book) In the Byzantine Rite, the liturgical book that contains the Proper of the Saints and of the fixed feasts for the whole year.

Mendicant Orders (MEHN-dih-kuhnt OR-derz): (Latin *mendicare:* to beg) Those religious communities, inspired by St. Francis of Assisi (1181-1216) and St. Dominic (1170-1221), whose members forfeit the right to own property and any possessions. Members of mendicant orders rely upon God's providence and the faithful's generosity. Cf. CCC 915, 2544-2545

Mene, Tekel, Upharsin (MAY-nay, TAY-kehl, ööp-HAR-seen): The three Aramaic words embedded on the palace wall during Belshazzar's feast (cf. Dn 5:25). Daniel was asked to interpret these strange words, which are descriptions of three Babylonian units: *mene,* "he has been measured"; *tekel,* "you are weighed"; *upharsin,* "[your kingdom] is divided."

Menology, also Menologion (meh-NAHL-uh-dzhee, meh-nuh-LO-yahn): (Greek *menos:* month + *logos:* an accounting or discourse) In the Eastern Church, a book containing the lives of the saints in accordance with the liturgical year; it corresponds to the martyrology and the *Acta Sanctorum* of the Western Church.

Menorah (meh-NOR-ruh): (Hebrew: candelabrum) The seven-branched candlestick used in the Jerusalem Temple. The Talmud prohibits an exact replica of the menorah. Currently, the menorah is a symbol of Jewish piety rather than an actual furnishing in a synagogue.

Mensa (MEHN-suh): (Latin *mensa:* table) The flat stone that forms the top of the altar. Previously, the mensa had to be constructed of a single piece of non-crumbling stone (Can. 1198). Current legislation repeats this requirement but does make allowances for "another material, worthy and solid" to be utilized, depending on the judgment of the episcopal conference (Can. 1236).

Mental Reservation or Mental Restriction (MEHN-tuhl reh-ser-VAY-shuhn, ree-STRIHK-shun): The practice, distinct from lying, that gives one's words a meaning different from what they ordinarily have, so as to conceal some legitimately confidential matter. Mental reservation is permissible when it is used to prevent others from learning what they have no right to know; it is not ethical to use in a court of law. CCC 2488-2489

Mercy, Divine (dih-VAIN MER-see): The attribute of God extending compassion to those in need. Both the O.T and N.T. illustrate that God desires to show mercy to the sinner. One must humbly accept mercy; it cannot be earned. As Christ has been merciful, so the faithful are mandated to exercise compassion to others, forgiving — in the words of Jesus — "seventy times seven times" (Mt 18:22). St. Faustina Kowalska of Poland was instrumental in propagating a widespread devotion to the Divine Mercy of God with her Chaplet and Novena of Divine Mercy, such that the Second Sunday of Easter is now celebrated as Divine Mercy Sunday. CCC 210-211, 270, 545, 589, 1037, 1439, 1829, 1846-1847, 2040, 2100, 2840

Mercy, Spiritual and Corporal Works of (SPIHR-ih-tshöö-uhl and KOR-per-uhl WERKS uhv MER-see): Works of charity done out of compassion or concern for those in distress and suffering. The corporal works are feeding the hungry, giving drink to the thirsty, clothing the naked, sheltering the homeless, visiting the sick and imprisoned, ransoming the captive, and burying the dead. The spiritual works are instructing the ignorant, correcting sinners, advising the doubtful, showing patience to sinners and those in error, forgiving others, comforting the afflicted, and praying for the living and dead. CCC 2447

Merit (MEHR-iht): The fruit of grace by which one is made "righteous" in God's eyes or grows in the righteousness already experienced. God gives freely to His sons and daughters, who cannot earn His grace but who can only humbly accept it. Luther asserted that man cannot perform any salutary acts because of Original Sin; however, the Church believes that when man is justified by faith in Christ, he can then perform supernatural works, making him a partner in

the work of redemption. (Cf. De Condigno, De Congruo.)
CCC 2006-2011; cf. 956, 1476, 1708, 2025-2027

Messiah (also Messias): See Christ

Metanoia (meh-tuh-NOI-yuh): (From Greek *metanoein:* to change one's mind, repent, be converted) N.T. term referring to conversion, entailing repentance of sin and a subsequent turning toward the Lord. Metanoia is essential to the Christian life and is necessary for spiritual growth. St. Paul speaks of the "new creation," involving a renewal of mind and heart through Baptism or sanctifying grace.

Metany (MEH-tuh-nee): In the East, an inclination of the head and shoulders (lesser metany) or a prostration to the ground (greater metany). Both are penitential gestures.

Metaphysics (MEH-tuh-fih-zihks): (Greek *meta:* after + *physika:* physics) The branch of philosophy dealing with first things, including the nature of being *(ontology),* the origin and structure of the world *(cosmology),* and the study of the reality and attributes of God *(natural theology).* Metaphysics within Catholic philosophy can be found in the writings of St. Augustine and St. Thomas Aquinas.

Metempsychosis (meh-TEHM-sai-KO-sihs): (Greek *meta,* change + *empsychoun:* to put a soul into) The belief that the human soul transmigrates from one body, either human or animal, to another. Also known as reincarnation, it is a characteristic belief of many Asian religions and is incompatible with Christian faith. **CCC 1013**

Methodism (MEH-thuh-dih-zuhm): The faith and practice of those Protestants who follow the teaching enunciated by John Wesley, along with his brother Charles Wesley and others in the first half of the eighteenth century. The name is taken from the methodical study and worship the Wesleys practiced in their "Holy Club," which met at Oxford University. Methodism teaches that there are four sources and guidelines for belief: the Bible, Tradition, experience, and reason. In accordance with most mainline Protestant bodies, the

Methodist Church recognizes only two sacraments (Baptism and the Lord's Supper) as being ordained by Christ.

Metropolitan (meh-truh-PAHL-ih-tuhn): 1. An archbishop who is the head of an ecclesiastical province. 2. The archdiocese that is the primary see of an ecclesiastical province.

Mexican American Cultural Center (MEHK-sih-kuhn uh-MEHR-ih-kuhn KUHL-tsher-uhl SEHN-ter): Founded in 1971 by the Texas Catholic Conference to provide research, education, publications, and leadership programs, both for Hispanics and for those ministering within the Hispanic community.

Micah (MAI-kuh): O.T. prophet. A contemporary of Isaiah, the sixth of the minor prophets, Micah lived in Judah in the latter half of the eighth century. His name, an abbreviation of Micahiah, is akin to that of Michael. He is a typical prophet, speaking for a God Who threatens disaster for the Jewish people because of their sins, and promising them freedom and prosperity under a new David in exchange for their repentance. Judah is called to take warning from the fall of Samaria. While Micah's chronology is not certain, it seems likely that the reform under Hezekiah was evidence of his success. He had a strong social conscience and felt solidarity with the oppressed poor (Mi 2, 3, 6:9-11). His most famous verse is 6:8, the definition of genuine religion: "To do only what is right, to love goodness, and to walk humbly with your God."

Middle Ages (MIH-duhl AY-dzhehz): The period between the fall of Rome (476) and the beginning of the Renaissance, about the end of the fifteenth century. (Some scholars contend that the Middle Ages began with the coronation of Charlemagne in 800.) Usually, the term is used negatively, referring to the eclipse of the ancient world; however, objectivity compels the acknowledgment that many great achievements in the arts and sciences occurred.

Midrash (MIHD-rahsh): (From Hebrew *darash:* to seek) An interpretation of Scripture by rabbis aimed at discovering the deeper meaning of the text, rather than the merely "literal" meaning. Catholic exegesis employs *midrash,* which dates from the second century B.C.

Migrant Ministries (MAI-gruhnt MIH-nih-streez): Begun in 1970 by Pope Paul VI and placed under the supervision of the Congregation for Bishops, the Pontifical Council for Migrants and Travelers was made autonomous in 1988 by Pope John Paul II. Among other tasks, it provides priests with specialized abilities and language skills, so that the Church might offer necessary services for the spiritual and temporal good of those faithful who are migrants, nomads, tourists, or travelers of any kind. **Cf. CCC 1911, 2241**

Military Chaplains (MIHL-ih-tehr-ee TSHAP-luhns): Priests or other ministers of religion whose ministry is to military personnel and their families. In some countries they are also military officers. In the U.S. the Military Ordinariate is a separate diocese (q.v.).

Military Ordinariates (MIHL-ih-tehr-ee or-dih-NEHR-ee-uhts): Special dioceses erected by the Holy See to serve the pastoral needs of military personnel and their families.

Millenarianism, also Millennialism (mih-leh-NEHR-ee-uhn-ih-zuhm, mih-LEHN-ee-uhl-ih-zuhm): The belief that Christ will return again to govern a temporal kingdom on earth for a thousand years. (See Chiliasm; Millennium.) **CCC 676**

Millennium (mih-LEHN-ee-uhm): A thousand-year reign of Christ and the just upon earth in grace before the end of the world. This belief of the Millenarians, Chiliasts, and some sects of modern times is based on an erroneous interpretation of Revelation 20. (See also Chiliasm.) **CCC 676**

Ministers (MIH-nihs-terz): (From Latin *minister:* servant) Those who function in some capacity in the celebration of the sacraments, including clergy and those who are instituted in the ministries of lector and acolyte. Although the term has been used more broadly since the Second Vatican

Council, referring to those who cooperate in the pastoral ministry of the clergy, Pope John Paul II, in *Christifideles Laici,* has urged caution in applying this term to those who are not ordained, so that there will be no confusion about the uniqueness of the respective vocations of the clergy and the laity. Cf. CCC 859, 874, 876, 878, 1142, 1553, 1579, 1584, 1592, 2122, 2686

Ministries (MIH-nih-streez): The norm concerning liturgical ministries articulated in *Sacrosanctum Concilium* that "in liturgical celebrations each person, minister or layman who has an office to perform, should carry out all and only those parts which pertain to his or her office by the nature of the rite and the norms of the liturgy" (n. 28). This makes clear what had long been true: There is a diversity of roles and ministries in liturgical celebration. The *First Apology* of Justin the Martyr (c. A.D. 150) confirms that there were readers, deacons, celebrant, and people present for the liturgy. The *Ordo Romanus Primus* and other sources from the Middle Ages indicate that there were as many as twenty ministers at liturgical celebrations. The Roman Pontifical after the Council of Trent attests to subdeacons and lectors carrying out liturgical roles. Today, it is not uncommon to find deacons assisting at liturgies with readers, acolytes, and cantors. The *General Instruction of the Roman Missal* considers these integral (nn. 103-104). The deacon is ordained; readers and acolytes are installed; the cantor functions without rites of installation. By custom, non-installed readers function ministerially at the liturgy. There may also be commissioned extraordinary ministers of Holy Communion when there is necessity. Women may be admitted as readers (lectors) and extraordinary ministers of Holy Communion but may not be formally installed as lectors or acolytes.

Ministry and Life of Priests, Decree on: See Presbyterorum Ordinis

Ministry of the Word (MIH-nih-stree uhv *th*uh WERD): 1. The spreading of the Gospel through evangelization and catechesis. 2. The Liturgy of the Word during the Sacrifice of the Mass, which contains, in part, the Scripture readings and homily. 3. The office of theologians as they plumb the depths of the Church's teaching and explain it to the faithful. Cf. CCC 132, 893, 903, 1596

Minor Orders (MAI-ner OR-derz): Lesser degrees of ministry received by candidates for the priesthood at regular intervals in the course of their studies. They were porter, lector, exorcist, and acolyte. The minor orders were abolished in 1972 and replaced by the ministries of lector and acolyte.

Miracle (MIHR-uh-kuhl): The transcending of a law of nature, resulting in an unexplained occurrence that glorifies God. A miracle communicates God's will ("prophetic") and His desire to save humanity ("salvific"). Jesus Himself worked many miracles, which play a common and important role in Scripture. CCC 156, 434, 515, 547-549, 1335, 2003

Miracle Plays (MIHR-uh-kuhl PLAYZ): A popular dramatic genre in the Middle Ages that presented the life of a saint, a religious historic event, a story from the Bible, or some teaching of the Faith, intended primarily as teaching aids to convey some moral or religious principle to the uneducated who would not otherwise be exposed to the Faith in an attractive or understandable fashion. They were usually presented by touring troupes of players outdoors, often in the courtyard or square before a cathedral. Miracle plays preceded mystery plays, which usually concentrated more on events from the O.T. or N.T. Many of the plays, in time, introduced verse, which remained the form of drama for centuries.

Miraculous Medal (mih-RAK-yöö-luhs MEH-duhl): The sacramental deriving from an apparition of Our Lady to Sister (now St.) Catherine Labouré on November 27, 1830, at the Daughters of Charity of St. Vincent de Paul Motherhouse in Paris. Mary directed St. Catherine to have a medal struck that corresponded to the image the French nun received during the vision. This devotion has had papal approbation; the Miraculous Medal continues to be worn by millions of persons the world over.

Mirari Vos (mih-RAH-ree VOS): The encyclical of Pope Gregory XVI (1832), condemning the social and political doctrines of the l'Avenir group in nineteenth-century France. L'Avenir tried to reconcile some of the ideas of the French Revolution with Catholicism, especially freedom of the press and freedom of worship. Later, Pope Pius IX condemned many of these same ideas in his *Syllabus of Errors* (1864). Church historians have held that Pius IX was condemning extreme liberalism in the *Syllabus* and not commonly accepted ideas belonging to democratic societies.

Miriam (MIH-ree-uhm): Sister of Moses and Aaron (cf. Ex 15:20; Nm 12:1, 15; 20:1; Mi 6:4) from whose name the N.T. name Mary is derived.

Miserere (mee-zay-RAY-ray): Psalm 51 (50), a penitential psalm, which in Latin begins, *"Miserere mei, Deus, secundum magnam misericordiam tuam"* ("Have mercy on me, O God, according to thy great mercy"). It was written by King David after he repented of adultery and of having had Uriah the Hittite killed so that he could take his wife Bathsheba (2 Sm 11 and 12). Psalm 51 (50) used to be prayed as the first psalm of Lauds in the weekday Office throughout the year and on many Sundays. It is now used on all Fridays to indicate the penitential character of the day.

Missal: See Roman Missal

Missiology (mih-see-AHL-uh-dzhee): (From Latin *missio:* sending off) The study of spreading the Christian Faith by: (1) analyzing doctrines and how to explain them to those who have either not heard them or rejected them; (2) considering how best to evangelize; (3) studying the vast cultures in which Christians are called to propagate the Faith.

Mission (MIH-shuhn): 1. The spreading of the Gospel to all nations. To be a Christian compels one to propagate the Faith. 2. An annex of a parish that often does not have enough parishioners to warrant a full-time pastor. 3. The visible and invisible extension of the processions of the Blessed Trinity.

The mission of the Son is the Incarnation, while that of the Holy Spirit is the indwelling in the hearts of the faithful.

Missionaries, also Missioners (MIH-shuh-nehr-eez, MIH-shuh-nerz): Religious and laypersons devoted to spreading the Gospel either to those who have not heard it or to those who have rejected it. The example of Christ is the impetus for all the faithful to take seriously their mandate of proclaiming the Faith in the daily events of life. CCC 828, 849-851, 854, 1122, 1533, 1565, 2044, 2419

Missionary Activity, Decree on the Church's: See Ad Gentes

Miter or Mitre (MAI-ter): (From Greek *mitra:* turban) The liturgical headdress proper to all bishops of the Latin Rite, including the Pope, consisting of two flaps, front and back, equal in size, and joined at the bottom by a headband; the flaps curve to a point at the top. A soft material joins these two flaps together, allowing for it to be folded when not in use. As we know it, the miter did not appear until the middle of the tenth century. At that time, the miter was worn only by the Pope at solemn liturgical functions. Antecedents of the miter were probably the headdress of the high priest of the Temple of Jerusalem and the head-covering worn by important officials in the Roman Empire. By the twelfth century, it became the custom for bishops to wear the miter. Later, others besides the Pope and bishops wore a miter. Today, its use is limited for the most part to bishops and abbots.

Mixed Marriage (MIHKST MEHR-ehdzh): Common term for a marriage between a Catholic and a non-Catholic. CCC 1633-1636

Modalism (MO-duhl-ih-zuhm): (Latin *modus,* manner) A third-century heresy concerning the Holy Trinity that regarded the Three Persons as three modes, or functions, of the one God, so making the Godhead a single Person. Cf. CCC 238-260

Moderator of the Curia (MAH-der-ay-ter uhv *th*uh KYÖÖ-ree-uh): An ecclesiastical office introduced after Vatican II. An administrative office for the coordination and supervision of offices and personnel of the diocesan curia.

Modernism (MAH-der-nih-zuhm): The term given a broad attempt by some thinkers at the beginning of the twentieth century to bring Catholic thought into line with the advances of current biblical, historical, philosophical, and scientific findings. In the process, some "modernists" ended up altering Catholic doctrine in their attempt to make it more palatable to contemporary men and women, thus earning the condemnation of Pope St. Pius X in his decree *Lamentabili* (September 8, 1907), and then his encyclical *Pascendi Dominici Gregis* (September 8, 1907). Prominent Modernists would include Maurice Blondel (1861-1949) in philosophy, Alfred Loisy (1852-1940) in Scripture, George Tyrrell (1861-1909) in theology, and Frederick von Heigel (1852-1925) in a variety of fields, all bound by the belief that a questioning, critical, accommodating theology was necessary if the Church was to reach twentieth-century humanity. In its extreme form, it doubted the divinity of Christ, posited the Church as a purely sociological enterprise, viewed Scripture as mere literature, and held that doctrines must change to suit the time. There is a question among historians as to whether Modernism was ever an organized, systematic movement, or more of a tendency popular at the turn of the last century. Whatever the case, St. Pius X attacked it with vigor; some opponents of Modernism, called "integralists," reacted with such excess that the successor of St. Pius X, Benedict XV (1914-1921), had to urge moderation.

Modes, Gregorian (Greh-GAW-ree-uhn MODZ): Musical "scales" used for Gregorian chant. The eight modes were divided into related authentic and plagal groups. In the authentic modes the cadential figure (final) appears at the lower portion of the range, while in plagal modes it is in the middle. Within the modes, there is only one accidental possible and that is the halftone lowering of the seventh note of the scale (Bb). (See also Gregorian Chant.)

Modes of Responsibility (MODZ uhv reh-spahn-sih-BIHL-ih-tee): The way by which one acts toward achieving true human fulfillment. These modes have been formulated by Germain Grisez and John Finnis and emphasize the responsibility that one has in loving God and neighbor.

Modesty (MAH-dehs-tee): The virtue promoting manners and harmony with others, enabling one to control conversations, dress, and external actions. A defect of modesty causes boorishness and coarseness, while excess in this virtue leads to excessive delicacy and fastidiousness. CCC 2521-2524, 2533

Mohammedanism or Muhammadanism: See Islam

Moicheia (moi-KAY-uh): The Greek noun for "adultery," occurring three times in the N.T. (Mt 15:19; Mk 7:21; Jn 8:3), which refers to the rending of the marital covenant when intercourse occurs with a third party. Adultery can also be committed in one's heart without the physical action (Mt 5:27-28).

Moleben (mo-LAY-behn): In the Byzantine Church, a service of prayer honoring a particular saint, the Blessed Virgin Mary, or Christ Himself. It may include prayers of thanksgiving, petition, and penance.

Molech, also Moloch (MAH-luhk): (Hebrew *melek:* king, with the vowels of *boshet:* shame) Literally, king of shamefulness, a name given by the Israelites to the Canaanite god who presided over the realm of the dead. It appears related to other divine names such as Muluk and Milcom, found in the Man texts and the Ugaritic tablets. Under Assyrian influence, the cult of this king-god grew in Palestine (2 Kgs 23:10, Jer 32:35). The sacrifice of children was central to the pagan ritual in the worship of Molech and is attested to from the archaeological finds of infant remains placed under the entrances to Canaanite homes as propitiatory offerings to Molech; in fact, it is suggested that *molk* may have been the term for a votive offering.

Molinism (MOHL-ih-nih-zuhm): The belief espoused by Luis Molina that stated that God directs human freedom so that if He desires that one make a specific choice, He will create the situation that will elicit such a choice. Molina asserted that God directs free choice without coercing the agent. This doctrine has been criticized because it seems, despite Molina's protestations, to make God force the choices that His creatures make. Cf. CCC 1730-1748

Monarchianism (mah-NAHR-kee-uhn-ih-zuhm): An understanding of the doctrine of the Trinity that stresses the unity or monarchy of the Godhead. Historically, this understanding was associated with the heresies that denied the reality of the Trinity in order to preserve the divine unity. The two notable heresies were *adoptionism* (which affirmed that Jesus was an ordinary human being upon whom God conferred a share of divine power) and *modalism* (which maintained that the One God adopted the successive roles of Father, Son, and Holy Spirit in the economy of salvation). By insisting on a Trinity of Persons in one nature, the Council of Nicaea (325) preserved the truth of the Godhead's unity while affirming the reality of three distinct Persons. Cf. CCC 238-260

Monastery (MAH-nuh-stehr-ee): The house of a religious community, usually — in current usage — of the cloistered or contemplative type. The typical monastery is constructed around a quadrangle (the cloister garth) and contains a church or chapel, a refectory, chapter hall, common room, workrooms, and individual rooms (cells) for the residents (monks or nuns). The entire physical property of the monastery, or at least some portion of it, is called the enclosure and is normally closed to the public. Cf. CCC 2691, 2696

Monasticism (muh-NA-stih-sih-zuhm): The form of life followed by those who withdraw from society in order to devote themselves totally to God through prayer, penance, and solitude. Two types of monasticism have emerged: anchoritic (in which the monks or nuns live as hermits and come together for prayer and some meals) and cenobitic (in which they live in community). St. Anthony (d. 357) is regarded as the Father of Monasticism, but another monk, St. Pachomius, formulated the first monastic rule. In Eastern Christianity, the most influential monastic rule is that of St. Basil, while in the West the Rules of St. Benedict and St. Augustine have prevailed. In both the East and the West, monasticism has proven to be a highly durable form of Christian life and has contributed enormously to the vitality of the Church and the wider culture. Important examples of anchoritic monasticism in the West are Carthusians and Camaldolese, while Benedictines and Cistericians stand out as representatives of the cenobitic type.

Monism (MO-nih-zuhm): (Greek *monos:* single) The philosophical belief that there is only one ultimate substance or principle, including within it all apparent diversity; thus, Monism would hold that all things are God, rather than having been created by God.

Monita Secreta (MO-nee-tuh seh-KRAY-tuh): The "secret orders" regarding the expansion of Jesuit authority allegedly given to Fr. Jerome Zahorowski, S.J., by the fifth general of the Society of Jesus. In 1611, Fr. Zahorowski was expelled from the Jesuits after the fraud became known.

Monk (MUHNK): (From Greek *monachos:* one who lives alone) One who withdraws from society in order to pursue a life totally dedicated to God in prayer, penance, and solitude. Monks are commonly distinguished from communities of clerics or friars who engage in some form of active ministry. While the term "monk" can refer both to men and women monastic religious, common English usage restricts it to men and prefers the term "nun" for women. **Cf. CCC 2687**

Monogamy (muh-NAH-guh-mee): The union of man and woman in the faithful, permanent life-giving bond of marriage, granting the couple friendship, intimacy, security, and stability and bestowing upon their children the love and fulfillment they need. Christ raised human marriage to the level of a sacrament. Polygamy (i.e., the taking of many wives) and polyandry (i.e., the taking of many husbands) are opposed to the will of God. "Serial polygamy" (i.e., taking partners whenever one desires) is prevalent today. Monogamy is the only legitimate form of sexual union recognized by the Church. Cf. CCC 1610-1611, 1645, 1664

Monophysitism (muh-NAH-fih-sih-tih-zuhm): A fifth-century heresy that claimed that Christ had only one nature, a composite of human and divine. Strong Monophysite sentiment lingered for about a thousand years, and Monophysite churches still continue today. CCC 467

Monotheism (MAH-no-thee-ih-zuhm): (Greek *monos:* single + *theos:* god) The belief that there is a single, personal, and transcendent God Who is distinct from the world that He has created. CCC 200-202, 222-227

Monothelism (muh-NAH-thuh-lih-zuhm): A seventh-century heresy that proposed that since Christ is one Person, He has only one will. It was an attempt to reconcile with the Monophysite Christians, who held that Christ had only one nature. Monothelism was condemned by the Council of Constantinople in 680. Cf. CCC 475

Monsignor (mahn-SEEN-yer): (Italian *monsignore,* my lord) A term of honor in addressing certain clerics. All bishops have a right to use it, but it is most commonly used to refer to those priests who have the title of "Chaplain of His Holiness," "Prelate of Honor of His Holiness" or "Protonotary Apostolic."

Monstrance (MAHN-struhns): (From Latin *monstrare:* to show) The sacred vessel (also called "ostensorium") used for the exposition and adoration of the Blessed Sacrament as well as solemn Benediction. The general form and shape of the monstrance is a round glass or crystal-covered opening through which the Sacred Host can be seen. The glass enclosure is frequently surrounded by rays or other decorations. These indicate the graces and spiritual blessings that flow from the Holy Eucharist upon those who adore and worship It. The glass enclosure, or "luna," is held up by a stem or base, allowing the monstrance to be placed on an altar or carried in procession, such as on the Solemnity of Corpus Christi.

Montana Case (mahn-TA-nuh KAS): The first instance in the United States of the Pope dissolving a marriage between a baptized person and a non-baptized person (1924). Also known as the "Helena Case" and later as dissolution in favor of the Faith, or Privilege of the Faith.

Montanism (MAHN-tuh-ih-zuhm): A second-century heresy whose adherents claimed to be oracles of the Holy Spirit and sole possessors of charismatic qualities. It persisted into the ninth century in some places.

Montessori Method (mahn-teh-SAW-ree MEH-thuhd): A technique for the education of children developed by Maria Montessori, an Italian physician and educator. It is based upon the belief that each child has an innate desire to learn and the ability to develop self-discipline by exercising personal freedom with limited control and direction. This theory led to the establishment of Montessori schools in Italy, Great Britain, and the United States.

Month's Mind (MUHNTHS MAIND): Unofficial but still popular name for a Mass celebrated for a deceased person on or close to the thirtieth day after death or burial. Some monastic communities and ethnic groups observed a full month of mourning. To mark the end of this period, a Mass was celebrated. Where the custom has not been abandoned, such an occasion provides an opportunity to offer consolation and assistance to the grieving family of the one who has died in Christ.

Morality (mo-RAL-ih-tee): (Latin *mores:* of manners or customs) Those principles governing whether an act is right or wrong, as understood through natural reason and in accordance with the teachings of Christ as they are revealed through Scripture and Tradition. **CCC 1691-2550**

Morality Play (mo-RAL-ih-tee PLAY): Dramatic work so designated for the moral struggle between virtue and vice that figures at the core of this genre of religious drama; *Everyman* (fifteenth century) is an example.

Moral Person (MOR-uhl PER-suhn): The 1917 C.I.C.'s term for a juridic person or kind of ecclesiastical corporation.

Moral Theology (MOR-uhl thee-AHL-uh-dzhee): The study of the ethical demands of the Gospel and those of faith, hope, and charity, which lead to conformity to Christ. It discerns the goodness or evil of actions according to the teachings of the Church. Faith, reason, Divine Revelation (i.e., Scripture and Tradition), and the natural law govern the norms of moral theology. It is closely connected to Canon Law and assists the faithful in knowing how to respond to the pressures of the modern world by making them aware of what the Church teaches on a variety of topics such as contraception, *in vitro* fertilization, and sharing with the needy. Cf. CCC 1749-1761

Moral Virtues (MOR-uhl VER-tshööz): The good habits that develop in one who has performed morally good acts. Moral virtues incline one to do good with ease, whereas intellectual virtues empower one to know the truth and supernatural virtues order one to seek God explicitly. The four fundamental "cardinal" virtues are prudence, justice, fortitude, and temperance. Prudence is the chief moral virtue. The moral virtues are requirements for the supernatural virtues that, in turn, strengthen the moral virtues. CCC 1805-1809

Moravian Church (mo-RAY-vee-uhn TSHERTSH): A community begun by John Hus, the priest-rector of the University of Prague, who rejected the spiritual authority of the Pope and appealed to the Bible only. The Moravian Church has no altars, baptizes infants, and observes the Lord's Supper six or seven times annually. Hus was burned at the stake for heresy in 1415.

Morganatic Marriage (mor-guh-NA-tihk MEHR-ehdzh): A marriage between a man of noble rank and a woman who is either a commoner or of lesser rank in the nobility.

Mormons (MOR-muhnz): Members of the Church of Jesus Christ of Latter Day Saints, founded in 1830 by Joseph Smith, who claimed to have discovered the "Book of Mormon," which was then added to the Bible as part of inspired Scripture. The beliefs of Mormons contain many elements of Protestantism, but they hold a modified view of the Holy Trinity, and in addition to having other doctrines that are incompatible with Christianity, they maintain that men may become gods in the same manner as was Jesus. Because of this, the Mormon religion is not considered a Christian denomination.

Morning Offering (MOR-nihng AW-fer-ihng): A prayer recited every morning that unites the one who utters it with the self-offering of Christ. That of the Apostleship of Prayer is fairly well-known: "O Jesus, through the Immaculate Heart of Mary, I offer You all my prayers, works, joys and sufferings of this day, for all the intentions of Your Sacred Heart, in union with the Holy Sacrifice of the Mass throughout the world, in reparation for my sins, for the intentions of all our associates, and for the general intention recommended this month."

Morning Star (MOR-nihng STAHR): A title used for Mary and found in the Litany of Loreto. This expression refers to the thought that Mary is the *stella matutina* ("morning star"), i.e., last star visible in the sky before the Sun of Justice, Jesus Christ.

Mortal and Venial Sin (MOR-tuhl and VEE-nee-uhl SIHN): A mortal sin is a violation of the law of God that concerns grave moral matter and is done with full knowledge, deliberation, freedom, and consent. Such an action concerns serious moral transgressions and not light or insignificant issues. The agent must know what the action is and also that the action is gravely immoral. The action must be chosen in full freedom, which means that the agent had the opportunity to refrain from performing the action, but chose not to do so. One mortal sin alters one's "fundamental option" in relation to God because it removes the love of God in our hearts. On the other hand, a venial sin either involves light moral matter or is done without adequate knowledge, full consent, or adequate freedom. Unlike venial sin, mortal sin destroys the love of God within us. Mortal sin can only be absolved through the Sacrament of Penance, and all mortal sins must be confessed in that sacrament according to their number and kind. A penance assigned by the confessor must be performed, and true contrition or attrition is required for their absolution. Confessing one's sorrow for mortal sins to God privately or confessing these sins at the Penitential Rite at the Eucharist is not sufficient for their absolution. (Cf. Mortal Sin; Venial Sin.) **CCC 1854-1864**

Mortal Sin (MOR-tuhl SIHN): The deliberate, conscious, free transgression of a moral law that involves serious matter, resulting in separation from God. Three requirements are necessary for a mortal sin: (1) grave matter (e.g., contraception, armed robbery, adultery); (2) sufficient reflection; (3) full consent of the will. Certain factors like habit, ignorance, and fear, can make the sin venial instead of mortal. However, humility dictates that one acknowledge that he is capable of mortal sin as long as he lives. Mortal sin is forgiven through the Sacrament of Penance and a perfect act of contrition. To die in unrepentant mortal sin merits eternity in hell. **CCC 1854-1861**

Mortification (mor-tih-fih-KAY-shuhn): The voluntary practice of self-denial, resulting in a freedom from sinful inclinations and a closer conformity to the suffering Christ. It promotes penance and enables one to become detached from material pleasures, so as to focus on the spiritual realm. **CCC 2015**

Mosaic Law (mo-ZAY-ihk LAW): The revelation to Moses on Mt. Sinai of a code embodying the civil, moral, and religious legislation found in the last four books of the Torah. Traditionally, Moses is considered the author of the Pentateuch; today, scholars assert that subsequent followers of the Mosaic Law helped to group these laws as we find them in the Torah. The Mosaic Law is known for its emphasis on love of God and neighbor (Dt 6:4-5).

Moses (MO-zuhs): While the name "Moses" appears some 771 times in the O.T. and a few more times in the N.T., the figure or person we know as Moses appears for the first time in Exodus 2. Here the birth of Moses is recorded, along with his much-storied discovery by Pharaoh's daughter among the reeds on the riverbank (Ex 2:3-10). After growing up as the adopted son of Pharaoh's daughter, Moses killed an Egyptian (Ex 2:12). Knowing he would be the victim of Pharaoh's wrath, Moses fled to the land of Midian, where he married Zipporah. Together, they had a son whom they named Gershom. While Moses was tending the flock of his father-in-law, Jethro, the Lord appeared to him in the form of a burning bush (Ex 3:2). At this point, God revealed His plan for Moses to lead the Israelites out of bondage in Egypt. But Moses considered himself a poor candidate to lead the Israelites to freedom, and therefore God gave Moses an assistant, his brother Aaron (Ex 3:16). Under the direction of Moses, the Israelites crossed over the Red Sea and eluded the pursuit of Pharaoh's charioteers. Following their heroic escape, the Israelites made their way to the Promised Land. But while out in the desert, Moses was summoned to the top of Mt. Sinai, where God gave him the Decalogue (Ex 20:1-17). In the N.T., Christ is presented as the New Moses, especially in St. Matthew's Gospel. Christ is the New Lawgiver, the One Who establishes the definitive covenant between God and man — a covenant sealed in the blood of the Lamb, His own blood.

Moslems: See Muslims

Motet (mo-TEHT): Musical composition in polyphonic style; a choral work with religious words that are not part of official liturgical texts.

Motive, Spiritual (SPIHR-ih-tshöö-uhl MO-tihv): The reason for an action that, in the Christian dispensation, is always derived from love of God and subsequently leads to increased holiness.

Motu Proprio (MO-töö PRO-pree-o): (Latin: by one's own motion) Common name given to a document written by the Pope on his own initiative and addressed to the entire Church.

Movable Feasts (MÖÖV-uh-buhl FEESTS): Feasts on the liturgical calendar that are not assigned a specific date because their celebration is based on means of calculating time other than chronological dates. Easter is the prototypical example. Its date depends on the lunar calendar. Because Easter moves every year, other feasts are subject to movement also. Some of these would be Ash Wednesday, Ascension, and Pentecost, along with the Sundays of Advent, Lent, and Easter.

Mozarabic Rite (mo-zuh-RA-bihk RAIT): One of the non-Roman Western liturgical rites proper to the Iberian Peninsula, celebrated through the eleventh century. Early references to this kind of Iberian liturgy derive from a letter of Pope Vigilius (c. 594) and Isidore of Seville's *De Ecclesiasticis Officiis.* Despite the efforts of Popes Alexander II and Gregory VII to abolish the Mozarabic Rites, pockets of this Moorish liturgical influence prevailed during the fourteenth and fifteenth centuries. Cardinal Ximenes, Archbishop of Toledo from 1495 to 1517, secured papal approbation for its use in the Toledo cathedral and in six parishes according to a newly printed Missal and Breviary. This rite contained the customary Liturgy of the Word but retained the reading from the O.T. as the First Reading at Mass, followed by a chant with clear Moorish influence. A series of nine prayers and rites followed, among which were two followed by the reading of names in the diptychs for intercessions, the kiss of peace, the *illatio* for transition to the Eucharistic Prayer (a chief characteristic of the rite), and an epiclesis (invocation of the Holy Spirit, especially significant when this was absent from the Roman Rite). The fraction (breaking) of the Host into nine pieces, seven of which were placed on the paten in the form of a cross, reflected Gallican and Celtic practices. Until 1992 this rite was reserved to quasi-private celebrations in a chapel in the Cathedral of Toledo but has now been extended by papal decree. Recent interest in research into this rite has been sparked by the possibility of reviving some of its features for an indigenous Spanish liturgy.

Mozzetta (mot-ZEH-tuh): (From Italian *mozzare:* to cut off) An elbow-length cape buttoning down the front, worn by the Pope, cardinals, bishops, abbots, and canons. It is worn over the rochet and the choir cassock. The Pope's mozzetta is of red satin, that of cardinals is scarlet wool, for bishops, purple wool; abbots wear a color of their Order, and canons wear gray or black with red or purple piping. The mozzetta dates all the way back to the thirteenth or fourteenth century. Originally a sign of jurisdiction, it may be worn by any prelate at any time.

Mundatory: See Purificator

Munera: See Offertory

Muratorian Fragment (möö-ruh-TOR-ee-uhn FRAG-mehnt): The oldest list of N.T. books, dating from no later than the eighth century, discovered by L. A. Muratori (1672-1750) in the Ambrosian Library in Milan and published in 1740. The manuscript is believed to reproduce a list dating from the late-second century, possibly compiled by St. Hippolytus.

Music, Church (TSHERTSH MYÖÖ-zihk): Music that is suitable not only at liturgical services but at paraliturgical functions as well. For music to be admitted into a liturgical celebration, it must be musically, liturgically, and pastorally appropriate (cf. Music in Catholic Worship). Music for paraliturgical functions is not as restrictive. **Cf. CCC 1156-1158**

Music, Liturgical (lih-TER-dzhih-kuhl MYÖÖ-zihk): Music intended and approved for use in liturgical services. Church music can be divided into two main branches: pieces suitable for liturgical services and pieces suitable for paraliturgical functions. To be suitable in liturgical services, a piece of music must be musically, liturgically, and pastorally appropriate. If a piece of music fails on just one of these counts, it may not be used. **Cf. CCC 1156-1158**

Music, Passion: See Passion Music

Musical Judgment: See Judgment, Musical

Music Coordinator (MYÖÖ-zihk ko-OR-dih-nay-ter): The person responsible for all music in a parish. This person must have a competence in both music and liturgy.

Music in Catholic Worship (MYÖÖ-zihk in KATH-uh-lihk WER-shihp): Published by the Bishops' Committee on the Liturgy in 1972, this work's most significant contribution to the Church was the delineation of a triple judgment to be applied regarding suitability. The triple judgment concerns a piece of music's pastoral, liturgical, and musical character.

Music Today, Liturgical (lih-TER-dzhih-kuhl MYÖÖ-zihk töö-DAY): A publication of the Bishops' Committee on the Liturgy in 1982. It reiterates and spells out in greater detail the principles enunciated in the U.S. Bishops' 1972 publication "Music in Catholic Worship."

Muslims (MØØZ-lihmz): Followers of the religion of Muhammad the Prophet, or Islam. The name "Muslim" literally means one who submits to Allah (God) and belongs to the community of Islam (q.v.). **CCC 841**

Mustum (MØØS-toom). (Latin: grape juice, vintage) Unfermented grape juice that contains no additives and has no alcohol content. Some alcoholic priests retain the privilege of using *mustum* at Mass since the faculty was revoked in 1983.

Myron (MAI-ruhn): (Greek: perfumed or scented oil) 1. The chrism consecrated by a bishop on Holy Thursday at the

Mass of Chrism and used throughout a diocese in sacramental ministrations. It may also be used by a bishop or designated priest in the consecration of churches and altars. 2. The oil that exudes from the bones of certain saints — for instance, St. Nicholas of Myra. 3. The oil that appears to stream from a holy icon, frequently bearing a sweet scent. **CCC 1183**

Mysteries of Faith (MIH-ster-eez uhv FAYTH): Supernatural truths whose existence cannot be known without revelation by God and whose intrinsic truth, while not contrary to reason, can never be wholly understood even after revelation. These mysteries are above reason, not against reason. Among them are the divine mysteries of the Trinity, Incarnation, and Eucharist. Some mysteries — e.g., concerning God's attributes — can be known by reason without revelation, although they cannot be fully understood. **CCC 2558**

Mysteries of the Rosary (MIH-ster-eez uhv *th*uh RO-suh-ree): Fifteen events in the life of Christ and His Blessed Mother that are meditated on during the recitation of the fifteen decades of the Rosary. The Joyful Mysteries are the Annunciation, the Visitation, the Birth of Our Lord, the Presentation, and the Finding of Jesus in the Temple. The Sorrowful Mysteries are the Agony in the Garden, the Scourging at the Pillar, the Crowning with Thorns, the Carrying of the Cross, and the Crucifixion and Death of Our Lord. The Glorious Mysteries are the Resurrection, the Ascension, the Descent of the Holy Spirit, the Assumption, and the Coronation of Mary as Queen of Heaven and Earth. The Joyful Mysteries are usually recited on Mondays and Thursdays; the Sorrowful, on Tuesdays and Fridays; and the Glorious, on Wednesdays, Saturdays, and Sundays.

Mystery (MIH-ster-ee): 1. The entire plan of God in which He saves — through the redemption wrought by Christ — those who are faithful to the Gospel. God also is a mystery; He acts in ways inconceivable to man. 2. Any reality that cannot be explained by reason but must be addressed from the standpoint of "supernatural" faith. **Cf. CCC 42, 122,**

206, 234, 280, 287, 295-301, 359, 385, 395, 512-560, 639, 654, 770-776, 813-816, 1028, 1067, 2558, 2779

Mystery, Paschal: See Paschal Mystery

Mystic (MIHS-tihk): A person who enjoys special gifts given through their practice of meditation and contemplation. (See Mysticism.)

Mystical Body of Christ (MIHS-tih-kuhl BAH-dee uhv KRAIST): The notion that the Church forms the Mystical Body of Christ combines a number of important truths. In the first place, membership in the Church entails an intimate communion with Jesus Christ that He Himself described as the relationship of vine and branches (cf. Jn 15:5). The communion of life between Christ and His disciples gives rise to the Church. This communion in Christ is properly identified as: (1) "bodily," in that it is like the unity formed by the members, or parts, of a body; and (2) "mystical," in that the reality of this unity is accessible, not to ordinary sense perception and knowledge, but to the eyes of faith. The Church forms a single body, united with Christ as the Head but with members who retain their diversity (1 Cor 12:1-11; Eph 1:18-23). The doctrine of the Mystical Body of Christ received a comprehensive formulation in the encyclical *Mystici Corporis* of Pope Pius XII (1943) and was reiterated at the Second Vatican Council (LG, n. 7). CCC 774, 776-777, 779, 787-796, 805-807, 1396

Mystical Sense of Scripture (MIHS-tih-kuhl SEHNS uhv SKRIHP-tsher): The "mystical sense" is sometimes called the typological meaning of a text. In biblical typology the figure, event, or person of an O.T. passage prefigures or anticipates a figure, event, or person in the N.T. That is, the type (O.T. reference) foreshadows, anticipates, or points to an antitype to be revealed at a future time (N.T.). For example, in the O.T. we note that manna was sent by God to feed and nourish Israel in the Exodus-journey from slavery (Egypt) into freedom (Palestine). That manna became a type of the Eucharist and so anticipates Jesus as the deeper manna, the Bread from heaven. Manna is the type; Jesus is the antitype. O.T. figures such as Adam, Melchizedek, and David are types for Christ, Who is *the* antitype or the fulfillment of the deeper reality to which their lives pointed. The antitype is usually "organically" related to its type just as the O.T. figures, persons, or events blossom forth into full flowering in the N.T. Thus the things *signified* by the O.T. types refer to their immediate historical referents, as well as to their antitypes to be revealed later in the N.T.

Mystical Theology (MIHS-tih-kuhl thee-AHL-uh-dzhee): Since the seventeenth century, there has been a tendency to distinguish the branches of theology in a way that was foreign to the unified vision of theology characteristic of classical and medieval theology. Dogmatic theology (whose object is things to be believed) was distinguished from moral theology (whose object is things to be done), and moral theology itself was distinguished from ascetical theology and mystical theology. According to the latter distinction, moral theology is concerned with the basics of Christian life. Ascetical theology studies the dynamics of ordinary purification in the person who is beginning in the practice of virtue, while mystical theology is concerned with the higher states of prayer attained through the gifts of the Holy Spirit and the special grace conferred upon the person who is far advanced along the way of perfection. Although these pragmatic divisions of the work of theology correspond to distinctions in the field of Christian belief and practice, they have contributed to a certain fragmentation in the unity of theology, to a marked intellectualization of dogmatic theology, and to the elevation of casuistry in moral theology. A more serious outcome of the division of moral, ascetical, and mystical theology has been the implication that the call to perfect charity is a selective rather than a universal one. In order at least partly to compensate for this weakness, many recent theologians prefer to include ascetical and mystical theology under the more comprehensive rubric of spiritual theology. It can only be hoped that theologians will continue to seek and give expression to an integral vision of the Christian Faith and life, in which the profound unity of dogmatic, moral, and spiritual theology will be clearly exhibited.

Mystici Corporis Christi (MIHS-tee-tshee KOR-por-ihs KRIHS-tee): Published on June 29, 1943, *Mystici Corporis Christi* is the encyclical in which Pope Pius XII teaches about the Church as the Mystical Body of Christ. He builds upon that description, saying that the Church is a "body" because it is one, undivided, and visible, with each member of the body having a proper role, drawing sustenance and being sanctified by the sacraments. He further teaches that the Church is the "body of Christ" because it was Christ Who founded it through preaching, by His suffering on the cross, and in sending the Holy Spirit on the day of Pentecost. Christ is the Head of the body, His Church, by reason of His pre-eminence as God, which gives Him the right to rule and govern the Church. This He does, invisibly in the hearts and minds of all, and visibly through the Pope and bishops. Through His governance Christ enlightens and sanctifies the Church, and by the graces that come from Him, He supports the Church in its mission of bringing His salvation to the world. The encyclical then teaches that the Church, the Body of Christ, is "mystical" because of that particular union which is between Christ and the Church, lifting it above any mere human society. This mystical union accomplishes many things in the lives of the faithful, bringing them closer to one another and to Christ through the virtues of hope, faith, and charity, with the indwelling of the Holy Spirit making their union more perfect. After a brief teaching about the Holy Eucharist as the symbol of unity, *Mystici Corporis Christi* warns about certain errors that can endanger faith, such as false mysticism and quietism, and then exhorts the faithful to penance and prayer. In his conclusion, Pope Pius XII commends the Church to the protection of the Blessed Virgin Mary, that she "may never cease to beg from Him that copious streams of grace may flow from its exalted Head into all the members of the Mystical Body."

Mysticism (MIHS-tih-sih-zuhm): According to the apt definition of Jean Gerson (1363-1429), mysticism is the "knowledge of God arrived at through the embrace of unifying love." Mystical knowledge has the same object as the knowledge of faith and theology, but its method is more intuitive and direct than discursive and scientific. A disciplined life given over to long periods of contemplation sets the stage for, though it does not ensure, an intimate knowledge and experience of God that He bestows through a special grace. Detachment, purification, and cultivation of stillness are fundamental in focusing the person's gaze on God. The struggle against distraction, sensuality, and absorption in the concerns of simply bodily life prepare the mystic for the experience of mystical states. Although the normal means by which human beings come to know God are through images and concepts, there is no reason to suppose that God could not bypass these ordinary vehicles in order to provide for a direct, spiritual intellection of Him that may be occasional or even permanent. Gerson's definition points to this harmonious ordering of the mystic's intellect and will toward the supremely perfect object of knowledge and love. Christian mysticism is distinctive in the prominence it gives to the notion of union over that of absorption. The mystic retains his or her personal identity in the relationship of mystical knowledge and love. The mystical relationship is thus a truly personal relationship between a created person and the triunely personal Creator. Hindu and Buddhist forms of mysticism, consistent with the pan-cosmic context out of which they arise, stress the absorption of the mystic in the impersonal unity underlying all reality.

Myth (MIHTH): (Greek: *mythos*) In ancient Greek literature (e.g., Homer, *Odyssey,* 11.56) "myth" designated a "word," "speech," later on "an account," "story," or "narrative," and eventually came to mean "rumor" or "fable." Contemporary scholars define myth as a symbolic form of thinking in the language, art, and science of the day in which the mind attempts to understand that which is beyond sensible experience. Narratives and stories of this nature answer primary questions: Who am I? Who is God (or the gods)? What are the origins of the universe, the tribe? What is good? In the N.T. the term invariably has a negative connotation. Typical use includes the notion that a story or teaching is unreliable, fanciful, of human origins alone, or just plain false (1 Tm 1:4; 4:7; 2 Tm 4:4; Ti 1:14; 2 Pt 1:16). Some scholars consider any religious attempt to express the inexplicable as mythological in one way or another. Regardless of the merits or drawbacks of such a position, the presence of mythological images and other elements need not carry any pejorative meaning. Various images from ancient Greek mythologies (thus prior to the pejorative use of the term) have found their way into N.T. passages expressing aspects of the Christian proclamation. In such instances, the N.T. authors are recasting or reshaping the conceptual material to fit the reality revealed to them. **CCC 285, 498**

N

Nag Hammadi (NAHG hah-MAH-dee): City about sixty miles south of Luxor, Egypt, where in 1945 there was discovered a Gnostic library of fifty-three texts preserved in thirteen papyrus codices written in Coptic; they are the product of a Gnostic sect that flourished in Egypt from the first to fourth centuries A.D. Significant for the sole witness of the "Gospel of Thomas," an apocryphal gospel that purports to present fourteen sayings of Christ, the Nag Hammadi Library provides modern scholars the opportunity for direct study of Gnostic literature, which previously was known only through the polemical writings of the Church Fathers, who in fact are shown through these texts to have given a relatively faithful portrayal of Gnostic thought and practice.

Nahum, Book of (BØØK uhv NAY-huhm): (Hebrew: comfort) O.T. prophetic book of three chapters containing the highly poetic "oracle on Nineveh," written ca. 660 B.C. by an author who calls himself Elkosh, probably a Judean. He takes the name of Nahum as witness to his attempt at consoling the people in the face of Israel's destruction and the humbling of Judah, as seen in the imprisonment of King Manasseh in Assyria, which was hoped by the downtrodden people to fall to Babylon.

Name, Christian (KRIHS-tshuhn NAYM): The former Code of Canon Law (1917) required that pastors see to it that those baptized were given a Christian name. The current code (1983) calls upon pastors, parents, and sponsors to be careful in selecting a name that is not antithetical to the Christian spirit (Can. 855). This change broadens the responsibility and repeats the counsel offered in the Rite of Christian Initiation of Adults (nn. 203 and 205). **CCC 2156-2159, 2165**

Name Day (NAYM DAY): The annual observance of one's patron whose memory is recalled in the liturgical calendar. Feast days or memorials are reserved to those who have been given the title "saint" or "blessed" by the Church. Name days are accorded the living who have been named after such patrons.

Names of God (NAYMZ uhv GAHD): In the O.T., some names for God were adapted from Canaanite usage, among them El, Elohim, El Elyon, El Shaddai. The most personal name of God, from the perspective of Israel, had to be Yahweh and its variants, Yah and Jo; this was the name revealed to Moses from the burning bush (Ex 3:13-15), but He reveals that His name is incommunicable. God's name is God Himself; thus, God revealed Himself: "I am Who am." CCC 206, 209-214, 231, 446

Narthex (NAHR-thehks): The portico of an ancient church or the vestibule leading to the nave of the church proper.

Nash Papyrus (NASH puh-PAI-ruhs): The only known pre-Christian biblical manuscript in Hebrew until the discoveries at Qumran brought to light even older Hebrew and Aramaic texts. A fragment of papyrus purchased in 1902 from an Egyptian dealer by the English archaeologist W. L. Nash, now in the library of Cambridge University, dating from 150 B.C., it is significant for its ancient witness to the text of the Ten Commandments, substantially in the form of Dt 5:6-21, and to the *Shema* of Dt 6:4-5.

National Association of Pastoral Musicians (NA-shuh-nuhl uh-so-see-AY-shuhn uhv PAS-ter-uhl myöö-ZIH-shuhnz): Organization founded in 1976 to help foster deeper spiritual participation in liturgical functions through improved celebrations. The organization strives to improve the musical and liturgical caliber of all persons and materials involved in the liturgy. It allows for dual membership for clergy and musicians, arranges educational programs, conducts regional and national conventions, and publishes materials dealing with musical and liturgical matters. The main office is located in Washington, D.C.

National Black Sisters' Conference [NBSC] (NA-shuh-nuhl BLAK SIHS-terz KAHN-fer-ehns [EHN BEE EHS SEE]): Organized in 1968, this group's membership is open to all women religious of African-American descent who are members of congregations or orders in the United States, or to any other women religious who are in agreement with the goals of the Conference. Among its purposes are to promote black Catholic vocations, to coordinate information for black Sisters, to assist in various apostolic projects, to improve black community schools, and to assist in the reform of prisons.

National Catholic Conference for Interracial Justice (NA-shuh-nuhl KATH-uh-lihk KAHN-fer-ehns for ihn-ter-RAY-shuhl DZHUHS-tihs): Organized in 1960 for the purpose of providing programs and resources that contribute to a better understanding among members of different races, with more than sixty member councils that encourage Catholics to fight against racial discrimination.

National Catholic Educational Association [NCEA] (NA-shuh-nuhl KATH-uh-lihk eh-dzhöö-KAY-shuh-nuhl uh-so-see-AY-shuhn [EEHN SEE EE AY]): Founded in 1904 for the purpose of providing leadership and support to those in the educational apostolate of the Catholic Church by promoting improved means of teaching, administration, and educational method in Catholic schools, assisting scholarly research in the fields of education and school administration, and facilitating the exchange of information of interest to those in the teaching apostolate.

National Catholic Welfare Conference [NCWC] (NA-shuh-nuhl KATH-uh-lihk WEHL-fehr KAHN-fer-ehns [EHN SEE DUH-buhl-yoö SEE]): Established for the purpose of organizing, unifying, and coordinating Catholic activities for the "general welfare of the Church," since 1967 its activities have been taken over by the United States Catholic Conference (USCC) and the National Conference of Catholic Bishops (NCCB), and since 2001, by the United States Conference of Catholic Bishops (USCCB).

National Conference of Catholic Bishops [NCCB] (NA-shuh-nuhl KAHN-fer-ehns uhv KATH-uh-lihk BIH-shuhps [EHN SEE SEE BEE]): When the National Catholic Welfare Conference was reorganized in 1967, its activities were divided between the National Conference of Catholic Bishops and the United States Catholic Conference. The NCCB focuses its activities on the internal work and concerns of the Church through several standing committees with permanent administrative staff members. As of 2001, the bishops have returned to a single entity.

National Council of Catholic Laity [NCCL] (NA-shuh-nuhl KAUN-sihl uhv KATH-uh-lihk LAY-ih-tee [EHN SEE SEE EHL]): An organization representing fifteen smaller organizations of Catholic laity, including the National Council of Catholic Men and the National Council of Catholic Women, for the coordination of programs and resources.

National Council of Catholic Men [NCCM] (NA-shuh-nuhl KAUN-sihl uhv KATH-uh-lihk MEHN [EHN SEE SEE EHM]): Established in 1920 for the extension of the lay apostolate through various programs dealing with such concerns as spiritual renewal, social action, family life, international affairs, and leadership, it gives representation of American Catholic laymen at various international meetings.

National Council of Catholic Women [NCCW] (NA-shuh-nuhl KAUN-sihl uhv KATH-uh-lihk WIH-mehn [EHN SEE SEE DUH-buhl-yoö]): Established in 1920 as a counterpart to the National Council of Catholic Men, to assist Catholic women in carrying out the Church's mission in the world and to represent American Catholic women within the universal Church.

National Council of Churches of Christ [NCCC] (NA-shuh-nuhl KAUN-sihl uhv TSHERTSH-ehz uhv KRAIST [EHN SEE SEE SEE]): (Full name adds "in the U.S.A.") Established in 1950 as the successor to the Federal Council of Churches, for the purpose of encouraging ecumenical endeavors and cooperation among the various denominations. The Catholic Church is not a member of the National Council of Churches, but cooperates with it in certain matters.

National Federation of Priests' Councils [NFPC] (NA-shuh-nuhl feh-der-AY-shuhn uhv PREESTS KAUN-sihlz [EHN EHF PEE SEE]): Founded in 1968 to be a national forum to address those issues affecting priestly life and ministry from the perspective of diocesan and religious priests, and for the promotion of justice in light of the teaching of the Church, in collaboration with the bishops' conference. It is composed of priests' councils in individual dioceses, but has its own national administrative officers.

Nationalism (NA-shuh-nuhl-ih-zuhm): Undue loyalty and devotion to one's nation, placing it above others, and the promotion of its culture above that of other nations.

National Parish (NA-shuh-nuhl PA-rihsh): A parish established for a specific group of people rather than on a territorial basis, such as a parish for an ethnic group.

Nativism (NAY-tih-vih-zuhm): School of political thought that holds that only persons born within a territory or country are trustworthy enough for full political participation in that territory.

Nativity (nuh-TIHV-ih-tee): (From Latin *nativitas:* "birth") The Church celebrates three birthdays in the liturgical calendar, that of Our Lord (December 25), Our Lady (September 8), and St. John the Baptist (June 24). Normally, liturgical commemorations of saints correspond to their dates of death that are, in reality, their "birthdays" into the life of heaven. When the Church observes literal "birthdays," it is a tacit statement that the person in question was born into this world without Original Sin; hence, Christ and His Mother, conceived without sin, and by common teaching, John the Baptist born without Original Sin, having been freed thereof by the presence of the Lord in His Mother's womb at the Visitation to John's mother, Elizabeth.

Natural Family Planning (NA-tsher-uhl FAM-ih-lee PLAN-ihng): The various methods that enable a married couple to know the wife's fertility. Natural family planning, which employs no artificial contraceptives, is moral, safe, effective, and contributes to the increased communication between husband and wife; it is advocated by the Church when there is a just reason for postponing a pregnancy. It may also be used to help the wife conceive. CCC 2368-2370

Naturalism (NA-tsher-uhl-ih-zuhm): The belief that all of reality is to be found in the world of nature, that natural law can explain all phenomena, and that all religious truth may be derived from the natural world.

Natural Law (NA-tsher-uhl LAW): Man's reasoned participation in God's eternal law. Natural law is promulgated by God and is the "objective order" established by Him; furthermore, man uses his reason to promulgate the dictates of natural law, which is autonomous. The development of society means an increase in the specific dictates of the natural law, so that what was once implicit gradually becomes explicit. The Catholic Church possesses the power to interpret and to help others understand the natural law, which is knowable by all human beings. CCC 1955-1956

Natural Rights (NA-tsher-uhl RAITS): The inviolable and universal privileges that man has because he possesses a rational soul. The Declaration of Independence acknowledges these rights and stresses the necessity of their protection. Pope John XXIII, in his 1963 encyclical *Pacem in Terris,* used the teachings of Pope Pius XII to emphasize the natural rights that all enjoy. These have been enumerated as the right to life, truth, moral and cultural values, economic and professional rights, participation in social life, choosing one's religion and state in life, free association and assembly, emigration and immigration, and legal protection of personal rights. CCC 2104, 2106, 2273, 2467

Natural Theology (NA-tsher-uhl thee-AHL-uh-dzhee): That knowledge of the existence and attributes of God that comes through human reason and the observation of nature, rather than through revelation. CCC 35-39, 47, 237, 286

Nature (NAY-tsher): 1. The character or set of qualities that makes something what it is in its essence. 2. The physical universe. 3. That which pertains to an individual apart from God's supernatural grace.

Nave (NAYV): The part of the church building between the entrance and the sanctuary where the congregation remains. There are two possible derivations. The first is from the Latin *navis,* meaning "ship" (the members of the Church are passengers on the ship of salvation). The second is from a corrupt form of the Greek *naos,* meaning "temple" (the Church is the new temple of salvation).

Nazarite (NA-zuh-rait): (Hebrew *nezir:* consecrated, set apart) Jewish sect especially dedicated to God by the taking of vows, specifically to refrain from using a razor to trim one's hair and beard, to abstain from intoxicating beverages, and to avoid any contact with a corpse; Samson serves as an obvious example of this sect (Jgs 13:5-7; 16:17). It was a common practice of Jews in the Hellenistic period to make similar vows as expressions of their dedication, as did St. Paul (Acts 18:18).

Nazorean or Nazarene (NA-zuh-ree-uhn, NA-zuh-reen): (Greek *nazoraios:* native of Nazareth, or Nazarite) A native of Nazareth, a small village in the territory of Zebulun, where Jesus lived with Mary and Joseph until the beginning of His public ministry (Mt 2:23; 21:11; Jn 18:7; Acts 10:37). The ambiguity in the use of this term by Matthew has led some to conjecture a possible theological meaning drawn from the O.T.; perhaps as the Greek equivalent of Nazarite (cf. Jgs 16:17), *nazoraios* might mean "holy to God" (cf. Mk 1:24; Lk 4:34; Jn 6:69); if the Hebrew *neser,* shoot, is meant, then the term may refer to Is 11:1. The early Christians were derisively called Nazoreans (Acts 24:5); similarly, in Modern Hebrew, the word for "Christian" is *nazri.*

Necromancy (NEHK-ruh-man-see): The practice of communicating with the dead, usually for the purpose of knowing the future, by magical means. The Church has condemned this aberration as evil because it demonstrates a mistrust of God and His providence. The faithful are encouraged to pray to the Holy Spirit for the wisdom and courage to persevere in the future, come what may. CCC 2116

Nehemiah, Book of (BØØK uhv nee-heh-MAI-uh): Historical book of the O.T. that presents the story of Nehemiah and his efforts to restore the Jews to their homeland from their captivity in the East. Having been the cup-bearer of the Persian King Artaxerxes I (464-424 B.C.), Nehemiah obtained the king's permission to go and rebuild Jerusalem, with even the help of a Persian subsidy; despite Samaritan opposition, Jerusalem was rebuilt and fortified in 445 B.C. Nehemiah returned in 432 B.C. to Jerusalem, where he enacted religious reforms, including observance of the Sabbath and the prohibition of religious intermarriage; these efforts at reform were carried on all the more intensely by the priest Ezra, who succeeded him.

Neighbor (NAY-ber): According to the O.T., a fellow member of the people of the covenant, but expanded in Christ's teaching to include all mankind. In the parable of the Good Samaritan (Lk 10:30-37), the concept of neighbor is active, rather than passive, which is reflected in the frequent teaching from Scripture that we are to "love our neighbors" as ourselves. Cf. CCC 1807, 1836

Nemours, Edict of (EE-dihkt uhv nuh-MÖÖR): The document signed by Henry III (1574-1589) that forbade Calvinists to impose their system of belief on the people of France, revoking concessions that had been made earlier.

Neophyte (NEE-o-fait): A newly baptized person. In the early Church, and to some degree today with the revival of the Rite for the Christian Initiation of Adults, the Easter season was used as a time of "continuing education" in the Faith as a necessary follow-up to the pre-baptismal catechesis of Lent.

Neo-Scholasticism (NEE-o-sko-LAS-tih-sih-zuhm): Movement begun in the late nineteenth century, most notably at the Catholic University of Louvain, in Belgium, and then extending into theological centers in Italy, France, and Germany, that sought the recovery of the works of the Scholastic masters, such as Peter Lombard, St. Albert the Great, St. Anselm, St. Bonaventure, and Bl. John Duns Scotus, for use in contemporary philosophy and theology. Particular attention was given to the philosophical and theological works of St. Thomas Aquinas, from which arose a particular school of neo-Thomism; the movement was strongly reinforced by Pope Leo XIII, who in his encyclical of 1879, *Aeterni Patris,* mandated that Scholasticism, in particular Thomism, be the foundation for all Catholic philosophy and theology taught in Catholic seminaries, universities, and colleges. Neo-Scholasticism stimulated a true intellectual renaissance in twentieth-century Catholic philosophy and theology, inspiring some of its greatest thinkers, among them, M.-D. Chenu, Henri de Lubac, Jacques Maritain, Étienne Gilson, and Paul Claudel.

Nesteia (nehs-TAY-uh): (Greek: fasting from food) Religious fast and abstinence as practiced in the rites of the Eastern Churches.

Nestorianism (neh-STOR-ee-uhn-ih-zuhm): A fifth-century heresy that taught that there were two separate Persons in the incarnate Christ, the one divine and the other human, as opposed to the orthodox doctrine that the incarnate Christ was of two natures in one Person, Who was at once God and man. Nestorianism was condemned in 431 by the Council of Ephesus. **CCC 466**

Ne Temere (NAY TAY-may-ray): Latin name ("not lightly") for the papal decree issued in 1908, making the canonical form of marriage obligatory for all Latin Rite Catholics throughout the world. **Cf. CCC 1631**

New American Bible (NÖÖ uh-MEHR-ih-kuhn BAI-buhl): English translation of the Bible, approved by the National Conference of Catholic Bishops for use by English-speaking Catholics of the U.S. in the Mass Lectionary and other liturgical books; it has most recently been revised in 1987, with significantly improved literary style and accuracy. The work of translation that resulted with the publication of the NAB in 1970 began in 1944 with the sponsorship of the Bishops' Committee on the Confraternity of Christian Doctrine, though the NAB differs greatly from that first Confraternity Edition by way of textual criticism, translation from texts in the original biblical languages, and the discovery of significant biblical manuscripts, previously unknown, particularly those of Qumran and other Dead Sea scrolls.

Nicaea, Councils of (KAUN-sihlz uhv nai-SEE-uh): Church councils held at Nicaea, a city of Bithynia, in Asia Minor; the first Council of Nicaea, convened by the Emperor Constantine, met from May to August, A.D. 325, and was the first ecumenical council of the Church; it settled the doctrinal question of the relationship that exists between the First and Second Persons of the Trinity, deciding in favor of Their sharing *homoousia,* the same substance; this council also condemned the Arian heresy. The Second Council of Nicaea, held in 787, was the seventh general council of the Church and the last recognized as ecumenical by the Orthodox Churches of the East; it responded to the iconoclasm controversy and defined the Church's teaching on the veneration of images and praying to the saints. Cf. CCC 242, 465, 476, 1170, 2131

Nicene Creed (NAI-seen KREED): The formal presentation of the chief doctrines of the Catholic Faith used as the Profession of Faith in the Mass; its recitation is prescribed as part of the Sunday liturgy. It was first formulated by the First Council of Nicaea in A.D. 325, in response to the Arian heresy and, therefore, incorporates the important theological term *homoousios;* its present form, however, is the product of the First Council of Constantinople, of A.D. 381, and is more accurately called the Nicene-Constantinopolitan Creed. CCC 195, 242

Nihil Obstat (NEE-kihl OB-staht): (Latin: nothing obstructs) The approval of a book or writing by an official Church censor before the issuing of an imprimatur.

Nimbus (NIHM-buhs): (Latin: cloud) The artistic depiction of a person's holiness, usually represented by a round white or gold image above the head of a saintly person. The nimbus is often called the "halo"; Mary and the saints often have a nimbus in art, while Christ's holiness is often represented by a threefold nimbus recalling the Blessed Trinity.

Ninety-Five Theses (NAIN-tee-FAIV THEE-seez): A series of statements by Martin Luther, outlining what he considered to be abuses in the Catholic Church. These statements numbered ninety-five and were posted on the main door of All Saints' Church in Wittenberg, Germany, on October 31, 1517.

Noble Guards (NO-buhl GAHRDZ): At one time the highest-ranking section of the papal military service, attending the Pope at special ceremonies and distinguished by their elaborate military costume, but disbanded by Pope Paul VI in 1968.

Nocturn (NAHK-tern): (From Latin *nocturnus:* of the night) Originally, the whole of the night office (Matins and Lauds). Later, a part of Matins (three nocturns on feasts, one nocturn on ferias). Among the monks, two nocturns were usual (up to twelve psalms and readings for Matins).

Nomocanons (no-mo-KA-nuhnz): Various collections of canons or legislation on ecclesiastical affairs gathered from both civil and ecclesiastical sources.

Non-Christian Religions, Declaration on the Relationship of the Church to: See Nostra Aetate

Nonconsummation (NAHN-kahn-suh-MAY-shuhn): The noncompletion of the act of sexual intercourse after marital consent has been exchanged. A nonconsummated marriage between baptized Catholics is considered sacramental but can be dissolved by the Holy See. **Cf. CCC 1640**

None (NON): (From Latin *ad [horam] nonam:* at the ninth [hour]) The canonical prayer offered at or around the ninth hour of the day, i.e., 3:00 P.M. Before the revision of the Divine Office at Vatican II, None was obligatory. After the revision, None was required only among contemplative religious. It has the following structure: "O God, come to my assistance. O Lord, make haste to help me"; a hymn (referring to the coming end of labor and imminent dusk as a portent of life's end); three brief psalms or three sections of a longer psalm; a brief selection from Sacred Scripture; verse, response, collect; "Let us bless the Lord. Thanks be to God."

Non Expedit (NON EHKS-pay-diht): (Latin: it is not expedient) Phrase used to indicate that a certain act or action should not be performed at a certain time. Used now as a response to petitions or requests to the Holy See.

North American College (NAWRTH uh-MEHR-ih-kuhn KAH-lehdzh): Founded in Rome on December 5, 1859, by the bishops of the United States, to serve as a residence and house of formation for American seminarians and graduate priests.

North American Martyrs (NAWRTH uh-MEHR-ih-kuhn MAHR-ters): The eight Jesuit missionaries who were tortured and martyred between 1642 and 1649 while engaged in evangelizing the native American population of present-day upstate New York and southeast Canada; canonized in 1930, their feast is October 19. Bl. Kateri Tekakwitha, the Lily of the Mohawks, is representative of the success of their efforts. They are venerated at two shrines: in Midland, Ontario, and in Auriesville, New York. The martyrs are René Goupil, Isaac Jogues, Jean Lalande, Jean de Brébeuf, Antoine Daniel, Gabriel Lalement, Charles Gamier, and Noël Chabanel.

North Door (NAWRTH DOR): That opening or portal of an iconostasis situated to the right of the celebrant as he stands facing the central altar or east in a church of the Byzantine Rite. The altar, whether it is actually geographic east or not, is considered the church's eastern point. Hence, all other points take their position from the altar. The door, then, to the celebrant's left would be the North Door; the nave, west; and the sanctuary, east. From the east rose Christ, the Sun of

Justice. Facing east at prayer is a common element in many faiths and has been retained as an orientation for the church building in the Byzantine ritual. The central doors of the icon screen are called the Holy or Royal Doors (q.v.), since Christ the King of Glory passes through in Word and Sacrament. Only a bishop, priest, or deacon may use the central doors; the northern and southern doors are commonly used by the deacons, lower clergy, and servers.

Nostra Actate (NO strah ay-TAH-tay): A declaration issued by the Second Vatican Council on "The Relation of the Church to Non-Christian Religions," urging all Christians to act in a spirit of charity by promoting fellowship and goodwill with those who do not hold to the Christian Faith. **Cf. CCC 839-845**

Novatianism (no-VAY-shuhn-ih-zuhm): Heresy that resulted in schism, promoted by Novatian (b. ca. A.D. 200), one of the first Christian theologians to write in Latin and the first man to establish himself as an antipope, in A.D. 251. He was a rigorist who held that the Church as a society of saints could have no place for mortal sinners, despite the attempt at repentance; he especially condemned the lapsed who had renounced the Faith during persecution, since pardon would compromise God's judgment. Condemned by Pope Cornelius and a Roman synod, he died in 258.

Novena (no-VEE-nuh): A period of nine consecutive days or one day for nine consecutive weeks in which a person prays according to a certain formula. Usually, these prayers are for a particular intention or in honor of a particular saint, or to highlight a mystery in Christ's life. The practice first developed in the seventeenth century, but the spirit of the novena stretches back much further, recalling the period of time (nine days) between the Ascension of Our Lord and the descent of the Holy Spirit at Pentecost.

Novice (NAH-vihs): According to the Code of Canon Law, a novice is one (male or female) who has begun a period of preparation and formation in the novitiate of a religious institute under the guidance of a master or mistress of novices. In a period that may last one or two years, novices discern if indeed they have vocations to religious life. This period of time allows superiors an opportunity to know the candidates and express a judgment about their suitability for religious life. At the conclusion of the novitiate period, novices either leave or make temporary vows of poverty, chastity, and obedience. The relevant canons in the Code of Canon Law are 646 and 652.

Novitiate (no-VIH-shee-eht): 1. The period of formation and probation of those desiring to enter a religious community. 2. The place at which religious novices reside; usually the novitiate is attached to the community's residence.

Novus Ordo Mass: See Order of Mass, New

Nuclear Deterrence, Morality of (mo-RAL-ih-tee uhv NÖÖ-klee-er dee-TER-ehnts): The debate over whether or not it is moral to build and possess nuclear weapons, which have tremendous destructive power, for the purpose of defending one's country and deterring one's enemies from aggression. Some justify such weapons as a necessary and last resort to defend the innocent, while others contend that such power will inevitably be abused; furthermore, this latter group claims that these weapons are indiscriminate because they could easily kill the innocent, even if they are directed at military targets. The Church has not condemned the possession of nuclear weapons, yet she gravely cautions that countries must work for an eventual verifiable disarmament. Cf. CCC 2315

Nullity: See Annulment.

Numbers, Book of (BØØK uhv NUHM-berz): Fourth book of the O.T. Pentateuch; its name translates the Septuagint title for this book, *arithmoi,* so called for the census accounts and other enumerations that occur throughout the book, although most of the book is devoted to legislation related to the Covenant and historical narrative that recounts the rebellious actions of God's Chosen People in their failure to trust God, Moses, and the priests.

Nun (NUHN): In its strictest sense, a woman who belongs to a religious order with solemn vows, but it is commonly used to refer to any woman religious. **Cf. CCC 924, 2687**

Nunc Dimittis (NØØNK dee-MEE-tihs): At the Presentation of the Infant Jesus in the Temple by His Mother, Mary, and foster father, Joseph, Simeon rejoiced in Christ as "a light for revelation to the Gentiles, and for glory to thy people Israel" (Lk 2:32). Near the end of Compline (Night Prayer), the *Nunc Dimittis* is used as the N.T. Canticle. Simeon, who had long awaited the consolation of the Lord, could now be dismissed — having seen the Infant Savior and held Him aloft.

Nunciature (NUHN-see-uh-tshcr): The official offices and often residence of a papal representative with the title of nuncio or pro-nuncio.

Nuncio (NUHN-see-o): The papal representative or ambassador to one of the countries that was a signatory to the Convention of Vienna in 1815, always named dean of the diplomatic corps in that country.

Nuptial Mass and Blessing (NUHP-shuhl MAS and BLEH sihng): The liturgical service consisting of a special Mass and blessing at which a couple exchange marital consent.

O

Oak, Synod of The (SIH-nuhd uhv *thee* OK): Theophilus, Patriarch of Alexandria at the dawn of the fifth century, had censured a group of Origenist priests. These priests turned to St. John Chrysostom, then Patriarch of Constantinople, who received them but withheld ecclesiastical communion with them. Incensed at even this show of prudence by the Constantinopolitan prelate, however, Theophilus organized thirty-six bishops (including more than twenty of his suffragans from Egypt) into a canonically illegal synod in a suburban area of Constantinople known as The Oak. After reciting a long (and at times comical) list of crimes alleged against the saint, the Synod fathers demanded John's presence, which he calmly denied them. (His messengers, incidentally, were beaten by Theophilus's synod.) Notwithstanding the clear illegality of their proceeding, the empress upheld the base condemnation of Chrysostom and ordered him into exile at the direction of the Synod of The Oak. An earthquake, among other things, convinced the authorities to recall the saint sometime later, but it was too late. The Greek Father had died in exile from his beloved Church in 407.

O Antiphons (O AN-tih-fahnz): Antiphons chanted before and after the Gospel Canticle of the Blessed Virgin Mary (the *Magnificat*) between December 17 and December 23 (late Advent). Each antiphon begins with the vocative "O" and continues with a title given to Christ, derived from the O.T. prophecies He fulfilled. The O Antiphons are as follows: December 17, *O Sapientia* (O Wisdom); December 18, *O Adonai* (O Lord of Might); December 19, *O Radix Jesse* (O Flower of Jesse's Stem); December 20, *O Clavis Davidica* (O Key of David); December 21, *O Oriens* (O Rising Dawn); December 22, *O Rex Gentium* (O King of Nations); December 23, *O Emmanuel.*

Oath (OTH): A solemn declaration in God's Name, either referring to past or present fact (assertory) or stating the sincerity of future actions (promissory). Oaths are to be taken only for an important and necessary reason, since they are discouraged by Holy Scripture (Mt 5:33-37; Jas 5:12). CCC 2149-2155

Oath of Succession (OTH uhv suhk-SEH-shuhn): An oath put to various national leaders by England's King Henry VIII obliging them to recognize the children of his wife Anne as lawful heirs and not those of his true wife, Catherine.

Obadiah (o-buh-DAI-uh): Shortest book in the O.T., only twenty-one verses long, but one of the most vigorous in its language and message, as it castigates the arrogance of the Edomites for their invasion of Judah, taking advantage of the fall of Jerusalem in 587 B.C.; Obadiah predicts their downfall when, on "The Day of the Lord," God will pass judgment on all the nations and Israel will be restored.

Obedience (o-BEE-dee-ehnts): (Latin *obaudire:* to listen, to hear with careful attention) The moral virtue by which one submits to the will or law of one in exercise of legitimate authority. Obedience may be demanded for a variety of reasons: a vow, a contract, religious piety, or the office of one in authority. As a virtue, obedience is pleasing to God because the sacrifice of one's will is chosen out of love for God. In the Bible, to obey is really to "hear" the expressed will of God by responding to it completely and without hesitation (Gn 22:18; Ex 15:26; Dt 4:1-6; 5:31-33; Mt 7:21; Mk 3:35; Jn 12:47; Rom 2:13). The very creed of Israel, recited by the Jewish people as their daily prayer, is the articulation of this faithful hearing that provokes obedience: "Hear, O Israel, the Lord our God, the Lord is one" (Dt 6:4). CCC 915, 1269, 1733, 1790, 1900, 2053, 2216-2217, 2240, 2251

Obedience of Faith (o-BEE-dee-ehnts uhv FAYTH): While the theological virtues of faith, hope, and charity bring the virtue of obedience to life, this is especially true of faith (Rom 1:5; 16:25-26; 2 Cor 10:5-6). Thus, God's sovereign will is revealed as dynamic in the very Person of Jesus Christ, such that faith is actually brought about in the person seeking God; the response to God's will is, in effect, obedience in the sense of a graced capacity to "hear" God and to respond without any reservation. Each Christian's first obedience must be to God (Acts 4:18-21; 5:27-32), so that the human respondent entrusts his whole self entirely to God, "making 'the full submission of intellect and will to God, who reveals' and willingly assenting to the Revelation given by him" (DV, n. 5). The authority of the Church likewise stems from the obedience owed to Christ, now delegated to His vicar and the Church hierarchy (Gal 1:11-12; 1 Cor 4:1-3). **CCC 143-149, 1831, 2087, 2098, 2135, 2340, 2716, 2825**

Oblates (AH-blayts): (From a form of the Latin *offerre:* to offer) 1. Those religious communities of men and women whose members are not solemnly professed but are dedicated to God under poverty, chastity, and obedience. 2. The young boys offered by their families to Benedictine communities. The Council of Trent forbade this practice for boys under ten. 3. Men and women who were not strictly professed but lived in religious communities while laboring at menial chores. 4. Members of "third orders" (secular orders) who are not solemnly professed but try to live poverty, chastity, and obedience in their particular state in life.

Oblation (ah-BLAY-shuhn): (Latin *oblatio:* offering) Gift to be offered, especially the offering of the Mass, at which the priest on behalf of the Church offers bread and wine to God, Who grants the priest the power to change them into the Body, Blood, Soul, and Divinity of Jesus Christ. **Cf. CCC 529, 1350**

Obreption (ahb-REHP-shuhn): (From Latin *obreptio:* act of stealing up on) A statement of falsehood about some matter contained in a petition for a rescript of some kind; attempt to receive a dispensation or other favor by fraud.

Obscenity (ahb-SEHN-ih-tee): (From Latin: disruptive) Oral, written, or visual materials that are against good manners, refinement, and the virtue of holy purity. Obscene materials involve the manipulation of others, usually women and children, contrary to chastity. Such materials are capable of great harm, especially against young people.

Obsession (ahb-SEH-shuhn): (From Latin *obsidere:* to besiege) An idea that persistently invades and engrosses the mind; an involuntary and irrational preoccupation with objects, persons, internal states, or emotions. In rare cases, obsessions may have a diabolical cause, but most often this condition is best treated by a combination of spiritual direction and psychological therapy.

Obsession, Diabolical (dai-uh-BAHL-ih-kuhl ahb-SEH-shuhn): Extraordinary state of mind in one who is seriously molested by evil spirits in an external manner more than simple temptation.

Occasion of Sin (o-KAY-zhuhn uhv SIHN): A person, place, or thing that is an attraction and enticement to sin; it may be either a situation that always leads to sin or one that usually leads to sin. One is obliged to avoid occasions of sin or, if they cannot be avoided completely, to make them as "remote" as possible. Cf. CCC 2847

Occult (ah-KUHLT): (From Latin: concealed) Something hidden or secret, but especially applied to the practice of magic through witchcraft or other "supernatural arts" (cf. Occultism). Cf. CCC 2117

Occult, Canonically (ka-NAH-nih-kuhl-ee ah-KUHLT): A canonical term literally meaning "secret," referring to a fact that is not provable in the external forum and yet is recognized by law.

Occult Compensation (ah-KUHLT kahm-pen-SAY-shuhn): The hidden taking of goods from one who has first unjustly taken possession of them when they actually belong to the first person. Although this practice is moral, it can easily lead to abuse; it can only be used as a last resort.

Occultism (ah-KUHLT-ih-zuhm): Practices involving ceremonies, rituals, chants, incantations, other cult-related activities, aimed at affecting the course of nature or knowing the future, that are associated with superstition, witchcraft, voodoo, Satanism, etc. The Church condemns these practices because they signal a desire to control the future rather than to trust in God's never-failing providence. **CCC 2117**

Occurrence (uh-KER-ehnts): The falling of two feasts on the same day of the liturgical calendar. When this happens, the higher-ranked feast is celebrated. A solemnity may be transferred to the closest day that is free on the liturgical calendar.

Octave (AHK-tehv): (Latin: eight) In liturgical usage, the practice of celebrating a major feast on the feast day itself and for seven days following. The entire period is called an octave and the eighth day the octave day. The practice has roots in the O.T. where feasts like Passover and Tabernacles are described as extended beyond the day itself. The celebration of an octave is signified by the use of the *Gloria* at Mass, the *Te Deum* at the Office of Readings, and the use of the word "today" in some prayers and prefaces that come from the day itself.

Ode (OD): (Greek *hodos:* way or road) In the Eastern liturgy, one of the nine sections of a canon, composed of a hirmos and a certain number of troparia, the last of which is called a Theotokion or Megalynarion, since it contains an invocation to the Mother of God.

Odor of Sanctity: See Sanctity, Odor of

Oecumenical: See Ecumenical

Offertory (AW-fer-taw-ree): The part of the Mass when the gifts of bread and wine are presented to the priest, who then places them on the altar for their transubstantiation into the Body and Blood of Christ. In the Tridentine Mass, or the Mass of Pope St. Pius V, the Offertory was considered one of the three principal parts of the Mass, along with the Consecration and Communion of the priest. In the Mass authorized by the Second Vatican Council, the Offertory is better termed the "Presentation of the Gifts." Along with the gifts of bread and wine, money or other gifts for the poor may be presented to the priest or deacon by the faithful. The prayers used at the Preparation of the Gifts are derived from Jewish table prayers. CCC 1333, 1350

Offertory Collection (AW-fer-taw-ree kuh-LEHK-shuhn): The taking up of monetary gifts at Mass at the beginning of the Liturgy of the Eucharist. In the past, the faithful brought money but especially the fruits of their toil — cattle, vegetables, fruits, etc. Each member of the Church is obliged to give according to his means and to be generous. CCC 1351

Office (AW-fihs): 1. The full cycle of canonical "Hours," called the Divine Office. 2. Any portion of the Divine Office. 3. The entire day's liturgy (Mass and Liturgy of the Hours all together). 4. Any public celebration of ecclesial prayer. 5. A ministry or function in the Church.

Office, Ecclesiastical (eh-KLEE-zee-AS-tih-kuhl AW-fihs): A function or position in the Church founded in either divine or ecclesiastical law and exercised in a stable manner for a spiritual purpose.

Office of the Dead (AW-fihs uhv *th*uh DEHD): The portion of the Liturgy of the Hours chanted or recited for the happy repose of the deceased. It is prayed on All Souls' Day and may be used after a death.

Official Catholic Directory of the United States (uh-FIH-shuhl KATH-uh-lihk duh-REHK-to-ree uhv *th*uh yoö-NAI-tehd STAYTS): An official annual publication listing all pertinent information concerning the Catholic Church in the United States, including all clergy, dioceses, parishes, institutions, religious orders and congregations, ordinations, necrology, and census information.

Oils, Holy (HO-lee OILZ): Used for liturgical purposes in the Church as a continuation of the practices described in the O.T. (Lv 8:12; 1 Sm 10:1, 16:13). These oils are blessed by the bishop for use in his diocese on Holy Thursday. Parishes generally conserve their oils in the aumbry, while priests usually keep their oils in an oil stock, a cylindrical metal case made with three separate compartments, each marked with the initials of the Latin name for the oil contained: *Oleum Sanctorum,* the oil of catechumens, used for Baptism; *Sacrum Chrisma,* sacred chrism, used in Baptism, Confirmation, the ordination of a priest, the consecration of a bishop, and in the dedication of churches and altars; *Oleum Infirmorum,* the oil of the sick, used in the Sacrament of the Anointing of the Sick. Cf. CCC 695, 1183, 1237, 1241, 1289, 1293-1294

Old Believers (OLD buh-LEEV-erz): Russian Orthodox Christians who dissented from the liturgical reforms carried out by Nikon, Patriarch of Moscow (1605-1681). These reforms brought Russian practice into line with Greek practice but were imposed by the assistance of State power and thus provoked opposition. The Old Believers were excommunicated in 1667. Almost two hundred years later, one sect of the Old Believers, the *Popoutsy,* were finally able to establish a hierarchy when they were joined by the deposed Bishop Ambrose of Bosnia. They were recognized by the State in 1881.

Old Catholics (OLD KATH-uh-lihks): A name given to several sects (Utrecht, Holland, Catholic Church; Polish National Church in the United States; and some German, Austrian, and Swiss Catholics) who left the Catholic Church because they rejected the dogma of papal infallibility defined by the First Vatican Council in 1870. They also do not accept papal primacy, obligatory auricular confession, a celibate clergy, compulsory fast days, indulgences, veneration of the saints, relics and images, sacramentals, mixed marriages, and pilgrimages. Further, they only accept the teaching of the first seven ecumenical councils.

Ombrellino (ahm-breh-LEE-no): (Italian: little umbrella) 1. The small canopy formerly required to be held over the Blessed Sacrament when it was exposed in the monstrance and moved from one place to another. 2. A large canopy, supported by six pole-bearers, was used when the Holy Eucharist was moved from one place to another during processions.

Omega Point: See Teilhardism

Omnipotence (ahm-NIH-po-tehnts): (From Latin: all + power) The unlimited power and authority of God, which He exercises in wisdom and love for the fulfillment of His divine will. CCC 268-278

Omnipresence (ahm-nih-PREHZ-ehnts): (From Latin: all + presence) Limitless presence of God in the universe He has created. Cf. CCC 239

Omniscience (ahm-NIH-shehnts): (Latin: all + knowledge) The unlimited knowledge of all things by God, in which there is no past, present, or future. Although He knows infallibly all that will happen, His knowledge does not take away human free will. CCC 214-217

Omophorion (ahm-o-FO-ree-ahn): (Greek: same light) Liturgical vestment worn by Byzantine, Armenian, and Coptic Rite bishops and archbishops in recognition of their hierarchical office. It consists of a broad strip of richly ornamented cloth, which is wrapped loosely around the neck so that one end hangs over the left shoulder in the front and the other over the left shoulder to the back; it corresponds to the pallium of the Latin Rite.

Only-Begotten One (OWN-lee bee-GAH-tehn WUHN): Jesus Christ, Son of God and Son of Mary, is the "Only-Begotten One," meaning that He and the Father are of the same substance and that Christ proceeds from the Father (no inequality is implied); that He obediently becomes flesh for "the life of the world"; that Christ is God but also our loving Savior and Brother. Cf. CCC 52, 246, 460, 467, 469

Onomasticon (o-no-MAS-tee-kahn): A list in alphabetical order of over three hundred geographical names mentioned in the Bible, compiled originally by Eusebius of Caesarea about A.D. 330, most commonly transmitted in its Latin translation, together with additions made by St. Jerome. Like the Medeba Map of Palestine, the mosaic floor of a church dating from the sixth century in modern Jordan, the onomasticon with its record of the traditional location of biblical sites is a valuable aid in the study of biblical geography and the science of biblical topography.

Ontologism (ahn-TAHL-uh-dzhih-zuhm): (Greek: being + study) A philosophical theory that holds that the knowledge of God is immediate and intuitive, and that all other human knowledge is dependent upon this. It was condemned by Pope Pius IX in 1861.

Ontology (ahn-TAHL-uh-dzhee): Branch of metaphysics (q.v.) studying the nature and relations of existence.

Oplatki (o-PLAHT-kee): A wafer-thin piece of unleavened bread, similar to a Communion host, blessed but not consecrated, which is exchanged among families at Christmas time. This Polish custom is derived from the Jewish Passover meal and is a symbol of the welcoming of Christ.

Optatam Totius (op-TAH-tahm to-TEE-øøs): (Latin: desired of all) The Decree on the Training of Priests of the Second Vatican Council, issued on October 28, 1965; it affirms that the true renewal of the whole Church depends on the training of priests prepared for "a priestly ministry animated by the spirit of Christ." The decree considers the fostering of priestly vocations, the important role of seminaries, the spiritual formation of those preparing for priesthood, the revision of seminary curricula, and the training for pastoral work.

Opus Dei (O-puhs DAY-ee): (Latin: work of God) 1. An association primarily of Catholic laity who seek to promote the universal call to holiness and the exercise of a personal apostolate in the ordinary circumstances of everyday life, particularly through one's ordinary work. Founded in Madrid by Bl. Josemaría Escrivá de Balaguer (beatified on May 17, 1992) on October 2, 1928, Opus Dei was accorded full pontifical approval on June 16, 1950, and was erected as a personal prelature by Pope John Paul II in 1982. Opus Dei is international in scope, serving the universal Church by its participation in the local church. The prelate has ordinary hierarchical jurisdiction, while the lay members remain subject to the local Ordinary of the diocese in which they live; they likewise retain full personal freedom and their own responsibility in all that pertains to their secular lives and work. Priests of the prelature are drawn solely from the lay membership and serve the membership and cooperators in the work, which may include non-Catholics. Diocesan priests who wish to share in the spirituality of the work may be associated with Opus Dei in the Priestly Society of the Holy Cross, while remaining fully under the jurisdiction of their own bishop. A specific ministry entrusted to the priests of Opus Dei by the Holy See is the spiritual direction of diocesan priests. Opus Dei embraces over seventy-five thousand lay members, thirteen hundred priests, and three hundred fifty seminarians. 2. The title used by the Benedictines for the Liturgy of the Hours in recognition of prayer as a special duty and privilege of monks, and one especially pleasing to God.

Orange, Councils of (KAUN-sihlz uhv o-RAHNZH): Two regional councils held in southern France in A.D. 441 and 529. The first dealt with general matters of discipline, and the second with Semi-Pelagianism (q.v.). (Cf. also Pelagianism.)

Orante (o-RAHN-tay): (Latin *orans:* praying) A figure depicted in early Christian art in the classical attitude of prayer, the *orante* has his or her hands lifted up, with palms facing outward, the elbows slightly bent. The physical demeanor of the *orante* is meant to convey an attitude of adoration and praise; as the hands are lifted up, so the *orante*'s mind and heart are raised to God. The palms are open to show an offering of thanks, but also to keep the sacred at a distance, lest the *orante* be guilty of profaning the presence of the sacred by approaching too closely. The most famous depiction of the *orante* is seen in the fresco painting of the three praying men in the Catacombs of Priscilla, Rome.

Orarion (o-RAHR-ee-ahn): The deacon's stole in the Byzantine Rite.

Orate, Fratres (o-RAH-tay, FRAH-trehz): (Latin: Pray, brethren) The formal invitation to prayer recited by the celebrant to the congregation before the Prayer over the Gifts at Mass. The priest asks the people to pray that his sacrifice and theirs may be acceptable to God.

Oratorio (O-ruh-TO-ree-o): (Latin, Italian: eloquence) Musical composition on sacred texts, employing soloists, chorus, and frequently an orchestra (e.g., Handel's *Messiah* or the Passion music of Bach); not liturgical but sometimes performed in a church with permission.

Oratory (O-ruh-to-ree): A place set aside by the bishop or diocese for divine worship. However, the bishop and certain liturgical laws may limit the liturgical ceremonies to be performed in an oratory, which is not strictly meant for solemn public use. There are three types: (1) *public,* for religious communities; (2) *semipublic,* for some specific groups; (3) *private,* for a family or individual.

Order (OR-der): (Latin *ordo:* row, rank) 1. The arrangement or sequence of certain parts that comprise a whole, or a particular level of reality. 2. The office of bishop, priest, or deacon, conferred sacramentally. 3. A religious community of men or women who have professed solemn vows. 4. A prescribed form of worship. Cf. CCC 299, 341, 1608

Order of Christian Funerals (OR-der uhv KRIHS-tshuhn FYÖÖ-ner-uhlz): The title given to the revised English translation and pastoral rearrangement of the *Ordo Exsequiarum* (post-Vatican II revision of the burial rites), developed by the International Committee on English in the Liturgy and authorized by the Holy See. It envisions three places of prayer (*stationes* in Latin): (1) wake service in the home of the deceased, funeral parlor, or church; (2) funeral liturgy (usually with Mass, though without Mass on those days that prohibit Mass or when a Funeral Mass is postponed to a later time); (3) committal. The current ritual provides for prayer at three other times: (1) with the family; (2) gathering in the presence of the body; (3) transferral to the church. The ritual also offers rites for the burial of children, Morning and Evening Prayer for the Dead from the Liturgy of the Hours.

Order of Mass, New (NÖÖ OR-der uhv MAS): (Latin *novus ordo:* new order) The texts and rites for the celebration of the Holy Eucharist in accord with the teaching of Vatican II and the documents issued by Pope Paul VI in 1969. These texts and rites include the Lectionary and Sacramentary (or Missal of Paul VI, as it is sometimes known). The Lectionary contains a three-year cycle of readings for Sundays, a two-year cycle for weekdays, and changes in the readings assigned for solemnities, feasts, and memorials. Modifications were also made in the Proper of the Seasons, the Proper of the Saints, the Common of Saints, Ritual Masses, Votive Masses, and other texts for Advent, Christmas, Lent, and Easter.

Orders, Holy: See Orders, Sacrament of Holy

Orders, Major: See Orders, Sacrament of Holy

Orders, Minor: See Minor Orders

Orders, Sacrament of Holy (SA-kruh-mehnt uhv HO-lee OR-derz): One of the seven sacraments, in which a bishop imposes hands and prays to confer spiritual power and grace to carry out the ordained ministry of the Church. Major Orders are comprised of the offices of deacon, priest, and bishop. CCC 1536-1600

Ordinariate (or-dih-NEHR-ee-uht): An ecclesiastical division similar to a diocese, yet not defined by geographic boundaries. Used almost exclusively to refer to military diocceses.

Ordinary (OR-dih-nerh-ee): A person placed in authority over a particular church (diocese) or its equivalent. Also, any person who possesses ordinary executive power, i.e., the power attached to an office. Bishops, major religious superiors, vicars general, and vicars episcopal are examples.

Ordinary Medical Treatments (OR-dih-nehr-ee MEH-dih-kuhl TREET-mehnts): Kinds of medical care that aim at continuing human life and promoting the good of one's life that are not "extraordinary" in themselves and, therefore, must be employed. Ordinary care: (1) is not extremely painful for the patient; (2) is not highly expensive; (3) is readily available; (4) is expected to be successful; (5) includes the "daily" maintenance of the patient (i.e., nutrition, hydration, hygienic procedures, protection from harm, and psychological support). **CCC 2279; cf. 2278**

Ordination (or-dih-NAY-shuhn): The act of consecrating or setting apart of men to be the sacred ministers for the worship of God and for the sanctification of all people. (Cf. Orders, Sacrament of Holy; Minor Orders, etc.) **CCC 1538**

Ordination of Women: See Women, Ordination of

Ordo (OR-do): (Latin: order, rank) A manual published annually by an archdiocese or diocese, or jointly by an archdiocese with its suffragan sees. It prescribes the dates of liturgical seasons and movable feasts, determining the rank and kind of festivity and liturgical colors to be used for the celebration of Mass and the Liturgy of the Hours. The ordo also lists penitential regulations, pastoral and liturgical notes, and a necrology of the clergy.

Ordo, Novus: See Order of Mass, New

Organ Transplants (OR-guhn TRANS-plants): Morally, the transplanting of organs from one person to another is permissible provided that: (1) it is done with the full consent of concerned parties and (2) it is not expected to result in the death or essential mutilation of the donor. Advances in methods and technology have increased the range of transplant possibilities in recent years. **CCC 2296**

Oriental Churches, Congregation for the (kahn-gruh-GAY-shuhn for *th*ee AW-ree-EHN-tuhl TSHERTSH-ehz): A Roman dicastery that oversees the matters of the Oriental Churches. The C.I.C. (Can. 360) identifies the Congregation for the Oriental Churches as the body that has jurisdiction over the matters of the Oriental Churches. A cardinal-prefect heads the congregation, with other members of the hierarchy as members of this congregation. Inside the congregation is a separate office for each of the twenty Eastern Catholic Churches. The congregation has all the faculties that are exercised individually for Latin Catholics in separate congregations for bishops, clergy, religious, and secular institutes, along with Catholic education.

Orientalium Ecclesiarum (O-ree-ehn-TAH-lee-øøm eh-klay-zee-AHR-øøm): The Decree on the Eastern Churches at the Second Vatican Council, issued on November 21, 1964, it asserts the equality of the Eastern Churches with the Western Church within the one Catholic Church. The document urges respect for and preservation of lawful liturgical rites and calls for an increased knowledge and understanding of the customs of the Eastern Churches. Significant features of this document include: article 18, which says marriages between Eastern Catholics and non-Catholic Eastern Christians before an Orthodox priest are valid; article 24, which urges unity through prayer; article 25, which allows for individual Eastern non-Catholics to become Catholics by a simple profession of faith. Articles 26-29 provide principles for worship by Catholics and non-Catholic Eastern Christians together. Article 27 establishes the circumstances under which Catholics may receive the sacraments from non-Catholic Eastern priests, and non-Catholic Eastern Christians from Catholic priests.

Original Sin (o-RIDZH-ih-nuhl SIHN): The sin of Adam and Eve (Gn 2:8—3:24), personal to them and passed on to all humans as a state of privation of grace. Despite that privation, the related wounding of human nature, and the weakening of natural human powers, Original Sin leaves unchanged all that humanity is by nature and potential. The scriptural basis for the doctrine was laid out by St. Paul in Rom 5:12-21 and 1 Cor 15:21 ff. Original Sin is remitted by Baptism and incorporation in Christ, through whom grace is given to persons. Pope John Paul II, while describing Original Sin during a general audience on October 1, 1986, called it "the absence of sanctifying grace in nature which has been diverted from its supernatural end." CCC 37, 215, 388-406, 409, 412, 1250, 1607, 1609, 1707, 2259, 2515

Orléans, Councils of (KAUN-sihlz uhv OR-lay-AHN): Six national, not ecumenical, councils held between 511 and 549 in the city of Orléans, France, at the direction of the first Christian king of the Franks, Clovis; legislation was enacted that gave structure to the Church in Gaul, promoted priestly celibacy, and encouraged charitable efforts by Christians.

Orphrey (OR-free): (From Latin *auriphrygium:* gold embroidery) A long, embroidered gold band that decorates sacred vestments.

Orthodox Church (OR-thuh-dahks TSHERTSH): That body of Eastern Christian believers who have a valid sacramental and hierarchical system but became separated from full communion with the Catholic Church by not acknowledging the Pope as Supreme Shepherd of the Church. Separation from the Catholic Church is traced to July 16, 1054, when Cardinal Humbert, the head of a papal delegation in Constantinople, placed a document of excommunication on the altar of Hagia Sophia, the cathedral church of Constantinople. The excommunication resulted in part from a disagreement between East and West over the *filioque* phrase ("and the Son") in the Creed. This led to a schism between East and West (cf. Schism, Eastern), which continues up to the present day. A symbolic gesture of reconciliation was offered by Pope Paul VI and Patriarch Athenagoras in 1966 when they mutually lifted the excommunications of their eleventh-century predecessors. While the Patriarch of Constantinople remains the visible head of Orthodoxy, Orthodoxy is now distinguished along national lines with many autonomous churches. The Orthodox accept only the first seven ecumenical councils (from Nicaea I to Nicaea II); they approve of the remarriage of divorced persons and are skeptical of the Catholic dogmas of purgatory, papal infallibility, and the Immaculate Conception. Cf. CCC 247, 836

Orthodoxy, Feast of (FEEST uhv OR-thuh-dahk-see): An observance in the Byzantine Rite on the First Sunday of Lent marking the definition of the Second Council of Nicaea (787), whereby the grounds for venerating images (icons) and relics was established. The Second Council of Nicaea distinguished between adoration, which is due to God alone (cf. latria), and veneration, which can be given to an icon or relic. The teaching of Nicaea II brought to an end the heresy of iconoclasm, or image-breaking.

O Salutaris (O sah-löö-TAH-rihs): (Latin: from the first two words of the hymn *O Salutaris Hostia,* "O Saving Victim") These words are taken from the last two verses of a hymn attributed to St. Thomas Aquinas (*Verbum Supernum Prodiens,* "The heavenly Word proceeding forth"). St. Thomas is thought to have written the hymn at the request of Pope Urban IV, who instituted the Feast of Corpus Christi. The last two verses of this hymn are often used at Exposition of the Blessed Sacrament. The words of the hymn are as follows: "O Saving Victim, op'ning wide / The gate of heav'n to men below: / Our foes press on from every side, / Thine aid supply, Thy strength bestow. / To Thy great Name be endless praise, / Immortal Godhead, One in Three, /O grant us endless length of days / In our true native land with Thee. Amen."

Osservatore Romano, L': See L'Osservatore Romano

Ostensorium (ah-stehn-SO-ree-uhm): (From Latin: show) Another name for the monstrance (q.v.), a vessel used to hold the Sacred Host during Eucharistic processions or Exposition and Benediction of the Blessed Sacrament.

Ostiarius (os-tee-AH-ree-øøs): (Latin: porter, doorkeeper) The ancient order of porter. The porter had the responsibility of taking care of the physical plant of the church building and thus the keys to the doors (hence the name). It was one of four minor orders (the other three being lector, exorcist, and acolyte) conferred upon candidates for the priesthood. Pope Paul VI suppressed the orders of exorcist and porter, along with the major order of subdeacon, in his Apostolic Letter *Ministeria Quaedam* of August 15, 1972.

Ostpolitik (AWST-paw-lih-TEEK): (German) The name given, when Communism dominated the countries of Eastern Europe, to the Holy See's policy of openness toward those governments, in an attempt to improve Church-State relations and to gain some religious freedom for those who lived under the Communist system.

Our Father: See Lord's Prayer

Our Lady (AUR LAY-dee): The title used for the Mother of God that has been common for many centuries to illustrate her close relationship with her Son, "Our Lord." The familiar French title *Notre Dame* means "Our Lady." (Cf. Mary, Blessed Virgin.)

Oxford Movement (AUKS-ferd MÖÖV-mehnt): A movement within the Church of England, or Anglican Church, that began in 1833 at Oxford University, through the efforts of Dr. John Keble to restore to that body some of the elements that had been lost after the Reformation: apostolic succession of the episcopacy, sacramental life, and restoration of liturgy and tradition, particularly with emphasis on the Fathers of the Church. Adherents came to include R. H. Froude, John Henry Newman, Edward B. Pusey, and R. Wilberforce; while they sought to return the Church of England to the apostolic origins of Christianity, many saw the movement as thinly disguised Romanism, deserving of censure by the Established Church. Aware that their view of Anglicanism as a distinct but full expression of Catholic Faith would never gain broad acceptance among their own, some of the leaders (e.g., W. G. Ward and F. Faber) left the Oxford Movement and became Catholics, the most notable dissenter being Newman, who was eventually made a cardinal.

P

Pacem in Terris (PAH-tshehm ihn TEH-rees): (Latin: Peace on Earth) Encyclical issued by Pope John XXIII in 1963, emphasizing the importance of peace and the maintenance and protection of human dignity. This letter teaches that if the kingdom of Christ is to be realized on earth, peace must exist between individuals, between individuals and governments, and between governments.

Pacifism (PA-sih-fih-zuhm): The belief that all war is immoral and contrary to the example and words of Our Lord (cf. Mt 5:39). Pacifists contend that no war is ever upright because it cannot be waged without an inner hatred. Catholic moral theology seeks to foster peace without counseling pacificism. Cf. CCC 2307-2314

Pactum Callixtinum (PAHK-tøøm kah-leeks-TEE-nøøm): (Latin: Pact of Calixtus) The agreement (also called the "Concordat of Worms") between Pope Calixtus II and Henry IV, who was the Holy Roman Emperor. Made in 1122 and confirmed by the First Lateran Council in 1123, the agreement ended the control that secular heads of State possessed over ecclesiastical appointments.

Paganism (PAY-guhn-ih-zuhm): Polytheistic religions, such as those of the ancient Roman or Greek civilizations, or nonrevealed religions, i.e., religions other than Christianity, Judaism, or Islam. CCC 522, 528, 781

Pain and Euthanasia (PAYN and yööth-uh-NAY-zhuh): The topic dealt with by Pope Pius XII in 1957 when answering the question of whether it was permissible to give pain-relief doses that might shorten the life of the patient. He said that such medicine could be administered provided: (1) there was no intention by anyone to end the patient's life; (2) no other means were available; (3) the dose was only given with the patient's consent; (4) the patient was devoid of outstanding obligations to himself or others; (5) the dose was proportionate to the condition of the patient. Today, medical advances have greatly eliminated the risk that certain medicines will shorten one's life. **CCC 2279**

Pain Bénit (PAN bay-NEE): (French: blessed bread) In certain cultures, the bread that is blessed and distributed to the faithful during certain times of the year, as a sign of belief in and love for Christ, and as a symbol of the unity of Christ's Body, the Church. It is a sacramental, not to be confused with the consecrated Host, which is the true Body of Christ.

Palatine (PAL-uh-tain): One of the seven hills of Rome, sacred to Pallas Athena, that served as residence to the emperors. The "Palatine Guard" came to mean imperial or papal administrative offices, while the "Palatine Library" refers to one section of the modern Vatican Library.

Palimpsest (PAL-uhm[p]-sehst): (Greek: to rub + again) A piece of parchment that has been rubbed clear of its original text so that the parchment could be reused because of the high cost of writing materials. One famous palimpsest contains some writings of Ephrem Syrus that had been written on parchments once containing the Old and New Testaments.

Pall (PAWL): 1. The piece of stiff linen, or cardboard covered with linen, usually between four and seven inches square, that covers the chalice at Mass so as to prevent dust and other particles from landing in the chalice. Often, the pall is either simply adorned with a cross or may have a colorful depiction of Our Lord, Our Lady, or some Eucharistic design. 2. The cloth that is spread over the coffin at funeral Masses, usually of the same color as the vestments used for the liturgy.

Pallium (PAL-yuhm): A circular band of white wool with two hanging pieces (front and back) decorated with six black crosses, worn over the shoulders by all metropolitan archbishops and by the Pope himself. Before the ninth century, the pallium was a ceremonial garment given to certain bishops as an honor. During the ninth century, all metropolitans wore it at pontifical liturgies. The ceremony for blessing the lambs from whose wool the pallia are woven takes place every year on January 21, the memorial of St. Agnes at the Church of Santa Agnese Fuori le Mura (outside the walls of the city of Rome). The *motu proprio* of Pope Paul VI entitled *Inter eximia episcopalis* contains provisions on the meaning and use of the pallium by metropolitan archbishops.

Palm Sunday (PAHLM SUHN-day): The secondary title (in parentheses) for the Sunday before Easter, the opening of Holy Week, Passion Sunday (the primary designation). On this day, two traditions and themes are merged. The first is the Jerusalem tradition of the blessing and procession with palms, recalling for the faithful the triumphant entry of the Savior into Jerusalem. The second tradition is the Roman one, with its solemn proclamation of the Passion, inaugurating Holy Week. Cf. CCC 560

Palms, Blessing of (BLEH-sihng uhv PAHLMZ): A ceremony that takes place on the Sunday before Easter (Passion [Palm] Sunday) before the principal Mass in which palm fronds are blessed before distribution to the faithful as a sacramental harbinger of Holy Week. Ideally, it should be done apart from the church where the Mass will be celebrated. This allows the congregation to process to the church, singing hymns to Christ the Messiah and King, recalling the triumphant entry of Christ into Jerusalem. The blessing has two forms. Following the Prayer of Blessing, the Gospel of the Lord's Entrance is proclaimed. At Masses without the procession, a solemn or simple entrance may be used.

Panagia (pa-nuh-DZHEE-uh): (Greek: all + holy, usually meaning Mary the Mother of God) 1. Encolpion or image taking the place of the pectoral cross for the Byzantine Rite bishop. 2. The Blessing at table in Eastern monasteries.

Pange Lingua (PAHN-dzhay LIHNG-gwah): (Latin: Sing, [my] tongue) Title, from the first words, of a hymn attributed to St. Thomas Aquinas honoring the Holy Eucharist, used particularly on Holy Thursday and in Eucharistic processions.

Pannykhidia (pan-ih-KEE-dyuh): (Greek: the whole night) A service for the departed in the Byzantine Rite. Originally, the pannykhidia was a vigil preceding a funeral. It could just as well be a separate memorial service today.

Pantheism (PAN-thee-ih-zuhm): (Greek: all God) The system of belief that all things are divine in nature and that God is identical with the universe, as opposed to the Catholic doctrine that God is present in all things as the cause of their being, without being identical with their substance. **CCC 285**

Pantocrator (pan-TAH-kruh-ter): (From Greek: ruler of all) Title given in the Eastern Church to Christ as the Ruler of Heaven and Earth; it corresponds to the Western title of Christ the King. In particular, the term is used of images of Christ depicted as Judge and Ruler; the most famous of these in the United States is the large mosaic of Christ the Judge behind the main altar and baldacchino (q.v.) of the Basilica of the National Shrine of the Immaculate Conception, Washington, D.C. **Cf. CCC 2749**

Papabile (pah-PAH-bi-lay): The Italian term referring to the one most likely to be elected the next Pope.

Papacy (PAY-puh-see): 1. The office of the Pope as head of the Church and sovereign of Vatican City State. 2. The duration of a particular Pope's reign. **Cf. CCC 100, 882, 892, 937, 1463, 2034**

Papal Blessing or Apostolic Blessing (PAY-puhl [a-pah-STAH-lihk] BLEH-sihng): The benediction given by the Pope at the end of liturgical and nonliturgical functions. Others may be delegated to give this blessing: cardinals, bishops, abbots, retreat masters, priests who attend the sick during their last hour, and newly ordained priests at their Solemn Mass of Thanksgiving.

Papal Chamberlain (PAY-puhl TSHAYM-ber-lehn): Honorary title bestowed on certain priests prior to 1968. Since that time, the title has been replaced by that of "Chaplain of His Holiness."

Papal Election (PAY-puhl ee-LEEK-shun): The Pope is elected by members of the College of Cardinals in a secret conclave or meeting convened ordinarily in secluded quarters of the Vatican Palace between fifteen and twenty days after the death of his predecessor. Cardinals under the age of eighty, totaling no more than one hundred twenty, are eligible to participate in the election. The conclave is usually in the Sistine Chapel, election is ordinarily by a two-thirds majority of the cardinals, and a candidate must be ordained a bishop before he is eligible to become Pontiff (q.v.). A Pope is elected for life. Ordinarily the first sign that a Pope has been elected is a plume of white smoke rising from the Vatican upon the burning of the last ballots.

Papal Flag (PAY-puhl FLAG): The official flag of the Holy See, which has two vertical stripes, yellow and white. On the white half, there is an illustration of the tiara (representing the threefold office of the Pope — teaching, sanctifying, and governing) with two crossed keys (denoting the "power of the keys" given by Jesus to St. Peter).

Papal Household (PAY-puhl HAUS-hold): A department or prefecture of the Roman Curia that manages the living arrangements of the Pope, both at home and on his travels.

Papal Letters (PAY-puhl LEH-terz): A generic term for any kind of official letter or document signed by the Pope.

Papal States (PAY-puhl STAYTS): The vast territories that, from 754 until 1870, were under the authority of the Pope. Today, the State of Vatican City (greatly reduced in size) is governed temporally by the Pope, according to terms of the 1929 Lateran Treaty.

Papal Theologian (PAY-puhl thee-uh-LO-dzhuhn): One especially proficient in theology appointed by the Pope to act as his special advisor in theological matters.

Pappas (PAH-puhs): The Greek term meaning "father," used for priests in the Greek-speaking Church. "Papa," designating the Pope, derives from this word.

Parable (PA-ruh-buhl): (From Greek *parabole:* comparison) The comparing of realities by placing them "side-by-side." Ancient rhetoric used this term for a figure of speech that Aristotle claimed could be used as proverbs or stories, in order to teach a message. Jesus used parables — which were often paradoxical and chosen from everyday events — to challenge His listeners. The Gospels are full of such parables (e.g., Mt 21:33-43; Mk 4:21-25; Lk 13:6-9). **CCC 546, 2607**

Paraclete (PA-ruh-kleet): (Greek *parakletos:* called to the side of, or advocate) The Holy Spirit. Several times the Gospel of St. John employs this title (14:16-17, 26; 15:26; 16:7-11), which is also translated as "Counselor," "Comforter," or "Consoler." The Paraclete will continue the saving work of Christ until His Second Coming. **CCC 692**

Paracletikes (pah-ruh-KLEET-uh-keez): The Byzantine Office of Consolation ("Paraclisis") prayed in honor of the Mother of God.

Paradise: See Eden, Garden of; Heaven

Paraekklesia (pah-ray-klay-ZEE-uh): (Greek: by the church) A side chapel or other addition to an Eastern Rite church building. It is similar to a "winter" chapel in Latin churches used to accommodate smaller groups.

Paraenesis (pah-reh-NEH-sihs): (Greek *parainein,* to advise) Advice or counsel; in particular, in biblical or patristic writers, the literary genre of preaching and exhortation. Examples include the Letter of James, the First Letter of Clement of Rome, and *The Shepherd of Hermas.*

Paraliturgical Actions (par-uh-lih-TER-dzhih-kuhl AK-shunz): Those rites, prayers, devotions, and ceremonies that are not part of the liturgy per se, but are associated with it in spirit. Devotions such as the Rosary, Stations of the Cross, and various novenas may be considered paraliturgical actions because they prepare us and dispose us to celebrate the Paschal Mystery in the Holy Eucharist. The Constitution on the Sacred Liturgy *(Sacrosanctum Concilium)* warmly commends these. Cf. CCC 1674-1675

Parallelism (PAR-uh-lehl-ih-zuhm): A literary device that repeats phrases and/or grammatical structures in succeeding lines, used in ancient literature such as the O.T. Parallelism is usually divided into four types: "synonymous," when a phrase is repeated but with different vocabulary (e.g., Ps 103:10); "antithetical," when the second phrase contrasts with the first (e.g., Ps 2:9); "synthetic," when the first phrase is developed and extended in the second by means of similar vocabulary (e.g., Ps 2:2); "staircase," when one or several words are taken from the first phrase and repeated in the second, then in the third, etc. (e.g., Jn 1:1-18).

Paraments: See Vestments

Parapsychology (PAR-uh-sai-KAH-luh-dzhee): The study of psychic phenomena such as clairvoyance and extrasensory perception (ESP). It is difficult to prove the existence of these powers. The Church continues to be cautious and exhorts all to seek the power found only in Christ through personal and liturgical prayer.

Parental Duties: See Parents, Duties of

Parenthood (PA-ruhnt-høød): The task that derives from the vocation of marriage in which husband and wife become father and mother. Parents are to love their children, providing for their human needs as well as their spiritual needs; hence, parents are the "first teachers" in the ways of the true Faith. As Pope John Paul II has written, the family is the "domestic church" in which adoration of God must occur. CCC 1250, 2221-2233

Parents, Duties of (DÖÖ-teez uhv PA-ruhnts): The teaching that parental obligations include providing for the physical needs of their children, such as adequate food, clothing, intellectual formation, and anything else necessary for life, and for the spiritual needs of their children, by having them baptized as soon as possible after birth, by seeing that they receive the sacraments of Penance, Holy Eucharist, and Confirmation at the proper times, by instructing them in the Faith, committing them whenever possible to Catholic schools, and by training them to form a correct conscience in their moral conduct. CCC 1250, 2221-2233

Parish (PA-rihsh): A stable community of the faithful established within a diocese by the bishop and entrusted to a pastor. CCC 2179, 2226

Parish Council (PA-rihsh KAUN-sihl): A representative group of members of a parish who advise the pastor on matters pertinent to the parish. It acts in an advisory capacity only.

Parishioner (puh-RIH-shuh-ner): One who is a member of a parish.

Parish Priest (PA-rihsh PREEST): The officially appointed leader or pastor of a parish.

Parish Team (PA-rihsh TEEM): 1. In Canon Law, a group of priests who share the ministry and pastoral care of a parish with one acting as moderator (Can. 517). 2. In the wide sense, the priests, religious, and laypersons who work together to fulfill the pastoral ministry of a parish under the authority of the pastor.

Parochial Administrator (puh-RO-kee-uhl ad-MIHN-ih-stray-ter): A priest appointed by the bishop to take the place of the pastor of a parish and fulfill the administrative and pastoral duties.

Parochial Mass (puh-RO-kee-uhl MAS): A Mass that the pastor is obliged to celebrate on a regular basis for all of the people entrusted to him in the parish (Can. 388). Also known as the *Missa pro populo,* or Mass for the People (q.v.).

Parochial Schools: See Schools, Parochial

Parochial Vicar (puh-RO-kee-uhl VIH-ker): A priest appointed by the bishop to assist a pastor in the exercise of his parochial duties. Formerly and often still known as assistant or associate pastor, or curate (Can. 545).

Parousia (PAHR-öö-SEE-uh): (Greek: presence) The Second Coming of Christ to earth (1 Cor 15:23), foretold by Jesus Himself, by St. Paul, and in several passages in the N T The *parousia* will happen swiftly and will introduce the General Judgment (q.v.). **CCC 1001**

Particular Church (pahr-TIHK-yöö-ler TSHERTSH): A term from Vatican II that describes certain divisions of the universal Church, such as dioceses, vicariates, and prelatures.

Particular Councils (pahr-TIHK-yöö-ler KAUN-sihlz): Gatherings of all the bishops of a given territory, e.g., plenary councils of all the bishops of a country, or provincial councils of all the bishops of a province (cc. 440-443).

Particular Judgment: See Judgment, Particular

Particular Law (pahr-TIHK-yöö-ler LAW): A Church law enacted for all the persons of a specific diocese or of a specific group, but not one that binds the entire Church (cc. 8, 12, 13).

Pascendi Dominici Gregis (pah-SHEHN-dee do-MEE-nee-tshee GRAY-dzhihs): The encyclical of September 8, 1907, in which Pope St. Pius X condemned modernism as "the synthesis of all heresies." He reiterated some of the chief doctrines of the Church concerning Scripture, the Magisterium, and the immutability of Divine Revelation.

Pasch (PASK): (From Hebrew *Pesach:* Passover) First great feast of the Jewish liturgical year, commemorating the passover of the Israelite homes by the avenging angel who killed only the firstborn of the Egyptians (Ex 11:1-10). The Pasch was celebrated at sunset on the fifteenth day of the month of Nisan (Dt 16:6), the first day of the Azymes (q.v.). A lamb was sacrificed, roasted, and eaten with bitter herbs and unleavened bread. The celebration of the exodus is symbolized by the garb and posture of the diners, prepared for flight at any moment (Ex 12:1-28). In patristic and medieval exegesis, the Pasch was considered as a symbolic type of Christ's sacrifice on the cross and the Eucharistic Sacrifice. **Cf. CCC 1096, 1164, 1363**

Paschal Candle (PAS-kuhl KAN-duhl): A large wax candle blessed after the Easter fire during the Service of Light, which begins the Easter Vigil. The paschal candle symbolizes the light of Christ rising in glory that scatters the darkness of sin and death. The paschal candle has a cross, alpha and omega, and the numerals of the current year on it. Grains of incense and stylized wax "nails" are implanted at the ends of the crossbars and in the center of the cross. The deacon carries the paschal candle into the darkened church, pausing three times to chant, "Christ our Light!" The congregation responds, "Thanks be to God!" each time. From its flame, the smaller candles of the faithful are lit; eventually, the deacon places the paschal candle near the pulpit or near the altar. By the illumination of the paschal candle, the deacon chants the *Exsultet*, or Easter Proclamation. During the fifty days of the Easter Season, the paschal candle remains lit. After the Solemnity of Pentecost, the paschal candle is returned to the baptistery, where the candles of the newly baptized infants are lit. At Masses of Christian Burial, the paschal candle is placed at the head of the casket to recall that the deceased person was given a share in the death and resurrection of Christ at Baptism. **Cf. CCC 1189, 1243**

Paschal Mystery (PAS-kuhl MIHS-ter-ee): (From *Pasch,* Hebrew *Pesach:* Passover) The passion, death, resurrection, and ascension of Christ, commemorated at each Holy Mass. Baptism and Holy Eucharist especially remind believers of the splendor and efficacy of the Paschal Mystery. **Cf. CCC 571-658**

Paschal Precept (PAS-kuhl PREE-sehpt): Church law requiring reception of the Eucharist in the Easter Season (also called the Easter Duty) unless, for a just cause, once-a-year reception takes place at another time. **CCC 2042**

Paschaltide: See Easter Season.

Paschal Precept: See Easter Duty.

Passion Music (PA-shuhn MYÖÖ-zihk): The musical form inspired by the Gospel accounts of Our Lord's passion. Some of this music employs only one or two voices, while other settings use many voices and instruments.

Passion of Christ (PA-shuhn uhv KRAIST): Paschal events in the life of Jesus Christ, including the Last Supper, His agony in Gethsemane, His arrest and trial, His scourging, His carrying of the cross, His crucifixion, and His death. **CCC 595-630**

Passion of the Martyrs (PA-shuhn uhv *th*uh MAHR-terz): (Latin *passio:* suffering) Also called martyr acts, the written account of the events surrounding a martyrdom; it usually includes the court proceedings with the testimony against the martyr and a detailed description of the martyr's suffering, death, and burial. It often ends with a depiction of the faithful who now come in pilgrimage to the tomb of the martyr; miracles obtained at the tomb are vividly described. The earliest such account in Latin is *The Acts of the Scillitan Martyrs* (A.D. 180); other notable passions include those of Perpetua and Felicity, Cyprian, Polycarp, and the Forty Martyrs of Sebaste.

Passion Sunday (PA-shuhn SUHN-day): The principal title for the Sunday before Easter, the Sunday that opens Holy Week. Palm Sunday, as it is also known, combines the Jerusalem custom of blessing palms and the Roman custom of proclaiming the Passion. **Cf. CCC 560**

Passiontide (PA-shuhn-taid): Before the revision of the liturgical calendar at Vatican II, the last two weeks of the Lenten Season were called Passiontide. Despite the suppression of the term "Passiontide," the focus of the scriptural texts has not been altered. It remains a more intensive consideration of the events leading up to the Lord's passion and death. To indicate this shift, the Preface of Passion I is used at Mass. Allowance is also made for the optional veiling of crosses and images to prepare for Holy Week.

Passion Week (PA-shuhn WEEK): Before the revision of the liturgical calendar at Vatican II, the week before Holy Week was called Passion Week. When Passiontide was suppressed by the reform, however, Passion Week as a term fell into disuse. The only designation that remains in use is Holy Week, the period from Passion Sunday (or Palm Sunday) to Easter.

Passover: See Pasch

Pastor (PAS-ter): (Latin: shepherd) 1. In the strict canonical sense, a residential bishop. 2. Generally used in reference to the priest charged with the care of souls of a parish. CCC 1560, 1585-1586, 2179

Pastoral Care of the Sick (PAS-ter-uhl KEHR uhv *th*uh SIHK): Subtitled "Rites of Anointing and Viaticum," this ritual is the 1983 English translation and arrangement of the Latin *Ordo unctionis infirmorum eorumque pastoralis curae.* The ritual contains Pope Paul VI's apostolic constitution that promulgated and confirmed the revised rites brought into existence at Vatican II. The revised rites changed the name of the sacrament from Extreme Unction to Anointing of the Sick. Part I of the ritual, entitled "Pastoral Care of the Sick," contains Offices for Visits to Sick Adults and Children, Communion of the Sick, and Anointing of the Sick (outside Mass and during Mass) and abbreviated rites for use in hospitals and institutions. Part II is entitled "Pastoral Care of the Dying." It includes the rites for three "last" sacraments (Penance, Anointing, and Viaticum), Emergency Anointing, and Christian Initiation for the Dying. Additionally, there is a complete Office for commending the dying and prayers for the dead. Part III offers suitable scriptural texts for all celebrations. An appendix includes the Rite of Penance. Cf. CCC 1499-1523

Pastoral Counseling: See Counseling, Pastoral

Pastoral Epistles (PAS-ter-uhl ih-PIH-suhlz): The Pauline letters of 1 and 2 Timothy and Titus, grouped together as "pastoral" because they are addressed to individual bishops, rather than to the local or universal Church, and deal with a set of pastoral issues from a common theological perspective.

Pastoral Judgment: See Judgment, Pastoral

Pastoral Ministry (PAS-ter-uhl MIHN-ih-stree): All those activities by which the clergy of the Church provide for the spiritual well-being of the faithful. Those members of the laity who have gifts and training in certain pastoral specialties may assist and share in this ministry, in accordance with Canon Law. **Cf. CCC 886, 890, 896, 927, 1560**

Pastoral Provision for the Common Identity (PAS-ter-uhl pro-VIH-zhuhn for *th*uh KAH-muhn AI-dehn-tuh-tee): Approved in 1981 by the Holy See on behalf of some clergy and laity of the Episcopal (Anglican) Church in the United States who were seeking full communion with the Catholic Church. It provides for exceptions to the rule of celibacy for those former Episcopalian married clergy who were found to be eligible for ordination as Catholic priests, and also a liturgical use for certain parishes erected to maintain an "Anglican common identity" within the Catholic Church. The first of these parishes was established in San Antonio, Texas, on August 15, 1983, under the patronage of Our Lady of the Atonement. The Pastoral Provision is commonly known as the Anglican Use.

Pastoral Theology (PAS-ter-uhl thee-AHL-uh-dzhee): The systematic study of the theory and practice by which the entire mission of the Church is carried out. It includes not only the study of the traditional branches of theology, but also the study of social and behavioral sciences, as well as aspects of history and anthropology, to provide a practical basis for the exercise of the pastoral ministry of the Church.

Paten (PAT-uhn): A dishlike sacred vessel used to hold the species of bread at Mass. By custom, the paten was made of gold or silver. The *General Instruction of the Roman Missal* does allow, however, for other materials, such as "ebony or other hardwoods" to be used in the making of patens — with preference given to those that "do not break easily or deteriorate" (n. 329). Patens should be blessed according to the *Rite of Dedication of a Church and an Altar* before they are used. The rite was drawn up by the Sacred Congregation for Divine Worship in 1977.

Pater Noster (PAH-tehr NOS-tehr): The first two words of the Lord's Prayer in Latin. The Gospel of St. Matthew (6:9-13) and the Gospel of St. Luke (11:2-4) record the seminal words of the prayer Our Lord gave to His disciples. In the early Church, catechumens were taught the Our Father either right before or after Baptism. The words of the Our Father in Latin are: *Pater noster, qui es in caelis: sanctificetur nomen tuum; adveniat regnum tuum; fiat voluntas tua, sicut in caelo, et in terra. Panem nostrum quotidianum da nobis hodie; et dimitte nobis debita nostra, sicut et nos dimittimus debitoribus nostris; et ne nos inducas in tentationem; sed libera nos a malo. Amen.* Cf. CCC 2762-2864

Patience (PAY-shuhnts): The virtue, connected to the cardinal virtue of fortitude, that enables one to endure suffering for love of God and neighbor. Patience allows one to grow in and respond to charity. CCC 736, 1825, 1832, 2219, 2447, 2613, 2822

Patriarch (PAY-tree-ahrk): The head of a branch of the Eastern Church, corresponding to a province of the Roman Empire. There are five official patriarchal sees: Rome, Constantinople, Alexandria, Antioch, and Jerusalem.

Patriarchs, Scriptural (SKRIHP-tsher-uhl PAY-tree-ahrks): The leaders of the Israelite tribes and heads of prominent families who appear in Genesis from Adam to Joseph. Honored as especially significant patriarchs are Abraham, Isaac, and Jacob; the patriarchal narratives in Genesis associated with them constitute the prologue to Israel's salvation history, and the period during which they lived is known as the Age of the Patriarchs. The title patriarch used for David (Acts 2:29) was simply one of honor. **CCC 61, 755, 839**

Patrimony, Canonical (ka-NAH-nih-kuhl PA-truh-mo-nee): 1. The stable temporal goods owned by a public juridic person in the Church (Can. 1291). 2. The unofficial term for property owned by a person who enters religious life — of which, in certain institutes, the member is able to retain ownership but not control.

Patrimony, Spiritual (SPIHR-ih-tshöö-uhl PA-truh-mo-nee): Pertaining to institutes of consecrated life, this term refers to the intentions of the founders for the mission of the institute as well as for the ends, spirit, characteristics, and approved traditions.

Patriotism, Christian (KRIHS-tshuhn PAY-tree-uh-tih zuhm): The respect that is due one's nation, its symbols and obligations, and the fulfillment of legitimate duties to society, recognizing that the authority of the State is morally legitimate when exercised for the well-being of all, and that it is required of citizens in order to promote and protect the common good.

Patripassionism (PAH-tree pa-see-uh-nih-zuhm): A third-century heresy that held that because the Father is no different from the Son, it was actually the Father Who suffered and died on the cross under the guise of the Son (cf. Sabellianism).

Patristics: See Patrology

Patrology (puh-TRAHL-uh-dzhee): The systematic theological study of the contents of the writings of ancient Christian authors who were accepted as orthodox during their lifetimes. Their authority is acknowledged throughout the Church and carries such weight that they have come to be called "Fathers of the Church" (hence the term "patrology"). Through their writings, these authors provided formulations of the Christian Faith that have become a standard by which to judge all subsequent theology. Important Eastern Fathers are Ignatius of Antioch, Clement of Alexandria, Origen, Athanasius, John Chrysostom, Gregory of Nyssa, Basil the Great, and Gregory Nazianzen. In the West, the names of the following stand out: Justin Martyr, Irenaeus, Tertullian, Ambrose, Jerome, Leo the Great, and Augustine of Hippo. The patristic period is commonly considered to have ended with Isidore of Seville (d. 636) in the West, and with John Damascene (d. 749) in the East. Cf. CCC 11, 78, 250, 688

Patron (PAY-truhn): 1. A benefactor or protector. In Church history, patrons were accorded variously considerable rights and privileges in regard to the institutions of which they served as patron. (Cf. Iuspatronatus, Advowson.) 2. Today, a nontechnical term referring to one who offers substantial support to an ecclesiastical enterprise, but who does so without expecting or receiving any notable temporal return. (Cf. Patron Saints.) Cf. CCC 1014, 2156, 2165

Patroness of the United States of America (PAY-truh-nehs uhv *the*e yöö-NAI-tehd STAYTS uhv uh-MEHR-ih-kuh): The Blessed Virgin Mary, under the title of Our Lady of the Immaculate Conception, is the patroness of the United States of America. This was determined by the Sixth Provincial Council of Baltimore in 1846.

Patron Saints (PAY-truhn SAYNTS): Saints who are recognized as the protectors and intercessors for persons, churches, dioceses, and the universal Church. The name taken at Baptism and Confirmation is frequently that of a patron. Parish churches and diocesan cathedrals are usually named after a patron saint. In some instances, a diocese may have more than one patron saint. The Third Eucharistic Prayer includes a commemoration for "the saint of the day or the patron saint." Cf. CCC 2156, 2165

Paul, St. (SAYNT PAWL): The "Apostle of the Gentiles" and perhaps the greatest missionary of the early Church. Through his missionary journeys, he helped to spread the Gospel throughout Greece and Asia Minor. He was born ca. A.D. 10 and was raised in Tarsus. As a devout Pharisee, Paul persecuted the Christian sect until, through a vision of Christ, he was converted and became a disciple. During his missionary journeys, he wrote letters to the communities he had founded. He was beheaded during a persecution of Christians in Rome ca. A.D. 62. Now part of the canon of the N.T., Paul's letters contain a lastingly powerful articulation of the Christian Faith. At the heart of his teaching is an affirmation that the sinful human race has been redeemed through the death and resurrection of Christ. Salvation comes to each person through faith in Christ and through conformity to Him, in the pattern of His death and resurrection.

Pauline Privilege (PAW-lain PRIHV-uh-lehdzh): A privilege in Canon Law whereby the marriage of two non-baptized persons is dissolved when, after their separation and divorce, one of the parties converts to Christianity and enters a subsequent marriage. The prior marriage is considered dissolved by the act of contracting the second marriage. The person who seeks the privilege must be baptized, but not necessarily in the Catholic Faith. In such cases, the petitioner usually seeks to marry a Catholic. It is also permissible for the converted party to marry a non-Catholic Christian or a non-baptized person. The Pauline Privilege is based on the teaching of St. Paul found in 1 Cor 7:12-15, whereby he allowed Christians to enter a second marriage if their non-Christian spouses had departed and refused to live peacefully with the Christian party. The Pauline Privilege is handled on the diocesan level. The bishop has the responsibility of asking the former spouse of the person petitioning for the privilege if he or she wishes to receive Baptism or is at least willing to resume peaceful cohabitation with the petitioner. This is called "interpellation" of the departed spouse. The bishop may dispense with the obligation of interpellation. In actuality, the Pauline Privilege is usually requested by people who are already divorced with no reconciliation possible. (Cf. cc. 1143-1150.) **Cf. CCC 1640**

Pax (PAHKS): (Latin: peace) The exchange of a sign of peace between those attending Mass, it comes between the recitation of the Our Father and the fraction (breaking of the Host) rite in the Western Eucharistic Liturgy. This gesture has ancient origins, going back as far as the second century according to the *First Apology* of Justin the Martyr. In the churches of the East, the sign of peace is exchanged before the Presentation of the Gifts. **Cf. CCC 1345**

Pax Christi (PAHKS KRIHS-tee): The international Catholic peace organization, begun in 1945 to reconcile France and Germany after World War II. Today, it exhorts all nations to seek peace "based on the natural law and on the justice and charity of Christ."

Peace (PEES): The condition of the heart and mind, within the very spirit, of one who is renewed and justified in Christ. This interior peace is the basis of all external peace within families, the community, society, and the world. It comes to the soul through the cross of Christ, which reconciles us to God and to one another. Peace is a quality that characterizes those who have received new life from God and entered into an eternal relationship with Him. Peace accompanies righteousness (Rom 14:7; Heb 12:11; Jas 3:18), grace (Phil 1:2; Rv 1:4), mercy (Gal 6:16; 1 Tm 1:2), love (Jude 2), joy (Rom 14:17; 15:13) and life (Rom 8:6). **CCC 2304-2305; cf. 736, 1424, 1468, 1716, 1784, 1829, 1832, 1909, 1941, 2015, 2302-2303, 2306-2317, 2442**

Peace, Kiss of (KIHS uhv PEES): 1. The sign of peace in use at Mass today was originally a kiss. It later developed into an embrace with an oral greeting of peace. 2. In the Middle Ages, there developed the custom of the priest kissing the altar. The gesture of peace in the Mass now is left to the determination of local episcopal conferences and is an optional rite. **Cf. CCC 1345**

Peace, Sign of: See Pax; Peace, Kiss of

Pectoral Cross (PEHK-ter-uhl KRAWS): (From Latin *pectus:* breast) A cross made of precious metal (sometimes decorated with jewels) suspended by a chain around the neck, worn over the chest by abbots, bishops, archbishops, cardinals, and the Pope. It is worn by prelates regardless of their attire, whether liturgical or not. The *Caeremoniale Episcopo-*

rum (Ceremonial of Bishops) stipulates exactly how the pectoral cross is used.

Pelagianism (puh-LAY-dzhee-uhn-ih-zuhm:) The heretical opinion held by Pelagius, a fifth-century monk, that one can "earn" one's own salvation by sanctifying oneself. He believed that one could reach perfection unaided by God's grace. This teaching diminishes the need for Christ's Redemption and the impact of Original Sin on the human race. **CCC 406**

Pelvicula (pehl-VIHK-yöö-luh): (Latin: little basin) Dish or plate, usually of glass, on which cruets are placed during Mass.

Penal Laws (PEEN-uhl LAWZ): The canons of the code that enumerate ecclesiastical crimes and the penalties applied as a result of their commission (C.I.C., Book VI).

Penal Process (PEEN-uhl PRAH-sehs): The procedure outlined in the code that must be followed by Church authorities when a person has been accused of an ecclesiastical crime and is being tried before a Church court (cc. 1717-1728).

Penalty (PEHN-uhl-tee): A punishment imposed on a person who has committed an offense.

Penalty, Ecclesiastical (eh-klee-zee-AS-tih-kuhl PEHN-uhl-tee): A punishment imposed on a person for the commission of an ecclesiastical crime as outlined in the Code of Canon Law, consisting of the deprivation of a temporal or spiritual benefit. Penalties are either medicinal (remedial) or expiatory (punishing), but are not to be confused with sacramental penances.

Penalty, Vindictive (vihn-DIHK-tihv PEHN-uhl-tee): Term in the 1917 code for one type of ecclesiastical penalty that is primarily ordered to punishment rather than being remedial in nature.

Penance or Penitence (PEH-nehnts, PEH-nih-tehnts): 1. Spiritual change that enables a sinner to turn away from sin. 2. The virtue that enables human beings to acknowledge their sins with true contrition and a firm purpose of amendment. (See Penance, Virtue of.) Confidence in God's mercy and forgiveness is fundamental to the Christian virtue of penance, along with a determination to be conformed to the passion, death, and resurrection of Christ through the practice of mortification. 3. Sacrament of Penance or Reconciliation (q.v.). 4. The form of amendment or expiation. CCC 1032, 1430-1439, 2043

Penance, Sacrament of (SA-kruh-mehnt uhv PEH-nehnts): Also called Confession or more recently the Sacrament of Reconciliation (although this latter term is more accurately the Rite of Reconciliation and not the name of the sacrament). The Gospels (Mt 16:19 and Jn 20:23) attest that Christ gave the Church the power to forgive sin. Historically, the Church has exercised this power in different ways. A few early sources (Jas 5:16 and the *Didache* 14:1) hint that confession of sins for forgiveness may have been public. If so, the practice did not perdure. Early evidence is that confession of sins was made privately and individually not to a priest but to a bishop. The penance the bishop assigned and the absolution he imparted were public, however. Those who had committed very serious sins (apostasy, murder, adultery, and sometimes fornication) were admitted to the Order of Penitents. Those in the Order of Penitents wore sackcloth and ashes, could not receive Holy Communion, and were remembered in the Church's prayer. Return to sacramental communion with the Church took place on Holy Thursday. Off the European continent, Irish monks began hearing individual confessions of the laity in their spiritual care. Sacramental absolution was given immediately after the confession of sins, and the confession of sins was not always limited to sins of a grievous nature. This form of the sacrament became very popular and spread throughout the Church. The Council of Trent required Catholics to confess all their mortal sins by species (type of sin) and number (approximate) to a priest. Following Vatican II, Catholics could celebrate the sacrament according to three rites: individually, communally with individual confession and absolution, and communally with general confession and general absolution (for use in emergency situations). The current Code of Canon Law obliges Catholics to confess all mortal sins by species and number at least once a year and encourages the frequent reception of the sacrament for sins not judged to be mortal. CCC 1422-1429, 1440-1470, 1480-1498; cf. 393, 433, 553, 755, 822, 827, 927, 980-982, 1020, 1210, 1259, 1385, 1395, 1401, 1415, 1532, 1622, 1851, 1861-1864, 2042, 2490, 2844

Penance, Virtue of (VER-tshöö uhv PEH-nehnts): The good habit that inclines one to be contrite for his sins, to avoid sin in the future, to atone for sins, and to turn completely to God. This virtue enables one to possess the proper attitude toward God as the All-Holy One and himself as one who fails. Cf. CCC 1430-1433

Penitent (PEH-nih-tuhnt): A person who seeks forgiveness of sins and reconciliation with the Church through the use of the Sacrament of Penance. In the early history of the Sacrament of Penance, one who belonged to the Order of Penitents was called a penitent. Now, a penitent is one who makes use of any one of the three forms of sacramental Penance: (1) Rite of Reconciliation of Individual Penitents; (2) Rite of Reconciliation of Several Penitents with Individual Confession and Absolution; (3) the Rite for Reconciliation of Several Penitents with General Confession and Absolution (this last for emergencies, with individual confession required when possible).

Penitential Books (peh-nih-TEHN-tshuhl BØØKS): Books compiled in the early Middle Ages and in use until about the eleventh century containing instructions for confessors such as prayers, questions, lists of sins, and appropriate penances.

Penitential Psalms (peh-nih-TEHN-tshuhl SAHMZ): Seven psalms (Pss 6, 32, 38, 51, 102, 130, and 143) that express sentiments of repentance and supplication. They have traditionally been grouped together for liturgical or private use.

Penitentiary, Sacred Apostolic (SAY-krehd a-pah-STAH-lihk peh-nih-TEHN-tshee-ehr-ee): The Church tribunal, whose deliberations are secret, having supreme authority over the Sacrament of Penance. It especially governs the "internal forum" of the Sacrament and, therefore, would grant absolution in reserved cases and dispensations to secret matrimonial impediments.

Pension (PEHN-shuhn): A portion of a parish's income set aside for the support of retired or disabled pastors. The pension, found in the 1917 Code of Canon Law, has been dropped in the revised code.

Pentateuch (PEHN-tuh-töök): The first five books of the Bible (Genesis, Exodus, Leviticus, Numbers, and Deuteronomy), called "Torah" in Jewish tradition. Although in the past it was attributed to the authorship of Moses, recent research has shown that several authors contributed to the composition of the Pentateuch and that these authors were themselves dependent on oral traditions stretching back to Moses himself. The chief sources of the Pentateuch — possibly taking shape as written documents and dating from different periods — are commonly distinguished as the Yahwist (J), the Elohist (E), the Deuteronomist (D), and the Priestly (P). While there is considerable debate about the details of this so-called "source theory," it is generally agreed among scholars that a variety of identifiable traditions have been woven into the final redaction (edition) of the Pentateuch. In these books of the Bible are recounted some of the most important events in the history of salvation: the creation of the world, the spread of sin, the divine intention to save the human race from the results of sin, the covenant with Abraham, the captivity of Israel in Egypt, their deliverance under the leadership of Moses, the giving of the Law, and the conquest of the Promised Land.

Pentecost (PEHN-tuh-kawst): (Greek: fiftieth day) 1. In Christian tradition, the day on which, as promised by Christ, the Holy Spirit was poured out on the Apostles and disciples in the form of tongues of fire (Acts 2:1-41). In the liturgical calendar, the feast of Pentecost is celebrated with great solemnity for the fifty days after Easter, as the culmination of the Paschal season that begins in Holy Week. 2. Pentecost or

Shavuot is also the name of a Jewish liturgical celebration, the "Feast of Weeks," which was originally a harvest feast and now chiefly commemorates the revelation of the Torah to Moses on Mt. Sinai. **Cf. CCC 696, 731-732, 767, 1076, 1287, 2623**

Pentecostal Churches (pehn-tuh-KAWST-uhl TSHERTSH-ehz): A number of Protestant assemblies, sects, and churches that grew out of the late-nineteenth- and early twentieth-century revivalist movement, exhibiting various charismatic phenomena, such as speaking in tongues and faith healing. The theology is characterized by Fundamentalist and Adventist themes, maintaining a literal interpretation of Scripture.

Pentecostalism, Catholic (KATH-uh-lihk pehn-tuh-KAWST-uhl-ih-zuhm): The practice by some Catholics of those forms of prayer and devotion found within the Pentecostalist movement that grew out of the Protestant revivalist movement of the late-nineteenth and early-twentieth centuries. Called charismatic, it differs from Protestant Pentecostalism by being grounded in the teaching and sacramental life of the Catholic Church, and so has not led to sectarian divisions. (Cf. Charismatic Renewal, Catholic.)

Pentecostarion (pehn-tuh-kaws-TA-ree-ahn): A Byzantine Rite book that contains the propers of the movable feasts in the period between Easter and the week after Pentecost.

People of God (PEEP-uhl uhv GAHD): A name for the Church, as it constitutes a people with Christ as its Head, the Holy Spirit as the condition of its unity, the law of love as its rule, and the kingdom of God as its destiny. Although it is a scriptural term, it was given new emphasis by the Second Vatican Council's Dogmatic Constitution on the Church *(Lumen Gentium)*. **CCC 781-786**

Perfectae Caritatis (pehr-FEHK-tay kah-ree-TAH-tihs): The Decree on the Up-to-date Renewal of Religious Life, promulgated by the Second Vatican Council, for the adaptation of religious life in all forms to the conditions of the modern world, without changing anything essential to the consecrated life.

Perfection (per-FEHK-shuhn): The attainment of authentic conformity to Jesus Christ, which will be complete only in heaven. Each follower of Jesus is to strive for perfection; receiving the sacraments and obeying the commandments leads to this sanctity. Cf. CCC 41, 213, 370, 825, 829, 1704, 1709, 1770, 1775, 1804, 1827, 1832, 1953, 2013-2015, 2028

Pericope (peh-RIH-kuh-pee): (From Greek *perikope:* extract, section) 1. Any passage of Scripture. 2. Since the sixteenth century, it especially refers to the biblical selection that follows a particular order in the Mass.

Periti (peh-REE-tee): (From Latin *peritus:* expert) 1. Court experts utilized in ecclesiastical tribunals. 2. Expert witnesses at ecclesial councils.

Perjury (PER-dzher-ee): (From Latin *per:* for worse +*jurare:* to swear) The deliberate lying or withholding of the truth when under oath. To take an oath means to call upon God as a witness; hence, to perjure oneself is to offend God gravely. CCC 2152; cf. 1756, 2153, 2163, 2476

Permanent Deacon: See Deacon, Permanent

Perpetual Adoration (per-PEH-tshöö-uhl a-do-RAY-shuhn): The continual exposition of the Blessed Sacrament, usually in the monstrance, for the adoration of the faithful. This devotion has enjoyed a long usage in the Church. It fosters love of our Eucharistic Lord and, subsequently, fraternal charity.

Persecutions, Religious (rih-LIH-dzhuhs per-seh-KYÖÖ-shuhnz): The Church has suffered persecution in one form or another throughout her history. Early Christians were the subject of persecution by the Jewish leadership in Jerusalem. Persecution of Christians broke out in the Roman Empire at various periods, particularly under the emperors Nero,

Decius, Diocletian, and Julian the Apostate. In later periods Christians were persecuted by the Persians, by barbarian peoples, by Muslims, and in Asia, Africa, and the Americas during missionary times. In modern times, anticlerical parties in Europe subjected Catholics to persecution. Unprecedented persecution of Christians occurred in the twentieth century in countries dominated by Communism. At various times, under the pressure of doctrinal disagreements and political turmoil, Christians have regrettably persecuted one another, notably in the aftermath of the Protestant Reformation in the sixteenth and seventeenth centuries. Christians have always seen persecution as a possible consequence of allegiance to Christ, since He Himself suffered persecution and death for our sakes. CCC 530, 675, 769, 1816

Person (PER-suhn): 1. In the canonical sense, one to whom Church law applies. One who has been baptized or makes a profession of faith becomes a person in the Church. 2. Juridical person is an aggregate of things or physical persons. Cf. CCC 203, 362, 1704, 2158, 2338-2345

Personal Prelature (PER-suhn-uhl PREHL-uh-tsher): An ecclesiastical entity established by the Holy See, similar to a particular church but composed of clerics who are incardinated into it.

Personalism (PER-suhn-uhl-ih-zuhm): A philosophic system in which persons are the only metaphysical realities and personal being is inherently communitarian. Sometimes contrasted with individualism.

Peschitto, The (*th*uh puh-SKEE-to): (From Syriac: simple) The official Syriac version of the Bible used by Syriac-speaking Christians from at least the fifth century A.D. The Peschitto manuscripts, many of which have survived, are important witnesses to the life of the Church in that period.

Peter, First Epistle of (FERST ih-PIH-suhl uhv PEE-ter): The first of two N.T. letters attributed to the authorship of St. Peter. Dating from around A.D. 66, this letter was written from Rome and sent to various eastern Churches by Silas

(Silvanus, 5:12), a frequent companion of St. Paul. The letter is a masterpiece of general spiritual direction. No class of Christians is left without some wise and gentle advice. The pagan slur against Christians as enemies of the State is rejected, and Christians are encouraged to be good citizens.

Peter, Second Epistle of (SEHK-uhnd ih-PIH-suhl uhv PEE-ter): The style of 2 Peter leads most scholars to doubt that St. Peter was the direct author of the second of two N.T. letters attributed to him. Since the letter appears to have been written at the very end of St. Peter's life (3:13-14), it may represent the record, made by a trusted friend, of his final instructions to the flock entrusted to his care.

Peter's Chains, Feast of (FEEST uhv PEE-terz TSHAYNZ): A feast celebrated in the former Roman Calendar on August 1. When it was celebrated, most of the Proper was taken from the texts of the Feast of Sts. Peter and Paul. This feast recalled the release of St. Peter from the bondage of chains. It was also celebrated to honor St. Paul and the martyrdom of the Seven Holy Maccabees. In the Middle Ages, this date was called "Lammas Day," when it was customary to consecrate bread baked from the first grain harvest or when the annual feudal tribute of lambs was due.

Peter's Chair, Feast of (FEEST uhv PEE-terz TSHEHR): A feast tracing its origins back to Rome in the fourth century, it is currently celebrated on February 22; previously, it was celebrated on January 18. The feast highlights the unity of the Church founded upon St. Peter. The readings for Mass on this feast are 1 Pt 5:1-4 and Mt 16:13-19.

Peter's Pence (PEE-terz PEHNTS): The annual collection, gathered near the Solemnity of Sts. Peter and Paul (June 29), that is used for the Pope's charities and the maintenance of the Holy See. Each bishop collects the sum given by his people and sends the amount to Rome.

Petition (peh-TIH-shun): One of the four purposes of prayer. In prayers of petition, persons ask of God the blessings they and others need. **CCC 2734**

Petrine Privilege (PEH-train PRIHV-lehdzh): Also called "Privilege of the Faith." The papal dissolution of a marriage between a baptized person and a non-baptized person. **Cf. CCC 1640**

Pew (PU): A long bench used for seating in a church.

Phantasiasm (fan-TAY-zee-az-uhm): A second-century heresy that claimed that Christ the man was only a phantom.

Pharisees (FEHR-uh-seez): A Jewish religious party whose membership was largely lay, in contrast to the Sadducees, who were mostly clerical. Apart from the N.T., our principal sources of information about the Pharisees are Josephus and the Talmud. Unlike the Sadducees, who regarded only the Torah as binding on the Jews, the Pharisees acknowledged the binding power of the oral traditions as well. They believed, as the Sadducees did not, in angels, spirits, and the resurrection of the dead. In the N.T., they epitomize opposition to Jesus, who censured them for merely external observance of the law. Nonetheless, some Pharisees became followers of Jesus (e.g., Nicodemus). After the fall of Jerusalem, they pass from view, but they exercised a profound influence on subsequent Judaism. **Cf. CCC 574-576, 579, 581, 588, 595-596, 993, 2054, 2285**

Phelonion (fuh-LO-nee-uhn): The outer vestment worn by priests in the Eastern Rites. The counterpart of the phelonion in the West is the chasuble.

Philemon, Epistle to (ih-PIH-suhl töö fih-LEE-muhn): St. Paul's letter to Philemon, occasioned by Paul's befriending and returning Philemon's slave, Onesimus. The letter is a masterpiece of persuasion. Paul seeks to transform the master-slave relationship from within, citing the deeper reality of being one body in Christ.

Philippians, Epistle to the (ih-PIH-suhl töö *th*uh fuh-LIH-pee-uhnz): A warm letter addressed by St. Paul to the Church where he began his missionary journey to Europe. In this letter, Paul's message stressed the urgency of doing God's will because the "Lord is at hand" (4:5). Paul looks forward with expectation to his "heavenly home" (3:20). Christ is the servant whom God vindicated, glorified, and made omnipotent over all things (2:5-11, 3:21). Having the mind of Christ (2:5) is of utmost importance for dealing with the problems facing the community within and without.

Philosophy (fuh-LAH-suh-fee): (Greek, *philein:* to love + *sophia:* wisdom) The study of that truth that is known by natural reason, rather than through Divine Revelation, concerning the fundamental questions about the nature of reality.

Photius (FO-tee-uhs): Layman who became patriarch of Constantinople in 858 and played an important role in events that eventually led to the East-West schism. In a dispute with Pope St. Nicholas I, he issued an encyclical in 867 defending the rights of Greek missionaries in Bulgaria. Accusing the Western Church of heresy for the inclusion of the *Filioque* phrase into the Creed, he "deposed" the Pope and declared him anathema. Although this so-called "Photian Schism" was perhaps motivated more by Photius's concerns for his own insecure position in Constantinople, it set the pattern for later events, especially in 1054, when the schism between the East and West occurred. **Cf. CCC 246-248**

Pietism (PAI-uh-tih-zuhm): A movement within German Lutheranism, originating in the teachings of the minister Philipp Jakob Spener (1635-1705), who sought to restore and enliven Christian fervor within the State church. Spener organized twice-weekly devotional meetings, called *collegia pietatis,* centering on Bible-reading and common prayer, in order to foster the inner spiritual life of the participants. When Frederick II founded the University of Halle in 1694, it became a Pietist center. The movement flourished in a variety of forms and influenced the development of similar movements elsewhere, notably John Wesley's Methodism in the Anglican Church.

Piety (PAI-uh-tee): (Latin *pietas,* from *pius:* dutiful) One of the seven gifts of the Holy Spirit, which enables one to practice reverence for parents and country. When piety is operative, one reverences other persons because of their connection to God. Cf. CCC 971, 1303, 1674, 1831, 2215, 2688

Pileus: See Zucchetto

Pilgrim and Pilgrimage (PIHL-gruhm, PIHL-gruhmchdzh): (Old French *pèlegrin*, from Latin *peregrinus:* foreigner) One who travels to a holy place to obtain some spiritual benefit, and the trip itself; the purpose of the pilgrimage may be to venerate a sacred object or religious relic, to be in the presence of a holy person, to do penance, or to offer thanksgiving in return for graces received (cf. Jgs 21:2, 1 Sm 1:3). The Ark of the Covenant was taken on pilgrimage to Jerusalem by David and his men (2 Sm 6-7), ritually followed by the procession of the Ark to the Temple (1 Kgs 8:1-10). These pilgrimages were consciously likened to the journey from Egypt to Zion (Ps 68). Although the pilgrimage, in the common experience, has lost much of its religious significance, all are still called to journey to the Father through the Son. CCC 769, 1013, 1419, 1438, 1674, 2101, 2691

Pious Foundation (PAI-uhs faun-DAY-shuhn): An aggregate or collection of goods, including money, that is intended for the pastoral apostolate, charitable apostolate, or other work of the Church, established as such by competent authority.

Pious Fund (PAI-uhs FUHND): A special fund created by the seventeenth-century Jesuit missionaries who evangelized northwestern Mexico. The fund was eventually confiscated by the Mexican government and only paid back to the Church in the nineteenth and twentieth centuries.

Pious Union: See Associations of the Christian Faithful

Pious Will (PAI-uhs WIHL): A donation of temporal goods, money, or other objects to the Church with a stipulation that it be used for a specific cause or that Masses or prayers be offered in return.

Pisa, Councils of (KAUN-sihlz uhv PEE-zuh): Two councils held at Pisa in 1409 and 1411 in response to the Western Schism. The first elected a third claimant to the papacy, and the second was declared schismatic and void.

Piscina (pih-SHEEN-uh): (Latin: basin) A place in the sacristy for the cleansing of sacred vessels and washing priests' hands.

Pistoia, Council of (KAUN-sihl uhv pih-STOI-yuh): A synod convened by Jansenist Bishop Ricci of Pistoia in 1768 and later condemned by the Pope.

Plain Chant (PLAYN TSHANT): (Latin: *planus,* flat, level + *cantus,* song) Also called plain song, an ancient monodic chant consisting of an unaccompanied melodic line, usually sung with Latin texts, used within the liturgy of the Church.

Plain Song: See Plain Chant

Planeta or Pianeta (plah-NEH-tuh, pyah-NEH-tuh): (Italian: planet; Latin *plane:* wholly) Latin and Italian words for the chasuble used at Mass, because the chasuble's length and width seemed to surround and linger about the priest's body.

Platform: See Predella

Pleroma (pluh-RO-muh): (Greek: plenitude) 1. Jesus Christ, the fullness of all things. 2. The abundance that comes to those who live in Christ Jesus (Col 2:9-10; Eph 1:22-23). 3. The Gnostic term meaning the fullness from which the world's Creator fell and to which all spirits trapped in matter must eventually return. Cf. CCC 5, 65-67, 423, 515, 824, 1042, 1953, 1974, 2013, 2055

Plumbator (PLUHM-uh-ter): (Latin *plumbum:* lead) A minor Vatican official whose duty is to affix the leaden seal to solemn pontifical documents.

Pluvial: See Cope

Pneumatomaci (nyöö-mah-TO-mah-chee): Fourth-century sect holding a belief similar to the Macedonian heresy, which denied the divinity of the Holy Spirit.

Polyglot Bible (PAH-lee-glaht BAI-buhl): (From Greek: many languages) An edition of the Scriptures containing translations into several languages from the original tongues. The six-volume Complutensian Polygot Bible (1522) featured Greek, Hebrew, and Latin translations of the O.T. and Greek and Latin translations of the N.T. Two-language ("diglot") Bibles have existed since the fifth century.

Polytheism (pah-lee-THEE-ih-zuhm): (Greek *poly:* many + *theos:* god) Belief in and worship of many gods or divinities, especially prevalent in pre-Christian religions. CCC 2112

Pontiff, or Supreme Pontiff (PAHN-tihf, suh-PREEM PAHN-tihf): (From Latin *pontem facere:* to build a bridge) The title of Supreme Pontiff originally referred to the Roman Emperor, who was also chief bridge-builder. The title was first used in reference to the successor of St. Peter by Gratian (A.D. 375). The Latin *Pontifex Maximus,* abbreviated P.M. or Pont. Max., often follows the writing of the Holy Father's name. CCC 882; cf. 100, 880-887, 891-892, 895, 937, 1369, 1463, 1559, 2034

Pontifical Biblical Commission (pahn-TIH-fih-kuhl BIII-blih-kuhl kuh-MIH-shuhn): The group of scholars established by Pope Leo in 1902 to safeguard Scripture from attacks and error. Throughout the years, the P.B.C. has responded to various inquiries concerning scriptural interpretation. Pope Paul VI reorganized the P.B.C. in 1971. Today, it promotes biblical studies by way of the research done by the P.B.C.

Pontifical Biblical Institute (pahn-TIH-fih-kuhl BIH-blih-kuhl IHN-stuh-tööt): Commonly called the Biblicum, from its Latin name, *Pontificium Institutum Biblicum;* founded by Pope Pius X in 1909 in Rome as an institute of higher biblical studies, the only such empowered by the Holy See to grant both the pontifical degrees S.S.L. and S.S.D. (the license and doctorate in Sacred Scripture); affiliated with the Gregorian University, with a separate campus in Jerusalem; the P.I.B. publishes the journal *Biblica,* of which the *Elenchus Biblicus* is an invaluable bibliographical tool.

Pontifical Institutes of Higher Learning (pahn-TIH-fih-kuhl IHN-stuh-tööts uhv HAI-er LER-nihng): Eighteen universities and theological faculties in Rome affiliate with the Holy See, thus designated as pontifical institutes. The universities offer general curricula in philosophy, theology, Canon Law, and Church history. Aside from the institutes whose names indicate their specialized areas of study, such as Scripture, Church music, and archaeology, San Anselmo is noted for liturgical studies and the Augustinianum for patristics. The pontifical institutes are empowered by the Holy See to grant one or several of the pontifical baccalaureate, license, and doctoral degrees. The *Annuario Pontificio* lists these pontifical institutes (they are commonly called by the Latin or Italian names in parentheses): (1) Pontifical Gregorian University; (2) Pontifical Biblical Institute (Biblicum); (3) Pontifical Institute of Oriental Studies; (4) Pontifical Lateran University; (5) Pontifical Urban University (Propaganda Fide); (6) Pontifical University of St. Thomas; (Angelicum); (7) Pontifical Athenaeum Salesianum; (8) Pontifical Institute of Classical Studies (Latinitas); (9) Pontifical Athenaeum of St. Anselm (San Anselmo); (10) Pontifical Athenaeum Antonianum; (11) Pontifical Institute of Sacred Music; (12) Pontifical Institute of Christian Archaeology; (13) Pontifical Theological Faculty of St. Bonaventure (Seraphicum); (14) Pontifical Institute of Spirituality (Teresianum); (15) Pontifical Theological Faculty of Mariology (Marianum); (16) Pontifical Institute of Arabic and Islamic Studies; (17) Pontifical Faculty of Educational Sciences (Auxilium); (18) Pontifical Athenaeum of the Holy Cross (Santa Croce).

Pontifical Mass (pahn-TIH-fih-kuhl MAS): A Mass celebrated by a bishop. In the postconciliar liturgical reform, these Masses are called "episcopal liturgies." Several documents — the motu proprio *Pontificalia Insignia* (1968), the instruction from the former Sacred Congregation of Rites, *Pontificalis Ritus* (1968), and *Caeremoniale Episcoporum* (1984) — treat pontifical Masses or episcopal liturgies.

Pontifical Right (pahn-TIH-fih-kuhl RAIT): Canonical term describing religious institutes that are under the authority of the Holy See.

Pontificals (pahn-TIH-fih-kuhlz): Common term for the special insignia worn by bishops and certain prelates during the Sacred Liturgy.

Pontifical Secrecy (pahn-TIH-fih-kuhl SEEK-ruh-see): The principle under which secret information about the Church is obtained and kept from being revealed because it could in some way hurt her universal mission.

Poor and Needy [The Poor] (PØØR and NEE-dee): 1. Those who are oppressed because of the lack of bodily necessities. The Church continues, as always, to assist the poor in their plight by appealing to the generosity of the faithful. 2. A reference to "spiritual poverty," which is the virtue of remaining detached from human possessions. Religious communities demand this from their members; however, all Christians are called to exercise some detachment from material things. **Cf. CCC 709, 716, 886, 1033, 1435, 1716, 1825, 2208, 2405, 2443-2449, 2544-2547**

Poor Box (PØØR BAHKS): Sometimes called the alms-box, a slotted box to collect alms for the needy; found in churches from the earliest days of Christianity.

Pope (POP): (Italian *papa*, from Greek *pappas*: father) The Bishop of Rome, the Vicar of Christ and successor of St. Peter, who exercises universal governance over the Church. He is elected by the College of Cardinals in a secret conclave. He is the visible symbol of the holiness and unity of the Church. (See also Appendix I, List of Popes). **CCC 882; cf. 100, 880-887, 891-892, 895, 937, 1369, 1463, 1559, 2034**

Pope Joan (POP DZHON): Alleged name of a woman falsely said to have been Pope from 855 to 858, actually years of the reign of Pope Benedict III. The myth was not heard of before the thirteenth century.

Pope Speaks, The *(th*uh POP SPEEKS): American bimonthly publication containing English translations of the more important papal and curial documents.

Popes: See Appendix I (List of Popes)

Popish Plot (POP-ihsh PLAHT): An unsuccessful attempt by Titus Oates and Israel Tonge in the seventeenth century to discredit the Catholics in England by bringing false charges before Parliament, claiming that there was a Jesuit-led plot to assassinate King Charles and to replace him with his brother James, the Duke of York. Although the Popish Plot was exposed as untrue, it led to increased persecution of English Catholics.

Populorum Progressio (pop-öö-LO-røøm pro-GREH-see-o): The encyclical letter *On the Development of Peoples* by Pope Paul VI in 1967, affirming the traditional Catholic teaching that, as a matter of justice, the wealthy are bound to help the poor to meet their needs. He applied this teaching not just to individuals, but also to nations, and outlined the relationship between the just development of the whole human family and the achievement of a stable peace in the world. **Cf. CCC 2315**

Porter (PAWR-ter): The lowest of the four traditional "minor" orders, suppressed in 1972, in which one "guarded" the door of the church to exclude unauthorized persons from entering during Mass.

Portiuncula (port-ee-ØØN-köö-luh): (Italian: a small portion) The place that some generous Benedictine monks gave to St. Francis of Assisi around the year 1210, in which he could welcome those who wanted to follow his new way of poverty and simplicity. St. Francis restored the small church on this land. Today, the church stands inside a grand basilica at Assisi. The Portiuncula Indulgence is granted to those who visit the church on August 2 or any other church possessing the privilege of this indulgence.

Positivism (PAH-sih-tih-vih-zuhm): The philosophy that teaches that the only reality is that which is perceived by the senses, and that the only truth is that which is personally experienced. It asserts that ideas about God, morality, or anything else that cannot be scientifically tested are to be rejected as nonsensical, or at least unknowable.

Possession, Demonic (dee-MAH-nihk po-ZEH-shuhn): The condition of one whose mind and body the devil has control. The N.T. records a number of instances of possession (Mt 8:16; Mk 1:34; Lk 7:21; Acts 5:16). The essential remedy against possession or harassment by an evil spirit is the power of the name of Jesus Christ. The invocation of this name summons the power of Christ's victory over Satan on the cross. "Exorcism," properly speaking, is the casting out of a demon, while "deliverance" is the driving away of evil spirits from a person not actually possessed. **Cf. CCC 1673**

Postcommunion (POST-kuhm-YOON-yuhn): Since the translation of the Roman Missal in 1974 and the 1985 translation of the Sacramentary, the title of this prayer is "Prayer After Communion," one of the three presidential prayers provided in each Mass "Proper" (or, on some saints' days, taken from "common" formularies), with the other two being the Opening Prayer (Collect) and the Prayer over the Gifts (Secret). The Prayer After Communion is a brief prayer that comes after a period of silent thanksgiving or hymn after the reception of Holy Communion.

Postulant (PAHS-tshöö-luhnt): (From French *postuler:* to solicit) A candidate for a religious order who is accepted for admission, but who enters the "pre-novitiate" period before entry into the novitiate. The specifics of the postulancy (duration, etc.) differ from one congregation to another.

Postulation (pahs-tshöö-LAY-shuhn): A type of canonical election whereby a person ordinarily prohibited from being elected because of some impediment is in fact elected by a two-thirds majority of the electors (cc. 180-183).

Postulator (pahs-tshöö-LAY-ter): The person charged with advancing the cause of a candidate's beatification or canonization, especially in reference to amassing the data on the candidate's life, as well as receiving testimony in regard to any possible miracles wrought through the candidate's intercession.

Poterion (po-TEHR-ee-ahn): The Eastern chalice.

Poverty (PAH-ver-tee): (Latin *pauper*: poor) 1. Condition of the poor, those deprived of basic necessities of life, for whom Vatican II and recent encyclicals have expressed the Church's "preferential option." 2. Known as "evangelical poverty," the voluntary renunciation of the ownership and use of material goods for the sake of seeking a life of more perfect union with God, and after the example of Christ and His Apostles. It is one of the three traditional vows made by those in consecrated religious life. Cf. CCC 544, 709, 716, 786, 852, 886, 915, 1033, 1397, 1435, 1716, 1825, 2208, 2405, 2439-2440, 2443-2449, 2544-2547

Power (PAU-er): The ability to exert authority, influence, or force over other persons or things. According to the Scriptures, all power comes from God (Ps 66:7). Divine power is manifest in creation and redemption, and ultimately in the life, death, resurrection, and glory of Jesus Christ. Cf. CCC 60, 124, 131, 405, 635, 649, 661, 664, 668, 703, 735, 798, 822, 1107, 1285, 1432, 1441, 1503-1504, 1520, 1550, 1566, 1615, 1624, 1642, 1704, 2057, 2090, 2472, 2520, 2584, 2848

Power of the Keys (PAU-er uhv *th*uh KEEZ): The authority and jurisdiction given by Christ to the Apostles and their successors. Hence, the Pope and bishops and their delegates have the power to "bind and loose" (Mt 16:14), not only in the confessional (internal forum) but also in their daily duties (external forum). CCC 553, 981-983

Pragmatism (PRAG-muh-tih-zuhm): (Greek *pragma:* a thing done) A theory that says there are practical consequences to any truth, and that these are a test of its truthfulness. Under this system truth is relative, and its validity cannot be determined by pure reason, but only through the acceptance of the fact that has been justified by its results.

Prayer (PREHR): The raising of the mind and heart to God in adoration, thanksgiving, reparation, and petition. Prayer, which is always mental because it involves thought and love of God, may be vocal, meditative, private, or personal, and public, social, or official. Its highest form is contemplation, a foretaste of the beatific vision (q.v.). The official prayer of the Church as worshipping community is called the liturgy. CCC 2558-2865; cf. 276, 435, 451, 520, 688, 741, 821, 958, 971, 1032, 1061-1065, 1073, 1124-1127, 1174-1178, 1352-1354, 1499, 1510, 1820, 2041, 2096-2097, 2205, 2252, 2424-2425, 2525

Prayer of the Faithful (PREHR uhv *th*uh FAYTH-fuhl): The intercessory prayers offered during Mass or at other liturgical prayer. The term grew out of the distinction between the prayers offered by and for the baptized and those offered by and for the catechumens. Two types of these prayers remain in the West. The first is the litany form of petitions offered by the deacon (or by another minister, in his absence) with a song or spoken response (for example, "Lord, hear our prayer"). The petitions are introduced by an exhortation by the priest or bishop celebrating the Mass and ended with a prayer by the celebrant. Suitable intercessory prayers are found in an appendix to the Sacramentary. The second kind is called the Roman type, an example of which is the Prayer of the Faithful used in the Liturgy of the Lord's Passion on Good Friday. These prayers are preceded by a statement of intention by the priest-celebrant, followed by a period of silence and a concluding prayer by the celebrant. Generally speaking, the proper formula of the Prayer of the Faithful consists of prayers for the Church, public authorities, the salvation of the world, the sick and deceased, and local needs (cf. *General Instruction of the Roman Missal,* nn. 69-71). Cf. CCC 1349

Prayer Over the Gifts (PREHR OVER *th*uh GIHFTS): One of the three "presidential" prayers provided in each set of Mass Propers (or on some saints' days, taken from "common" formularies), along with the Opening Prayer (Collect) and the Prayer After Communion. In the preconciliar liturgy, the Prayer Over the Gifts was known as the "Secret" prayer because the priest offered it silently with the exception of the last few words, *"per omnia saecula saeculorum . . .* for ever and ever." The celebrant's invitation ("Pray, brethren, . . .") and the congregation's response ("May the Lord accept. . .") serve as an introduction or prelude to the Prayer Over the Gifts. **CCC 1350**

Prayer, Mystical: See Mysticism

Preaching (PREE-tshihng): A stable ecclesiastical office of communicating God's Word, held by the Pope and bishops by divine law and others by ecclesiastical law (cc. 762-772). **CCC 76-77, 94, 132, 651, 875, 1122, 1151, 1716**

Pre-Cana: See Cana Conferences

Precept (PREE-sehpt): (From Latin *praeceptum:* instruction) 1. An order issued by an ecclesiastical superior to one under his authority (Can. 49). 2. More broadly, a command or order given to an individual or a community in a particular case, establishing law for concerned parties. Preceptive documents are issued by the Pope, departments of the Roman Curia, bishops, and other competent authority in the Church. **Cf. CCC 1650, 1968, 1973, 2036-2037, 2041-2043, 2048**

Precepts of the Church: See Commandments of the Church.

Precious Blood, Feast of the (FEEST uhv *th*uh PREH-shuhs BLUHD): Early in the nineteenth century, some religious orders celebrated feasts in honor of the Precious Blood. In 1859, Pope Pius IX decreed that the Feast of the Precious Blood would be celebrated in the universal Church. In 1914, Pope Pius X made July 1 the date for the Feast, observed until the reform of the liturgy following Vatican II. Now, a

Votive Mass of the Precious Blood may be celebrated at the discretion of the priest-celebrant.

Predella (pray-DEHL-luh): (Italian: platform, stool) The floor of the platform on which an altar stands. On the old high altars, the top of the gradines (q.v.), where the candlesticks and flower vases rested on the predella.

Predestination (pree-dehs-tih-NAY-shuhn): 1. The belief that God knows the outcome of all events by virtue of His omniscience. Because He lives in the "eternal," the Creator knows what choices His children will make. 2. The theory that human freedom is negated because God knows the result of human actions. This opinion has been condemned by the Church. Although God does know how each person will choose, He does not deny the individual the choice; rather, He knows what will be chosen. CCC 257, 600, 1007, 2012, 2782, 2823

Preface (PREH-fuhs): (Latin *praefatio:* introduction or formula) A formal proclamation of praise by the priest celebrating the Mass. Currently, the term "Preface" refers to the exhortation "Lift up your hearts," which is uttered by the priest, and concluding with the words immediately before the *Sanctus* ("Holy, holy, holy Lord."). At one time, before the Council of Trent (1545-1563), there were numerous prefaces in use. The Council of Trent eliminated all but eleven of them due to theological and literary problems. At the beginning of the twentieth century, several more prefaces were approved (for the Dead, St. Joseph, Christ the King, Sacred Heart). With the revision of the Missal called for by Vatican II, the number of prefaces jumped to more than eighty, with the allowance for national episcopal conferences to request more. In the United States, special prefaces exist for Thanksgiving Day and Independence Day, for example. With the addition of Eucharistic Prayers for Masses of Reconciliation and Masses with Children, the number of approved prefaces was increased yet again. The number of prefaces continued to rise with the publication of the *Collection of Masses of the Blessed Virgin Mary.* CCC 1352

Prefect, Apostolic or Vicar Apostolic (a-pah-STAH-lihk PREE-fehkt, VIH-ker a-puh-STAH-lihk): A priest or bishop given authority over a territorial division of the Church that has not been erected as a diocese.

Prefecture, Apostolic (a-pah-STAH-lihk PREE-fehk-tsher): Territorial division of the Church erected by the Holy See and under the authority of a prelate who is generally not a bishop (Can. 371).

Preferential Option (PREH-fer-EHN-shuhl AMP-shun): Apparent favor shown to the poor in the Church's ministry (cf. Poverty, 1.), shown by Christ in the Gospels and particularly expressed in documents since Vatican II, but sometimes erroneously stated in terms of Marxist-Leninist class warfare (cf. Liberation Theology). **Cf. CCC 2729, 2732**

Prelate (PREH-luht): (From past participle of Latin *praeferre:* offered as a model) 1. A cleric with some form of ecclesiastical jurisdiction, which may be temporary. 2. A cleric who holds a minor, major, or honorary permanent rank in the Church.

Premoral Evil (pree-MOR-uhl EE-vuhl): The concept in some systems of modern moral theology in which an "evil" does not have moral significance because it occurs proportionately to the goods and evils involved. If this evil becomes disproportionate, it then is changed into a moral evil. This notion is vague and seems to permit evils that have been classified as such by the Magisterium.

Presanctified, Mass of the (MAS uhv *th*uh pree-SANK-tih-faid): A term derived from the Greek *(leitourgia ton prohegiasmenon)* to indicate a Eucharistic Liturgy without a consecration. In this kind of a liturgy, Hosts consecrated at a prior Mass would be distributed to the faithful. As far back as the late seventh century in the East, there is evidence of a Presanctified Mass. In the West, it came later, through the Gelasian Sacramentary. The present Good Friday Liturgy of the Lord's Passion is no longer associated with this term, even though the Hosts distributed on Good

Friday are consecrated the evening before at the Mass of the Lord's Supper.

Presbyter (PREHZ-bih-ter): (Greek *presbyteros:* elder) One who exercises oversight in a community. In a practice rooted in the O.T., elders functioned as the leaders of various Jewish communities at the time of Christ. Since the earliest Christian communities were composed mostly of converts from Judaism who simply adapted patterns of leadership from the Jewish community, elders came to exercise governance in these communities (see Acts 11:30 and 15:23). In the early Church, the pastoral responsibility of the elders overlapped with that of the overseers or bishops. By as early as A.D. 110, however, the bishops came to exercise leadership over the elders. As a sign that they have assumed the roles fulfilled by the elders, priests are often referred to as "presbyters" today. Cf. CCC 896, 1516, 1526, 1530, 1537-1538, 1554, 1567-1568, 1590, 1593

Presbyteral Councils (prehz-BIH-ter-uhl KAUN-sihlz): Another name for Priests' Councils (q.v.).

Presbyterian Churches (prehz-bih-TEER-ee-uhn TSHERTSH-chz): Those Protestant denominations that adhere to the Westminster Confession and Catechism (1643), based upon the teaching of John Calvin (1509-1564) and John Knox (1513-1572). The name refers to the system of church governance, which is by "presbyters," although there is some divergence of opinion among Presbyterians whether both ministers and elders are to be considered presbyters.

Presbyterorum Ordinis (prez-bih-teh-RO-røøm OR-dee-nihs): The document, the Decree on the Ministry and Life of Priests, issued on December 7, 1965, by the Second Vatican Council, explicating the very essence of the priesthood and how priests are to live their divine calling. Cf. CCC 1562-1568

Presbytery (PREHZ-bih-ter-ee): (Greek *presbyteros*, elder) Not to confuse the Christian priesthood with the Hebrew priesthood of the O.T. and the many variations of the pagan priesthood in existence at the time, the early Christians used this term when referring to their priests (cf. Acts 15:2, 6; Jas 5:14). There are three chief meanings for presbytery: (1) the part of the church building set aside for the exclusive use of the clergy; (2) the ancient custom of identifying those priests who assisted the bishop in governing his diocese, a kind of college of consultors; (3) it may refer to the house where the parish clergy reside. In the United States it is much more common to call this residence the rectory. Cf. CCC 877, 1354, 1369, 1567-1568, 1595

Prescription (pree-SKRIHP-shuhn): (Latin: a rule preordained, something mapped out) 1. A means of acquiring property through actual possession for an unspecified period of time (Can. 1268). 2. In penal law of the C.I.C., a statute of limitations after which a criminal action cannot be made.

Presence of God (PREH-sehnts uhv GAHD): The manifestation of God in one's life and, objectively speaking, in the world. He shows Himself especially in the Holy Eucharist, along with Sacred Scripture, the Church, the Pope and ordained ministers, the assembled body of believers, and in His creation. CCC 208, 1148, 2144, 2565

Presence, Real (REEL PREH-sehnts): The dogma of the Catholic Church that teaches that when bread and wine (matter) are consecrated (form) by a duly ordained priest who has the proper intention, the Body, Blood, Soul, and Divinity of Jesus Christ becomes really, truly, and substantially present — still under the appearances of bread and wine. Adoration is to be given to the Sacred Species. CCC 1373-1379

Presentation of the Blessed Virgin Mary (preh-sehn-TAY-shuhn uhv _th_uh BLEH-sehd VER-dzhihn MEH-ree): Placed on the liturgical calendar for November 21, a memorial that recalls the presentation of Mary in the Temple when she was three years old. There is a reference to this event in the apocryphal Book of James. In the East, this feast can be traced as far back as the eighth century; it came somewhat later in the West. In 1585, Pope Sixtus V authorized the feast for the entire Church. **CCC 529**

President, or Presider (PREH-zih-dehnt, pree-ZAI-der): (From Latin *praesedere*) A more recent designation given to the priest celebrating the Mass. The Missal of Pope Paul VI refers to the priest celebrating the Mass simply as the "priest" or the "celebrant." Some liturgists today dislike these two words so they substitute the word "presider" as if to say that the priest is not the only one who celebrates the Mass. The traditional terminology does not make this claim, however. Without denigrating the priesthood of all the faithful, the term "priest" or "celebrant" makes clear the unique and indispensable role of the ordained minister in the Holy Sacrifice of the Mass. Besides, "president" or "presider" is too passive a concept for what actually occurs and takes place in the Eucharistic Liturgy. We must be careful not to be Pelagian in this matter; yet there is no Mass without a validly ordained priest, who does not merely oversee the sacred mysteries as some kind of head chef but really and truly celebrates them as one who offers sacrifice. **Cf. CCC 1142, 1184, 1348, 1369, 1411**

Presidential Prayers (preh-zih-DEHN-tshuhl PREHRZ): The three main prayers offered by the priest celebrating the Mass, also known as the Mass Propers. These three are: the Opening Prayer (Collect), the Prayer Over the Gifts (formerly known as the Secret), and the Prayer After Communion (Postcommunion). These presidential prayers are said aloud by the priest only. All three prayers are found in the Sacramentary, along with those presidential prayers that form the "Ordinary" of the Mass.

Press, Catholic: See Catholic Press

Presumed Death (pree-ZÖÖM'D DEHTH): Canonical process whereby a person is declared free to marry based on the moral certitude of the bishop that the other party is dead although physical proof of death is lacking (Can. 1707).

Presumption (pree-ZUHMP-shuhn): The affirmation of the truth or falsehood of a probable fact based on certain and determined facts directly related to the issue. The Code of Canon Law contains presumptions of law and presumptions of fact. CCC 2091-2092

Preternatural Gifts (PREE-ter-NA-tsher-uhl GIHFTS): Exceptional gifts, beyond the exigencies and powers of human nature, enjoyed by Adam and Eve in the state of original justice: immunity from suffering and death, superior knowledge, integrity, or perfect control of the passions. These gifts were lost as a result of Original Sin; their loss, however, implied no impairment of the integrity of human nature. Cf. CCC 374-384

Prevenient Grace (pree-VEEN-yuhnt GRAYS): The assistance given by God to help one turn to Him and recognize that He alone is man's salvation. The Church teaches that no one "earns" this grace, but one must accept it if he is to enjoy a relationship with God and, subsequently, eternal life. Cf. CCC 490-493

Pride (PRAID): The first of the seven deadly, or capital, sins. As distinct from the holy recognition that one's self-worth is grounded in God and His goodness, pride designates the acceptance of glory, attention, credit, and honor that is self-centered and perverse. Christian Tradition affirms that some of the angels rebelled against God because of pride and thus fell from grace. Pride causes one to turn away from dependence on God and fosters a sinful self-reliance. CCC 1866, 2514; cf. 1784, 2094, 2317, 2540, 2728

Prie-Dieu (PREE-dyøø): (French: pray God) A kneeler or bench suitable for kneeling in prayer.

Priest (PREEST): The man ordained by a bishop to the ministry of presbyter. He is to be "another Christ" by offering the Sacrifice of the Mass; he also reconciles sinners to God, preaches the Gospel, anoints the sick, baptizes, and witnesses marriages. CCC 1544-1554, 1557, 1562-1568, 1572, 1580, 1592, 1595; cf. 877, 983, 1120, 1142-1143, 1175, 1256,

1312-1314, 1411, 1461-1467, 1495, 1516, 1530, 1630, 1673

Priesthood, Ministerial: See Priest

Priesthood of the Faithful (PREEST-hØØd uhv *th*uh FAYTH-fuhl): The office that each layperson enjoys by virtue of Baptism. Those baptized join themselves with the Great High Priest and offer their lives totally to God. The priesthood of the faithful and the priesthood of the ordained differ both in essence and degree. CCC 784, 941, 1119, 1141, 1143, 1268, 1273, 1546-1547, 1591

Priests' Associations (PREESTS uh-SO-see-AY-shuhnz): Those associations of priests that were encouraged by the Second Vatican Council in *Presbyterorum Ordinis* as a means of encouraging the bond and cooperation that should exist among priests, to strengthen their spiritual lives and to build up the Body of Christ. Proper associations should "foster holiness," and priests are to "refrain from establishing or participating in associations whose ends or activity cannot be reconciled with the obligations proper to the clerical state."

Priests' Councils (PREESTS KAUN-suhlz): Sometimes called presbyteral councils, representative bodies of priests of a diocese, made up of *ex officio* members and others elected by the diocesan priests. They are generally consultative in nature, meant to advise the bishop on current problems.

Priests, Decree on the Ministry and Life of: See Presbyterorum Ordinis

Priests, Decree on the Training of: See Optatam Totius

Primacy of the Pope (PRAI-muh-see uhv *th*uh POP): The character enjoyed by the Pope, as Vicar of Christ and successor of St. Peter — the supreme visible judge, legislator, ruler, and teacher in the Church. Cf. CCC 882

Primary Option (PRAI-meh-ree AHP-shun): The life-choice of a person for or against God that shapes the basic orienta-

611

tion of moral conduct. A primary option for God, unfortunately, does not preclude the possibility of serious sin.

Primate (PRAI-muht): Now an honorary title used in some countries by the archbishop or bishop of the oldest see (Can. 438).

Primatial Liturgy (prai-MAY-shuhl LIH-ter-dzhee): Liturgical usages or variations on the Roman liturgy of the primatial sees of various countries, only four of which have survived (Lyons, Braga, Toledo, Milan).

Prime (PRAIM): Literally "first," from the Latin title of this part of the Divine Office, *ad primam,* "at the first hour of the day." Prime began in monastic communities as an additional prayer before the morning work period. Prime consisted of the reading of the martyrology (or saint of the day), a selection from the monastic Rule, and a prayer that we might "prosper for the work of our hands." In the reform of the Divine Office following Vatican II, Prime was suppressed and the obligation to pray it was removed. However, some monastic communities continue to use the Office of Prime because the *Psalterium Monasticum (Monastic Psalter)* makes allowances for its celebration.

Principalities (prihn-sih-PAL-ih-teez): In the N.T., "principalities" refers to one of several metaphysical beings quite hostile to God and humans. Along with the "principalities" (Greek *archai:* cf. Rom 8:38; 1 Cor 15:24; Eph 1:21, 3:10, 6:10-12; Col 1:16, 2:10, 15) are the "powers" (Greek *dynameis;* Rom 8:38; 1 Cor 15:24; Eph 1:21; 1 Pt 3:22; 2 Thes 1:7); "cosmological powers" (Greek *exousiai;* 1 Cor 15:24; Eph 1:21, 3:10; Col 1:15); "dominions" (Greek *kuriotes;* Eph 1:21; Col 1:16), and "thrones" (Greek *thronoi;* Col 1:16). The clarity of the N.T. witness helps us see that these beings were created through Christ and for Him (Col 1:16). Given their hostility to God and humans due to sin, Christ's ultimate rule over them (1 Cor 15:28; 1 Pt 3:22; etc.) expresses the reign of the Lord over all that is in the cosmos — a witness grounded in O.T. texts and completely reaffirmed in the N.T. This lordship of Christ, which reveals God's tremendous plan of salvation in the conquering of sin and death at the cross, now takes place in the Church (Eph 3:10). Cf. CCC 331

Prior (PRAI-er): The superior of some religious houses. Religious communities vary greatly in the role played by the prior. Benedictines and Cistercians have two kinds of priors who are dependent on the nearest abbey and one type who is an independent superior.

Prioress (PRAI-er-ehs): The woman religious superior who governs her community, much as a prior is superior over friars or monks.

Priory (PRAI-er-ee): The houses of monastic orders that are governed by priors or prioresses. Some priories are "conventual" (i.e., autonomous but not an abbey) or "simple" or "obedientiary" (i.e., dependencies of abbeys).

Priscillianism (prih-SIHL-yuhn-ih-zuhm): The fourth-century heresy, combining Docetism, Manichaeism, and Modalism, that rejected the preexistence and humanity of Jesus. Originated by Priscillian, a leader of a Spanish ascetic movement, who was executed for sorcery in 386, Priscillianism was condemned by the Councils of Toledo (340) and Braga (563).

Private Mass (PRAI-vuht MAS): A Mass celebrated by the priest alone or with the assistance of a sole server. Out of devotion, a priest may choose to celebrate a Mass without a congregation, as the Sacramentary calls it, or it may be a Mass for which a stipend was taken and there would not be a congregation to attend. The *General Instruction of the Roman Missal* treats such Masses in nn. 252-272. The revised Code of Canon Law treats this matter in Can. 837 and Can. 906. These canons reflect the principles found in *Sacrosanctum Concilium,* the Constitution on the Sacred Liturgy. Basically, these canons assert that a Mass with a congregation is preferable to a Mass without one, but in no way does the C.I.C. prohibit priests from offering Masses without a congregation, as some have falsely alleged or interpreted.

Private Revelation (PRAI-vuht reh-vuh-LAY-shuhn): Divine Revelation or public revelation must be accepted with the assent of faith as part of the Deposit of Faith. Private revelation, on the other hand, stems from apparitions or locutions that, although approved by Church authority as "worthy of belief," do not require the acceptance of the faithful. The content of such revelations may never be in contradiction to public revelation, which is found in the Sacred Scriptures and in Sacred Tradition.

Privation (prai-VAY-shuhn): A canonical punishment that consists of removal from ecclesiastical office (Can. 184).

Privilege (PRIHV-uh-lehdzh): 1. A special concession by authority, granting a favor (cc. 76-84; cf. Portiuncula, Privilege of the Faith). 2. A sacramental dispensation based on Holy Scripture (cf. Pauline Privilege, Petrine Privilege).

Privileged Altar (PRIHV-uh-lehdzh'd AL-ter): A term found in the 1917 Code of Canon Law (cc. 916-918). It refers to an altar where a plenary indulgence can be gained for a soul in purgatory by virtue of a Mass being offered there for that intention. When Pope Paul VI's apostolic constitution *Indulgentiarum Doctrina* appeared in 1967, it suppressed privileged altars (norm 20).

Privilege of the Faith (PRIHV-lehdzh uhv *th*uh FAYTH): Dissolution of the marriage of a baptized person and a nonbaptized person by the Holy Father. Cf. CCC 1640

Probabiliorism (prah-buh-BIHL-yaw-rih-zuhm): The moral system asserting that the "more probable" opinion of a varied set of acceptable positions regarding the binding character of a law should be accepted and promoted. If the reasons for being free from a law are more probably true, one is freed from the law's obligations. However, probabiliorism maintained that if it was probable that the law did not bind, one still had to follow it unless it was more probable that the law did not bind.

Probabilism (PRAH-buh-buhl-ih-zuhm:) The moral system contending that a "probably true" moral opinion is to be permitted. Probabilism maintained that "a doubtful law does not bind in conscience." Later moralists, called "rigorists," asserted that probabilism was too lax and advocated probabiliorism instead. Probabilism eventually degenerated into voluntarism (q.v.) because of the lack of objective criteria in determining whether an obligation was probable, more probable, or less probable.

Pro-Cathedral (pro-kuh-THEE-druhl): A church used on a temporary basis or as a quasi-permanent substitute for a diocesan cathedral. The need for a pro-cathedral may be prompted because the cathedral is insufficient in size and because it may be far removed from the majority of people in the diocese.

Process, Due: See Due Process

Process, Penal: See Penal Process

Processional Cross: See Cross, Processional

Procession, Divine (dih-VAIN pro-SEH-shuhn): The inter-Trinitarian origins of the Son and the Holy Spirit. "Generation" is the eternal procession of the Son from the Father, while "spiration" is the eternal procession of the Holy Spirit from the Father and the Son. The Divine Persons are distinct from one another in the One God; the processions ("relations") distinguish each Person. The Father's distinguishing attribute is paternity; the Son's, filiation; the Holy Spirit's, procession ("spiration").

Processions (pro-SEH-shuhnz): Sacred parades, either inside or outside the church, in which clergy and faithful travel from one place to another, giving praise, thanks, and worship to God (especially by adoring the Blessed Sacrament, honoring Our Lady or the angels and saints, asking pardon for sins, etc.). The O.T. presents many processions performed by the Israelites, especially that of Passover. Some processions are "ordinary" (such as the Corpus Christi procession with the Blessed Sacrament), while others are "functional" (e.g., procession of the casket at a Funeral Mass and entrance procession during the liturgy). Cf. CCC 1378, 1674

Procurator (PRAH-kyøø-ray-ter): (Latin: caretaker) 1. One who acts on behalf of another person or group in canonical trials. 2. The member of a religious order or religious institute appointed to represent the institute to the Holy See. 3. Title sometimes used for the financial officer of certain religious communities or other ecclesiastical entities.

Profanity (pro-FA-nih-tee): The disrespectful use of God's name, which, if done in anger and without reflection, is venially sinful, but if directed against God, deliberate, or causing scandal, is gravely wrong. CCC 2120

Profession of Faith (pro-FEH-shuhn uhv FAYTH): A public act by which personal belief is expressed through the recitation of a creed. By this means, a person attests to the community his faith in the teachings of the Church. The recitation of the Nicene Creed at Mass is the commonest form of profession of faith. On certain occasions, solemn professions of faith are required of persons who are about to undertake special responsibilities within the community of the Church (see Can. 883). Cf. CCC 14, 189, 978, 1229

Profession, Religious (rih-LIH-dzhuhs pro-FEH-shuhn): The public vows, taken by members of a Church-approved religious community consecrated to God, observing the three evangelical counsels: poverty, chastity, obedience. Temporary vows (between three and six years) precede perpetual profession — the sign that one is a full-fledged member of the institute. Cf. CCC 873, 915, 925, 944

Prokimenon (pro-kee-MEH-nahn): In the Byzantine Rite, versicles from the Psalms chanted by the reader before the Epistle.

Pro-Life (PRO-LAIF): Activities that promote and defend the dignity of human life, especially that of the preborn child. Initially, the term was used, after the Supreme Court's *Roe* v. *Wade* decision (1973) legalized abortion-on-demand, to signify opposition to this ruling. Now, the term has come to be used to designate activities to defend life from conception to natural death. "Pro-life" is in opposition to the "quality of life" argument, which asserts that only life that has some obvious value should be protected. Cf. CCC 1935, 2158, 2235, 2267, 2297, 2304

Promise of God (PRAH-mihs uhv GAHD): The covenant established by God with the Israelites and fulfilled in Christ. To inherit the promise, one must be united to Christ in the Holy Spirit for the glory of the Father. CCC 60, 212, 215, 422, 484, 652, 705-706, 1063-1065, 2787

Promoter of Justice (pro-MO-ter uhv DZHUHS-tihs): Tribunal official who acts as a prosecuting attorney at penal trials, and at contentious trials as well if the public good is at stake.

Promoter of the Faith (pro-MO-ter uhv *th*uh FAYTH): An official of the Congregation for the Causes of Saints who is part of the process leading to sainthood and whose duty is to raise all reasonable objections to the canonization of the candidate; frequently called "devil's advocate" in the past, in an irreverent and perhaps inappropriate attempt at humor.

Promulgation (prah-muhl-GAY-shuhn): The official method of making laws known to the community. Church laws are ordinarily promulgated by publication in the *Acta Apostolicae Sedis.*

Pro-Nuncio (pro-NØØN-see-o): (Latin: exchanged messenger) Papal representative or ambassador to a country that has diplomatic relations with the Holy See as well as to the Catholic Church in the same country.

Proofs, Judicial (dzhöö-DIH-shuhl PRÖÖFS): Documents, witness testimony, expert testimony, presumptions, and declarations that are admitted by the judge in a canonical trial in order to assist in demonstrating the truth of the issue.

Propaganda, Congregation of: See Evangelization of Peoples, Congregation for the

Propagation of the Faith and Sacred Congregation for the Evangelization of Peoples: See Evangelization of Peoples, Congregation for the

Propagation of the Faith, Society for the (suh-SAI-uh-tee for *th*uh prah-puh-GAY-shuhn uhv *th*uh FAYTH): An international organization founded under the inspiration of Pauline Jaricot in Lyons, France, in 1822, with the goal of assisting missions and missionaries with prayers and financial aid. Today it serves as the organ of the Holy See for worldwide collection of alms and their distribution among all Catholic missions. Its United States headquarters are located at 366 Fifth Avenue, New York, NY 10001.

Propers of the Mass (PRAH-pers uhv *th*uh MAS): Those parts of the Mass that change from day to day, as opposed to the Ordinary of the Mass, which remains the same for the most part. The propers include the Scripture readings, as well as the antiphons for the entrance and Communion rites, in addition to the Opening Prayer, Prayer Over the Gifts, and Prayer After Communion.

Property, Ecclesiastical (eh-klee-zee-AS-tih-kuhl PRAH-pertee): Real or movable property owned by an ecclesiastical juridic person.

Prophecies of Nostradamus (PRAH-fuh-sees uhv NO-strah-DAH-møøs): So-called predictions contained in *Centuries,* a supposed "future history of the world" in rhyme by Michel de Notredame (1503-1566), French astrologer-physician for King Charles IX, who won notoriety because some predicted events seemed to come true. The "prophecies" are vague and symbolic, subject to various interpretations, and to believe in their accuracy (or that of the "prophecies" below) is to refute or undercut the power of God (cf. Divination).

Prophecies of St. Malachy (PRAH-fuh-seez uhv SAYNT MAL-uh-kee): Supposed prophecies listing designations of one hundred two Popes and ten antipopes, falsely attributed to St. Malachy, Bishop of Armagh (d. 1148); actually forgeries by an unknown writer in the sixteenth century. The first seventy-five "prophecies" are fairly accurate because they were actually history, but from then on the list becomes vague, fanciful, and subject to wide interpretation; e.g., "interpreters" allege there will be only two Pontiffs after Pope John Paul II before the end of the world.

Prophecy, True (TRÖÖ PRAH-fuh-see): The expression and deliverance of a message from God that constitutes a true judgment of the present, in the light of the future, arrived at in obedience to the will of God and under divine authority. The term refers to any message from God, including predictions of the future. CCC 2004

Prophet (PRAH-feht): The individual who speaks in the name of God, in obedience to God, and delivers a message that is not one's own but God's is, properly speaking, a prophet. Among the chief prophets of the O.T. are Isaiah, Jeremiah, Ezekiel, and Daniel. John the Baptist is the great prophet of the N.T. CCC 64, 201, 218, 522-523, 719, 762, 1964, 2100, 2380, 2543, 2581, 2584, 2595

Prophetical Literature of the Bible (pro-FEH-tih-kuhl LIHT-er-uh-tsher uhv thuh BAI-buhl): Those books of the O.T. comprising the four major prophets (Isaiah, Jeremiah, Ezekiel, and Daniel) and the twelve minor prophets (Hosea, Joel, Amos, Obadiah, Jonah, Micah, Nahum, Habakkuk, Zephaniah, Haggai, Zechariah, and Malachi).

Prophetism (PRAH-fuh-tih-zuhm): The special charism that God imparts to certain individuals empowering them to be spokesmen of revelation. Moses, the prophets, John the Baptist, the Apostles, and other singular figures in the Scriptures are the recipients of this gift. The formal property of the charism of prophecy is that the prophet delivers not his own message but the Word of God. The prophet's gifts and personality provide the vehicle by which the Word of God is communicated. Cf. CCC 2004

Propitiation: See Satisfaction

Proportionalism (pruh-POR-shuh-nuhl-ih-zuhm): The moral doctrine asserting that an action is judged on whether the evils resulting are proportionate to the goods that result. If the evils outweigh the goods, the act is reprehensible; however, if the opposite is true, the act is upright. Proportionalism differs from consequentialism in that the former admits that the inherent morality of the act and the agent's intention must also be considered. Critics submit that proportionalism does not offer an objective criterion for determining when evils are proportionate or disproportionate; furthermore, it does not consider the intrinsic nature of human acts or encourage Christians to grow in virtue.

Propositions, Condemned (kuhn-DEHM'D prah-puh-ZIH-shuhnz): A set of eighty liberal and modernist propositions designated as contrary to the Catholic Faith by Pope Pius IX in the encyclical *Quanta Cura* in 1864. Included in this "Syllabus of Errors" were pantheism, naturalism, rationalism, latitudinarianism, socialism, communism, and liberalism. Other condemned propositions concerned interpretation of the Bible, Church-State relations, papal temporal authority, Christian marriage, and liberal political views.

Proselyte (PRAH-suh-lait): (From Greek *proselytos:* stranger, one who approaches) Claims about God's universal supremacy, as the Creator, the only God, etc., all naturally flow into the notion of mission to others. We find such convictions throughout the O.T. (Is 42:6 ff., 45:14 ff., 56:1-8, 66:19; Jonah, etc.). Thus anyone who converts to the one true God and becomes a Jew in the full and legal sense is a proselyte. In classical Judaism, conversion included circumcision, a ritual bath, and the offering of a sacrificial victim. From the second century B.C. to around the fourth century A.D., many Gentiles were attracted to elements of Judaism (monotheism, sexual ethics, Sabbath observance, knowledge of God through ancient writings, etc.). The N.T. offers limited evidence concerning Jewish attempts to convert Gentiles (Mt 23:15); many converts to Judaism became Christians (e.g., Acts 6:5).

Proskomide (pro-sko-MEE-day): 1. The credence table or table for the offerings. It is the same as the altar of prothesis in the Eastern Church. 2. The service of preparation performed there.

Prosphora (PRAHS-for-ah): 1. The offering made by the congregation in the celebration of the Divine Liturgy of the Byzantine Rite. 2. In a restricted sense, the prosphora is the loaf out of which the priest will carve the part to be consecrated.

Prostitution (prahs-tih-TÖÖ-shuhn): The practice of selling one's body in sexual "favors" for money or other return. It is contrary to "fidelity," one of the goods of marriage, disrupts the harmony within families, and often frustrates the procreative dimension of marital intercourse. Prostitution encourages immorality and lust, spreading diseases that threaten the collective health of society. **CCC 2355**

Protestant (PRAH-tuh-stuhnt): A name originating at the Second Diet of Speyer (1529) when several princes and cities objected to the reversal of a previous decision to allow each prince or city to choose to be either Lutheran or Catholic. The term came to designate all those groups and individuals who espoused the anti-Catholic reformation in the sixteenth century.

Protestantism (PRAH-tuh-stuhnt-ih-zuhm): A name given to the movement of protest and reform inspired by Martin Luther in Germany and later taken up by John Calvin in France, Ulrich Zwingli in Switzerland, and King Henry VIII in England. The official response of the Church to Protestantism occurred at the Council of Trent (1545-1563). Eventually, the Protestant movements took on the form of independent or national churches, the predecessors of modern denominations. The major groups within Protestantism today are Baptists, Methodists, Lutherans, Presbyterians, Disciples of Christ, Pentecostals, and Quakers.

Prothesis (pro-THEE-sihs): 1. The preparation of the offerings performed at a side altar in the Eastern Church. 2. The side altar itself.

Protocanonical Books of Scripture (pro-to-ka-NAH-nih-kuhl BØØKS uhv SKRIHP-tsher): Those books admitted to the canon of Scripture with little or no debate, having achieved canonical status early (and thus called *homologoumena,* or agreed upon) and distinguished from the deutero-canonical books, which were under discussion until doubts about their canonicity could be resolved (called *antilogomena,* disputed; or *amphiballomena,* doubtful).

Protoevangelium (pro-to-ay-vahn-DZHEHL-ee-øøm): The "first gospel," Gn 3:15, which refers to the coming of Jesus Christ as promised by God. After Original Sin, the Lord promised Eve that her offspring would crush Satan, thereby defeating sin and spiritual blindness.

Protomartyr (PRO-to-mahr-ter): A title frequently given to St. Stephen, the first martyr (Acts 7:60), or to the first martyr of a specific nation. The Feast of St. Stephen is December 26. Placing the feast of martyred Stephen so close to the Solemnity of Christmas is not accidental. Having celebrated the beginning of our redemption with Christ's birth, the very next day the Church bids us contemplate the prospect of our entrance into eternal glory.

Protonotary Apostolic (pro-to-NO-ter-ee a-pah-STAH-lihk): 1. One of seven minor prelates of the Roman Curia whose duty it is to sign or notarize papal documents. 2. The highest honorary title accorded a priest.

Proverbs, Book of (BØØK uhv PRAH-verbz): The oldest of the sapiential books of the O.T., some parts of which may go back to Solomon (to whose authorship the book is attributed in Jewish tradition). Although there is no logical order to the arrangement of the Proverbs, there are basic recurrent themes: the value of wisdom, parents as a source of wisdom, cautions against evil men and women, and warnings against idleness, greed, arrogance, and gullibility.

Providence of God (PRAH-vih-dehnts uhv GAHD): The plan, an act of divine wisdom, by which God orders all things to their true end. It is, like God's will, eternal and involves God's act of preserving and governing His creation. While everything is ordered by God as the First Cause, He nevertheless allows His creatures to choose freely — even to choose moral evils. No sin or physical defect can obstruct God's plan. CCC 302-314, 321-324, 395, 1040, 2215, 2547, 2738, 2830

Providentissimus Deus (pro-vee-dehn-TIH-see-møøs DAY-øøs): (Latin: Most Provident God) The encyclical, beginning a new approach to Catholic biblical studies, issued by Pope Leo XIII in 1893, reiterating the beliefs that the Church is the only true interpreter of Sacred Scripture. This letter, called the "Magna Carta of Biblical Studies," states that God is the author of Scripture and that He influenced the intellect and will of the human writers. Experts are encouraged to use biblical tools in the study of Scripture and are to become familiar with the ancient languages used in Scripture. Pope Leo XIII exhorted the faithful to read Scripture "with reverence and piety."

Province (PRAH-vihnts): 1. A grouping of two or more dioceses together with a metropolitan archbishop as the head. 2. A territorial division of a religious institute.

Provincial (pruh-VIHN-shuhl): The major religious superior of a regional division or province of a religious institute, subject to the superior general of the institute, with the responsibility of administering the province and fostering fidelity to the constitutions of the institute by making regular visitations to the houses of the province.

Provision, Canonical (ka-NAH-nih-kuhl pro-vih-zhuhn): The canonical term for the formal filling of an ecclesiastical office (cc. 146-156).

Provisors, Statute of (STAT-shööt uhv pro-VAI-zerz): A law passed by King Edward III of England in 1351 that purported to annul any episcopal appointments made in the realm without the king's consent.

Proxy Marriage (PRAHK-see MEHR-ehdzh): A marriage in which the parties are not present to each other when consent is exchanged. A proxy, or stand-in, represents one or both of the parties (Can. 1105).

Prudence (PRÖÖ-duhnts): (Latin *prudentia:* foresight in practical matters) The exercise of the knowledge of what things ought to be avoided. One of the cardinal virtues, prudence is an intellectual and moral virtue that, although conferred by God, enables a person to control conduct in the light of consequences. CCC 1788, 1805-1806, 1835, 1906

Psalm, Responsorial (reh-spahn-SOR-ee-uhl SAHM): The text and melody of the psalm chanted after the First Reading during the Sacred Liturgy. The cantor or choir intones the refrain, and the faithful repeat it. Then, the cantor or choir sings the verses of the psalm, while the faithful respond again with the end of each verse.

Psalmody (SAHLM-uh-dee): The different methods and arrangements for singing the Psalms, of which there are three main types: (1) responsorial, in which the congregation repeats a refrain in response to verses recited by a leader or cantor; (2) antiphonal, in which two groups within the congregation alternate the verses of the Psalm; (3) direct, in which all sing or recite the Psalm together. Cf. CCC 1156, 1176-1177, 2585-2589, 2657

Psalms, Book of (BØØK uhv SAHMZ): The O.T. book attributed by Tradition to the authorship of David and containing one hundred fifty religious songs and poems. Many of the Psalms are hymns of praise and thanksgiving. Others are songs of petition or repentance, while still others are expressions of messianic expectations. The Psalms are perhaps one of the most important constituents of Christian worship. They make up the bulk of the Liturgy of the Hours, distributed over a four-week cycle. They also figure prominently at the celebration of the Eucharist and the other sacraments. In addition, they are particularly appropriate for private prayer and meditation.

Psalter (SAHL-ter): (Latin *psalterium,* from Greek *psalterion*) 1. The Book of Psalms (q.v.). 2. Any book containing a collection of psalms for devotional purposes.

Pseudo-Isidore (SYÖÖ-do-IH-zih dor): (Greek *pseudo:* false) Writings attributed to Isidore Mercator (d. A.D. 850), listing ninth-century decretals, but not likely his actual work, distinguished from his genuine writings by the designation of Pseudo-Isidore.

Publican (PUH-blih-kuhn): (Latin *publicanus:* tax farmer) A man involved in the collection of taxes for the Roman government. The government farmed out, for a fixed yearly sum, the right to collect taxes. The amount charged for this right was reckoned on the basis of the estimated revenues. The fee charged was lower than the anticipated return. The tax collector was expected to pay the fixed price, whether he succeeded in collecting that amount or not. He could, however, keep any money above the amount established by the government. Those engaged in this work were private businessmen. The agreement was struck between the government and the chief tax-gatherer, who in turn would employ tax-gatherers who would do the actual tax-gathering. As can be easily surmised, such a system was susceptible of abuses and corruption. That abuses did materialize is clear from the contempt in which publicans were held as a very general rule. The Jews had further reasons to disdain publicans. For one thing, publicans functioned in behalf of the foreign invaders, the Romans, which seemed disloyal. Besides, their role was reprehensible because it required Jewish publicans to be in close contact with Gentiles, an activity judged to be defiling. In N.T. times in Palestine, it was customary to farm out only customs duties, not regular taxes. Although publicans were, as a rule, bracketed with the lower elements of society, e.g., sinners and Gentiles (Mt 9:10 f., 18:17), the N.T. does, on occasion, present publicans in a favorable light. It notes, for instance, that publicans were among those who came to be baptized by John the Baptist (Lk 3:12; 7:29), that Levi was a publican (Mt 9:9), and that Jesus told a parable that showed a publican in a good light (Lk 18:9-14).

Public Propriety (PUH-blihk pro-PRAI-uh-tee): A diriment impediment to marriage that arises between a man and the blood relatives in the first degree of the direct line of a woman with whom he is living in public concubinage. The same is true for the woman and the blood relatives of the man (Can. 1093).

Public Revelation: See Revelation

Pulpit (PUHL-piht): (Latin *pulpitum:* platform) A raised stand of wood or stone from which the Sacred Scriptures are proclaimed and the homily is delivered. It first came into general use in the Middle Ages. Today, the pulpit is commonly but not exclusively found in the sanctuary of the church. In a few instances, the pulpit is placed in the nave of the church for greater visibility or audibility. The present *General Instruction of the Roman Missal* does not demand that the homily be given at the pulpit, allowing for it to be offered either at the chair or the lectern (n. 136). The revised *Ceremonial of Bishops* permits the bishop to preach his homily at his chair or another suitable place (n. 120).

Punishment Due for Sin (PUH-nihsh-muhnt DÖÖ for SIHN): Consequence of any offense against God and neighbor, either: (1) eternal, the punishment of hell to which one becomes subject by commission of mortal sin; or (2) temporal, a consequence of venial sin and/or forgiven mortal sin, not everlasting, and remittable in this life by means of penance. Temporal punishment unremitted during this life is remitted by suffering in purgatory. **CCC 2061**

Purgatory (PER-guh-tor-ee): The state or condition of cleansing for one who dies in God's friendship ("state of grace"), but who still has sins or temporal punishment for which to atone. Neither the nature nor the duration of purgatory is specified in Catholic doctrine; however, the existence of purgatory is a dogma of the Faith. The faithful are encouraged to assist the "poor souls" by their prayers and penances. CCC 1030-1032, 1472

Purification of the Blessed Virgin Mary (pyøør-ih-fih-KAY-shuhn uhv *th*uh BLEH-sehd VER-dzhihn MEH-ree): The commemoration of Mary's having been ritually cleansed according to the Jewish law after the birth of Our Lord. Celebrated on February 2, the feast is now called the Presentation of Jesus in the Temple ("Candlemas Day") and dates in the Western Church from the seventh century. Candles are blessed on this day to remember Simeon's prophecy about Jesus as a "light to the nations" (cf. Lk 2:32).

Purificator (PYØØR-ih-fih-kay-ter): (Latin *purus*, clean + *facere*, to make) A small linen cloth usually marked with a cross in the center, used in cleansing the vessels after Holy Communion.

Purim (PØØR-ihm): According to popular etymology, the word derives from the Hebrew word for "lot" *(pur,* plural *purim)*. The actual origins of the word, however, remain obscure; some suggest that it may have a Babylonian root. The term designates a Jewish festival celebrated in the spring (February-March) on the fourteenth of the Jewish month of Adar. The celebration commemorates the deliverance of the Jews in Persia from the persecution of Haman, as recounted in the Book of Esther. The feast seems to have more of a national and secular coloration than a religious one. It has also been suggested that Purim may represent an adaptation by the Jews of an original Persian or Mesopotamian holiday.

Puritanism (PYØØR-ih-tuhn-ih-zuhm): The doctrine held by those in the Church of England who objected that the reforms of Elizabeth I and of her successors did not go far enough to eliminate all traces of Roman Catholicism. Their desire to "purify" the Church of England did not succeed to the extent that they had hoped, so many fled to Holland. Subsequently, a group of Puritans founded the Plymouth Colony in Massachusetts.

Putative Father (PYÖÖ-tuh-tihv FAH-ther): (Latin *putare:* to think) Joseph, the foster father of Jesus, who was thought by outsiders to be the natural father of Christ; hence, St. Joseph is the "putative father" of Our Lord.

Putative Marriage (PYÖÖ-tuh-tihv MEHR-ehdzh): A marriage that is actually invalid because of the presence of an undispensed impediment or a defect of consent but yet was contracted in good faith by one or both parties.

Pyx (PIHKS): (Greek *puxis:* box) A sacred vessel in which the Blessed Sacrament is placed in order to be brought to the sick and homebound. Originally made of wood, the pyx today is a flat container made of metal. Priests and those properly deputized to bring Holy Communion to the sick and homebound may have their own pyx. Sometimes a pyx with a large Host in it is found in the tabernacle. In this instance, the pyx contains the Host to be placed in the monstrance for Exposition and Benediction.

Q

Q Document (KYÖÖ DAHK-yöö-mehnt): The hypothetical written source, containing the various sayings of Jesus, upon which the Synoptic Evangelists relied (along with "oral tradition") when composing their Gospels under divine inspiration. In 1838, C. H. Weisse contended for the existence of "Q" (from German *Quelle,* source). While accepted by Catholic and Protestant scholars, this theory now has been severely criticized, in part because of the failure to discover any evidence of such a source.

Qoheleth: See Ecclesiastes, Book of

Quadragesima (kwah-druh-DZHAY-zee-muh): (Latin: fortieth) The forty days of Lent, a penitential period in the Church. Cf. CCC 540, 1095, 1438

Quadragesimo Anno (kwah-druh-DZHAY-zee-mo AH-no): On the fortieth anniversary of Pope Leo XIII's epochal encyclical on social justice, *Rerum Novarum,* May 15, 1931, Pope Pius XI issued an encyclical letter known by this title. In essence, its teaching reaffirmed that of the earlier document, but it had a sense of added urgency, coming as it did during the worldwide depression. Pius XI, echoing Leo, rejected both the economic extremes of unbridled, cutthroat capitalism and collectivist, statist socialism. It also encouraged a restructured society, based on a respect for the trades, the laborer, and the owner, holding up as a model the unified, organic society common to the Middle Ages. While supporting the right of private property, it also posited that government and the wealthy had the duty to ameliorate social evils, and that the worker had the right to a wage that would enable him to support his family "in reasonable and frugal comfort." CCC 1928-1942, 2425-2426, 2832

Quaestor (KWAYS-tor): (Latin: investigator, treasurer) One designated to collect alms for the poor.

Quakers (KWAY-kerz): The popular name for members of the Religious Society of Friends, founded by George Fox (1624-1691), who taught that each person should follow an "inner light," which would be a guide. The term "Quaker" came into being first in a scornful way, when Fox told a certain Justice Gervase Bennett that he should "tremble at the Word of God." Quakers do not practice any of the traditional outward forms of Christianity, including sacraments.

Quanta Cura (KWAHN-tuh KÖÖ-ruh): The encyclical, issued on December 8, 1864, by Pope Pius IX, promulgating the *Syllabus Errorum,* which condemned eighty liberal and modernistic theses.

Quarantine (KWAW-ruhn-teen): Originally a strict fast lasting for forty days, which was a specific penance assigned by a confessor, but then came to be applied to partial indulgences, referring to the amount of temporal punishment removed by the particular penance. With the revision of indulgences in 1967, the term ceased to be used with this meaning.

Quasi-Domicile (KWAY-zai DOH-mih-sail): (From Latin: almost + dwelling) Temporary residence in a territory, status acquired by actually living there for three months or going there with the intention of living there for at least three months (Can. 102).

Quasi-Parish (KWAY-zai PA-rihsh): A temporary community of the faithful, with its own pastor but not yet erected to the full status of a parish, with the consequent degree of stability (Can. 516).

Queenship of Mary (KWEEN-shihp uhv MEH-ree): The liturgical commemoration of Mary as Queen of Angels and Men, Queen of Heaven and Earth, celebrated on August 22.

Quiet, Prayer of (PREHR uhv KWAI-eht): A form of contemplation that cannot be achieved by human effort but is a gift from God, although it presupposes a life of virtue. It directs the human will toward God and brings an experience of peace and heightened awareness of God's presence. **Cf. CCC 2713, 2717**

Quietism (KWAI-eh-tih-zuhm): Doctrine promoted by Miguel Molinos, similar to pantheism, stating that sanctity could be obtained by doing as little as possible; one had to remain "passive" by praying in a meditative way, which would eliminate all desires. Then a kind of mystical death would be achieved, and one would find oneself "in God." Since the person's will would now be destroyed, one could not commit sin. This belief has no rightful place in Christian spirituality and has never been approved by the Church.

Quinisextum Council (kwee-nee-SEHKS-tøøm KAUN-sihl): (Latin: fifth-sixth) Also known as the Trullan Synod, a meeting of Eastern bishops held in 691 in Constantinople, in order to complete the work of the fifth (553) and sixth (680) general councils. It enacted canons on various disciplinary matters, but its decisions were rejected by Pope St. Sergius I because Rome had not been represented and some of the canons put forth were contrary to Roman practice. This action contributed to the growing rift between the Eastern and Western Churches.

Quinquagesima (kwihn-kwah-DZHAY-zee-muh): (Latin: fiftieth) The Sunday before Lent, the fiftieth day before Easter. This was the last of the pre-Lenten Sundays in the liturgical calendar before Vatican II. In the reform authorized by Vatican II, Quinquagesima was eliminated so as not to overshadow the complete impact of Lent.

Quinquennial Report (kwihn-KWEH-nee-uhl ree-PORT): A report on all aspects of a diocese, which a bishop is required to complete and submit every five years to the Holy See.

Quinque Viae (KWIHN-kway VEE-ay): (Latin: five ways) The five "proofs" for God's existence advanced by St. Thomas Aquinas in his *Summa Theologiae* (Part 1, question 2, article 3). Simply put, the five ways are: (1) all the motion in the world points to an unmoved Prime Mover; (2) the subordinate agents in the world imply the First Agent; (3) there must be a Cause Who is not perishable and Whose existence is underived; (4) the limited goodness in the world must be a reflection of Unlimited Goodness; (5) all things tend to become something, and that inclination must have proceeded from some Rational Planner. St. Thomas attempts to demonstrate that the God Christians worship is the Cause of the world. CCC 31-35, 286

Quire: See Choir

Quirinal (KWEER-ih-nuhl): One of the seven hills of Rome upon which a papal residence was built in the sixteenth century as a summer palace for the Popes. It was also the location of many papal conclaves. In 1870, it became the residence for Italy's kings and, since 1946, Italy's presidents.

Qumran Community (KØØM-rahn kuh-MYÖÖ-nih-tee): The group of ascetical Jews, consisting of priests and laymen, married and celibate, who lived near Wadi Qumran between 125 B.C. and A.D. 70. Probably Essenes, the Qumran Community was considered fanatical; the members believed themselves to be the "remnant of Israel." The Dead Sea Scrolls, other archaeological findings, and the writings of the period show this community to have prayed daily from the Psalter, performed purificatory washings symbolizing repentance, celebrated a religious meal of bread and wine, and shared property together.

Qumranites (KØØM-ruh-naits): The Jewish religious community, with a library now known as the Dead Sea Scrolls, that apparently lived near the Dead Sea, seven to eight miles south of Jericho, a location known as Khirbet Qumran. The Qumranites were probably Essenes and lived there from 125 B.C. until A.D. 70.

Qumran Movement (KØØM-rahn MÖÖV-mehnt): The Jewish "separatist" movement, probably composed of Essenes, whose members lived near the Dead Sea from approximately 125 B.C. to A.D. 70 and whose library (i.e., the Dead Sea Scrolls) was found in 1947 near the Wadi Qumran.

Quo Vadis (kwo VAH-dihs): The question, recorded in the apocryphal Acts of Peter (c. A.D. 190), that St. Peter asked Jesus during the persecution under Nero (ruled 37-68). As St. Peter was escaping Rome, he saw Christ and said: *"Domine, quo vadis?"* ("Lord, where are You going?"). Jesus said that He was going to Rome to be crucified again, since Peter was apparently unwilling to die for Him. Peter then followed Him and was crucified with his head downward as a sign of his unworthiness to be martyred in precisely the same manner as his Lord. Henryk Sienkiewicz wrote the novel *Quo Vadis* in 1895.

R

Rabat (RA-bee or ruh-BAHT): (From French *rabattre,* to pull down) The piece of black cloth attached to the Roman collar and worn under the clerical shirt or cassock of a seminarian, deacon, or priest. The monsignor's and bishop's rabat is purple, a cardinal's is red, and the Pope's is white.

Rabbi (RA-bai): (Aramaic: my master) The term *rabboni* is an emphatic form of "rabbi." Originally, the word was employed as a respectful honorific form of address. In several of the Gospels, it is so used to address Jesus. This was the fashion in which students of a scribe would address their teacher. Right after the N.T. period, in the early Christian era, the word was used by Jews as a title and as such was combined with a scholar's name, thus: Rabbi Judah-ban-Nasi. At a still later time, the word "rabbi" began to be used as a common noun with the meaning, "a teacher." By this time, the force of the suffix "i" ("my") was no longer felt. Cf. CCC 581

Rabdos (RAHB-dos): The Eastern bishop's staff, or crozier.

Raccolta (ruh KOL-tuh): (Italian: collection or harvest) The official Roman Catholic prayer book, first published in 1807 by Telesforo Galli in Rome, containing all the indulgences attached to prayers and pious works. The Raccolta was used prior to the Second Vatican Council. Today, the *Enchiridion Indulgentiarum (Enchiridion of Indulgences)* contains the indulgenced prayers and the normal conditions for obtaining plenary and partial indulgences.

Race (RAYS): Distinction based on the color of skin. The Church has maintained that all humans are created equal and endowed with a rational soul (intellect, will, memory). Any prejudice and mistreatment on the basis of race is to be roundly rejected. Cf. CCC 1935, 2113

Racism (RAY-sih-zuhm): A prejudicial attitude about members of particular racial groups, which can lead to discriminatory behavior against individuals. Racism is contrary to the Gospel message because it violates justice by denying the legitimate value and rights of others, and it is contrary to the law of charity because it falsely justifies doing harm to others. Cf. CCC 1935, 2113

Ransom (RAN-suhm): The term has a strict meaning in its original sense — the cost for release from detention or incarceration. In the O.T., it expresses God's salvific response to Israel's predicaments; in the N.T., it is God's response to the sinner who is in bondage or "incarcerated by sin" (Mt 20:28; Mk 10:45). The verb can refer to the action of paying the ransom (figuratively, 1 Pt 1:18) and means to set free, redeem, or rescue (Lk 24:21; Ti 2:14; Acts 28:19). The noun means "redeemer," in the sense of one who effects freedom from slavery (e.g., Moses [Acts 7:35]). The notion of ransom paid by a ransomer touches upon the very core of the mystery of salvation: We are dead to God, prisoners to the bondage of sin until we are freed, ransomed by Christ's precious Blood. His Blood communicates life to us (Jn 6:53 ff.; 1 Cor 10:16); it is an offering for our sins (Rom 3:25), which "redeems" us (Eph 1:7) and draws us near to God (Eph 2:13), effecting eternal redemption (Heb 9:12). **Cf. CCC 440, 601-602, 605, 608, 622, 786**

Rapture (RAP-tsher): The gathering up of the saved at Christ's Second Coming. St. Paul writes: "And the dead in Christ will rise first; then we who are alive, who are left, shall be caught up together with them in the clouds to meet the Lord in the air" (1 Thes 4:16-17). **Cf. CCC 1001**

Rash Judgment (RASH DZHUHDZH-mehnt): A hastily formed opinion, favorable or not, on the moral status of another. At times, judgments must be made concerning another's actions so as to promote the common welfare (e.g., voting for a candidate). Yet the judgment must be reached in charity and after painstaking investigation. Rash judgment, against which Christ warned (cf. Mt 7:1-2), is neither charitable nor just. **CCC 2477, 2478**

Rationalism, Theological (thee-uh-LAH-dzhih-kuhl RA-shuhn-uhl-ih-zuhm): The notion that human reason is sufficient, without Divine Revelation, to know truths about God and other spiritual realities. Theological rationalists believe that reason supersedes faith. The Church, in the constitution *Dei Filius* of the First Vatican Council, asserted that reason is sufficient when proving God's existence but that not all about God can be known by reason; hence, faith gives solidity to reason and informs it. Reason can help one know that the rational soul is immortal; but faith and Divine Revelation are needed to know and accept what Christ has handed on to the Apostles. Cf. CCC 35-39, 47, 50, 156-159, 237, 274, 286, 1706

Ratio Studiorum (RAT-see-o stöö-dee-OR-øøm): The "plan of studies" of a religious institute or community, usually used by those in a religious province, to be followed by all candidates and students. For example, the *Ratio Studiorum* of the Jesuits presents the curriculum for candidates for vows and orders, as well as students at lower levels.

Reader: See Lay Reader

Readings, Cycle of (SAI-kuhl uhv REED-ihngs): The Church calendar assigns a three-year cycle of Scripture readings for Sundays. A two-year weekday cycle, a one-year cycle for feasts of saints, and readings for ritual Masses and Masses for particular intentions are also designated. These readings are contained in a book called the Lectionary. The present English Lectionary was approved in 1970. A second edition, basically the same as the first, was published in 1981, with yet a third revision mandated in 2001. If three readings are required, the first is usually from the O.T., the second from the N.T. (Letters, Acts, Revelation), and the third reading always a selection from a Gospel. If two readings are required, the first is from the O.T., Letters, Acts, or Revelation; the second reading is a passage from one of the Gospels. The Sunday Lectionary arranges the texts in a three-year cycle. Thus the same text is read only once every three years. Each year is designated A, B, or C. Year C is a year whose number is equally divisible by three. Thus 1990 is year A, 1991 is year B, 1992 is year C, and so forth.

Real Presence: See Presence, Real

Reason, Age of: See Age of Reason

Recension (ree-SEHN-shuhn): (Latin *recensere,* to assess) Revision of a biblical text based on critical examination of the sources. Clearly, from the significance of such a revision, there must be a substantial reason for a recension to be made, with the attempt always at transmitting the intended words of the inspired writer.

Rechabites (REH-kuh-baits): An order or group of people devoted to a nomadic way of life. This group dwelt in the Judean desert in Jeremiah's time but later, during Nebuchadnezzar's campaign in Judah, took refuge within the confines of the city of Jerusalem. The origins of the order remain obscure. In Jer 35:6 they are reported as maintaining "Jonadab, the son of Rechab, our father." The ambiguity of the phrase does not quite make clear whether Jonadab or Rechab founded the order. Verse 19 asserts that Jonadab in fact was the founder, leaving unexplained why in that case they should be called Rechabites. The rule the Rechabites lived by was one of unadulterated nomadism. They eschewed wine and were not to build or live in houses. They lived in tents. Neither were they ever to sow seeds (Jer 35:6-7), which was judged to be a degrading occupation for a man. This rule of life reflects the difference of outlook between those given to pastoral pursuits on the one hand and those engaged in agricultural enterprises on the other. It is a conflict that was encountered widely in the Near East of those times. In the literature of Sumer, the farmer is preferred to the shepherd; just the opposite is the Cain and Abel account, in which the shepherd is favored. Elsewhere in the O.T., the naturalness and simplicity of the nomadic life is commended. The Rechabites espoused the desert nomadic values as a religion. It has been remarked that the Rechabites could not have been very numerous, since Jeremiah assembles the whole group in a single room of the Temple. There is no sound basis for affirming the survival of the Rechabites beyond the Babylonian exile. In the middle of the nineteenth century, the name "Rechabites" was assumed in New England by a society whose members were pledged to total abstinence from alcohol.

Recidivist (reh-SIH-dih-vihst): One who habitually commits the same sin and who, despite his claims of sorrow, makes little improvement. Recidivism opposes the virtue of penance, which inclines one to make a break with sin. Recidivists need to be dealt with charitably and firmly and implored to beg God for fortitude and patience so as to bear the temptations they encounter. Cf. CCC 1865

Recollection (reh-kuh-LEHK-shuhn): 1. Meditation or concentration on God and spiritual entities, enabling one to develop as a Christian disciple (as in "Day of Recollection"). Distractions are avoided as much as possible by one seeking to be recollected. 2. The stage in the spiritual life in which the faculties of one's rational soul (intellect, will, memory) are quiet, allowing for God's grace to work uninhibited. Cf. CCC 1185, 1199, 2711, 2721

Reconciliation (reh-kuhn-sihl-ee-AY-shuhn): (Latin: recovery) 1. The effect of Christ's saving passion, death, and resurrection, which restores man to God. Complete reconciliation with God will occur only at the Parousia (q.v.). 2. A term often used for the Sacrament of Penance because it emphasizes the desired effect of that encounter with Christ. CCC 1422-1429, 1440-1470, 1480-1498; cf. 393, 433, 553, 755, 822, 827, 927, 980-982, 1020, 1210, 1259, 1385, 1395, 1401, 1415, 1532, 1622, 1851, 1861-1864, 2042, 2490, 2844

Reconciliation, Rite of: See Penance, Sacrament of

Reconciliation Room (re-kuhn-sihl-ee-AY-shuhn RŌŌM): Place where the Sacrament of Penance is celebrated (cf. Confessional), offering the option of receiving the Sacrament anonymously or face-to-face.

Reconventio (ray-kawn-VEHNT-see-o): (Latin: recontract) Canonical term for the canon law equivalent of what in civil law would be called a counterclaim (Can. 1482).

Records, Sacramental (SA-kruh-mehn-tuhl REH-kerdz): Registers kept by the Church that record the reception of the sacraments by persons. The principal record is the baptismal record, which notes the reception of the Sacraments of Confirmation, Matrimony, and Orders.

Recourse, Hierarchical (hai-er-AHRK-ih-kuhl REE-kors): Canonical process whereby a person can appeal an administrative decree of a superior to that person's superior or superiors.

Rector (REHK-ter): (Latin: guide or pilot) 1. A priest charged with the pastoral care of a church that is neither a parish church nor a church entrusted to a religious community. 2. The person in charge of a seminary. 3. The person in charge of certain pontifical faculties, universities, or colleges. 4. The local superior of Jesuit communities.

Recusants (REHK-yöö-zuhnts): (From Latin: to refuse) Name given those tenacious Catholics in England who refused to accept the Church of England during the reign of Elizabeth I (1558-1603) and beyond. A law of 1593 used the term as synonymous with "traitor." Some recusants were martyred, some imprisoned, some harassed, some stripped of property and voting rights, and some forced into exile. One bright spot in centuries of oppression is that exiled Catholic scholars established centers of learning at Douai and Rheims, where priests were formed, and where the Scriptures were translated into English. Prejudice against the recusants came to an end during the reign of George II, when the Second Relief Act of 1791 repealed many anti-Catholic proscriptions.

Redditio of Creed (reh-DEET-see-o uhv KREED): This phrase, meaning "the return of the Creed," refers to the Profession of Faith during the baptismal ceremony via the question-and-answer format.

Redeemer: See Redemption of Man

Redemption of Man (ree-DEHMP-shuhn uhv MAN): The deliverance of humanity from sin and the restoration of grace due to the passion, death, and resurrection of Jesus Christ. The redemption is God's free gift to mankind and cannot be earned. Theologically speaking, the Father could have chosen another way to reconcile the world to Himself; yet it was most fitting that His Son demonstrate His obedience and die for the salvation of mankind. Christ's salvific act proves that death has no power over man. Now, through the redemption, the human race is once again united to the Godhead. CCC 55, 64, 494, 508, 517, 571, 573, 601, 605, 613, 616, 634-635, 776, 1067

Red Mass (REHD MAS): The yearly celebration of the Eucharistic Sacrifice that commemorates the opening of the annual session of the Sacred Roman Rota in Rome, the Supreme Court in Washington, D.C., and other judicial bodies throughout the world. The "Red" refers to the red vestments used to honor the Holy Spirit, Who is the Source of the seven gifts so necessary to the judiciary.

Refectory (rih-FEHK-tuh-ree): The word commonly used in religious communities for a dining room.

Reformation (reh-for-MAY-shuhn): A complex movement of the sixteenth and seventeenth centuries that divided Western Christians into two distinct groups: Catholics, marked by adherence to the Roman Pontiff and the historic formulations of the Faith, and a group of other Christian bodies, loosely united as "Protestants." A number of factors had weakened the Church in the late medieval period: the decline of religious learning and fervor after the Black Death, the disruptions of the Avignon papacy and the schism of the West, conciliarism, the worldliness and corruption of many churchmen, nominalism, and other unhealthy theological trends. Movements toward spiritual renewal and even a renewal council (Lateran V, 1517) had limited influence. The Reformation is generally dated from the publication of certain theses by Martin Luther on October 31, 1517. Central to Luther's teaching is the affirmation of Original Sin as sinful concupiscence that remains after Baptism (corruption of man) and an acceptance of man by God without interior regeneration of man (justification by faith alone, man at once sinner and justified). Opposition by Catholic theologians led Luther to harden his position, especially the rejection of any teaching authority of the Church, either papal or conciliar, and the rejection of traditional teaching on the sacraments. He held for a real presence of Christ in the Eucharist, but denied transubstantiation. Luther did not want to start a new church, but after the rejection at the Diet of Augsburg (1530) of the Protestant party's bid for acceptance as a valid form of Catholic life, Lutheranism became more clearly a separate denomination. It spread rapidly throughout much of Germany and Scandinavia. Nonreligious factors also influenced the situation. Some German princes saw the new religion as a way of expressing independence from the Catholic emperor, and many were anxious to seize the wealth and lands of the Church. Besides the Lutheran or Evangelical tradition, early Protestantism had several other strands. Ulrich Zwingli (1458-1531) began preaching about reform even before he was influenced by Lutheran teaching. He led the reform movement in Zurich and later in some other parts of Switzerland. His views, especially on the sacraments, were more extreme than Luther's. The groups led by Zwingli and his successor H. Bullinger eventually merged with those led by Calvin (1509-1564) at Geneva to form the Reformed or Calvinistic tradition. A distinctive element of Calvin's thought (although not commonly held by modern Calvinists) is his teaching on predestination: that some humans are created for heaven, others for hell. His book, *Institutes of the Christian Religion,* in five versions between 1536 and 1559, is a kind of *Summa* of Calvinistic beliefs and helped assure him a significant place in the history of Western Christianity. Written in Latin and translated by Calvin into French, it soon appeared in other languages and helped fix the influence of the Reformed tradition not only in Switzerland but also in parts of France, the Low Countries, and Scotland. The Anabaptists, the third Protestant tradition, are not an organized denomination but a loose association of more radical Protestants. They put great stress on inner religious experience, rejecting both ecclesiastical and civil authority. They rejected infant Baptism as invalid, insisting on "believer's" Baptism; hence, their name Anabaptists, or "Re-baptizers." Fiercely persecuted and always small in number, they survive in a number of Mennonite and Amish communities. The reform in England followed a complex course. Henry VIII broke with Rome but wanted to retain Catholic doctrine and worship. Under Edward VI, only nine years old when he succeeded his father, the regents introduced more Protestant elements. Mary Tudor (1553-1558) strove mightily — sometimes too mightily — to restore the old religion. The long reign of Elizabeth (1558-1603) saw the triumph of the new Anglicanism: with some Catholic elements but more Calvinistic than the settlement of Henry VIII. These two elements — Catholicism and Calvinism — exist in a kind of tension in Anglicanism. Sometimes Catholic forms seem to advance (e.g., under the Caroline [King Charles] divines); at other times, Calvinistic themes are more dominant (e.g., under Oliver Cromwell or after the Revolution of 1688). Only in recent decades have the polemics of the Reformation era been muted, and the first tentative efforts at ecumenism begun. **Cf. CCC 406, 1400**

Regina Coeli (ray-GEE-nuh TSHAY-lee): The first words of the Latin version of the antiphon of the Blessed Mother, chanted in the Divine Office or Liturgy of the Hours at the conclusion of Compline. It is used from the period beginning Holy Saturday through the Saturday following Pentecost. The *Regina Coeli*, or Queen of Heaven, is recited during the Easter Season in place of the *Angelus* three times a day: at 6:00 A.M. or the first thing in the morning, at 12:00 noon, and again at 6:00 P.M. It is recited while standing. The words of the antiphon are as follows: "Queen of Heaven, rejoice, Alleluia, / Because He Whom thou didst merit to bear, Alleluia, / Has risen as He said, Alleluia, / Pray to God for us, Alleluia." (When the *Regina Coeli* is prayed in place of the *Angelus*, the following responsory and prayer are added: "Rejoice and be glad, O Virgin Mary, Alleluia, / The Lord has truly risen, Alleluia. / Let us pray. O God, Who by the Resurrection of Thy Son, Our Lord Jesus Christ, didst grant joy to the whole world: grant, we beseech Thee, that through the intercession of the Virgin Mary, His Mother, we may lay hold of the joys of eternal life. Through the same Christ Our Lord. Amen.")

Regulae Iuris (RAY-göö-lay YØØR-ihs): Latin for "Rules of Justice," a series of thirty-nine canonical maxims developed over a period of time to express the fundamental principles that helped shape the practice of Canon Law.

Reign of God, The *(th*uh **RAYN uhv GAHD):** The term "reign" is synonymous with "kingdom." The "reign of God" thus includes the notion of kingship or the exercise of royal power and rule in a kingdom (Lk 19:12; 1 Cor 15:24; Heb 18; Rv 1:6, 7:12). In particular, the kingdom or reign of God (or of heaven) communicates the salvation that has come with power and might, which we are to witness in the final days. Those who hear this message can find meaning for it in Jesus' parables (e.g., Mk 4:1-9, 10-12, 13-20; also, vv. 21-25, vv. 26-29, and especially vv. 30-32). (Cf. Kingdom of God.)

Reinstatement (ree-ihn-STAYT-mehnt): A canonical procedural act whereby a person who was injured by an unjust judicial sentence can be reinstated to the status he or she had before the sentence was issued.

Relativism (REHL-uh-tih-vih-zuhm): A theory of ethics teaching that all moral judgments differ according to circumstances. This is contrary to Catholic teaching, which states that while culpability may vary, certain actions or attitudes are always wrong and other actions or attitudes are always right, without regard to circumstances.

Relics, Sacred (SAY-krehd REHL-ihks): Bodies of the saints, parts of the bodies, something used by the saints, or objects touched to the bodies of the saints that have enjoyed for centuries the reverence offered by the Church. There are three kinds: first-class (part of a saint's body); second-class (something used by the saint); third-class (an object touched to a first-class relic). First-class relics of martyrs are placed in an altar when it is consecrated. **Cf. CCC 1674**

Relief Services, Catholic (KATH-uh-lihk ree-LEEF SER-vih-sehs): Association that assists needy countries by way of monies and supplies. Begun in 1943 by the U.S. bishops, it is supported by the contributions of the lay faithful in the U.S.

Religion (reh-LIH-dzhuhn): Term used by St. Thomas Aquinas for that part of the virtue of justice by which man publicly and privately worships God. Today, religion has come to mean any contact with the transcendent reality that is close to human existence. Religion can be "private" (i.e., one follows practices and beliefs similar to organized religion) or "public" (i.e., communities adhere to creeds and customs in worshipping God), "traditional" (i.e., "primitive" beliefs and practices like those of the Native Americans) or "major" (i.e., "world" religions that dominate the scene today like Christianity or Hinduism). **Cf. CCC 238, 842-843, 1807, 1969, 2095-2096, 2104-2105, 2117, 2125, 2135, 2137, 2144, 2244, 2467, 2566**

Religious Discourse (rih-LIH-dzhuhs DIHS-kors): The way in which various sects use language to convey their spiritual beliefs and practices. Often creeds, prayers, invocations, and stories are used to put forth their understanding of God and the transcendent. Philosophical theology concerns itself with the issues of religious discourse in the Christian context.

Religious Institute: See Institute, Religious

Religious Liberty: See Liberty, Religious; Dignitatis Humanae

Religious Life: See Perfectae Caritatis

Religious Life, Decree on the Up-to-date Renewal of: See Perfectae Caritatis

Religious Orders (rih-LIH-dzhuhs OR-derz): Communities of men and women who profess solemn vows of poverty, chastity, and obedience. These orders are varied in spiritual

charisms and apostolates. (Cf. Orders, Sacrament of Holy.)
CCC 916, 925-927, 933

Reliquary (REHL-ih-kweh-ree): A receptacle, varying in size and shape, containing the relics of a saint or other sacred object. Most reliquaries have a glass lid that allows for the viewing of the object.

Remnant (REHM-nuhnt): Biblical idea referring to the survivors of some calamity who nonetheless retain their faith in God and await their deliverance. The idea is developed especially by the prophets (e.g., Am 5:15, Is 10:20-22) and appears in the N.T. as well (notably Rom 9:25-27).

Renewal, Charismatic: See Charismatic Renewal, Catholic

Renunciation (ree-nuhn-see-AY-shuhn): 1. The explicit disavowal of Satan and sin by the parents, godparents, and any adult to be baptized, thereby rejecting all that is contrary to the Gospel. 2. The sacrifice of material goods to which one has a right, enabling one to live a truly spiritual life in union with God. Renunciation is a necessary component of the Christian life and offers the freedom to "live in Christ." One must be careful that renunciation does not lead to arrogance or even an attitude of independence from God. Cf. CCC 618, 736, 1237, 1427, 1615, 1808, 2015, 2103, 2306, 2544, 2556, 2715, 2745

Reparation (reh-per-AY-shuhn): Making amends for the harm done by sin. One atones to God for sin by prayer and penance; one also repairs for sins done to others by the same means and often by restoring to the other what was damaged (material goods, the other's reputation, etc.). Reparation or satisfaction is essential when being forgiven by God for sins committed. CCC 1414, 2412, 2454, 2487, 2509

Repentance (ree-PEHN-tehnts): Contrition for sins and the resulting embrace of Christ in conformity to Him. Both Old and New Testaments record numerous examples of repentance for sin. Jesus acknowledged that He had come to call sinners to repentance. True repentance occurs through Baptism, faith, charitable works, and frequent reception of the Sacraments of Penance and Holy Eucharist. CCC 1451-1454; cf. 393, 982, 1259, 1433, 1492, 1861, 1864

Repository: See Reservation of the Blessed Sacrament

Reproductive Engineering (ree-pro-DUHK-tihv ehn-dzhih-NEER-ihng): A general term for a variety of techniques, usually having to do with a deficiency in human fertility and conception. There are certain interventions that are morally acceptable, provided that the sperm and egg are joined in the womb after an act of natural sexual intercourse. Illicit techniques are those that involve masturbation or join the sperm and egg outside the womb. Cf. CCC 2374-2379

Requiem (REH-kwee-ehm): A Mass offered for the repose of the soul of one who has died in Christ. It derives its name from the first word of the Gregorian (Latin) entrance chant (or Introit) at Masses for the dead: *"Requiem aeternam dona eis, Domine . . ."* ("Eternal rest grant unto them, O Lord . . ."). The revised Rite for Funerals refers to the requiem as the Mass of Christian Burial; however, it would not be uncommon to hear people employ the former usage. Cf. CCC 1680-1690

Reredos (REH-ruh-dahs): (Alteration of French for "behind the back") The screen of stone or wood at the back of the altar and connected to it by means of the predella (q.v.). Since the twelfth century, the reredos has been in use; often it serves as a backdrop for decorated panels depicting religious scenes.

Rerum Novarum (REH-røøm no-VAH-røøm): (Latin: of new matters) The 1891 encyclical issued by Pope Leo XIII, "On the Condition of Human Labor." The Pontiff, wishing to lessen the prevalent poverty, called for the renewal of capitalism and the practice of subsidiarity. He recognized a limited right to own private property; workers, he said, must be paid just wages and be allowed to form labor unions. *Rerum Novarum* has been acknowledged as the beginning of the social justice movement in the Church.

Rescript (REE-skrihpt): Written reply; an administrative act or "writing back," issued to a competent superior in response to a request for a privilege, dispensation, or some other favor. Papal dispensations are in the form of rescripts.

Reservation of the Blessed Sacrament (reh-zer-VAY-shuhn uhv *th*uh BLEH-sehd SA-kruh-mehnt): 1. The practice of keeping the Blessed Sacrament in the tabernacle, for two reasons: (a) so that the sick may receive Holy Communion and (b) for the adoration of the faithful. 2. Specifically, the removal of the Holy Eucharist from the tabernacle at the conclusion of the Mass of the Lord's Supper on Holy Thursday evening and the reposition of the Eucharist in a repository chapel. Cf. CCC 1378-1379

Reserved Censure (ree-ZERV'D SEHN-sher): (From Latin: punishment) A canonical penalty that can be removed only by a specific authority in the Church. In the new code, all reserved censures are reserved to the Holy See. Reservations are made because of the serious nature and social effects of certain sins and censures. Cf. CCC 1463

Residence (REH-zih-dehnts): The obligation assumed by certain officeholders in the Church that they will reside in the territory over which they have authority.

Resignation (reh-zihg-NAY-shuhn): A means by which a person ceases to hold ecclesiastical office. With the exception of the papacy, all resignations must be accepted by a competent superior.

Res Iudicata (REHZ yöö-dee-KAH-tuh): (Latin: matter settled) A definitive judicial sentence that, because of its nature, is presumed to be so firm that it admits of no further appeal.

Respondent (reh-SPAHN-duhnt): A common though unofficial term for the other party to a canonical trial.

Responsibility, Modes of: See Modes of Responsibility

Responsorial Psalm: See Psalm, Responsorial

Responsory (reh-SPAHN-sor-ee): (From Latin *responsorium*)
A chant or spoken response to a liturgical reading taken from
the Scriptures or related to the season of the Church year. At
Mass, the Responsorial Psalm may be either sung or recited.
In the Divine Office, the responsory follows the reading from
Sacred Scripture and the nonbiblical passage at the Office of
Readings. Cf. CCC 1096

Restitution (reh-stih-TÖÖ-shuhn): An act whereby an injury done to the property or person of another is repaired or
restored, insofar as is possible. The willingness to make restitution is a sign of sincere contrition and purpose of amendment, and receiving absolution from sin can be made con-
tingent upon it. Cf. CCC 2412, 2454, 2487

**Resurrection of Christ (reh-zuh-REHK-shuhn uhv
KRAIST):** A basic truth of the Christian Faith and an essential part of the teaching of the Church from the earliest days.
The Gospels all give witness to Christ's resurrection (Mt 28:1-
20; Mk 16:9-20; Lk 24:1-9; Jn 20:1-18), and it is professed
in all of the ancient Creeds. St. Paul proclaims that "if Christ
has not been raised, then our preaching is in vain and your
faith is in vain" (1 Cor 15:14). The doctrine occupied the
central place in St. Peter's sermon on Pentecost, and has been
upheld constantly by the solemn teaching authority of the
Catholic Church. On the third day after His death and burial,
the Lord Jesus rose from the dead through His own power,
because of the union of the human and divine natures in the
one divine Person of Christ. When Holy Scripture says that
Christ was raised by God (Acts 2:24) or by the Father (Gal
1:1), it is to be understood that these statements refer to His
human nature, but the cause of the resurrection was the hypostatic union of Christ's humanity with the Godhead. The
resurrection of Christ is objective in that He walked out of
the tomb, still bearing the wounds of His suffering, but from
the moment of the resurrection His body was in a state of
glory, which is attested to by the circumstances of His appearances recorded in the Gospels and in Acts, in which He

is no longer bound by time or space. Although our redemption comes through the merits of Christ's sacrificial death upon the cross, the resurrection of Christ is seen as the completion of the redemptive act and so is associated with His death as a complete whole. Also, the risen Christ is seen as the "first fruits of those who have fallen asleep" (1 Cor 15:20), and so is the model for the bodily resurrection of all the faithful on the last day. CCC 272, 627, 638-648, 651-656, 991; cf. 519, 658, 992-1004, 1163, 1166-1167, 1337, 2174, 2191

Resurrection of the Body (reh-zuh-REHK-shuhn uhv *th*uh BAH-dee): With the Trinity and the Incarnation, a central tenet of Catholic (and of all Christian) belief. It is important to distinguish the biblical notion of resurrection from the Hellenistic concept of the soul's immortality. Greek philosophy and many religious movements within Hellenism held that the soul was incorruptible and "naturally" enters into divine immortality at death. The basic truth from Holy Scripture is that the whole person (body, mind, and spirit) will be resurrected on the "last day." The O.T. anticipates and prepares for the N.T. teaching on the resurrection of the body in statements about God's great power to make "the dead live" or "bring down to Sheol and raise up" (1 Sm 2:6; Wis 16:13). God restores to life (Ps 30:3). The bringing back to life of dead children (1 Kgs 17:22; 2 Kgs 4:35, 13:21), as well as the above examples, prepares us for Christ's resurrection in the N.T. Passages such as Is 25:8 ("He will swallow up death for ever") and Is 26:19 ("Thy dead shall live, their bodies shall rise") certainly anticipate something like the N.T. teachings on resurrection. A greater degree of explicitness concerning belief in the resurrection is achieved in passages such as 2 Mc 7:9-26; 12:41-46; Dn 12:2-3. Except for the Sadducees, most Jewish groups believed in the resurrection of the body (e.g., Pharisees, Acts 24:15). The resurrection of the body is the preeminent sign that the final age of salvation has arrived. The general resurrection (Mt 11:22, 12:41, etc.) is consistent with such a belief. In John's Gospel, the teaching is more clear (Jn 5:28 ff.; 6:39, 44, 54), and Paul is quite explicit about the resurrection of the body (e.g., 1 Cor 15), the hope of all who believe. In summary, those who live and die "in Christ" are hidden with Christ in God, but when Christ comes again they will appear with Him in glory (Col 3:3-4). **CCC 366, 556, 988-1013, 1038, 1524, 2301**

Retable (ree-TAY-buhl): A frame (reredos) or ledge (gradine), at the back of the altar, used to support decorated panels, etc.

Retablo (ray-TAH-blo): (Spanish: retable) 1. Painted representation of Christ and/or individual saints on a wooden panel, hung in Spanish or Mexican churches. 2. The reredos itself.

Retreat (ree-TREET): Period observed in prayer, meditation, and worship of God taken annually by priests, deacons, religious, and many laypersons. The practice of retreats hails from the O.T.; Christ Himself also spent forty days in the desert to pray in preparation for His public ministry. The Jesuits were among the first to include the making of retreats in their rule of life.

Retribution (reh-trih-BYÖÖ-shuhn): The reward or punishment due to good or sinful actions; however, retribution is normally associated with punishment for sin. **CCC 1021-1022, 2016**

Retroactive Force of Law (reh-tro-AK-tihv FORS uhv LAW): A specific indication by a competent ecclesiastical authority that a newly promulgated law has an effect on past actions.

Revelation (reh-vuh-LAY-shuhn): 1. God's activity in making Himself and His purposes known to humankind through Christ, the prophets, and Apostles. 2. The content that is communicated and handed on. Revelation has an interpersonal structure and point. God reveals to human beings His intention to draw them into union with Him. In the course of doing so, He discloses the mystery of His own inner Trinitarian life and the true destiny of human beings. With revelation, therefore, comes a body of knowledge otherwise inaccessible to human discovery. The knowledge of God's own self-description and of His grace-filled purpose for humanity throws light on and draws to itself all the other knowledge that human beings can acquire by observation and inquiry. The divinely chosen vehicles of revelation are human beings who, through special grace, are inspired to speak and write on God's behalf. Paramount among these is Jesus Christ — the very Word of God — Who communicates, definitively and unsurpassably, all that the Triune God wants mankind to know about Himself and His saving purposes. The normative source of revelation is the Scripture as encompassed within the living Tradition of the teaching and worshipping community of Christ's followers. The human response to revelation is faith, chiefly in God Himself and secondarily in the human bearers and sources of revelation. By extension, the term "revelation" is also used to refer to what can be known about God through an understanding of His creation and through experience of human life in the world. Although this extended sense is commonly designated "general revelation," it should not be viewed as a genus with several species, of which revelation through Christ and the Apostles is one form (so-called "special revelation"). Revelation, properly speaking, is God's free, direct communication of Himself and His purposes, casting light on other putative revelations. CCC 35-38, 50-83, 101, 105, 124, 157-158, 1960; cf. 129, 142-143, 150-152, 156, 176, 201-214, 237-248, 272, 287, 337, 386-390, 438, 502, 516, 544, 561, 647-648, 651, 687-688, 732, 992, 1048, 1701, 1814, 1846, 2059-2060, 2070-2071, 2085, 2143, 2419, 2779

Revelation, Book of (BØØK uhv reh-vuh-LAY-shuhn): This, the last book of the N.T., has also been called by its Greek name, Apocalypse. The earliest Christian writers considered it to be the work of St. John the Apostle. Modern scholars, noting differences in style and vocabulary, are skeptical of this attribution. The book is composed of two unequal parts. The first three chapters are spent on pastoral letters for the benefit of seven churches in Asia Minor: Ephesus, Smyrna, Pergamum, Thyatira, Sardis, Philadelphia, and Laodicea. Each letter, while sent to the bishop of the respective church, is clearly addressed through him (the message-deliverer) to the congregation. The message is one of encouragement and rebuke; when criticism is called for, it is expressed in such strong words as could have come only from one of high standing and authority. A comparative study of four topics (Christ, Satan, the Holy Spirit, the Jews) will show that these letters reflect the outlook of the Fourth Gospel. The remaining nineteen chapters are less pastoral in tone, and less concerned with existing religious problems. They contain a number of vivid visions, symbolic of tribulations coming upon believers from a political source. These visions are organized in the same highly structured way as the seven initial letters and the seven miracles of the Fourth Gospel: seven seals, seven trumpets, seven plagues, seven bowls. The city on the seven hills, called "Babylon," is indubitably Rome, and the number refers without doubt to Nero. He had shed the blood of St. Paul, St. Peter, and many others who were dear to St. John; he had declared war on the Jewish freedom fighters; his Roman troops had already overrun Galilee and were besieging Jerusalem, if indeed they had not already taken it. The reference to the "new Jerusalem" can best be understood if the destruction of the old Jerusalem had passed or was at least obviously imminent. The Jewish apocalyptic tries to view events as God sees them, simultaneously, without the historian's respect for time. This explains the montage that is frequently encountered in such writings. The woman of the Apocalypse, for example, can be understood by Jews as Israel and by Christians both as the Blessed Virgin Mary and Holy Mother Church. The woman in the heavens is crowned with twelve stars (Israel and the tribes, or the Apostles on Pentecost); she brings forth her Son (the Messiah), destined to shepherd the nations. The devil tries in vain to devour her Son, and He ascends into heaven. The sufferings of Jesus had been experienced by Israel and are relived by the Church as she strives to bring forth other Christs; her efforts are also resisted by the devil, incarnate in the Roman persecutors, but he will not prevail.

Revelation, Dogmatic Constitution on Divine: See Dei Verbum

Revelation, Private: See Private Revelation

Revelation, Public: See Public Revelation

Reverend (REH-ver-ehnd): Literally meaning "one who is to be revered," it is a title of respect tendered to clergy and Religious, usually modifying the title used in direct address (e.g., "Reverend Father," "Reverend Mother").

Reverential Fear (reh-ver-EHN-shuhl FEER): That kind of mental trepidation, or fear, induced in a person that is inspired when he or she seeks to avoid the sense of anger, disappointment, or rejection of a loved one if an act is or is not completed. Most often applied in marriage nullity cases.

Rheims or Reims (REEMZ, REM [also, REHNS]): (Anglicized or French original) The Douay-Rheims Bible, an English translation of the Bible, published in two parts in different cities at different times. The N.T. books were published in 1582 in the city of Rheims. The O.T. was published between 1609 and 1610 in Douay (France). The principal translators were Gregory Martin (d. 1582), Thomas Worthington, Richard Bristowe, and William Allen, all from Oxford. The translation sought to avoid heretical tendencies found in other English-language translations of the day (Protestant translations). It was not from the original Hebrew/Aramaic and Greek O.T. texts, nor from the original Greek of the N.T., but from the Latin Vulgate. This translation achieved a high standard of consistency and influenced the language found in the Authorized Version translation (1611). It remained the standard English-language Bible of Catholics for three and a half centuries.

Riddels: See Dossal

Rights, Ecclesial (eh-KLEE-zee-uhl RAITS): Rights that persons acquire by the very fact that they are members in communion with the Catholic Church. A right is something to which one is entitled, and in the Church there are certain rights common to all of the faithful, others common to the laity, and still others that are acquired because of sacred orders or because of an ecclesial office held. The 1917 code stated that Baptism constituted a person as a member of the Church with all of the rights and duties proper to Christians. It did not list what these rights and duties might be, with the exception of stating that Catholics had a right to the sacraments and were not to be denied them without just cause. This code concentrated on the rights of certain groups in the Church (the clergy, religious, hierarchy) and certain officeholders. The revised Code of Canon Law still contains the rights proper to certain groups and to officeholders, but before listing these, it enumerates several fundamental rights of all the faithful (cc. 208-223) and especially the laity (cc. 224-231). These rights are interspersed with various fundamental obligations. The enumeration of the rights and duties of the faithful was taken from the proposed *Lex Ecclesiae Fundamentalis (Fundamental Law of the Church)*, which was studied but not included in the code. The statements on rights in the *Lex* were, in great part, inspired by the documents of Vatican II. The first canon in the section (Can. 208) states that by virtue of Baptism, there exists a true equality among all Christians. It distinguishes between fundamental spiritual equality and the fact that people differ in their capacities and in their roles in the life of the Church. Equality and capacity are not the same and the fact that some have authority roles in the Church and some do not does not mean that this differentiation is based on inequality. Concerning the ecclesial rights of all the faithful, the following are found in the canons: (1) the right to make known needs and desires, especially spiritual ones, to the pastors of the Church (Can. 212.2); (2) the right and sometimes the duty to express one's opinion of matters pertaining to the good of the Church, both to Church authorities and other Christians (Can. 212.3); (3) the right to spiritual assistance, especially the Word of God and the sacraments (Can. 213); (4) the right to worship according to one's own rite and to follow one's own form of spiritual life (Can. 214); (5) the right to found and govern associations for religious and charitable purposes and the right to assembly (Can. 215); (6) the right to promote and sustain apostolic activity according to one's state and condition (Can. 216); (7) the right to a Christian education (Can. 217); (8) the right to academic freedom for those engaged in teaching and research in the sacred sciences, with due respect for the Magisterium (Can. 218); (9) the right to choose freely one's state in life (Can. 219); (10) the right to one's good reputation and the right to privacy (Can.

220); (11) the right to defend and vindicate one's rights before a competent ecclesiastical court, the right to be judged, if called into court, according to the norms of the law, and the right not to be punished by ecclesiastical penalties, except according to the norms of law (Can. 221). These general ecclesial rights of all the faithful, clergy and laity alike, are to be understood within a specific context, i.e., the fundamental obligation of all Catholics to build up the Church according to the teaching and discipline of the Magisterium. Following the canons on the rights of all, the code then considers specific rights of the laity. These are preceded by a statement of the fundamental obligation and right of the laity to participate in the mission of the Church (Can. 225). The first specific right pertains to married persons. Describing marriage as a vocation, the canon states that married couples have a special duty to build up the Body of Christ through their marriage. They have both the obligation and the right to educate children given them by God (Can. 226). The other rights pertain to the laity in general: (1) The right to the same civil liberties enjoyed by all citizens (Can. 227); (2) the capacity (rather than the right) to assume ecclesiastical offices and functions that they are capable of exercising according to the norms of law (Can. 228); (3) the capacity of acting as experts and advisors to the bishops, provided they have been properly trained (Can. 228); (4) the right to a Christian education and the right to study the sacred sciences at ecclesiastical institutions (Can. 229); (5) the capacity to fulfill certain liturgical functions, including the distribution of Communion, presiding over the Liturgy of the Word, and conferring Baptism when there is a need and they have been properly deputed (Can. 230); (6) the right, for those employed in the service of the Church, to a decent remuneration, pension, social security, and health benefits (Can. 231). All of the canons on ecclesial rights are relatively broad in their approach. Their practical application and more specific meaning in real life hinges on the evolving understanding of the meaning of the Church as the "People of God," as well as on the development of tribunal structures and jurisprudence that will help spell out the meaning of these rights in actual situations.

Rights, Natural: See Natural Rights

Right to Die (RAIT töö DAI): The claim that one may end his life when and in whatever way he desires. Some suggest that one may reject painful medical treatments; others assert that one may actively take his own life (or the life of another who desires to die). The Church teaches that one may refuse "extraordinary" care (i.e., burdensome, painful, expensive care); however, there is no "right" to die. Only God can give and take life because He alone is the Master of life. **Cf. CCC 2278-2279**

Right to Life (RAIT töö LAIF): The just claim that innocent human beings have to be spared any deliberate assaults on their earthly existence. Each person has the duty to preserve his health and life because God has granted that life, which only He can give and take. The Church teaches that man has the right to receive "ordinary" treatment (i.e., non-burdensome, not extremely expensive, non-risky measures); "extraordinary" medical treatments need not be taken to preserve earthly life. Violations against innocent persons are direct attacks on God. (Cf. Right to Die.) **CCC 2264, 2270, 2273, 2322; cf. 2278-2279**

Rights of the Human Person: See Natural Rights

Rigorism (RIH-gor-ih-zuhm): The term referring to the "Tutiorism" approach found in moral theology, which holds that one must follow the law unless one is "morally certain" that it does not apply. The Church has condemned this theory as too restrictive of human freedom.

Ring (RIHNG): A circular band of metal symbolic of one's dedication to Christ (e.g., a woman religious) or to one's spouse. Cardinals, abbots, and bishops wear rings, as does the Pope, whose ring ("the Fisherman's Ring") is a gold seal ring depicting St. Peter in a boat; the Pope's name is engraved on the ring. There are also "rosary rings" that have ten beads and often a crucifix, enabling one to recite this prayer. **Cf. CCC 1574**

Ripidion (rih-PIH-dee-ahn): A fan used to ventilate the consecrated Species in the Byzantine Rite. If the fan is adorned with a six-winged cherub, it is called a hexapterygon.

Risorgimento (rih-sor-dzhee-MEHN-to): (Italian: revival) Title of the movement devoted to unifying Italy. Count Victor Cavour founded a newspaper by this name in 1847. Initially, the movement enjoyed papal support; however, Pope Pius IX opposed it after the 1848 revolution.

Rite (RAIT): 1. Ceremonies surrounding the Sacred Liturgy and the sacraments (e.g., Rite of Election, Rite of Confirmation). 2. A particular division within the Catholic Church pertaining to geographical and cultural differences (e.g., Latin Rite, Chaldean Rite, Maronite Rite). **Cf. CCC 1125, 1131, 1201, 1203, 1208**

Rite, Alexandrian (al-ehk-ZAN-dree-uhn RAIT): The liturgy of Alexandria is attributed to St. Mark and is the parent of all the Egyptian liturgies. It was probably an adaptation of the Antiochene Rite (from Antioch), which was finalized by St. Cyril in the fifth century. The liturgy of St. Mark is no longer used, since it was used in Greek only by the Melkites, who later replaced it with the Byzantine Rite. It was adapted by the Copts and Ethiopians, who developed modified versions of it in their own languages (Coptic and Geez). The present liturgy for the Catholic Patriarchate of Alexandria is that of the Coptic Rite. **Cf. CCC 1203**

Rite, Antiochene (an-TEE-o-keen RAIT): The rite of the early Christian community of Antioch (cf. Acts 8-11), which spread to Jerusalem and from there all over after it had been translated into Greek and Aramaic. As this rite crystallized in the Patriarchate of Antioch, it had much influence on other rites (e.g., the Byzantine and Alexandrian). In ancient classic form, the outline of this rite can be found in Book 8 of the *Apostolic Constitutions,* a fourth-century Syrian source. The liturgy of Antioch is sometimes called the West Syrian Rite, which developed after the condemnation of Nestorius (431). Christians following this rite in union with Rome developed what is called the Chaldean Rite. The influence of the Antiochene liturgy can be seen in India in both the Malankar and Malabar Rites, and the liturgy of St. James, followed by the Christians in Iraq and Syria. Cf. CCC 1297

Rite, Armenian (ahr-MEEN-ee-uhn RAIT): When the Armenian Church was organized in the fourth century, the liturgical practice of Cappadocia was introduced, as were some Syrian customs, and this became the basis of the Armenian Rite. The Lectionary reflects that of fifth-century Jerusalem. In the course of time, various influences have been felt on the rite: the Byzantine in the rite of preparation; Antiochene Syrian usage in the litany after the Epiclesis; and many Romanisms left by the Crusaders. This rite is used by Armenians united with Rome, who after Vatican II have purified their rite of most Roman usages. Cf. CCC 1203, 2678

Rite, Byzantine (BIH-zuhn-teen RAIT): One of several divisions or categories of churches within the universal Church, specific to the East. The Byzantine Rite traces its origin to the ancient capital city of the eastern half of the Roman Empire, Istanbul or Constantinople, formerly Byzantium. The Byzantine Rite shares its Tradition with the churches of Antioch, Alexandria, and Jerusalem. When Emperor Constantine moved his capital to Byzantium in 330, the city became the "New Rome," and its sphere of influence was secured. Next to the Roman, it is the second-most-used rite and is shared by Eastern Christians, both Catholic and Orthodox (since 1054, the time of the Great Schism between East and West). Traditionally, Baptism is administered by immersion, Confirmation (called Chrismation) immediately follows, and the Eucharist is given to the newly baptized. Leavened bread is used for the Divine Liturgy, of which there are two, that of St. John Chrysostom and that of St. Basil the Great. An ancient liturgy of St. James of Jerusalem is no longer used but reflects its roots from Jerusalem itself. Cf. CCC 281, 335, 1203, 1300, 1320, 1481, 1587, 1690, 2619, 2678, 2760

Rite, Celtic: See Celtic Rite

Rite, Chaldean: See Chaldean Rite

Rite, Coptic: See Coptic Rite

Rite, Georgian Byzantine: See Georgian Byzantine Rite

Rite, Latin: See Latin Rite

Rite, Malabar: See Malabar Rites

Rite, Melkite: See Melkite Rite

Rite, Mozarabic: See Mozarabic Rite

Rite, Religious (rih-LIH-dzhuhs RAIT): A liturgical usage celebrated by members of certain older religious institutes such as the Carmelites, Carthusians, Dominicans, and Norbertines. After Vatican Council II, most religious institutes adopted the revised liturgical practices as their own.

Rite, Roman: See Roman Rite

Rite, Russian (RUH-shuhn RAIT): That usage of the Byzantine Rite proper to those national groups situated in the former Soviet Union or tracing their ethnic origin thereto. Its main language remains Church Slavonic, since none of the "Russian" Churches has an extant contemporary translation of the liturgical services in the modern Russian vernacular. The vast majority of Russians are Eastern Orthodox. There is a Pontifical Russian College in Rome for the training of deacons and priests in the Byzantine Rite usages particular to the Russian Orthodox. Since 1968, the college has also been open to accept Russian Orthodox seminarians and clergy to reside and study there as well. An apostolic exarch resides in France for Russian Catholics throughout the world.

Rite, Ruthenian: See Ruthenian Catholics

Rite, Syrian: See Syrian Rite

Rite of Christian Initiation of Adults (RAIT uhv KRIHS-tshuhn ih-nih-shee-AY-shuhn uhv uh-DUHLTS): The process, instituted by Pope Paul VI on January 6, 1972, by which adults are received into full communion with the Catholic Church. There are four stages: (1) *Pre-Catechumenate* ("Inquiry"), which begins in the summer or September and attempts to answer questions, inviting the catechumens (the unbaptized) and the candidates (those who have been baptized as non-Catholics or Catholics who have never practiced) to begin personal prayer and provide a focus for the entire process; (2) *Catechumenate,* a period of intellectual and spiritual formation with an emphasis on Sacred Scripture; (3) *Election,* the various rites beginning on the First Sunday of Lent (scrutinies, presentation, anointing) leading to the Easter Vigil; (4) *Final Initiation,* when the catechumens receive Baptism, Confirmation, and Holy Eucharist, while the candidates receive Confirmation and Holy Eucharist. (The Sacrament of Penance is received before the Easter Vigil for the candidates and after the Vigil for the catechumens.) *Mystagogia* is a post-baptismal catechesis occurring during the Easter Season. CCC 1232-1233

Rite of Constantinople (RAIT uhv kahn-stan-tih-NO-puhl): The largest of the four main patriarchal liturgical branches of the Eastern Churches, used by both Catholic and Orthodox Eastern Christians, with its primary liturgical languages being Greek and Church Slavonic. Although its roots are in Antioch, its name is derived from the capital city of the ancient Byzantine Empire.

Rites, Chinese (tshai-NEEZ RAITS): A variety of ancient practices of the Chinese that were tolerated for a time by Catholic missionaries sent to evangelize them. The majority of the practices involved Confucianism, ancestor worship, and technical terms referring to God. Roman investigation of the customs began in 1693, followed by condemnation in 1715 and 1742 by Popes Clement XI and Benedict XIV respectively. Two centuries later Pope Pius XII indicated that some practices might be open to reconsideration.

Rites, Sacred Congregation of (SAY-krehd kahn-greh-GAY-shuhn uhv RAITS): The section of the Roman Curia that directed the ritual and pastoral dimensions of divine worship such as the Mass, the Liturgy of the Hours, and the

Sacraments. Pope Sixtus V instituted the Congregation in 1588; on March 1, 1989, with the approval of Pope John Paul II, the Congregation was united to the Congregation for the Sacraments and is now called the Congregation for Divine Worship.

Ritual (RIH-tshöö-uhl): 1. A liturgical ceremony performed with words, gestures, and sacred objects under the auspices of the Holy See. 2. Book, authorized by the Holy See, containing the ceremonies and prayers used during sacred rites.

Rochet (RAH-tsheht): (Apparently from an old Franco-Germanic word for coat) White linen knee-length garment, similar to a surplice, derived from the alb, worn by the Pope and other prelates under the mozzetta or mantelletta.

Rogation Days (ro-GAY-shuhn dayz): Special days of penance and prayer, similar to the Ember Days, that were replaced in 1969 by periods of prayer extending for one to several days. The two times of rogation days were the Feast of St. Mark (April 25) and the Monday, Tuesday, and Wednesday before Ascension Thursday.

Rogito (ro-DZHEE-to): (Italian: diminutive of "funeral pyre") The official collection of documents that certify the death and burial of a Roman Pontiff.

Roman Catholic (RO-muhn KATH-uh-lihk): The name often used to designate adherents to the Pope as Vicar of Christ and the bishops in union with him; the expression seems to have first appeared in the sixteenth century or later under the influence of those (especially Anglicans) who wished to suggest that the Church of Rome (i.e., the Catholic Church) was but one of many branches of the Church Universal.

Roman Collar (RO-muhn KAH-lehr: In common parlance, the clerical collar worn by clergy and seminarians as street dress in non-Catholic countries. (See Dress, Clerical.)

Roman College (RO-muhn KAH-lehdzh): Founded by St. Ignatius Loyola in 1551, the Collegium Romanum is now known as the Pontifical Gregorian University and awards doctorates in Sacred Theology (S.T.D.) and Canon Law (J.C.D.), along with licenses in both disciplines. Other Roman ecclesiastical universities such as the "Angelicum" and the "Lateran" are also referred to as the Roman College.

Roman Congregations (RO-muhn kahn-greh-GAY-shuhnz): The departments of the Roman Curia that, with the Secretariat of State, the Roman Rota, and other commissions, assist the Pope in the governance of the Church. Each congregation is headed by a cardinal prefect and a secretary (usually an archbishop). The congregations are involved with the following concerns: the Doctrine of the Faith, Eastern Churches, Divine Worship, Clergy, Religious and Secular Institutes, Bishops, Evangelization of Peoples, Causes of Saints, Seminaries, and Catholic Institutions.

Roman Law (RO-muhn LAW): 1. In general, the laws that prevailed in ancient Rome from the period of the kings until the period of the post-Christian emperors. 2. The compilation of Roman laws known as the *Corpus Iuris Civilis,* codified under the Emperor Justinian.

Roman Missal (RO-muhn MIH suhl): Literal translation of *Missale Romanum,* the title of the book that contains the introductory documents and prayer texts for the celebration of Mass according to the Roman Rite. The Missal of the pre-Vatican II rite ("the Missal of Pope St. Pius V" or "Tridentine Missal," as it is sometimes called) contained all elements of the "propers" (Introit, Collect, Epistle, Gradual/Tract, Alleluia, Gospel, Offertory Verse, Secret, Communion Verse, Postcommunion) as well as the "ordinary," or Order of Mass. The Roman Missal promulgated by Pope Paul VI in 1970, containing the revised liturgy of Mass, corresponding to the directives of Vatican II, actually consists of two books: (1) the Roman Missal properly so-called (in the United States and Canada, this book is entitled the Sacramentary), containing the three proper "presidential prayers" for each Mass (Opening Prayer, Prayer Over the Gifts, Prayer After Communion) and, for convenience, the Entrance and Communion Antiphons, as well as the complete Order of Mass; (2)

the Lectionary for Mass, containing the now greatly expanded selection of Scripture readings (a three-year cycle of O.T., N.T., Gospel readings, and intervening chants for Sundays; and a two-year cycle of first readings with a daily Gospel for weekdays; as well as readings for sanctoral, ritual, and votive celebrations). By a special indult of 1984, extended through the Apostolic Letter *Ecclesia Dei* of 1988, permission to use the former Roman Missal (in its 1962 edition) has been granted by the Holy See under certain conditions.

Roman Missal, General Instruction of the (DZHEHN-er-uhl ihn-STRUHK-shuhn uhv *th*uh RO-muhn MIH-suhl): The introductory document that prefaces the Roman Missal (or Sacramentary) and sets forth: (1) the historical context in which the Second Vatican Council mandated the revision of the Eucharistic liturgy; (2) the theological orientation necessary to understand the Eucharist as the action of Christ within the community of His Church; (3) an extensive presentation of the various elements constituting the Eucharist and the rubrics governing its proper celebration. The United States edition of the Roman Missal (Sacramentary) contains an appendix of explanations, modifications, and adaptations. Important related documents are also to be found in the front of the Missal after the *General Instruction:* Directory for Masses with Children, General Norms for the Liturgical Year, and the Calendar (both the General Roman Calendar and the Proper Calendar for Dioceses of the United States). Cf. CCC 2760

Roman Rite (RO-muhn RAIT): The manner of celebrating the sacraments and other ecclesiastical ceremonies and the recitation of the Liturgy of the Hours authorized by the Diocese of Rome and mandated for use in most dioceses of Western Catholicism. The Roman Rite, altered somewhat by the Second Vatican Council, is the most widely used rite in Christendom. Cf. CCC 1203, 1233, 1298-1299, 1320, 1513, 1531

Roman Stations (RO-muhn STAY-shuhnz): Churches within the city of Rome where the early Popes celebrated Mass on special days, in time becoming a Lenten devotion.

Tradition has it that clergy and congregation assembled in one place and processed to another where the Holy Sacrifice of the Mass was offered. At the head of these processions, a relic of the True Cross was carried aloft. This practice continues to the present day. Now, a list of which stational churches and on what days they will be used is published in advance.

Romans, Epistle to the (ih-PIH-suhl to *th*uh RO-muhnz): St. Paul's letter to the Christians at Rome, written probably in the winter of A.D. 57-58 and intended to introduce Paul to these Christians in preparation for his first visit there. In this letter, Paul outlines the message of the Gospel: Salvation comes through Christ and the cross, is rooted in God's righteousness and love, and is available to all human beings who believe. Justification and salvation are not attained by fulfilling the law but only through faith in Jesus Christ. The Gospel is God's salvific work made known in Christ (1:17), and access to salvation is through Baptism into Christ (6:3-11).

Rome (ROM): (Italian *Roma)* Capital city of modern Italy, the seat of government and principal city of the ancient Roman Empire, Rome was inhabited, according to tradition, as early as 753 B.C.; in fact, all Roman history was dated from the traditional year of the city's settlement (in Latin, *Ab Urbe Condita),* so that Christ is said to have been born A.U.C. 753. There were likely Etruscan settlers on the seven hills several centuries earlier, as is reflected in the very name of *Roma,* derived from the Etruscan word for city, *Rom.* As vicar of Christ, St. Peter enjoyed a most privileged position within the early Christian communities, and his immediate successors were recognized for the central role they played in Church governance (e.g., *Letters of Clement of Rome).* Hence, one understands the central place of Rome in the life of the Church today and the significance of the Church of (at) Rome, presiding over the Church Universal and focused upon the ministry of the Bishop of Rome. Since the founding of the Church there by St. Peter, Rome has been the center of all Christendom. The entire area of the sovereign Vatican City-State is confined within the city of Rome. By way of the Lateran Pact with the Italian government of 1929, more recently reaffirmed by both sides, additional properties apart from Vatican City are also considered as territorial parts of the Vatican. CCC 834-835; cf. 185, 194, 877, 882, 892, 1559, 1900

Rood-Screen (RÖÖD SKREEN): (From Old English *rod:* cross) A crucifix with the figures of Our Lady and St. John the Evangelist at the foot of the cross, placed in medieval English churches on a wooden beam near the sanctuary. The rood-screen, located beneath the cross, often contained paintings and carvings of the saints.

Rosary (RO-zuh-ree): The popular prayer composed of the fifteen Joyful, Sorrowful, and Glorious Mysteries, said to have been given by Our Lady to St. Dominic in the thirteenth century, which offers the opportunity for reflection on the events in the life of Christ and how Mary was called to cooperate in His saving work (see Mysteries of the Rosary). The Rosary is usually prayed using beads; the liturgical commemoration of Our Lady of the Rosary is October 7. CCC 971, 2678, 2708; cf. 1674

Rose Window (ROZ WIHN-do): A circular stained-glass window, used in Gothic architecture, with tracery radiating from the center. Rose windows are generally located in the transepts, behind the altar, or above the church's entrance.

Rosh Hashanah (ROSH hah-SHAH-nah): The Jewish New Year remembrance observed on the first and second days of the Jewish month Tishri (September-October). The shofar, often a ram's horn (but it may be from any animal except the cow), is blown during the commemoration, probably alluding to the proclamation with trumpets at a king's coronation and on the day that God will be known as King.

Rota, Sacred Roman (SAY-krehd RO-muhn RO-tuh): The highest appeal court in the Church, situated in Rome. It primarily reviews marriage nullity cases from around the world.

Royal Doors: See Holy or Royal Doors

Rubrics (RÖÖ-brihks): Liturgical directives that guide the administration of the sacraments. Rubrics may be either obligatory or directive (which allow for interpretation). The word "rubric" is derived from the Latin word meaning "red"; the rubrics are written in red in the Missal so as to distinguish them from the text of the Mass.

Rule, Religious (rih-LIH-dzhuhs RÖÖL): The basic regulations of a religious institute, encompassing its daily order and discipline. Cf. CCC 347

Russian Rite: See Rite, Russian

Ruth, Book of (BØØK uhv RÖÖTH): Book of the O.T. containing a charming short story about married love, offering a glimpse of the acceptance by the good-hearted Jew (in this case, Obed) of the righteous Gentile (in this case, the Moabite woman Ruth).

Ruthenian Catholics (röö-THEE-nee-uhn KATH-uh-lihks): Those Catholics of the Byzantine Rite who trace their ethnic origin to that geographical area that for the most part was designated the Transcarpathian Province of the former Soviet Union. Evangelized by the Greek brothers Sts. Cyril and Methodius in 963, this group of Eastern Christians lapsed into orthodoxy at the time of the Eastern Schism (1054) but returned to communion with Rome at the Union of Uzhorod on April 24, 1646. In 1949 the Ruthenian Church in Eastern Europe was forcibly returned to the Russian Orthodox, but the majority of churches became restored to Catholic communion at the time of the Dubcek regime in Czechoslovakia in 1966. Since that time, an apostolic administrator governs the Church in Presov. Hundreds of thousands of Ruthenian Catholics emigrated from the former Austro-Hungarian Empire at the turn of the twentieth century and were given their first bishop in 1925 in the person of the late Bishop Basil Takach, who resided in Pittsburgh. Today the former diocese of Pittsburgh for the Ruthenians has become an archdiocese with a metropolitan archbishop residing there and suffragan sees in Passaic, New Jersey, Parma, Ohio, and Van Nuys, California. Within the jurisdiction of the

Ruthenians also fall Hungarian and Croatian Catholics of the Byzantine Rite. A separate jurisdiction for the Ukrainians was also established in 1925 with the late Bishop Constantine Bohachevsky as their first bishop in the United States. The Ukrainians trace their evangelization to Prince Vladimir in Kiev in the year 988. Following the schism of 1054, many Ukrainians resumed Catholic unity at the Synod of Brest-Litovsk in 1596. From August 1907 until his death on March 24, 1916, Bishop Soter Ortynsky served as the Ordinary common to both Ruthenian and Ukrainian Catholics in the United States. The Ukrainian Catholics today have a metropolitan archbishop residing in Philadelphia, Pennsylvania, with suffragan sees in Chicago, Illinois, Stamford, Connecticut, and Parma, Ohio.

S

Sabaoth (SAH-bah-ot): (Hebrew plural of *saba:* host) The word's most notable occurrence is in one of the divine names — "Yahweh of Hosts" or "Yahweh, God of Hosts" — a title for God encountered often in the prophets. Basically, "hosts" means an army, whether of Israelites or angels or all the forces of the universe. It is translated in the *Sanctus* or "Holy, Holy" as "power and might."

Sabbatarianism (sa-buh-TEHR-ee-uhn-ih-zuhm): A seventeenth- and eighteenth-century movement within the English and Scottish Reformation communities that advocated a strict observance of Sunday as the Sabbath, based upon principles found in the O.T. Although the prohibition of all recreation and many other activities on Sunday was made part of the law, by the late nineteenth century the influence of the Sabbatarian movement was greatly decreased.

Sabbath (SA-buhth): The seventh day of the Jewish week. The word is related to a Hebrew verb meaning "to cease" or "to rest." At least from the time of the monarchy in Israel, the Sabbath was observed as a day of rest. Gradually, the details of this observance came to be expressed with great care and attention. The rigoristic observance of the Sabbath was criticized by Jesus (see Mt 12:2-4). In time, the early Christians took to celebrating the first rather than the seventh day of the week, in commemoration of the Lord's resurrection from the dead as well as the coming of the Holy Spirit on Pentecost. CCC 345, 348, 582, 2168-2176, 2189-2190

Sabellianism (suh-BEHL-ee-uh-nih-zuhm): Third-century heresy that held that Christ was no different from God the Father.

Sacrament: See Sacraments, Seven; Sacraments of Initiation

Sacramentals (sa-kruh-MEHN-tuhlz): Sacred signs, whether objects (e.g., scapulars, holy water) or actions (e.g., blessings), possessing a likeness to the sacraments and whose effects are obtained by the prayer of the Church (Can. 1166). The sacraments were instituted by Christ and effect grace by virtue of themselves; the sacramentals are instituted by the Church and impart grace according to the disposition of the recipients and the intercession of the Church. CCC 1667-1676

Sacramental Theology (sa-kruh-MEHN-tuhl thee-AHL-uh-dzhee): The study of the belief and practice of the seven sacraments and how they increase the grace within one's life. The sacraments involve matter (object), form (words), intention, gestures, sacred places, vestments, time, etc.; they are seen as linked to Christ because He instituted them. Sacramental theology is connected to other theological subfields such as liturgiology, Canon Law, and moral theology.

Sacramentarians (sa-kruh-mehn-TEHR-ee-uhnz): The name given to Zwingli and other Reformers by Martin Luther because of the former's belief that the bread and wine of the Eucharist were only symbolically Christ, thus only in a metaphorical or "sacramental" sense. Luther believed in the Real Presence but only as consubstantiation or impanation. The Catholic position, of course, is the Real Presence through transubstantiation, defined by the Fourth Lateran Council (1215) and reiterated by the Council of Trent (1545-1563).

Sacramentary (sa-kruh-MEHN-ter-ee): The English edition of the *Missale Romanum,* containing the directives, prayers, and rubrics for the Sacrifice of the Mass. The Lectionary possesses the readings used during the liturgy. Both volumes are available in Latin and the vernacular.

Sacraments, Seven (SEH-vuhn SA-kruh-mehnts): The unique signs instituted by Christ that give the grace they signify. They are Baptism, Penance, Holy Eucharist, Confirmation, Holy Orders, Matrimony, and Anointing of the Sick. As long taught by the Church, the sacraments are defined by name and number; they produce grace *"ex opere operato"* (i.e., any sacrament administered properly with no obstacles gives grace, regardless of the holiness of the minister). CCC 774, 1084, 1113-1131; cf. 698, 738-740, 747, 775-776, 780, 790, 798, 815, 947, 950, 977, 987, 1045, 1074-1076, 1088, 1108, 1132-1133, 1140, 1150, 1178, 1183, 1210-1212, 1269, 1275, 1324, 1374, 1418, 1420-1421, 1425, 1509, 1533-1535, 1680, 1692, 2003, 2030, 2691, 2839

Sacraments of Initiation (SA-kruh-mehnts uhv ih-nih-shee-AY-shuhn): The three sacraments that enable one to be fully prepared to spread the Gospel. These three are Baptism ("rebirth"), Confirmation ("recommitment" or "sealing"), and Holy Eucharist ("nourishment"). CCC 1212, 1275

Sacrarium (sak-REH-ree-uhm): (From Latin: sacred place) Another name for the piscina, a basin with the drain leading directly into the ground, for disposing of water used sacramentally.

Sacred Art and Furnishings (SAY-krehd AHRT and FER-nih-shihngz): The Church has from earliest times utilized external beauty as an expression of the invisible glory of God, in painting, sculpture, mosaics, architecture, vesture, etc. Even the catacombs are decorated with murals, as later basilicas with mosaics, and medieval cathedrals with sculpture and stained glass. The arts in the service of the Church reached a great synthesis in the Middle Ages; however, surely another high point was achieved in the Baroque era, although such display is not always to contemporary taste. Because much nineteenth- and twentieth-century art did not continue the high standards set by previous eras, the Vatican II Constitution on the Sacred Liturgy (*Sacrosanctum Concilium*) encourages Ordinaries to strive after "noble beauty rather than mere sumptuous display" (n. 124), probably a thrust at neo-historic styles copied in the nineteenth century. Unfortunately, this has often been misinterpreted, as if such simplicity excludes any art or images at all, even though the same constitution says that sacred images are to be retained (n. 125). It would seem that, regardless of style (all architectural styles are permitted: cf. n. 123), a church edifice ought to have at least an image of the Crucified One over or near the altar, a

Madonna, and an image of the patron saint, with the possibility of other images, e.g., the life and teaching of Our Lord, the mysteries of the Faith, the saints of the Church, and all or any of these depicted in such wise that they be recognized, i.e., not so abstract as to be meaningless. Of course, how much pictorial representation is possible would depend on the architecture of the structure and the financial resources to pay for good art. But this dimension of teaching and also of externalizing the glory of God ought not to be neglected. The principal furnishings of the Church discussed in the section "Arrangement and Furnishing of the Church" of the *General Instruction of the Roman Missal* are, in order of importance, the altar, the lectern, the chair, the tabernacle, and images. All of these items "should be truly worthy and beautiful, signs and symbols of heavenly realities" (n. 288). CCC 1159-1162, 1180-1184

Sacred College of Cardinals: See College of Cardinals, Sacred

Sacred Heart Enthronement (SAY-krehd HAHRT ehn-THRON-mehnt): Acknowledgment of the sovereignty of Jesus Christ over the Christian family, expressed by the installation or picture of the Sacred Heart of Jesus (q.v.) in a place of honor in the home, accompanied by an act of consecration.

Sacred Heart of Jesus (SAY-krehd HAHRT uhv DZHEE-zuhs): Symbol of the love of Christ for the human race. A strong impetus for this devotion occurred when St. Margaret Mary Alacoque enjoyed visions of the Sacred Heart between 1673 and 1675. The Sacred Heart of the God-Man reminds all of the compassion and mercy of the Almighty. Cf. CCC 478

Sacred Heart, Promises of the (PRAH-mih-suhz uhv *th*uh SAY-krehd HAHRT): Twelve promises to those devoted to the Sacred Heart of Jesus, communicated by Christ to St. Margaret Mary Alacoque in a private revelation in 1675: (1) all graces necessary to their state in life; (2) peace in their homes; (3) comfort in all afflictions; (4) secure refuge in life and death; (5) abundant blessings on all their undertakings; (6) infinite mercy for sins; (7) tepid souls turned fervent; (8) fervent souls mounting in perfection; (9) blessing everywhere a picture or image is honored; (10) gift to priests of touching the most hardened hearts; (11) promoters' names written in His heart; (12) the grace of final penitence to those who receive Holy Communion on nine consecutive First Fridays.

Sacred Liturgy, Constitution on the: See Sacrosanctum Concilium

Sacred Meal (SAY-krehd MEEL): A gathering around food possessing a religious meaning, which for Catholics culminates in the Holy Sacrifice of the Mass. The sacred meal is, for Christians, the Last Supper. The agape (q.v.) was a fellowship meal held immediately prior to the offering of the Holy Eucharist in early Christian times.

Sacred Places (SAY-krehd PLAY-sehz): Places such as churches or oratories, designated by Church authority for divine worship or for the burial of the faithful. Cf. CCC 1179-1186, 1198-1199

Sacred Roman Congregations: See Roman Congregations

Sacred Times (SAY-krehd TAIMZ): Sundays of the year, holy days of obligation, and days and seasons of penance that are so designated by Church authority. Cf. CCC 1163-1167, 1438, 2042, 2177

Sacred Vessels (SAY-krehd VEH-suhlz): The *General Instruction of the Roman Missal,* nn. 327-334, describes sacred vessels as those "requisites for the celebration of Mass" that "hold a place of honor, especially the chalice and paten" (n. 327). Other vessels described concern the celebration of the Eucharist or the worship of the Eucharist outside of Mass. Among these are the ciborium (the vessel that resembles the chalice with a cover containing the Eucharistic Bread), the pyx (the container for the large Host used in exposition from a monstrance), the monstrance (the large vessel for exposing the large Host for Exposition and Benediction) (n. 329).

The *General Instruction* asserts that "for the consecration of hosts one rather large paten may properly be used; on it is placed the bread for the priest as well as for the ministers and the faithful" (n. 331). In preconciliar legislation, vessels for the Eucharistic Bread were to be made of precious metal (particularly gold or silver). The present instruction states that "sacred vessels are to be made from noble metal. If they are fabricated from metal that produces rust, or from a metal less noble than gold, then generally they shall be gold-plated on the inside" (n. 328); other suitable materials for these vessels may be determined by the judgment of the Conference of Bishops, with the confirmation of the Apostolic See, and that "in the common estimation of the region are regarded as noble, e.g., ebony or other hard woods as long as such materials are suited to sacred use," with preference "to be given always to materials that do not break easily or deteriorate" (n. 329). Chalices should "have a cup of nonabsorbent material" (n. 330). The exact dimensions and design of sacred vessels are left to the artist's discretion and creativity: "The artist may fashion the sacred vessels in a shape that is in keeping with the culture of each region, provided each type of vessel is suited to the intended liturgical use and is clearly distinguishable from those designed for everyday use" (n. 332). Following liturgical custom, such vessels are consecrated or blessed according to the prescribed rite. This may now be done by any priest and should be done for all such vessels, whatever their material (see n. 333).

Sacred Writers (SAY-krehd RAI-terz): The human persons, especially the four Evangelists, who wrote the books of Sacred Scripture, inspired by the Holy Spirit. Their testimony concerning God's revelation is infallible. **Cf. CCC 102, 107**

Sacrifice (SA-krih-fais): The act of offering to God, and often the subsequent destruction or consumption of some gift. It runs deep throughout the history of the world; Scripture is full of such offerings. The greatest sacrifice is the very offering of Christ Himself to the Father through the Holy Spirit, which sacrifice is perpetuated at each Holy Mass. **Cf. CCC 901, 1334, 2099-2100**

Sacrifice of the Mass (SA-krih-fais uhv _th_uh MAS): The offering of the combined Liturgies of the Word and the Eucharist at which bread and wine are changed into the Body, Blood, Soul, and Divinity of Jesus Christ. The Mass is a true and proper sacrifice; it is the "unbloody" sacrifice in which Christ joins the liturgical offering to His own offering on Calvary. The elements of a true sacrifice are present at Mass: a sense-perceptible offering (bread and wine) is destroyed (consecrated into a wholly different reality) by an authorized minister (duly ordained priest), in order to worship God (the Mass is the solemn worship of God by priest and faithful). CCC 611, 618, 1088, 1113, 1323, 1330, 1358, 1362-1372, 1382, 1410, 1414, 1419, 2031

Sacrilege (SA-krih-lehdzh): Violent, disrespectful treatment of persons, places, and objects dedicated to God. Receiving the sacraments unworthily (i.e., in mortal sin) is also sacrilegious. CCC 2118, 2120, 2139

Sacristan (SA-krihs-tuhn): One who is responsible for the good order and proper maintenance of sometimes not just the sacristy but the entire church building. The sacristan should see to it that the church is clean, that the altar and sanctuary are prepared for liturgical ceremonies, that vestments are ready to be used, candles are lit, etc. Sometimes the work of the sacristan overlaps with that of the sexton.

Sacristy (SA-krihs-tee): (Latin _sacristia_) A room adjacent to the sanctuary or near the main entrance to the church. The sacristy stores the items necessary (books, vestments, sacred vessels, etc.) for all liturgical ceremonies to take place in the church or on church property. It is also the place where ministers in the sanctuary vest and unvest. The sacristy is equipped as well with a sink and sacrarium.

Sacrosancta (sah-kro-SAHNK-tah): The decree, referred to as _Haec Sancta,_ issued by the Council of Constance (1414-1418), and later condemned by Pope Pius II (1458-1464), that claimed that even the Supreme Pontiff is subject to the authority of a general council.

Sacrosanctum Concilium (sah-kro-SAHNK-tøøm kon-TSHEEL-ee-øøm): The first document promulgated at the Second Vatican Council (December 4, 1963). A culmination of the liturgical renewal under way for at least several decades, *Sacrosanctum Concilium* establishes the principles for, among other things, making possible the "full, conscious, and active" participation in the Eucharistic Sacrifice by all the faithful (n. 14). There are twelve separate sections of the document, touching on topics such as the nature of the Sacred Liturgy, its promotion, true reform, the Holy Eucharist, the other sacraments and sacramentals, the Divine Office, the Liturgical Year, Sacred Music, and Sacred Art and Furnishings. The liturgy is referred to here as the source and summit of the Christian life (cf. n. 10). This document has easily had the most far-reaching and visible impact on the Catholic Faith in the postconciliar period. While there have been many other changes in ecclesial life following Vatican II, it is widely argued that this document has authorized the most profound shifts in how the Church becomes conscious of her foremost duty: i.e., how she prays. In some quarters, the changes wrought by *Sacrosanctum Concilium* have been understood, interpreted, and carried out well, and the transition from a preconciliar liturgy to a postconciliar liturgy has been relatively harmonious. In other quarters, however, the changes brought on by *Sacrosantum Concilium* have been understood, interpreted, and carried out poorly, and the transition to postconciliar liturgy has been nothing short of traumatic. To this day, the liturgical life of some Catholic communities continues to suffer from distorted, misinterpreted readings of *Sacrosanctum Concilium* and so-called appeals to the "spirit" of the document. Sadly, this has prevented one of the principal aims of *Sacrosanctum Concilium* from being realized: the true interiorization of the sacred mysteries. In time, though, a sound catechesis and increased respect for the authority of the Church will help to remake the abuses into genuine encounters of holiness, grace, and peace.

Sadducees (SA-dzhoo-seez): One of several distinct groups within Judaism during the N.T. era. The Sadducees existed from around the second century B.C. to the first century A.D. The English term is from the N.T. Greek *saddukaios* (cf. Mt 3:7; 16:1, 6, 11 ff.; 22:23, 34; Mk 12:18; Lk 20:27; Acts 5:17, 23:6-8), which is a transliteration of the Hebrew *tzaddiquim*, meaning "righteous ones." The Sadducees rejected any belief in the immortality of the soul and life after death (Mk 12:18; Acts 23:8) or the notion of fate; did not believe in angels, spirits, or the resurrection (Acts 23:8); and accepted as Sacred Scripture only the Torah (not the prophets or their writings). They were mostly wealthy people and priests from powerful families, greatly influenced by Hellenism at the expense of what other first-century Jewish groups would hold as authentic religion. They probably had significant control over the Sanhedrin and systematically worked at fostering positive relations with the Romans. They rejected rabbinic interpretations of the Law. Scholars speculate that the friendly relationship between the Roman occupation forces and the Sadducees led other Jewish groups to exterminate the Sadducees during or after the Jewish wars (A.D. 66-70). **Cf. CCC 535, 993**

Saint (SAYNT): (Latin *sanctus, -a*: consecrated, holy) 1. A person in heaven, whether or not canonized, who lived a life of great charity and heroic virtue. Saints now live forever with God and share in His glory. 2. Any person, according to St. Paul, who follows Christ (cf. Col 1:2). **CCC 828; cf. 61, 867, 946-962, 1161, 1172-1173, 1195, 1331, 1477, 2030, 2156, 2683**

St. Joseph's Oratory (SAYNT DZHO-sehfs OR-uh-tor-ee): A popular place of pilgrimage near the summit of Mt. Royal, overlooking the city of Montreal, Quebec, Canada. It began as a small wooden chapel in 1896 through the efforts of Bl. André Bessette of the College of Notre Dame of the Holy Cross in recognition of the patronage of St. Joseph, who was declared the patron saint of Canada in 1624. From its foundation, the Oratory quickly acquired a reputation as a place of miraculous cures, many of which were attributed to Bl. André. Crowded with crutches and other testimonials of favors received through St. Joseph's intercession, the original chapel has been enlarged three times. The present church, built in the neo-Classic style in 1918, stands as a testimony to the faithful, the miracles performed, and St. Joseph's patronage of Canada and the universal Church.

St. Peter's Basilica (SAYNT PETERZ buh-SIHL-ih-kuh): The largest church edifice in the world, built above the traditional site of the martyrdom and burial of St. Peter, Christ's appointed vicar and the first Pope of the Catholic Church. Though within the modern city of Rome today, more specifically at the heart of Vatican City, the site of St. Peter's in ancient times was outside the city limits and, therefore, appropriate by Roman custom to serve as a burial ground, a fact confirmed only in recent years by the archaeological excavations beneath the Renaissance basilica. The Piazza di San Pietro, with its still more ancient Egyptian obelisk at its core, is likely laid out over the site of Nero's forum, which, despite tradition, was a far more commonly used place than the Roman Colosseum for the persecution and martyrdom of the early Christians. The literary evidence suggests that St. Peter was martyred by crucifixion, head downward out of deference to the Lord, in this forum, and that his body was quickly and discreetly removed to a nearby Christian burial place. After a brief removal of his remains to the Catacombs of St. Sebastian, they were returned to the burial place closer to his martyrdom, and here Constantine built the first basilica in the fourth century in honor of St. Peter, Prince of the Apostles. Recent archaeological research confirms the belief that Peter's remains are in fact still entombed immediately beneath the high altar of the present basilica. Because of its proximity to the papal palace of the Vatican, though not the cathedral of the Bishop of Rome (St. John Lateran is the cathedral), St. Peter's Basilica is used for most of the major ceremonies of the Catholic Church, the coronations or, more recently, the installations of Popes, their funerals, canonizations of saints, and the papal Masses on major feasts, such as Christmas and Easter. The last two of the twenty-one ecumenical councils of the Church have been held in St. Peter's Basilica.

Saints, Cult of (KUHLT uhv SAYNTS): The veneration, called *dulia,* of holy persons who have died and are in glory with God in heaven; it includes honoring them and petitioning them for their intercession with God. Liturgical veneration is given only to saints officially recognized by the Church; private veneration may be given to anyone thought to be in heaven. Veneration of saints is essentially different from *latria,* the adoration given to God alone; by its very nature, however, it leads to worship of God. CCC 61, 956, 1172-1173, 1477, 2683

Saints, Invocations and Veneration of (ihn-vo-KAY-shuhnz and veh-ner-AY-shuhn uhv SAYNTS): Calling upon the saints for help (invocation) and giving them praise and honor as holy people (veneration). CCC 61, 956, 1172-1173, 1477, 2683

Saints, Patron: See Patron Saints

Sakkos (SAH-kos): The outer garment of a Byzantine bishop. The omophorion (q.v.) is wrapped over the sakkos.

Salt, Liturgical Use of (lih-TER-dzhih-kuhl YÖÖS uhv SAHLT): Before the reform of the liturgy, salt had a more prominent usage. It was used during the scrutinies of catechumens and at the Baptisms of infants. It was also used in the blessing of holy water and in the rite of consecration of a church and an altar. In the liturgy in use now, salt may be mixed with newly blessed holy water (cf. Rite for Blessing and Sprinkling with Holy Water). This recalls the salt scattered over the water by the prophet Elisha. Salt in the Scriptures represents wisdom and integrity of life (Mt 5:13; Col 4:6). Salt is no longer used in Christian initiation.

Salvation (sal-VAY-shuhn): The result of being released from death through the passion, death, and resurrection of Christ, which brings us to the newness of life in heaven. Humans have sinned; however, God promised the Redeemer, Who gave up His life on the cross, yet rose glorious so that His followers could enter eternal life. CCC 169, 456-457, 519, 600-602, 617, 620, 830, 980, 1019, 1066; cf. 54, 56, 95, 107, 122, 218, 313, 331-332, 402, 431, 511, 588, 776, 780-781, 816, 851, 874, 969, 1058, 1129, 1256-1261, 1277, 1477, 1565, 1603, 1696, 1739-1742,

1811, 1816, 1889, 1949, 2036, 2091, 2250, 2448, 2575, 2744, 2851

Salvation History (sal-VAY-shuhn HIS-tuh-ree): The entire way in which God has acted in creating the world and bringing it to fulfillment. God unfolds His plan gradually and through human persons. He created humans, who sinned; the Savior, Jesus Christ, was sent to suffer, die, and rise. Then the Holy Spirit was sent at Pentecost to continue the saving action of God. The Lord works in mysterious ways, yet His goal is obvious: to bring humanity to experience the beatific vision forever. Cf. CCC 280, 332, 430-431, 668, 1080, 1103

Salvation Outside the Church (sal-VAY-shuhn out-SAID *th*uh **TSHERTSH):** A teaching tempering the doctrine, found in the writings of St. Paul, many of the Church Fathers, the Popes, and general Councils, that one cannot be saved if one purposely remains outside the Church. This must be understood to mean that if one knows that the ordinary means of salvation, as willed by Christ, is that one must be incorporated into Christ's Mystical Body through Baptism and then subsequently nourished and sanctified by those sacraments instituted by Our Lord, then one has an absolute obligation to act upon this knowledge. If an individual is invincibly ignorant of that, there would be no guilt, and so could be saved by God through extraordinary means. This salvation, however, is still accomplished through Jesus Christ and His Church, even if that fact is not known by the one being saved. CCC 846-848; cf. 588, 1129, 1256-1261, 1949, 2448

Salve Regina (SAHL-vay ray-DZHEE-nuh): Familiar prayer "Hail, Holy Queen," dating from the eleventh century. Attributed to various authors, it was added to the Liturgy of the Hours by Pope St. Pius V in the sixteenth century. Cf. CCC 966

Samuel, First and Second Books of (FERST and SEH-kuhnd BØØKS uhv SAM-yöö-uhl): Included in the Vulgate as the first two of the four Books of Kings, the two Books of Samuel were originally one composition. The title is taken from the name of the central character, the priest, prophet, and judge Samuel, a most significant figure in this transitional period of Israel's history. In his lifetime, the twelve tribes became a unit, instituted under the one kingship (1 Sm 8:5-9). God led David to the heights of leadership and promised him a lasting "house." The basic religious idea of these books is "election," that God has chosen and made firm a people of His own and one in whom there would be carried out His salvific will toward the eventual salvation of all (cf. the Prophecy of Nathan in 2 Sm 7). As Samuel announced the new king of Israel, David, so St. John the Baptist is called the "new Samuel" who announced the King of all, the Messiah, the fulfillment of every messianic prophecy, such as that contained in 2 Samuel 7, Christ the Lord.

Sanation (sa-NAY-shuhn): (Latin *sanatio:* healing or curing) A "healing" or "retroactive validation" that is an administrative act whereby a competent ecclesiastical superior decrees that an act which was invalid for some reason is made valid without repeating the formalities of the act.

Sanctification (sank-tih-fih-KAY-shuhn): The process by which one grows in holiness (i.e., conformity to Christ). This occurs through the infusion of sanctifying grace, which enables one to be a friend of God. The seven sacraments are the primary means by which one experiences a more profound indwelling of the Holy Spirit. CCC 1123, 1152, 1540, 1668, 1677, 1989, 1995, 1999-2001; cf. 703, 767, 819, 824, 827, 893, 902, 928, 1070, 1174, 1637, 1670, 2187, 2427, 2807-2815, 2818, 2858

Sanctifying Grace (SANK-tih-fai-ihng GRAYS): The "habitual" life of God given to one at Baptism and reinforced when receiving the other sacraments, in prayer, and through the performance of charitable works. Through sanctifying grace, God enlivens the whole person and enables one to be authentically converted to the Lord. CCC 824, 1266, 1999-2001, 2023-2024

Sanctity (SANK-tih-tee): (Latin *sanctitas:* holiness) Sacred state of blessedness, holiness, or sainthood. **Cf. CCC 257, 1257, 1700, 1703, 1711, 1718, 1720-1722, 1727, 1731, 1769, 1818, 1855, 1863, 1874, 1934, 2548**

Sanctity, Odor of (O-der uhv SANK-tih-tee): Term using sweetness of smell metaphorically for the condition of sainthood, but sometimes understood literally because of olfactory phenomena associated with the remains of some holy people.

Sanctity of Life (SANK-tih-tee uhv LAIF): The Church's constant teaching that human life is valuable and possesses inherent dignity. In *Casti Connubii,* Pope Pius XI emphasized that innocent human life must never be taken. Each person is made in the *imago Dei* ("the image and likeness of God") and is destined to share in the divine life of the Blessed Trinity; hence, human life must be protected from assaults and esteemed as a gift from the Creator. This teaching is given full expression in *Evangelium Vitae,* one of the encyclicals of Pope John Paul II. **CCC 2259-2283**

Sanctuary (SANK-tshöö-ehr-ee): According to the *General Instruction of the Roman Missal,* the sanctuary (*presbyterium*) is where the priest and servers have places to perform their proper function, whether it is leading in prayer, announcing the Word of God, or ministering at the altar (nn. 294-295). The sanctuary should be set off from the rest of the church by a raised floor, special shape, or decoration (n. 295). **Cf. CCC 1183, 1674, 2691**

Sanctuary Lamp: See Lamp

Sanctus (SAHNK-tøøs): (Latin: holy) A hymn of praise at the conclusion of the preface and prior to the recitation of the canon or Eucharistic Prayer. The first part is based on a song of praise sung by the angels before the throne of God in heaven (Rv 4:9-11, echoing Is 6:3). The second part recalls the praise offered to Christ upon His triumphal entry into Jerusalem (Mk 11). At Masses without music (such as a daily Mass), the *Sanctus* is usually not sung or chanted. But at

Masses with music (especially Sunday Masses), the *Sanctus* is sung or chanted. The following are the words to this prayer: "Holy, holy, holy Lord, God of power and might. Heaven and earth are full of your glory. Hosanna in the highest. Blessed is he who comes in the name of the Lord. Hosanna in the highest." **Cf. CCC 559**

Sandals (SAN-duhlz): The special ceremonial shoes formerly worn by the Pope and bishops during Pontifical Solemn Masses. Developed from the shoes worn by Roman officials, sandals were of the liturgical color of the day. They are not worn when using the Missal of Pope Paul VI but would be worn if the Tridentine Rite were employed.

Sanhedrin (san-HEH-drihn): (Greek *synedrion:* assembly) The highest court and governing council of the ancient Jewish nation, composed of seventy-one members presided over by the high priest of the Temple in Jerusalem, operating from the second century B.C. until the destruction of Jerusalem in A.D. 70. **Cf. CCC 591, 596**

Sapiential Books (sap-ee-EHN-tshuhl bøøks): Seven books of the O.T. generally classified as "wisdom literature": Job, Psalms, Proverbs, Ecclesiastes (Qoheleth), the Song of Songs, Wisdom, and Sirach (Ecclesiasticus).

Sardica, Council of (KAUN-suhl uhv SAHR-dih-kuh): A council of Greek and Latin bishops, held in A.D. 343, which drafted canons to facilitate reforms necessitated by the Arian heresy.

Sarum Use (SEHR-uhm YÖÖS): (From the name of an ancient city near Salisbury, England) The adaptation of the Roman liturgy for use at the cathedral of Salisbury in the thirteenth century. Eventually this adapted liturgy spread to the rest of England, to Wales, and parts of Ireland before the Reformation. In time, a Sarum Breviary came into being and was used in the Province of Canterbury. From the Sarum Use, the Prayer Book of Edward VI (1549) developed.

Satan: See Devil and Evil Spirits

Satanism (SAY-tuhn-ih-zuhm): Worship of the devil, a blasphemous inversion of the order of worship that is due to God alone. CCC 2113, 2116-2117

Satisfaction (sa-tihs-FAK-shuhn): The action, endowed with God's grace, by which one repairs for one's own sins or the sins of others. Christ has made the full satisfaction for sin by His death and resurrection. Each faithful disciple is invited to join Jesus by offering with Him to the Father through the Holy Spirit the gift of his entire self. CCC 1414, 2412, 2454, 2487, 2509

Saul: See Paul, St.

Scala Sancta (SKAH-luh SAHNK-tuh): (Latin: holy stairs) The steps, composed of marble and numbering twenty-eight, that are believed to be the stairs of Pilate's praetorium in Jerusalem that Jesus ascended for His interrogation. Presently, the steps are in Rome near St. John Lateran Basilica and were supposedly brought from Jerusalem by St. Helena around A.D. 326.

Scamnum (SCAHM-nøøm): (Latin: stool) Another name given to the *sedilia,* or bench on which the ministers sat during parts of the High Mass. It has been replaced by the celebrant's chair (presidential chair) and other seats for ministers in the sanctuary.

Scandal (SKAN-duhl): The act of soliciting another to sin by words or deeds. Direct scandal occurs when one willfully seeks to draw another to sin; indirect scandal takes place when another person's sin is not intended but is foreseen by one's actions. It may also occur when a non-sinful action draws another to sin. CCC 2284-2287, 2326; cf. 589, 1938, 2282, 2353-2355, 2489

Scapular (SKAP-yöö-ler): (From Latin *scapula:* shoulder blade) One of the Church's sacramentals: a garment covering the chest and back of one wearing it, extending almost to the feet. Many religious wear a scapular as part of their habit. Laypeople who wear a scapular use a much shorter version; this consists of two small pieces of cloth, approximately two and a half by two inches, connected by two long cords placed over the head and resting on the shoulders. There are eighteen scapulars approved for use in the Church today. The most popular, most indulgenced, and most widely used is the scapular of the Carmelite Order, known as the "brown scapular."

Scapular Medal (SKAP-yöö-ler MEH-duhl): Medallion with a representation of the Sacred Heart on one side and the Blessed Virgin Mary on the other, approved by St. Pius X in 1910. It may be worn on a chain or carried in place of the scapular by one already invested.

Scapular Promise (SKAP-yöö-ler PRAH-muhs): According to a legend of the Carmelite Order, the Blessed Virgin Mary appeared to St. Simon Stock at Cambridge in 1251 and declared that wearers of the brown Carmelite scapular would be saved from hell and taken to heaven by her on the first Saturday after death. The Church has never ruled on the legend's validity, but essentially it shows great belief in the intercession of Mary and the power of sacramentals in the Christian life.

Schism (SIH-zuhm): (Greek: split) The formal and deliberate break of a group from ecclesiastical unity. Schism is a serious separation and a sin, not against the teachings of the Church (i.e., heresy) but against unity. **CCC 817-819, 2089**

Schism, Eastern (EES-tern SIH-zuhm): The separation between the ancient patriarchal sees in the East and Rome in the West, culminating in 1054. Also known as the "Great Schism," it resulted from long-standing conflicts between the Latin and Greek Churches over political, cultural, and some religious issues. Attempts to reunite the Eastern and Western Churches have not been successful, although there has been some modest reconciliation in recent years.

Schism, The Great Western: See Western Schism, The Great

Schoenstatt Movement (SHEHN-staht MÖÖV-mehnt):
The international movement founded by Pallotine Fr. Joseph Kentenich in 1914 at Schoenstatt, Germany, seeking to nurture the Christian life in its members by emphasizing devotion to Our Lady. Five secular institutes have developed; in 1926, the Schoenstatt Sisters were begun by the founder.

Schola Cantorum (SKO-luh kahn-TOR-øøm): 1. The school, established in the fifth century, for singers and other liturgical musicians who are instructed in vocal and instrumental techniques, along with musical composition. 2. The group of vocalists who usually sing more difficult works during liturgical functions.

Scholastic (skuh-LAS-tihk): 1. A student of medieval philosophy, which is most often associated with St. Thomas Aquinas (1225?-1274). St. Thomas stressed the importance of both faith and reason in delving into the mysteries of God and Catholic dogma. He continues — as directed by the Second Vatican Council — to hold pride of place in Catholic theology and philosophy. 2. A member of the Society of Jesus (Jesuits) who has finished his novitiate and embarked upon the final preparation for the priesthood.

Scholasticism (skuh-LAS-tih-sih-zuhm): The method of philosophical and theological investigation that uses analogy, definition, and synthesis of these findings so as to penetrate the depths of revealed truth. It has enjoyed a long history of adherence by notables like St. Augustine, St. Albert, and St. Thomas Aquinas; however, today its followers have been greatly reduced in number.

Schools, Catholic (KATH-uh-lihk SKÖÖLZ): From the time of the founding of a Franciscan school in Florida in 1606, Catholic schools spread throughout the territories as they were settled, to teach reading, mathematics, and the principles of the Catholic religion. With the growth of the public school system, it was necessary to establish the legal right of Catholic schools to exist, which was accomplished by the United States Supreme Court decision in *Pierce* v. *Society of Sisters* in 1925. The Code of Canon Law, following the lead of the Second Vatican Council, reminds Catholic parents of their obligation to entrust their children to Catholic schools. Cf. CCC 2229

Schools, Parochial (puh-RO-kee-uhl SKÖÖLZ): Elementary or secondary schools, supported by the local parish or a group of parishes, that teach not only academics but also the essentials of the Faith. Parochial schools are known for their discipline and scholarship and have benefited millions of persons. The Third Plenary Council of Baltimore decreed in 1884 that every parish should have a school, if possible.

Scotism (SKO-tih-zuhm): The system of Scholastic philosophy developed by the Franciscan Bl. John Duns Scotus (1265-1308), which contrasts with Thomism by assigning primary importance to love and the will rather than knowledge and reason.

Scotula: See Bugia

Scribe (SKRAIB): (Hebrew *sofer;* Latin *scriba*) A member of the class composed of well-educated Jews who explained and studied the Law. Although scribes were not priests, some were members of the Sanhedrin. They believed Jesus to be a threat to their authority and took part in planning His death. In the N.T. a scribe who was an expert in the Scriptures enjoyed the title "rabbi." Cf. CCC 572, 574-575, 581, 2054, 2285

Scripture, Holy: See Bible

Scruple (SKRÖÖ-puhl): The fear that one has sinned when in fact no sin has occurred. Scrupulosity results from rigorism or a psychological dysfunction. Often, one with scruples believes that an action concerns grave matter when it really does not. In confession, the priest needs to exercise patience and firmness with one who has scruples.

Scrutiny (SKRÖÖ-tih-nee): 1. Technical term for the evaluation of a seminarian prior to ordination (Can. 1051). 2. Part of the RCIA (Rite of Christian Initiation of Adults) that judges candidates' readiness for Baptism. 3. An individual ballot in a canonical election.

Seal: See Lamb

Seal of Confession (SEEL uhv kuhn-FEH-shuhn): The obligation of a priest never to reveal anything told to him in sacramental confession (Can. 984). CCC 1467, 2490

Second Vatican Council: See Vatican Council II

Secret Marriage (SEE-kreht MEHR-ehdzh): A marriage celebrated according to all the norms of law, including canonical form, but without the usual publicity so that it is not known to the public and is recorded only in the secret diocesan archives (cc. 1130-1133).

Secret of the Mass (SEE-kreht uhv *th*uh MAS): A designation employed in the pre-Vatican II Rite for the Prayer Over the Gifts. It came to be known as such because the celebrant offered the prayer in silence with the exception of the last part, *"per omnia saecula saeculorum"* ("forever and ever" or, literally, "through all ages of ages"). In the post-Vatican II rite, the entire prayer is proclaimed aloud by the priest. Currently, the prayer is known by its function, Prayer over the Gifts, or in Latin, *"super oblata."*

Secret Societies (SEE-kreht suh-SAI-eh-teez): Organizations that forbid their members to disclose their purposes, rituals, or activities to nonmembers. Because the beliefs of most secret societies are founded upon some form of deism, and so are incompatible with the Catholic Faith, membership in such organizations traditionally has been forbidden by the Church.

Secular Institute: See Institute, Secular

Secularism (SEK-yöö-ler-ih-zuhm): A system of thought that rejects any reference to God or religion and seeks to improve the human condition solely through science, social organization, and human reason.

Secularization (sek-yöö-ler-ih-ZAY-shuhn): The canonical process whereby a member of a religious institute is separated from it.

Sede Vacante (SAY-day vuh-KAHN-tay): (Latin: vacant seat) The period of time when the Apostolic See or a diocesan see is without a shepherd.

Sedia Gestatoria (SAY-dee-uh dzhehs-tuh-TOR-ee-uh): (From Latin *sedes:* chair + *gestare:* to carry) The portable throne used to carry the Pope during processions and public ceremonies. Pope John Paul I was the last Pontiff to use the *sedia gestatoria*. Pope John Paul II has not used the throne because of the connotations of worldly splendor associated with it.

Sedilia (seh-DIH-lee-uh): (Latin: seats) Benches used for the clergy and assistants during liturgical celebrations. *Sedilia* can be found in the catacombs and, in some places, were carved into the south sanctuary wall.

See (SEE): (From Latin: chair, or throne) Another name for a diocese or archdiocese. Cf. CCC 194, 919

Semi-Arianism (SEH-mee-EHR-ee-uhn-ih-zuhm): An attempt, led by Basil, fourth-century Bishop of Ancyra, to bridge the gap between Arianism and orthodox theology. It held that the Son was like the Father though not His divine equal.

Seminarian (sehm-ih-NEHR-ee-uhn): One who is a candidate for the priesthood by virtue of his participation in an ecclesiastically approved program of formation and studies. The seminary prepares men spiritually, intellectually, and apostolically for the reception of the sacrament of Holy Orders.

Seminary (SEHM-ih-nehr-ee): (From Latin *seminare:* to sow, plant seed) The ecclesiastical center of formation that trains men for the reception of Holy Orders.

Semi-Pelagianism (SEH-mee-puh-LAY-gee-uhn-ih-zuhm):
A French variation on Pelagianism that held that the human will both deserved and made God's grace efficacious.

Semite (SEH-mait): Those persons considered to be descendants of Shem, son of Noah, and who came from Asia and Africa. Scholars today believe that the original home of the Semites was probably Arabia. Arabic, Aramaic, and Hebrew are Semitic languages.

Senses of Scripture (SEHN-sehz uhv SKRIHP-tsher): The Bible, composed by men who were chosen by God, "is inspired of God and profitable for teaching, for reproof, for correction, and for training in righteousness, that the man of God may be complete, equipped for every good work" (2 Tm 3:16). The human authors of Scripture, writing what God wanted, nevertheless used their own intellectual and literary gifts. Therefore, as is taught in *Dei Verbum* (DV), the Dogmatic Constitution on Divine Revelation, "it follows that the interpreter of Sacred Scriptures, if he is to ascertain what God has wished to communicate to us, should carefully search out the meaning which the sacred writers really had in mind, that meaning which God had thought well to manifest through the medium of their words." This *literal sense* is essential to the proper interpretation of Scripture, not as a word-for-word literalism, but as seeking the mind and intention of the inspired author. This includes a knowledge of the original languages of the Bible, literary forms, context, facts of culture, history, geography, and other influences upon the writer. This literal sense of Scripture also encompasses the *sensus plenior* ("the fuller sense"), whereby God sometimes intends a deeper sense than is evident from a solitary text; rather, the fuller apprehension of the truth is possible when later revelation is applied to that which came earlier, thus communicating something more profound than that which is apparent at first. The *typical sense* of Scripture not only involves the meaning that a passage has in itself, but refers to some truth or event of which it is a "type" or "foreshadowing." This can be seen in the exodus of the Israelites from Egypt as a type of our deliverance from sin, or the bronze serpent on the rod of Moses foreshadowing Jesus

Christ on the cross. This use of typology can be found in Scripture itself (for example, Jn 3:14; Rom 5:12-14; 1 Pt 3:20-21), and can show the unity of the O.T. and N.T. in revealing God's plan for the salvation of mankind. The *accommodated sense* of Scripture involves placing an interpretation upon a passage that has no strict connection to it. This may be done to make some moral or allegorical point, but if proper caution is not taken, it can distort the primary meaning of the words. An accommodation must never contradict the literal sense of the original text, nor can it be used as a proof of some particular doctrine. (See also Interpretation, Scriptural.) **CCC 115-119**

Sentence (SEHN-tehnts): The written decision of the judge in a case presented to an ecclesiastical court (cc. 1612-1613).

Separation (seh-per-AY-shuhn): The physical parting of a husband and a wife from each other without divorce or annulment, for adultery or other causes provided in Canon Law (cc. 1151-1155). **CCC 2383**

Septuagesima (sehp-töö-uh-DZHAY-zee-muh): (Latin: seventieth [day before Easter]) The third Sunday before Lent or the ninth Sunday before Easter was considered the septuagesima. It marked a transition from the post-Epiphany Sundays to the Lenten Season. Violet vesture was worn, and the Alleluia was omitted from Masses and Offices. However, fasting was not prescribed. The septuagesima was suppressed in the reform of the liturgical calendar because it was thought to mitigate or reduce in significance the full impact of Lent.

Septuagint (sehp-TÖÖ-uh-dzhihnt): The Greek translation, begun in Alexandria, Egypt, in the third century B.C. and completed in 100 B.C., of the Hebrew O.T. The Septuagint includes several books not found in the Hebrew Scriptures. The symbol LXX ("seventy") refers to this translation, representing the seventy-two Jewish scholars who translated the Hebrew Scriptures for the benefit of the Greek-speaking Jews. When citing O.T. passages, the early Church often used the Septuagint. **Cf. CCC 213**

Seraph (SER-uhf): One of the angels present at God's throne who constantly praise Him. The prophet Isaiah (6:1-7) writes that the seraphim have six wings; one of them touched Isaiah's lips with a hot coal. The seraphim form the highest choir of angels.

Sermon: See Homily

Sermon on the Mount (SER-muhn awn *th*uh MAUNT): The discourse of Jesus in Mt 5:1—7:29, comprising the first of five collections of Jesus' sayings arranged by Matthew into extended discourses, is traditionally known as the Sermon on the Mount. It begins with the Beatitudes and ends with the parable of the house built on rock. Among its chief themes are that Jesus Himself perfectly fulfills the law and that the new law He gives is in certain instances more challenging than the old law (e.g., with respect to divorce and retaliation). Christ commends genuine piety over exterior display, and appropriate concern over anxiety. The contents of the Sermon on the Mount have always been taken with the greatest seriousness by the Church because they express the solemn teaching of Christ Himself. CCC 577, 1454, 1724, 1965-1966, 1968, 2153, 2262, 2336, 2608, 2830

Servant of Yahweh (SER-vuhnt uhv YAH-way): A number of individuals and groups in the O.T. are described as servants of the Lord. For example, Moses is the servant of the Lord *par excellence* in the Deuteronomic writings (e.g., Dt 34:5; Jos 1:1-2; cf. also Rv 15:3), and the title is extended to his successor Joshua (Jos 24:29; Jgs 2:8). Prophets collectively are the Lord's servants (2 Kgs 17:3; 21:10; 24:2; cf. also Rv 10:7), and individual prophets are identified as the Lord's servants (e.g., Elijah in 2 Kgs 9:36; Isaiah in Is 20:3). The king is also said to be the Lord's servant, and this is especially so in the case of David (cf. 2 Kgs 19:34; 20:6; Ps 18:1; 36:1; 78:70; 89:4, 21; 132:10; 144:10). Those who worship the Lord are His servants, both collectively (cf. Ps 134:1; 135:1) and as individuals who depend on the Lord and who place complete trust in Him (Ps 31:17). The title "Servant of Yahweh," also called the "Suffering Servant of Yahweh," applies particularly to a figure found in four poetic texts of the Book of Isaiah. These four Servant songs or Servant poems are found in that portion of the Book of Isaiah (Chs. 40-55) attributed to an anonymous prophet who wrote during the Babylonian Exile and who is known as 2 Isaiah or Deutero-Isaiah. The poems themselves say little that might lead to a clear determination of the Servant's identity. In the first poem, the Lord points him out as "my servant whom I uphold, my chosen one with whom I am pleased" (Is 42:1). The figure is also called "my servant" in the second poem (49:3, 6) and in the fourth (52:13; 53:11). Outside the Servant poems themselves, it is clear in texts of 2 Isaiah that Israel in exile is the Lord's chosen servant, whom the Lord Himself strengthens and upholds (Is 41:8-9; 44:1-2, 21; 45:4). Within the poems, in Is 49:3 the Servant is called "Israel, through whom I show my glory," though Is 49:4-6 complicates this identification by indicating that the Servant has a mission to Israel. The identification is further complicated by the opposition that the Servant faces and the oppression to which he is subjected, especially in the fourth poem (Is 52:13—53:12). Very early on, Christians came to recognize Jesus as the fulfillment of the Servant poems, understanding Jesus as the Servant of the Lord.

Server, Altar (AL-ter SER-ver): One who assists the celebrant at Mass and other liturgical rites. Servers may carry candles, the missal, the processional cross, the thurible with incense, and the aspergillum with holy water. The Second Vatican Council distinguishes between altar servers and "acolytes," who are officially instituted in their ministry and must be males according to Pope Paul VI's *Ministeria Quaedam*.

Service (SER-vihs): 1. The exercising of one's duty toward God and neighbor. The first three commandments encompass one's responsibility of serving the Lord through prayer and worship; the final seven commandments are concerned with one's vocation to serve others through charitable works and good example. 2. Any liturgical rite without the Mass (e.g., the Good Friday liturgy).

Servile Work (SER-vail WERK): Activity that is performed by physical exertion. The Church forbids servile work on

Sundays and holy days of obligation unless it is necessary for the good of society or for the welfare of a family.

Seven Dolors: See Sorrows of the Blessed Virgin Mary

Seven Gifts of the Holy Spirit: See Gifts of the Holy Spirit, The Seven

Seven Joys of the Blessed Virgin Mary (SEH-vehn DZHOIZ uhv *th*uh BLEH-sehd VER-dzhihn MEH-ree): The traditional rendering of seven joyful events in the life of Our Lady. This devotion, begun in the Middle Ages, includes the following occurrences: the Annunciation, the Visitation, the Nativity, the Adoration of the Magi, the Finding of Jesus in the Temple, the Appearance of the Risen Lord to Mary, and the Assumption and Coronation of Mary.

Seven Last Words of Christ (SEH-vehn LAST WERDZ uhv KRAIST): Words spoken by Jesus on the cross: (1) "Father, forgive them; for they know not what they do"; (2) to the penitent thief, "Truly I say to you, today you will be with me in Paradise"; (3) to Mary and the beloved disciple, "Woman, behold your son . . . Behold your mother"; (4) "My God, my God, why hast thou forsaken me?"; (5) "I thirst"; (6) "It is finished"; (7) "Father, into thy hands I commit my spirit."

Sexagesima (sehks-uh-DZHAY-zee-muh): (Latin: sixtieth [day before Easter]) The second Sunday before Lent or the eighth Sunday before Easter was designated the sexagesima. In the reform of the liturgical calendar, the sexagesima was suppressed in order not to diminish Lent in any way.

Sex and Christianity (SEHKS and krihs-tshee-AN-ih-tee): The connection between two realities that some consider to be strained but the Church has always supported. Human sexuality impinges on one's whole being and is a powerful force that must be directed toward God and His plan. Christianity teaches that sexuality is truly expressed in the celibate commitment (priesthood, consecrated life, dedicated single state) or in sacramental marriage (which has the purpose of sharing love and procreation). All are called to shun impure thoughts, desires, words, and actions, thereby respecting the gift of maleness and femaleness created by God. Promiscuous sex, highly encouraged by some today, has repeatedly been demonstrated to be the cause of disease and, especially in the Christian context, is a grave sin against God.

Sexism (SEHKS-ih-zuhm): Discrimination against individuals on the basis of gender. Although the term is used extensively by feminists to protest any differentiation between the sexes, Catholic teaching affirms that there are differences in the roles of men and women that are not discriminatory. **Cf. CCC 369, 2334, 2393**

Sext (SEHKST): That part of the Divine Office that is said at midday.

Sexuality (sehk-shoo-AL-ih-tee): All that comprises the experience of men and women living within society, exercising those masculine and feminine roles proper to each. **CCC 369-373, 1605, 2332-2337; cf. 355, 383, 2351-2357, 2360-2363, 2370, 2380, 2388-2390, 2393-2395, 2522**

Shekinah: See Glory

Shema (SHMUH): The title and first Hebrew word of the Jewish declaration of belief: "Hear, O Israel! The Lord our God is one Lord" (Dt 6:4). The Shema, which was written on the phylacteries and mezuzah, was identified by Jesus as the most important commandment (cf. Mk 12:29).

Shepherd, Good (GOOD SHEH-perd): Jesus identifies Himself as the Good Shepherd in Jn 10:11-18, specifying in verse 11 that "the good shepherd lays down his life for the sheep." As the Good Shepherd, He adds in verse 14, "I know my own and my own know me." The Good Shepherd metaphor in Jn 10:11-18 is but part of the pastoral imagery presented in John 10. The chapter begins with the parable of the sheepfold (10:1-6), where Jesus distinguishes between the true shepherd, who enters the sheepfold through the gate to lead out the sheep he knows by name, and the thieves and robbers who climb into the sheepfold by another way and are not recognized by the sheep. Explaining this imagery, Jesus first identifies Himself as the gate through which the sheep are safely led to pasture (10:7-10), and then identifies Himself as the Good Shepherd. The imagery of John 10 has its background in the pastoral imagery of the O.T. In a society where the care and feeding of sheep and other domesticated animals was a matter of everyday economic importance involving a significant portion of the population, metaphors involving sheep and shepherding were immediately accessible and easily understandable. John 10 is an effective vehicle of Johannine Christology. The description of the Good Shepherd as one Who knows His sheep and Who is known by them is connected in Jn 10:14-15 to the mutual knowledge that exists between Jesus and the Father. That communion of knowledge underlies the mutual knowledge of the sheep and the Good Shepherd, for it stems from Jesus' loving fulfillment of the Father's command (Jn 10:17-18). Thus the Good Shepherd is the one Who willingly lays down His life for the sheep. Cf. CCC 160, 754

Showbread (SHO-brehd): The twelve loaves of bread, referred to in Lv 24:59, that were set out each Sabbath in two piles of six on the golden table in the Temple. On the Sabbath, the priests ate the cakes placed there the previous Sabbath. This use of the showbread seems to be of pagan origin. In St. Mark's Gospel (2:26), Jesus refers to the incident of King David and his troops eating this bread when other food was unavailable (1 Sm 21:2-7).

Shrine (SHRAIN): A church or other sacred place approved by the local Ordinary to which the faithful go to make pilgrimages (Can. 1231).

Shrine, Crowned (KRAUN'D SHRAIN): A shrine approved by the Holy See as a place of pilgrimage. The approval permits public devotion at the shrine and implies that at least one miracle has resulted from devotion there. Among the best known crowned shrines are those of the Blessed Virgin at Lourdes and Fátima. Shrines with statues crowned by Pope John Paul II in 1985 in South America were those of Our

Lady of Coromoto, patroness of Venezuela, in Caracas; and Our Lady of Carmen of Paucartambo in Cuzco, Peru.

Shroud of Turin, Holy (HO-lee SHRAUD uhv TØØ-rihn): The linen cloth housed in the Cathedral of St. John the Baptist in Turin, Italy, which is claimed by some to be the burial garment of Jesus. Tests were performed in 1988, which indicated that the cloth is of medieval origin; however, some scholars contended that the testing procedure was riddled with errors. The Holy See stresses that since acceptance of the Shroud is not a matter of faith, one may either believe or disbelieve in its authenticity.

Shrovetide (SHROV-taid): Restricted originally to the day before Ash Wednesday, Shrove Tuesday. This day was set aside for confessing one's sins in the Sacrament of Penance as a prelude to the Lenten discipline. Later liturgical commentaries and devotional literature refer to Shrovetide as a period extending anywhere from one to six days.

Shrove Tuesday: See Shrovetide

Sick, Sacrament of the Anointing of the: See Pastoral Care of the Sick

Sign (SAIN): Something that gives direction but, more importantly, points beyond itself to some spiritual reality that may not be attained easily or perceived readily. 1. In the Gospels, particularly the Gospel of John, Jesus refers to His miracles as signs. 2. A rich theology of sign is present in the Church's liturgical and sacramental life. Signs may be gestures (standing, kneeling, bowing, prostration, etc.), actions (blessing oneself, anointing with chrism, etc.), liturgical vesture (alb, stole, chasuble, etc.), sacred vessels (chalice, ciboria, etc.), and ecclesiastical art (stained glass, bells, Book of the Gospels, etc.). Without these signs, the Faith would be unknowable and opaque. With them, it is possible for Catholics to enter into the mysteries behind the signs and thereby be caught up into the life of Christ and the Church. We refer to the sacraments as signs because they both cause and effect grace through the act of signifying. **CCC 1146-1148; cf.**

575, 628, 694-695, 699, 701, 775, 1084, 1123, 1130-1131, 1149-1152, 1157-1158, 1161, 1189, 1235, 1238, 1241, 1243, 1293-1301, 1333-1336, 1412, 1507, 1574, 1667-1668, 2260

Sign of Jonah (SAIN uhv JO-nuh): In Mt 12:28-42, 16:1-4, and Lk 11:29-32, Jesus replies to the Pharisees' demand that He produce a sign from heaven to lend credibility to His claims by declaring that no sign will be given "except the sign of Jonah." This seems to point to His resurrection on the third day. (Cf. Jonah, Sign of.) **Cf. CCC 994**

Sign of the Cross (SAIN uhv *th*uh KRAWS): The ritual gesture whereby we acknowledge the triune nature of God, i.e., Three Persons in One God. We profess our faith in the Father, Son, and Holy Spirit. With right hand cupped, we make the Sign of the Cross by touching first the forehead, then the breast, and finally both shoulders. This gesture is used privately as a devotional practice and is used publicly when the Church celebrates the Holy Eucharist, for example. The Sign of the Cross is also used in the Rite of Baptism (traced by celebrant, parents, and godparents) and Confirmation (the bishop or priest traces the Sign of the Cross with chrism on the forehead). **CCC 2157**

Signs of the Times (SAINZ uhv *th*uh TAIMZ): Contemporary events, trends in culture and society, the needs and aspirations of people — all the factors that form the context in and through which the Church must carry on its saving mission. The Second Vatican Council speaks of these signs and the relationship between them, a kind of manifestation of God's will, positive or negative, and also speaks about subjecting them to judgment and action corresponding to the demands of divine revelation through Scripture, Christ, and the experience, traditions, and Magisterium of the Church. **CCC 1788**

Simar: See Zimarra

Simony (SIH-muh-nee): The selling or purchasing of spiritual things, which is forbidden both by natural law and ecclesiastical law. The term is derived from the story of Simon Magus (Acts 8:18-24), in which he attempted to purchase spiritual powers from the Apostles. **CCC 2118, 2121**

Simple Feast (SIHM-puhl FEEST): A term used before the reform of the calendar and the Sacred Liturgy in the West, referring to the least important grade of feast. By decree of the Sacred Congregation of Rites in 1961, simple feasts became commemorations. Now many of the former simple feasts are designated optional memorials.

Simulation (sim-yöö-LAY-shuhn): The intentional falsification of a canonical or liturgical act so that there is the appearance of the act, all the while lacking validity.

Sin (SIHN): The deliberate, free, knowledgeable transgression of Divine Law, which is a refusal to strive for sanctity and may either drive all charity from one's soul ("mortal sin") or partially expel charity ("venial sin"). Sin entered the world through the disobedience of Adam and Eve. The O.T. considers sin to be "missing the mark," while sin in the N.T. is viewed as straying from the loving Father. The Redemption wrought by Christ has conquered sin. All sins are forgivable, except the sin against the Holy Spirit (q.v.). **CCC 1849-1850; cf. 211, 270, 277, 286-288, 311-312, 385-387, 392-393, 398, 400, 410-411, 430-431, 457, 523, 536, 549, 602-604, 606-618, 615, 705, 761, 814, 817, 827, 943, 953, 977-978, 985, 987, 1006, 1008, 1213, 1237, 1263-1264, 1420, 1426, 1431, 1434-1441, 1459, 1472-1473, 1488, 1609, 1708, 1739, 1741, 1851-1854, 1865-1869, 1949, 1989-1990, 1999, 2057, 2097, 2516, 2844, 2846, 2852**

Sin, Actual: See Actual Sin

Sindon: See Shroud of Turin

Sin, Mortal and Venial (MOR-tuhl and VEE-nee-uhl SIHN): Distinction grounded in Scripture: "All wrongdoing is sin, but there is sin which is not mortal" (1 Jn 5:17). A mortal sin is a violation of God's law that concerns grave moral matter and is done with full knowledge, deliberation, freedom, and consent. A venial sin involves lighter moral matter or is done without sufficient knowledge, full consent, or adequate freedom. CCC 1854-1864

Sin, Occasion of: See Occasion of Sin

Sin, Original (uh-RIH-dzhih-nuhl SIHN): The free disobedience of Adam and Eve, which closed the gates of heaven and brought with it many serious ramifications. Original Sin was the refusal to respond to God's love and to obey His commands. This transgression affected the state of "original justice." Thus sanctifying grace was lost, along with the other preternatural gifts that God gave to Adam and Eve: immortality, freedom from illness, keen intellect, and strong will. Original Sin has ushered in an "inner disordering" called "concupiscence," which is an inclination to evil. Only Jesus and Mary have been spared Original Sin. CCC 37, 215, 388-406, 409, 412, 1250, 1607, 1609, 1707, 2259, 2515

Sin, Reserved (ree-ZERV'D SIHN): A sin that could be absolved only by a bishop. Found in the 1917 Code of Canon Law but dropped from the revised code.

Singing (SIHNG-ihng): The worship of God in song at liturgical functions by the celebrant, cantor, choir, congregation, or a combination of these. Singing during the sacred functions has been a mainstay since the early Church. CCC 1156-1158, 1162, 1191

Singing, Congregational (kahn-greh-GAY-shuh-nuhl SIHNG-ihng): Participating at a sacred function by virtue of the singing of the congregation. Each musical work must be a combination of the "artistic" and the "sacred." The Second Vatican Council encouraged the use of sacred music that is simple enough for the congregation to sing, yet dignified and appropriate for use in the sacred setting.

Sins Against the Holy Spirit: See Holy Spirit, Sins Against the

Sins That Cry to Heaven for Vengeance (SIHNZ *th*at KRAI to HEH-vuhn for VEN-dzhuhnts): Willful murder; sins against nature; oppression of the poor, widows, and orphans; defrauding laborers of their wages. Cf. CCC 1867

Sirach (SIH-rak): A long sapiential book of the O.T., also called Ecclesiasticus, written in Hebrew at the beginning of the second century B.C., then translated into Greek shortly after 132 B.C. It is a deuterocanonical book, not accepted as inspired by Jews and Protestants, but included in the Catholic canon. The author is actually the grandson of Sirach, who identifies himself (50:27) as "Jesus, son of Eleazar, son of Sirach." Perhaps many of the author's counsels had come from his grandfather. Sirach contains the most complete and systematic presentation of the ideals of Jewish spirituality. In a paternal, but not paternalistic, way, it shows loving concern for the well-being of the coming generation. It offers guidance in almost every area of life. If it seems chauvinistic in being addressed only to men, perhaps we should keep in mind that it is no small part of wisdom to recognize that they are most in need of this kind of instruction.

Sister (SIH-ster): Any woman religious, in popular speech; strictly, the title applies only to women belonging to institutes whose members never professed solemn vows. Most of the institutes whose members are properly called Sisters were established during and since the nineteenth century. Women who take solemn vows, or belong to institutes whose members formerly professed solemn vows, are properly called nuns. Cf. CCC 918, 924

Sisterhood (SIH-ster-hood): Generic term referring to the whole institution of life of women religious in the Church, or to a particular institute of women religious. Cf. CCC 918, 924

Sisters, Renewal of Religious Life of: See Perfectae Caritatis

Sistine Chapel (SIHS-teen TSHAP-uhl): The principal chapel of the Vatican palace, referred to as the "Pope's Chapel" and used for the consistory of cardinals when electing a Pope; it boasts murals by Michelangelo and Raphael.

Sistine Choir (SIHS-teen KWAIR): The special choir whose official title is Il Collegio dei Capellani Cantori della Capella Pontificia, which sings at papal ceremonies and popularized *a cappella* singing in the sixteenth century.

Situation Ethics: See Ethics, Situation

Slander (SLAN-der): The communicating or attributing of falsehoods about another, often using elements that are true and false and purposely omitting details in order to damage the other's reputation. The virtue of justice demands that one guilty of slander restore the other's reputation by denouncing what was said and stopping the spread of the slander. Also, it is beneficial if the slanderer apologizes to the person accused. The Church has held that slander is distinct from telling what should be told about another and that it cannot be justified. **CCC 2477, 2479, 2507**

Sloth (SLOTH): One of the seven capital sins, which is marked by a spiritual laziness preventing one from doing his legitimate duties. Sometimes called *acedia* (Greek: not caring), sloth is a kind of sorrow for a spiritual good, rendering one unwilling to do the good that one can. While charity compels one to do good, sloth neglects the good and can be seriously wrong when one omits grave responsibilities to God, oneself, or others. **CCC 1866, 2094, 2733, 2755**

Social Communication, Decree on the Means of: See Inter Mirifica

Social Encyclicals: See Encyclicals, Social

Socialism (SO-shuhl-ih-zuhm): Various political and social systems that oppose individualism and emphasize one's duties to others. Most forms of socialism spring from Marxism and non-Christian sources that are hostile to religion, especially Christianity. Communism, a kind of socialism, exalts the State over the person in every facet of life. Recently, some socialists, such as those representing African political movements, claim to be striving for a balance between radical Marxism and unmitigated capitalism. Cf. CCC 1907, 1929-1933, 1944, 2284-2301

Society (suh-SAI-eh-tee): The sum of interactions between persons, existing to promote the common good, so that its members might develop and flourish. In the medieval and Reformation periods, society was to promote "true religion"; however, society is viewed today as having its own goals, other than those of the Church. Religion assists society by imbuing its adherents with the spirit to contribute to society's welfare by living upstanding, moral lives. Cf. CCC 1897-1904, 1918-1923, 2238-2243, 2255-2256, 2288; cf. 1907, 2104-2105, 2208-2210, 2273, 2433

Society of Apostolic Life (suh-SAI-eh-tee uhv a-pah-STAH-lihk LAIF): A grouping of people who live a common life and pursue an apostolate but who do not take public vows (cc. 731-746). CCC 930

Society, Religious: See Congregation; Order

Socinianism (so-SIHN-ee-uhn ih-zuhm): A form of Unitarianism that denied the doctrine of the Trinity, the virgin birth, and the redemption of mankind. The term is taken from the Latinized name of Lelio Sozzini (1525-1562) and his nephew Fausto (1539-1604), both of whom propagated these views among the Reformed communities in Geneva, Italy, and in Poland.

Sociology (so-see-AHL-uh-dzhee): The study of the development, structure, and function of groups of people, and of those institutions and relationships that form society.

Sodality (so-DAL-ih-tee): An organization, usually of laypeople, that promotes pious or charitable acts (Can. 298).

Sodepax (SO-deh-pahks): A common name for the Joint Commission on Society, Development, and Peace, which was an agency both of the World Council of Churches and the Pontifical Commission for Justice and Peace. Established in 1968, it was replaced by another agency in 1980.

Solemnity (so-LEHM-nih-tee): The highest rank of liturgical celebration. (See Feasts of the Church.)

Solesmes (so-LEHM): The French village that is home to the Benedictine Abbey known for its monks' work in restoring Gregorian chant melodies to their original form. The famed Abbot Prosper Guéranger was responsible for coordinating the publishing of the *Liber Usualis*.

Solideo: See Zucchetto

Solitude (SAHL-ih-tööd): The permanent or temporary withdrawal from others in order to seek a deeper relationship with God. Physical solitude is intended to lead to spiritual solitude, in which the soul is attentive to God alone. Cf. CCC 538, 917, 920, 2602, 2620, 2691

Sollicitudo Rei Socialis (so-lih-tshee-TÖÖ-do RAY-ee so-shee-AHL-ihs): The encyclical letter *On Social Concern* written by Pope John Paul II in 1987, which outlines the duty of all persons and nations to consider the interdependence of all people when making personal and political decisions, remembering especially the widening gap between rich and poor, and to work in solidarity for universal justice. Cf. CCC 1939-1942, 1948, 2402, 2407, 2437-2442, 2495, 2831

Solitary: See Hermit

Solomon (SAHL-uh-muhn): The youngest son of David and Bathsheba, who became the third king of Israel (961-922 B.C.) and is remembered for his poetry, managerial skills, and building the Temple in Jerusalem. He failed to centralize the government. By his intermarriage to many women of pagan cultures, Solomon angered God (1 Kgs 11:1-8). After his death, Israel suffered from a divided kingdom. Cf. CCC 283, 590, 697, 2580

Song, Leader of (LEED-er uhv SAWNG): One who encourages, through singing and appropriate hand gestures, the participation of the assembled community during liturgical rites. The leader of song is to direct the sung prayer of the assembly. Often the cantor assumes the role of song leader.

Song of Songs (SAWNG uhv SAWNGZ): Known also as the Canticle of Canticles and the Song of Solomon, a clutch of long songs and fragments of love poems, apparently the composition of more than one author. Through the mouth of lovers, the book praises love in courtship and in marriage. The goodness and propriety of marriage is celebrated through a series of rich images drawn from a blend of nature and love. The book reveals the warm and innocent satisfaction the ancient Hebrews drew from the physical and emotional relationships of man and woman. There was some reluctance to receive the Song of Songs into the canon of Jewish Scriptures, but it was eventually accepted as ceremonial. Beginning with the Jewish period and onward, there has been an almost irresistible tendency to allegorize the work. For the Jews, Yahweh was seen as the lover, Israel as the beloved. For some of the Fathers and other Christian commentators, the bride was the Church. At times the figure of the bride has been felt to have a layered meaning: Israel, the Church, the Virgin Mary, and the individual believer. In recent times the urge toward allegorical interpretation of the Song of Songs seems to have abated.

Songs of Ascent (SAWNGZ uhv uh-SEHNT): The category of O.T. Psalms (120-134) that were probably used by pilgrims as they "went up" to the Temple for the New Year commemoration.

Son of Man (SUHN uhv MAN): One N.T. title for Christ, referring to His emptying of self and His humility, usually occurring in self-reference by Jesus and found only in the Gospels. This title is used when Christ predicts His coming passion. "Son of God" particularly refers to Jesus' glory as a Divine Person. Cf. CCC 53, 211, 331, 440, 460, 649, 653, 661, 664, 697, 1038, 1384, 1441, 2173, 2613

Sorcery (SOR-ser-ee): A kind of black magic in which evil is invoked by means of diabolical intervention; a violation of the virtue of religion. Cf. CCC 2115-2117

Sorrows of the Blessed Virgin Mary (SAH-roz uhv *th*uh BLEH-sehd VER-dzhihn MEH-ree): Also called the Seven Dolors of Our Lady, the Seven Sorrows are an expansion upon the five Sorrowful Mysteries of the Rosary. Traditionally, they include the prophecy of Simeon (Lk 2:34) that a sword would pierce Mary's heart by reason of her Son's being a sign of contradiction to the world; the flight into Egypt (Mt 2:13); and the loss of the Child Jesus in the Temple (Lk 2:46). The final four involve Mary in her Son's passion and death: the *via dolorosa* (or way of the cross); the crucifixion; the descent from the cross; and the entombment in the Holy Sepulcher. The Latin Rite chapel in the Church of the Holy Sepulcher in Jerusalem has as its focus a very moving sculpture that portrays Mary with her heart pierced by seven small swords. The liturgical calendar celebrates the memorial of Our Lady of Sorrows on September 15, appropriately the day following the Feast of the Triumph of the Cross.

Soteriology (so-teer-ee-AHL-uh-dzhee): (From Greek *soter:* savior) The study of the passion, death, and resurrection of Christ and how it redeems and subsequently saves the disciples of Jesus. Soteriology explores how the merits of Christ are granted to human beings, how one is justified and sanctified, and the nature of the human condition and human destiny. Cf. CCC 1949-2051

Soutane: See Cassock

Soul (SOL): The "animating" principle, created directly by God, which together with the body contributes to the unity of man. The human soul is immaterial, rational, and immortal; it is independent of matter and enables man to enjoy a relationship with God. Cf. CCC 33, 327, 362-367, 382, 992, 1004, 1060, 1503, 1934, 2332

Spiritism (SPEER-ih-tih-zuhm): The attempted communication with the souls of the deceased, often using séances, table-tapping, ouija boards, or witchcraft. In 1 Sm 28:8, King Saul communicated with the departed Samuel. Christian theologians contend that these communications arise from demons committed to harming the Church. Catholics have long prayed for the dead; however, the Church condemns spiritist superstition and practices related to Satanism. Cf. CCC 2111, 2115-2117

Spiritual Communion: See Communion, Spiritual

Spiritual Exercises of St. Ignatius Loyola (SPIHR-ih-tshöö-uhl EHK-ser-sai-zehz uhv SAYNT ihg-NAY-shuhs loi-O-luh): Written by the founder (d. 1556) of the Society of Jesus (Jesuits), these exercises were intended primarily as a guide for his spiritual sons in making their annual month-long religious retreat. Directed to the amendment of one's life and the achievement of personal sanctification, the Exercises develop a particular point of meditation and resolution for each of the four weeks: (1) the consequences of sin; (2) Christ as exemplar for the Christian; (3) amendment in imitation of Christ; (4) the reward of eternal life. Given their great practicality and sound psychology, the Spiritual Exercises of St. Ignatius have long had an appeal beyond the confines of Jesuit life; in fact, many non-Jesuit spiritual directors today employ the principles of the Ignatian Exercises in directing retreats. Cf. CCC 1438

Spirituality (spihr-ih-tshöö-AL-ih-tee): The way an individual responds through grace to the call of Christ and His invitation to discipleship. This always involves conversion, or change of heart, on the part of those called by Christ. We are thus called to renounce sin and unite ourselves to the Lord's preeminent victory over sin and death, His Paschal Mystery. While this call is intensely personal, it simultaneously brings us into communion with the Church, the Body of Christ. Through Baptism and the other sacraments, we are linked ever more deeply to our Savior and to all those redeemed by the Blood of His Cross. Although the Faith admits of many different spiritualities (e.g., Ignatian and Franciscan), a single spirituality can be discerned in the life of every believer. Traditionally, it rests on personal prayer, the sacraments, and the virtues. Engaged in these, it now becomes possible for us in the Catholic Tradition to pursue holiness, the goal of everyone who bears the name Christian. Cf. CCC 89, 131, 1374, 1392, 2014, 2684, 2687, 2693, 2697

Spiritual Works of Mercy: See Mercy, Spiritual and Corporal Works of

Spiritual Works of Mercy (SPIHR-ih-tshöö-uhl WERKS uhv MER-see): Acts of charity extending from compassion for victims of a kind of spiritual deprivation. These works of mercy especially focus on the spiritual welfare of the one in need. They are: instructing the ignorant, converting sinners, advising the perplexed, comforting the sorrowful, showing patience to sinners and those who err, forgiving others, and praying for the living and the dead. (Cf. Mercy, Spiritual and Corporal Works of.) **Cf. CCC 2447**

Sponge (SPUHNDZH): Called for in the ritual of the Eastern Churches, it is used to wipe the diskos (q.v.) clean of any consecrated particles of the Body of Christ. A sponge may be also used to remove excess oils following the anointings at Baptism, Confirmation, the Anointing of the Sick, or the solemn consecration of an altar, church, or sacred vessel.

Sponsor (SPAHN-ser): A person who gives special assistance to one who is about to be baptized or confirmed. Also called godparent. **Cf. CCC 1311, 2156**

Spoon, Liturgical (lih-TER-dzhih-kuhl SPÖÖN): A spoon used by the priest in the Byzantine Rite to dip a particle of the Host into the chalice and to give Holy Communion to a recipient.

Spouse of Christ (SPAUS uhv KRAIST): 1. As St. Paul develops the theme in his Epistle to the Ephesians, the Church is especially understood as the spouse of Christ (Eph 5:22-33). 2. A professed religious woman, by reason of her vowed chastity, is also called a bride of Christ, the symbolism of which was traditionally emphasized by the elaborate ceremony reminiscent of a wedding used for the entrance into convent life. The nun would dress as a bride on that day and would continue to wear a wedding ring symbolic of her intimate union with the Lord. **CCC 796**

Spouses of the Blessed Virgin Mary (SPAUS-ehz uhv *th*uh BLEH-sehd VER-dzhihn MEH-ree): 1. St. Joseph, as the betrothed of Mary, is described in the Gospel as "her husband, an upright man unwilling to expose her to the law" (Mt 1:18-19; cf. Lk 1:27, 2:5), who decided in view of her pregnancy "to divorce her quietly." Through angelic intervention, it was made clear to Joseph that "that which is conceived in her is of the Holy Spirit" (Mt 1:20). With that assurance, Joseph lived with Mary in a chaste and virginal relationship and is justifiably called the spouse of the Blessed Virgin Mary. In the Gospels, Jesus is typically called the carpenter's son, in recognition of Joseph as the human foster father of the Son of God. 2. By reason of the Annunciation and Incarnation, the Holy Spirit is also considered the Spouse of the Blessed Virgin Mary, since it is by Him that she conceived her Child. **Cf. CCC 437, 484-486**

Staff: See Crosier

Stained Glass (STAYN'D GLAS): An art form, dating from the twelfth century, used to decorate churches, buildings, and homes. By using colors and the arrangement of the pieces, stained glass provides an eloquent and descriptive means of expressing God's presence.

State of Grace (STAYT uhv GRAYS): The condition whereby one enjoys the friendship of God. One who possesses "sanctifying" or "habitual" grace is enabled to know, love, and serve God and others in reference to Him. The state of grace is relinquished upon committing mortal sin but may be regained through the Sacrament of Penance or perfect contrition. **Cf. CCC 1310, 1319, 1415, 1861**

Stational Churches, Days: See Stations, Roman

Stations (Way) of the Cross (STAY-shuhnz [WAY] uhv *thuh* KRAWS): A devotional practice that reconstructs the events in the life of our Lord from His trial to His entombment. These are recalled in fourteen stations or places. Sacred Scripture, reflection, meditative silence, vocal prayer, mental prayer, and formulary prayer may be used at each of the stations. The stations may be prayed individually or corporately; they may be indoors (as in a church or chapel) or outdoors, as in a cemetery or on the grounds of a shrine or place of pilgrimage. Indulgences are attached to observing this devotion. It is not uncommon, for example, that parishes offer this devotion to their parishioners on the Fridays of Lent and Good Friday. The stations are: (1) Jesus is condemned; (2) Jesus carries His Cross; (3) Jesus falls the first time; (4) Jesus meets His mother; (5) Simon of Cyrene helps carry the Cross; (6) Veronica wipes Jesus' face; (7) Jesus falls a second time; (8) Jesus meets the women of Jerusalem; (9) Jesus falls the third time; (10) Jesus is stripped of His garments; (11) Jesus is nailed to the Cross; (12) Jesus dies on the Cross; (13) Jesus' Body is taken down from the Cross; (14) Jesus' Body is laid in the tomb. Some modern stations add a fifteenth for Jesus' resurrection. Cf. CCC 1674, 2669

Stations, Roman (RO-muhn STAY-shuhnz): Churches in the city of Rome where (mostly the early) Popes would celebrate the liturgy at least on special days; eventually, this came to be observed principally as a Lenten devotion. Usually the stational observance would begin with clergy and congregation gathering at one place *(collecta)* and processing with accompanying litanies and prayers to the day's station *(statio)* for the Eucharist. During Lent, at the head of these processions, a relic of the True Cross was carried aloft. Today a list is published in Rome at the beginning of Lent proclaiming which churches will be stational and on which day, a necessary practice because of scholarly debate about the historical precedent of using some of the churches and also because some Roman churches are closed for periodic repairs. More famous examples of stational observance include St. Mary Major at Midnight Mass on Christmas and St. John Lateran for Easter (with the large baptistery building used at the Easter Vigil for initiation). The Lenten station days are carried on in a modified fashion today, although the Pope normally celebrates Ash Wednesday only by processing from the Church of San Anselmo on the Aventine (home of the Benedictines) to the home of the Order of Preachers at Santa Sabina (also on the Aventine) for Mass. **Cf. CCC 1674**

Status Animarum (STAH-toøs-ah-nee-MAH-roøm): (Latin: state of souls) The name for the official report filed with the Holy See by each diocese giving the overall condition of the Church within that territory.

Statutes (STA-tshööts): Virtually the same as decrees (q.v.), they almost always designate laws of a particular council or synod rather than pontifical laws.

Stephanos (STEH-fah-nos): 1. The episcopal miter used in the East. 2. The crowns used in the Eastern marriage ceremonies.

Sterilization (stehr-ihl-ih-ZAY-shuhn): The temporary or permanent prevention of conception by medication, procedure, or operation. Vasectomies (for males) and tubal ligations (for females) are intended to be permanent, while the Pill, the condom, and other contraceptives are usually meant to render the marital act(s) infertile for a specific duration. The Church has condemned "direct" sterilization (i.e., performed so as to prevent children) as mutilation; however, "indirect" sterilization (i.e., done to correct a pathology, foreseeing that conception is not possible) is permissible. Sterilization and subsequent acts of marital intercourse are gravely wrong. The Sacrament of Penance is available for those offending God in this matter. **CCC 2399**

Stewardship (STÖÖ-werd-shihp): The proper and profitable management of that with which a person is entrusted. In Christian terms, this would refer to both physical and spiritual things, which are to be used and administered responsibly, because all things ultimately belong to God. **Cf. CCC 373, 2280, 2402, 2404, 2417, 2457**

Sticharion (stih-KAHR-ee-ahn): In the Churches of the East, a silk or linen embroidered vestment worn by the priest under the phelonion. It is the equivalent of the alb in the Western Church.

Stichon (STEE-kon): 1. A scriptural quotation, often from the Psalms, used in the East. 2. The prayer inspired by the scriptural quotation.

Stigmata (stihg-MAH-tuh): (Greek *stigma:* mark) A collective noun for the scars that correspond to the wounds suffered by Christ in His passion and crucifixion and appear as abrasions of the skin on certain individuals of unusual personal holiness; usually these marks are external, visible, and painful, consisting of wounds to the forehead, hands, and feet, which bleed profusely. The Church considers the three hundred recorded manifestations of the stigmata as signs of particular favor by the Lord, Who allows the stigmatist a privileged, physical participation in His own suffering. Perhaps the most famous stigmatic is St. Francis of Assisi; other stigmatics in modern times have included Theresa Neumann of Germany and the Italian Padre Pio.

Stipend (STAI-pehnd): A common term for the offering given to a priest for celebrating a Mass or performing some other sacramental ceremony (cc. 945-959).

Stock (STAWK): The term usually applied to a container for oils used for the various sacraments. The oil stocks are generally three in number, corresponding to the types of holy oil: chrism, oil of catechumens, oil of the sick.

Stole (STOL): A liturgical vestment in the form of a long, narrow strip of cloth worn by deacon, priest, or bishop around the neck. The *General Instruction of the Roman Missal* declares that priests and bishops wear the stole around their necks and hanging in front of them. Deacons wear the stole over their left shoulders and drawn across the chest to the right side (n. 340). The color of the stole is determined by the liturgical color prescribed for the particular celebration.

The stole is worn at all sacramental celebrations, at many sacramentals, and at various prayer services.

Stole Fee (STOL FEE): A common but unofficial term for a voluntary offering made to a priest for the celebration of a sacrament.

Stone, Altar: See **Altar Stone**

Stoup (STŌŌP): A vessel used to contain holy water. See **Font**.

Stylite (STAI-lait): (Greek *stylos,* pillar) A hermit whose particular form of asceticism consisted of his removal from society by living atop a pillar. Food and other necessities were usually obtained by way of a basket maneuvered via ropes and pulleys. Stylites were quite common in the Eastern Church, the most famous of which was Simon Stylites; but their way of life did not survive beyond the early centuries of the Church. Cf. CCC 920-921

Subdeacon (suhb-DEE-kuhn): Appearing as early as the third century in Rome and in Africa, not until the thirteenth century did the subdiaconate come to be understood as one of the major orders (before the diaconate and the priesthood). At the subdeacon's ordination, he promised obedience to the bishop and faithful recitation of the Divine Office, as well as the obligation of celibacy. At the celebration of Holy Mass, the subdeacon chanted the Epistle, assisted the deacon with the bread, water, and wine, and removed the sacred vessels from the altar following the distribution of Holy Communion. In 1972, the *motu proprio* of Pope Paul VI *Ministeria Quaedam* suppressed the subdiaconate. Therefore, it currently does not exist in the Latin Church (although it does in the East); allowance, however, is given to episcopal conferences should they decide in favor of treating acolytes as subdeacons.

Subdelegation (suhb-dehl-uh-GAY-shuhn): The act whereby one who has delegated power of governance allows another to act on this power (Can. 137).

Subpedaneum (suhb-peh-DAH-nay-øøm): (Latin: that which goes under the feet) 1. The footstool or pillow placed under the Holy Father's feet when seated on his throne. Pope John Paul II, unlike his recent predecessors, does not make use of the *subpedaneum.* 2. The platform or predella upon which a priest stands when offering the Holy Sacrifice.

Subreption (suhb-REHP-shuhn): The concealing of certain truths or other information from ecclesiastical authority, usually in connection with a petition for a rescript.

Suburbicarian Dioceses (suh-ber-bih-KEHR-ee-uhn DAI-uh-seez-ehz): The seven dioceses nearest to Rome, whose bishops are always cardinals, with duties that include working within the various congregations or commissions of the Holy See.

Suffering and Euthanasia (SUHF-fer-ihng and YÖÖ-thuh-nay-zhuh): A Greek word meaning "easy death," euthanasia refers to the premature ending of the life of one who is enduring, or anticipating, great suffering. Because it is a Christian belief that suffering can be an opportunity for a person to experience spiritual growth and grace and is a means of participating in the suffering of Christ, and because it would usurp God's divine authority over life and death, euthanasia is never morally permissible. However, there is no moral requirement that extraordinary means must be used to prolong an individual's life. Cf. CCC 1435, 1473, 1499-1505, 1508, 1521, 2276-2277

Suffragan Bishop (SUHF-ruh-guhn BIH-shuhp): Any diocesan bishop of a province other than the metropolitan (archbishop).

Suffrages (SUHF-ruh-dzhehz): Prayers or Masses offered for special intentions, particularly for the dead. Cf. CCC 958, 1032, 1055, 1684-1690

Summa Theologiae (SÖÖM-uh tay-o-LO-dzhee-ay): The seminal work of St. Thomas Aquinas (1225?-1274), the "Angelic Doctor," in which he applied Aristotelian philosophy to Church teaching without compromising established faith and morals. There are three parts to this treatise: (1) God as Creator; (2) God as the Good and the End of Angels and Men; (3) God as the Way Who Is Needed to Redeem the World.

Sunday (SUHN-day): (Latin *dies solis:* day of the sun) Sometimes, Sunday is referred to as the day of the Lord. In Christianity, Sunday replaced Saturday as the day to honor and worship the Lord. Our Lord rose from the dead on Sunday, and "the breaking of the bread" (Acts 20:7) was held on Sunday. Additionally, Sunday is revered because it is the first day of creation (Justin the Martyr and St. Isidore of Seville) and the day the Holy Spirit descended upon the Apostles at Pentecost (Acts of the Apostles). Later on, Sunday came to be regarded as a day of rest and freedom from servile work. The current Code of Canon Law (Can. 1247) stipulates that Catholics are bound to attend Mass on Sunday (or its vigil) and should "abstain from those labors and business concerns which impede worship to be rendered to God, the joy which is proper to the Lord's Day or the proper relaxation of mind and body." CCC 1163, 1166-1167, 1193, 2190; cf. 1343, 2174-2177, 2184-2188, 2193-2194

Sunday Obligation (SUHN-day ah-blih-GAY-shuhn): The duty of the faithful to participate in the Eucharistic Sacrifice on Sundays and holy days of obligation (cc. 1245, 1248). Cf. CCC 1389, 2042, 2180-2183

Supererogation, Works of (WERKS uhv söö-per-ehr-o-GAY-shuhn): Good works that are helpful in developing one's spiritual and moral life but which are not strictly required by morality (e.g., evangelical counsels of poverty, chastity, and obedience; corporal works of mercy).

Supernatural (SÖÖ-per-NA-tsher-uhl): Above the natural; that which exceeds and is not due or owed to the essence, exigencies, requirements, powers, and merits of created nature. While humans have no claim on supernatural things and do not need them in order to exist and act on a natural level, they do need them in order to exist and act in the higher order or economy of grace established by God for their salvation. Cf. CCC 91-93, 153, 179, 367, 950, 1722, 1727, 1812-1813, 1840-1841, 1998

Suppedaneum: See Subpedaneum

Suppressed (suh-PREHST): An organization, action, devotion, juridic person, or other official ecclesiastical entity that is foreclosed by competent Church authority.

Supreme Moderator (suh-PREEM MAH-der-ay-ter): The highest authority of a religious institute or society of apostolic life (Can. 622).

Surplice (SER-plihs): (From Old French: over the fur) A loose white linen or cotton vestment worn over the cassock or religious habit, used by clergy and laity when serving in some capacity at liturgical functions. Originally, it was substituted for the alb because it was to be worn over the fur coats that were customary in cold northern countries.

Suspension (suh-SPEHN-shuhn): An ecclesiastical penalty applied only to clerics whereby the cleric is forbidden to exercise all or some of the powers of his Sacred Order (cc. 1333, 1334).

Swedenborgianism (swee-dehn-BOR-dzhee-uhn-ih-zuhm): A system of speculative mystical theology that derives its name from its founder, Emanuel Swedenborg (1688-1772). Swedenborg, the son of Jesper Swedberg, Lutheran Bishop of Skara, grew up in a well-to-do and thoroughly religious household. Bishop Swedberg showed an unusual and relatively unhealthy proclivity toward the primeval spirit forms of the Nordic imagination; he was not reluctant to invoke spirits, good and evil alike, in his typically florid fashion from the pulpit. Out of this environment, Emanuel Swedenborg developed his theories of the basic spiritual structure of the universe. He claimed to have had a number of visions in 1745, wherein Christ instructed him in the spiritual sense of Scripture and then commissioned him to share this privileged knowledge with others. Combining pantheism and theosophic concepts, Swedenborg attempted in his *Arcana Coelestia* (1756) to propose the basic tenets of his new church, which, he held, was eventually to supplant Christianity itself. He refused to acknowledge a belief in the Trinity, Original Sin, Christ's resurrection, and the sacraments, except Baptism and the Eucharist. In the United States, his congregations are found primarily in southeastern Pennsylvania and in Delaware, where Swedenborg's thought found a natural reception among the Swedish colonists. The Swedenborgian Cathedral for the United States is located in Wilmington, Delaware.

Swiss Guards (SWIHS GAHRDZ): A body of Swiss men organized in 1505 with the responsibility of protecting the Pope. They are identified by their distinctive uniform, designed by Michelangelo, and while they are trained in the use of modern arms, they seldom carry anything other than a sword.

Syllabus of Errors (SIHL-uh-buhs uhv EHR-erz): The series of eighty propositions condemned in *Quanta Cura* by Pope Pius IX on December 8, 1864. This document condemned the liberal and modernistic errors of the age.

Symbol (SIHM-buhl): (From Greek *symbolon:* sign) A token, pledge, or sign by which we can experience some reality through another reality. Most often, symbol is used in connection with the liturgy. Through symbols, we can participate in the saving mysteries of Christ's passion, death, and resurrection. This is preeminently true in the celebration of the Eucharistic Sacrifice. The Word of God and the bread and wine are symbols that make present again the redemption won for us on Calvary by Christ. A symbol, in the religious sense, is cognitive and evocative. As such, it bids us look beyond what our senses tell us is present and available to us and elicits from us a belief in a more transcendent, mysterious reality that the senses cannot apprehend. **Cf. CCC 522, 697, 1145-1152, 1189**

Symbolism (SIHM-buh-lih-zuhm): A method or mode of analysis that bids us look beyond what is immediately apparent and consider deeper, more overarching realities. Symbolism is operative in many different fields (e.g., literature, history, art). Theology and liturgy are not excluded either. Sacred Scripture contains symbolic references, i.e., figures, events, and realities that point beyond themselves to hidden or transcendent verities. The symbolic value of the liturgy cannot be underestimated. The crucifix is always much more than a corpus nailed to vertical and horizontal pieces of wood. The Eucharist is always much more than a wafer over which the words of institution have been said by a priest. **Cf. CCC 375, 694-696, 701, 1177, 1202, 1220, 1293**

Synagogue (SIHN-uh-gahg): (Greek *synagoge:* assembly) The assembly place for the Jews, dating from the time of Ezra. The synagogue provided a place for readings from the Torah, hymns, and prayers; it was viewed as a "study home." Jesus Himself frequented the synagogue. **Cf. CCC 442, 1338, 2586, 2599, 2701**

Synapte (sihn-AP-teh): The two successions of prayers during the Byzantine Divine Liturgy.

Synaxis (sih-NAK-sihs): Derived from the Greek term for assembly or congregation, it may refer to liturgical prayer with or without the celebration of the Holy Eucharist. **Cf. CCC 1329, 1566**

Synderesis (also Synteresis) (sihn-duh-REE-sihs): 1. The knowledge of the first principle of moral action, i.e., that good should be pursued and evil avoided. 2. The core in one's soul where mystical marriage or "union" occurs. **Cf. CCC 1780**

Synod (SIH-nuhd): An official gathering of clergy and/or laity: (1) A synod of bishops is a gathering of representatives of episcopal conferences from all over the world; (2) a diocesan synod is a gathering of clergy, religious, and lay representatives from throughout a diocese. **Cf. CCC 887**

Synod of Bishops (SIH-nuhd uhv BIH-shuhps): First chartered by Pope Paul VI in 1965, an assembly of bishops chosen from throughout the world, with the task of meeting for deliberation when requested by the Pope, who is the president of the synod.

Synod of The Oak (SIH-nuhd uhv *thee* OK): Illegal synod called by Emperor Theophilus in the fifth century to censure St. John Chrysostom for receiving priests censured by the emperor. (Cf. Oak, Synod of The.)

Synoptic Gospels, The *(thuh sih-NAHP-tihk GAH-spuhlz):* There is an impressive agreement — verbal and sequential — among the first three Gospels, Matthew, Mark, and Luke. For purposes of comparison, these Gospels can be put into parallel columns. This ordering of materials is known as a "synopsis." As a result, Matthew, Mark, and Luke have come to be known as the Synoptic Gospels. The extensive similarity of content and arrangement among these Gospels, alongside some notable dissimilarities that they exhibit vis-à-vis one another, gives rise to what has become known as the Synoptic Problem — i.e., the problem of the literary relationships among the three texts. To date, no universally accepted solution to the Synoptic Problem has been devised. (Cf. Synoptic Question.) **Cf. CCC 1338, 2053**

Synoptic Question, The (*thuh* sih-NAHP-tihk KWES-tshuhn): Since the time of J. Griesbach (1776), the first three Gospels (Matthew, Mark, and Luke) have been called the Synoptic Gospels because they provide a "synoptic" view of the life and teaching of Christ; i.e., they offer a presentation of these materials from a more or less similar point of view. The "question" or "problem" arises when these Gospels are compared with one another. Such a comparison reveals a notable concordance in form and content but a surprising divergence in details. Several explanations for this situation have been proposed, but none rises above the level of hypothesis.

Synteresis: See Synderesis

Syrian Rite (SEER-ee-uhn RAIT): Two branches of the liturgical rite, Eastern and Western, but having similar basic structures and common formulae. The East Syrian liturgies have strong Semitic influences; the West Syrian liturgies embrace the following rites: Syro-Antiochene, Maronite, Byzantine, and Armenian. Cf. CCC 1203, 2678

T

Tabernacle (TA-ber-na-kuhl): The receptacle in which the Blessed Sacrament is reserved in churches, chapels, and oratories. It is to be immovable, solid, locked, and located in a prominent place. CCC 1183, 1379

Tabernacle Veil: See Veils, 2.

Talitha Koum (TAHL-ee-thuh KØØM): The Aramaic words, meaning "Little girl, get up," used by Jesus and found in Mk 5:41 when He spoke to Jairus's dead daughter. *Talitha* (literally, "ewe lamb") was a term of endearment used when addressing a small girl.

Talmud (TAHL-møød): (Hebrew: learning) A collection of teachings on the Torah, regarded as authoritative by Jews. The Talmud contains the Mishnah (oral rabbinic teaching on the Torah) and the Gemara (commentary on the Mishnah). Two versions of the Talmud survive, both originally composed in Aramaic: the Jerusalem Talmud, containing the teaching of the Palestinian rabbis, and the Babylonian Talmud, deriving from the rabbis at Babylon and generally regarded as the more important of the two versions.

Tametsi (tuh-MEHT-see): (Latin: even though) The title of the decree issued by the Council of Trent (1563) concerning the form of marriage. According to this decree, a marriage between two baptized persons, even non-Catholics, was valid only if contracted in the presence of the parish priest, the local Ordinary, or a priest delegated by either of these, and two witnesses. A decree clarifying the stipulations of *Tametsi* was promulgated by the Holy See in 1908. Cf. CCC 1631

Tantum Ergo (TAHN-tøøm EHR-go): The last two verses of the Latin hymn *Pange Lingua,* written by St. Thomas Aquinas for the Office of the Solemnity of Corpus Christi. When the English version of St. Thomas's hymn is used, it begins with the words "Down in adoration falling." The *Tantum Ergo* is sung while the congregation adores the Sacred Host during Exposition of the Blessed Sacrament and in procession to the Altar of Repose on Holy Thursday following the Mass of the Lord's Supper.

Teaching of the Twelve Apostles (TEETSH-ihng uhv *th*uh TWEHLV uh-PAH-suhlz): Also known by its Latin title, *Didascalia Apostolorum*, this ancient Christian church order dates from third-century Syria and treats a variety of subjects: the duties of bishops, liturgy, widows and deaconesses, conduct in times of persecution, etc.

Te Deum (TAY DAY-øøm): An ancient Latin hymn, inserted into Matins and used now at the conclusion of the Office of Readings in the Liturgy of the Hours. The *Te Deum* is not used every day but on Sundays (except during Lent), solemnities, and feasts. The spirit of the hymn is joyful thanksgiving.

Teilhardism (tay-AR-dih-zuhm): An evolutionary theory propounded by the French Jesuit Pierre Teilhard de Chardin (1881-1955), holding that there are four stages of development in the universe: (1) evolution from elements to organized matter; (2) evolution from organized matter to life; (3) evolution from living things to rational beings; (4) evolution from individual rational beings to a society with Christ as Lord (the so-called "omega point"). Teilhardism is not strictly scientific, philosophical, or theological, but is a mystical consideration of science and religion, seeking to reconcile the two. The Vatican has issued warnings that this theory contains some ambiguities and errors and is not completely consonant with Catholic doctrine.

Temperance (TEHM-per-ehnts): The cardinal virtue that moderates the drive for sensual pleasure. It enables one to pursue the necessary relationship with God if perfection is to be attained. Mary is the example *par excellence* of temperance. CCC 1809, 2730; cf. 1805, 1838, 2290, 2341, 2407, 2517, 2521

Temple in Jerusalem, The (*th*uh TEHM-puhl ihn dzhuh-RÖÖ-suh-lehm): It was revealed to King David that the

Temple of the Lord was to be built on Mt. Moriah in Jerusalem (2 Chr 3:1). On this spot, his son, Solomon, built the first of the three Temples of Jerusalem (1 Kgs 5-7). It consisted of three areas: a vestibule, the Holy Place or Sanctuary, and the Holy of Holies. Solomon's Temple was destroyed by the Babylonians in 587 B.C. The second Temple was built by Zerubbabel (Ezr 5:2-8). Then, in 20 B.C., Herod the Great began the construction of the third structure to be built on this site. It was in this Temple that Zechariah, the father of John the Baptist, offered incense. Here also Mary and Joseph brought the infant Jesus. Later, Christ preached and taught in the Temple. Following the Jewish revolt against Roman rule, the Temple was destroyed by the Emperor Titus in A.D. 70. Today, the Muslim Mosque of Omar, commonly known as the Dome of the Rock, stands upon the outcropping of rock believed to have been the foundation of the altar of the Temple and, by Muslims, to have been the site of Muhammad's ascent into heaven. Cf. CCC 593, 2580

Temporal Goods: See Goods, Temporal

Temporal Power (TEHM-per-uhl PAU-er): In ecclesiastical parlance, the jurisdiction or authority a Church official enjoys in secular or civil affairs. Pastors and parochial administrators, for example, possess this power over the material goods, properties, and functioning of the parish or school. Temporal power is distinguished from spiritual power, which is the authority over spiritual matters such as the administration of the sacraments and the celebration of liturgical services. As head of the Vatican City State, the Pope is supreme in secular matters in that sovereignty. His dominion over the Papal States ended in 1870 when they became part of Italy. In 1929, the Holy See and the Italian government signed a concordat resolving the status of the Church's temporalities.

Temptation (tehm[p]-TAY-shuhn): In Christian usage, any incitement to sin arising from the world (the actions or inducements of others), the flesh (our own weaknesses and desires), and the devil (suggestions by the fallen angels). According to Scripture, God allows us to be tempted, but never beyond our powers to resist with the help of His grace (cf. 1 Cor 10:13). The trial of temptation provides the occasion for moral and spiritual growth. Fidelity to the practices of the Faith and perseverance in prayer afford the chief means by which one is strengthened against temptation. **Cf. CCC 538-540, 566, 1808, 2113, 2119, 2157, 2340, 2612, 2732-2733, 2753-2755, 2846-2849, 2863**

Tenebrae (TEHN-uh-bray): (Latin: darkness) The combination of Matins and Lauds for Holy Thursday, Good Friday, and Holy Saturday in the former Divine Office, which was celebrated on the evening before these days. The term "Tenebrae" refers to the evening setting for these services of the Word and the progressive extinguishing of the church lights during them. In the Middle Ages this custom became stylized, so that a candle stand (often termed a "hearse") for fifteen candles (the number of the psalms prayed each day) was used, one candle being extinguished after each psalm was sung. The main focus during these services was on Christ's suffering, death, and descent among the dead. The Tenebrae custom is technically suppressed in the present edition of the Liturgy of the Hours; however, it is possible to celebrate a combination of the Office of Readings and Morning Prayer on Good Friday and Holy Saturday mornings.

Terce (TERS): (From Latin *tertius:* third) The third hour of the Divine Office, prayed at midmorning.

Terna (TER-nuh): Latin term for the list of three names of possible candidates for bishop submitted for consideration by the Holy Father.

Tertiaries (TER-shee-ehr-eez): (Latin *tertius:* third) Sometimes called "Third Order," referring to laity living in the world seeking Christian perfection in their state in life in accordance with the spirit of a particular religious order. Although Tertiaries are not religious, they may be full members of a religious order, and are subject to the superior general of the institute. Usually they do not wear habits or live in community, but they do have a share in the spiritual benefits of the good works of the order to which they are affiliated. Tertiaries of the various Orders of Friars Minor are now called Secular Franciscans.

Testament (TEHS-tuh-mehnt): (Latin *testamentum;* Greek *diatheke)* An agreement or last will. When this term is used in the Bible, it must be taken to mean "covenant." **Cf. CCC 861**

Tetragrammaton (teh-truh-GRA-muh-tahn): (Greek: four letters) The four consonants (YHWH) of God's proper name, Yahweh. **Cf. CCC 206, 210-213, 446**

Thanksgiving (thanks-GIH-vihng): 1. Expression of gratitude to God for His goodness and the blessings He grants; one of the four ends of prayer. 2. Holiday celebrated in gratitude to God since the time of the first English settlers in the U.S., now usually observed on the last Thursday of November. **Cf. CCC 224, 795, 983, 1167, 1328, 1333, 1352, 1358-1360, 2062, 2603-2604, 2637-2638, 2781, 2807**

Thaumaturge (THAW-muh-terdzh): (Greek: wonderworker) A title conferred on saints notable for the number and magnitude of the miracles attributed to them. St. Gregory Thaumaturgus (A.D. 213-268) is probably best known by this title, but it has also been conferred on St. Nicholas of Ban (d. 350), St. Anthony of Padua (d. 1231), and St. Vincent Ferrer (d. 1419).

Theism (THEE-ih-zuhm): (Greek *theos* + *ismos:* God-belief) Philosophy that admits the existence of God and the possibility of divine revelations. God is transcendent and also active in the world. Because it is a philosophy rather than a system of theology derived from revelation, it does not include specifically Christian doctrines like those concerning the Trinity, Incarnation, and Redemption.

Theocracy (thee-AHK-ruh-see): A political system in which divine law is the source of all civil law. The Chosen People lived under such a polity in the O.T. with the interplay of priests, prophets, and kings anointed to govern Israel.

Theodicy (thee-AH-dih-see): (Greek *theos:* God + *dike:* judgment) A study of God as He can be known by natural reason, rather than from supernatural revelation, with its primary focus on attempting to make compatible God's omnipotence with the existence of evil. The term was first used by Gottfried Leibnitz (1646-1716).

Theologian (thee-uh-LO-dzhuhn): One who engages by profession in the study, teaching, and defense of the science of God, the whole body of revealed and human knowledge in the light of God's nature and purposes, and under the guidance of faith in Him. Normally, one who wants to become a theologian must undergo a long period of study in order to gain a mastery of the contents of the chief sources of Christian teaching and a skill in dealing with the principal issues these sources pose. It is customary for the theologian to be certified by an accredited faculty of theology, to possess a doctoral degree, and to receive the *mandatum* from the local bishop certifying his orthodoxy.

Theological Virtues (thee-uh-LAH-dzhih-kuhl VER-tshööz): The supernaturally infused "good habits" of faith, hope, and charity, having God as their object and motive. Faith enables one to accept the truths revealed by God on the basis of His authority; hope allows one to anticipate eternal life by trusting in God and His grace; charity impels one to love God, oneself, and others for His sake. Acts of faith, hope, and charity assist one in growing in holiness and in becoming more cooperative by obeying God and His plan. CCC 1812-1829, 1840-1841

Theology (thee-AHL-uh-dzhee): (Greek: science of God) Disciplined reflection, carried on in the light of faith, concerning the whole body of revealed and human knowledge. Theology has been called "faith seeking understanding." Theology seeks to discern and exhibit the internal intelligibility of Revelation and to show its connection with other fields of learning and science. The rapid expansion of knowledge has led to specialization within theology. CCC 94

Theophany (thee-AH-fuh-nee): (Greek *theophaneia:* manifestation of God) The actual appearance of God (e.g., when He appeared to Moses on Mt. Sinai) or the medium of that appearance (e.g., in the forces of nature). CCC 707

Theosis: See Deification

Theotokion (thay-o-TO-kee-ahn): A commemoration for the Mother of God in the Byzantine liturgy.

Theotokos (thay-o-TO-kos): (Greek: God-bearer) The pre-eminent title given to the Blessed Mother in the Oriental Church. This title has very ancient roots, stretching as far back as the third century. It was not until the Council of Ephesus in 431, however, that this title became official in the Church. CCC 495

Thessalonians, First and Second Epistles to the (FERST and SEHK-uhnd ih-PIH-suhlz töö *th*uh THEH-suh-LO-nee-uhnz): Two N.T. letters addressed to the Church at Thessalonica, the first of which was written by St. Paul around A.D. 50 and the second of which was by him or in his name. First Thessalonians is the earliest affirmation of the salvific meaning of Christ's death, resurrection, and return in glory, and is meant to allay the anxiety of Christians about the death of some of their number before the return of Christ. The main concern of 2 Thessalonians is to correct misinformation concerning "the day of the Lord." Both letters are thus chiefly concerned with matters of eschatology, and are remarkably similar in structure, vocabulary, and themes.

Third Order (THERD OR-der): Generally, an association of laypeople connected to consecrated religious who follow a particular Rule and spirituality in either the First or Second Order (respectively, male and female religious). The most famous are those of the Franciscans, Dominicans, and Carmelites.

Thomas, Gospel of (GAHS-puhl uhv TAH-muhs): A work dating from around A.D. 140, discovered in 1945 in Nag Hammadi in Egypt as part of a twelve-volume library of papyri belonging to a Gnostic sect. Despite its title, the book differs from the N.T. Gospels in that it is a collection of alleged sayings of Jesus emphasizing the importance of knowledge.

Thomism (TO-mih-zuhm): The philosophy based on St. Thomas Aquinas (1225?-1274), which is mandated to be the dominant philosophy used in Catholic educational institutions. Pope John Paul II combines Thomism and Christian phenomenology when writing about contemporary issues such as the need to defend the dignity of the human person.

Thomism, Transcendental (tran-sehn-DEHN-tuhl TO-mih-zuhm): The twentieth-century philosophical system that combines the philosophy of St. Thomas Aquinas with the "transcendental" character of Kantian philosophy. Immanuel Kant asserted that many Catholic teachings exceeded what man can meaningfully contemplate; self-critical awareness about reality is a must. Modern transcendental Thomists such as Joseph Marechal, Karl Rahner, and Bernard Lonergan accent some of Kant's philosophy but insist against him that a correct understanding of knowledge does enable one to ask meaningful questions about God and human beliefs.

Throne (THRON): The seat of a bishop, from which he presides, officiates, or celebrates the rites of the Church. **CCC 1137**

Thrones (THRONZ): One of the nine choirs of angels.

Thurible (THER-ih-buhl): A metal vessel capable of holding burning charcoal. When incense is added to the burning charcoal, it produces rising smoke, which signifies prayer ascending to heaven. A thurible can be used at the Holy Sacrifice of the Mass, the recitation of the Divine Office, and Benediction of the Blessed Sacrament. It also goes by the name of censer.

Thurifer (THER-if-fer): The minister who tends the thurible during a liturgical ceremony.

Tiara (tee-AH-ruh): The crown or ceremonial headdress worn by the Supreme Pontiff of the Catholic Church. Made of silver or gold cloth and decorated with precious stones, it has three crowns or diadems, representing the tripartite rule of the Vicar of Christ: his universal episcopate, his supremacy of jurisdiction, and his temporal influence. Since the papacy of Paul VI, the tiara has not been used by the Holy Father. However, a future Pope could decide to wear the tiara for nonliturgical but public functions.

Tierce: See Terce

Time (TAIM): A measurable interval during which something exists, happens, or acts, with change defining past, present, and future. God is unchangeable and is therefore outside of time, whereas creation is changing and so is measured by time. Cf. CCC 205, 338, 484, 600, 672, 1007, 1042, 1076, 1163-1165, 2184-2187, 2194

Time, Computation of (kahm-pyöö-TAY-shuhn uhv TAIM): Means of computing periods of time according to the norms of Canon Law (cc. 200-203).

Timothy, First Epistle to (FERST ih-PIH-suhl töö TIHM-uh-thee): The first of two N.T. letters addressed by St. Paul to Timothy, who had oversight of the churches in Macedonia. Along with 2 Timothy and the letter to Titus, 1 Timothy is considered one of the Pastoral Epistles, addressed not to a local Church or the universal Church but to an individual to provide instruction for the execution of pastoral duties. In the first chapter of 1 Timothy, St. Paul warns Timothy of the danger of false teachers who propound erroneous doctrines about the authentic role of the old law for Christians, and instructs him about liturgy, women's roles, and the selection of ministers. The letter presents a set of instructions to guide Timothy in a number of areas.

Timothy, Second Epistle to (SEHK-uhnd ih-PIH-suhl töö TIHM-uh-thee): The second of two N.T. letters addressed by St. Paul to Timothy who had oversight of the churches of Macedonia. This pastoral epistle continues the line of thought initiated in 1 Timothy concerning the dangers of false teachers. The letter commends endurance and steadfastness in suffering.

Tithe *(TAITH):* A percentage of one's income given as an offering to God. The traditional amount of ten percent is based upon the law found in Lv 27:30, which prescribed that one tenth of all produce, animals, and plants be set aside and given back to the Lord. It is one of the precepts of the Church that all members must give support, in accordance with their circumstances, to her work and ministry. **Cf. CCC 2449**

Titular Sees (TIH-työö-ler SEEZ): Dioceses where the Church once flourished but which later were overrun by pagans or Muslims and now exist only in name or title. Bishops without a territorial or residential diocese of their own (e.g., auxiliary bishops) are given titular sees.

Titulus (TEE-tøø-løøs): (Latin: title) 1. In classical times, an inscription that might denote a boundary line or indicate ownership of a particular building. Homes used for worship by early Christians were recognized by the titulus. 2. The sign placed on the cross, which said in Latin, Greek, and Hebrew, "Jesus of Nazareth, King of the Jews."

Titus, Epistle to (ih-PIH-suhl töö TAI-tuhs): With 1 and 2 Timothy, one of the pastoral epistles of the N.T. This letter was written by St. Paul to Titus, who had responsibility for the church at Corinth. Paul's concern is with the influence of false teachers who tried to subvert the Gospel he preached.

Tobit, Book of (BØØK uhv TO-biht): An O.T. book concerned particularly with the problems and tribulations of life in the Diaspora (non-Palestinian areas inhabited by Jews). The message of the books is that God will heal and protect those who are pious and compassionate. While Tobit is part of the Catholic (and Eastern Orthodox) Bible, it does not appear in the Jewish or Protestant canons.

Tones (TONZ): In the Eastern churches, a method of eight standard melodies with variations for plain chant.

Tonsure (TAHN-sher): The custom of shaving part (or all) of the hair on the head, originating with monastic observance in the fourth and fifth centuries. This custom was retained until the reform of minor orders after the Second Vatican Council. When it was in use, tonsure symbolized admission to the clerical state.

Torah (TOR-uh): From the Hebrew root meaning "to instruct," the term came to be used for the written collection of the Law, i.e., the Pentateuch, the first five books of the Bible. Cf. CCC 702

Totalitarianism (to-tal-ih-TEHR-ee-uhn-ih-zuhm): A system in which the State maintains total control over the life and conduct of its citizens. It is contrary to Catholic teaching, not only because of the official atheism and restricted religious practice usually associated with totalitarianism, but also because it violates the rights of individuals and families to pursue their own good ends within the general principle of seeking the good of society. Cf. CCC 2244, 2257, 2414, 2425, 2455, 2499

Totemism (TO-tehm-ih-zuhm): The phenomenon in some religions involving a "totem," high tower, or sacred object to which was attributed special religious or magical powers. Some primitive peoples associated themselves with a plant or animal thought to possess strength. The totem might be untouchable or touchable, sacred or secular. Some speculate that the Israelites employed totems; however, not enough evidence has been gathered to support this opinion.

Toties Quoties (TO-see-ayz KWOT-see-ayz): (Latin: as often as) Canon Law term meaning that a plenary indulgence could be obtained as often as the conditions were met. Church law now states that a plenary indulgence may be gained only once a day, except for the hour of one's death, when yet another may be obtained. Cf. CCC 1471, 1478-1479

Tract (TRAKT): 1. A chant sung in the Tridentine liturgy that took the place of the Alleluia on penitential days. 2. A pamphlet or monograph on some religious subject. The Oxford Movement in the nineteenth century produced tracts that interpreted Anglican doctrine from a Catholic point of view, thus earning its participants the name Tractarians. Some of the Tractarians converted to Catholicism, among them John Henry Cardinal Newman.

Tradition (truh-DIH-shuhn): (From Latin: handing over) In the religious sense, the teachings and practices handed down, whether in oral or written form, separately from but not independent of Scripture. Tradition is divided into two areas: (1) Scripture, the essential doctrines of the Church, the major writings and teachings of the Fathers, the liturgical life of the Church, and the living and lived faith of the whole Church down through the centuries; (2) customs, institutions, and practices that express the Christian Faith. The Council of Trent (1546) affirmed both the Bible and Tradition as divine sources of Christian doctrine. Vatican II states, "It is clear . . . that in the supremely wise arrangement of God, sacred Tradition, Sacred Scripture, and the Magisterium of the Church are so connected and associated that one of them cannot stand without the others. Working together, each in its own way under the action of the one Holy Spirit, they all contribute effectively to the salvation of souls" (DV, n. 10). Cf. CCC 75-84, 95, 97, 113, 120, 126, 174, 1124, 2651

Traditionalism (truh-DIH-shuh-nuhl-ih-zuhm): A nineteenth-century theory that states that individual reason is untrustworthy, and so truth can be known only by Divine Revelation, and is transmitted solely through Tradition. This is contrary to the Catholic teaching that maintains that certain truths can be known by the proper exercise of human reason. Traditionalism is known also as "fideism" because of this denial of the capacity of reason to ascertain truth, thus placing an undue stress on faith. Cf. CCC 35-39, 47, 50, 156-169, 237, 274, 286, 1706

Traditores (trah-dee-TOR-ayz): (Latin *tradere:* to hand over or betray) The technical term first applied at the Council of

Arles (314) for those priests and other clerics who willingly surrendered sacred vessels and biblical and liturgical texts to the pagan authorities, who threatened persecution for non-compliance.

Traducianism (trah-DÖÖ-shuhn-ih-zuhm): An erroneous teaching of the fifth century that holds that individual human souls originate by derivation from the souls of their parents, in a way analogous to the generation of individual bodies. The heretical proponents of traducianism maintain that God does, in fact, create individual souls, but with reliance on the parents' souls, which provide the matter for this divine activity, just as the bodies of the parents provide the matter for the divine creation of the body of their offspring. Heresy enters with the denial of God's creation of the soul *ex nihilo,* whereby His divine activity presupposes no prior object upon which He works. Both Tertullian and St. Augustine at times appear to subscribe to theories of traducianism, although ultimately St. Augustine, judging that Scripture does not give an adequate answer to the questions posed by traducianism, refuses to endorse the traducianist theory of creation. Pope Anastasius (d. 498) condemned traducianism as a heresy, while Pope Gregory the Great (d. 604) held the question as yet unresolved.

Training of Priests: See Optatam Totius

Transcendence (tran-SEHN-dehnts): The relationship between a superior and a lesser thing. In reference to God, transcendence describes Him as surpassing the universe because He is its Creator and is not dependent upon it in any way. When considering the transcendence of God, we must also keep in mind His immanence, which describes His closeness to His creation. CCC 42, 212, 239, 300, 1028

Transfiguration (trans-fihg-yøø-RAY-shuhn): The occasion described in the first three Gospels (Mt 17:1-13; Mk 9:2-13; Lk 9:28-36) when the divine glory of Christ was shown in a comprehensible way to the Apostles Peter, James, and John, through a change in His outward appearance and the presence with Him of Moses and Elijah. CCC 554-556, 568

Transfinalization, Transignification (trans-FAI-nuhl-ih-ZAY-shun, tran-SIHG-nih-fih-KAY-shun): Terms coined to express the sign value of consecrated bread and wine with respect to the presence and action of Christ in the Eucharistic Sacrifice, and the spiritually vivifying purpose of the Eucharistic Meal in Holy Communion. The theory behind the terms has strong elements of existentialism and semiotics; it has been criticized for its openness to interpretations at variance with the doctrine of transubstantiation and the abiding presence of Christ under the appearances of bread and wine after Mass and Communion have been completed. If used as substitutes for transubstantiation, the terms are unacceptable. Cf. CCC 1373-1381

Transitional Deacon: See Deacon, Transitional

Translation (trans-LAY-shun): A largely archaic word used to refer to the removal of relics from one place to another, the movement of a feast day, or the transfer of a bishop.

Transubstantiation (tran-suhb-stant-see-AY-shuhn): A term adopted by the Fourth Lateran Council in 1215 to describe the change of the substance of bread and wine into the substance of the Body and Blood of Christ, so that only the accidents of bread and wine remain, when consecrated by a validly ordained priest. "The way Christ is made present in this sacrament [Holy Eucharist] is none other than by the change of the whole substance of bread into His Body, and of the whole substance of the wine into His Blood [in the Consecration of the Mass] . . . this unique and wonderful change the Catholic Church rightly calls transubstantiation" (Pope Paul VI, encyclical *Mysterium Fidei,* 1965). CCC 1373-1377, 1413

Treasury of the Church (TREH-zher-ee uhv *th*uh TSHERTSH): The superabundant merits of Christ and the saints from which the Church draws to confer spiritual benefits, such as indulgences. CCC 1476; cf. 1477-1478

Tree of Jesse (TREE uhv JEH-see): The family tree of Jesus Christ, which traces His lineage to Jesse, father of King David (cf. 1 Sm 16:18-22, Is 11:1), thereby establishing Christ as the proper fulfillment of messianic prophecy (2 Sm 7). In medieval art and in the stained-glass depictions of the Jesse Window, the various biblical ancestors of the Lord are frequently shown seated on the branches of the tree, while Jesse forms the very roots and Jesus is seated with Mary on the highest branches.

Trent, Council of (KAUN-sihl uhv TREHNT): The challenges offered by the sixteenth-century Protestant Reformers prompted many in the Church to call for a general council. Disputes arose not only about whether to have the Council, but also about its location (imperial or papal territory), membership (bishops or a "summit meeting" of various Christian leaders), and purpose (doctrine or discipline). It finally opened on December 13, 1545, as the nineteenth ecumenical council, concerned both with doctrine and discipline. A number of events interfered with the work of the Council: wars, deaths of Popes (therefore, the need to be reconvened), change of location (in Bologna 1547-1548). At one point, the Council was suspended for about ten years. Its final session was December 4, 1563, but the task of implementation took many additional years. Careful doctrinal decrees, rooted in Sacred Scripture and Tradition, summarized Church teaching on a number of fundamental issues (especially the role of Scripture, Original Sin, justification, and the sacraments), both in terms of ancient errors and the views of the reformers. The reform of the liturgy resulting from the Council gave to most parts of the Latin Church a uniform liturgical practice that was not significantly changed until Vatican II. Perhaps the most important disciplinary action of the Council was the establishment of the seminary system. The reforms of the Council and especially its doctrinal formulations set the tone for Catholic life for four centuries. It squarely faced the issues of the day, but for a number of reasons did not treat some significant theological issues: faith and revelation, papal primacy, and the nature of the Church. These received needed treatment at Vatican I and II.

Tribunals (trai-BYÖÖ-nuhlz): The courts of the Church established to decide cases of dispute in matters of Canon Law. Tribunals are to be established in every diocese. **Cf. CCC 911, 1629**

Tribunals, Roman (RO-muhn trai-BYÖÖ-nuhlz): The three tribunals or courts of the Roman Curia: the Roman Rota, the Tribunal of the Apostolic Signatura, and the Penitentiary.

Tridentine (TRAI-dihn-teen): The adjective that relates to the Council of Trent, as in its decrees or in the Roman Missal or Catechism that resulted from the impetus provided by that Council. Today its most frequent use is in reference to that form of the Mass codified by Pope St. Pius V after the Council of Trent and sometimes used by indult of the local bishop by communities desirous of this liturgical usage that immediately preceded the reforms initiated by the Second Vatican Council.

Triduum (TRIH-döö-øøm): (Latin *tres:* three + *dies:* day[s]) A three-day period set aside for special prayer and devotion in relation to some solemnity or feast. A triduum can be observed publicly or privately, and may also be kept for the purpose of petitioning God for some grace.

Triduum, Paschal (PAS-kuhl TRIH-döö-øøm): A period of three days for the most exalted liturgical celebration of the year, beginning with the Mass of the Lord's Supper on Holy Thursday evening and concluding with Vespers on Easter Sunday, recalling the passion, death, and resurrection of Christ, along with His institution of the Holy Eucharist and Holy Orders. **Cf. CCC 1168**

Trination (trai-NAY-shuhn): The faculty for priests to celebrate the Holy Sacrifice of the Mass "three times on Sundays and Holy Days of Obligation, provided there is a genuine pastoral need." This faculty is found in *Pastorale Munus,* the 1964 *motu proprio* of Pope Paul VI, which spells out the powers and privileges of diocesan bishops.

Trinity, The Most Holy *(th*uh MOST HO-lee TRIH-nih-tee): The central doctrine of the Christian Faith, which states that the one God is Father, Son, and Holy Spirit, Three Persons sharing one nature. The Three Persons are co-equal, co-eternal, and consubstantial, and are to receive the same worship. CCC 232-267; cf. 684, 689, 732, 813, 1066, 1077-1109, 2205, 2655

Triodion (trai-O-dee-uhn): The Byzantine Rite's "Book of Three Odes," which contains the proper parts of the daily services beginning twenty-two days before Lent and extending through the Midnight Office of Holy Saturday night. The Lenten canons usually contain three rather than the customary nine odes.

Triple Candle (TRIH-puhl KAN-duhl): A type of three-branched candle used at the Easter Vigil liturgy on Holy Saturday night until 1955, when the Paschal Candle currently in use was restored to its original and preeminent position.

Triple Judgment (TRIH-puhl DZHUHDZH-mehnt): Three criteria employed in making a determination concerning the suitability of a musical piece during a liturgical celebration. A musical piece under consideration for use should be musically, liturgically, and pastorally appropriate. These criteria are found in the 1972 document of the Bishops' Committee on the Liturgy, "Music in Catholic Worship." (Cf. Judgment, Triple.)

Triptych (TRIHP-tihk): Three painted panels joined by hinges; usually the central panel is the largest and depicts the most important scene of the painting, often a significant event from the life of Our Lord, Our Lady, or one of the saints. The side panels often portray other participants in the central event, angels in adoration, the patrons of the artwork, or a combination of these. In the Middle Ages, triptychs were frequently placed above the high altar of a church. During Passiontide, the side panels were closed to bring a more somber atmosphere to the sanctuary or chancel and to deny the congregation the joy derived from the artwork, which would be inappropriate during that penitential season.

Trisagion (tree-SAH-[g]yahn): In the Byzantine Rite, a hymn used at the liturgy with these words: "Holy God. Holy and Mighty One. Holy and Immortal One. Have mercy on us."

Triumphalism (trai-UHM-fuhl-ih-zuhm): The concept that one is saved by means of the graces God has given through the Catholic Church. Triumphalism has been rejected by the Church as erroneous because Christ offers His grace to all; hence, one is primarily saved by responding to the gift of God by faith, prayer, good works, and obedience. True, the Catholic Church possesses the fullness of the Faith, but one is called to accept humbly the redemptive merits of Jesus. Cf. CCC 169, 456-457, 519, 588, 620, 776, 780, 816, 1019

Triumph of the Cross (TRAI-uhmf uhv *th*uh KRAWS): The feast observed every September 14, which recalls two events: (1) the exposition for veneration of the True Cross in Jerusalem by Emperor Heraclius in 629; (2) the dedication of the Basilica of the Resurrection, built by Emperor Constantine over the Holy Sepulcher.

Troparion (tro-PAHR-ee-ahn): In the Byzantine liturgy, a commemoration for a saint or feast day; it is variable and is sung.

Truce of God (TRÖÖS uhv GAHD): Truce or agreement enacted by the Council of Elne in 1027, forbidding the waging of war on Sundays and later expanded to include the holy seasons of Advent and Lent.

Trullo, Council of (KAUN-suhl uhv TRØØ-lo): A synod of Eastern bishops held in 691 to enact disciplinary decrees implementing the second and third Councils of Constantinople.

Tunic (TÖÖ-nihk): A liturgical garment originally worn by the subdeacon. In the Reformation period, those not admitted to the subdiaconate such as servers, crossbearers, and thurifers could wear this kind of vesture, too. Up until 1960, a bishop at pontifical ceremonies wore a tunic, along with a dalmatic, under his chasuble. It is not in general use today.

Tutiorism (TÖÖT-see or-ih-zuhm): The moral principle that only the most certain moral opinion may be followed in case of doubt. In the "absolute" tutiorist system, one must heed only the most certain opinion; in the "mitigated" tutiorist framework, one may follow the most probable opinion.

Typikon (TIH-pih-kahn): In the Eastern Rites, a liturgical manual that spells out the regulations and how they are to be observed when praying the Divine Office and the Eucharistic Liturgy.

Typological Sense of Scripture (tai-puh-LAH-dzhih-kuhl SEHNS uhv SKRIHP-tsher): A way of reading the Bible as a unified whole, with Christ at the center. Christians discern in O.T. persons and events prefigurements, or "types," of persons and events that occur in the new dispensation. Thus, King David points to Christ, the King of the New Israel; the passage of Israel to Egypt points to the passover of Christ, and so on. Indeed, the employment of the typological reading of Scripture implies that the "real" meaning of earlier events is to be found in those consummations in the later events and persons to which they point. This standard way of reading Scripture as a typologically and narrationally unified book, with Jesus Christ at its center, is clearly reflected in the organization of the Lectionary, and, indeed, in the very pattern of the liturgy itself. The contemporary community is thus taken up into an overarching narrative of cosmic significance, embracing everything that has happened in the history of salvation from the very beginning, and moving under God's providential care to its consummation. **CCC 117; cf. 128, 130**

U

Ubiquitarianism (yöö-bih-kwih-TEHR-ee-uhn-ih-zuhm): (Latin *ubique:* wherever, everywhere) The view, proposed by Martin Luther and accepted by some of his followers (though not normative for the Lutheran confessions), that Jesus Christ is present everywhere in His human nature; Luther appealed to this notion in his writings on the Eucharist, in order to defend the Real Presence of Christ.

Ultramontanism (uhl-truh-MON-tahn-ih-zuhm): French movement of the seventeenth century that stressed devotion and service to the Holy See in reaction to Gallicanism (q.v.).

Umbanda (øøm-BAHN-duh): An Afro-Brazilian cult that synthesizes African, native Indian, Catholic, and spiritualist elements. It is nominally monotheistic; however, it practices its ritual at *centros* that are dedicated to various deities with roots in West Africa but that are now associated with Catholic saints. The primary ritual is the *consulta,* during which mediums seek to help those who have come to them for assistance. Umbanda presents a great pastoral problem for the Church in Brazil, because many of the practitioners of Umbanda consider themselves Catholics.

Unam Sanctam (ÖÖ-nahm SAHNK-tahm): (Latin: one holy) Controversial papal bull promulgated by Pope Boniface VIII in 1302 as the formal response to King Philip the Fair of France, who had threatened royal interference in ecclesiastical affairs. It is of the greatest significance in its development of the "two swords" theory that both spiritual and temporal authority govern the world. He is not arguing for Caesaropapism, where there is one united authority alone; rather, he affirms unambiguously the right and duty of the Church to pass judgment on the political arena in matters of morals, in which matters the temporal sword must yield to the spiritual. Most debated is the formal declaration of the last sentence: "We declare, state, and define that for salvation it is altogether necessary that every human creature be subject to the Roman Pontiff." Clearly, the Second Vatican

Council, in *Lumen Gentium, Unitatis Redintegratio, Nostra Aetate,* and *Gaudium et Spes,* has made allowance for a most broad interpretation and application of this doctrine, as have other magisterial documents before and since.

Unction (UHNK-shuhn): (From Latin *ungere:* smear, anoint) The Sacrament of the Sick, or the Anointing of the Sick, was formerly known as Extreme Unction. As such, it was the last anointing before death. Anointings are used in other sacraments: Baptism, Confirmation, and Holy Orders. In Baptism, there are two anointings, first, the oil of catechumens is used, and then sacred chrism is administered. In Confirmation and Holy Orders, the anointing in each of these sacraments is with sacred chrism. Cf. CCC 695, 1241-1242, 1289-1295, 1300, 1499-1525

Uniate Churches (YÖÖ-nee-uht TSHERTSH-ehz): Churches of the East that have entered back into communion with the Holy See. As such, these Churches have preserved their own liturgies, rites, laws, disciplines, and ecclesial structures. This term is often used by Eastern Orthodox in a derogatory manner.

Uniformity, Acts of (AKTS uhv yöö-nih-FOR-mih-tee): A series of laws, passed in England in the sixteenth century, to compel uniformity in following Anglican religious usages and forbidding Catholic liturgical practice.

Unigenitus (öö-nee-DZHEHN-ee-tøøs): (Latin: only-begotten) Formal constitution of Pope Clement XI, promulgated on September 8, 1713, condemning one hundred one propositions of Pasquier Quesnel (1634-1719), published in his *Réflexions,* based on previously condemned Jansenist theology. Quesnel asserted that no grace is given outside the Church, that grace is irresistible, that without grace one is incapable of any good, and that all acts of a sinner, even prayer and the Mass, are sins. Although he never accepted this condemnation, Quesnel nevertheless received the Last Rites of the Church on his deathbed.

Union, Mystical: See Mysticism

Unitarianism (yöö-nih-TEHR-ee-uhn-ih-zuhm): A system of belief that denies the doctrine of the Trinity, teaching that God is a single Person, and, while professing a belief in the teachings of Jesus, denies His divinity. Unitarianism has no creed and generally rejects traditional Christian doctrines.

Unitatis Redintegratio (öö-nee-TAH-tihs ray-dihn-tay-GRAHT-see-o): The Decree on Ecumenism promulgated by the Second Vatican Council on November 21, 1964, outlining the Catholic principles and practice of ecumenism. It urges all Christians to pray and work for the unity of the Church, according to the mind of Christ. The decree encourages dialogue among all Christians, always in a spirit of charity and understanding, but without obscuring the true meaning of Catholic doctrine. Cf. CCC 816, 819-822, 1636

United States Catholic Conference [USCC] (yöö-NAI-tehd STAYTS KATH-uh-lihk KAHN-fer-uhns [YÖÖ EI IS SEE SEE]): A public policy agency of the hierarchy in the United States that shared administrative structures with the National Conference of Catholic Bishops (NCCB) until 2001. Its task was to develop policies and programs (under the directions of the NCCB), which are then presented to the bishops for discussion and approval. Those policies approved were then implemented by the various departments of the USCC.

Unity (YÖÖ-nih-tee): The condition of being one. (1) When applied to persons, it is achieved through common beliefs, desires, and goals; (2) when applied to the Church, it is a work of the Holy Spirit; (3) when applied to God, it describes His Divine Nature, which has made itself known as Three Persons, one in substance and being. Cf. CCC 254-255, 360, 362-368, 382, 775, 791, 795, 813-819, 820-822, 1045, 1396, 1416, 1702, 1878, 1890

Universal Law: See Law, Universal

University, Pontifical (pahn-TIH-fih-kuhl yöö-nih-VER-sih-tee): A university erected by the Holy See and under its direct supervision. It has its own constitution and statutes, which must be approved by the Holy See. A pontifical university differs from a Catholic university in that the latter is not necessarily erected by the Holy See. There are several pontifical universities throughout the world. They specialize in the teaching of the sacred sciences of theology, Canon Law, and philosophy. The most prominent are the pontifical universities in Rome.

Univers, L' (LÖÖ-nee-vehr): A nineteenth-century French newspaper, under the editorship of Louis Veuillot (1813-1883), with the purposes of opposing Catholic liberals, condemning the principles of the French Revolution, and urging a union between Church and State for a return to the more authoritarian prerevolutionary society.

Urbi et Orbi (ØØR-bee eht OR-bee): (Latin: to the city and to the world) A blessing given by the Roman Pontiff upon his election, and annually at Christmas and Easter. It is accompanied by a message or allocution for the world, coupled with salutations in many languages.

Urim and Thummim (ØØR-ihm and TÖÖM-ihm): (Hebrew: lights and integrity, although this meaning is debated) Two objects, possibly stones, used by Israelite priests to obtain divine answers to their questions (Lv 8:9); they were kept in the high priest's breastplate (Ex 28:30). It is suggested that one represented "yes" (thummim) and the other "no" (urim), since questions were asked in expectation of such a response (1 Sm 14:41; 28:6).

Ursacrament [also Ursakrament] (ØØR-sa-kruh-mehnt): (German: original sacrament) Term introduced by Edward Schillebeeckx and Karl Rahner to designate the Church as the original or fundamental sacrament, from which the seven sacraments proceed; the doctrine of the Incarnation is introduced with Christ seen as the "Sacrament of encounter with God": the presence of grace in the Church and under the sacramental form is seen to parallel the incarnate presence of the divine in the human form of Jesus. **Cf. CCC 747, 774-776, 780, 1045, 1108, 1140**

Usury (YŌŌ-zher-ee): The practice of lending money at an excessive rate of interest. Because it is taking advantage of the need of another person, it is contrary to the natural law, and insofar as it might harm one who is poor, it is a sin against charity. In Jewish tradition and in the Church through the Middle Ages, the charging of interest was forbidden altogether; however, by the eighteenth century the Church recognized the legitimacy of receiving an equitable interest on loans. **CCC 2269, 2449**

Utraquism (YŌŌ-truh-kwih-zuhm): The doctrine held by the "Calixtin" followers of John Huss (1372-1415) that not only required receiving the Host at Holy Communion but also insisted that one must receive from the chalice. Utraquism was condemned by the Councils of Constance (1415) and Basel (1432).

V

Vagi (VAH-dzhee): (Latin: wanderers) The homeless, persons with no fixed abode. Cf. CCC 2447

Vaison, Councils of (KAUN-suhlz uhv vay-ZON): Two synods, one disciplinary and the other liturgical, held at Vaison, near Avignon, France, in A.D. 442 and 529.

Valentinianism (val-uhn-TIHN-ee-uhn-ih-zuhm): A Gnostic heresy that arose in Egypt in the second century, dividing mankind into three categories, only the first of which, its adherents, were assured salvation. Cf. CCC 285

Valid (VAL-ihd): With reference to an ecclesiastical act, real; with canonical, spiritual, or social consequences. Cf. CCC 1306, 1312, 1411, 1483, 1576-1577, 1622-1623, 1638, 1958, 2033, 2261, 2312, 2477

Validation of Marriage: See Convalidation

Vandalism (VAN-duh-lih-zuhm): The destruction of persons or objects, in opposition to justice and charity, which often results from an intense anger or psychological immaturity. When repenting of vandalism, one must make satisfaction through restitution.

Vatican (VA-tih-kuhn): (Latin *vaticanus,* from *vates canunt:* the soothsayers proclaim) In antiquity, the *mons vaticanus* was a religious site associated with the taking of auguries and auspices; it was at the end of the circus of Nero; and since it was outside the original city walls, it was appropriate as a necropolis to which the Christians brought their dead, many of whom had been persecuted in the nearby circus. Among those interred here was St. Peter, and so the Basilica of St. Peter was built atop his grave. Since the end of the Avignon captivity in 1377, the Vatican has served as the chief residence of the Popes, and so the term "Vatican" often serves to denote the Holy See, the papal provenance of Church policies or pronouncements. Located within the Vatican are most of the offices of the Papal Curia, the residences of some cardinals and other Church officials, the Swiss Guard, and the Vatican Museums and Library.

Vatican City, State of (STAYT uhv VA-tih-kuhn SIH-tee): Recognized as an independent, sovereign State by the Lateran Treaty of 1929, the State of Vatican City occupies 108.7 acres, with a population of 1,000, all of whom are citizens of the city-state. It survives as the last remnant of the once-vast Papal States, suppressed by Garibaldi and incorporated into the Republic of Italy in the mid-nineteenth century. Beginning with the building program of Pope Nicholas V in 1447, the Popes have initiated construction over the centuries to bring the Vatican to its present form; it includes the Vatican Palace, its gardens, the Piazza and Basilica of St. Peter, and, as a sovereign State, its own government buildings including post offices and a bank. In addition, the Vatican mints its own coins and issues passports and automobile license plates. The Pope governs Vatican City as sovereign ruler, though most of the civil responsibilities are delegated to an archbishop who serves as governor of the city-state.

Vatican Council I (VA-tih-kuhn KAUN-sihl WUHN): The twentieth ecumenical council and the first held within the Vatican, lasting from December 1869 to July 1870 and never officially adjourned. Among its achievements was the proclamation of papal infallibility as a dogma of the Church. Cf. CCC 293, 812

Vatican Council II (VA-ti-kuhn KAUN-sihl TÖÖ): The twenty-first ecumenical council of the Catholic Church, which was opened on October 11, 1962, at St. Peter's Basilica by Pope John XXIII. Approximately twenty-five hundred bishops participated over a period of three years. The threefold mandate given to the Council by the Pope consisted of renewal, modernization, and ecumenism, with the program to achieve these objectives contained in the sixteen documents that were promulgated. Cf. CCC 111, 597, 748, 816, 1232, 1388, 1513, 1557, 1571, 1656, 2068

Vaudois: See Waldenses

Veils (VAYLZ): 1. In the celebration of the Divine Liturgy of the Byzantine Rite, the Offerings are covered with three veils: the chalice veil, the veil over the diskos, and the aer, which covers them both. 2. In the Latin Rite, the tabernacle veil covers the locked receptacle for the reserved Blessed Sacrament. 3. The humeral veil, a long strip of cloth, is used by a priest to hold the monstrance with the Holy Eucharist in a procession or Benediction of the Blessed Sacrament.

Velum: See Humeral Veil

Venerable (VEH-ner-uh-buhl): The canonical title given to a deceased person who, though not beatified or canonized, has been judged to have lived the heroic virtues.

Veneration of the Saints (veh-ner-AY-shuhn uhv *th*uh SAYNTS): Devotion to the saints, who are invoked in recognition of their presence before God and thus capable of intercession on behalf of the living and those suffering in purgatory; they are particularly honored as patron saints because of their example in this life. The O.T. sentiment of 2 Mc 15:12, that the holy ones pray for the community, reechoes in Heb 12:1, where the holy people of the O.T. are called a "cloud of witnesses." Rooted in the Pauline doctrine of the Mystical Body of Christ, the earliest testimony of such veneration is the reverence accorded to the martyrs of the early Church. Since the fourth century, the veneration of saints has expanded to include all God's holy ones who enjoy the beatific vision and continue to intercede on our behalf; in their diversity, the saints offer an inexhaustible source of imitation and inspiration to Christians. The reverence shown the saints, called *dulia,* must be distinguished from *latria,* the worship and adoration given to God alone. CCC 1090

Venia (VEE-nee-uh): Act of satisfaction performed by religious after the commission of a venial fault.

Venial Sin (VEE-nee-uhl SIHN): Disobedience to God involving light moral matter or done without adequate knowledge, freedom, and full consent of the will. God detests all sin; however, the love of God can exist in one who has committed venial sins (but not mortal sins). Venial sin is remitted through the Sacrament of Penance, Holy Communion, acts of charity and penance, etc. CCC 1862-1863; cf. 1458

Veni, Creator Spiritus (VAY-nee, kray-AH-tor SPEE-ree-tøøs): (Latin: "Come, Creator Spirit") Hymn addressed to the Holy Spirit, for centuries part of the Divine Office, commonly sung at papal elections, episcopal consecrations, and ordinations to Holy Orders, and for invoking the Holy Spirit's presence in the conferring of Confirmation and at councils, synods, and canonical elections; though the authorship is debated, it is likely the work of Rabanus Maurus (776-856). Cf. CCC 291, 700

Veronica (Vuh-RAH-nih-kuh): (Latin *vera:* true + Greek *eikon:* image) 1. A likeness of Christ. 2. The name of a woman said to have given Him a cloth on which He caused an imprint of His face to appear. Veneration at Rome of a likeness depicted on cloth dates from about the end of the tenth century; it figured in a popular devotion during the Middle Ages, and in the Holy Face devotion practiced since the nineteenth century. A faint, illegible likeness said to be of this kind is preserved in St. Peter's Basilica. The origin of the likeness is uncertain, and the identity of the woman is unknown. Up to the fourteenth century there were no known art representations from the legendary incident concerning a woman who wiped the face of Christ with a cloth while He was being led to Calvary.

Versicle (VER-sih-kuhl): The first part of a pair of phrases or sentences commonly taken from the Psalter, joined together and sung or said antiphonally at the liturgy. The classic opening versicle and response to Morning and Evening Prayer are: "God, come to my assistance" and "Lord, make haste to help me," the versicle sung by the leader and the response sung by all. A series of versicles and responses follows the *Te Deum* when this is included in the Office of Readings. In the revised *Ceremoniale Episcoporum (Ceremonial of Bishops)*, the "Second Form" of episcopal blessing offered is introduced by two versicles with responses: "Blessed be the name of the Lord," "Now and for ever." "Our help is in the name of the Lord," "Who made heaven and earth."

Vespers (VEHS-perz): (From Latin: evening) The evening service of the Divine Office, also known as Evening Prayer, or among Anglicans as Evensong. Cf. CCC 1175

Vestments (VEHST-mehnts): (Latin *vestimentum* from *vestire:* to clothe) The garments worn at liturgy and other religious functions by the clergy. In the Catholic Church their design and color have been prescribed in liturgical and canonical legislation. Their origins from customary secular usage trace back to the fourth century, with a fairly stable usage in place by the ninth century. All liturgical services have prescribed vesture for the ministers, a chief example of which is the new Order of Mass. The *General Instruction of the Roman Missal* (n. 297) states that the diversity of liturgical roles is demonstrated by the diversity of liturgical vestments. "At the same time the vestments should also contribute to the beauty of the rite" (n. 297). The vestment common to all ministers at Mass is the alb (with cincture and amice, if needed) (n. 298). The chasuble is the vestment proper to the priest celebrant; it is worn over the alb and stole (n. 299). The dalmatic, worn over the alb and stole, is the proper vestment of the deacon (n. 300). Priests wear the stole around the neck, hanging down; deacons wear the stole over the left shoulder fastened on the right side (n. 302). A cope is worn by the priest "in processions [e.g., with palms on Passion Sunday] and other services in keeping with the rubrics of each rite" (n. 303). "The beauty of a vestment should derive from its material and design rather than from lavish ornamentation. Representations on vestments should consist only of symbols, images or pictures portraying the sacred" (n. 306). The *Instruction* states that traditional colors for vestments are retained in the present reform: (1) white for the seasons of Easter and Christmas, feasts of the Lord, of Mary, angels, and most saints; also for feasts of All Saints, John the Baptist, John the Evangelist, Chair of St. Peter Apostle, and Conversion of St. Paul; (2) red on Passion Sunday, Good Friday, Pentecost, birthday feasts of Apostles and Evangelists, and celebrations of martyrs; (3) violet, for the seasons of Lent and Advent, offices for the dead; (4) black is optional for Masses for the dead; (5) rose is optional on Laetare and Gaudete Sundays. In addition, "the conference of bishops may choose and propose to the Apostolic See adaptations suited to the needs and cultures of peoples" (n. 308). Cf. CCC 1161, 1672, 1685

Viaticum (vai-A-tih-kuhm): (Latin: provision for a journey) The administration of the Holy Eucharist to those about to die. The present *Rites of Anointing and Viaticum* contain a special chapter on the "Celebration of Viaticum" (ch. 5, nn. 175-211), which is introduced by the statement: "The celebration of the Eucharist as Viaticum, food for the passage through death to eternal life, is the sacrament proper to the dying Christian. It is the completion and crown of the Christian life on this earth, signifying that the Christian follows the Lord to eternal glory and the banquet of the heavenly kingdom" (n. 175). Two rites are provided for Viaticum, one within Mass and the other outside Mass (containing introductory rites, Liturgy of the Word, Liturgy of Viaticum, concluding rites). CCC 1331, 1392, 1517, 1524-1525

Vicar (VIH-ker): (Latin *vicarius:* substitute, deputy) One who performs acts of ecclesiastical authority in an ecclesiastical office in the name of another. Cf. CCC 882, 894, 1560, 1778

Vicar, Judicial (dzhöö-DIH-shuhl VIH-ker): The chief judge and head of the tribunal of a diocese.

Vicar Forane (VIH-ker for-AYN): (From Latin: deputy outside) Priest given limited authority over a certain area of a diocese (cf. Dean).

Vicar General (VIH-ker DZHEHN-er-uhl): Priest or bishop appointed by the bishop of a diocese to serve as his deputy, with ordinary executive power, in the administration of the diocese.

Vicar of Christ (VIH-ker uhv KRAIST): (Latin *vicarius:* one who serves in place of another + *Christi)* Title used almost exclusively of the Bishop of Rome as successor of Peter and, therefore, the one in the Church who particularly takes the place of Christ, but used also of bishops in general and even of priests. First used by the Roman Synod of A.D. 495 to refer to Pope Gelasius; more commonly in Roman curial usage it refers to the Bishop of Rome during the pontificate of Pope Eugene III (1145-1153). Pope Innocent III (1198-1216) asserted explicitly that the Pope is the Vicar of Christ; it was further defined at the Council of Florence in the *Decree for the Greeks* (1439) and Vatican Council I in *Pastor Aeternus* (1870). The Second Vatican Council, in *Lumen Gentium,* n. 27, calls bishops in general "vicars and legates of Christ." All bishops are vicars of Christ for their local churches in their ministerial functions as priest, prophet, and king, as the Pope is for the universal Church; the title further denotes that they exercise their authority in the Church not by delegation from any other person, but from Christ Himself. **CCC 882, 894, 1560**

Vicar of Peter (VIH-ker uhv PEE-ter): Never an official papal title, formally rejected by Pope Innocent III, since it implies that the vicar holds his office in place of Peter, rather than as his successor; thus, to serve as a vicar of Peter would contradict the papacy as the office of the Vicar of Christ, since it would suggest that papal authority was not of divine, but human, origin. Correctly termed, the Pope is the successor of Peter, who was the first Vicar of Christ.

Vicariate, Apostolic (a-pah-STAH-lihk vih-KEHR-ee-uht): A territorial division of the Church established, usually, in a mission country that does not have its own hierarchy, and under the authority of a prelate.

Vice Chancellor (VAIS TSHAN-suh-ler): A cleric or layperson appointed by the bishop to assist the chancellor (Can. 482).

Vienne, Council of (KAUN-suhl uhv vee-EHN): The fifteenth ecumenical council, convoked in 1311, which dealt with the suppression of the Knights Templar, unrest in the Holy Land, and Franciscan disputes concerning poverty.

Vigil (VIH-dzhihl): (From Latin: awake) 1. A watch on the eve of a religious feast. Liturgical services consisting of psalms, readings, and silent prayer were common in earliest Christianity as attested to in Pliny's Letter to Trajan (c. 112) and in Egeria's Diary (late fourth century); often the vigils lasted all night and ended with the Eucharist. Vigils of particular importance were those for Easter and Pentecost. A connection between keeping vigil and the Liturgy of the Hours is clear in the evolution of Matins and preserving a Saturday evening Vigil of the Resurrection, which looked toward the Eucharist on Sunday, the day of the Resurrection. The present revision of the Liturgy of the Hours contains an Appendix for "Canticles and Gospel Readings for Vigils." The Gospel texts provided are the accounts of the post-Resurrection appearances from the four Evangelists (Mt 28:1-11, 16-20; Mk 16:1-20; Lk 24:1-2, 13-35, 35-53; Jn 20:1-18, 19-31, 21:1-14). 2. The celebration of Mass on evenings preceding important feasts. Those that perdure in the present liturgy are vigils for Christmas, Easter, Pentecost, Birth of John the Baptist, Sts. Peter and Paul, and the Assumption. **Cf. CCC 281, 647, 1095, 1217, 1238, 1254**

Vigil Light (VIH-dzhihl LAIT): A candle burned as an act of devotion, or for a particular intention, in a shrine or before a holy image. The flame is said to "keep vigil" when the person cannot be present.

Vincent de Paul, St. (SAYNT VIHN-sehnt duh PAWL): French saint (1581-1660), ordained to the priesthood in 1600. A noted preacher, he was the founder of the Congregation of Priests of the Mission and the Daughters of Charity. He is most remembered for his great love and charity toward the poor; his work continues in the numerous St. Vincent de Paul Societies that have been established. He was canonized in 1737 and was declared the patron saint of charitable works and organizations that serve the poor.

Vindictive Penalties (vihn-DIHK-tihv PEHN-uhl-teez): More severe canonical penalties in the 1917 Code of Canon Law that were punitive in intention. (Cf. Penalty, Vindictive.)

Virgin Birth of Christ (VER-dzhihn BERTH uhv KRAIST):
An article of faith, as in the Nicene Creed: "By the power of
the Holy Spirit, He was born of the Virgin Mary"; thus,
with no human father, Jesus Christ was born uniquely of a
virgin mother (Mt 1:18-25; Lk 1:26-38); this is the constant
teaching of the Church and a basic norm of orthodox Christianity. Jesus Christ has but one Father, and the eternal origin of the Son is unique to His procession from the Father. It
is appropriate that the principle of the New Creation, the
Holy Spirit, should inaugurate the New Creation through
the virginal conception of Christ, which in turn makes the
radical introduction of the adopted sonship of all those born
anew in Christ. Cf. CCC 487-507, 510, 723

Virginity (ver-DZHIHN-ih-tee): The state of perpetual abstinence from sexual intercourse. As an evangelical counsel,
virginity has as its motive the search for the perfect love of
God alone. Christian teaching affirms the fundamental goodness of sexual love within marriage, and so virginity is not to
be seen as the avoidance of something evil, but rather a voluntary renunciation, which is a particular vocation from God,
and for which He provides the necessary grace. Cf. 922, 1618-
1620, 2349

Virgin Mary (VER-dzhihn MEH-ree): Mary, the Mother
of Jesus, was a virgin before, through, and after the conception and birth of Christ, *ante partum, in partu, et post partum,*
according to the consistent teaching of the Church from antiquity; thus, it is held that Mary's virginity was perpetual.
Although some misunderstand the reference to the "brethren of the Lord" (cf. Mk 3:31-35) as violating her virginity,
actually this reference is probably to close relations or cousins. Jesus Christ remains the only Son of Mary, while her
maternity encompasses all who are born again in Christ, "the
first-born among many brethren" (Rom 8:29). CCC 496-
499, 502-503, 506, 510, 723

Virtue (VER-tshöö): A good habit of the intellect or will
that enables one to perform an action with ease. Some are
infused (e.g., theological virtues: faith, hope, charity) while
others are developed by practice (e.g., cardinal virtues: pru-

dence, justice, fortitude, temperance). Virtue brings to fulfillment the powers and abilities that one possesses. CCC 1803-1804, 1833; cf. 25, 153, 798, 1266, 1697, 1784, 1805-1844, 1863, 1942, 1948, 2223, 2284, 2290, 2337, 2341-2349, 2468-2469

Virtues, Moral: See Moral Virtues

Virtues, Theological: See Theological Virtues

Visions (VIH-zhuhnz): Not illusions or hallucinations but a charism through which an individual perceives someone or something that is naturally invisible. Several of the saints (among them St. Teresa of Ávila and St. John of the Cross) claimed to have had visions. St. Thomas divided visions into corporeal, imaginative, and intellectual. Like other charisms, visions are for the spiritual good of people. However, they are not necessary for salvation or holiness. Cf. CCC 67

Visitation, Episcopal (ih-PIHS-kuh-puhl vih-zih-TAY-shuhn): Official visits by the diocesan bishop to all institutions under his jurisdiction, to be made at least every five years.

Visitation of Mary (vih-zih-TAY-shuhn uhv MEH-ree): Mary's journey to Ain Karem, a town in the Judean hills, to visit her pregnant relative, Elizabeth (Lk 1:39-56), with the annunciation of Jesus' birth (Lk 1:26-38) preparing the way logically and theologically for the visitation, as Gabriel announced to Mary that Elizabeth's unusual pregnancy was a sign that "with God nothing will be impossible" (Lk 1:37). In response to Gabriel's annunciation, Mary declares her willingness to cooperate with God's word and to go to the assistance of Elizabeth, with whom she spends three months, and then leaves not long before the birth of John the Baptist (Lk 1:56). The visitation also serves as the first encounter between the two unborn sons, Jesus and John the Baptist, who leaps in his mother's womb at the sound of Mary's greeting (Lk 1:41-44), fulfilling the prediction that "he will be filled with the Holy Spirit even from his mother's womb" (Lk 1:15). Just as Mary learns of Elizabeth's condition by divine mediation, so Elizabeth learns of Mary's pregnancy through this first prophetic act of John the Baptist. Filled with the Holy Spirit, Elizabeth blesses Mary: "Blessed are you among women and blessed is the fruit of your womb!" (Lk 1:42), while Mary responds with the *Magnificat,* her canticle of praise (Lk 1:46-55). The Feast of the Visitation is celebrated on May 31; the Visitation serves as the Second Joyful Mystery of the Rosary. **Cf. CCC 717**

Visitator, Apostolic (a-pah-STAH-lihk VIH-zih-tay-ter): A special representative assigned by the Holy See to visit and report on the conditions of a diocese, religious institute, or other ecclesiastical entity.

Vitalism (VAI-tuhl-ih-zuhm): (Latin: *vitalis,* of life) The contemporary ethical system that states that all human life must be preserved, regardless of cost or burden to the patient or his family. The Church recognizes that medical treatments have their limits; hence, extraordinary measures need not be accepted. The charge of vitalism is used in debates by advocates of euthanasia who attempt to disparage another's legitimate concern for human life. **Cf. CCC 2278-2279**

Vitandus (vee-TAHN-døøs): (Latin: one to be avoided) Term from the 1917 Code of Canon Law describing an excommunicated person who was not to be associated with in any way. Not retained in the revised code.

Vocation (vo-KAY-shuhn): (From Latin *vocare:* to call) The calling from God to follow a particular way of life. The Second Vatican Council, in *Lumen Gentium* and *Gaudium et Spes,* emphasizes the universal call to holiness, that general call of God to all the baptized to a life of grace and union with Him; this vocation is the call that gives human life its destiny and meaning. In particular, vocation is understood as God's call to a distinctive state of life, viz., married, single, religious, or priestly; the Sacraments of Matrimony and Holy Orders are thus designated sacraments of vocation. Although the term has this broad meaning, it has come to refer more specifically to the calling to religious life or the priesthood; thus it is common to speak of a religious vocation and the necessary discernment by the competent Church authorities of the authentic call to priestly or religious life. CCC 1, 27, 44, 898-900, 1583, 1603-1604, 1716-1724, 1974; cf. 30, 307, 373, 490, 521, 539, 542-543, 762, 784, 804, 831, 863, 1121, 1260, 1533, 1607, 1656, 1699-1703, 1877-1886, 1907, 1962, 1998, 2030, 2085, 2226, 2232, 2331, 2337-2359, 2369, 2392, 2442, 2461, 2820

Voluntarism (VOL-uhn-ter-ih-zuhm): The moral theory holding that the malice of an action is determined by the agent's intention. Peter Abélard took this position, as do some contemporary theologians. On the other hand, St. Thomas Aquinas wrote that there are three factors that determine the morality of a human act: the object; the end; the circumstances. Cf. CCC 1749-1761

Von Balthasar, Hans Urs (HAHNZ ØØRS fon BAHL-tuh-zahr): Swiss priest and theologian (1905-1988) whose theology gives clarity to the distinctive work of God in Christ, and its ramifications for the life and ministry of the Church within contemporary culture. He founded *Communio,* a journal of Catholic scholarship, and was honored by Pope John Paul II for his service to the Church, finally being named a cardinal one month before his death, which occurred before his investiture, hence never becoming a member of the College of Cardinals.

Votive Mass (VO-tihv MAS): In general, this term refers to Mass formularies in the Roman Missal for special occasions or in honor of aspects of the mystery of God or the saints. In the present Sacramentary, "Masses and Prayers for Various Needs and Occasions" are divided into three types: ritual Masses (celebration of certain sacraments), various needs and occasions (as the need arises), and "votive Masses of the Mysteries of the Lord or in honor of Mary or a particular saint or of all the saints, which are options provided for the faithful's devotion" (n. 329). The priest may choose to use these texts when no other solemnity, feast, or memorial occurs on that day. The Sacramentary contains the following Mass formulas: Holy Trinity, Holy Cross, Holy Eucharist, Holy Name, Precious Blood, Sacred Heart, Holy Spirit, Blessed Virgin

Mary, Angels, St. Joseph, Apostles, Peter, Paul, An Apostle, All Saints.

Votive Offerings (VO-tihv AW-fer-ihngs): (Latin *votum:* wish, vow) O.T. term that pertains to a voluntary offering made to God but not required by the Law. The technical term in Hebrew for such an offering is *neder* (vow). The Book of Deuteronomy (Dt 12:5-6, 11) specifies the place where votive offerings were to be made. In Christian usage, votive offerings are freewill gifts of money or other goods in light of some spiritual request. They are also the donation made when candles or vigil lights are lit to signify an intention. **Cf. CCC 1566**

Votive Office (VO-tihv AH-fihs): Similar to votive Masses in the sense that these can substitute for the regular daily office on particular occasions. The *General Instruction of the Liturgy of the Hours* states that "for a public cause or out of devotion [except on solemnities and certain feasts] . . . a votive office may be celebrated, in whole or in part: e.g., on the occasion of a pilgrimage, a local feast, or the external solemnity of a saint." The clearest example in the present edition of the Liturgy of the Hours is the Office for the Dead.

Vow (VAU): A free and deliberate promise made to God concerning a possible and better good to be fulfilled by the person making it. **CCC 2102-2103**

Vulgate (VUHL-gayt): The Latin translation of the Bible from the Greek and Hebrew by St. Jerome. The Vulgate was declared the official edition of the Bible for the Latin Church and derives its name from the Latin term *versio vulgata,* meaning "popular" or "widespread."

W

Waldenses (wahl-DEHN-seez): Christian sect that takes its name from its founder, Peter Valdez, a rich merchant of Lyons, who in 1173 gave away his possessions and became an itinerant lay preacher. Valdez and his followers, also called the "Poor Men of Lyons" and the "Vaudois," preached against clerical worldliness and the heresy of the Cathars. Despite the informal approbation granted to them in 1179 by Pope Alexander III and their fidelity to Church teaching, the Waldensians, along with the Cathars, were excommunicated in 1184 at the Council of Verona. Their increasingly heterodox views concerning the number of the sacraments and the invalidity of sacraments administered by unworthy clergy, and their rejection of purgatory or devotion to the saints, made them objects of persecution by both the Church and secular authorities. Their "proto-Protestantism" brought them into contact with the Reformers of the sixteenth century; with their adoption of a formal Confession of Faith and their repudiation of the Catholic Church at the Synod of Chanforans (1532), the Waldensians in effect became a Reformed Protestant sect. Today they number about twenty thousand members, centered chiefly in the Piedmont region of northern Italy.

War, Morality of (mor-AL-ih-tee uhv WAHR): The discussion about whether an armed conflict can ever be just. The traditional criteria for a just war may be stated thus: (1) The agent's intention must be just; (2) the means used must be proportionate, just, and discriminate; (3) the war must be a last resort; (4) a proportion between the goods and evils must result; (5) there must be a reasonable prospect for success; (6) the war's cause must be just. A war is just only if it is morally certain that all the criteria are met. **CCC 2304, 2307-2317**

Water (WAH-ter): Used extensively throughout O.T. Jewish ceremonies, in Christian usage water is the essential matter for the Sacrament of Baptism. Also, in imitation of Our Lord's example, it is used in the devotional practice of the washing of feet on Holy Thursday, and is specially blessed as holy water for the blessing of persons and objects, and for the use of the faithful in their homes. CCC 694, 1213-1225; cf. 256, 344, 536-537, 701, 720, 766, 782, 1011, 1094, 1137, 1147, 1179, 1185, 1189, 1228, 1238-1240, 1257, 1262, 1278, 1284, 1299, 1345, 1429, 1668, 2345, 2557, 2560-2561, 2652, 2686, 2691, 2790, 2813, 2835

Week of Prayer for Christian Unity (WEEK uhv PREHR for KRIHS-tshuhn YÖÖ-nih-tee): Eight days of prayer, January 18-25, for unity of all Christians in the Church established by Christ. Coined by Fr. James Wattson, S.A., of Graymoor, New York, it started in 1908 as the Chair of Unity Octave. It has become more strongly an ecumenical and even interfaith exercise in recent years.

Western Schism, The Great *(th*uh GRAYT WEHS-tern SIH-zuhm): A disruption in Catholic unity lasting from 1378 until 1417, resulting from rival claims to the papacy. After the election of Urban VI in 1378, thirteen of the cardinal electors challenged him, and then chose Clement VII, who returned to Avignon in France. In an attempt to correct the situation, a third Pope, Alexander V, was elected at the Council of Pisa. After a time of great confusion and bitter politics, the schism was ended when the Council of Constance (1414-1418) elected Pope Martin V. The rivals either resigned or eventually died.

Wine, Liturgical Use of (lih-TER-dzhih-kuhl yöös uhv WAIN): In accord with the example of Christ, unleavened bread and grape wine are used in the celebration of the Eucharist. The *General Instruction of the Roman Missal* states that "the wine for the Eucharist must be from the fruit of the vine (see Lk 22:18), natural, and pure, i.e., not mixed with any foreign substance" (n. 322). The 1983 Code of Canon Law reiterates this prescription and says that the Eucharist "must be offered with bread and wine, with which a small quantity of water is to be mixed" (Can. 924, 1). "The wine must be natural wine of the grape and not corrupt" (Can. 924, 3). With regard to the distribution of the Eucharist under both species, the code states: "Holy Communion is to be given under the form of bread alone or under both kinds in accord with the norm of the liturgical laws or even under the form of wine alone in case of necessity" (Can. 925). Cf. **CCC 1333-1335, 1375-1376, 1413**

Winter Chapel (WIHN-ter TSHA-puhl): Small side chapel in a Latin Rite church designed to accommodate a smaller congregation. (Cf. Paraekklesia.)

Wisdom (WIHZ-duhm): As one of the seven gifts of the Holy Spirit, wisdom, with knowledge, perfects the use of judgment; knowledge perfects the judgment of practical reason, while wisdom perfects the judgment of speculative reason. In the Bible, wisdom is the name for the personification of God's wise dealings and plan for the world and the human race, manifest in both creation and redemption. **CCC 283, 1303, 1831, 2500; cf. 216, 272, 295, 299, 339, 369, 1950, 1954**

Wisdom, Book of (BØØK uhv WIHZ-duhm): Last of the seven sapiential books of the O.T., written in Greek by a Jew of Alexandria, ca. 100 B.C.; it is called deuterocanonical because it was not included in the Jewish canon of the Bible. In Syriac, it is called "The Book of the Great Wisdom of Solomon"; thus, the author presumes to speak in the name of Solomon, though he appears to address those Jews so enamored of Greek science and philosophy that they were tempted to abandon the ancient practices of their religion from the time of Solomon. Absent from earlier Jewish thought, but important for Christian theology, are these tenets of the Book of Wisdom: God can be naturally known to exist by pondering the origin of the universe; the human soul is immortal and survives the death of the body; and with God there is divine wisdom, through which He made the universe. The author takes a transcendental view of the world: The first wisdom is in God; human beings participate in wisdom; and the first manifestation of wisdom in them is their recognition of God.

Witness (WIHT-nehs): 1. One who gives testimony concerning something of which one has direct knowledge or acquaintance. 2. In its Christian sense, witness refers to the Apostles, martyrs, and the first disciples of Christ who bore witness to His resurrection. More widely, it describes every Christian who is called to bear witness, by word and deed, to the hope that comes from Our Lord Jesus Christ. **Cf. CCC 30, 642, 688, 857, 929, 932-933, 995, 1816, 2044, 2058, 2087, 2226, 2464, 2471-2473, 2476, 2506**

Women, Ordination of (or-dih-NAY-shuhn uhv WIH-mehn): The exclusion of women from ordination is found in the expressed will of Christ, Who called men alone to be His Apostles, and it has been the constant tradition and teaching of the Church that women are ineligible to receive the Sacrament of Orders. This is not a reflection on the dignity of women, but rather because of the relationship between Christ as Spouse and the Church as Bride. In 1976, the declaration of the Congregation for the Doctrine of the Faith, *Inter Insigniores,* dealt with this matter in a detailed and authoritative manner, followed by the irreformable document of Pope John Paul II, *Ordinatio Sacerdotalis,* in 1994. **CCC 1577-1578**

World Council of Churches (WERLD KAUN-sihl uhv TSHERTSH-ehz): An international organization founded in 1948, representing one hundred forty-seven Protestant and Orthodox bodies. Resulting from ecumenical concerns among various Christian denominations, it has sought to bring about reconciliation, although some of its social and doctrinal positions have provoked controversy and criticism. The Catholic Church is not a member of the WCC, but it does cooperate with the organization, especially in the area of social justice.

Wreath, Advent (AD-vehnt REETH): A popular, though not strictly speaking liturgical, custom whereby a circlet made of evergreen boughs and adorned with four candles is suspended from the ceiling, or placed on a stand, with the candles lighted in succession to mark the passage of the four weeks of Advent. By tradition, but not of necessity, the candles are of the color of the Advent vestments: usually three purple and one rose (for the third Sunday, *"Gaudete,"* or "Rejoice,"

Sunday). Originally a focal point for prayer in the home, and still placed in the refectory of many monastic and religious communities, the Advent Wreath has become a standard decoration of the worship space during this preparatory season for Christmas. The new *Book of Blessings* provides for a formal blessing of the Advent Wreath as part of the General Intercessions on the First Sunday of Advent. The Spanish *Bendicional* has an alternative approach, in which the Blessing of the Wreath and Lighting of its First Candle take place at Vespers or at the beginning of the Vigil Mass of the First Sunday of Advent. In both rituals, the lighting of the subsequent candles on the following weeks takes place in silence or during the opening hymn with no further words or ceremonies. A form for blessing the Advent Wreath at home and prayers to be used at the candle-lighting each evening are given in *Catholic Household Blessings and Prayers.*

Y

Yahweh (YAH-way): (Hebrew name of God) God's proper name revealed to Moses during the Exodus (Ex 3:11 ff.); in this moment of revelation, Israel came to know more precisely the identity of God as the One Who delivered His Chosen People from slavery in Egypt. The Yahwist tradition, eager to show Yahweh as God of the whole human race and not just of Israel, cites use of this name in the time of Enosh, grandson of Adam (Gn 4:26). According to the priestly tradition, though God appeared to Abraham, Isaac, and Jacob, He did not identify Himself to them by this name (Ex 6:23). The Elohist tradition appears to confirm this by use of the name Elohim in preference for Yahweh in Genesis, before the revelation of the name in Exodus 3. All the traditions are one in maintaining that Moses did not encounter a new God in the burning bush; rather, He is the "God of the fathers." As diacritical marks to indicate the sounds of vowels in Hebrew were introduced only late in the history of the language, God's name originally appeared in Hebrew as the grouping of four consonants, YHWH; thus, the actual pronunciation of the name can only be conjectured. For this reason some attempt a reconstruction of the name as Jehovah, using the same four consonants, but with the vowels of *Adonai* ("Lord"), the vowels of which were written under the consonants YHWH in late manuscripts to prevent the unconscious sacrilege of saying the sacred name. The actual meaning of the name has never been firmly established. While the most common is "I am Who am," such an abstraction is more appropriate to Hellenistic speculation than to the theology of the primitive Hebrew Bible; the rabbis often suggest the name means "I am" in the sense of "I am here for you, on your behalf, ready to be of assistance." Some modern interpreters suggest, "I am Who act passionately," compatible with the vigorous, dynamic image of God; others suggest "I am Who speak," with emphasis on the revealing character of God; while the most intriguing is "I am the One Who cause to be whatever comes to be," which stresses the biblical view of God as Creator and Sustainer. **CCC 206, 210-213, 446; cf. 211, 446-447, 2666**

Yom Kippur: See Atonement, Day of

Youth, Impediment of (ihm-PEH-dih-mehnt uhv YŌŌTH): Canon 1083 of the 1983 Code of Canon Law (q.v.) establishes that boys must be at least sixteen years old and girls at least fourteen years old to enter sacramental marriage validly. In Roman Law, and throughout much of the history of Canon Law, the minimum ages for marriage were fourteen for boys and twelve for girls, which are roughly equivalent to the ages of puberty. The 1917 code raised the minimum ages as above. They would have been raised higher still with the appearance of the 1983 Code, except for the great difficulty in arriving at a suitable universal age, given the fact that the Code of Canon Law operates in a wide variety of cultures and economic conditions. Because the minimum ages were determined by ecclesiastical law, it is within the power of the diocesan bishop to dispense from this matrimonial impediment. On the other hand, the conference of bishops may establish a higher age for the licit celebration of marriage. The Church's concern for the marriage of the very young extends considerably beyond the establishment of the impediment of youth. Canon 1072, for example, directs pastors to discourage persons from marrying when they are merely younger than the customary age for marrying in that area or community. The good sense behind this canon is self-evident. Canon 1071 requires the pastor (or other official witness) for a proposed marriage to seek the permission of the diocesan bishop when it is a question of marrying persons who are under eighteen if their parents are unaware of the marriage or are reasonably opposed to it. And more broadly yet, Canon 1063 urges pastors to develop a system of marriage preparation suitable for, among others, young people, in order to help them grow in their understanding of the fullness of Christian marriage. Warning of the dangers of immature weddings can be an integral part of such preparation programs.

Youth Organization, Catholic: See Catholic Youth Organization

Z

Zeal (ZEEL): The charity and resulting effort that enable one to serve God and others in the furthering of the Mystical Body of Christ. When one is animated with zeal, he acknowledges the treasure of the Faith and seeks to defend it and share it with those who have not heard it or those who have but are not living its demands. CCC 579, 2442

Zechariah, Book of (BØØK uhv zeh-kuh-RAI-uh): One of the twelve minor prophets, a contemporary of Haggai, who wrote the first eight chapters of his prophecy 520-518 B.C. In the first and authentic part of this book, there are eight nocturnal visions intended to encourage hope in the Messiah among the people with the promise of great blessings attendant upon his advent. The final six chapters, attributed to Deutero-Zechariah, continue to emphasize the Messianic theme, with the assurance of the end of oppression by the Gentiles; though a son of David, the Messiah will be poor.

Zelanti (zeh-LAHN-tee): (Latin *zelantes:* eager ones) Franciscans in the Franciscan Controversy of the thirteenth century who opposed any modification of the Franciscan Rule as it was established by St. Francis of Assisi in 1221 and revised by him in 1223. They were opposed in their zeal by the *Relaxati* (or Lax) who favored a relaxation of the rigors of their rule.

Zeon (ZEE-ahn): A sacred vessel used in the liturgy of the Byzantine Rite. The zeon is a small metal container out of which hot water is poured into the chalice before receiving Holy Communion.

Zephaniah, Book of (BØØK uhv zeh-fuh-NAI-uh): The ninth of the minor prophets, Zephaniah was a direct descendant of King Hezekiah of Judah, of Judean origin, and born ca. 660 B.C. He saw the Scythian invasion of Palestine as the instrument of God's judgment on Judah and, in a sense, on the whole world (Zep 1:2-3), with the blame lying in their attraction to pagan rituals. With obvious influence from Amos and Hosea, he also censures the people for their lack of concern for ethical standards (Zep 1:8-9); he places a great emphasis, perhaps more than any other prophet, on the Day of the Lord and the consequent ruin and devastation. The book does have an optimistic ending; God will renew the faithful remnant in Judah and will rejoice over them (Zep 3:9-20).

Ziggurat (ZIH-guh-rat): (Assyrian: pinnacle or height) A temple tower of the Assyrians and Babylonians, built as a terraced pyramid, with each level smaller than the one just below it; it probably served as a model for the Tower of Babel (Gn 11).

Zimarra (zih-MAH-ruh): (Italian: robe, cloak) The cassocklike attire that used to be worn by all prelates but is now reserved for bishops, cardinals, and the Pope. It is like a house cassock but has a small shoulder cape *(pellegrina)* attached to the collar. Pope Pius IX decreed that the zimarra would be standard attire for prelates at papal audiences.

Zone (ZON): Belt worn by an Eastern Rite priest over the sticharion.

Zucchetto (zöö-KEH-to): Derived from the popular Italian idiom *zucca* ("pumpkin"), used as slang for "head," the zucchetto is a small skullcap worn by ecclesiastics, especially prelates. The Holy Father wears a white zucchetto made of watered silk. The cardinals use scarlet, and bishops use purple. Priests of the monsignorial rank may wear black with purple piping. All others may wear simple black, including abbots who do not have episcopal dignity.

Zwinglianism (ZWIHNG-lee-uh-nih-zuhm): The teaching of the Swiss Protestant Ulrich Zwingli (1484-1531). Although Martin Luther believed in a Real Presence of Christ in the Eucharist, Zwingli maintained that it was only symbolic. The Swiss Reformation became increasingly Calvinistic, but Zwingli had a great influence on Protestant theology.

Appendix I

List of Popes
Bracketed dates are dates of installation.

1. St. Peter (Galilean, d. c. 64 or 67)
2. St. Linus (67-76)
3. St. Anacletus or Cletus (76-88)
4. St. Clement 1(88-97)
5. St. Evaristus (Greek, 97-105)
6. St. Alexander I (105-115)
7. St. Sixtus 1(115-125)
8. St. Telesphorus (Greek, 125-136)
9. St. Hyginus (Greek, 136-140)
10. St. Pius 1(140-155)
11. St. Anicetus (Syrian, 155-166)
12. St. Soter (166-175)
13. St. Eleutherius (Greek, 175-189)
14. St. Victor I (African, 189-199)
15. St. Zephyrinus (199-217)
16. St. Calixtus I (217-222)
17. St. Urban 1(222-230)
18. St. Pontian (July 21, 230 — September 28, 235)
19. St. Anterus (Greek, November 21, 235 — January 3, 236)
20. St. Fabian (January 10, 236 — January 20, 250)
21. St. Cornelius (March 251 — June 253)
22. St. Lucius I (June 25, 253 — March 5, 254)
23. St. Stephen I (May 12, 254 — August 2, 257)
24. St. Sixtus II (Greek, August 30, 257 — August 6, 258)
25. St. Dionysius (July 22, 259 — December 26, 268)
26. St. Felix I (January 5, 269 — December 30, 274)
27. St. Eutychian (January 4, 275 — December 7, 283)
28. St. Caius (Dalmatian, December 17, 283 — April 22, 296)
29. St. Marcellinus (June 20, 296 — October 25, 309)
30. St. Marcellus I (May 27, 308 or June 26, 308 — January 16, 309)

31. St. Eusebius (Greek, April 18, 309 or 310 — August 17, 309 or 310)
32. St. Melchiades or Miltiades (African, July 2, 311 — January 11, 314)
33. St. Sylvester I (January 31, 319 — December 31, 335)
34. St. Mark (January 18, 336 — October 7, 336)
35. St. Julius I (February 6, 337 — April 12, 352)
36. Liberius (May 17, 352 — September 24, 366)
37. St. Damasus I (Spanish, October 1, 366 — December 11, 384)
38. St. Siricius (December 15 or 22 or 29, 384 — November 26, 399)
39. St. Anastasius I (November 27, 399 — December 19, 401)
40. St. Innocent I (December 22, 401 — March 12, 417)
41. St. Zosimus (Greek, March 18, 417 — December 26, 418)
42. St. Boniface I (December 28 or 29, 418 — September 4, 422)
43. St. Celestine I (September 10, 422 — July 27, 432)
44. St. Sixtus III (July 31, 432 — August 19, 440)
45. St. Leo I (the Great, September 29, 440 — November 10, 461)
46. St. Hilary (November 19, 461 — February 29, 468)
47. St. Simplicius (March 3, 468 — March 10, 483)
48. St. Felix III (actually II, March 13, 483 — March 1, 492: because St. Felix of Rome, a martyr, was erroneously considered by early historians to have been a Pope, Felix II and his successors were all incorrectly numbered)
49. St. Gelasius I (African, March 1, 492 — November 21, 496)
50. Anastasius II (November 24, 496 — November 19, 498)
51. St. Symmachus (November 22, 498 — July 19, 514)
52. St. Hormisdas (July 20, 514 — August 6, 523)
53. St. John I (August 13, 523 — May 18, 526)
54. St. Felix IV (actually III, July 12, 526 — September 22, 530)

55. Boniface II (September 22, 530 — October 17, 532)
56. John II (January 2, 533 — May 8, 535)
57. St. Agapitus I (May 13, 535 — April 22, 536)
58. St. Silverius (June 1 or 8, 536 — November 11, 537 [d. December 2, 537; abdicated after being deposed, March 537])
59. Vigilius (March 29, 537 — June 7, 555)
60. Pelagius II (April 16, 556 — March 4, 561)
61. John III (July 17, 561 — July 13, 574)
62. Benedict I (June 2, 575 — July 30, 579)
63. Pelagius II (November 26, 579 — February 7, 590)
64. St. Gregory I (the Great, September 3, 590 — March 12, 604)
65. Sabinian (September 19, 604 — February 22, 606)
66. Boniface III (February 19, 607 — November 12, 607)
67. St. Boniface IV (August 25, 608 — May 8, 615)
68. St. Deusdedit or Adeodatus I (October 19, 615 — November 8, 618)
69. Boniface V (December 23, 619 — October 25, 625)
70. Honorius I (October 27, 625 — October 12, 638)
71. Severinus (May 28, 640 — August 2, 640)
72. John IV (Dalmatian, December 24, 640 — October 12, 642)
73. Theodore I (Greek, November 24, 642 — May 14, 649)
74. St. Martin I (July 649 — September 16, 655 [exiled June 17, 655])
75. St. Eugenius I (August 10, 654 — June 2, 657)
76. St. Vitalian (July 30, 657 — January 27, 672)
77. Adeodatus II (April 11, 672 — June 17, 676)
78. Donus (November 2, 676 — April 11, 678)
79. St. Agatho (June 27, 678 — January 10, 681)
80. St. Leo II (August 17, 682 — July 9, 689)
81. St. Benedict II (June 26, 684 — May 8, 685)
82. John V (Syrian, July 23, 685 — August 2, 686)
83. Conon (October 21, 686 — September 21, 687)
84. St. Sergius I (Syrian, December 15, 687 — September 8, 701)
85. John VI (Greek, October 30, 701 — January 11, 705)

86. John VII (Greek, March 1, 705 — October 18, 707)
87. Sisinnius (Syrian, January 15, 708 — February 4, 708)
88. Constantine (Syrian, March 25, 708 — April 9, 715)
89. St. Gregory II (May 19, 715 — February 11, 731)
90. St. Gregory III (Syrian, March 18, 731 — November 741)
91. St. Zachary (Greek, December 10, 741 — March 22, 752)
92. Stephen II (March 26, 752 — April 26, 757)
93. St. Paul I (April [May 29] 752 — June 28, 767)
94. Stephen III (August 1 [7], 768 — January 24, 772)
95. Adrian I (February 1 [9], 772 — December 25, 795)
96. St. Leo III (December 26 [27], 795 — June 12, 816)
97. Stephen IV [V] (June 22, 816 — January 24, 817)
98. St. Paschal I (January 25, 817 — February 11, 824)
99. Eugenius II (February [May] 824 — August 827)
100. Valentine (August 827 — September 827)
101. Gregory IV (827 — January 844)
102. Sergius II (January 844 — January 27, 847)
103. St. Leo IV (January [April 10] 847 — July 17, 855)
104. Benedict III (July [September 29] 855 — April 17, 858)
105. St. Nicholas I (the Great, April 24, 858 — November 13, 867)
106. Adrian II (December 14, 867 — December 14, 872)
107. John VIII (December 14, 872 — December 16, 882)
108. Marinus I (December 16, 882 — May 15, 884)
109. St. Adrian III (May 17, 884 — September 885)
110. Stephen V [VI] (September 885 — September 14, 891)
111. Formosus (October 6, 891 — April 4, 896)
112. Boniface VI (April 896)
113. Stephen VI [VII] (May 896 — August 897)
114. Romanus (August 897 — November 897)
115. Theodore II (December 897)
116. John IX (January 898 — January 900)
117. Benedict IV (January [February] 900 — July 903)
118. Leo V (July 903 — September 903)
119. Sergius III (January 29, 904 — April 14, 911)
120. Anastasius III (April 911 — June 913)

121. Landus (July 913 — February 914)
122. John X (March 914 — May 928)
123. Leo VI (May 928 — December 928)
124. Stephen VII [VIII] (December 928 — February 931)
125. John XI (February [March] 931 — December 935)
126. Leo VII (January 3, 936 — July 13, 939)
127. Stephen VIII [IX] (July 14, 939 — October 942)
128. Marinus II (October 30, 942 — May 946)
129. Agapitus II (May 10, 946 — December 955)
130. John XII (December 16, 956 — May 14, 964)
131. Leo VIII (December 4 [6], 963 — March 1, 965)
132. Benedict V (May 22, 964 — July 4, 966)
133. John XIII (October 1, 965 — September 6, 972)
134. Benedict VI (January 19, 973 — June 974)
135. Benedict VII (October 974 — July 10, 983)
136. John XIV (December 983 — August 20, 984)
137. John XV (August 985 — March 996)
138. Gregory V (Saxon, May 3, 996 — February 18, 999)
139. Sylvester II (French, April 2, 999 — May 12, 1003)
140. John XVII (June 1003 — December 1003)
141. John XVIII (January 1004 — July 1009)
142. Sergius IV (July 31, 1009 — May 12, 1012)
143. Benedict VIII (May 18, 1012 — April 9, 1024)
144. John XIX (April [May] 1024 — 1032)
145. Benedict IX (1032 -- 1044: forcibly removed in 1044; if this action was not legitimate, then Sylvester III was an antipope)
146. Sylvester III (January 20, 1045 — February 10, 1045)
147. Benedict IX [second time] (April 10, 1045 — May 1, 1045: resigned; then removed at synod in December 1046; if these actions were not legitimate, then Gregory VI and Clement II were antipopes)
148. Gregory VI (May 5, 1045 — December 20, 1046)
149. Clement II (Saxon, December 24, 1046 — October 9, 1047)
150. Benedict IX [third time] (November 8, 1047 — July 17, 1048; d. c. 1055)
151. Damasus II (Bavarian, July 17, 1048 — August 9, 1048)

152. St. Leo IX (Alsatian; February 12, 1049 — April 19, 1054)
153. Victor II (Swabian, April 16, 1055 — July 28, 1057)
154. Stephen IX [X] (French, August 3, 1057 — March 29, 1058)
155. Nicholas II (French, January 24, 1059 — July 27, 1061)
156. Alexander II (October 1, 1061 — April 21, 1073)
157. St. Gregory VII (April 22 [June 30], 1073 — May 25, 1085)
158. Bl. Victor III (May 24, 1086 — September 16, 1087)
159. Bl. Urban II (French, March 12, 1088 — July 29, 1099)
160. Paschal II (August. 13 [14], 1099 — January 21, 1118)
161. Gelasius II (January 24 [March 10], 1118 — January 28, 1119)
162. Calixtus II (French, February 3 [9], 1119 — December 13, 1124)
163. Honorius II (December 15 [21], 1124 — February 13, 1130)
164. Innocent II (February 14 [23], 1130 — September 21, 1143)
165. Celestine II (September 26 [October 31], 1143 — March 8, 1144)
166. Lucius II (March 12, 1144 — February 15, 1145)
167. Bl. Eugenius III (February 15 [18], 1145 — July 8, 1153)
168. Anastasius IV (July 12, 1153 — December 3, 1154)
169. Adrian IV (English, December 4 [5], 1154 — September 1, 1159)
170. Alexander III (September 7 [20], 1159 — August 30, 1181)
171. Lucius III (September 1 [6], 1181 — September 25, 1185)
172. Urban III (November 25 [December 1], 1185 — October 20, 1187)
173. Gregory VIII (October 21 [25], 1187 — December 17, 1187)
174. Clement III (December 19 [20], 1187 — March 1191)

175. Celestine III (March 30 [April 14], 1191 — January 8, 1198)

176. Innocent III (January 8 [February 22], 1198 — July 16, 1216)

177. Honorius III (July 18 [24], 1216 — March 18, 1227)

178. Gregory IX (March 19 [21], 1227 — August 22, 1241)

179. Celestine IV (October 25 [28], 1241 — November 10, 1241)

180. Innocent IV (June 25 [28], 1243 — December 7, 1254)

181. Alexander IV (December 12 [20], 1254 — May 25, 1261)

182. Urban IV (French, August 29 [September 4], 1261 — October 2, 1264)

183. Clement IV (French, February 5 [15], 1265 — November 29, 1268)

184. Bl. Gregory X (September 1, 1271 [March 27, 1272] — January 10, 1276)

185. Bl. Innocent V (French, January 21 [February 22], 1276 — June 22, 1276)

186. Adrian V (July 11, 1276 — August 18, 1276)

187. John XXI (Portuguese, September 8 [20], 1276 — May 20, 1277)

188. Nicholas III (November 25 [December 26], 1277 — August 22, 1280)

189. Martin IV (French, February 22 [March 23], 1281 — March 28, 1285)

190. Honorius IV (April 2 [May 20], 1285 — April 3, 1287)

191. Nicholas IV (February 22, 1288 — April 4, 1292)

192. St. Celestine V (July 5 [August 29], 1294 — December 13, 1294 [resigned, d. 1296])

193. Boniface VIII (December 24, 1294 [January 23, 1295] — October 11, 1303)

194. Bl. Benedict XI (October 22 [27], 1303 — July 7, 1304)

195. Clement V (French, June 5 [November 14], 1305 — April 20, 1314)

196. John XXII (French, August 7 [September 5], 1316 — December 4, 1334)

197. Benedict XII (French, December 20, 1334 [January 8, 1335] — April 25, 1342)

198. Clement VI (French, May 7 [19], 1342 — December 6, 1352)

199. Innocent VI (French, December 18 [30], 1352 — September 12, 1362)

200. Bl. Urban V (French, September 28 [November 6], 1362 — December 19, 1370)

201. Gregory XI (French, December 30, 1370 [January 5, 1371] — March 26, 1378)

202. Urban VI (April 8 [18], 1378 — October 15, 1389)

203. Boniface IX (November 2 [9], 1389 — October 1, 1404)

204. Innocent VII (October 17 [November 11], 1404 — November 6, 1406)

205. Gregory XII (November 30 [December 19], 1406 — July 4, 1415 [resigned, d. October 18, 1417]

206. Martin V (November 11 [21], 1417 — February 20, 1431)

207. Eugenius IV (March 3 [11], 1431 — February 23, 1447)

208. Nicholas V (March 6 [19], 1447 — March 24, 1455)

209. Calixtus III (Spanish, April 8 [20], 1455 — August 6, 1458)

210. Pius II (August 19 [September 3], 1458 — August 14, 1464)

211. Paul II (August 30 [September 16], 1464 — July 26, 1471)

212. Sixtus IV (August 9 [25], 1471 — August 12, 1484)

213. Innocent VIII (August 29 [September 12], 1484 — July 25, 1492)

214. Alexander VI (Spanish, August 11 [26], 1492 — August 18, 1503)

215. Pius III (September 22 [October 1, 8], 1503 — October 18, 1503)

216. Julius II (October 31 [November 26], 1503 — February 21, 1513)

217. Leo X (March 9 [19], 1513 — December 1, 1521)

218. Adrian VI (Dutch, January 9 [August 31], 1522 — September 14, 1523)

219. Clement VII (November 19 [26], 1523 — September 25, 1534)

220. Paul III (October 13 [November 3], 1534 — November 10, 1549)

221. Julius III (February 7 [22], 1550 — March 23, 1555)

222. Marcellus II (April 9 [10], 1555 — May 1, 1555)

223. Paul IV (May 23 [26], 1555 — August 18, 1559)

224. Pius IV (December 25, 1559 [January 6, 1560] December 9, 1565)

225. St. Pius V (January 7 [17], 1566 — May 1, 1572)

226. Gregory XIII (May 13 [25], 1572 — April 10, 1585)

227. Sixtus V (April 24 [May 1], 1585 — August 27, 1590)

228. Urban VII (September 15, 1590 — September 27, 1590)

229. Gregory XIV (December 5 [8], 1590 — October 16, 1591)

230. Innocent IX (October 29 [November 3], 1591 — December 30, 1591)

231. Clement VIII (January 30 [February 9], 1592 — March 3, 1605)

232. Leo XI (April 1 [10], 1605 — April 27, 1605)

233. Paul V (May 16 [29], 1605 — January 28, 1621)

234. Gregory XV (February 9 [14], 1621 — July 8, 1623)

235. Urban VIII (August 6 [September 29], 1623 — July 29, 1644)

236. Innocent X (September 15 [October 4], 1644 — January 7, 1655)

237. Alexander VII (April 7 [18], 1655 — May 22, 1667)

238. Clement IX (June 20 [26], 1667 — December 9, 1669)

239. Clement X (April 29 [May 11], 1670 — July 22, 1676)

240. Bl. Innocent XI (September 21 [October 4], 1676 — August 12, 1689)

241. Alexander VIII (October 6 [16], 1689 — February 1, 1691)

242. Innocent XII (July 12 [15], 1691 — September 27, 1700)

243. Clement XI (November 23, 30 [December 8], 1700 — March 19, 1721)

244. Innocent XIII (May 8 [18], 1721 — March 7, 1724)

245. Benedict XIII (May 29 [June 4], 1724 — February 21, 1730)

246. Clement XII (July 12 [16], 1730 — February 6, 1740)

247. Benedict XIV (August 17 [22], 1740 — May 3, 1758)

248. Clement XIII (July 6 [16], 1758 — February 2, 1769)

249. Clement XIV (May 19, 28 [June 4], 1769 — September 22, 1774)

250. Pius VI (February 15 [22], 1775 — August 29, 1799)

251. Pius VII (March 14 [21], 1800 — August 20, 1823)

252. Leo XII (September 28 [October 5], 1823 — February 10, 1829)

253. Pius VIII (March 31 [April 5], 1829 — November 30, 1830)

254. Gregory XVI (February 2 [6], 1831 — June 1, 1846)

255. Pius IX (June 16 [21], 1846 — February 7, 1878)

256. Leo XIII (February 20 [March 3], 1878 — July 20, 1903)

257. St. Pius X (August 4 [9], 1903 — August 20, 1914)

258. Benedict XV (September 3 [6], 1914 — January 22, 1922)

259. Pius XI (February 6 [12], 1922 — February 10, 1939)

260. Pius XII (March 2 [12], 1939 — October 9, 1958)

261. John XXIII (October 28 [November 4], 1958 — June 3, 1963)

262. Paul VI (June 21 [30], 1963 — August 6, 1978)

263. John Paul I (August 26 [September 3], 1978 — September 28, 1978)

264. John Paul II (Polish, October 16 [22], 1978 —)

Appendix II

Councils of the Church and Their Teachings

The most solemn and official assembly of all bishops of the world (thus "ecumenical," or universal) that, when summoned by the Bishop of Rome, constitutes the highest teaching authority in the Church. These meetings are usually convoked at pivotal, critical moments in the life of the Church and are charged with discussing and then articulating formal statements on doctrine or discipline. At times throughout Church history, secular rulers, theologians, superiors of religious orders, and most recently, representatives of other creeds are also invited to attend. Catholics recognize twenty-one ecumenical councils, listed as follows, with the Orthodox Churches accepting only the first seven. Of necessity, what is offered below contains only the most salient points; for a fuller treatment, the reader should consult the proper entry for each council within the body of the Dictionary.

1. **Nicaea I, 325**
   Condemned Arianism and declared the Son "consubstantial" with the Father.

2. **Constantinople I, 381**
   Condemned Macedonians and declared the Holy Spirit consubstantial with the Father and the Son.

3. **Ephesus, 431**
   Condemned Nestorians and Pelagians and declared the divine maternity of the Blessed Virgin Mary.

4. **Chalcedon, 451**
   Condemned Monophysitism and declared the two natures of Christ.

5. **Constantinople II, 553**
   Condemned the Three Chapters and reaffirmed the teachings of the earlier councils, clarifying that the two natures of Christ are inseparable and unconfused.

6. **Constantinople III, 680**
    Condemned Monothelitism and censured Honorius, proclaiming that Christ, having two natures, had two wills, human and divine, the former becoming subjected to the latter through obedience.

7. **Nicaea II, 787**
    Condemned iconoclasm, recommending the cult of sacred images and the seeking of the intercession of saints.

8. **Constantinople IV, 869**
    Ended the Greek schism, deposed Photius, and reaffirmed the teachings of the earlier councils.

9. **Lateran I, 1123**
    Issued decrees on simony, celibacy, and lay investiture; confirmed the Concordat of Worms, clarifying the relationship between Church and State.

10. **Lateran II, 1139**
    Ended the papal schism and enacted reforms regarding simony, marriage, collective and individual unfaithfulness of religious to vows, tithes, cease-fire from wars during Lent and the Easter octave, usury, jousts, laying violent hands on a cleric, ecclesiastical offices and honors, arson, and war tactics.

11. **Lateran III, 1179**
    Condemned the Albigenses and Waldenses and regulated papal elections; enacted and upheld previous reforms regarding eligibility for reception of Sacred Orders, excommunications without warning, simony, ecclesiastical benefices, rules for religious, rules for clerical continence.

12. **Lateran IV, 1215**
    Planned a crusade, mandated annual reception of Holy Communion, repeated the condemnation of the

Albigenses, enacted new reforms and upheld previous ones.

13. **Lyons I, 1245**
Deposed Frederick II, clarified positions on Church-State issues, and planned a crusade.

14. **Lyons II, 1274**
Reunited the Church with the Greeks in some measure, and legislated certain new disciplinary reforms, confirming and intensifying old ones.

15. **Vienne, 1311-1312**
Abolished the Knights Templar and enacted or upheld reforms.

16. **Constance, 1414-1418**
Ended the Great Schism; condemned Wyclif, Hus, and Jerome of Prague; advanced the cause of ecclesiastical reform.

17. **Basel-Ferrara-Florence, 1431-1445**
Effected to some degree union with Greeks, Armenians, and Copts, and continued to press for reforms.

18. **Lateran V, 1512-1517**
Treated of the Neo-Aristotelians, sought peace among Christian rulers and enacted/upheld reforms.

19. **Trent, 1545-1563**
Condemned Protestantism, promulgated the canon of Scripture, defined the nature of the means of justification, the sources of revelation, and the number and significance of the sacraments, legislated the institution of seminaries and the codification of the Mass, and mandated disciplinary reforms.

20. **Vatican I, 1869-1870**
Condemned errors such as rationalism and fideism, and defined papal infallibility.

21. **Vatican II, 1962-1965**
    Promulgated sixteen documents on such topics as: the liturgy, social communication, ecclesiology, Eastern Catholic churches, ecumenism, episcopacy, religious life, training of priests, education, non-Christian religions, Divine Revelation, the laity, religious liberty, missionary activity, ministry and life of priests, and the Church in the modern world.

Appendix III

Church-Related Abbreviations

AA: *Apostolicam Actuositatem:* Decree on the Apostolate of the Laity.

A.A.: *Augustiniani Assumptionis:* Augustinians of the Assumption (Assumptionists).

AAS: *Acta Apostolicae Sedis:* Acts of the Apostolic See.

Abb.: Abbacy, Abbot.

Abp.: Archbishop.

Acts: Acts of the Apostles (N.T. [New Testament]).

A.D.: *Anno Domini:* in the year of Our Lord.

ad lib.: *ad libitum:* at your own choice.

Adv.: *Adversus:* Opposing.

AG: *Ad Gentes:* Decree on the Church's Missionary Activity.

A.I.D.: Artificial Insemination by a Donor.

AIDS: Acquired Immune Deficiency Syndrome.

A.I.H.: Artificial Insemination by the Husband.

A.J.: Apostles of Jesus.

Am: Book of Amos (O.T. [Old Testament]).

A.M.D.G.: *Ad majorem Dei gloriam:* to the greater glory of God

A.M.E.: African Methodist Episcopal (Church).

Ap.: Apostle, Apostolic.

A.U.C.: *Ab Urbe Condita:* from the founding of the city (of Rome).

A.S.C.: Adorers of the Blood of Christ.

A.S.C. J.: Apostles of the Sacred Heart of Jesus.

A.S.S.P.: Angelic Sisters of St. Paul.

A.V.: Authorized Version (of the Bible).

B., Bl.: *Beatus, — a:* Blessed.

Bar: Book of Baruch (O.T.).

B.C.: Before Christ.

B.C.E.: Before the Common or Christian Era (used by some non-Christians).

BCL: Bishops' Committee on the Liturgy.

B.C.L.: Bachelor of Canon (or Civil) Law.

B.F.C.C.: Brothers of Christian Community.

B.G.S.: Little Brothers of the Good Shepherd.

Bp.: Bishop.

Bro.: Brother.

B.V.M.: Blessed Virgin Mary.

B.V.M.: Sisters of Charity of the Blessed Virgin Mary.

Can., cc.: Canon, canons.

CARA: Center for Applied Research in the Apostolate.

CCC: *Catechism of the Catholic Church.*

CCCB: Canadian Conference of Catholic Bishops.

CCD: Confraternity of Christian Doctrine.

C.C.V.I.: Sisters of Charity of the Incarnate Word.

C.D.F.: Congregation for the Doctrine of Faith.

C.D.P.: Sisters of Divine Providence.

C.E.: Common or Christian Era.

CEF: Citizens for Educational Freedom.

cf.: *confer:* compare.

C.F.A.: *Congregatio Fratrum Cellitarum seu Alexianorum:* Alexian Brothers.

C.F.C.: Congregation of Christian Brothers.

C.F.I.C.: Congregation of Franciscans of the Immaculate Conception.

C.F.R.: Franciscan Friars of the Renewal.

C.F.X.: *Congregatio Fratrum S. Francisci Xaverii:* Xaverian Brothers.

C.H.M.: Congregation of the Humility of Mary.

1 Chr: First Book of Chronicles (O.T.).

2 Chr: Second Book of Chronicles (O.T.).

C.I.C.: *Codex Iuris Canonici:* Code of Canon Law.

C.I.C.M.: *Congregatio Immaculati Cordis Mariae:* Congregation of the Immaculate Heart of Mary (Missionhurst; Scheut Missionaries).

C.J.: *Congregatio Josephitarum Gerardimonensium:* Josephite Fathers (of Belgium).

C.J.D.: Canons of Jesus the Lord.

C.J.M.: Congregation of Jesus and Mary (Eudists).

C.M.: Congregation of the Mission (Vincentians or Lazarists).

C.M.F.: *Cordis Mariae Filii:* Missionary Sons of the Immaculate Heart of Mary (Claretians).

C.M.I.: Carmelites of Mary Immaculate.

C.M.M.: *Congregatio Missionariorum de Mariannhill:* Missionaries of Mariannhill.

CMRS: Conference of Major Religious Superiors.

CMSM: Conference of Major Superiors of Men.

C.N.: Capuchin Sisters of Nazareth.

C.N.D.: Congregation of Notre Dame.

CNS: Catholic News Service.

C.O.: *Congregatio Oratorii:* Oratorians.

COCU: Consultation on Church Union.

Col: Letter to the Colossians (N.T.).

1 Cor: First Letter to the Corinthians (N.T.).

2 Cor: Second Letter to the Corinthians (N.T.).

C.P.: Congregation of the Passion (Passionists).

CPA: Catholic Press Association.

C.P.M.: *Congregatio Presbyterorum a Misericordia:* Congregation of the Fathers of Mercy.

C.PP.S.: *Congregatio Missionariorum Pretiosissimi Sanguinis:* Society of the Precious Blood.

C.R.: Congregation of the Resurrection.

C.R.I.C.: Canons Regular of the Immaculate Conception.

C.R.L.: Canons Regular of the Lateran.

C.R.M.: Clerics Regular Minor (Adorno Fathers).

CRS: Catholic Relief Services.

C.R.S.P.: Clerics Regular of St. Paul (Barnabites).

C.S.: Missionaries of St. Charles (Scalabrians).

C.S.B.: Congregation of St. Basil (Basilians).

C.S.B.: Congregations of St. Bridget.

C.S.C.: *Congregatio Sanctae Crucis:* Congregation of Holy Cross.

C.S.F.: Congregation of the Holy Family.

C.S.J.: Congregation of St. Joseph.

C.S.J.: Sisters of St. Joseph.

C.S.J.P.: Sisters of St. Joseph of Peace.

C.S.P.: Congregation of St. Paul (Paulists).

C.S.S.: Congregation of the Sacred Stigmata (Stigmatine Fathers and Brothers).

C.S.S.F.: Congregation of Sisters of St. Felice Cantalicio (Felicians).

C.SS.R.: *Congregatio Sanctissimi Redemptoris:* Congregation of the Most Holy Redeemer (Redemptorists).

C.S.Sp.: *Congregatio Sancti Spiritus:* Holy Ghost Fathers.

C.S.V.: Clerks of St. Viator (Viatorians).

C.V.I.: Sisters of the Incarnate Word and Blessed Sacrament.

C.Y.O.: Catholic Youth Organization.

DAS: *Divino Afflante Spiritu:* Encyclical on Bible research (Pope Pius XII).

D.C.: Daughters of Charity.

D.C.L.: *Doctor Canonicae (Civilis) Legis:* Doctor of Canon (Civil) Law.

D.D.: *Divinitatis Doctor:* Doctor of Divinity.

DH: *Dignitatis Humanae:* Decree on Religious Liberty.

D.H.M.: Daughters of the Heart of Mary.

D.H.S.: Daughters of the Holy Spirit.

D.M.: Daughters of Mary of the Immaculate Conception.

D.Min: Doctor of Ministry.

Dn: Book of Daniel (O.T.).

D.N.J.C.: *Dominus Noster Jesus Christus:* Our Lord Jesus Christ.

D.O.M.: *Deo Optimo Maximo:* To God, the Best and Greatest.

DS: Denzinger-Schönmetzer, *Enchiridion Symbolorum.*

Dt: Book of Deuteronomy (O.T.).

DV: *Dei Verbum:* Dogmatic Constitution on Divine Revelation.

D.V.: *Deo volente:* God willing.

D.W.: Daughters of Wisdom (Montforts).

Eccl: Book of Ecclesiastes (O.T.).

Enarr.: *Enarratio:* Analysis or description.

Eph: Letter to the Ephesians (N.T.).

Er.Cam.: *Congregatio Monachorum Eremitarum Camaldulensium:* Monk Hermits of Camaldoli.

Est: Book of Esther (O.T.).

et. al.: *et alii (aliae, alia):* and others.

Ex: Book of Exodus (O.T.).

Ez: Book of Ezekiel (O.T.).

Ezr: Book of Ezra (O.T.).

F.C.: *Fratres Caritas:* Brothers of Charity.

F.C.J.: Faithful Companions of Jesus.

F.F.P.: Faith Foundation Program.

F.D.C.C.: Canossian Daughters of Charity.

F.D.N.S.C.: Daughters of Our Lady of the Sacred Heart.

FDLC: Federation of Diocesan Liturgical Commissions.

F.D.P.: *Filii Divinae Providentiae:* Sons of Divine Providence.

F.I.: Franciscans of the Immaculate.

F.I.C.: Brothers of Christian Instruction.

F.M.A.: Daughters of Mary Help of Christians (Salesian Sisters).

F.M.I.: Daughters of Mary Immaculate (Marianist Sisters).

F.M.M.: Franciscan Missionaries of Mary.

F.M.S.: *Fratres Maristarum a Scholis:* Marist Brothers.

F.M.S.I.: Sons of Mary, Health of the Sick.

F.P.O.: Franciscans of Primitive Observance.

Fr.: Father or Friar.

F.S.C.: *Fratres Scholarum Christianarum:* Brothers of the Christian Schools (Christian Brothers).

F.S.C.G.: Daughters of the Sacred Heart of Jesus.

F.S.C.J.: Sons of the Sacred Heart, Verona Fathers.

F.S.M.: Franciscan Sisters of Mary.

F.S.P.A.: Franciscan Sisters of Perpetual Adoration.

F.S.S.J.: Franciscan Sisters of St. Joseph.

F.S.S.P.: Priestly Fraternity of St. Peter's.

Gal: Letter to the Galatians (N.T.).

GE: *Gravissimum Educationis:* Declaration on Christian Education.

Gn: Book of Genesis (O.T.).

G.N.S.H.: Grey Nuns of the Sacred Heart.

GS: *Gaudium et Spes:* Pastoral Constitution on the Church in the Modern World.

Hb: Book of Habakkuk (O.T.).

Heb: Letter to the Hebrews (N.T.).

Hg: Book of Haggai (O.T.).

Hos: Book of Hosea (O.T.).

I.B.V.M.: Institute of the Blessed Virgin Mary.

I.C.: Institute of Charity (Rosminians).

ICEL: International Committee (Commission) on English in the Liturgy.

ICET: International Consultation on English Text.

I.C.M.: Missionary Sisters of the Immaculate Heart of Mary.

I.H.M.: Servants of the Immaculate Heart of Mary.

IHS: Jesus (from Greek IHSOYS) or "By this sign conquer" (from Latin *In Hoc Signo*).

IM: *Inter Mirifica:* Decree on the Means of Social Communication.

I.M.C.: *Institutum Missionum a Consolata:* Consolata Society for Foreign Missions.

I.N.R.I.: *Iesus Nazarenus, Rex Iudaeorum:* Jesus of Nazareth, King of the Jews.

Is: Book of Isaiah (O.T.).

I.T.C.: International Theological Commission.

I.W.B.S.: Sisters of the Incarnate Word and Blessed Sacrament.

Jas: Letter of James (N.T.).

Jb: Book of Job (O.T.).

J.C.D.: *Juris Canonici Doctor:* Doctor of Canon Law.

J.C.L.: *Juris Canonici Licentiatus:* Licentiate in Canon Law.

J.D.: *Juris Doctor:* Doctor of Law.

Jdt: Book of Judith (O.T.).

Jer: Book of Jeremiah (O.T.).

Jgs: Book of Judges (O.T.).

Jl: Book of Joel (O.T.).

J.M.J.: Jesus, Mary and Joseph.

J.O.C.: *Jeunesse Ouvrière Chrétienne:* Young Christian Workers (Jocists).

Jn: Gospel According to John (N.T.).

1 Jn: First Letter of John (N.T.).

2 Jn: Second Letter of John (N.T.).

3 Jn: Third Letter of John (N.T.).

Jon: Book of Jonah (O.T.).

Jos: Book of Joshua (O.T.).

J.U.D.: *Juris Utriusque Doctor:* Doctor of Both (Civil and Canon) Laws.

Jude: Letter of Jude (N.T.).

1 Kgs: First Book of Kings (O.T.).

2 Kgs: Second Book of Kings (O.T.).

K.G.H.S.: Knight Grand Cross of the Holy Sepulcher.

K.H.S.: Knight of the Holy Sepulcher.

KJV: King James Version (of the Bible).

K.M.: Knights of Malta.

K. of C.: Knights of Columbus.

K.P.IX: Knight of Pius IX.

K.S.G.: Knight of St. Gregory.

K.S.S.: Knight of St. Sylvester.

Lam: Book of Lamentations (O.T.).

L.B.S.F.: Little Brothers of St. Francis.

L.C.: Legionaries of Christ.

L.C.M.: Sisters of the Little Company of Mary.

LCWR: Leadership Conference of Women Religious.

LG: *Lumen Gentium:* Dogmatic Constitution on the Church.

Lk: Gospel According to Luke (N.T.).

LL.B.: *Legum Baccalaureus:* Bachelor of Laws.

LL.D.: *Legum Doctor:* Doctor of Laws.

L.S.P.: Little Sisters of the Poor.

Lv: Book of Leviticus (O.T.).

LWF: Lutheran World Federation.

M.Afr.: Missionaries of Africa (formerly White Fathers).

Mal: Book of Malachi (O.T.).

M.C.: Missionaries of Charity.

1 Mc: First Book of Maccabees (O.T.).

2 Mc: Second Book of Maccabees (O.T.).

M.C.C.J.: *Missionarii Comboniani Cordis Jesu:* Comboni Missionaries of the Heart of Jesus (Verona Fathers).

M.C.D.P.: Missionary Catechists of Divine Providence.

M.C.M.: Cordi Marian Sisters.

M.C.S.T.: Missionary Catechists of St. Thérèse of the Child Jesus.

M.Div.: Master of Divinity.

M.F.I.C.: Missionary Franciscans of the Immaculate Conception.

M.F.V.A.: Franciscan Missionaries of the Eternal Word.

M.E.P.: *Société des Missions Étrangers de Paris:* Paris Foreign Mission Society.

M.H.M.: Mill Hill Missionaries.

M.H.S.H.: Missionary Helpers of the Sacred Heart.

Mi: Book of Micah (O.T.).

M.I.C.: *Congregatio Clericorum Regularium Marianorum sub titulo Immaculatae Conceptionis Beatae Mariae Virginis:* Marian Fathers and Brothers.

Mk: Gospel According to Mark (N.T.).

MM: Martyrs.

M.M.: Catholic Foreign Mission Society (Maryknoll Missioners).

M.O.P.: Missionaries of the Poor.

M.P.F.: Religious Teachers Fillippine.

M.P.V.: Religious Teachers Vernerini.

M.S.: Missionaries of Our Lady of La Salette.

M.S.A.: Missionaries of the Holy Apostles.

M.S.B.T.: Missionary Servants of the Blessed Trinity.

M.S.C.: Missionaries of the Sacred Heart.

M.S.F.: *Congregatio Missionariorum a Sancta Familia:* Missionaries of the Holy Family.

Msgr.: Monsignor.

M.S.S.: Missionaries of the Blessed Sacrament.

M.SS.C.: Missionaries of the Sacred Hearts of Jesus and Mary.

Mt.: Mount.

Mt: Gospel According to Matthew (N.T.).

M.T.: Missionary Servants of the Most Holy Trinity.

n., nn.: number, numbers.

NA: *Nostra Aetate:* Declaration on the Relationship of the Church to Non-Christian Religions.

Na: Book of Nahum (O.T.).

NAB: New American Bible.

NAPM: National Association of Pastoral Musicians.

NAWR: National Assembly of Women Religious.

NBSC: National Black Sisters Conference.

NCCB: National Conference of Catholic Bishops.

NCCC: National Council of Churches of Christ (in the U.S.A.).

NCCIJ: National Catholic Conference for Interracial Justice.

NCCL: National Council of Catholic Laity.

NCCM: National Council of Catholic Men.

NCCW: National Council of Catholic Women.

NCEA: National Catholic Educational Association.

NCRLC: National Catholic Rural Life Conference.

NCWC: (Former) National Catholic Welfare Conference.

NEB: New English Bible.

Neh: Book of Nehemiah (O.T.).

N.F.P.: National Family Planning.

NFPC: National Federation of Priests' Councils.

Nm: Book of Numbers (O.T.).

NOBC: National Office for Black Catholics.

NRSV: New Revised Standard Version.

N.T.: New Testament.

O.A.R.: Order of Augustinian Recollects.

Ob: Book of Obadiah (O.T.).

O.C.: Order of Carmelites.

O.Carm.: *Ordo Carmelitorum:* Order of Carmelites.

O.Cart.: *Ordo Cartusiensis:* Carthusian Order.

O.C.D.: *Ordo Carmelitorum Discalceatorum:* Order of Discalced Carmelites.

O.Cist.: *Ordo Cisterciensis:* Cistercian Order.

O.C.S.O: Order of Cistercians of the Strict Observance (Trappists).

O. de M.: *Ordo Beatae Mariae de Mercede:* Order of Mercy (Mercedarians).

OE: *Orientalium Ecclesiarum:* Decree on the Eastern Churches.

O.F.M.: Order of Friars Minor (Franciscans).

O.F.M. Cap.: Order of Friars Minor Capuchin (Capuchins).

O.F.M. Conv.: Order of Friars Minor Conventual (Conventuals).

O.F.M.I.: Franciscan Friars of Mary Immaculate.

O.H.: *Ordo Hospitalarius S. Joannis de Deo:* Hospitaler Order of St. John of God.

O.L.M.E.: Our Lady's Missionaries of the Eucharist.

O.L.V.M.: Victory Noll Sisters.

O.M.: Minim Fathers.

O.M.I.: Oblates of Mary Immaculate.

O.M.V.: Oblates of the Virgin Mary.

O.P.: Order of Preachers (Dominicans).

O.Praem.: Order of Premonstratensians (Norbertines).

O.R.C.: Order of Canons Regular of the Holy Cross.

O.R.S.A.: Augustinian Recollects.

O.S.: Oblates of Wisdom.

O.S.A.: Order of Hermits of St. Augustine (Augustinians).

O.S.A.: *Opus Sanctorum Angelorum*: Work of the Holy Angels.

O.S.B.: Order of St. Benedict (Benedictines).

O.S.B.M.: *Ordo Sancti Basilii Magni:* Order of St. Basil the Great (Basilians of St. Josaphat).

O.S.C.: *Ordo Sanctae Crucis:* Order of the Holy Cross (Crosier Fathers).

O.S.Cam.: Order of St. Camillus (Camillians).

O.S.F.: Order of St. Francis: Franciscan Brothers; also various congregations of Franciscan Sisters.

O.S.F.S.: Oblates of St. Francis de Sales.

O.S.J.: Oblates of St. Joseph.

O.S.M.: Order of Servants of Mary (Servites).

O.S.P.: Order of St. Paul the First Hermit (Pauline Fathers).

O.Ss.S.: Brigittine Monks.

O.SS.T.: *Ordo Sanctissimae Trinitatis Redemptionis Captivorum:* Order of the Most Holy Trinity (Trinitarians).

O.S.T.R.: Oblates of St. Thérèse Reformed.

O.S.U.: The Ursulines.

O.T.: Old Testament.

OT: *Optatam Totius:* Decree on the Training of Priests.

P.A.: Protonotary Apostolic.

P.B.C.: Pontifical Biblical Commission.

P.B.V.M.: Sisters of the Presentation of the Blessed Virgin Mary.

PC: *Perfectae Caritatis:* Decree on the Up-to-Date Renewal of Religious Life.

P.C.C.: Poor Clares Collettines.

P.C.P.A.: Poor Clares of Perpetual Adoration.

Phil: Letter to the Philippians (N.T.).

Ph.D.: Doctor of Philosophy.

P.H.J.C.: Poor Handmaids of Jesus Christ.

Phlm: Letter to Philemon (N.T.).

P.I.B.: *Pontificium Institutum Biblicum:* Pontifical Biblical Institute.

P.I.M.E.: *Pontificium Institutum pro Missionibus Externis:* Pontifical Institute for Foreign Missions (Missionaries of SS. Peter and Paul).

P.M.: Sisters of the Presentation of Mary.

PO: *Presbyterorum Ordinis:* Decree on the Ministry and Life of Priests.

Pont. Max.: *Pontifex Maximus:* Supreme Pontiff.

PP., Pp.: *Papa:* Pope.

Prv: Book of Proverbs (O.T.).

Ps(s): Book of Psalms (O.T.).

P.S.S.J.: Poor Sisters of St. Joseph.

1 Pt: First Letter of Peter (N.T.).

2 Pt: Second Letter of Peter (N.T.).

q.v.: *quid vide:* which see (reference).

R.A.: Religious of the Assumption.

R.C.: Roman Catholic.

r.c.: The Religious of the Cenacle.

R.D.C.: Religious of Divine Compassion.

Rev.: Reverend.

R.G.S.: Religious of the Good Shepherd.

R.I.P.: *Requiescat in pace:* may he (she) rest in peace.

R.J.M.: Religious of Jesus and Mary.

R.M.I.: Religious of Mary Immaculate.

R.N.D.M.: Sisters of Our Lady of the Missions.

RNS: Religious News Service.

Rom: Letter to the Romans (N.T.).

R.P.: *Reverendus Pater:* Reverend Father.

R.S.C.: Religious Sisters of Charity.

R.S.C.J.: Religious of the Sacred Heart of Jesus.

R.S.H.M.: Religious of the Sacred Heart of Mary.

R.S.M.: Sisters of Mercy.

R.S.V.: Revised Standard Version (of the Bible).

R.V.M.: Religious of the Virgin Mary.

Ru: Book of Ruth (O.T.).

Rv: Revelation to John (Apocalypse or Book of Revelation, N.T.).

S, or St.; SS. or Sts.: Saint; Saints.

S.A.: *Societas Adunationis:* Franciscan Friars of the Atonement.

S.A.C.: *Societas Apostolatus Catholici:* Society of the Catholic Apostolate (Pallottines).

S.A.C.: Sisters of the Guardian Angel.

SC: *Sacrosanctum Concilium:* Constitution on the Sacred Liturgy.

S.C.: Brothers of the Sacred Heart.

S.C.: Servants of Charity.

S.C.: Sisters of Charity.

S.Ch.: Society of Christ.

Sch.P. or S.P.: *Ordo Clericorum Regularium Pauperum Matris Dei Scholarum Piarum:* Order of Regular Poor Clerics of the Mother of God of the Pious Schools (Piarists).

S.C.J.: *Congregatio Sacerdotum a Corde Jesu:* Congregation of the Sacred Heart (Sacred Heart Fathers and Brothers).

S.C.S.J.A.: Sisters of Charity of St. Joan Antida.

S.D.B.: Salesians of Don Bosco.

S.D.S.: Society of the Divine Savior (Salvatorians).

S.D.V.: Society of Divine Vocations (Vocationists).

S.E.C.: Sisters of the Eucharistic Covenant.

S.F.: *Congregatio Filiorum Sacrae Familiae:* Sons of the Holy Family.

S.F.O.: Secular Franciscan Order (formerly Third Order).

Sg: Song of Songs (Canticle of Canticles, Song of Solomon, O.T.).

S.G.: Brothers of St. Gabriel.

S.H.C.J.: Society of the Holy Child of Jesus.

S.H.F.: Sisters of the Holy Family.

S.H.S.: Sisters of the Holy Spirit.

Sir: Book of Sirach (or Ecclesiasticus, O.T.).

S.I.W.: Sisters of the Incarnate Word.

S.J.: *Societas Iesu:* Society of Jesus (Jesuits).

S.L.: Sisters of Loretto.

1 Sm: First Book of Samuel (O.T.).

2 Sm: Second Book of Samuel (O.T.).

S.M.: Society of Mary (Marists or Marianists).

S.M.A.: *Societas Missionum ad Afros:* Society of African Missions.

S.M.B.: *Societas Missionaria de Bethlehem:* Society of Bethlehem Missionaries.

S.M.I.: Sisters of Mary Immaculate.

S.M.M.: *Societas Mariae Montfortana:* Company of Mary (Montfort Missionaries).

S.M.O.M.: Sovereign Military Order of Malta.

S.M.S.M.: Marist Missionary Sisters.

S.N.D.: Sisters of Notre Dame.

S.N.DdeN.: Sisters of Notre Dame de Namur.

S.N.J.M.: Sisters of the Holy Names of Jesus and Mary.

S.O.Cist.: Cistercians of the Common Observance.

S.O.L.M.: Sisters of Our Lady of Mercy.

S.O.L.T.: Society of Our Lady of the Most Holy Trinity.

S.P.: Servants of the Paraclete.

S.P.: Sisters of Providence.

S.P.S.: St. Patrick's Missionary Society.

Sr.: Sister.

S.S.: Society of St. Sulpice (Sulpicians).

S.S.A: Sisters of St. Ann.

S.S.C: Franciscan Servants of the Sacred Heart.

SS.CC.: *Congregatio Sacrorum Cordium:* Fathers of the Sacred Hearts (Picpus Fathers).

S.S.C.M.: Servants of the Holy Heart of Mary.

S.S.E.: Society of St. Edmund.

S.S.F.: Society of St. Francis.

S.S.J.: Sisters of St. Joseph.

S.S.J.: *Societas Sancti Joseph SSmi Cordis:* St. Joseph's Society of the Sacred Heart (Josephites).

S.S.L.: *Sacrae Scripturae Licentiatus:* Licentiate in Sacred Scripture.

SSma, -mae, -mi, -mus: Most Holy, Most Sacred.

S.S.N.D.: School Sisters of Notre Dame.

S.S.P.: Society of St. Paul (Pauline Fathers and Brothers).

S.T.: *Missionarii Servi Sanctissimae Trinitatis:* Missionary Servants of the Most Holy Trinity (Trinity Missions).

S.T.B.: *Sacrae Theologiae Baccalaureus:* Bachelor of Sacred Theology.

S.T.D.: *Sacrae Theologiae Doctor:* Doctor of Sacred Theology.

S.T.L.: *Sacrae Theologiae Licentiatus:* Licentiate in Sacred Theology.

S.T.M.: *Sacrae Theologiae Magister:* Master of Sacred Theology.

S.U.: Society of the Sisters of St. Ursula.

S.V.: *Sacra Virgo:* Consecrated Virgin.

S.V.: *Sorores Vitae:* Sisters of Life.

S.V.D.: *Societas Verbi Divini:* Society of the Divine Word.

S.X.: *Societas Xaveriana:* Xaverian Missionary Fathers.

Tb: Book of Tobit (O.T.).

1 Thes: First Letter to the Thessalonians (N.T.).

2 Thes: Second Letter to the Thessalonians (N.T.).

Ti: Letter to Titus (N.T.).

1 Tm: First Letter to Timothy (N.T.).

2 Tm: Second Letter to Timothy (N.T.).

T.O.C.: Third Order Carmelite.

T.O.R.: Third Order Regular of St. Francis.

T.O.S.F.: Tertiary of the Third Order of St. Francis.

UR: *Unitatis Redintegratio:* Decree on Ecumenism.

USCC: United States Catholic Conference.

USCCB: United States Catholic Conference of Bishops.

V.A.: Vicar Apostolic.

V.E.: *Verbo Encarnado*: The Word Incarnate.

Ven.: Venerable.

viz.: *videlicet:* namely.

V.F.: Vicar Forane.

V.G.: Vicar General.

vs.: *versus:* against.
V.S.C.: Vincentian Sisters of Charity.
V.T.: *Vetus Testamentum:* Old Testament.
WCC: World Council of Churches.
W.F.: White Fathers (changed to M.Afr.)
Wis: Book of Wisdom (O.T.).
Y.C.M.: Young Christian Movement.
Zec: Book of Zechariah (O.T.).
Zep: Book of Zephaniah (O.T.).

Appendix IV

Terms of Address for Ecclesiastical Persons

The following titles are the standard forms for referring to ecclesiastical persons in the English language:

The Pope: His Holiness Pope N. (with number).
(Speaking to: "Holy Father"; "Your Holiness.")

Cardinals: His Eminence N. Cardinal N.
(Speaking to: "Your Eminence"; "Cardinal.")

Bishops and Archbishops: His Excellency N.N.
(In writing, one uses in the address: "The Most Reverend N.N., [Arch]Bishop of N."; in speaking: "Your Excellency"; sometimes archbishops are also referred to as "Your Grace.")

Abbots: The Right Reverend Abbot N.N.
(Speaking to: "Father Abbot.")

Monsignori: The Reverend Monsignor N.N.
(Speaking to: "Monsignor.")

Priests: The Reverend [Father] N.N.
(Speaking to: "Father.")

Abbess or Superior of Religious Women: [Reverend] Mother.
(Speaking to: "Mother.")

Women Religious: [Reverend] Sister.
(Speaking to: "Sister.")

Male Religious (not ordained): [Reverend] Brother.
(Speaking to: "Brother.")